INSTRUCTOR'S

STRATEGIC MARKETING PROBLEMS

INSTRUCTOR'S MANUAL
Roger A. Kerin
Southern Methodist University

NINTH EDITION

Strategic Marketing Problems

CASES AND COMMENTS

Roger A. Kerin
Robert A. Peterson

Acquisitions editor: Whitney Blake
Assistant editor: Anthony Palmiotto
Production editor: Theresa Festa
Manufacturer: Victor Graphics, Inc.

Copyright ©2001 by Prentice-Hall, Inc., Upper Saddle River, New Jersey, 07458. All rights reserved. Printed in the United States of America. This publication is protected by copyright, and permission should be obtained from the publisher prior to any prohibited reproduction, storage in a retrieval system, or transmission in any form or by any means, electronic, mechanical, photocopying, recording, or likewise. For information regarding permission(s), write to: Rights and Permissions Department.

ISBN 0-13-027776-2

10 9 8 7 6 5 4 3 2 1

TABLE OF CONTENTS

Preface 1

Exercises in Financial Analysis and Marketing Decision Making 5

Opportunity Analysis and Market Targeting

    Quetzal Collections, Inc. 28
    Jones Blair Company 34
    Tyler Pet Foods, Inc. 47
    Curtis Automotive Hoist: Market Opportunities in the European Union 59
    Frito-Lay's Dips 72
    South Delaware Coors, Inc. 86

Product and Service Strategy and Brand Management

    Zoecon Corporation: Insect Growth Regulators. 100
    Ms-Tique Corporation 115
    Manor Memorial Hospital: Downtown Health Clinic 126
    Procter & Gamble, Inc.: Scope 141
    Frito-Lay Company: Cracker Jack 156
    Swisher Mower and Machine Company: Evaluating a Private Brand Opportunity 179

Integrated Marketing Communications Strategy and Management

    Throckmorten Furniture, Inc. (A) 193
    Throckmorten Furniture, Inc. (B) 202
    Cadbury Beverages, Inc.: Crush Brand 209
    Drypers Corporation: National Television Advertising Campaign 233
    Price Waterhouse 254
    Godiva Europe 265

Marketing Channel Strategy and Management

    Dell Computer Corporation: The Higher Education Market 276
    Amway Japan Limited 288
    Goodyear Tire and Rubber Company 300
    Hendison Electronics Corporation 313
    Chesterton Carpet Mills, Inc. 323

Pricing Strategy and Management

Southwest Airlines 332
Burroughs Wellcome Company: Retrovir 357
Afton Industries 375
Augustine Medical, Inc.: The Bair Hugger Patient Warming System 388
Seagram in Taiwan: Scotch and Cognac Pricing 405
Texas Instruments: Global Pricing in the Semiconductor Industry 418

Interactive Marketing and Electronic Commerce

Peapod: Moving to the Internet 428
Amazon.com: Winning the Online Book Wars 444
Arrow Electronics, Inc. 459
Vector Marketing Corporation: "CUTCO, The World's Finest Cutlery" 477

Marketing Strategy Reformulation: The Control Process

Pharmacia & Upjohn, Inc.: Rogaine Hair Regrowth Treatment 491
3M Telecom Systems Division: Fibrelok Splice 521
The Circle K Corporation 529
Marshall Museum of Art 544

Comprehensive Marketing Programs

Frito-Lay, Inc.: SunChips Multigrain Snacks 566
United States Census Bureau: Marketing Services Office 599
Biopure Corporation 609
CIMA Mountaineering, Inc. 628
Blair Water Purifiers India 643

NOTE

Case teaching notes included in the Instructor's Manual reflect the judgments, opinions, and the analyses of the authors or specific case writer where indicated. Teaching notes were prepared to assist the instructor in class preparation, examining case issues, and promoting class discussions. They are not designed to illustrate appropriate or inappropriate handling of the situation presented in the case or the merits of the decision(s) made by the company or its executives.

PREFACE

Strategic Marketing Problems: Cases and Comments, Ninth Edition, and the **Instructor's Manual** were prepared to provide students and faculty with an interesting, informative, contemporary, and decision-oriented tool for the study and teaching of marketing management concepts and practices. The book was prepared for use in an MBA first-course in marketing or marketing management and in the capstone undergraduate strategic marketing, marketing policy, marketing strategy, or marketing management course.

The Casebook

This edition of *Strategic Marketing Problems: Cases and Comments* seeks a balance between marketing management content and process. The book consists of eleven chapters and 42 cases. The first chapter provides an overview of fundamental concepts in formulating marketing strategy. **Appendix A: A Sample Marketing Plan**, contains tips for writing a marketing plan and an annotated version of the actual 5-year marketing plan for Paradise Kitchens, Inc., and its principal product line, Howlin Coyote Chili. Chapter 2 provides an overview of financial analysis for marketing management. Chapter 3 provides an introduction to marketing decision-making and case analysis. The remaining eight chapters focus on major topics in strategic marketing. A synopsis of each chapter follows.

Chapter 1, **Foundations of Strategic Marketing Management**, provides an overview of the strategic marketing management process. Principal emphasis is placed on defining an organization's business, mission and objectives, identifying opportunities (including SWOT analysis), formulating product-market and marketing mix strategies, budgeting, developing contingency plans, and considering ethical issues.

Chapter 2, **Financial Aspects of Marketing Management**, provides an overview of concepts from managerial accounting and managerial finance useful in marketing management. Primary emphasis is placed on such concepts as cost structure, relevant versus sunk costs, margins, cost-volume-profit analysis, liquidity, operating leverage, discounted cash flow, and preparing a pro forma income statement. Exercises at the end of this chapter can be used to give students practice in applying these concepts.

Chapter 3, **Marketing Decision Making and Case Analysis**, introduces a systematic process for marketing decision-making and provides an overview of various aspects of case analysis. Decision analysis is introduced and described in the chapter.

Chapter 4, **Opportunity Analysis and Market Targeting**, focuses on identification and evaluation of marketing opportunities. Market segmentation, market targeting, business definition and distinctive competency, and market potential and profitability issues are considered in the text and cases.

Chapter 5, **Product and Service Strategy and Brand Management**, focuses on the management of the organization's offering. New offering development, life cycle management, product or service positioning, product mix decisions, brand equity and brand valuation, brand growth strategy are considered in the text and cases.

Chapter 6, **Integrated Marketing Communications Strategy and Management**, raises issues in the design, implementation, and evaluation of an integrated communications mix. Decisions concerned with communication objectives, strategy, budgeting, programming, and effectiveness, in addition to sales management, are addressed in the text and cases.

Chapter 7, **Marketing Channel Strategy and Management**, introduces a variety of considerations in marketing channel selection and modification, and trade relations. Specific decision areas introduced in the text and cases include direct versus indirect distribution, dual distribution, disintermediation, and cost-benefit analyses of channel choice and evaluation.

Chapter 8, **Pricing Strategy and Management**, highlights concepts and applications in price determination. Emphasis is placed on demand, cost, and competitive influences on selecting or modifying pricing strategies for products and services in the text and accompanying cases.

Chapter 9, **Interactive Marketing and Electronic Commerce**, is new to this edition. The text and cases focus on marketing opportunity analysis, different Internet business models, formulating a customer value proposition, and strategic and operational challenges facing incumbent and new entrant companies in the marketspace.

Chapter 10, **Marketing Strategy Reformulation: The Control Process**, focuses on the appraisal of marketing action for the purpose of developing reformulation and recovery marketing strategies. Considerations and techniques applicable to strategic and operations control are introduced in the text and cases.

Chapter 11, **Comprehensive Marketing Programs**, raises issues in developing integrated marketing strategies. Attention is placed on marketing strategy decisions for new and existing products and services. Issues related to marketing mix sensitivities, marketing strategy implementation and marketing organization are introduced.

Appendix B contains a full-length actual case and a "student analysis" of the case. This feature is welcomed by students who like to see the nature and scope of a thorough written case analysis.

A **Subject, Company, Brand Index** allows students and faculty to identify the use of important concepts across text and case material.

The case selection represents a broad overview of contemporary strategic marketing problems. Fully 76 percent of the cases are dated since 1995 and 40 percent are dated since 1998. Of the 42 cases included, 30 deal with consumer products and services; 12 cases have a business-to-business marketing orientation. Nine cases introduce marketing issues in the international and global arena. Marketing of services and in the not-for-profit sector are addressed in four cases, and four cases deal with electronic commerce. Sixty-one percent of the cases are new, revised, or updated cases for this edition and many have spreadsheet applications imbedded in the case analysis. All text and case material has been classroom tested.

The cases provide an opportunity to apply marketing concepts and practices in a wide variety of industry settings. These industry settings include the soft drink, semiconductor, pharmaceutical, housewares, computer, snack food, confectionery, footwear, pet food, public accounting, health care, cosmetics, industrial equipment, automotive, disposable diaper, beer, book, grocery and convenience store retailing, airline and industries among others.

Equally important, the cases require thoughtful student analysis. Every case has a decision orientation and almost all of the cases necessitate meaningful numerical and financial analysis. Yet, the cases are not so lengthy as to be unduly burdensome. The average case length is approximately 15 pages. Students will need three to four hours to properly prepare most of the cases. The cases can be easily taught in a 75-minute class period.

Instructor's Manual

The **Instructor's Manual** is designed to assist instructors in preparing for class case discussions and developing a rigorous case-oriented marketing management course.

Comprehensive Teaching Notes

Our experience in teaching cases has led us to conclude that thorough case teaching notes are a must for instructors. Therefore, we have paid particular attention to developing notes that will assist instructors in analyzing and teaching the cases in this book. We believe the teaching notes in the **Instructor's Manual** are among the best available. A new addition to this edition is the inclusion of **PowerPoint Slides** for each chapter and case.

Many of the teaching notes contain figures and exhibits that are suitable as transparency masters. Experience suggests that these figures and exhibits prove useful in integrating important points in the case and motivating the class discussion. Each teaching note contains five parts:

Synopsis. The synopsis is an overview of the case, including the principal issues to be addressed and decisions to be made.

Teaching Objectives/Suggestions. This part of the note specifies (1) what the student is expected to experience/learn from the case, and (2) how the instructor might teach the case. A list of discussion/assignment questions is also provided. These questions can be posed to students prior to or during a class discussion. In addition, the suitability of the case for examination or group presentation purposes is also discussed.

Areas for Discussion/Analysis. This part of the note contains a detailed case analysis. This analysis is typically oriented around the discussion/assignment questions and follows the format described in the Case Analysis Worksheet given in Chapter 3 of the casebook. We have found that the repetitive use of this general format is a valuable learning objective apart from the cases themselves.

Epilogue. Where possible, the actions or decisions made by the principal(s) in the case are provided as well as the rationale for a decision or action. This feature is particularly well received by students.

Summary Points. The last part of the note provides selected observations or conceptual generalizations drawn from the case. We have found that the learning experience is enhanced if students can see the broader implications of the case problem and analysis. Therefore, instructors might consider highlighting these points for students at the conclusion of the case discussion. In short, the instructor will be telling students what they should have learned from the case.

Every effort has been made to assure that the teaching notes are comprehensive and numerically error-free. Suggestions for improving case teaching notes are welcome.

Case teaching notes reflect the judgments, opinions, and analyses of the authors or specific case writer where noted based on information contained in the case. The teaching notes were prepared to assist the instructor in examining issues present in the case and are not designed to illustrate appropriate or inappropriate handling of the decision or issue faced by the organization. In some instances, all of the factors bearing on the decision or issue are not described in the case. Therefore, the decision or analysis presented in a teaching note may differ from the decision or analysis made by the organization. Instructors should consider these factors when describing what happened or a company's decision at the conclusion of a class case discussion.

Acknowledgments. We wish to thank the case writers who have shared their teaching notes and insights with us. Each is acknowledged on the first page of the teaching note for their case. We also wish to thank previous adopters of the text for (1) calling our attention to new material for the teaching notes, (2) suggestions on how the cases could be revised and taught, (3) correcting errors in the teaching notes. Their attention to these matters is sincerely appreciated.

EXERCISES IN FINANCIAL ANALYSIS AND MARKETING DECISION MAKING

The exercises or problems following Chapter 2 were prepared to give students an opportunity to apply text material to straightforward problems in financial analysis. Chapter 2 covers material dealing with (a) fixed and variable costs, (b) relevant costs, (c) margins, (d) break-even analysis, (e) liquidity, (f) operating leverage, (g) discounted cash flow, and (h) preparation of pro forma income statements.

It is recommended that Chapter 2 and the problems be assigned early in the course. Students are typically assigned the text material and several problems for one 75-minute class session. The instructor would then provide an overview and have the class prepare the answers to the questions following each problem. Each problem is accompanied by text that is designed to elaborate on the answers themselves. We have found it useful for instructors to provide commentary for students on what they have calculated so they come to better appreciate the meaning and implications of their financial analyses.

PROBLEM 1: STUDIO RECORDINGS, INC.

Purpose

The purpose of this problem is to introduce students to simple calculations involved in break-even analysis. Specific topics addressed are (a) the determination of fixed and variable cost, and (b) profit impact analysis.

Assignment

1. **Calculate the contribution per CD unit**

Selling price to CD distributor		$9.00
Less: Variable cost		
CD Package and disk (direct material/labor)	$1.25/unit	
Songwriter's royalties	$0.35/unit	
Recording artists' royalties	$1.00/unit	
Total variable cost		2.60
Contribution per CD unit		$6.40

2. **Calculate the break-even volume in CD units and dollars**

Total Fixed Cost:	Advertising and promotion	$275,000
	Studio Recordings, Inc. overhead	250,000
	Total	$525,000

    Contribution per CD unit (from #1 above) $6.40

    Contribution margin   ($9.00 - $2.60)/$9.00 = .711 or 71.1%

    $$\text{Break-even volume in units} = \frac{\$525,000}{\$6.40} = 82,031.25 \text{ units}$$

    $$\text{Break-even volume in dollars} = \frac{\$525,000}{.711} = \$738,396.62$$

    $$= 82,031.25 \times \$9.00 = \$738,281.25$$

    (difference is due to rounding the contribution margin percent)

3. Calculate the net profit if 1 million CDs are sold

	Total Sales (1,000,000 units x $9.00)	$9,000,000
Less:	Total Variable Cost (1,000,000 units x $2.60)	2,600,000
Less:	Total Fixed Cost	525,000
	Net Profit	$5,875,000

4. Calculate the necessary CD unit volume to achieve a $200,000 profit

Profit objective = $200,000

Fixed cost = $525,000

Contribution per Unit = $6.40

$$\frac{\$525,000 \text{ Fixed Cost} + \$200,000 \text{ Profit Objective}}{\$6.40 \text{ Contribution per Unit}} = 113,281.25 \text{ units}$$

PROBLEM 2: VIDEO CONCEPTS, INC. (A)

Purpose

The purpose of this problem is to introduce students to distinctions among investment, fixed, and variable costs in the context of calculating contribution margins, breakeven points, and market share requirements. As such, it is similar to problems 1 and 4.

Assignment

1. **What is VCI's unit contribution and contribution margin?**

Selling price for VCI:	$20.00	Suggested retail price
	− 8.00	Retailer margin (40% of
	$12.00	suggested retail price)

   Variable cost per unit
   - Copy Reproduction ($4,000/1000) — $4.00
   - Label & Package Mfg. ($500/1000) — .50
   - Royalties ($500/1000) — .50

   Total variable cost per unit — $5.00

   Unit contribution = $12.00 − $5.00 = $7.00

   Contribution margin = $\dfrac{\$7.00}{\$12.00}$ = .583 or 58.3%

2. What is the breakeven point in units? In dollars?

Fixed Costs:
    Distribution rights for film $125,000
    Label design   5,000
    Advertising   35,000
    Package design   5,000
    $175,000

$$\text{Breakeven points in units} = \frac{\$175,000}{\$7.00} = 25,000 \text{ units}$$

$$\text{Breakeven points in dollars} = \frac{\$175,000}{.583} = \$300,172$$

3. What share of the market would the film have to achieve to earn a 20 percent return on VCI's investment the first year?

20 percent return first year $150,000 (investment) x .20 = $30,000

Fixed cost plus required return $175,000 + $30,000 = $205,000

Units required to achieve return $\dfrac{\$205,000}{\$7.00} = 29,286 \text{ units}$

Market share required $\dfrac{29,286 \ (\text{B/E Unit Volume})}{100,000 \ (\text{Est. Mkt. Size})} = .293 \text{ or } 29.3\%$

PROBLEM 3: AMERICAN THERAPEUTIC CORPORATION

Purpose

The purpose of this problem is to introduce students to basic calculations involved with incrementalism and the implications of the concept. Specifically, an incremental increase in advertising expenditures and a 10% decrease in price are posed for analysis. As such, it is similar to problems 1 and 4.

Assignment

1. What absolute increase in unit sales and dollar sales will be necessary to recoup the incremental increase in advertising expenditures for Rash-Away? Red-Away?

$$\text{Rash-Away: Contribution Margin} = \frac{\$2.00 - \$1.40}{\$2.00} = 30\%$$

$$\text{Absolute Increase in Units Sales} = \frac{\$150,000}{\$.60} = 250,000 \text{ units}$$

$$\text{Absolute Increase in Dollar Sales} = \frac{\$150,000}{.30} = \$500,000$$

$$\text{Red-Away: Contribution Margin} = \frac{\$1.00 - \$.25}{\$1.00} = 75\%$$

$$\text{Absolute Increase in Unit Sales} = \frac{\$150,000}{\$.75} = 200,000 \text{ units}$$

$$\text{Absolute Increase in Dollar Sales} = \frac{\$150,000}{.75} = \$200,000$$

2. How many additional sales dollars must be produced to cover each $1.00 of incremental advertising for Rash-Away? Red-Away?

$$\text{Rash-Away:} \quad \frac{\$1.00 \text{ incremental advertising}}{30\% \text{ contribution margin}} = \$3.33$$

Sales	$3.33
Variable Costs (70%)	2.33
Contribution Margin (30%)	$1.00
Incremental Fixed Cost	1.00
Profit	0

Red-Away: $\dfrac{\$1.00 \text{ incremental advertising}}{75\% \text{ contribution margin}} = \$1.33$

Sales	$1.33
Variable Costs (25%)	0.33
Contribution Margin (75%)	$1.00
Incremental Fixed Cost	1.00
Profit	0

Note: The instructor should highlight the difference in sales dollars necessary to recoup incremental expenditures. Specifically, the instructor should note that when the contribution margin is small, large increase in sales volume are required before noticeable increases in profit are observed as evident in the Rash-Away situation. Alternatively, when the contribution is large, small increases in sales volume are required as is evident in the Red-Away situation.

The size of the contribution margin influences expenditures such as advertising. This is one reason why we see substantially larger advertising expenditures for such consumer products as cosmetics and soft drinks, but smaller expenditures for industrial equipment.

3. **What increase in absolute unit sales and dollar sales will be necessary to maintain the level of total contribution dollars if the price for each product is reduced by 10 percent?**

Rash-Away:
Current Contribution Dollars = 1,000,000 units x $.60 = $600,000

New Price and Contribution with 10% Price Reduction =
 $1.80 Unit Price
 1.40 Unit Variable Costs
 $ .40 Unit Contribution or 22.22% Contribution Margin ($.40/$1.80)

$.40(x) = $600,000, where x = units
 x = 1,500,000 units

Increase in Unit Sales = **500,000** (1,500,000 - 1,000,000 = 500,000)

.2222(x) = $600,000, where x = dollars
 x = $2,700,000 (rounded since contribution margin is actually 22.2222%)

Increase in Dollar Sales = $700,000 ($2,700,000 − $2,000,000)

<u>Red-Away</u>
Current Contribution Dollars = 1,500,000 units x $.75 = $1,125,000

New Price and Contribution with 10% Price Reduction =
$.90 Unit Price
.25 Unit Variable Costs
$.65 Unit Contribution, or 72.22% Contribution Margin ($.65/$.90)

$.65(x) = $1,125,000, where x = units
x = 1,730,769 units

Increase in Unit Sales = 230,769   (1,730,769 - 1,500,000 = 230,769)

.7222 (x) = $1,125,000, where x = dollars
x = $1,557,692 (rounded since contribution margin is actually 72.2222%)

Increase in Dollar Sales = $57,692 ($1,557,692 − $1,500,000)

Note: Some instructors might wish to elaborate on these calculations from a managerial perspective. In the Rash-Away example, unit sales must increase by 500,000 units which represents a percentage change in quantity of 50 percent. In the Red-Away example, unit sales must increase by 230,769 units which represents a percentage change in quantity of 15.4 percent.

The percentage change in quantity relative to a percentage change in price allows for the calculation of an implicit price elasticity of demand:

Rash-Away: $E_{qp} = \dfrac{50\%}{-10\%} = -5$

Red-Away: $E_{qp} = \dfrac{15.4\%}{-10\%} = -1.54$

From a managerial perspective, the price elasticity of -5 for Rash-Away indicates that demand for this product must be quite elastic before a price reduction can be profitable. If management does not believe that demand is sufficiently price elastic for Rash-Away, then the alternative of reducing its price by 10 percent is not economically justified given its unit variable costs. (For an extended discussion of this topic, see Kent B. Monroe, <u>Pricing: Making Profitable Decisions</u> 2nd ed. New York: McGraw-Hill, Inc., 1990, pp. 179-180.)

PROBLEM 4: DIVERSIFIED CITRUS INDUSTRIES

Purpose

The purpose of this problem is to provide a straightforward exercise dealing with (a) trade margins, (b) the determination of variable costs, particularly coupons, (c) break-even analysis as it relates to relevant and sunk costs, and (d) break-even share of market when the "served market" is a consideration.

Assignment

1. At what price will Diversified Citrus Industries be selling their product to wholesalers?

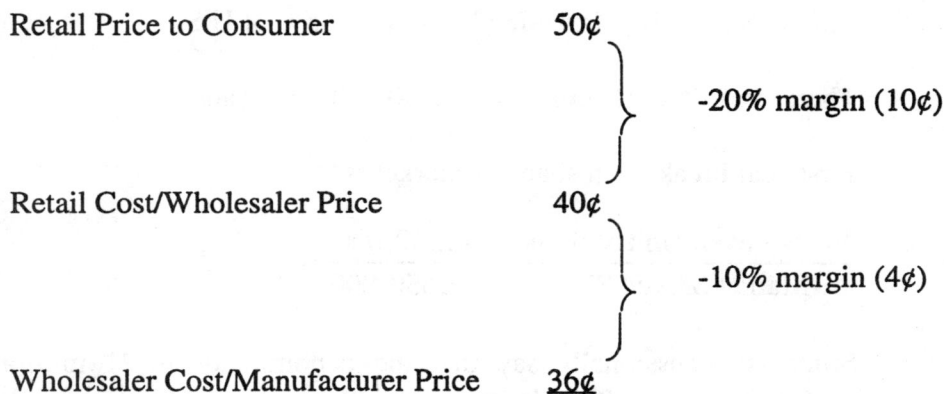

2. What is the contribution per unit for ZAP?

Unit Selling Price = $.36

Unit Variable Costs:

Material	$.18	
Labor	.06	
Coupon	.04	.28
(1/5 x 20¢ = 4¢)		

      Contribution per unit = $.08

13

3. **What is the break-even unit volume in the first year?**

   Total Fixed Costs:

Advertising	$250,000	
Overhead	90,000	$340,000

   Contribution per unit $.08

   $$\text{Break-even Unit Volume} = \frac{\$340,000}{\$.08} = 4,250,000 \text{ units}$$

   Note: Students should not include the $300,000 for research and development. This cost is a **sunk cost**.

4. **What is the first year break-even share-of-market?**

   Total U.S. Market Size = 21 million 8-oz. cans

   Market Served by Marketing Program = 65% of U.S.

   Therefore, .65 x 21 million = 13,650,000 8-oz. cans

   First year break-even share-of-market is:

   $$\frac{\text{Break-even Unit Volume}}{\text{Market Served Size}} = \frac{4,250,000}{13,650,000} = .31 \text{ or } 31\%$$

Note: Students occassionally say that the denominator is 21 million units, not 13,650,000 units. **This is incorrect.** Students should be reminded that since the marketing program for ZAP is only directed at a portion of the total market, this portion is the **relevant served** market. It is sometimes instructive to ask students: "What if the 'market size' for breakfast drinks **globally** was, say, 50 million eight-ounce cans. Would the denominator then be 50 million?"

PROBLEM 5: VIDEO CONCEPTS, INC. (B)

Purpose

This problem introduces studens to the concept of product cannibalism and the importance of focusing on the contribution of a product-line additon to fixed costs rather than simply its incremental sales. The problem is similar to problem 6. Consequently, they can be assigned independently or in tandem to reinforce each other.

Assignment

1. **Should VCI add new Model LXR to its line of VCRs? Why?**

    Present product line contribution

Product	Selling Price	Unit Variable Cost	Units Sold	Contribution
LX1	$175.00	$100.00	2,000	$150,000
LX2	$250.00	$125.00	1,000	125,000
LX3	$300.00	$140.00	500	80,000
			Total 3,500	$355,000

    Note: LX1 present contribution is ($175.00 − $100.00) x 2,000 = $150,000

    If LX4 is added to the present product line, it will cannibalize the sales of the present product line as shown below:

Total product sales of LX4	300 units	
Cannibalized sales (60%)	180 units	
From LX1 (10%)		18 units
From LX2 (30%)		54 units
From LX3 (60%)		108 units
Incremental Sales (40%)	120 units	

    Product contribution if LX4 added

LX1	($175.00 − $100.00) x 1982 =	$148,650
LX2	($250.00 − $125.00) x 946 =	118,250
LX3	($300.00 − $140.00) x 392 =	62,720
		$329,620
LX4	($375.00 − $225.00) x 300 =	$ 45,000
Total product line contribution		$374,620

The addition of the LX4 model does increase product line contribution by $19,620 (Original Contribution = $355,000 vs. New Contribution = $374,620). However, VCI will incur an incremental fixed cost of $20,000 to add the LX4 model to the line. Therefore, VCI incurs a loss of $380: $19,620 − $20,000 = −$380. The decision? Do not introduce LX4 because incremental contribution does not cover incremental fixed cost.

PROBLEM 6: DYSK COMPUTER, INC.

Purpose

The purpose of this problem is to introduce students to basic calculations required to perform a cannibalism analysis when a new product is being added to the product line. In addition, contribution analysis is again emphasized.

Assignment

1. Should Mr. Leonard add the DC6900-X model to the line?

This problem can be approached in two ways.

Approach 1.

Given:

Product	Unit Selling Price	-	Unit Variable Cost	=	Unit Contribution
DC6900-Omega	$5,900	-	$2,200	=	$3,700
DC6900-Alpha	$2,500	-	$1,200	=	$1,300
DC6900-X	$3,900	-	$1,800	=	$2,100

Fixed cost for introducing the DC6900-X in the First Year = $2,000,000.

Therefore:

    1. The DC6900 line will **lose** $1,600 in unit contribution each time a sales is diverted away from the DC6900-Omega to the DC6900-X. This occurs because the DC6900-X contribution is $2,100 and the DC6900-Omega contribution is $3,700.

    2. The DC6900 line will **gain** $800 in unit contribution each time a sale is diverted away from the DC6900-Alpha to the DC6900-X. This occurs because the DC6900-X contribution is $2100 and the DC6900-Alpha contribution is $1,300.

    3. Given that the problem states that 30% of the DC6900-X sales (.3 x 500,000 units), or 150,000 units will be cannibalized from the DC6900-Omega, the total contribution **lost** will be $1,600 x 150,000 units = $240,000,000.

4. Given that the problem states that 20% of the DC6900-X sales (.2 x 500,000 units), or 100,000 units will be cannibalized from the DC6900-Alpha, the total contribution **gained** will be $800 x 100,000 units = $80,000,000.

5. Given that the problem states that the DC6900-X will sell an additional 250,000 units at a $2,100 unit contribution, then incremental net new volume will be $2,100 x 250,000 = $525,000,000.

6. The net financial effect of the DC6900-X will be:

Net New Volume	$525,000,000
+ Gain from DC6900-Alpha	80,000,000
	$605,000,000
- Loss Due to Cannibalism from DC6900-Omega	240,000,000
- Less Fixed Cost of Introduction	2,000,000
	+ $363,000,000

Approach 2.

Product	Next Year Unit Volume	Unit Contribution	Contribution Dollars
DC6900-Alpha	500,000	$1,300	$ 650,000,000
DC6900-Omega	250,000	$3,700	925,000,000
	750,000		$1,575,000,000
+DC6900-X			
Cannibalized Vol.	250,000	$2,100	$ 525,000,000
Incremental Vol.	250,000	$2,100	525,000,000
	1,250,000		$1,575,000,000
Less Original Forecast For:			
DC6900-Alpha	600,000	$1,300	$780,000,000
DC6900-Omega	400,000	$3,700	$1,480,000,000
	1,000,000		$2,260,000,000
Less Fixed Costs			$2,000,000
			$363,000,000

In summary, Dysk should add the DC6900-X model as it will make a $363 million profit before tax.

PROBLEM 7: SPORTS NUTRITION COMPANY

Purpose

The purpose of this problem is to introduce students to the mechanics of present value analysis. Specific emphasis is placed on calculating discounted cash flow using two different discount rates – 20 percent and 15 percent – and employing the decision rule when interpreting net present value: An investment should be accepted if the net present value is positive and rejected if it is negative.

Instructors should note that the 20 percent discount rate factors need to be calculated, whereas the 15 percent discount rate factors are shown in Chapter 2: Exhibit 2.3. This was done purposely so that students can actually do the calculations rather than simply applying given discount factors. However, the instructor should expect that a student might have actually consulted his/her finance text or some other source to obtain the discount rates.

Assignment

1. **Should the company proceed with the development of the product if the discount rate is 20 percent? Why?**

Year	Cash Flow	Discount Factor (Rounded)	Discounted Cash Flow
0	($17,500,000)	1.000 [$1/(1+.20)^0$]	($17,500,000)
1	$ 6,100,000	.833 [$1/(1+.20)^1$]	$ 5,081,300
2	$ 7,400,000	.694 [$1/(1+.20)^2$]	$ 5,135,600
3	$ 7,000,000	.579 [$1/(1+.20)^3$]	$ 4,053,000
4	$ 5,500,000	.482 [$1/(1+.20)^4$]	$ 2,651,000
		Net Present Value	($ 579,100)

<u>No.</u>

This analysis indicates that the net present value is negative. Therefore, it is not advisable to proceed with the development of the product when the discount rate is 20 percent.

2. **Does the decision to proceed with development of the product change if the discount rate is 15 percent? Why?**

Year	Cash Flow	Discount Factor (Exh. 2.3)	Discounted Cash Flow
0	($17,500,000)	1.000	($17,500,000)
1	$ 6,100,000	.870	$ 5,307,000
2	$ 7,400,000	.756	$ 5,594,400
3	$ 7,000,000	.658	$ 4,606,000
4	$ 5,500,000	.572	$ 3,146,000
		Net Present Value	$ 1,153,400

Yes.

This analysis indicates that the decision is to proceed with the development of the product when the discount rate is 15 percent. With a 15 percent discount rate, the net present value becomes positive.

PROBLEM 8: CENTURY OFFICE SYSTEMS, INC.

Purpose

The purpose of this problem is to provide students with an opportunity to prepare a **pro forma** income statement. Specific topics include (a) the preparation of a **pro forma** income statement, (b) consideration of changes in net profit before taxes assuming a projected sales do not materialize, and (c) further application of break-even analysis.

Assignment

1. Prepare a pro forma income statement for the Home Office Systems group given the information provided.

This question is designed to get students thinking about how a **pro forma** income statement is formatted, address cost allocation issues, and consider fixed versus variable cost elements of various activities. The following information is provided:

a.	Sales forecast	$25,000,000
b.	Product line direct material and labor costs	50% of the sales
c.	Freight costs	8% of sales
d.	Indirect manufacturing overhead	$ 600,000
e.	Administrative overhead	$ 300,000
f.	Sales force expenses	
	• Sales allocation (40% of $7.5 million)	$ 3,000,000
	• Commissions	15% of sales
g.	Advertising/sales promotion expenses	
	• Trade advertising & sales promotion production and media costs	$ 300,000
	• Co-op advertising production costs	$ 100,000
	• Co-op advertising allowances	5% of sales
h.	Staff salaries & benefits	$ 250,000

The **pro forma** income statement, given the information provided, is shown in Exhibit 1. Students should recognize that:

a. Many costs have both a fixed and a variable component as was the case with sales force and advertising expenses.

b. Costs are often allocated based on negotiation. This was done with allocation of indirect manufacturing and administrative overhead costs. An instructor might note that the allocation process sometimes is arbitrary and that cost allocation can spell the difference between a profitable or unprofitable venture.

c. Costs are both programmed and committed. Examples of committed costs are general and administrative expenses. Programmed costs are often marketing expenses.

2. Prepare a pro forma income statement for the Home Office Systems group if annual sales of only $20 million materialize.

The purpose of this question is to focus student attention on a "what if" scenario. The **pro forma** income statement with a $20 million sales forecast is shown in Exhibit 2. Students should recognize two points after completing this assignment question:

a. A 20 percent projected decline in sales does not necessarily produce a 20 percent cost reduction. Many costs are fixed. While total cost of goods sold and freight expenses decrease by 20 percent (these costs are variable), all general and administrative costs remain and marketing expenses decline by only 13.5 percent since they are largely fixed.

b. Students might be directed to the fact that the other scenarios are possible. For instance, if sales are unchanged at $25 million, but cost of goods sold increases as a percent of sales from 50 percent to 60 percent of sales, gross margin again becomes $10 million ($25 million - $15 million), other costs remain unchanged and an identical loss of $150,000 results.

3. At what level of dollar sales will the Home Office Systems group break-even?

This question is designed to provide an opportunity to perform a break-even analysis given a more elaborate context. In order to perform a break-even analysis, students must explicitly identify the variable and fixed costs of the Home Office Systems group. The variable costs in this example are all expressed as a percent of sales and total 78 percent of sales:

Cost of Goods Sold	50 percent of sales
Sales commissions	15 percent of sales
Cooperative Advertising Allowances	5 percent of sales
Freight Expenses	8 percent of sales
TOTAL	78 percent of sales

Fixed costs include both committed and programmed costs and include:

Sales Force Allocation	$ 3,000,000
Manufacturing Overhead	$ 600,000
Administrative Overhead	$ 300,000
Production and Media Costs for:	
Trade & Sales Promotion	$ 300,000
Co-op Advertising	$ 100,000
Staff Salaries & Benefits	$ 250,000
TOTAL	$ 4,550,000

The **contribution margin** for the Home Office Systems group is 22 percent (1-.78). Therefore, the break-even dollar sales figure is:

$$\frac{\text{Break-even}}{\text{Sales}} = \frac{\text{Fixed Cost}}{\text{Contribution Margin}} = \frac{\$4,550,000}{.22} = \$20,681,818$$

A **pro forma** income statement which confirms the break-even sales allocation is shown in Exhibit 3. Students should recognize from this exercise that:

a. Break-even calculations and **pro forma** income statement analysis complement each other. That is, cost-volume-profit relationships underlie much of what appears in **pro forma** income statements and vice-versa.

b. Contribution margin can be calculated both in an aggregated fashion as shown below:

$$\text{Contribution Margin} = \frac{\text{Total Sales - Total Variable Cost}}{\text{Total Sales}}$$

Alternatively, contribution margin can be computed on a unit basis:

$$\text{Contribution Margin} = \frac{\text{Unit Selling Price - Unit Variable Cost}}{\text{Unit Selling Price}}$$

An aggregate contribution margin is typically applied in the case of multiple products and services. A unit contribution margin only applies to individual products and services.

EXHIBIT 1

PRO FORMA INCOME STATEMENT

HOME OFFICE SYSTEMS

Sales		$25,000,000
Cost of Goods Sold		12,500,000
Gross Margin		$12,500,000
Marketing Expenses		
Sales Expenses	$6,750,000	
Advertising/Sales Promotion Expenses	1,650,000	
Freight Expenses	2,000,000	10,400,000
General and Administrative Expenses		
Administrative Overhead	$ 300,000	
Manufacturing Overhead	600,000	
Staff Salaries & Benefits	250,000	1,150,000
Net Profit Before (Income) Tax		$ 950,000

EXHIBIT 2

PRO FORMA INCOME STATEMENT

HOME OFFICE SYSTEMS

Sales		$20,000,000
Cost of Goods Sold		10,000,000
Gross Margin		$10,000,000
Marketing Expenses		
Sales Expenses	$6,000,000	
Advertising/Sales Promotion Expenses	1,400,000	
Freight Expenses	1,600,000	9,000,000
General and Administrative Expenses		
Administrative Overhead	$ 300,000	
Manufacturing Overhead	600,000	
Staff Salaries & Benefits	250,000	1,150,000
Net Profit Before (Income) Tax		($ 150,000)

EXHIBIT 3

PRO FORMA INCOME STATEMENT

HOME OFFICE SYSTEMS

Sales		$20,681,818
Cost of Goods Sold		10,340,909
Gross Margin		$10,340,909
Marketing Expenses		
Sales Expenses	$6,102,272.70	
Advertising/Sales Promotion Expenses	1,434,090.90	
Freight Expenses	1,654,545.40	9,190,909
General and Administrative Expenses		
Administrative Overhead	$ 300,000	
Manufacturing Overhead	600,000	
Staff Salaries & Benefits	250,000	1,150,000
Net Profit Before (Income) Tax		0

QUETZAL COLLECTIONS, INC.

Synopsis

Quetzal Collections, Inc. is an importer and distributor of authentic South American and African artifacts and Southwestern Indian jewelry and pottery. The firm has maintained an exclusive distribution policy marketing its lines through specialty dealers, "showings," and a "few exclusive department stores." This policy was presumably adopted because of limited supplies of product.

In recent years, Quetzal's product line has gained in popularity, the number of importers has increased, customers are sending out their own buyers to purchase items, "nonauthentic" items and replicas are being distributed by less exclusive stores and less reputable dealers at lower prices, and the company is experiencing greater difficulty in obtaining authentic items.

Quetzal has been approached by a mass merchandise store concerning the possibility of carrying its complete line. The tentative contract called for a purchase of items at 10% below existing prices with an initial purchase of $750,000. The contact would mean that Quetzal would have to triple its production of replicas. A possibility of selling $4 million annually was quoted by store representatives. Quetzal is faced with the decision of whether to accept this offer. A more fundamental issue implicit in Quetzal's decision is the linking of distinctive competencies with the "marketing opportunity."

Teaching Objectives

Three teaching objectives should be emphasized in this case:

1. Students should recognize the importance of business definition and distinctive competence when assessing marketing opportunities.

2. Success requirements often differ between different market segments.

3. The attractiveness of a marketing opportunity depends on competitive activity, buyer requirements, demand/supply relationships, political forces, and organizational capabilities.

Teaching Suggestions

This short case has been used in a variety of contexts. It is placed in the Opportunity Analysis and Marketing Targeting section because it raises basic issues in business definition, identifying a firm's distinctive competency, and assessing a marketing opportunity. The case can also be used in the Marketing Channel Strategy and Management portion of the course since it raises issues related to channel modification in a changing environment.

Specific questions that might be posed to students prior to or during class discussion include:

1. How might one describe the product-market matrix for Quetzal's products?

2. How would one define Quetzal's business?

3. How would accepting the mass merchandiser's offer affect Quetzal's business definition?

4. What is Quetzal's distinctive competency?

5. What is the apparent relationship between Quetzal and its distributors and how might the contract affect it?

6. Under what conditions should Quetzal accept the offer?

Areas for Discussion/Analysis

A. How Might One Describe the Product-Market Matrix for Quetzal's Products?

The market for Quetzal's product line is essentially a narrow one due to the specialty type of product: authentic South American and African artifacts would most likely appeal to fairly upper middle class collectors of such items. Jewelry and replicas are not so clear-cut as evidenced somewhat by the recent popularity among the "mass market." However, is this Quetzal's target market? Probably not. Some instructors might identify this phenomenon as evidence of the "trickle-down" theory at work. The nature of the product-market matrix for the general product type is described below. Quetzal would be presumably satisfying the authentic/collector group.

Product (Offering)	Market "Mass"	"Collectors"
Authentic Artifacts		X
Non-Authentic Replicas	X	

B. How Would One Define Quetzal's Business? How Might Accepting the Contract Affect Quetzal's Business Definition?

1. Quetzal's business definition can be defined by **customer group, buyer needs,** and the **means for satisfying buyer needs**.

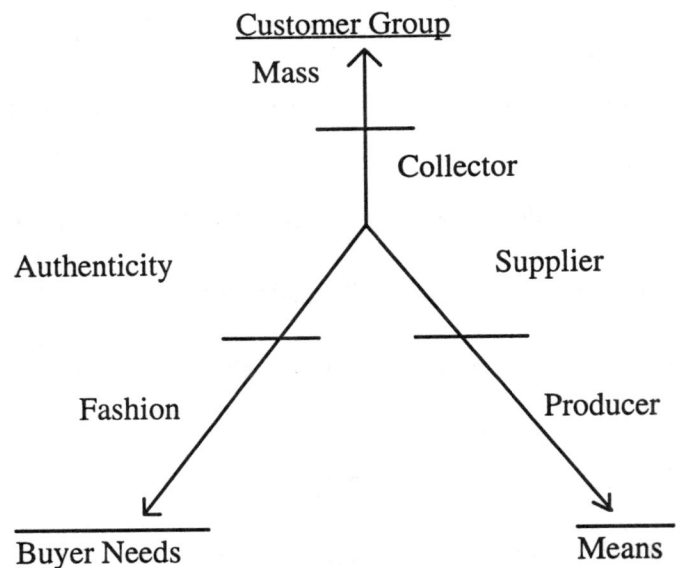

Quetzal's business would seem to be defined as a **supplier of authentic artifacts to collectors**.

2. If Quetzal should accept the contract offer, then its business might be redefined as a **producer of fashionable items to the mass market**.

C. What is Quetzal's Distinctive Competency?

1. As described in Chapter 1, a firm's distinctive competency relates to its principal strengths and skills. These strengths and skills become **distinctive** when (a) they are imperfectly imitable by competitors and (b) make a significant contribution to the benefits perceived by customers and by doing so, create value for them.

2. Quetzal's distinctive competency lies in its ability to provide: (1) specialized buying skills which virtually "guarantee" the authenticity of its items, (2) provide a sufficiently wide assortment of these items to be the sole source of supply for many of its retail distributors, and (3) the ability to obtain a sufficient supply of items. For these reasons, Quetzal has established a national reputation and a competitive advantage.

D. What is Quetzal's Relationship with Existing Distributors?

1. Quetzal's relationship with existing distributors is based on its distinctive competences described above. **Supply of authentic items** would seem to be a major concern for distributors. Also distributors would seem to be adequately suited for the "authentic/collector" market served by Quetzal. Despite the increase in importers, Quetzal is apparently holding its own; sales volume continues to increase, about 20% per year over the past decade.

2. Independent buying of Indian jewelry and replicas by large specialty stores and distributors is a problem. However, it might be questionable if these buyers are obtaining the quality product provided by Quetzal. Rather, these buyers might be securing added supplies of lower quality jewelry and replicas to satisfy the demand. The fashion cycle in jewelry as opposed to South American/African artifacts is important to consider particularly with respect to the mass market versus collector market. Note, too, that artifacts and replicas might also be affected by a fashion cycle among non-collectors.

E. Under What Conditions Should Quetzal Accept the Contract?

1. The contract provisions raise a conflict in Quetzal's channel strategy. Quetzal might consider the contract providing:

   a. The mass merchandise department store channel will become important in the future.

   b. Items are available or quickly procurable in such amounts that satisfying the new channel will not jeopardize existing dealers.

   c. The contract will have little or no negative effect on existing dealers.

2. How important are mass merchandise department stores apt to become to Quetzal? Given the nature of the product (artifacts), the market, and the implied expensiveness, it would seem that slow turnover, knowledgeable salespeople for selling, and reasonably large assortment (depth and width) would be characteristic of this line. All of these characteristics imply that artifacts would not be major items of importance to the "typical" mass merchandiser. However, replicas might become a major item in these types of outlets. They are fashionable, have reasonably high turnover, display space near other jewelry is probably available, and high margins would presumably exist.

3. Are items available or quickly procurable? As long as Quetzal subscribes to the "authenticity" strategy, then it seems that adequate supplies will be a problem. However, can Quetzal sell different items to mass merchandisers? Probably not; the original line is what is being sought through the contract. Other sources are available for lower quality (non-authentic and decorative) items and probably at a cheaper price.

4. Will the contract have an effect on existing dealers? Yes, and probably negative. Although dealer discontent will vary by competitive situation in market areas, a more important issue is the implied question of adequate supplies and dealer competitive advantage. The possibility exists of some existing dealers seeking alternative sources of supply if a shortage occurs, competitive bargaining at the retail level, and potential lost sales volume.

5. Finally, a question arises as to the future environment and the industry as a whole. If Quetzal refuses the contract, another firm will most likely get it. This will have a deleterious effect on Quetzal providing (1) the market served by mass merchandisers has a future (see above) and (2) the market is consistent with Quetzal's competitive strengths. In neither case does this apparent market potential fit with Quetzal's ability or wishes.

E. Epilogue

Quetzal Collections, Inc. (disguised name) did not accept the contract. Recognizing the future problems in obtaining authentic artifacts from foreign countries, Quetzal adopted a novel approach for securing supplies. It began a program of evaluating artifacts for estates and purchasing authentic artifacts from estates. The skills of its buyers in determining authenticity were thus transformed into a **service**. Moreover, the business definition was not changed, but enhanced.

In mid-2000, the company commissioned the development of a web site. The web site featured dealer and department store locations that carried its products and listed dates and locations of company-sponsored showings. The company has elected not to sell products with its web site.

F. Summary Points

1. Business definition is an important consideration in evaluating marketing opportunities.

Quetzal's business definition
Customer Group: Collector
Customer Needs: Authenticity
Technology/Means: Supplier (Buyer)

"Opportunity" requires...
Customer Group: "Mass Market"
Customer Needs: Fashion
Technology/Means: Producer of Replicas

It is clear that the "opportunity" is outside Quetzal's business definition.

2. Success requirements and distinctive competency must match to create a marketing opportunity.

3. Attractiveness of a market opportunity depends on

- Competitive Activity
- Buyer Requirements
- Demand/Supply Relationships
- Political Forces
- Organizational Capabilities

4. Under what conditions might Quetzal accept the contract?

- Mass merchandise department store channel will become important in the future.

- Items are available or quickly procurable in sufficient amounts that satisfying the new channel will not jeopardize existing distributors.

- The contract will have little or no negative effect on existing distributors.

None of these conditions exist.

JONES BLAIR COMPANY

Synopsis

Jones Blair Company (JBC) markets paint and allied products in over 50 counties in Texas, Oklahoma, New Mexico, and Louisiana. The company is facing a situation where overall paint demand has plateaued and competition from mass merchandisers and national paint companies is increasing. These factors combined with JBC's premium price has placed the company in a position where sales growth is likely to decline unless remedial action is taken.

Company president Alexander Barrett is faced with the question of where and how to deploy corporate marketing efforts among the various architectural paint coatings segments served by the company. Company executives are in disagreement over whether emphasis should be placed on the urban (Dallas-Ft. Worth area) versus rural market and the household versus professional painter segment. Proposals related to how JBC might proceed - increased advertising, reduced prices, more sales representatives - are raised for consideration.

An underlying issue, much broader in scope, is where and how JBC will compete in the future. For example, even though the urban segment now accounts for 60 percent of paint volume, by 1999-2000 the rural segment could equal or exceed the urban segment if current growth rates are extrapolated. Similarly, even though the household segment currently accounts for a majority of paint sales in JBC's trade area, this segment is likely to become even more "congested" with private brands and other regional/local paint firms seeking a piece of the pie in the near future. This long-run (say 5 year) view makes for a richer analysis than the simpler short-run issue described above. Moreover, the long-run issue described above casts the entire problem in a different light.

Teaching Objectives

As a case on Opportunity Analysis and Market Targeting, JBC seeks to achieve five objectives. First, students should recognize that a "market" can be segmented in a variety of ways, e.g., by geography and by end users. Second, the attractiveness of a market segment is affected by demand characteristics, extent of competitive activity, buyer requirements and organizational capabilities. Third, students should be introduced to the **"majority fallacy"** concept, i.e., larger segments may be less profitable because they attract disproportionately heavy competition. Fourth, competitive position, as measured by "market share," is influenced by the definition of the "market." Finally, financial and quantitative analysis is necessary to make a thorough opportunity and market targeting decision.

Teaching Suggestions

This case is most suitable for early sessions in the opportunity analysis and market targeting portion of the course. It is recommended, however, that students be exposed to basic concepts of financial analysis in Chapter 2 before being assigned the case.

This case is suitable as an examination exercise early in the course. Specific questions that might be posed to students prior to or during class discussion are:

1. How might one characterize the architectural paint coatings industry and Jones Blair's trade area?

2. How might one segment Jones Blair's market area?

3. Which segment(s) represent opportunities for Jones Blair?

4. What is Jones Blair's competitive position in its market area?

5. Which segment or segments should Jones Blair pursue?

6. What strategy should Jones Blair adopt to reach the segment(s) sought?

Areas for Discussion/Analysis

A. How might the architectural paint industry be characterized?

1. Paint might be viewed as a durable good which is infrequently purchased.

2. The industry is mature as evident by paint being a commodity item, the proliferation of private brands, and gradual slowing of overall volume growth of 1 to 2 percent annually.

3. Competition is increasing at both the manufacturing and retail levels leading to further concentration in the manufacturing sector and vertical integration at the retail level. Also, the industry is facing increased competition from substitute products: aluminum and vinyl siding, interior wall coverings and wood paneling.

4. #2 and #3 indicate that market share gains rather than sales volume gains through primary demand are required. Given the lack of product differentiation (commodity product), share gains are likely through being the low cost producer (lower price) or through company differentiation and performance factors, e.g., service, distribution, segmentation.

B. **How might the Jones Blair market area be characterized?**

1. The Jones Blair Company market area is following the same pattern as the industry as a whole:

   a. Overall dollar sales volume is experiencing an average annual increase of 1% to 2%.

   b. Mass merchandisers - private brands account for 50% of household or do-it-yourselfer sales in DFW, the major urban area in the trade area.

2. Differential growth between urban/rural area is evident from case Exhibit 3:

   a. Dallas-Ft. Worth (urban) dollar volume is flat, or declining slightly.

   b. Rural dollar volume is increasing at average annual increase of about 21% per year, including the recent 15.5% increase between 1995 and 1996.

4. Still, the DFW urban area accounts for a majority of dollar paint and sundry sales; 60 percent or $48 million in 1996.

C. **How might one segment Jones Blair's market area?**

The case makes it apparent that the architectural paint market can be segmented by geography and by end user as follows:

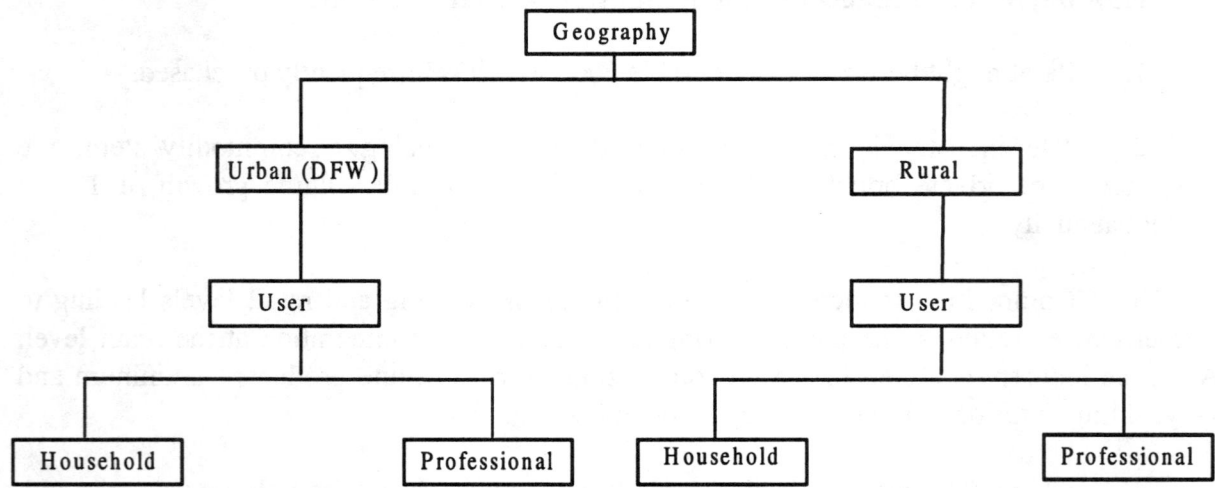

36

D. Which segment(s) represent opportunities for Jones Blair?

Both a quantitative and qualitative analysis are required to address this question in a thorough manner.

1. Quantitative Appraisal

   a. Case notes that the market size is $80 million.

   b. Case notes that 60 percent of sales volume is in the urban area.

   c. Case notes that households account for 70% of the dollar volume in DFW and 90% of the dollar volume in rural areas.

Applying these percentages:

	End User		
Geography	Household	Professional	
Urban (DFW)	$33.6 MM (42%)	$14.4 MM (18%)	$48 million (60%)
Rural	$28.8 MM (36%)	$3.2 MM (4%)	$32 million (40%)
	$62.4 million (78%)	$17.6 million (22%)	$80 million (100%)

At first glance, the household segment (versus professional) or the urban segment (versus rural) offer the most promise given their size.

   d. However, further consideration of these data indicate that:

   - The urban market exhibits little growth (case Exhibit 1) while the rural market is growing rapidly.

   - Household segment volume is probably overstated since 50 percent of the volume in the urban/household segment is captured by mass merchandisers/private brands with a decided price advantage.

   - If private brand dollar volume is removed, then the effective size of the urban/household segment is $16.8 million, or close to the $14.4 million urban/professional painter segment.

2. Qualitative Appraisal

   a. Each of the four segments differs according to buyer requirements and the extent of competitive activity These factors affect the attractiveness of each segment.

   b. Buyer requirements in

   - Urban/Household Segment: Price sensitivity due to heavy price emphasis by mass merchandisers; large number of paint outlets, and outlets carry multiple brands, hence ease of purchase and opportunity for comparative shopping; probably small purchases. Product quality is important, but how knowledgeable is the typical household buyer?

   - Rural/Household Segment: Same as urban do-it-yourselfer, but fewer opportunities for comparative shopping and no mass merchandisers.

   - Rural/Professional Segment: Same as urban/professional.

3. Based on this analysis, it would seem that the **Urban/Professional Segment** and the **Rural/Household and Rural/Professional Segments** represent the principal opportunities for Jones Blair.

E. **What is Jones Blair's Competitive Position in its Market Area?**

Both a quantitative and qualitative analysis are required to address this question.

1. Quantitative Appraisal (DFW) market.

   a. Case notes that JBC sales are distributed evenly between DFW and non-DFW accounts. Hence, 50 percent of JBC sales went to the urban (DFW) market.

   b. Case notes that 70 percent of JBC urban (DFW) sales went to professionals; therefore 30 percent of urban (DFW) sales went to household, or do-it-yourself buyers.

   c. Case notes that 70 percent of JBC rural sales went to households; therefore 30 percent of rural sales went to professional painters in rural areas.

   d. Given that JBC dollar sales volume was $12 million in 1996, JBC's competitive position can be assessed against market size computations as shown in Exhibit 1 in this note.

EXHIBIT 1

JONES BLAIR'S COMPETITIVE POSITION (MARKET SEGMENT SHARES)

	End User Segments		
Geographic Segments	Household	Professional	
Urban	$\dfrac{\$1.8MM}{\$33.6MM} = 5.4\%$ $\dfrac{\$1.8MM}{\$16.8MM} = 10.7\%$ *	$\dfrac{\$4.2MM}{\$14.4MM} = 29.2\%$	$\dfrac{\$6MM}{\$48MM} = 12.5\%$
Rural	$\dfrac{\$4.2MM}{\$28.8MM} = 14.6\%$	$\dfrac{\$1.8MM}{\$3.2MM} = 56.3\%$	$\dfrac{\$6MM}{\$32MM} = 18.75\%$
	$\dfrac{\$6MM}{\$62.4MM} = 9.6\%$	$\dfrac{\$6MM}{\$17.6MM} = 34\%$	$\dfrac{\$12MM}{\$80MM} = 15\%$

*Note: JBC has a market share of 10.7% among non-mass merchandiser paint sold in the urban/household segment.

2. This analysis reveals that while JBC captures 15 percent of the total market, market shares vary dramatically by segment, i.e., JBC has:

    a. 34 percent of the professional painter market

    b. 18.75 percent of the rural market, but more noteworthy

    c. 56.3 percent of the rural/professional market and

    d. 5.4 percent to 10.7 percent of the urban/household market

3. Qualitative Appraisal

    a. JBC is the premium-priced paint in its outlets; it loses at the point of purchase among price shoppers in outlets with multiple brands (typically urban outlets).

    b. JBC's channels (hardware/paint stores, lumber yards) are eroding particularly in urban areas, but holding their own in rural areas despite the presence of Wal-Mart in some rural markets.

    c. JBC faces less overall competition in rural markets, despite Wal-Mart's presence.

    d. Only Wal-Mart currently competes in rural areas, but not in all markets.

F. Which segment or segments should Jones Blair pursue?

1. The previous analysis indicates that JBC prioritize the market segments in order of importance:

    a. Rural/Household Segment

    b. Urban/Professional Segment

    c. Rural/Professional Segment ⎦ These segments may be reversed.

    d. Urban/Household Segment

2. This priority **does not** mean that JBC overlook some segments. Rather, it highlights the importance of the rural/household segment and downgrades the importance of the urban/household segment as an opportunity segment.

G. **What strategy should Jones Blair adopt to reach the segment(s) sought?**

Four approaches are outlined in the case:

- Do nothing different - no change in focus or increase in expenditures

- Increase advertising to the household segment by $350,000 with an emphasis on corporate brand advertising

- Price reduction of 20 percent across-the-board

- Add additional sales reps at a direct cost of $60,000 each

1. **Do Nothing**

    a. **Pros**

    - JBC had been profitable - don't "rock the boat"

    - Primary demand in rural areas will carry JBC given rural distribution

    b. **Cons**

    - JBC's profitability is more illusionary than real - no **real** growth

    - Current situation is a result of a "do nothing" approach

    - Failure to act in the short-term might have long-term negative results, e.g., failure to attack growth segments thus losing the initiative

2. **Increase Advertising to Household Segment by $350,000 for Corporate Brand Awareness (Pull Strategy)**

    a. **Pros**

    - DFW (urban) households account and rural households account for a total of 78 percent of total paint purchased in the JBC market area (see the earlier analysis).

    - Awareness levels are lower than national paint brands and mass merchandiser brands. There is some evidence of an awareness - last brand purchase link (case Exhibit 6).

    - Industry research indicates that advertising affects purchase behavior in terms of where to shop and what brand to buy.

b. **Cons**

- Even though there appears to an advertising - last brand purchase linkage, it also appears that household do-it-yourselfers choose a store for paint first, than a brand (see case Exhibit 2). This suggests emphasis on cooperative advertising featuring stores and brands, not corporate brand advertising.

- Current funds allocated to advertising/sales promotion equals 3 percent of sales or $360,000. Assuming a modest increase in sales volume, then this amount will remain unchanged next year. The added $350,000 represents a doubling of expenditures.

- Given that the vice-president of finance has said that JBC's contribution margin is 35 percent, then the incremental dollar volume to break even on this expenditure can be calculated as follows:

$$B/E = \frac{\$350,000 \text{ (Incremental Expenditure)}}{.35 \text{ (Contribution Margin)}} = \$1,000,000$$

$$B/E = \frac{\$350,000}{(.35-.095)} = \$1,372,549,$$ where .095 or 9.5% is the return on sales

- These figures indicate that JBC must capture an additional 1.6 market share point (1 point = $624,000) of the household market to recoup this expenditure in one year.

- How likely is this given that fewer than 1 in 4 customers are shopping for paint in any one year?

3. **A 20 percent across-the-board price reduction**

    a. **Pros**

    - Will achieve parity with national brands in stores where JBC is one of 2 or 3 brands.

    - Might attract the more price sensitive household buyer and professional painter.

b. **Cons**

- Dealers might not favor such an approach since it will eliminate customary price lines.

- Profit consequences are severe:

    JBC Contribution is 35% or .35 x $12 MM = $4,200,00

    A 20% reduction in price translates into a reduction in contribution dollars:

	Current	Price Reduction (20%)
Sales	$1.00	$.80
Var. Cost	.65	.65
Contribution	$ .35	$ .15 (New Contribution = .15/.80 = 18.75%)

    JBC will need sales of $22.4 million to match the $4,200,000 contribution:

    $4,200,000/.1875 = $22,400,000, or increase sales by almost twofold!

4. **Add sales representatives to increase retail distribution or call on professional painters.**

    a. Before an analysis of this option is performed, it should be recognized that adding one sales representative will require an incremental increase in sales of $171,428 ($235,294 with a 9.5% profit):

    $$\frac{\text{Cost of One Rep}}{\text{Contribution Margin}} = \frac{\$60,000}{.35} = \$171,428$$

    b. Furthermore, the revenue from one professional painter and one retail outlet should be computed:

    - 1 Prof. Painter in DFW =

    $$\frac{\$4.2\text{MM Sales}}{400 \text{ Prof. Painters}} = \$10,500 / \text{Yr.}$$

- 1 Prof. Painter in Rural Areas =
  $$\frac{\$1.8\text{MM Sales}}{200 \text{ Prof. Painters}} = \$9,000 / \text{Yr.}$$

- 1 Outlet in DFW (based on current performance and 40% of JBC 200 outlets in DFW):
  $$\frac{\$1.8\text{MM}}{80 \text{ outlets}} = \$22,500 / \text{Yr.}$$

- 1 Outlet in Rural Areas (based on current performance and 60% of JBC 200 outlets in rural areas):
  $$\frac{\$4.2\text{MM}}{120 \text{ outlets}} = \$35,000 / \text{Yr.}$$

(These averages are for illustrative purposes only. Given the account/sales distribution shown in case Exhibit 4 they may be low due to the skewed distribution. For example, even though a DFW outlet averages $22,500/Yr., only 19 percent of DFW outlets sells this amount; 81 percent sell over $25,000/Yr. Similarly, there is likely to be great variance in sales among professional painters given the range from one person operations to the larger painting firms.)

 c. Add sales rep(s) to focus on adding new outlets.

  Most likely successful if emphasis placed on rural areas since it is unlikely JBC will be little more than one among 2 to 3 brands in urban area outlets. Growth in rural areas also suggests potential new outlets might be willing to handle JBC rather than convincing established dealers to convert to JBC.

 d. Add rep(s) to focus on attracting professional painters.

  Most likely successful if emphasis placed on professional painters in rural areas given that JBC has numerous "exclusive dealers" in rural areas who will welcome added sales support. Likely successful, too, if focus is on painters in the trade area of exclusive dealers in the urban DFW area.

 e. The issue boils down to:

- which will be easier to attract? New store accounts or new professional painters?

- which favors a long-run source of market dominance?

It would seem that professional painters would be easier to attract, but as the case states, "distribution is a key success requirement." Thus, rural dealers should be pursued both with a new rep and the current sales force.

H.　Recommended Action

1. It would seem that JBC should actively pursue the rural household and professional painter segment with secondary emphasis on the urban professional painter segment. The urban household do-it-yourself segment does not appear to represent an opportunity segment in a comparative sense.

2. The rural household and professional painter segment should be sought through new outlet development with secondary emphasis on the rural professional painter segment. A "push" strategy with sales representation will be necessary.

3. Invest in one or two new sales reps with primary emphasis on building the rural store business and recruiting the professional painter business.

I.　Epilogue

Jones Blair Company adopted the actions described above. This decision has placed Jones Blair in a strong position in rural areas which had yet to be dominated by mass merchandisers including Wal-Mart. Jones Blair efforts in 1997 focused on recruiting new outlets in rural areas and was extremely successful as it set a new annual record for new outlets. The company hired one new salesman to specifically pursue the professional painter market. This individual recorded sales of about $400,000 in 1997 (Note the estimated break-even was $235,294 with a 9.5% profit). Jones Blair has avoided any price reductions. In fact, prices were increased 4 percent across-the-board with no measurable decline in gallonage. Advertising and promotion was budgeted at 3 percent of sales in 1998 - no change from 1997.

J.　Summary Points

1. A market opportunity analysis can be enhanced if the "market" can be structured into its component parts or segments:

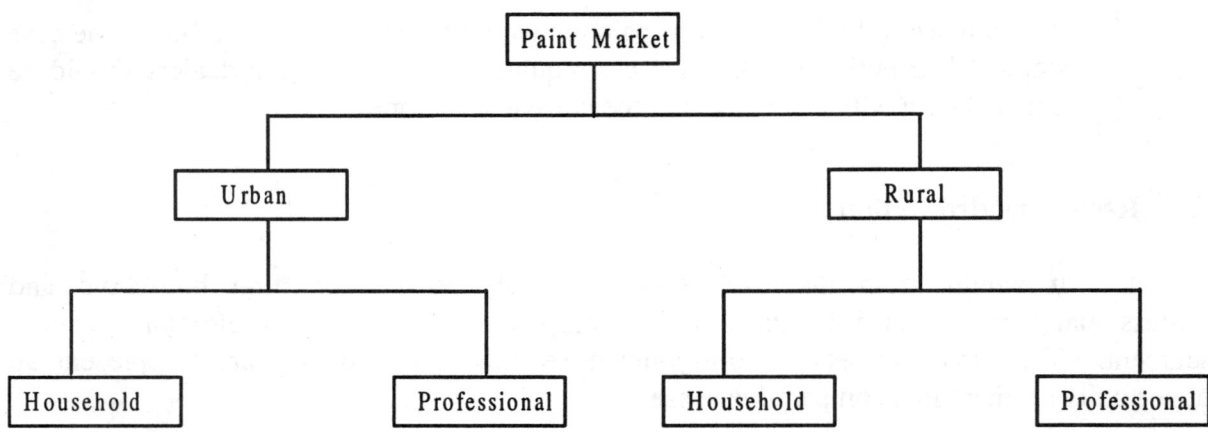

2. "Market share" can have different interpretations depending on the definition of the "market." For example, market share calculations can be made for the (a) "urban" or "rural" market, (b) the "professional" or "household" market, (c) the "total" market, (d) or, more specifically, the non-mass merchandise paint sold in the urban/household segment.

3. Market targeting decisions require both a quantitative and a qualitative analysis. A quantitative appraisal requires a market potential and profitability analysis. A qualitative appraisal requires an assessment of buyer requirements and competitive activity.

4. Cost-volume profit analysis is a useful tool for matching incremental costs and incremental revenues.

TYLER PET FOODS, INC.

Synopsis

The opportunity for Tyler Pet Foods to pursue a market development strategy for "Show Circuit Frozen Dog Dinner" is described in this case. Food brokers had approached Tyler Pet Foods about the possibility of entering the household dog food market in Boston. They had heard of a similar product being sold in the freezer section of selected supermarkets in the southwestern United States and believed that a great potential existed in selling Show Circuit in Boston-area supermarkets. The company has been successful in selling Show Circuit to the kennel market and contracted a consulting firm to develop a market entry program for introducing the product on a limited basis through supermarkets to the household dog food market in the Boston metropolitan area.

The case allows students to explore aspects of market structure and segmentation, the product itself, the positioning and pricing of the product, market segment potential and the nature of the promotion strategy for introducing the product. The apparent decision facing the company is to accept, reject, or modify the proposed introductory marketing program. An implicit question is whether the household dog food market represents an opportunity for the company.

Teaching Objectives

This case has four objectives:

1. To expose students to the highly competitive pet food industry and marketing practices in the dog food market.

2. To determine from product characteristics and market data the "market niche" and potential for Show Circuit Frozen Dog Dinner in the household dog food market.

3. To illustrate how market segmentation, product positioning, and pricing can affect sales potential for an innovative new product.

4. To evaluate both qualitatively and quantitatively the likelihood of profitable results from a proposed market development strategy.

Teaching Suggestions

This case is a proven vehicle to get students to think about market structure, market segment potential, product positioning and pricing, and the promotion program for a market entry strategy. The case can be assigned early in the course to illustrate aspects of market opportunity analysis or later in the course to illustrate the challenge of developing a comprehensive marketing program. The case has been used in both undergraduate and graduate classes. The case works best as a class discussion case for graduate courses. However, instructors have used the case for examination purposes or as a group presentation assignment in undergraduate courses.

A major teaching issue in the case arises from students' preoccupation with the consultants' program. This focus leads to a superficial discussion. Experience suggests that the class discussion and student analysis proceeds more satisfactorily if the potential markets for the product are isolated, competition and potential in these markets is evaluated, and product benefits examined. Once this is accomplished, the match between the market niche and promotional strategy can be evaluated in addition to other elements of the marketing mix.

Specific questions that might be used to direct students include:

1. How would you describe the household dog food market?

2. How might one segment the dog food market and where does Show Circuit fit?

3. How might Show Circuit be positioned in the dog food market?

4. What is the market potential for Show Circuit?

5. What are the marketing program economics of Show Circuit?

6. What does an appraisal of the introductory promotion program tell us?

7. Should the promotion program be accepted, rejected or modified?

Areas for Discussion/Analysis

A. **How would you describe the household dog food market?**

1. Dog food sales in the United States total $5.6 billion at manufacturer's prices. Nevertheless, fewer than one-half of dogs are regularly fed prepared dog food.

2. About 55 percent of total dog food sales are made in supermarkets. The remaining 45 percent is sold through pet superstores, discount and mass merchandisers,

warehouse clubs, pet stores, Internet companies, and veterinarians. These percentages also apply to the Boston market.

3. There are about 50 dog food manufacturers and 350 dog food brands sold in the U.S. However, five companies — Ralston Purina, Kal Kan Foods, Nestle USA, Heinz, and Nabisco — capture 83 percent of supermarket dog food sales.

4. The household dog food industry consists of four categories of food. These categories and the percent of total dog food sales of each are shown below:

Category	Percent of Dog Food Sales
Dry Dog Food	58.6%
Canned Dog Food	23.7%
Dog Biscuits/Treats	15.5%
Semi-Moist Dog Food	2.2%
	100.0%

5. Dog food manufacturers about 2 percent of their sales for advertising. Annual advertising spending for established brands is $7 to $8 million for nationwide media promotion. Spending for introductory marketing programs for new products/brands is substantially higher. Heinz spent $30 million to introduce Reward, a premium canned dog food. Ralston Purina spent $25 million to $30 million to introduce Nature's Course, a premium dry dog food. Alpo Lite, a line extension for Alpo canned dog food, was launched with $10 million in advertising.

B. How might one segment the dog food market and where does Show Circuit fit?

1. Due to the unusual characteristics of Show Circuit, it is important that the student determine the target market(s) for the product. These markets may include: (1) extreme dog lovers, (2) dog owners concerned more with nutrition than convenience and storage, and (3) owners of pedigree dogs. Marketing Ventures Unlimited, the consultants hired to prepare a marketing plan for Show Circuit, suggest that the target market for advertising should be singles and marrieds between the ages of 21 and 50 with a household income greater than $25,000. Where would these people purchase dog food? In supermarkets, mass merchandisers, pet food stores or from veterinarians? These questions are important since the case states that 55 percent of dog food sales are made in supermarkets; 45 percent in the latter outlets. The initial reaction to this analysis is that the target market(s) might be quite small and the distribution program misdirected. Moreover, Show Circuit might be a "specialty-type" product.

2. Further analysis of the market should examine major dog food categories (Exhibit 2 in the case) and how Show Circuit "fits." An attribute-market matrix is a useful illustration

for an in-class discussion. Students can use this format to determine the **positioning** of Show Circuit in terms of an attribute comparison.

Dog Food Category

Product Attributes	Dry	Semi-Moist	Canned	Treats
Ease of Preparation				
Nutrition				
Palatability				
Price				
Storage				
Appearance				

Is the product most similar to one dog food category? Or is it between two categories? Is there (can there be) a frozen dog food category as the consultants' report maintains?

C. How might Show Circuit be positioned in the dog food market?

1. Students usually conclude that Show Circuit "fits" the canned dog food segment based on the previous analysis; however, the product is occasionally positioned as somewhere between canned and semi-moist. This analysis is consistent with consultants' program in that canned foods are considered to be prime competitors (see ad in Exhibit 5 in the case). The consultants belief that dry foods are a competitor is not supported however (see the ad in Exhibit 4 in the case).

2. The positioning issue is also relevant in terms of market (category) concentration. According to case Exhibit 2, five brands capture 84.6 percent of the canned market; five brands capture 92.2.5 percent of the semi-moist market. Assuming these percentages also apply to the Boston market, then the opportunity for Show Circuit is reduced.

3. Positioning has direct implications for pricing. The consultants believe that Show Circuit's quality suggests a "premium price." However, premium pricing is a relative term; that is, premium to what? Case Exhibit 3 shows that the price per ounce for canned food ranges from 10¢ (for Mighty Dog) to 4.8¢ for Cycle and Alpo. Case Exhibit 3 shows that the price per ounce for semi-moist dog food ranges from 5.8¢ for Gaines Burgers to 4.6¢ for Moist & Meaty. If Show Circuit is positioned as a canned dog food, a suggested premium price to the consumer for a 15-ounce tub would be $1.50 (10¢ x 15 oz.) to be comparable with Mighty Dog. Alternatively, if Show Circuit is positioned as a semi-moist dog food, then a suggested premium price to the consumer for a 15-ounce tub would be 87¢ (5.8¢ x 15 oz.) to be comparable with Gaines Burgers.

Pricing can also be examined from the perspective of Bil Jac, a frozen dog food sold in selected supermarkets in Dallas, Texas. This product carried a retail price of $2.29 for a two-pound packagae (or 7.2¢ per ounce) and $4.19 for a five-pount package (or 5.2¢ per ounce). Clearly, Bil Jac is priced higher than Cycle and Alpo in the canned category, but lower than Mighty Dog. Bil Jac is priced higher than Gaines Burgers' 3.75 pound package. On average, Bil Jac is priced at 6.2¢ per ounce which translates to a Show Circuit price of 93¢ per 15-ounce tub (6.2¢ x 15 oz.).

D. What is the market potential for Show Circuit?

1. The previous analysis comes full circle to a fundamental question: "**Where** and **what** is the market potential for Show Circuit?" Students might approach this question in different ways. A convenient approach is to divide the dog food market into its four categories and apply national statistics to the Boston market using a variation of the chain ratio method described in Chapter 4 to estimate market sales potential.

2. The case states that the Boston market has 1.5 percent of the dog population. Since the total dog food market, at manufacturers' prices, is $5.6 billion, the Boston market can be estimated to have a dog food potential of $84 million (.015 x $5.6 billion). This total must be carved into the various types or categories of dog food. Furthermore, since Show Circuit will be sold only through supermarkets, the totals must be reduced further (55% of dog foods are sold by supermarkets). Given these data, Exhibit 1 in this note can be constructed. As indicated, dog food sales potential sold through supermarkets in Boston is an estimated $46.23 million.

3. Depending upon how Show Circuit is targeted, its Boston market potential will vary. If Show Circuit is targeted at canned food, then market potential is $10.95 million, if as a semi-moist food, then the market potential is $1.02 million.

E. What are the marketing program economics for Show Circuit?

1. Marketing program economics for Show Circuit will depend on a student's targeting/positioning analysis and recommendation, the suggested list price chosen, and the choice of introductory market entry advertising and promotion strategy (see case Exhibit 7).

2. Exhibit 2 in this note shows the estimated contribution for Show Circuit on a per case and per tub basis, assuming Show Circuit is priced on the high-end of the canned and semi-moist dog food categories. Exhibit 2 does not include the coupon cost (which is variable) since this cost is part of the promotion strategy. If the coupon cost is included, then the coupon redemption will cost 12¢/case or 1¢/tub. These figures are based on the consultants' estimate that 1 in 10 coupons distributed would be redeemed with each coupon valued at 10¢. [**Note:** A 10% redemption rate seems high, but can be used for analysis purposes.]

EXHIBIT 1

ESTIMATING TOTAL AND CATEGORY DOG FOOD SUPERMARKET SALES POTENTIAL

IN BOSTON AT MANUFACTURERS' PRICES

Dog Food Category	National (U.S.)* Sales Data	x	Percent of Dogs/ People in Boston**	=	Estimated Boston Dog Food Sales	x	Percent of Boston Dog Food Sold Through Supermarkets***	=	Boston Area Supermarket Dog Food Sales
Dry	$3.282 Bill. (58.6% of Total)		1.5%		$49.23 Mill.		55%		$27.10 Mill.
Canned	$1.327 Bill. (23.7% of Total)		1.5%		$19.91 Mill.		55%		$10.95 Mill.
Semi-Moist	$.123 Bill. (2.2% of Total)		1.5%		$1.85 Mill.		55%		$1.02 Mill.
Treats	$.868 Bill. (15.5% of Total)		1.5%		$13.02 Mill.		55%		$7.16 Mill.
Totals	$5.6 Bill.		1.5%		$84.01 Mill.		55%		$46.23 Mill.

*Category percentages based on case Exhibit 2; U.S. dog food sales at manufacturer prices were $5.6 billion given in case.

**Assume a relationship between the percentage of dogs in a geographical area and the percentage of total food consumed.

***Supermarkets account for 55% of dog food sales.

EXHIBIT 2

ESTIMATED SHOW CIRCUIT CONTRIBUTION AT ALTERNATIVE SUGGESTED LIST PRICES PER CASE OF 12 AND 15-OUNCE TUB

Show Circuit:		Premium Priced Canned Dog Food		Premium Priced Semi-Moist Dog Food	
		Case	Tub	Case	Tub
	Price to Consumer	$18.00	$1.50	$11.16	$0.93
	Price to Retailer (assuming 25% retailer gross profit margin)*	$13.50	$1.125	$8.37	$0.698
Less:	Broker Commission ((7% of price to retailer)*	($0.945)	($0.079)	($0.586)	($0.049)
Less:	Production + Freight + Packaging Costs (all variable)*	($6.37)	($0.531)	($6.37)	($0.531)
	Contribution	$6.185	$0.515	$1.414	$0.118

*Given in the case

3. A simple break-even analysis can be performed using the two price (contribution) estimates and the two promotion spending levels of $400,000 and $600,000, plus the need to pay a slotting fee of $30,000, given in the case. Representative calculations are shown in Exhibit 3 in this note.

4. Sometimes students will conclude that the break-even dollar sales volume is small given the size of the Boston market. For instance, these students might calculate a break-even share-of-market using either the $84 million market estimate for Boston or the $46.23 million figure for Boston supermarket sales as the denominator:

$$\text{Breakeven Share-of-Market} = \frac{\text{Show Circuit B/E Estimate}}{\text{Boston Market Size Estimate}}$$

Based on break-even figures in Exhibit 3 in this note, the break-even share-of-market estimate will be in the range of 1.1 percent to 8.1 percent. **Such a calculation is incorrect.**

5. A correct calculation is to compute the break-even share-of-market based on supermarket sales of the category that is targeted and the positioning of Show Circuit. Using the figures shown in Exhibits 1 and 3 in this note, the correct break-even share-of-market calculation would show that the share-of-market percent necessary to break-even is much larger. For example,

- If Show Circuit is positioned as a premium-priced canned dog food and $630,000 ($430,000) in promotion and fees is spent to introduce the product, then

    B/E Share-of-Market @ $630,000 = $1,375,097 ÷ $10.95 million = 12.6%

    B/E Share-of-Market @ $430,000 = $938,561 ÷ $10.95 million = 8.6%

- If Show Circuit is positioned as a premium-priced semi-moist dog food and $630,000 ($430,000) in promotion and fees is spent to introduce the product, then

    B/E Share-of-Market @ $630,000 = $3,729,212 ÷ $1.02 million = 366%

    B/E Share-of-Market @ $430,000 = $2,545,334 ÷ $1.02 million = 250%

It is clear from this analysis that the semi-moist dog food category will to be unprofitable for Show Circuit. However, there exists a possibility for the canned dog food segment. A lot depends on the quality of the introductory promotion program and the amount spent.

EXHIBIT 3

BREAK-EVEN CALCULATIONS FOR SHOW CIRCUIT AT DIFFERENT CONTRIBUTION AND ADVERTISING AND PROMOTION SPENDING LEVELS

	Advertising and Promotion Strategy Expenditure + Slotting Fee	
Contribution/Case	$430,000	$630,000
Premium-priced canned dog food: $6.185	B/E(cases) = $\dfrac{\$430{,}000}{\$6.185}$ = 69,523	B/E(cases) = $\dfrac{\$630{,}000}{\$6.185}$ = 101,859
	B/E ($) = 69,523 × $13.50 = $938,561	B/E ($) = 101,859 × $13.50 = $1,375,097
	$430,000	$630,000
Premium-priced moist dog food: $1.414	B/E(cases) = $\dfrac{\$430{,}000}{\$1.414}$ = 304,102	B/E(cases) = $\dfrac{\$630{,}000}{\$1.414}$ = 445,545
	B/E ($) = 304,102 × $8.37 = $2,545,334	B/E ($) = 445,545 × $8.37 = $3,729,212

F. **What does an appraisal of the introductory promotion program tell us?**

1. The evaluation of the introductory promotion program follows directly from the previous discussion. The apparent promotion objectives are to (1) create awareness of a new brand, (2) obtain distribution through grocery outlets, (3) motivate trial through coupon redemption and through the emotional impact of TV. These are stated in the MEDIA PLAN section of consultants' proposal. More subtle points must be also examined such as the program's positioning strategy.

2. **Positioning Strategy.** The proposal states that Show Circuit will be positioned as "the finest dog food available at any price and the only thing you would feed your dog if he were truly a member of the family." This may be true, but it is not clear that the benefit-cost comparison is in Show Circuit's favor.

Examining the appeals in the program indicate that the product is positioned against **canned** and **dry** foods (see Exhibits 4 and 5 in the case). This is not entirely consistent with the positioning analysis addressed earlier, at least for dry food. Furthermore, it might be questioned whether the appeals used are desirable, believable or exclusive enough to generate interest in the product. This has implications for the coupon program.

3. **Media Scheduling and Placement.** The program planned seems to miss a sizable portion of the target markets with the daytime TV scheduling. Aren't most 21-50 single/married people working? Other issues include? (1) What is the effect of insertions in *Better Homes & Gardens*? (2) How intensive is the TV schedule?

4. **Trade Program.** A major issue here is whether the proposed program will gain distribution. Trade promotion materials emphasize the popularity of dog food, the acceptance of Show Circuit by dog breeders, and the consumer advertising. A major problem is that brokers must deal with frozen food buyer and not the pet food buyer. Therefore, education is necessary. How receptive will the frozen food buyers be given that (1) typically competition for freezer space is severe, and (2) many frozen food items are not specialty items and those that are would probably have higher margins. Not only is distribution in question, but space is also important. If adequate space is not available, will the impulse buyer be reached?

5. **Coupon Program.** As discussed earlier, an extension on the break-even analysis discussed earlier can be applied to the coupon program. The consultants estimated that 1 in 10 coupons distributed would be redeemed with each coupon valued at 10¢. On average, then, coupon redemption will cost 1¢/tub or 12¢/case. Since this is a variable cost, coupon redemption should be subtracted from the contribution. Therefore, the new contribution per case will be 12¢ less. This will increase the break-even volume.

6. **Advertising Spending Level.** It is also appropriate to consider the advertising and promotion expenditure itself, excluding slotting fees. The $400,000 expenditure for the Boston market is equivalent to $20 million for a national introduction (.015X = $400,000; X

= $26.67 million). A $600,000 expenditure for the Boston market is equivalent to $40 million for a national introduction. As described in the case, Heinz spent $30 million to introduce Reward; Ralston Purina spent $25 million to $30 million to introduce Nature's Course. Neither product pioneers a "new category" - frozen food dog food. Therefore, it would seem that Show Circuit is underspending at the $400,000 level for the introduction which further places the market entry in jeopardy. The $600,000 spending level seems more appropriate. However, the analysis of the marketing program economics described in E. above indicates this amount is likely to be unprofitable.

G. Epilogue

The company accepted Marketing Ventures' program proposal. The introductory advertising and promotion program budgeted at $430,000 was begun with Show Circuit retail-priced at 99¢ per tub and distribution was obtained through chain supermarkets. Although precise figures are not available, it is estimated that about 4,000 cases were sold in a three month promotion period. At this rate, Tyler Pet Foods could not break-even on the venture. About 140 coupons were redeemed in the three month promotion period. This failure plus other factors not described in the case prompted Tyler Pet Foods to go out of business shortly after this case was written.

H. Summary Points

1. A market opportunity analysis can be enhanced if the "market" can be structured into its component parts or segments:

U.S. Dog food Market

```
            ┌─────────────┬─────────────┬─────────┐ ........
         Boston
         ┌────┴────┐
    Pet Stores,   Supermarkets
      Other    ┌────┬────┬────┐
            Treats Canned Dry Semi-Moist
```

2. One of the most important decisions any organization makes is the choice of markets it elects to serve. The choice commits the organization to ...

- A set of customers

- A set of competitors

3. The requirements for an effective market segment are:

- Measurability
- Accessibility
- Substantiability
- Durability
- Defensibility
- Responsiveness to marketing action - Product/Service, Promotion, Distribution, Price

It is not apparent that Marketing Ventures considered these factors.

4. Break-even analysis and break-even share-of-market analysis is only a source of information when the "market" is carefully defined and quantified. When the "market" is properly defined and quantified, a simple break-even analysis serves as a powerful tool for assessing the likely profitability of a marketing program.

CURTIS AUTOMOTIVE HOIST: MARKET OPPORTUNITIES IN THE EUROPEAN UNION

Synopsis

Mark Curtis, president of Curtis Automotive Hoist, is considering his company's entry into the European market in 1998. Curtis Automotive Hoist, a Canadian manufacturer of surface hoists, has experienced rapid growth in North America but future prospects in this market may be limited given the current distribution system. A French firm is interested in licensing the Curtis design but the firm is also considering a joint venture with the firm or setting up its own manufacturing facility.

This case addresses decisions faced by many small companies that wish to expand their operations. The first decision is whether to gain a greater share of the existing market in North America or expand into a new, but unfamiliar market (Europe). Case information allows for a discussion of the new European Union. The second decision is the market entry strategy into Europe (local manufacturing, joint venture, licensing) and the pros and cons of each strategy.

This case raises numerous issues. First, students are exposed to subtleties in business-to-business marketing, including "buy classes" (new buy, modified rebuy), the purchase of capital goods, and buying center roles. Second, opportunities and risks involved in marketing in the European Union environment are introduced. Third, students are challenged to estimate market potentials and profitability of options given incomplete information.

Teaching Objectives

This case has four teaching objectives:

1. To evaluate the opportunities and threats in entering international markets.

2. To understand the strengths and weaknesses of a company within the context of home and foreign markets.

3. To understand the implications of alternative international market entry strategies.

4. To develop an appreciation for many market entry decisions based on a limited amount of information.

This teaching note is based on an analysis plan prepared by Professor Gordon H. G. McDougall, Wilfrid Laurier University.

Teaching Suggestions

This case is best suited or use as an exercise in market opportunity and targeting analysis. However, some instructors might assign the case later in the course. This case is suitable for undergraduate and graduate students and can be used for examination or group presentation purposes.

Two possible approaches to teaching this case are (1) to go through the questions listed below in sequence which allows for a relatively logical progression to the decision or (2) to start by asking "which is the most promising market?" and then have students defend their point of view. After the arguments in favor of Europe are heard, the instructor can move to a discussion of the market entry strategies for Europe and then to the decision for next year.

Some instructors may wish to play a proactive role in the class discussion by introducing Exhibit 1 in this note to students. This exhibit presents what we call a "strategic issues map" that portrays the issues in the case in a two-step format: (1) where to compete, and (2) how to compete.

Specific questions that can be posed to students either before or during a class discussion are:

1. What factors have contributed to Curtis Automotive Hoist's success to date?

2. Which opportunity, greater penetration of the U.S. market or entering Europe, would you recommend Curtis pursue?

3. If Curtis was entering the European market, what entry strategy would you recommend? Why?

4. What approach should Curtis Automotive Hoist take for the next year?

Areas for Discussion/Analysis

A. What factors have contributed to Curtis Automotive Hoist's success to date?

1. Curtis Automotive Hoist (CAH) has done exceptionally well in the hoist market. In the last three years CAH has dramatically increased its sales and share in a highly competitive market. As shown in Exhibit 2 in this note, CAH now holds 45 percent of the scissor hoist market based on industry (case Exhibit 3) and CAH (case Exhibit 2) unit sales history.

EXHIBIT 1

CURTIS AUTOMOTIVE HOIST: STRATEGIC ISSUES MAP

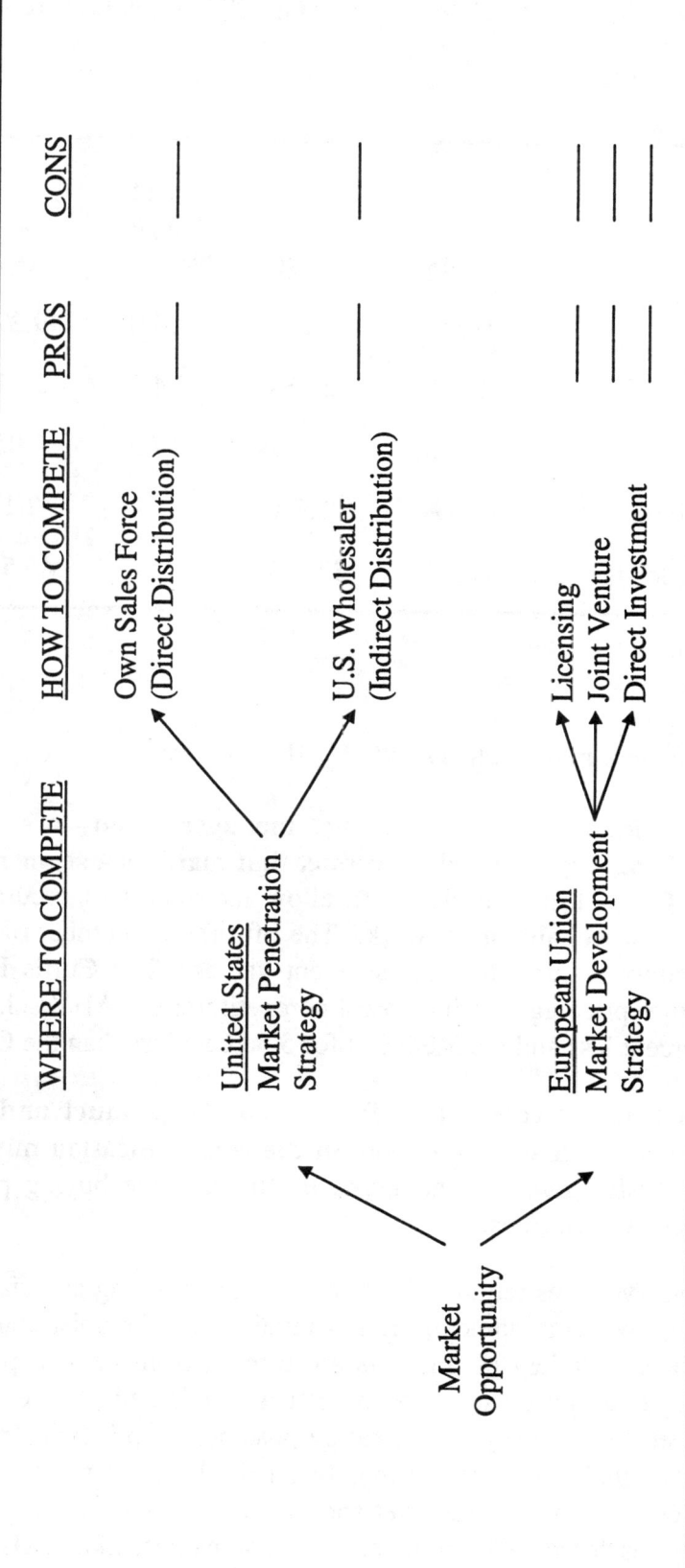

EXHIBIT 2

TOTAL HOIST MARKET AND CURTIS AUTOMOTIVE HOIST (CAH) SHARE
(UNITS)

	1995	1996	Percent Change '95-'96	1997	Percent Change '96-'97
Total Hoists*	48,234	50,187	4.0	49,272	(1.8)
Scissor Hoists*	2,170	2,258	4.1	2,316	2.6
CAH Sales**	723	847	17.2	1,054	24.4
CAH Share of Total Hoists	1.5%	1.7%	–	2.1%	–
CAH Share of Scissor Hoists	33.3%	37.5%	–	45.5%	–

* From Case Exhibit 3
** From Case Exhibit 2

2. Numerous factors have contributed to CAH's success:

- **A president and marketing manager who are dedicated to manufacturing a superior product that matches a segment's needs.** The basic Curtis Lift is designed to allow mechanics to accurately and easily perform wheel alignment work. The lift offers a number of design, quality, and safety features that the segment values. The Curtis Lift is sold at a premium price against its closest competitors; the AHV scissor lift sold for 20 percent less and the Mete Lift for 5 percent less than the Curtis Lift.

- **A marketing strategy that focuses on the product and uses personal selling as the main component of the communication mix.** This strategy is successful given the nature of the market, the buying process, and the competitive activities.

- Because vehicles require different types of servicing at different times (e.g., tune-up, wheel alignment, muffler repair, etc.), the hoist market has evolved to where a variety of products are offered from general purpose hoists to very specialized hoists. The market is dominated by two large U.S. firms who sell the majority of general purpose hoists (primarily inground and two post surface) and compete mainly on the basis of price. Those two firms hold 60 percent of the market and the largest, AHV with 40 percent, has its own sales force. The remaining 14 companies, like CAH, operate within product segments or regions and use only wholesalers or a combination of wholesalers and company sales force. The overall market can be viewed as having two basic products, general purpose hoists which are sold primarily on the basis of price, and specialty hoists which are sold on a differentiated, nonprice basis (e.g., quality, design). Like many markets, it allows for dominant, price-driven competitors and niche players. **Curtis is obviously a niche player that is now "dominating" a niche.**

The buying process is probably a new task or modified rebuy. The process is complicated by the fact that with respect to chains, head office approval (at times a long and arduous task) is required before the service manager/decider in the garage/service center can consider a particular brand. The decider (and there may be influencers, initiators, etc., involved in the process) is likely to spend some time examining alternatives because of the investment involved. The deciders may or may not have some experience with hoists but probably their knowledge is limited when they start the decision process. The buying criteria are formed as they go through the information gathering, alternative evaluation stages.

The implications of the above are that: (a) personal selling can have a major impact on the buying process, and (b) the salesperson needs to recognize and appreciate the complexities of the process.

3. The competitors who appear to be either dominant or gaining in this market use price and/or product and personal selling to achieve their goals. In particular, AHV holds a 40 percent share based on marketing standard products with a company sales force that emphasizes price ("a hoist is a hoist"). CAH is gaining share by focusing on a segment with a differentiated product using a combination of company sales force and wholesalers/distributors.

4. A closer examination of CAH's sales by channel (as shown in Exhibit 3 in this note) reveals the impact of personal selling. The company sales force, four salespeople plus Mr. Gagnon, focused primarily on chains and accounted for 25 percent of company sales (units). The Canadian distributors, who handled only one hoist, the Curtis Lift, accounted for 15 percent of sales. In total, Canadian sales were 422 units. The U.S. wholesaler, who handles five hoists including the Curtis Lift, sold 632 units. Assuming the U.S. market is 10 times larger than the Canadian market (the case makes reference to this figure), if the Curtis Lift achieved the same level of sales in the U.S. as Canada, sales in the U.S. would be about 4,220 units (10 x 422). To realize greater sales in the U.S., CAH will have to alter its strategy.

EXHIBIT 3

CURTIS AUTOMOTIVE HOIST SALES BY CHANNEL (1997)

Channel	Units*	Sales ($)	Avg. retail price times percentage received by CAH
Company sales force (direct)	264	2,901,360	(100% x $10,990)
Canadian distributors	158	1,389,136	(80% x $10,990)
U.S. wholesaler	632	5,417,630	(78% x $10,990)
Total	1,054	$9,708,126	

*Case notes that 25% of CAH sales were through its own sales force; 60% of sales were in the United States in 1997 (p. 99).

B. Which opportunity, greater penetration of the U.S. market or entering Europe, would you recommend Curtis pursue?

1. The U.S. opportunity depends on the new relationship CAH establishes with the U.S. wholesaler. Ideally, Mark Curtis and/or Pierre Gagnon could visit the U.S. wholesaler, show the wholesaler the potential for Curtis Lift sales in the U.S., encourage the wholesaler to "push" the Curtis Lift, and the wholesaler responds positively. Practically, this is not likely to happen.

2. The U.S. wholesaler has "control" of this channel as the Curtis Lift is a small portion of its total sales and a small share (20%) of its lift sales. It is possible that the wholesaler may push the Curtis Lift a bit harder (the contribution for the wholesaler is $2,417.80 per unit; total contribution is $1,528,049.60). CAH can justify more effort from the wholesaler and some may be forthcoming.

3. Another option for CAH is to strike a deal with the U.S. wholesaler to let CAH market the product in the Northeastern United States. The market potential there is around 1,003 units if CAH could sell at the equivalent Canadian rate (14.07 units per million population) or 198 if sales were at the equivalent U.S. rate (2.39 units per million population) (See Exhibit 4 in this note). It is likely that CAH sells most of the scissor units in Canada so that the 14.07 units/million reflects an upper market potential.

The Northeastern United States constitute about 31 percent of the U.S. population (83/264) and is about 2.8 times the size of the Canadian market (83/30). At the Canadian (14.07) level, this market offers CAH the potential to increase sales by 805 units (1,003 minus 198) which is a 127 percent increase (805/632) over existing sales. At issue is the reaction of the U.S. wholesaler.

EXHIBIT 4

ESTIMATED MARKET POTENTIAL IN THE NORTHEASTERN UNITED STATES

BASED ON POPULATION

Market	Population	Vehicles	Curtis Lift Unit Sales	Curtis Lift Sales Per Million Population	Curtis Lift Sales Per Million Vehicles
Canada	30,000,000	14,000,000	422	14.07 (422/30)	30.14 (422/14)
U.S.	264,000,000	146,000,000	632	2.39 (632/264)	4.32 (632/146)

Market	Population	Projected Curtis Lift Sales At Canadian Level (14.07)	At U.S. Level (2.39)
New England	13,000,000	183	31
Mid-Atlantic	38,000,000	370	91
Mid-Eastern	32,000,000	450	76
Total		1,003	198

4. The cost side of directly entering the Northeastern United States depends on the wholesaler reaction on CAH's level of commitment. Assuming the wholesaler agrees to the idea, CAH might start with a similar sales group to Canada (a marketing manager, three sales support staff, and four salespeople). The cost would be $460,000 (see case Exhibit 2).

Based on case Exhibit 2, students can estimate CAH unit contribution by dividing 1997 Contribution ($2,718,000) by 1997 Unit Sales (1,054). **This figure is $2,578.75.** Unit contribution is a rough estimate since cost of sales will likely differ between direct sales and distributor sales. Recognizing this, an estimated unit break-even for a CAH Northeastern U. S. market entry using its own sales force is:

$$B/E = \frac{\$460,000}{\$2,578.75} = 178.4 \text{ units}$$

5. Applying a similar logic to the European market, the market potential varies from 5,206 to 884 units for Europe in total and from 4,140 to 620 in the five "primary" countries (see Exhibit 5 in this note). The market appears to offer less direct competition for the scissor type lift than North America.

6. On the surface, the U.S. opportunity looks more promising because: CAH knows this market; its environment (culture, economic, language, etc.) is very similar to Canada's; and there is a sizable opportunity that could keep CAH "busy" for years. The caveat is the U.S. wholesaler's reaction to any proposal. The possible downside is that the wholesaler refuses to allow CAH to service the Northeast market and, if CAH persists, the wholesaler could drop the Duncan line.

7. Europe is unknown to CAH and the preliminary report is very sketchy. While the market is "bigger," the cost of entering and servicing the European market may be prohibitive for CAH without a partner. This suggests either a joint venture or licensing agreement with the French firm, Bar Maisse.

At some point, the issue of skill transfer should be discussed. CAH has an excellent product, which can be transferred with little difficulty to other markets. However, CAH's skill in marketing, particularly personal selling, will be difficult to transfer to the European market because of the language and cultural differences. This negates part of CAH's competitive advantage or competence in Europe.

C. If Curtis was entering the European market, what entry strategy would you recommend? Why?

The three entry options are: local manufacturing or direct investment, joint venture, or licensing. Both the licensing and joint venture can be pursued with a company, Bar Maisse, that seems to complement CAH. Bar Maisse specializes in wheel alignment, it has produced a sophisticated product, and, based on a limited sample, it makes quality products.

EXHIBIT 5

ESTIMATED MARKET POTENTIAL IN EUROPE

		Units/Millions
CAH Sales Rate (see Exhibit 4 in this note)	- Canada - per million population	14.07 (A)
	- U.S. - per million population	2.39 (B)
	- Canada - per million vehicles	30.14 (C)
	- U.S. - per million vehicles	4.32 (D)

Market	Population (millions)	Vehicles (millions)	Unit Potential Based on:			
			A	B	C	D
Europe	370.0	N/A	5206	884	–	–
Germany	81.5	41.1	1147	195	1239	178
France	58.0	29.3	816	139	883	127
Italy	57.2	32.3	805	137	973	140
United Kingdom	58.3	24.3	820	139	732	105
Spain	39.2	16.2	552	94	488	70

The discussion of the three options should incorporate the general advantages and disadvantages of each option. Then, options can be reviewed in the context of CAH's goals, strengths, and weaknesses. The typical criteria used to evaluate the options are: investment required, other resources required, level of control, level of risk, and potential return on investment.

1. Licensing

Licensing is particularly appealing to firms with technology/product/manufacturing expertise who lack the resources, desire, or experience to enter foreign markets. There are virtually no risks and the only costs are in signing the agreement and checking on the implementation. The major disadvantages are loss of control, potential returns from marketing and manufacturing may be lost, and the licensee may turn itself into a competitor when the agreement expires. Further drawbacks are that the licensor, e.g., CAH, learns nothing about the foreign market. In summary, licensing is a low cost-method of potentially making relatively "easy" money in the short term.

- For CAH, the **major benefits to licensing** with Bar Maisse are:

    - Bar Maisse appears to be a quality organization and will probably manufacture a quality lift (a concern of Mr. Curtis).

    - Bar Maisse provides market and other expertise that CAH lacks in Europe.

    - CAH has no financial risk exposure.

    - CAH makes some "easy" money (assume the selling price is equivalent to $11,000, CAH has a 5% royalty fee, and say 1,000 units are sold, then Duncan makes $550,000; stated another way, CAH makes $550 for every unit sold).

- For CAH, the **disadvantages to licensing** with Bar Maisse are:

    - Licensing is likely to produce the lowest financial return of the three market entry strategies.

    - CAH learns little about the European market (although this does not appear to be a major concern).

    - In three years, Bar Maisse can terminate the agreement and produce a "similar" hoist.

2. Joint Venture

A **joint venture** provides a more extensive form of participation in foreign markets. The major advantages are the sharing of risk and the combined strengths of the two partners.

Joint ventures allow the partner to gain access to market knowledge and build its expertise in this area. The main disadvantages are the costs of control and coordination in working with a partner and the potential for conflict. Over time, many joint ventures are dissolved because the partners perceived inappropriate allocation of costs versus returns (i.e., each partner felt the other was contributing too little and getting too much).

- For CAH, the **major benefits of a joint venture** with Bar Maisse are:

    - CAH would gain market knowledge (may not be important).

    - A "pretty good" match exists between the two companies.

    - CAH will probably earn more money than it would with licensing. While it is difficult to determine the investment acquired, on a per unit basis current contribution is about $2,580. If CAH has a 50-50 joint venture, then CAH "makes" $1,290/unit versus $550 on licensing. For 1,000 units sold, a joint venture will produce $740,000 more than the licensing option.

- For CAH, **negative features of a joint venture** are:

    - CAH will have to make an investment (although money does not appear to be a problem).

    - Pierre Gagnon, a valued CAH executive, may have to move to France.

    - CAH and Bar Maisse may not get along. CAH knows very little about Bar Maisse, its management, goals, style of operation, or even its size. There is a reasonable argument that CAH should have some discussions with Bar Maisse before any agreement is signed. This may not happen as Mark Curtis has a "bias for action."

3. **Direct Investment or Local Manufacturing**

Direct investment involves setting up a plant in Europe. If this option was accepted, the country data contained in the case becomes relevant for site location. The advantages of direct investment are: (1) control is maintained, (2) market knowledge is gained, and (3) all profits accrue to the firm. The disadvantages include: (1) the investment required, (2) the commitment of other resources, and (3) all risks are borne by CAH.

For CAH, the major advantage is that direct investment guarantees entry and a presence in the European Union. The other advantage is that CAH "runs its own show" which may be important to Mr. Curtis as he wants to maintain a quality image. The disadvantages are numerous and the major ones are: CAH has no knowledge or expertise that can be transferred to the European market setting, CAH will have to invest a minimum of $550,000 ($250,000 + $200,000 + 10% interest on $1,000,000), and Pierre Gagnon would head the European division.

A rough guesstimate of fixed costs are $1,000,000 (based on Canadian experience). At a contribution per unit of $2,580, the European division would require 387 units to break-even. If CAH sold 1,000 units, profits would be $1,580,000. However, CAH is ill-suited at this time to consider direct investment as an entry strategy to the European Union. There is no indication that Mr. Curtis is committed to international expansion (an important criteria for company success) but rather he is committed to growth. This goal can be achieved closer to home.

D. What approach should Curtis take for the next year?

1. The approach taken depends on the reaction of the U.S. wholesaler to CAH's proposals to achieve a greater share of the U.S. market. It also depends on the results of the further discussions with Bar Maisse. If the wholesaler expresses a willingness to "push" the Curtis Lift, then CAH can assist in this process by providing seminars, information, etc., for the distributor's sales force and possibly working with the sales force on the large chains.

2. If the U.S. wholesaler is reluctant to push and is not interested in letting CAH into the northeast, then CAH has a problem and Europe becomes more attractive to achieve its growth objectives. The probable scenario is that the U.S. wholesaler will let CAH into the northeast providing it gets a commission on every unit CAH sells in the area. The attractiveness of this for CAH depends on the size of the commission.

3. With respect to Europe, CAH should discuss matters further with Bar Maisse. At a minimum, if CAH decides to go "full speed ahead" in the U.S. then a licensing agreement will provide some returns. This is probably the only feasible option under the "full speed ahead" scenario because CAH does not appear to have management depth. A lower commitment to the U.S. could allow CAH to consider the joint venture in Europe. All things considered, the "best" strategy for CAH, at this time, is a licensing agreement for Europe.

E. Epilogue

Curtis Automotive Hoist (a disguised name) officials have elected to focus their attention on trying to get the U.S. wholesaler to "push" the CAH product line harder. European expansion plans have been put on hold until the effort directed at the U.S. wholesaler and the results can be determined.

F. Summary Points

1. The central issue for Curtis Automotive Hoist is whether to pursue a ...

    ... Market penetration strategy in North America
      or
    ... Market development strategy in Western Europe

2. There are four principal market development entry strategies for foreign markets ...

   ... Exporting
   ... Licensing
   ... Joint Ventures
   ... Direct Investment

Each strategy option has distinct advantages and disadvantages that must be acknowledged before a strategic decision can be made.

3. Assessing market potential in foreign markets is often a difficult task requiring estimates based on incomplete data.

4. A profitability analysis must be performed for a complete assessment of a strategic option. A simple break-even analysis often provides valuable insights into the potential profitability of a firm's entry strategy. Equally relevant in this regard is the financial commitment or exposure.

FRITO-LAY'S DIPS

Synopsis

In late, 1986, Frito-Lay executives had just completed the planning review for Frito-Lay's Dips. The major issue raised was where and how Frito-Lay's Dips could be developed further. One viewpoint was that Frito-Lay should pursue a market penetration strategy and build market share in the "chip dip" category where it has a strong presence. An opposing view was that Frito-Lay should pursue a market development strategy using its new sour cream-based French Onion Dip to enter the "vegetable dip" category. The sour cream dip had been introduced in 1986, and had been placed in the salty snack (chip) location in supermarkets.

The case provides an extensive review of Frito-Lay's efforts to date in the "chip dip" category. Industry and company research on the "vegetable dip" category is also provided. At the time of the case, Frito-Lay does not have a presence in the "vegetable dip" category given its emphasis on Mexican and Cheese dips.

The primary issue posed to students focuses on the emphasis to be placed on "chip vs. vegetable dip" categories. A related issue is on adopting a **line extension** strategy vs. a **brand extension** strategy for the sour cream dip. Issues related to market segmentation and profit contribution are also raised for consideration.

Teaching Objectives

This case has three teaching objectives:

1. To force students to consider alternative ways of segmenting the dip market and assessing market segment size.

2. To examine the pros and cons of a line extension and franchise extension as a matter of product policy.

3. To perform basic financial and profitability analyses and the brand level.

Teaching Suggestions

This case can be used either in the Opportunity Analysis or Product Strategy and Brand Management section of a course. Moreover, the case would make for an excellent mid-term examination.

Specific questions that can be posed to students either before or during a class discussion are:

1. How would you characterize the dip category in general?

2. How might the dip category be segmented?

3. What is Frito-Lay's competitive position within the segments it pursues?

4. What sales volume and market share(s) will be required of the dip line to preserve its profit contribution given budgeted promotion expenses?

5. What are the pros/cons of focusing attention on the "chip dip" segment?

6. What are the pros/cons of focusing attention on the "vegetable dip" segment?

Some instructors may wish to assign additional reading for this case. Two suggestions are Edward M. Tauber, "Brand Leverage: Strategy for Growth in a Cost-Control World," *Journal of Advertising Research* (August-September, 1988), pp. 26-30, and Peter H. Farquhar, et al., "Strategies for Leveraging Master Brands," *Marketing Research* (September, 1992), pp. 32-43.

Areas for Discussion/Analysis

A. How would you characterize the dip category in general?

1. Overall, dips are a popular category with 1985 retail sales of $620 million (case Exhibit 1). However, real growth is flat. Dollar volume growth (10% annually) has come about through price increases and new cheese-based dips which have taken away volume from other dip flavors.

2. It is plausible that **shelf-stable** cheese-based dips have spurred dip dollar growth as evidenced by Frito-Lay's cheese dips introduction in 1984 and competitor new products (see case Exhibit 2).

3. Competitive activity has increased overall. Dip competitors spent $58 million for consumer advertising alone (excluding trade promotion) in 1985 which was 25% higher than 1984. Furthermore, new product activity increased in 1985. Given flat real growth, this means that considerable brand switching is occurring. The sales decline in Frito-Lay's cheese dips from $55 million in 1984 to $48 million in 1985 is one example of this happening (see case Exhibit 2). It is noteworthy that Frito-Lay spent three times more on advertising and promotion in 1985 than it did in 1984 (see case Exhibit 5).

B. **How might the dip category be segmented?**

1. Exhibit 1 in the case shows one approach to segmenting the dip category based on **product characteristics**. However, at least two other segmentation schemes are possible (see Exhibit 1 in this note).

2. Most notably, the dip category can be segmented into "chip dips" and "vegetable dips" reflecting **usage characteristics**. The case states that about 33% of dip usage is for vegetables which represents $207 million in 1985 retail sales; 67% is for chip usage or $413 million in 1985 retail sales. This segmentation scheme is useful because it directly relates to the decisions at hand.

3. A third segmentation scheme is based on **flavors**. The case states that 50% of total dip retail sales are accounted for by sour cream-based dips, 25% by cheese dips, 10% by bean and picante dips, and 15% by cream cheese dips.

4. Segmentation based on usage and flavor show that "chips" and sour cream-based flavors are the dominant segments within the dip category.

C. **What is Frito Lay's competitive position within the segments it pursues?**

1. Competitive position, as measured by market share, can be computed using the different segmentation schemes and information contained in case Exhibit 1. It is clear that Frito-Lay's competitive position varies greatly depending on how the dip category is segmented (see Exhibit 2 in this note). For example, Frito-Lay captures

- almost 3/4's of shelf-stable dips (73.0%)
- almost 1/3 of the "chip dip" segment (32.7%)
- almost 1/2 of cheese dips (47.7%)
- almost all of the Mexican (bean/picante) dip segment (96.7%)

2. Competitive position can be assessed in terms of its marketing/distribution effort as well. Frito-Lay has recently adopted an aggressive stance with respect to new product introduction (a full line of cheese dips) and advertising and merchandising (A&M) expenditures. A&M expenditures increased almost three-fold between 1984 and 1985 and doubled again between 1985 and 1986 (planned). The emphasis on A&M has also changed from "push" marketing to in the trade to "pull" marketing focusing on the consumer. Distribution is a Frito-Lay **distinctive competency** and Frito-Lay's Dips has benefited from its location near salty snacks. Moreover, Frito-Lay's strong national market share in salty snacks is an added strength given the link between "chips" and "dips".

3. Frito-Lay's Dips is firmly entrenched in the **shelf-stable dip** segment. This is a segment that Frito-Lay has (presumably) pioneered. This unique feature is a benefit to consumers and certainly fits the firm's distribution and sales system for salty snacks. Yet, it may be a **limiting** factor as well. As Ann Mirabito, product manager, notes: "Consumer research tells us that products in a metal can are seen as being overly processed, filled with

EXHIBIT 1

ALTERNATIVE SEGMENTATION SCHEMES FOR DIPS

Usage Segmentation

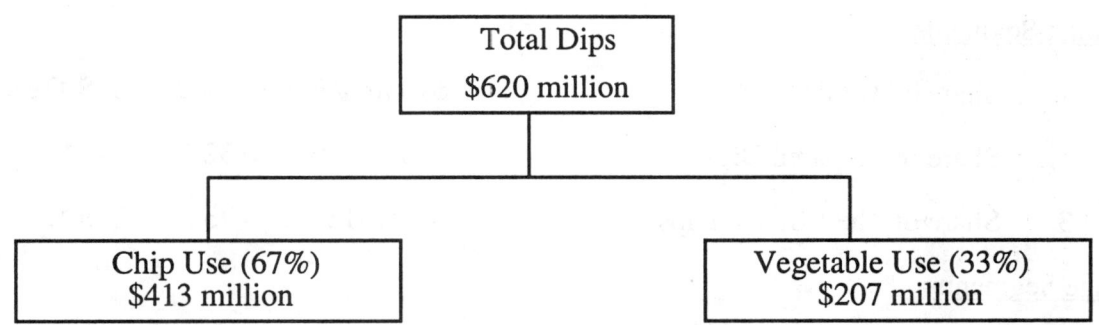

Flavor Segmentation

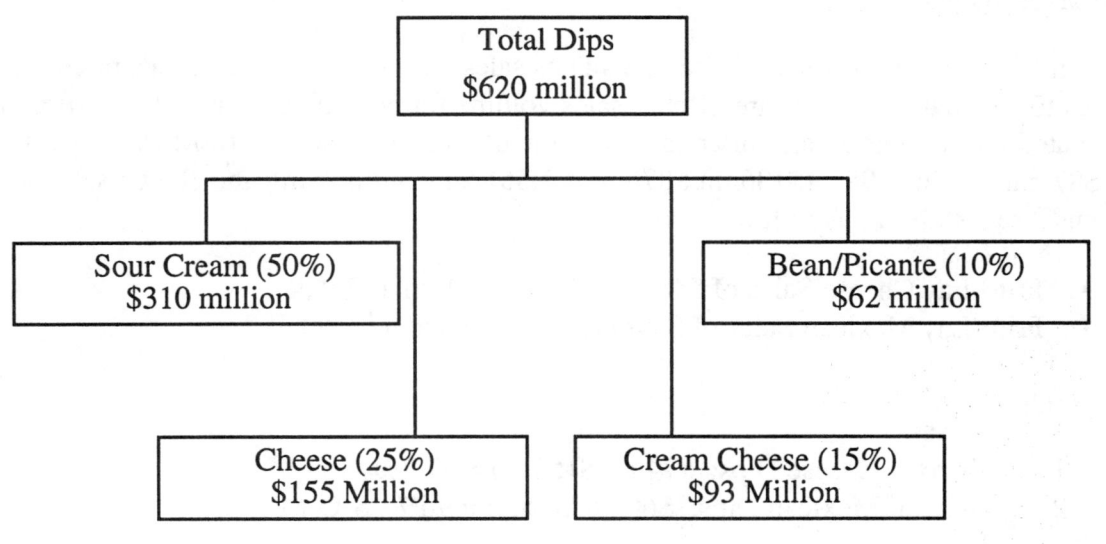

EXHIBIT 2

FRITO-LAY'S DIPS COMPETITIVE POSITION IN MARKET SEGMENTS BASED ON MARKET SHARE
(BASED ON RETAIL PRICES)

Product Segments

1. Share of Total Dips: $135mn/$620mn = 21.8% S-O-M

2. Share of Prepared Dips: $135/$420mn = 32.1% S-O-M

3. Share of Shelf-Stable Dips: $135/$185mn = 73.0% S-O-M

Usage Segments

1. Share of "Chip Dips": $135/$413mn = 32.7% S-O-M (note Frito-Lay competes almost exclusively in this segment).

2. Share of "Vegetable Dips": Assumed to be very small since refrigerated salad dressings (e.g., Marie's) and dip mixes/refrigerated dips dominated this segment and sour cream dips were more popular for vegetable dipping.

Flavor Segments

It is necessary to convert Frito-Lay's Dips sales volume at manufacturer's prices to retail prices to calculate market share. Retail sales volume for bean/picante and cheese dips can be estimated by dividing retail dollar sales volume of $135 million by Frito-Lay's sales volume of $87 million in 1985 ($135mn/$87mn = 1.55) and multiplying the flavor sales volume (from Case Exhibit 2) as follows:

- Frito-Lay Cheese Sales of $48mn x 1.55 = $74mn at Retail
- Frito-Lay Mexican Sales of $39mn x 1.55 = $60mn at Retail

Therefore,

1. Share of Cheese Dips: $74mn/$155mn = 47.7% S-O-M
2. Share of Mexican Dips: $60mn/$62mn = 96% S-O-M

Note: Frito-Lay has no cream cheese dip and just introduced a sour cream dip.

preservatives, and having a metallic taste." Thus, a question remains as to how large this segment can grow given (1) refrigerated (fresher?) dips, (2) dip mixes that use fresh ingredients, and (3) some preference for homemade dips (20% of all dip volume is homemade).

    4.   Frito-Lay's Dips are profitable. The case states that dips have a gross margin of 47% and a 10% profit contribution. However, certain differences between Mexican Dips and Cheese Dips exist. As shown in Exhibit 3 in this note, Mexican Dips are the major profit contributor with a higher gross margin, fewer marketing expenses, and a higher profit contribution than Cheese Dips. Moreover, Mexican Dips have a higher contribution margin than Cheese Dips. Exhibit 4 in this note, which is based on the 1986 forecast of revenues and expenses, shows a different picture. That is, **Frito-Lay's Dips will incur a decline in profitability given the current strategy and resource allocation.**

    D.   **What sales volume and market share(s) will be required of the dip line to preserve its profit contribution given budgeted promotion expenses?**

    1.   Case Exhibit 8 shows that the advertising and merchandising expenditures for dips will be $4,728,510 in 1986. Exhibit 3 in this note showed that the 1985 profit contribution was 10.3% which Frito-Lay wished to preserve. Therefore it is possible to calculate the sales volume assuming general and administrative overhead remains at $6,572,000 (from case Exhibit 3):

Fixed Costs

Promotion Expenses (case Exhibit 8)	$ 4,728,510
G&A Overhead (case Exhibit 3)	6,572,000
	$11,300,510

Sales volumes required to achieve 10.3% profit contribution:
$11,300,510/.103 = $109.7 million

    2.   A sales volume of $109.7 million is about 26% higher than 1985 sales of $87 million and about 11% higher than forecasted revenues for 1986.

    3.   Sales volume of $109.7 million at Frito-Lay prices translates to $170 million at retail prices ($109.7mn x 1.55). Market share of total dips will be 27.4% and 40.5% of prepared dips.

EXHIBIT 3

1985 SALES, EXPENSE, AND PROFIT PERCENTAGE BREAKDOWN

	Mexican Dips	Cheese Dips	Total Dips
Net Sales	100.0%	100.0%	100.0%
Gross Margin	49.0	45.0	47.0
Marketing Expense:			
Selling	22.5	22.9	22.7
Freight	3.75	3.78	3.77
Cons. Advtg.	.15	.18	.17
Cons. & Trade Promo.	2.2	2.8	2.5
Total Mktg. Expense	28.6	29.6	29.2
Gen. & Admin. O'hd.	7.1	7.8	7.5
Profit Contribution	13.3%	7.8%	10.3%
Contribution Margin*	22.8%	18.5%	20.5%

*Contribution Margin calculated as follows: Gross Margin - (Selling + Freight).

EXHIBIT 4

FRITO-LAY'S DIPS 1986 SALES, EXPENSE AND PROFIT FORECAST
($000's)

	Mexican Dip	Cheese Dip	Sour Cream Dip	Total Dips
Net Sales	$40,602	$48,296	$10,000	$98,898
Gross Margin	19,895	21,733	4,500	46,128
Marketing Expense:				
Selling	9,135	11,060	2,270	22,465
Freight	1,523	1,825	377	3,726
Cons. Advtg.	523	627	0	1,170
Cons. & Trade Promo.	1,237	1,530	761	3,528
Total Marketing Expense	12,418	15,063	3,408	30,889
Gen. & Admin. Overhead	2,883	3,767	--	6,650
Profit Contribution	$ 4,594	$ 2,903	$1,092	$ 8,589
Profit %	11.3%	6.0%	10.9%	8.7%

Note:
1. Gross margin, selling, and freight expense for Mexican and Cheese Dips based on Exhibit 3 percentages in this note. Sour cream dip and gross margin given in case; selling and freight expense based on total dips percent.

2. Consumer advertising, consumer and trade promotion expenditures for Mexican and cheese dips obtained from case Exhibit 8 and allocated on the basis of 1985 sales for each product. Sour cream dip expenditure obtained from Exhibit 8.

E. **What are the pros and cons of focusing attention on the "chip dip" segment?**

1. **Pros**

    - Frito-Lay has a well established competitive position based on location near salty snacks (a "natural carrier") and sales/distribution effort. They know how to market "chip dips."

    - A linkage between Frito-Lay potato chips (O'Grady's, Lay's, Ruffles) and sour cream-based dips exists; about 50% of salty snack volume is captured by potato chips. Note: Mexican Dips complemented Tostitos and Fritos and Cheese Dips complemented tortilla chips (e.g., Doritos, Tostitos). In short, the formula works in the chip dip business, at least for Frito-Lay.

    - The focus on "chip dips" has resulted in highly respectable market shares (see Exhibit 2 in this note).

    - The focus on "chip dips" has proven to be a profitable target market strategy - at least historically (see Exhibit 3 in this note). However, profitability will suffer in 1986 given pro forma revenue and expenses (see Exhibit 4 in this note).

    - Penetration of chip dips is low. Presently, 20% of chips are eaten with dips; 45% of all households used dips in 1985. Frito-Lay has a 20% penetration with its dips; therefore, there is an opportunity to make further inroads.

    - Frito-Lay's usage frequency for shelf-stable dips per year is 3.6 times while the frequency for all shelf-stable dips was 4 times per year. Thus, volume gains from increased use frequency is possible.

    - Competition in the chip segment is heating up given new competitive products and increased advertising/promotion dollars. It may be "wise" to continue attention here and use the sour cream dip as a **line extension** to fill-out the line for **chip dips**.

    - The chip segment is the dominant segment with 67% of dip dollar volume in 1985. **Assuming** 2/3 of sour cream volume is for chips, then the chips segment is where to be. Alternative estimates of sour cream potential for Frito-Lay's French Onion Dip are shown in Exhibit 5 in this note for both chips and vegetable dipping. Note that the estimates range from $73 million to $114 million for sour cream vegetable dipping.

    Cons

    - The chip segment is congested and likely to become more so in the near future. Further gains in market share for Mexican/Cheese dips might be overly costly.

EXHIBIT 5

ALTERNATE ESTIMATES OF SOUR-CREAM DIP POTENTIAL FOR CHIP AND VEGETABLE DIPPING

Estimate 1:

1. Case states 67% of dips used for chips; 33% of dips for vegetables.

2. **Assuming** sour-cream dip usage follows this pattern and **given** that sour-cream dollar volume is $310 million (Exhibit 1 in this note), then sour-cream volume estimate for
   - chip dipping: $310 million x .67 = $208 million
   - vegetable dipping: $310 million x .33 = $102 million

Estimate 2:

1. Frito-Lay's sour-cream dip is a prepared dip; prepared sour-cream dip dollar volume from case Exhibit 1 is $220 million.

2. **Assuming** the 2/3, 1/3 split on chip/vegetable dip usage holds, then sour-cream volume for
   - chip dipping: $220 million x .67 = $147 million
   - vegetable dipping: $220 million x .33 = $73 million

Estimate 3:

1. **Given** the 2/3, 1/3 split on chip/vegetable usage and total dip volume of $620 million;

2. **Given** that bean/picante (Mexican) dips are not used with vegetables and 25% of cream cheese and 85% of cheese-based dip volume is linked to chip usage; then

3. Sour cream volume for chips and vegetables for 1985 can be deduced as follows using the dollar volume figures in Exhibit 1 in this note:

Flavor

Usage	Bean/Picante	Cream Cheese	Cheese	Sour Cream
Chip	$62 mm	$23 mm	$132 mm	$196 mm
Vegetable	0	$70 mm	$23 mm	$114 mm
Totals	$62 mm	$93 mm	$155 mm	$310 mm

- Heavy investment of promotion dollars might preserve market share; however, profit contribution might suffer if volume gains are not realized (see Exhibit 4 in this note).

- Over emphasis on chip dips might be myopic given that 1/3 of dips are purchased for vegetable dipping.

- Trend data "suggest" possible concerns about nutritional value and salt content of prepared foods (e.g., chips). Vegetable or natural foods might be preferred in the near future.

- A financial analysis of Frito-Lay's Dips, excluding for the moment sour cream, indicates that Mexican and Cheese Dips must achieve sales of $102,321,450 at Frito-Lay prices given the advertising and promotion expenditures planned and a 10.3% profit contribution.

    Fixed Costs:

Promotion Expenses (case Exhibit 9)	$ 3,967,110
Gen., Admin., Overhead (no change from case Exhibit 3)	6,572,000
	$10,539,110

    Contribution Margin (Exhibit 3 in this note) 20.5%

    Profit Contribution (Exhibit 3 in this note) 10.3%

    $$B/E = \frac{\$10,539,110}{.103} = \$102,321,450$$

Therefore, an 18% increase in sales is necessary. Is this possible given the recent sales history of Frito-Lay's Mexican Dips and Cheese Dips, the share of Mexican Dips (97% from Exhibit 2 in this note) and Cheese Dips (48% from Exhibit 2 in this note), even with, say, a 10% price increase? Moreover, adjusting to retail sales volume indicates that sales must reach $160,151,470.

F. What are the pros and cons of focusing attention on the "vegetable dip" segment?

A decision to pursue vegetable dipping is an example of a **brand extension**. A brand extension strategy involves taking a well-established brand name into a product category that is new to the company. Sometimes this strategy is called **brand leveraging** because it can build on customer awareness and goodwill.

According to Tauber (*Business Horizons*, March-April, 1981), a brand extension can be successful if three criteria are satisfied: (1) Perceptual Fit, (2) Competitive Leverage, and (3)

Benefit Transfer. **Perceptual fit** means that prospective buyers perceive the new item (i.e., sour cream dip) to be congruent with the parent brand (i.e., Mexican and Cheese dip). **Competitive leverage** means that the parent brand provides an advantage that competitors already in the category do not have (e.g., strong sales and distribution system, advertising/promotion skills, etc.). **Benefit transfer** means that the benefit(s) provided by the parent brand is the same one being offered by the new item **and** this benefit is desired. Tauber also notes that "brand extension always carries greater risk when a brand name is used almost synonymously with a specific product."

Given this background, the pros and cons of pursuing the vegetable dip segment are outlined below.

1. **Pros**

   - Frito-Lay has not actively pursued this segment which represents 1/3 of dip sales volume, or $207 million at retail prices.

   - Frito-Lay's French Onion Dip is a means for reaching this segment given that sour cream dips are preferred over cheese dips for vegetable dipping.

   - "More" attention to vegetable dipping will expand the served market beyond chip dips only.

   - There are fewer, less powerful competitors (e.g., Marie's) relative to Frito-Lay's size and marketing strength.

2. **Cons**

   - Reaching vegetable dip consumers may be a problem. The sour cream dip will probably have to be located in (near) the produce section of supermarkets given research which shows dips should be situated near their "natural carrier." Frito-Lay has limited experience dealing with produce buyers (competitive leverage). Sales costs could increase to 25% of sales from 22.7% of sales.

   - Can the vegetable segment be aggressively pursued with a single item? Will a full line of sour cream-based be needed as was the case with Frito-Lay's cheese dips? It is not clear that the costs associated with an active product development program for vegetable dips is warranted given the market size.

   - Concern about the shelf-stable dip packaging might be issue since consumers are sensitive to the taste issue.

   - **If** Frito-Lay **actively** pursues vegetable dipping which would include placement in the produce section, then the economics must be considered. As shown below, the contribution margin for a vegetable dip focus will become 16.2%:

Sales		100.0%
Gross Margin		45.0%
Variable Mktg. Expense:		
Selling	25.0%	
Freight	3.8	28.8
Contribution		16.2%

If Advertising-to-Sales is, say, 3% which is allocated for Mexican/Cheese Dips, and G&A Overhead is charged at 7.5% of sales, then the profit contribution falls to 5.7% for the sour cream dip. A 7.5% profit contribution is lower than cheese dips and **much** lower than Mexican dips. If Frito-Lay spends 7.6% of sales on advertising for sour cream dips as it did in 1986, then sour cream would contribute little or no profit:

Sales		100.0%
Gross Margin		45.0%
Variable Marketing Expense		
Selling	25.0%	
Freight	3.8%	28.8%
Advertising & Promotion		7.6%
G & A Overhead		7.5%
Profit Contribution		1.1%

G. What strategy should be adopted?

1. On balance, it would seem that Frito-Lay should more actively pursue the "chip dip" category treating the sour cream dip as a **line extension**.

2. Active (aggressive) pursuit of the "vegetable" dip category does not seem wise from a marketing and profit impact perspective.

3. It would seem that Frito-Lay could advertise the use of sour cream dip for vegetable dipping. However, shelf placement would remain among salty snacks.

H. Epilogue

Frito-Lay executives opted to treat sour cream dips as a line extension and continued to pursue the chip dip segment. However, the company did experiment with shelf placement by using end-of-aisle displays apart from salty snacks. It also devoted limited dollars to promoting sour cream dip for vegetable dipping. Neither proved to be successful according to Frito-Lay executives.

I. Summary Points

1. Market segmentation is important not only for identifying a marketing opportunity, but also for assessing market position. Segmentation bases possible in this case included (1) product form, e.g., mix vs. refrigerated, (2) usage, e.g., for chips or vegetables, and (3) flavors, e.g., cheese, sour-cream, etc. Each approach provides a different perspective on market opportunity and position.

2. Profitability analysis is central to performing a marketing opportunity assessment. Profitability analysis includes an assessment of product costs (gross margin) **and** present and future marketing expenditures.

3. Subtle factors must be considered in the decision whether to pursue different segments. For example, issues in this case related to shelf placement in supermarkets (near produce, salty snacks), different buyers for snack foods vs. produce, and different delivery systems (e.g., warehouse vs. store door delivery). Oftentimes subtleties can make the difference between success and failure.

4. Case illustrates the concept of market evolution and a changing competitive environment through time. Market evolution reflected in changing consumer tastes, and eating habits spurred primary demand for dips which Frito-Lay benefited from. The company's swift response with cheese dips illustrates the benefits of being "first to market" in a product-market segment. However, success attracts imitators as a product-market evolves and necessitates a search for new opportunities.

5. A firm's **distinctive competency** can be used to achieve a dominant competitive position. At the same time, it can limit a firm. In this case, Frito-Lay's vaunted sales/delivery system through store-door route sales people -- a distinctive competency -- was a limiting factor given different buyers and different delivery systems for vegetable dips.

6. Case illustrates a fundamental issue in product/brand management; namely, the issue of pursuing a **line** extension versus a **brand** extension. The vegetable dip opportunity involved treating Frito-Lay's sour-cream dip as a franchise extension. Three questions are therefore posed:

    a. Is the new item congruent with the parent brand (perceptual fit)?

    b. Does Frito-Lay have the leverage over competitors in terms of marketing skill (competitive leverage)?

    c. Is the benefit provided by the parent brand the same as the one being offered by the new item and is the benefit desired (benefit transfer)?

It is not obvious that the sour cream extension meets these criteria for a **brand** extension.

SOUTH DELAWARE COORS, INC.

Synopsis

South Delaware Coors, Inc. represents an interesting marketing case situation for three reasons: the issue in the case is clear-cut while data needed to solve the issue requires conceptualization and insight; the case contains elements common to most feasibility decisions (estimates of industry demand, market share, investments, costs, and resulting performance are required); and the case is ripe with learning potential for the student in terms of developing actionable decisions based on research information.

Two issues are present in the case. The first is a decision on what research should be conducted by Manson and Associates to allow Larry Brownlow to estimate the feasibility of a Coors beer distributorship for a two-county area in Delaware. This issue is evident, even stressed, throughout the case. The second issue is a decision on whether or not the distributorship is feasible or, in other words, a go/no-go decision by Brownlow regarding his application. This issue is largely implicit in the case.

Teaching Objectives

This case is designed to teach students: (1) To make a feasibility decision, the market researcher usually needs estimates of industry demand, market share, investments, costs, and performance; (2) It is important to conceptualize data before marketing research is conducted, i.e., the researcher must anticipate research results and how such results will solve the research problem; (3) Effort spent in the problem formulation stage of marketing research can often reduce later costs of performing research; (4) Secondary data is the appropriate starting point for marketing research; (5) The cost of information is real and usually constrained in most marketing research problems; (6) Cheap information may not be the most economical when quality of information is compared; (7) Break-even analysis is often a required tool in feasibility studies; (8) Because the research budget has excess funds available, this is not sufficient reason to conduct extraneous research.

Finally, the case provides the opportunity to stress two other objectives not usually found in conventional case situations. If the first and recommended method of use is utilized by the instructor, the case will provide students with the experience of living with past

---

This note is adapted from notes prepared by Professor James E. Nelson and Doctoral Student Eric J. Karson, University of Colorado at Boulder.

decisions and the experience of group decision-making. These experiences should be part of a student's formal marketing education but are too often lacking in a conventional case.

Teaching Suggestions

Two methods of use are possible. The first begins with the instructor assigning the case in the usual manner. Early in the class discussion, students would be encouraged to analyze the case situation in terms of the consumer, competition, and the relative merits of each of the nine research studies. Some students will likely rush headlong into a decision on which research should be conducted; this should be avoided until the analysis is complete. This step in the classroom usage should take not more than 20 minutes.

When the instructor is satisfied that students understand the case situation, the discussion should be stopped with a statement similar to "All right. What I want you to do now is quickly divide into groups of three. Assume you are advisers to Larry who must make a decision in the next 15 minutes regarding what research should be conducted. When your group has decided, send a representative to me for further instructions."

When each group's representative approaches, he or she should be asked to identify which research studies the group has decided Larry should have conducted. The instructor then hands copies of the requested studies' research results (Exhibit 1 in this note) and charges the group with the responsibility of analyzing the data and recommending whether or not Larry should apply for the distributorship. The representative then returns to the group and members perform analyses they consider appropriate. The instructor should feel free to observe closely the decision process occurring at each group but should provide little or no input if requested. Students must make the decision.

Near the end of the period, the instructor should call for written go/no-go decisions from each group as supported by analyses members see fit to include. The instructor can then evaluate each group's decision-making process before the next class period, at which time decisions can be returned, discussed, and learning objectives presented. Class periods of 75 minutes minimum would be required to use this method.

An alternative method of use is more conventional and can be accomplished in shorter class periods. Here, the instructor would assign the case and pass out all research results before class discussion. Student analyses would center again about the consumer, competition, and the relative merits of each research study but with full knowledge of research results. Additional discussion would center on the feasibility of the distributorship and appropriate methods of analysis.

This second method of use is a far less powerful learning experience for the student. Of the course objectives outlined earlier in this note, only 1, 4, 6, and 7 are likely to be realized with this method.

Areas for Discussion/Analysis

Once students have a framework for analysis, the decision-making process should proceed relatively easily. The framework used in this note is organized about the consumer and estimates of demand, market share, investments, costs and performance. All data references in the following quantitative analyses come from the Appendix in this note.

A. Consumer Analysis

Students should be able to deduce that nearly every beer drinking consumer in the market area will try Coors when it becomes available. Perceived risk is slight, the product will be widely available at competitive premium prices, latent demand likely exists, extensive informative advertising including word-of-mouth will likely occur, and existing brand loyalty is likely low among most present buyers of beer.

However, Coors' market share will eventually stabilize at a level similar to those at the national or regional level. Students should spend some time identifying this permanent market segment, where it would expect to buy Coors, and what product and other purchase features these consumers would consider important in buying Coors.

The typical purchase will likely occur almost exactly as typical Budweiser, Miller, Busch, or other purchases occur. If a planned purchase, the consumer will buy from the same source as last time unless new stimuli interfere. In the absence of specials, price at all outlets of a given type will be so close as to make comparison shopping meaningless. Impulse or emergency purchasing will occur from the nearest source with little regard to price or brand, depending on the nature of the consumer and purchase situation. For most consumers, Coors will be purchased as a convenience good, along with groceries and other regularly purchased household consumables. The specialty and unsought good status Coors may presently enjoy will soon disappear after introduction.

B. Industry Demand

It is possible for students to estimate industry demand in two manners. The first involves results of Studies A and B and could be termed a "per capita" approach. Students need merely take the 1991 per capita consumption figures from Table A (for Delaware) and multiply these data by population estimates from Table B. Their estimates for 1991 should be around 231,750 people living in the two counties, 162,250 of whom are age 21 and over. Multiplying 231,750 people by 28.9 gallons per capita consumption will produce an industry demand total of around 6.7 million gallons in 1991 (multiplying 162,250 people over age 21 by 41.9 gallons will produce an estimate of 6.9 million gallons).

The second manner of estimating involves Study E data and could be termed a "taxes paid" approach. Totaling taxes paid by the six distributors for 1988 and 1989 yields $228,000 and $306,000, respectively. Dividing each of these figures by 6 cents, the tax per gallon, provides consumption estimates of around 4.8 and 5.1 million gallons. Students will need to extend these results to 1991; a range of 5.6 to 5.8 million gallons for their estimates can be expected.

Which method is better? The first study's sources of data are not identified nor do we know the accuracy of the computer models used to make projections. The second method uses an unbiased source (the Delaware Department of Revenue) but relies on students to extend 1988 and 1989 data to 1991. Their methods of projection may be less accurate than Manson's computer models. The second is cheaper than the first ($200 vs. $2500). The second provides data specifically for the two-county market area while the first uses consumption averages generated for the entire state. Students frequently take both approaches to estimate industry demand and strike an average between the disparate results. Students might discuss the wisdom of such a strategy -- is more information always better?

C. Market Share Projections

Table C, containing market share projections, is straight-forward and needs little explanation here. Some evaluation of the accuracy of Manson and Associates' market share projections could be undertaken if time permits.

Table C data are crucial to making a sales projection for the distributorship.

D. Investments

Larry's estimates of capital needed to start the business are outlined in the case. Little quarrel with the figures as given can be voiced. However, Larry has neglected to estimate what investments in cash and accounts receivable will be required and has, therefore, understated his capital requirements.

Estimates of the additional funds needed can be derived from Table F. Table F shows the typical wholesaler of wine, liquor, and beer examined by Robert Morris Associates had 11.1% of its assets in cash and 14.8% in receivables. Allowing for an efficient operation, Larry has underestimated the needed capital by some 26%. Thus, a better estimate of capital required would be $800,000/.74 or about $1,080,000.

Students will comment and often object to the validity of data in Table F on bases noted at the bottom of the table. Certainly the data have the potential for non-representativeness but students should be made to consider what alternative data sources are available given the facts in the case. Larry is too busy to seek out other sources and Coors management will provide no cost or performance information.

E. Costs

Estimates of fixed costs are reasonably straightforward and are given in the case. However, Larry has estimated no expenditures for interest payments, advertising, and travel. No data in the case bear on travel expenditures or advertising; interest costs can be estimated only by the student. If total capitalization is $1,000,000 and Larry provides only about $400,000, a first-year interest charge of $70,000 is reasonable. The other first-year expenses are $160,000 for salaries and $90,000 for fixed or semi-fixed expenses. Thus, total fixed costs will be at least $320,000 plus travel and advertising expenses, both of which will be substantial.

To estimate variable costs, Tables F and I are needed. Table F shows the cost of goods sold averages 77.1% of sales; Table I shows an average wholesale price for the seven competing brands of about $3.16 per six pack. Multiplying $3.16 by 1.77 produces a wholesale price of $5.59 per gallon.

In addition to selling beer in bottles and cans, the distributorship will also sell kegs in a ratio of 1 gallon of keg beer to 3 gallons of beer in bottles and cans. The case states that keg beer prices at the wholesale level were about 45% of prices for beer in bottles and cans. These two facts can be combined with wholesale costs and prices for beer in bottles and cans to produce an overall weighted average contribution per gallon of $1.10. Relevant figures appear in Exhibit 1 in this note.

EXHIBIT 1

ESTIMATES OF WHOLESALE COSTS AND PRICES

Beer	Weight	Wholesale Cost per Gallon ($)		Wholesale Price per Gallon ($)	
Bottles and Cans	3	4.31	←77.1%-	5.59	
Kegs	1	1.94		2.52	) 45%
	weighted average =	3.72		4.82	

Performance

To conclude on the feasibility of the distributorship, students should first calculate a break-even point and compare this figure to industry demand and expected market shares. From data in the case and this note the break-even gallonage and break-even market share can be calculated (assuming the estimated Delaware market size conforms to Study E estimates, say, 5.7 million gallons). This is done below:

$$\text{Break-even} = \frac{\text{FixedCosts}}{\text{UnitSellingPrice} - \text{UnitVariableCosts}}$$

$$= \frac{\$320,000}{\$4.82 - \$3.72} = 291,000 \text{ gallons}$$

$$\text{Market share} = \frac{291,000 \text{ gallons}}{5,700,000}, \text{ or about } 5.0\%$$

Students should also perform similar calculations to determine quantities and market shares based on the operation earning a suitable return on investment and spending, say, $100,000 on advertising and travel. Market shares here should be between 7% and 9%.

Comparison of these market shares with those forecast in Table C show the distributorship to be a feasible operations (how accurate are those forecasts?). However, missing from the present analysis is consideration of incentive costs. A five percent incentive based on sales revenues and a narrowing of prices and costs could easily make the distributorship a break-even operation.

Some students will prepare pro forma income statements for 1990 and later years. Others will calculate cash flows. Many will use spread sheet analyses, with results shown for several scenarios based on varying degrees of optimism in their assumptions.

Analysis Summary

Based on the analysis in this note, Larry would be well advised to apply for the distributorship. **Crucial data used to come to this conclusion result from Research Studies C, E, F, and I and a total cost of $4,250.** The remaining five studies are not needed. Students are usually interested to learn what was the class average amount spent on marketing research compared to $4,250. The instructor should be able to provide this comparison.

Because the total cost of the required studies is low relative to the budgeted amount and because students will inadequately conceptualize the problem, requests for extraneous research will usually occur. Students may frequently argue that consumer and retailer research, Studies G and H respectively are needed to estimate feasibility. At first glance, this may appear to be so.

However, consumer and retailer data as derived from these studies are largely **irrelevant, given Coors' national experience** (unless the student has reason to believe Delaware residents or market conditions differ **greatly** from those of the rest of the U.S.). Restating, extensive research on attitudes and intentions of consumers and retailers will yield less valid data than measures of actual experience of similar groups of people.

Finally, several students may comment on the **ethics** of Manson and Associates regarding their making a research proposal totaling $18,550 when only $4,250 worth of research was needed. If time permits, a discussion of this topic will be worthwhile. However, there is not sufficient data in the case on which to determine Manson and Associates' intent in proposing "excess" research. Time also might be spent discussing the ethics of Larry's taking the proposal and executing several of the studies himself. Often several students would have Larry conducting studies E, F, and I.

Student Learning Experience

At least two levels of learning are present in business case analysis. The first or lowest level of learning would be called "methods of problem solving" or something similar. That is, marketing instructors attempt through case analyses to teach students methods of problem solving applicable to real world situations in which students will find themselves after graduation. South Delaware Coors, Inc. provides this level of learning through introducing students to considerations present in feasibility analyses and, to some degree, in data collection.

A second or higher level of learning is possible. This is the development of "principles" that can be similarly learned and carried over to the business world. Principles which are potentially learnable from the case are course objectives 1
through 8 listed at the start of this note. To encourage this sort of learning, the instructor should devote a few minutes at the start of the next class session to summarize what was done in the previous meeting and to present objectives for the case as what has hopefully been learned by the student.

Part of the student learning potential with South Delaware Coors, Inc. was also mentioned earlier as the student's exposure to group decision-making. Groups or committees in marketing make large numbers of decisions in the areas of new product development, pricing, marketing strategy, and marketing policy, for examples. Thus, the instructor should also devote discussion or lecture time at the start of the next session to the group aspect of making a decision (if the class used this method in analyzing the case).

The topic could be titled, "What sorts of things happen when, instead of an individual, a group makes a decision?" These things, among others, do: (1) The decision takes longer; (2) More variety in reasoning occurs; (3) Conflict and differences of group opinion occur; (4) Communication is needed; (5) Feelings toward others in the group develop; (6) A group spirit evolves; (7) Equal participation is difficult to achieve; and (8) Social pressures toward conformity exist. Other things happen in group problem-solving and the instructor should feel free to note and discuss them. For more background on group decision processes, see parts 5-8 of N.R.F. Maier's **Problem Solving and Creativity in Individuals and Groups**, Brooks/Cole Publishing Company, Division of Wadsworth Publishing Company, 1970. The instructor can greatly aid the relevancy of the discussion here by presenting interpretations of what he or she observed occurring in the groups during the decision-making process.

Final Research Report Tables

The Appendix presents final report tables for all research Manson and Associates proposed. The instructor should reproduce each table before the class discussion separately in sufficient quantity to satisfy demands of class groups.

Summary Points

A good way to end discussion often has been for the instructor to present the eight learning objectives listed in the second section of this note as a short lecture to students. The eight points noted in the paragraph before last could also serve as a short lecture.

APPENDIX

EXAMPLES OF FINAL RESEARCH REPORT TABLES

TABLE A: NATIONAL AND DELAWARE RESIDENT CONSUMPTION PER CAPITA, 1988-1992 (GALLONS)

	U. S. Consumption		Delaware Consumption	
Year	Based on Entire Population	Based on Population over Age 21	Based on Entire Population	Based on Population over Age 21
1988	24.1	35.0	26.7	38.3
1989	24.6	35.9	27.2	39.3
1990	24.6	36.0	27.2	39.4
1991	26.1	38.3	28.9	41.9
1992	25.8	37.9	28.6	46.5

Source: Study A

TABLE B: POPULATION ESTIMATES FOR 1986-1996 FOR TWO DELAWARE COUNTIES IN MARKET AREA

County	Entire Population (000)					
	1986	1988	1990	1992	1994	1996
KENT	106.3	109.5	112.2	114.9	117.8	119.1
SUSSEX	110.7	114.0	116.8	119.6	122.6	124.0

County	Populaton Age 21 and Over					
	1986	1988	1990	1992	1994	1996
KENT	69.4	72.3	75.2	77.0	78.0	81.0
SUSSEX	77.5	81.5	85.3	87.0	90.1	90.1

Source: Study B

TABLE C: COORS MARKET SHARE ESTIMATES FOR 1990-1995*

Year	Market Share (%)
1990	8.9
1991	8.7
1992	8.7
1993	8.8
1994	8.8
1995	8.8

Source: Study C.
*Includes imports

TABLE D: LIQUOR AND BEER LICENSE ESTIMATES FOR MARKET AREA FOR 1990-1995

Type of License	1990	1991	1992	1993	1994	1995
All beverages	330	340	350	365	385	405
Retail Beer and wine	55	60	60	65	65	70
Off-premise beer only	210	220	225	230	235	245
Veterans beer and liquor	12	12	13	13	12	12
Fraternal	20	20	20	20	20	20
Resort beer and liquor	25	25	31	32	34	36

Source: Study D.

TABLE E: BEER TAXES PAID BY BEER WHOLESALERS IN THE MARKET AREA, 1988 AND 1989

Wholesaler	1988 Tax Paid ($)	1989 Tax Paid ($)
A	40,300	42,840
B	31,680	33,660
C	40,320	42,840
D	83,520	88,740
E	60,480	64,260
F	31,680	33,660

Source: Study E.

Note: Delaware beer tax is 6 cents per gallon.

TABLE F: FINANCIAL STATEMENT SUMMARY FOR 510 WHOLESALERS OF WINE, LIQUOR, AND BEER IN FISCAL YEAR 1988

Assets	Percentage	Ratios	%
Cash and equivalents	11.1	Quick	.6
		Current	1.6
Accounts and notes		Debts/worth	1.6
receivable net	14.8		
Inventory	33.6	Sales/receivables	49.2
All other current	1.9	Cost sales/inventory	11.9
Total Current	61.1	Percentage profit before	
Fixed assets net	24.1	taxes based on total assets	6.3
Intangibles net	5.3		
All other noncurrent	9.5		
Total	100.0		
Liabilities		**Income Data**	
Notes payable --		Net sales	100.0%
short-term	11.8	Cost of sales	77.1
Current maturity		Gross profit	22.9
long-term debt	3.7	Operating expenses	20.3
Account and notes		Operating profit	2.6
payable -- trade	15.5	All other expenses net	.4
Income taxes payable	1.1		
All other current	7.7	Profit before taxes	2.2%
Total current	39.7		
Long-term debt	17.6		
All other noncurrent	2.1		
Net worth	40.1		
Total Liabilities			
and net worth	100.0		

Source: Study F (Robert Morris Associates, 1989).

Interpretation of Statement Studies Figures

    RMA recommends that Statement Studies data be regarded only as general guidelines and not as absolute industry norms. There are several reasons why the data may not be fully representative of a given industry:

    1. The financial statements used in the Statement Studies are not selected by any random or statistically reliable method. RMA member banks voluntarily submit the raw data they have available each year, with these being the only constraints: (a) The fiscal year-ends of the companies reported may not be from April 1 through June 29, and (b) their total assets must be less than $100 million.

    2. Many companies have varied product lines; however, the Statement Studies categorize them by their primary product Standard Industrial Classification (SIC) number only.

    3. Some of our industry samples are rather small in relation to the total number of firms in a given industry. A relatively small sample can increase the changes that some of our composites do not fully represent an industry.

    4. There is the chance that an extreme statement can be present in a sample, causing a disproportionate influence on the industry composite. This is particularly true in a relatively small sample.

    5. Companies within the same industry may differ in their method of operations which in turn can directly influence their financial statements. Since they are included in our sample, too, these statements can significantly affect our composite calculations.

    6. Other considerations that can result in variations among different companies engaged in the same general line of business are different labor markets; geographical location; different accounting methods; quality of products handled; sources and methods of financing; and terms of sale.

    For these reasons, RMS does not recommend the Statement Studies figures as absolute norms for a given industry. Rather the figures should be used only as general guidelines and in addition to the other methods of financial analysis. RMA makes no claim as to the representativeness of the figures printed in this book.

TABLE G: CONSUMER QUESTIONNAIRE RESULTS

	Yes	No
Consumed Coors in the past:	62.1%	37.8%

Attitudes toward Coors	%
Strongly like	10.7
Like	38.1
Indifferent/no opinion	18.9
Dislike	18.4
Strongly dislike	13.9
Total	100.0

Usually buy beer at	%
Liquor stores	5.7
Taverns and bars	10.6
Supermarkets	65.2
Corner grocery	18.5
Total	100.0

Weekly beer consumption	%
Less than 1 can	28.8
1-2 cans	37.2
3-4 cans	14.0
5-6 cans	10.4
7-8 cans	6.8
9 cans and over	2.8
Total	100.0

Features considered important when buying beer	%
Taste	23.3
Brand Name	32.6
Price	31.7
Store location	5.5
Advertising	1.0
Carbonation	1.2
Other	4.7
Total	100.0

Intention to Buy Coors:	%
Certainly will	70.0
Maybe will	11.2
Not sure	6.9
Maybe will not	1.8
Certainly will not	10.1
Total	100.0

Semantic Differential Scale - Consumer

	Extremely	Very	Somewhat	Somewhat	Very	Extremely	
Masculine							Feminine
Healthful							Unhealthful
Cheap							Expensive
Strong							Weak
Old-fashioned							New
Upper-class							Lower-class
Good taste							Bad taste

Key: ——— Coors .... Ideal — — Miller — . — Miller Lite — .. — Budweiser

Source: Study G.

TABLE H: RETAILER QUESTIONNAIRE RESULTS

Brands of beer carried

Beer sales

	%		%
Budweiser	99	Budweiser	28.7
Miller Lite	99	Miller Lite	12.4
Miller	99	Miller	8.2
Busch	87	Busch	6.4
Bud Light	99	Bud Light	6.1
Old Milwaukee	72	Old Milwaukee	6.0
Michelob	95	Michelob	5.8
Others	91	Others	26.4
		Total	100.0

Semantic Differential Scale - Retailer

	Extremely	Very	Somewhat	Somewhat	Very	Extremely	
Masculine							Feminine
Healthful							Unhealthful
Cheap							Expensive
Strong							Weak
Old-fashioned							New
Upper-class							Lower-class
Good taste							Bad taste

Key: ——— Coors · · · · Ideal — — Miller — · · Miller Lite — · Budweiser

Intention to Sell Coors	%
Certainly will	88.7
Maybe will	5.7
Not sure	4.0
Maybe will not	1.6
Certainly will not	0.0
Total	100.0

Source: Study H.

TABLE I: RETAIL AND WHOLESALE PRICES FOR SELECTED BEERS IN THE MARKET AREA

Beer	Wholesale[a] Six-Pack Price (dollars)	Retail[b] Six-Pack Price (dollars)
Budweiser	3.29	3.49
Miller Lite	3.29	3.49
Miller	3.29	3.49
Busch	2.57	2.73
Bud Light	3.29	3.49
Old Milwaukee	2.68	2.85
Michelob	3.68	3.91

Source: Study I.

[a]Price that the wholesaler sold to retailers.

[b]Price that the retailer sold to consumers.

Note: The wholesale gallon price is about 1.77 times the 6-pack price.

ZOECON CORPORATION: INSECT GROWTH REGULATORS

Synopsis

In January, 1986, executives at Zoecon Corporation met to assess future opportunities for Strike ROACH ENDER, a new product containing an adulticide and an insect growth regulator (IGR). The product had just completed a six month test market with mixed results. Company executives are faced with the decision of what to do next. Three options are presented: (1) Expand distribution to a 19 city area where 80 percent of roach control products are sold, (2) Focus attention on the professional pest control market (e.g., Pest Control Operators), and/ or (3) Contact the makers of Raid, d-Con, or Black Flag for the purpose of including the IGR chemical. Combinations of these options are possible.

The case raises a variety of issues. For example, product related qualities that affect the diffusion of new products must be considered. Market size estimates must be calculated based on product category, distribution channels, and the geographic scope of market coverage. Sales volume estimates using trial and repeat purchase data must be determined as well as profitability. Equally important, the issue of whether to distribute the product through supermarkets, PCOs, and/or a third-party insecticide marketer needs to be considered by Zoecon executives. In this regard, issues related to **dual distribution** are raised for consideration.

Teaching Objectives

This case has five objectives:

1. To expose students to unique problems faced by a firm introducing an innovative product concept - "birth control" for roaches.

2. To hone student analytical skills relating to market size estimation, volume forecasting using product trial and repeat purchase behavior, and profit determination.

3. To illustrate important differences in marketing to end consumers (households) and industrial buyers (professional pest control operators).

4. To introduce the idea of "third-party" distributors as an alternative marketing channel to reach markets.

5. To raise for consideration issues related to dual distribution.

Teaching Suggestions

This case can be assigned as a product strategy decision, a channel choice issue, or to illustrate joint product-channel management issues.

This case is suitable for both undergraduate and graduate courses. Moreover, it has been shown to be an effective examination case given the variety of issues addressed and as a group presentation case. A class discussion would benefit from raising the following questions either before or during the discussion:

1. How would you characterize the Premise Insecticide Market?

2. How do insect growth regulators "fit" each segment? What was learned from Zoecon's flea IGR introduction?

3. What has been learned from the Strike ROACH ENDER test market?

4. What are the pros and cons of the options available for Zoecon's Strike ROACH ENDER?

5. Assuming Zoecon pursues a third-party distribution arrangement, what specific information should be contained in a presentation to d-Con, S. C. Johnson & Sons, or Boyle-Midway?

As an assignment with the case, some instructors might ask students to read: John Quelch, "Why Not Exploit Dual Marketing?" *Business Horizons* (January-February 1987), pp. 52-60. As a postscript, instructors might read excerpts from "Adios, la Cucaracha," *Forbes* (September 21, 1987), pp. 174-175. This article describes the novel ways firms, including Zoecon, are trying to combat cockroaches. The "pest-mortem" at the end of this note, written by a Zoecon executive, also makes for a good wrap-up.

Areas for Discussion/Analysis

A. How would you characterize the Premise Insecticide Market?

1. The premise insecticide market is composed of two primary segments: (1) consumer and (2) professional pest control. Characteristics of each segment are summarized in Exhibit 1 in this note.

2. Clearly, the consumer and professional pest control segments are very different. Notable differences exist in promotion, distribution and product packaging as well as market size.

EXHIBIT 1

CHARACTERISTICS OF THE PREMISE INSECTICIDE MARKET

Characteristic	Consumer Segment	Professional Pest Control Segment
1986 Market Size (Mfr. Prices)	$440 million*	$118.26 million**
Annual Mkt. Growth	10%	8%
Mfr. Gross Profit	55%	51%
Regionality	Southern 14 states, 50% of sales	Presumably same
Seasonality	Prime sale months: May-October	Presumably same
Major Competitors	Raid (45% S-O-M) Black Flag (12% S-O-M) d-Con (10% S-O-M)	None given in case Presumably same producers
Distribution	Supermarkets (70% of Sales) Drug stores (9% of Sales) Others (21% of Sales)	14,000 PCOs. Orkin and Terminix are largest. Mfrs. sell through distributors to PCOs
Promotion	Emphasizes media Advertising (Pull Strategy)	Emphasizes Trade Advertising + Personal Selling (Push Strategy) About 27% of Sales
Application Segments	Aerosols + Foggers (74% of Sales) Liquid Sprays (14% of Sales) Others (12% of Sales)	Bulk (cases + pallets)
Insect Treatment	Ant + Roach (40% S-O-M) Flying Insects (20% S-O-M) Fleas (11% S-O-M) Other (29% S-O-M)	Roach, Flea, Ant (52% S-O-M) Termites (21% S-O-M) Other, e.g., Rodents (27% S-O-M)

*1985 Market Size = $400 million. Estimated 1986 Market Size = $440 million ($400 MM x 1.10). Note that this figure can be adjusted to reflect Zoecon's "served market;" that is roach, flea, ant.

**Market Size at Manufacturers' Prices Computed as Follows: 1986 Revenues = $2.5B revenue x .06 (chemical cost percent = $162 million.
1986 Mfg. Sales = $162 million x 73% (27% distributor margin) = $118.26 million. Note that this figure can be adjusted to reflect Zoecon's "served market" of roach, flea, ant.

B. How do insect growth regulators "fit" each segment? What was learned from Zoecon's flea IGR introduction?

1. This question is an important one to pose early in the class discussion. It is designed to get students thinking about the unique qualities of IGRs vs. conventional insect adulticides. Moreover, this question can be used to draw important conclusions from Zoecon's experience with its flea IGR, STRIKE Flea Ender.

2. Students should recognize that IGRs are quite different from insect adulticides. Most importantly, they affect the normal sequence of metamorphosis and prevent insects from entering adulthood, hence the reproductive period. With time, an insect infestation should be controlled, if not eliminated, due to sexually impotent insects. Insect adulticides, by comparison, only kill live insects or force insects to avoid treated areas for a period of time. When an adulticide is included with an IGR, this combination serves to reduce the effect of the IGR because insects avoid treated areas ... but insects are killed.

3. Acceptance of IGRs will depend on a number of product related factors, based on the discussion in Chapter 6: Product Strategy and Management. These factors and a rating of IGRs vis-a-vis adulticides for the consumer and PCO market are shown below (+ = better than adulticide; - = worse than adulticide).

Product Factor	Consumer Segment	PCO Segment
1. Relative Advantage		
• Short-term	-	-
• Long-term	+	+
2. Compatibility	-	+
3. Simplicity (of use)	-	+
4. Immediacy of Benefit	-	-
5. Felt Need	+	+

For the consumer segment, this analysis indicates that IGRs are better than adulticides for long-term treatment of insects and they do satisfy a felt need (insect elimination). However, IGRs do not satisfy "quick-kill" needs; they may not be compatible with the "chase and squirt" behavior of consumers, and their application differs from adulticides since "only a few tenths of a milligram per square foot are required" and the scheduled (120 day) application. Perhaps the major difference between IGRs and adulticides lies in the immediacy of the benefit, namely dead bugs! While a few dead insects might be seen, it is unlikely that the same result from, say, Raid, Black Flag, or d-Con will exist. The real effect of an IGR will not be seen for 120 days.

Two potential positive factors, not found in the consumer segment, may exist in the PCO segment. PCOs typically spray premises; therefore, a "chase and squirt" mentality is not present. PCOs will also know (hopefully) how to apply the IGR. Moreover, they might benefit from the need for less chemicals **and** the scheduled reapplication after 120 days.

4. Given the potential inhibiting product factors mentioned, what accounted for the successful introduction of PRECOR (flea IGR) to PCOs, vet clinics, and pet stores, and Strike FLEA ENDER in supermarkets?

    a. PRECOR's introduction was probably assisted by knowledgeable vets and pet store owners who could explain the benefits plus application to consumers.

    b. The benefits of a flea IGR can be seen in about 23 days versus 120 days for a roach IGR.

    c. Strike FLEA ENDER achieved an 18 percent market share (given b. above) after two years, but has not achieved its profit objective (presumably the company average 25 percent before tax profit on sales).

C. What has been learned from the Strike ROACH ENDER tests market?

1. It is instructive to review the test market strategy at this point in the discussion.

    a. **Geographic Scope:** Four city test (Charleston, SC; Beaumont, TX; Charlotte, NC; New Orleans, LA) which contained 5.3 percent of the 22 million households in the 19 city market area (Southern tier of states) where 80 percent of roach insecticides are sold.

    b. **Timing:** Six month test (May-October, 1985) during peak period for insecticides.

    c. **Test Market Objectives:** (1) to determine consumer acceptance of the product, (2) to qualify the trade and consumer marketing program.

    d. **Target Consumer Segment:** Primary Segment -- "End Problem Permanently"; Secondary Segment -- "Product That Lasts." Focused on 25-54 year old women in 3+ person households.

    e. **Product Positioning:** "Scientific breakthrough with unique qualities."

    f. **Price Strategy:** "Skimming Strategy" with prices 50-75% higher than existing insecticides, due to unique compound and long-term benefit.

    g. **Advertising/Trade Promotion Strategy:** "Pull Strategy" to consumers (TV + newspaper + couponing) plus sell-in activity to supermarket buyers (discounts + sales aids + in-store displays).

    h. **Distribution Strategy:** Focus on supermarkets where 70% of insecticides purchased (selective distribution).

Overall, the test market strategy represents a "typical" introductory program for a consumer packaged good.

2. Test market data indicate the following:

   a. 57% of the households in the test market were aware of the product at the end of the test.

   b. 6 percent of households tried the product; 30 percent of trial households repurchased during the test period.

   c. Average trial households purchased 1.3 units; repeat households purchased 3.5 units.

   d. 66% of purchases were aerosol sprays; 34% foggers. Same breakdown for trial and repeat households.

   e. 11,700 cases (12/case) of aerosol sprays shipped; 6,300 cases (12/case) of foggers shipped.

3. Several observations/conclusions can be drawn from the test market.

   a. It would seem that the advertising was effective in creating awareness for the product; however, it was not effective in stimulating trial, e.g., interest in the product.

   b. Repeat purchase behavior (30% of trial households) would seem quite good given a repurchase cycle of four months (120 days). This is, households buying in the third month (July) for the first time would not necessarily engage in repeat purchasing. Therefore, a six month test (measurement) might not properly gauge repeat purchasing.

   c. Using trial/repeat purchase data, Strike ROACH ENDER produced sales of $498,374.37, but generated a loss of $1.2 million (see Exhibit 2 in this note).

   d. Strike ROACH ENDER achieved a market share of 17.2% of the ant and roach product category, or possibly 34% of the roach category (see Exhibit 3 in this note).

EXHIBIT 2

TEST MARKET SALES AND PROFIT ASSESSMENT

I. **Package Economics** (From Case Exhibit 4)

Package	Sales Mix	Price	Contribution
Aerosol	66%	$3.14	$1.73
Fogger	34%	$2.79	$1.53

Weighted Avg. Unit Price: .66($3.14) + .34(2.79) = $3.021

Weighted Avg. Unit Contribution: .66($1.73) + .34(1.53) = **$1.662** (55%)

II. **Sales and Profit Analysis**

Trial: 1.17 million HH x .06 trial rate x 1.3 units x $3.021/unit = $275,696.46

Repeat: 70,200 trial HH x .30 repeat rate x 3.5 units x $3.021/unit =   222,677.91

Total Sales	$498,374.37
Contribution (%)	x .55
Contribution	$274,105.90
Less: Case Exhibit 6 Expenditures	1,478,000.00
Loss	($1,203,894.10)

Note: Students sometimes conclude that the sales estimate of $498,374.37 represents 75% of annual sales since 75% of total insecticide sales occur in the May-October period. They conclude that annual sales would be $664,499.16 ($498,374.37 = .75x, x = $664,499.16). This calculation does not materially affect the conclusion.

EXHIBIT 3

ESTIMATED TEST MARKET SHARE ASSESSMENT

I. Given in case (see also Exhibit 1 in this note):
- Market size was $400 million at manufacturers' prices in 1985.
- 10% annual growth rate; therefore 1986 estimated market size is $440 million.
- 40% of sales for ant and roach products
- 80% of total roach sales in 19 city (southern tier) market
- 5.3% of households in 19 city market exposed to test market effort
- 70% of insecticides sold through supermarkets
- 75% of insecticides sold during the May-October period
- 74% of insecticides sold in aerosol and fogger form

II. Estimated market size in test cities:

$440 MM x .40 x .80 x .053 x .70 x .75 x .74 = $2,899,142

III. Estimated market share of ant and roach products:

$498,374.37/$2,899,142 = 17.2% market share

Assuming ant and roach products sales are evenly split (50/50), then the market share might be as high as 34%.

Note: The market share estimate of 17.2% is the same if sales are annualized (see Exhibit 2 in this note): $664,499.16/$3,865,523 = 17.2%.

D. **What action(s) should Zoecon pursue with regard to Strike ROACH ENDER?**

1. Five actions are possible given case information:

    a. **Expand distribution to 19 city consumer market.**

    b. **Focus exclusively on professional pest control (PCO) market.**

    c. **Pursue opportunity to sell hydroprene chemical to a third-party, namely the makers of d-Con, etc. and pursue PCO market.**

    d. **Expand consumer marketing and PCO marketing effort.**

    e. **Sell to marketers of d-Con, etc. and pursue PCO market.**

Note that marketing under the Strike name to the consumer and selling hydroprene to the makers of d-Con, Black Flag, and Raid would be infeasible.

2. **Expand distribution to 19 city consumer market**

    a. **Pros:**

    - Repeat purchasing (repeat rate) indicates the product was adopted by a reasonable (30 percent of households (even with the replacement cycle issue mentioned earlier).

    - The product did capture a potentially high market share.

    - Margin structures indicate that a consumer marketing approach produces the highest gross (contribution) margin -- 55 percent.

    b. **Cons:**

    - Despite heavy promotion, which produced a 57 percent awareness level, the trial rate was only 6 percent of households. This suggests that the advertising/promotion was ineffective in generating interest in the product. Advertising copy/appeal needs attention.

    - Assuming Zoecon pursues the 19 city market, spends at the same levels for advertising/promotion, and generates the same trial/repeat, a loss would result (see Exhibit 4 in this note).

    - All things considered, the introduction of roach IGRs might require a long-term investment, but can Zoecon afford it given its well-entrenched competitors?

EXHIBIT 4

FORECASTING SALES AND PROFIT OF A 19 CITY INTRODUCTION

I. Assuming that all test market data would remain the same for expanded distribution, then forecasted sales in the 19 city market composed of 22 million households would be $9,271,142:

Trial: 22 million HH   x   .06 (trial)   x   13 units   x $3.021/unit   = $5,184,036
+
Repeat: 1.32 million HH   x   .30 (repeat)   x   3.5 units   x $3.021/unit   = $4,187,106

                                     Total Sales $9,371,142

II. Contribution dollars would be $5,154,128:

$9,371,142 x .55 (contribution) = $5,154,128

III. Expenditure levels can be estimated several ways.

     A. Assuming expenditures are based on a per capita approach and the test market cities contained 5.3% of household population, then advertising and promotion expenditures for the 19 city market would be, say 20 x $1,016,000 = $20,320,000.

     B. Assuming expenditures are based on a per city approach and spending in 5 of 19 cities (test market cities) or about 1/4 of cities for advertising and promotion was $1,016,000, the total spending would be, say 4 x $1,016,000 = $4,064,000.

     C. Assuming Zoecon adopts the industry "rule of thumb" that $10 million are necessary to launch a new product when consumers were familiar with the brand name (which might be the case since Strike FLEA ENDER was distributed in 19 city market), then spending for advertising and promotion would be $10 million.

3. **Focus exclusively on professional pest control (PCO) market**

   a. **Pros:**

   - Zoecon is already selling its roach IGR to PCOs under the GENCOR trade name.

   - IGRs appear to require educating buyers and PCOs seem to be doing this. Moreover, Zoecon's PRECOR (flea IGR) was successfully introduced this way.

   - Margin to PCOs was 51 percent. While lower than the consumer market, this figure is higher than selling to marketers of insecticides, e.g., Raid with 50 percent.

   - If Zoecon **does not** spend additional $500,000 to promote GENCOR to PCOs and spends at the 27 percent of sales rate, then profit before any assignable overhead would be 24 percent:

Selling Price	100%
Gross Profit	51%
Minus Marketing Expenses	27%
Profit before Overhead	24%

   b. **Cons:**

   - PCO market is small compared to consumer market (see Exhibit 1 in this note) -- $440 million vs. $118.26 million at manufacturer prices. Note these figures have to be adjusted downward to reflect the served market.

   - Dollar profit potential is limited if $500,000 additional promotion is spent.

4. **Pursue opportunity to sell hydroprene chemical to a third party, e.g., d-Con.**

   a. **Pros:**

   - Means to reach consumer market without marketing expenses

   - This practice has worked in the past with Zoecon flea IGR (PRECOR) in d-Con Flea Stop, Raid Flea Killer Plus. Also arrangement with Black Flag (Roach Motel).

   - Margin (50%) similar to PCO market (51%).

b. **Cons:**

- Possibly foreclose Zoecon from further marketing under the Strike brand name (for roach IGRs).

- Developing such arrangements has not been easy.

- Depending on how the test market results are read, there may be a lack of interest.

- Margins for a third-party arrangement (50%) are lower than marketing to consumers by Zoecon (55%).

5. **Expand consumer marketing and PCO marketing effort**

   a. **Pros:**

   - Possibility that PCO use will enhance sales of Strike ROACH ENDER once the benefits of IGRs are observed.

   - Possible scale economics are possible given larger production runs when serving two markets.

   b. **Cons:**

   - Could be very expensive given test market experience.

   - To what extent is the benefit transferable between PCO and consumer market?

6. **Sell to makers of d-Con, etc. and pursue PCO market.**

   a. **Pros:**

   - Same as pros in #3 and #4.

   b. **Cons:**

   - Same as cons in #3 and #4.

E. **What specific information should be contained in a presentation to d-Con, S. C. Johnson & Sons, or Boyle-Midway?**

   1. Students should be asked how they would "package" a presentation to a third-party distributor. Elements of the presentation are shown in Exhibit 5.

EXHIBIT 5

ELEMENTS OF A PRESENTATION TO A THIRD-PARTY DISTRIBUTOR

I. **Unique Qualities of IGRs**
   A. Safe for humans and animals (pets)
   B. Long-term effect
   C. When combined with adulticide, provides immediate and long-term control.

II. **Consumer Acceptance of IGRs**

   A. Proven Acceptance for Fleas: d-Con Flea Stop, Raid Flea Killer Plus, Strike FLEA ENDER (18% market share after 2 years)

   B. Proven Acceptance for Roaches: Strike FLEA ENDER achieved 30% Repeat Purchase Rate in 6-Month Test Market. Estimated market share of 17.2% to 34%.

III. **Benefit of Well-Known Brand**

   A. Well-known brand (Raid, Black Flag, d-Con) could possibly increase trial rate given customer franchise.

   B. Introductory marketing expenses might not be as high as with "new brand" plus "new product."

F. **Epilogue**

The following is a "pest-mortem" prepared by Monty Allen, Vice-President - Insect Control Group, at Zoecon Corporation.

In January 1986 the decision was made to a) continue the Gencor presence in the PCO market, but at normal levels of ad and promotional support, and b) to substantially close the Strike brand down and license hydroprene marketing rights to the consumer market to one of the "big three" household insectcide companies.

The rationale was as follows. In the PCO markets, there was no evidence that extra-normal levels of marketing support would accelerate sales growth. Furthermore, no competitive IGR's were expected in the PCO market for several years. In the consumer market, the Strike line of products, led by methoprene-containing Strike Flea Ender, had never approached profitability. The launch of Roach Ender to 19 markets or nationally would keep the Strike brand unprofitable for at least three more years, according to projections. The projected losses would be material to Zoecon and would not allow Zoecon to meet the objective of "high financial return". The forecaster eventual profitability even had a low probability of occurrence because of the large resources and brand franchises held by Raid, Black Flag, and d-Con. They would not and had not been idle against a new entrant. The licensing option would transfer the early year investment losses to the licensee-marketer for a shot at a significant competitive edge in the marketplace. Zoecon would reap immediate profits from the sale of Gencor to the marketer at the cost of not fully controlling the efforts that help determine the success of the compound in one of the biggest market arenas available.

For Zoecon this course was the best one of take (short-term "sure thing" vs. long-term "high risk-high reward") because of new investment options in pharmacological compound development for large and small animal applications. Sandoz, being a major pharmaceutical firm, offered Zoecon an access to such compounds.

As a hedge strategy to enable Gencor to be in the market in 1986 in the event this option was chosen, three Zoecon executives had been negotiating a license arrangement prior to January 1986 with Black Flag. Those negotiations were quickly concluded, an agreement signed, and in May 1986 Black Flag Roach Ender began selling at retail. By late 1985 it became widely known that the next probable IGR in the consumer market would be introduced by Raid in 1988 or 1989. Black Flag was therefore very interested in access to the first IGR as a competitive strategy against Raid.

At the end of 1986 Black Flag Roach Ender had captured 8% market share in the roach products category of the household insecticide market. In late 1986 Black Flag licensed the Flea Ender trademark from Zoecon to launch a methoprene containing product line. That was introduced in 1987. By August 1987 that line had captured 15% of the flea products category. In late summer of 1987, Roach Ender was struggling at 7% category share. A non-IGR, non-aerosol alternative to roach control, introduced in 1985, was taking the roach products market by storm and hurting all prior product forms. Combat brand roach bait stations had captured 25% share of the roach category by late 1987. Combat, marketed by the Shulton Division of American Cyanamid, is the story of the 1980's in this market. It is a marketing story, not so much a technology story, and therein lies another case....

G. Summary Points

1. Choice of a product-market target or segment to serve is a central decision in strategic marketing as it will determine the composition of the marketing mix and ultimately, profitability.

2. The adoption of novel new products by a market is influenced by a variety of product-related factors, including

- **Relative advantage** over competing offerings (adulticides)

- **Compatibility** with existing ways of doing things (killing insects)

- **Simplicity of use** (households vs. professional

- **Immediacy of the Benefit** (dead roaches)

- **Felt Need** (need to eliminate roach infestation)

3. Sometimes the "product" is not fixed, but rather a variable that can be manipulated by the producer. For example, Zoecon's IGR could be marketed as (a) an IGR chemical only, (b) IGR + adulticide, (c) in bulk to PCOs, (d) in an aerosol or fogger to consumers, and so forth, hence the term "product market."

4. Multiple channels exist for the distribution of Zoecon's IGR:

- Through distributors to PCOs

- Through supermarkets to consumers

- Through "third-party distributors" who include it in their products.

5. A strategy of dual distribution provides an opportunity to reach different markets simultaneously. Oftentimes the "product" differs, however.

MS-TIQUE CORPORATION

Synopsis

In January 2000, Phoebe Masters, the newly-appointed product manager for hand and body lotions at Ms-Tique Corporation, is faced with the decision whether to add a 5-1/2 ounce or 10-ounce aerosol package alongside the existing tube container of the firm's Soft and Silky brand of women's shaving gel. The apparent decision involves the determination of whether to conduct a market test on the two aerosol packages to determine which package will be most profitable when sold with the tube container. However, as the case unfolds, the whole matter of an aerosol container being a viable line extension at all emerges to cloud the decision.

The case provides an opportunity to deal with the twin issues of uncertainty (market response) and the amount at stake (financial loss) in a straightforward manner. Specifically, case information allows the student to assess qualitative (focus group) information, convert "source of volume" projections into dollar figures, construct a payoff table, compute the expected monetary value of the two aerosol packages, and calculate the value of "perfect information." In addition, issues related to "relevant costs" are introduced for consideration.

Teaching Objectives

This case is designed to achieve five major teaching objectives:

1. Introduce students to a common issues in product management; namely the role of packaging in the marketing mix and product life cycle management.

2. Give students an opportunity to interpret qualitative (focus group) information and quantitative "source of volume" data when assessing a new product introduction.

3. Provide an opportunity to utilize decision analysis, calculate the cost of perfect information, and perform a sensitivity analysis when making a marketing decision.

4. Introduce students to the product cannibalism concept with line extensions and illustrate how cannibalism can affect product line profitability.

5. Allow students to identify relevant and sunk costs in a marketing decision.

Teaching Suggestions

This case should be used in that portion of the course where the instructor wishes to introduce an application of decision analysis applied to test marketing and product line management. However, the case has been used as an assignment after Chapter 3: Marketing Decision Making and Case Analysis, because it raises the value of "perfect information" issue in a test market setting. The case has been assigned as an in-class examination after completion of the Product-Service Strategy and Brand Management chapter and as a portion of a final examination because of the clear-cut problem raised and answer.

This case has been taught in both undergraduate and graduate courses with equal success; however, undergraduate students seem to be less willing to "work with the numbers" in the case. Better graduate students particularly enjoy the case problem and respond favorably to the application of decision analysis. They particularly welcome the "sensitivity analysis" discussed later in the teaching note. Previous experience teaching the case indicates that instructors should consider bringing examples of women's shaving creams and gels to class as props.

Specific questions that may be posed to students prior to or during the case discussion include:

1. Based on Soft and Silky's sales performance through 1999, results from the focus group studies, and the performance of analogous products, should the aerosol container concept be pursued further?

2. What are the economics of the 5 1/2-ounce tube container, 5 1/2 ounce aerosol container, and the 10-ounce aerosol container?

3. Assuming the research firm's four forecasts for the combined products shown in Exhibit 5 are reasonable, what incremental contribution can be expected in 2000 for the Soft and Silky brand for each forecast?

4. What are the pros/cons of commissioning the test market recommended by the research firm and Heather Courtwright?

5. What action would you take in this situation?

Areas for Discussion and Analysis

A. **Based on Soft and Silky's sales performance through 1999, results from the focus group studies, and the performance of analogous products, should the aerosol container concept be pursued further?**

   1. **Yes**

      a. S&S's unit sales volume plateaued growth suggests that the brand might be in the mature stage of its cycle. Perhaps a packaging change is necessary to stimulate growth since aerosols have become so popular and the women's shaving market is growing at a rate of 3 to 5 percent annually since 1994.

      b. But, where will the source of volume growth come from? Former users of soap and water; S&S; or users of competitor creams and gels? Focus group studies indicate that shaving cream users like the aerosol can - 1/4 said they would switch over to S&S's aerosol can irrespective of can size. It is unlikely that current S&S users will purchase more (at least there is no data to support a counter-agreement).

      c. A marketing research firm studied case studies in which marketers of men's shaving cream had introduced a new package. As shown in case Exhibit 5, the research firm projected a unit (ounces) increase in sales volume for the S&S brand (S&S was projected to sell 1,953,668 5 1/2-ounce tubes in 2000 or 10,745,174 ounces. All projections were greater than this figure).

      d. Customers and noncustomers were unanimously in favor of the aerosol can. The 10-oz. size can was most preferred.

   2. **No**

      a. Twenty percent of the present S&S users say they would switch to the 10-oz. can. Since the 10-oz. can is almost **twice** the size of the present 5 1/2-oz. tube, this could reduce the turnover of S&S in stores.

      b. Furthermore, the retail store's margin for the 5 1/2 -oz. aerosol can will be $1.40/can compared with $1.58/can for the 5 1/2-oz. tube container (see calculations in Exhibit 1 in this note). Slower turnover plus lower margin are not in the best interest of supermarket health and beauty aid buyers. However, a higher retail margin for the 10-oz aerosol can ($1.70) exists. Even so, the larger retail margin does not compensate for an almost doubling of the container size.

c. Couple a. and b. above, health and beauty aid buyers in retail stores might think twice about giving the aerosol container shelf space.

3. Instructors should expect students to make reference to the $10,000 supplier's set-up charge as a relevant cost for producing S&S in an aerosol container. But is this $10,000 a relevant cost pertaining to the test market which focuses on identifying the consumer acceptance of a 5-1/2 oz. can versus a 10-oz can? The case notes that the $10,000 set-up charge will occur if either can size is produced. As stated in Chapter 2, **relevant costs are future expenditures unique to the decision alternatives under consideration.** Since this cost is not unique to the decision alternatives, it is not a relevant cost for assessing the merits (or profitability) of the alternatives; that is, choosing between the 5-1/2 oz. can versus the 10-oz. can.

Furthermore, the $10,000 set-up charge does not differ between the decision alternatives of whether to test market the aerosol can or introduce the aerosol can without a test market. This cost will be incurred in either instance; hence, it is not a relevant cost.

The $10,000 supplier set-up charge might be viewed as a relevant cost only in reference to the decision alternative of whether to introduce the aerosol can at all versus doing nothing; that is staying with the tube. In this instance, the "cost" of doing nothing can be estimated to be the "lost contribution," of $9,508 reflected in the forecasted decline in tube sales [1999 tube ounces of 10,780,000 (1,960,000 units x 5.5 oz. tubes) minus 2000 forecasted ounces of 10,745,174 given in the case times the tube contribution per ounce of $.273 equals $9,508.] In short, it's a "push."

The entire matter of relevant costs can be discussed or addressed in a broader context as well. For example, the cost of the test market ($30,000) is a relevant cost. However, the $35,000 already spent on consumer research is not a relevant cost, but rather a **sunk cost** as it relates to the decision at hand.

B. **What are the economics of the 5 1/2-oz. tube container, 5 1/2-oz. aerosol container, and the 10-oz. aerosol container?**

1. The case states that the retail margin is 40 percent and the jobber margin is 20 percent. Furthermore, the suggested retail prices are given and the cost per delivered aerosol unit is given.

2. Contribution per unit and contribution per ounce is calculated in Exhibit 1 in this note. The 10-oz. aerosol can has a higher unit contribution than the tube container. However, on a per ounce basis, both the 5 1/2-oz. and the 10-oz. aerosol have lower contribution figures. The 5 1/2-oz. tube container has a higher contribution/ounce. [Note: Expect some students to "complain" that Heather

EXHIBIT 1

CALCULATION OF CONTRIBUTION BY PACKAGE

	5 1/2 oz. Tube	5 1/2 oz. Aerosol	10 oz. Aerosol
Retail Price	$3.95	$3.50	$4.25
Less: Retail Margin (40%)	1.58	1.40	1.70
Jobber Price	$2.37	$2.10	$2.55
Less: Jobber Margin (20%)	.47	.42	.51
Soft & Silky Price/Unit	$1.90	$1.68	$2.04
Variable Cost/Unit*	.40	.24	.29
Contribution/Unit	$1.50	$1.44	$1.75
Contribution/Oz.	$1.50 / 5.5 = $.273	$1.44 / 5.5 = $.262	$1.75 / 10 = $.175

*5 1/2-oz. tube container variable cost is equal to the cost of goods sold ($784,000) given in case Exhibit 1 divided by the 1,960,000 unit volume given in the case, or $784,000 ÷ 1,960,000 units = $.40. Variable cost/unit for aerosol containers is the estimated delivered cost given in the case.

Note: Some students might view the estimated delivered cost per unit of the aerosol containers as fixed since a 100,000 unit volume commitment exists. This cost will be at the very least a step-variable cost should the aerosol can be launched.

Courtwright's suggested retail prices for the aerosols are too low since the 5-1/2 oz. tube is priced at $.72/oz. at retail — see case Exhibit 3. By comparison, the 5-1/2 oz. and 10-oz. aerosols are priced at $.63/oz. and $.425/oz., respectively. They may be correct; however, Courtwright believes the retail prices reflect competitive realities in the category and the brand can retain its premium image even at the lower prices.

3. An analysis of container economics indicates that every time a current S&S tube buyer switches to the aerosol, a loss in contribution/ounce occurs. It would seem that the incremental volume gains will have to compensate for the lower contribution/ounce of the aerosol container. But will this happen? The analysis should then turn to the volume projections discussed in the case and summarized in case Exhibit 5.

C. **"Assuming" that the research firm's four forecasts for the combined products shown in Exhibit 5 are reasonable, what incremental contribution can be expected in 2000 for each forecast?**

1. Exhibit 2 in this note calculates the incremental contribution for the S&S product line when a 5-1/2 oz. aerosol or a 10-oz. aerosol container is introduced alongside the 5-1/2 oz. tube container. [Note: Some students will subtract the $10,000 set-up charge for the aerosol container from the incremental contribution. This is "ok" and will not alter the conclusion, only the dollar values.]

2. Some students might calculate the incremental contribution differently as portrayed in Chapter 2, but the numbers are identical (except for rounding):

   a. Low Estimate (5 1/2-oz. Aerosol Container)
   New Volume   Cannibalization
   [300,000 x $.262] – [2,145,174 x ($.273 – $.262)]
   $78,600   – $23,597   = $55,003

   b. High Estimate (5 1/2-oz Aerosol Container)
   New Volume   Cannibalization
   [500,000 x $.262] – [2,345,174 x ($.273 – $.262)]
   $131,000   – $25,797   = $105,203

   c. Low Estimate (10-oz. Aerosol Container)
   New Volume   Cannibalization
   [800,000 x $.175] – [1,745,174 x ($.273 – $.175)]
   $140,000   – $171,027   = ($31,027)

   d. High Estimate (10-oz Aerosol Container)
   New Volume   Cannibalization
   [1,500,000 x $.175] – [1,145,174 x ($.273 – $.175)]
   $262,500   – $112,227   = $150,273

EXHIBIT 2

INCREMENTAL PRODUCT LINE CONTRIBUTION BY FORECAST
(all figures rounded to nearest dollar)

A. Low Estimate for 5 1/2-Ounce Aerosol Package Addition

5 1/2-oz. Tube Package Volume	8,600,000	x	$.273	=	$2,347,800
5 1/2-oz. Aerosol Package Volume:					
Cannibalized Volume	2,145,174	x	$.262	=	562,036
Net New Volume	300,000	x	$.262	=	78,600
					$2,988,436
Less Original Forecast Tube Volume:	10,745,174	x	$.273	=	-2,933,433
Incremental Contribution					$ 55,003

B. High Estimate for 5 1/2-Ounce Aerosol Package Addition

5 1/2-oz. Tube Package Volume	8,400,000	x	$.273	=	$2,293,200
5 1/2-oz. Aerosol Package Volume:					
Cannibalized Volume	2,345,174	x	$.262	=	614,436
Net New Volume	500,000	x	$.262	=	131,000
					$3,038,636
Less Original Forecast Tube Volume:	10,745,174	x	$.273	=	-2,933,433
Incremental Contribution					$ 105,203

C: Low Estimate for 10-Ounce Aerosol Package Addition

5 1/2-oz. Tube Package Volume	9,000,000	x	$.273	=	$2,457,000
10-oz. Aerosol Package Volume:					
Cannibalized Volume	1,745,174	x	$.175	=	305,405
Net New Volume	800,000	x	$.175	=	140,000
					$2,902,405
Less Original Forecast Tube Volume:	10,745,174	x	$.273	=	-2,933,433
Incremental Contribution					$ -31,028

D. High Estimate for 10-Ounce Aerosol Package Addition

5 1/2-oz. Tube Package Volume	9,600,000	x	$.273	=	$2,620,800
10-oz. Aerosol Package Volume:					
Cannibalized Volume	1,145,174	x	$.175	=	200,405
Net New Volume	1,500,000	x	$.175	=	262,500
					$3,083,705
Less Original Forecast Tube Volume:	10,745,174	x	$.273	=	-2,933,433
Incremental Contribution					$ 150,272

3. As can be seen, except for the low estimate for the 10-oz. aerosol container, the addition of an aerosol produces a higher incremental contribution than not adding the aerosol; that is, doing nothing. Looking back at the discussion under A.3, the forecasted volume for the 5-1/2 oz. tube container alone resulted in a loss in contribution of $9,508 for 2000.

D. What are the pros/cons of commissioning the test market recommended by the research firm and Heather Courtwright?

1. **Pros**

    a. The data gathered appear too sketchy and raise several questions:

        1. Are men's shaving cream products the same as women's?

        2. There is no documentation presented to support the "source of volume" forecasts shown in case Exhibit 5.

    b. There appears to be a potential for an **actual loss** in contribution to the S&S line if the 10-ounce aerosol is introduced alongside the 5-1/2-oz. tube and the low forecast becomes reality.

    c. In short, there is considerable uncertainty present and the amount at stake is very real in a financial sense. This suggests a test market might be necessary.

2. **Cons**

    a. If one "assumes" that the forecasts are correct (reflected in the calculated payoffs) and the probabilities are accurate, then the Expected Monetary Value or **EMV** for the two aerosol package sizes can be calculated, but more importantly, the **EMV: Perfect Information** can be computed (see the discussion in Chapter 3).

    b. Exhibit 3 in this note shows the calculations indicating that the 10-ounce package is the best alternative and the value of perfect information is $25,809. This figure is lower than the $30,000 cost of the test market which is a relevant cost. This suggests that the test market cost exceeds the cost of perfect information. Therefore, the test market should not be commissioned. [Note: If students do subtract the $5,000 set-up charge, all of the dollar numbers are reduced by $5,000. The EMV: Perfect Information amount of $25,809 remains the same; hence the decision does not change.]

EXHIBIT 3

CALCULATION OF EXPECTED MONETARY VALUE AND THE VALUE OF PERFECT INFORMATION

(All Numbers Rounded)

Payoff Table

Aerosol Container

	Low Estimate P = .3	High Estimate P = .7
5 1/2-Ounce Package	$55,003	$105,203
10-Ounce Package	-$31,027	$150,273

$$EMV_{5\ 1/2\text{-oz. package}} = .3(\$55,003) + .7(\$105,203) = \$90,143$$

$$EMV_{10\text{-oz. package}} = .3(-\$31,027) + .7(\$150,273) = \$95,883*$$

Value of Perfect Information

$$EMV_{Certainty} = .3(\$55,003) + .7(\$150,273) = \$121,692$$

$$EMV_{Best\ Alternative} = \underline{\$95,883}$$

$$EMV_{Perfect\ Information} = \underline{\$25,809}$$

E. **What action would you take in this situation?**

1. There appears to be adequate justification for and against the test market recommendation and, indeed, the aerosol line extension. It depends on the "believability" of the "source of volume" forecasts, hence the payoffs, and the probabilities. If any of these change, then the conclusion could change.

2. In a classroom setting, the instructor should push students to consider the sensitivity of the decision analysis to the probabilities: "Would your views change if the probability of the low estimate were .5?"

3. This kind of question will allow the student ample opportunity to illustrate how one might develop a "break-point" where the decision **would** change. This is done below where the student sets the aerosol package size alternatives equal to each other and solves for **P** using simple algebra.

5-1/2 oz. Aerosol Can		10-oz. Aerosol Can
P(55,003) + 1−P(105,203)	=	P(−31,027) + 1−P(150,273)
55,003P + 105,203 − 105,203P	=	−31,027P + 150,273 − 150,273P
−50,200P + 105,203	=	−181,300P + 150,273
131,100P	=	45,070
P	=	.344

In words, if the probability of the low estimate is greater than .344, then the 5 1/2-ounce aerosol package should be chosen on the basis of contribution. This analysis demonstrates to students how sensitive the analysis and decision is to the probabilities.

F. **Epilogue**

Phoebe Masters did not expect this decision to greet her on her first day on the job as Product Manager for Soft & Silky at Ms-Tique Corporation (a disguised name). In her view, aerosols seemed like a natural line extension given their emergence as the dominant package for women's shaving gels. The economics, however, were working against her given the suggested retail price points recommended by Heather Courtwright. She felt that the focus groups should have offered participants a higher range of prices given the "value-added" benefits over the existing S&S product and tube package. Add to this, she was not very confident in the source of volume (cannibalized and net new volume) estimated by the marketing research firm.

On the other hand, she felt the S&S shaving gel was in need of a volume boost even though she was facing a limited manufacturing capacity. When she made an inquiry about the cost of "outsourcing" the tube container, she realized this too would be expensive and no impactful "product news" would result to increase sales in her view.

She said the market test was "throwing good money after bad" adding that "aerosols were a better bet than tube containers." She decided to introduce the 10-ounce aerosol container in all stores that stocked S&S shaving gel in April, 2000 at a suggested retail price of $4.95. At a suggested retail price of $.495/oz., S&S was comparatively priced on a per ounce basis with Aveeno, the premium-priced aerosol gel sold by Ryoelle Labs, a division of S. C. Johnson, the marketer of Skintimate. This price meant that S&S aerosol would produce a contribution of $.211/oz. which was still less than the tube container.

As of this writing (June 2000), the new 10-ounce aerosol was producing a seasonally-adjusted unit volume of 270,000 cans, or 2.7 million ounces. This figure was higher than the 10-oz. aerosol package high estimate of 2,645,174 ounces projected by the marketing research firms. She also believed the cannibalism rate for the tube container was less than that projected by the marketing research firm (44% of the total volume).

G. Summary Points

1. Decision analysis is a useful tool for identifying and specifying decision alternatives, uncertainties, and outcomes. It is particularly useful for considering "what if" situations so common in formulating competitive marketing strategy.

2. Marketing research information has a cost that must be absorbed by the manager. The cost exists in real dollars as well as the "opportunity cost" involved in gathering it.

3. The value of "perfect information" can be calculated and serves to highlight the benefit-cost trade-offs in planning research expenditures.

4. Product cannibalism potential must be considered when new package designs or line extensions are added to the product line. Careful assessment of unit volume, dollar volume, and profitability is necessary. Oftentimes one cannot "have one's cake and eat it too!"

5. Carefully consider the "unit of analysis" when conducting any kind of quantitative or financial analysis. Package sizes often differ which in turn can distort quantitative or financial analyses.

MANOR MEMORIAL HOSPITAL: DOWNTOWN HEALTH CLINIC

Synopsis

In mid-April, 2000, Ms. Sherri Worth, assistant administrator at Manor Memorial Hospital and director of the hospital's Downtown Health Clinic (DHC) became aware of a study being done to determine market demand for a competitive clinic located five blocks north of the DHC. News of the potential competitor struck a chord of concern for three reasons. First, the service area of the competitive clinic would cut into DHC's service area and attract potential and current patients. Second, the competitor - MEDCENTER - was known to be an aggressive, marketing-oriented, privately-owned clinic that had a successful location in the suburbs. Third, DHC had not achieved break-even in any month since its opening on May 1, 1999, and had a cumulative loss of $238,488 over eleven months. Dr. Mahon, Manor Memorial Hospital's administrator has asked Ms. Worth to prepare a concisely written analysis of DHC's position and specify and evaluate the alternatives for DHC assuming MEDCENTER would or would not open a facility.

This case raises a variety of considerations in service management and marketing including high fixed costs, uneven demand, customer (patient) mix, and the subtle issue of a product-service mix profitability. For example, DHC has a congestion problem during lunch hours part because the majority of patient visits are for personal illnesses and exams and this service has the lowest revenue per visit. The case emphasizes these points as well as offering alternatives for overcoming DHC's poor profitability. These alternatives include expanded hours designed to focus on employment examinations and the addition of gynecology services to focus on female office workers. Qualitative and quantitative information is provided to thoroughly assess DHC's position and potential.

Teaching Objectives

This case has three teaching objectives:

1. Provide students with an opportunity to apply marketing concepts and tools in a service industry and specifically health care.

2. To illustrate problems encountered by many service organizations such as uneven demand, a fixed capacity, and high operating leverage.

This teaching note benefited from insights provided by Professor Greg Bonner, Villanova University.

3. To illustrate how different product-service portfolios can produce different levels of contribution and profitability.

Teaching Suggestions

The best way to approach this case in a class discussion setting is to focus attention initially on DHC's present operating and financial situation and the reasons for this situation. The discussion can then move toward determining DHC's situation if nothing is done. After students come to recognize DHC's predicament, then attention can focus on the "what if" types of analysis related to the remedial options, e.g. expand hours, add gynecology services, etc.

A "red herring" issue present in the case in the MEDCENTER threat. While a competitor might affect the DHC somewhat, a closer examination reveals that its impact would be limited. Support for this view is found in Case Exhibit 6 which shows patient origin. A plot of the distance/direction origin figures reveals that very few patients are coming from the intersection of the service areas shown in Case Exhibit 1. Insightful students point out that the distance/direction statistics indicate that probably 10 percent of present patients would be lost. Therefore, the real focus in the case is on managing DHC better.

Experience with this case indicates it is an excellent examination vehicle, particularly toward the end of the course. It has been used as a group analysis and presentation case as well with excellent results in both undergraduate and graduate courses.

Specific questions that can be posed to students prior to or during a class discussion are:

1. How would you describe the consumer decision process for patronizing an ambulatory health care facility?

2. How would you characterize the DHC's performance after being open eleven months from a financial, marketing, operations, and hospital-wide perspective?

3. What is your prognosis for the DHC next year assuming the 8% increase in average service charges and the reduction in bad debt expense occurs, but nothing else?

4. What strategic changes, if any, should DHC consider to improve its performance?

5. How might DHC bring about any changes suggested?

Areas for Discussion/Analysis

A. How would you describe the consumer decision process for patronizing an ambulatory health care facility?

    1.   There is little case information dealing with this question. However, students will draw an analogy with their family/personal physician and note that:

        a.   A visit to a physician is probably spur of the moment given an illness or emergency - little preplanning.

        b.   Case Exhibit 3 indicates that individuals who do not have a regular physician will patronize such a facility: 77% (198/256) of those individuals who would use/try the DHC did not have a regular physician (excluding gynecologist). Furthermore, 70% (168/240) of the females surveyed would use/try the DHC while 55% (88/160) of the males would do so.

    2.   However, employment/insurance physical examinations can be preplanned to some extent as can selected worker's compensation visits. More importantly, these health care services are likely to be employer or other initiated rather than being patient initiated. A matrix showing the link between initiator and type of service is instructive and is similar to a product/service - "market" matrix:

Initiator

Service	Individual	"Other" (employer, insurance co. etc.)
Personal Illness	X	
Worker's Compensation		X
Employ/Ins. Exam		X
Emergency	X	

    3.   Such a matrix should illustrate that companies or employers may have a say (i.e. influence, perhaps decision-maker) where an individual obtains selected health care services. This analysis is supported by Dr. Mahon's interest in designing a PPO Program (Preferred Provider Organization) using the DHC and Ms. Worth's efforts to work with downtown businesses or scheduling examinations.

    4.   Furthermore, this matrix suggests a segmentation scheme - individuals vs. businesses - useful in directing marketing efforts.

B. **How would you characterize the current DHC's performance after being open eleven months from a financial, marketing, operations, and hospital-wide perspective?**

1. **Financial Perspective.**

   a. The DHC is losing money as Case Exhibit 5 clearly shows. The DHC has failed to reach break-even volume and has a cumulative (11 month) loss of $238,488.

   b. When the month of May (start-up) data is eliminated because of its atypical and probably non-recurring costs, the 10 month experience indicates that the DHC has an:

   Average Contribution Margin Per Month = 83.5%

   Average Fixed Cost Per Month = $37,670

   c. Therefore, the monthly break-even volume of patient visits can be calculated two ways given the average patient revenue per visit of $67.90 (given in the case):

   $$\text{Breakeven (\$)} = \frac{\$37,670}{1 - \frac{.165}{1.00}} = \frac{\$37,670}{.835} = \$45,113.72$$

   $$\text{Breakeven (visits)} = \frac{\$37,670}{\$67.90 - \$11.20} = \frac{\$37,670}{\$56.70} = 664 \text{ visits/month}$$

   (Note: $45,113.72 / $67.90 = 664 visits/month

   d. If the average revenue per visit, the contribution margin, and the average fixed costs/month remain unchanged, then the DHC must have 7,968 visits/yr. (664 x 12) to break-even, i.e. become self-supporting.

   e. The DHC appears to be holding to its expenditure budget (see Case Exhibit 2). The problem appears to be a lack of patient visits necessary to cover fixed cost, or in the service mix which produces the $67.90 revenue/visit.

2. **Marketing Perspective.**

   a. Case Exhibit 5 shows that the DHC has received 3,490 visits in the first eleven months and is expected to have an additional 410 visits in April, or

3,900 visits in the first year of operation - roughly 50% short of its target break-even volume of 7,968 visits.

b. Virtually all (97%) of DHC's volume is due to first use (trier) visits according to case information with 133 visits being repeat visits.

c. Most (53%) patient visits are for personal illness/examinations. Personal illness/exams present a problem because (1) they produce the lowest average charge ($50) per visit (2) appear to be causing congestion during lunch hours and (3) would seem to have little referral potential for Manor Memorial Hospital. Moreover, it is virtually impossible to schedule/manage demand for this service.

d. Finally, Exhibit 1 in this note shows the potential for personal illness/exams given case information and the DHC capture rate. This exhibit shows that 5,249 potential visits are possible in any given year and DHC has a capture rate of 39.4%. This exhibit is important for two reasons: (1) the potential for personal illness/exam visits is not as large as it appears on first glance and (2) other services must be emphasized both to build volume and revenue since personal illness has a low visit charge. Nevertheless, an opportunity exists to increase this service category if the DHC staff wishes to do so. Unfortunately, such a move might exacerbate the congestion problem.

3. **Operations Perspective**

   a. DHC may be approaching a capacity problem due to uneven daily demand since 70% of visits occur during the lunch period (11:00 a.m. - 2:00 p.m.).

   b. For illustrative purposes, during the peak month of February, 2000, 463 visits occurred over a 21 day period (Case Exhibit 5). This translates to 22 visits /day and 15 visits (.7 x 22) during the lunch period, or 5 visits/hr. (15/3).

   c. **Assuming** DHC reaches its 664 monthly break-even visit volume (over 21 days), then 7 visits (664/21 ≅ 32; 32 x .7 = 22; 22/3 = 7) per hour would occur during the lunch period, or **one every 8-9 minutes**! Is this possible or preferable?

   d. In other words, if the DHC meets its assumed 32 visits per day at full capacity (see note on the bottom of Case Exhibit 2), then overcrowding will occur during the lunch period and the implicit assumption of a 15 minute visit will be halved!

EXHIBIT 1

MARKET POTENTIAL ESTIMATE IN FIVE BLOCK SERVICE AREA AND DHC CAPTURE RATE FOR PERSONAL ILLNESS/EXAMS

Market (Visit) Potential Estimate (Case Exhibit 3)

11,663	Office Workers
x .5	Intention to Use
5832	(rounded)
x .9	Avg. visit/worker
5,249	rounded

Computation of Visits Per Worker For Personal Illness (Case Exhibit 3)

Visits	Percent Freq.	Wt. Avg.
Every Other yr.	.60 x .5	= .30
1x/Yr.	.25 x 1	= .25
2x/Yr.	.10 x 2	= .20
≥ 3x/Yr.	.05 x 3	= .15
		.90

Market (Visit Capture Rate For Personal Illness/Exams)

Actual Visit Volume for 11 months (case Exhibit 5)	3,490
Forecasted April Visits	+ 410
Total Year Visits	3,900
Personal Illness/Exam Visits (53% of visits)	x .53
Total Pers. Illness/Exam Visits	2,067
Potential Visits (see above)	÷ 5,249
	39.4% capture

4. **Hospital-wide Perspective**

   a. It appears that the DHC has led to referrals of privately insured referrals to Manor Memorial Hospital. Furthermore, the service mix indicates that DHC is satisfying downtown employers' specific health care needs as evidenced by physical exams, workers' comp., and possibly emergency services.

   b. Still, the $30,000 incremental net profit produced by referrals (referenced in the case) does not cover the operating losses from DHC.

C. **What is your prognosis for the DHC next year assuming the 8% increase in average service charges and the reduction in bad debt expense occurs, but nothing else.**

   1. In effect, this question forces students to consider what will happen if DHC does nothing to change its operations/marketing.

   2. Exhibit 2 in this note shows that only personal illness/exams volume increases by 20% (2,067 x 1.2). Other services remain stable at last year's levels. The contribution margin increases to 85.5% due to the 2% reduction in bad debt. Personnel and professional expenses increase by 5% [Personnel = $15,050 (avg. 10 mo. personnel cost) x 1.05 x 12; Professional (Physician) Services = 260 days x 8 hrs. x $69.30 ($66 x 1.05)]. Facility, miscellaneous, and amortization expense remain at last year's average monthly (10 month) levels; professional fees are assumed to remain at $43,720, as shown in case Exhibit 2.

   3. Exhibit 2 in this note shows:

      a. DHC will incur a projected $165,300 loss at a 4,313 visit volume. This is obviously better than last year. However, Dr. Mohan's belief that the DHC will break-even next year is suspect.

      b. The $70.86 average charge is higher than last year's $67.90, but only 4% higher, not 8% higher. This occurs because the service mix is being further dominated by personal illness/exams. This point should be emphasized for students and should make them sensitive to service mix profitability.

   4. Equally relevant is the fact that personal illness/exam visits will cause further congestion and probably have limited potential for referrals to Manor Memorial Hospital.

D. **What strategic changes, if any, should DHC consider to improve its performance?**

   1. When this question is posed to students either as a study question or during a class discussion, the immediate reaction is for students to recommend increased hours, add a gynecologist, etc. Should this happen, the instructor should ask students "why?" and turn their thinking to more fundamental issues.

EXHIBIT 2

REVENUE AND FINANCIAL ANALYSIS OF DO NOTHING OPTION

SERVICE REVENUE PER VISIT CALCULATION

Type of Visit	Projected Visits[a]	Prop. of Visits	Avg. Chg.[b]	Wtd. Avg. Chg (Col. 2 x Col. 3)
Personal Illness/Exam	2,480	.58	$ 54.00	$31.32
Worker's Compensation	975	.23	$ 84.24	19.38
Employment/Insurance Exams	741	.17	$101.52	17.26
Emergency	117	.02	$144.72	2.90
	4,313	1.00		$70.86

[a] Projections made by Ms. Worth.

[b] Assumes 8% across-the-board increase in service charges.

PROJECTED INCOME STATEMENT (May 1, 2000 - April 30, 2001)

Gross Revenue (4,313 visits x $70.86)		$305,619
Less: Variable Costs (14.5%)		44.315
Contribution (85.5%)		$261,304
Less Fixed Expenses:		
Personnel (5% increase)	$189,630	
Professional Services (5% increase)	144,144	
Professional Fees	43,720	
Facility + Misc.	33,786	
Amortization	15,324	426,604
Net Loss		($165,300)

2. It would seem that DHC should attempt to:

   a. **Change the Service Mix.** DHC must decrease the number of personal illness visits **relative** to other service visits. Such action will increase the average charge per visit and increase the dollar contribution per visit.

   b. **Alter Demand By Day-Part.** DHC must reduce the current and potential congestion during the 11:00 - 2:00 p.m. lunch period. A change in the service mix will help in this regard, e.g., insurance/employer physical exams can be scheduled. Expanded hours should also help.

   c. **Pursue Services That Have Repeat Potential.** The current service mix does not appear to have great potential for repeat business on a regular basis. Rather the DHC should pursue services that make it a convenient alternative to a primary care physician practice. Gynecology services seem to be useful in this regard.

   d. **Pursue Services with Referral Potential.** Ideally, DHC should pursue services that will produce privately-insured patients for Manor Memorial Hospital. In addition, the referrals should produce short-stays (low number of in-patient days) and high profit margins. One might argue that gynecology services might have high referral potential for obstetrics (delivery of babies) at Manor Memorial Hospital.

E. **How might DHC bring about any changes suggested?**

   1. Case information, based on Ms. Worth's observations, indicate that DHC has four alternatives. They are:

   a. **Do Nothing** (This alternative was addressed under C. above and in Exhibit 2).

   b. **Expand Operating Hours** (This alternative involves adding part-time personnel, another physician).

   c. **Adding Gynecology Services** (This alternative involves adding a gynecologist to the DHC professional staff).

   d. **Expanding Operating Hours and Adding Gynecology Services** (This alternative is a combination of b and c).

2. **Do Nothing**

   a. **Pros** - There are none.

   b. **Cons**

   - Will not make DHC self-supporting (see Exhibit 2 in this note)

   - DHC will become primarily a convenient, low-cost handler of personal illness cases and exams

   - Minimal referral potential - probably stay at current levels

3. **Expand Operating Hours**

   a. **Pros**

   - Should reduce congestion during lunch hours

   - Should stimulate employment physical visits

   - Should modify DHC service mix and raise average revenue per visit (see Exhibit 3 in this note)

   - Might increase total visits of all types given increased access to DHC

   - Appears to be consistent with suburban ambulatory health care facilities and particularly MEDCENTER - the potential competitor

   b. **Cons**

   - Expensive alternative

   - Not apparent that large volume gains will occur given Ms. Worth's estimates

   - Will produce an annual loss of $315,059 (see Exhibit 3 in this note)

   - Not apparent that referrals and repeat visits will be stimulated

   - Appears to be the same thing - but more of it!

EXHIBIT 3

REVENUE AND FINANCIAL ANALYSIS OF EXPANDED HOURS OPTION

SERVICE REVENUE PER VISIT CALCULATION

Type of Visit	Projected Visits[a]	Prop. of Visits	Avg. Chg.[b]	Wtd. Avg. Chg (Col. 2 x Col. 3)
Personal Illness/Exam	2,480	.50	$ 54.00	$27.00
Worker's Compensation	975	.20	$ 84.24	16.85
Employment/Insurance Exams	1,380	.28	$101.52	28.43
Emergency	117	.02	$144.72	2.89
	4,952	1.00		$75.17

[a] Projections made by Ms. Worth.

[b] Assumes 8% across-the-board increase in service charges.

PROJECTED INCOME STATEMENT (May 1, 2000 - April 30, 2001)

Gross Revenue (4,952 visits x $75.17)		$372,242
Less: Variable Costs (14.5%)		53,975
Contribution (85.5%)		$318,267
Less Fixed Expenses:		
Personnel (5% increase + 1/3 more hours)	$252,208	
Professional Services (5% increase)	288,288	
Professional Fees	43,720	
Facility + Misc.	33,786	
Amortization	15,324	633,326
Net Loss		($315,059)

4. **Add Gynecology Services**

    a. **Pros**

    - Provides a source of repeat patients
    - Provides a foundation for referrals - possibly obstetrics given child-bearing ages of female patients
    - Should modify service mix and raise average revenue per visit
    - Given appointments, should not add to congestion
    - Different from MEDCENTER - a source of differentiation

    b. **Cons**

    - Additional cost of another physician (gynecologist)
    - Is the visit potential as high as Ms. Worth projects?
    - Will women patronize DHC for this service - fundamentally different from conventional services provided by ambulatory health care facilities. It's risky!
    - Will produce an annual loss of $41,969, but might be overcome by referral revenue/profit (see Exhibit 4 in this note)

5. **Expanding Operating Hours and Adding Gynecologist**

    a. **Pros**

    - Combination of Pros for both individual alternatives
    - Most expensive alternative and possibly most risky (see Exhibit 5 in this note)

    b. **Cons**

    - Combination of Cons for both individual alternatives.
    - Most expensive alternative and possibly most risky (see Exhibit 5 in this note).

EXHIBIT 4

REVENUE AND FINANCIAL ANALYSIS OF GYNECOLOGIST OPTION

SERVICE REVENUE PER VISIT CALCULATION

Type of Visit	Projected Visits [a]	Prop. of Visits	Avg. Chg. [b]	Wtd. Avg. Chg (Col. 2 x Col. 3)
Personal Illness/Exam	2,480	.39	$54.00	$21.06
Worker's Compensation	975	.15	$84.24	12.64
Employment/Insurance Exams	741	.12	$101.52	12.18
Emergency	117	.02	$144.72	2.89
Gynecology	2,000	.32	$104.00	33.28
	6,313	1.00		$82.05

[a] Projections made by Ms. Worth.

[b] Assumes 8% across-the-board increase in service charges; gynecology visit charge given.

PROJECTED INCOME STATEMENT (May 1, 2000 - April 30, 2001)

Gross Revenue (6,313 visits x $82.05)		$517,982
Less: Variable Costs (14.5%)		75,107
Contribution (85.5%)		$442,875
Less Fixed Expenses:		
Personnel (5% increase)	$189,630	
Professional Services (5% increase)	144,144	
Professional Fees	43,720	
Gynecologist [a]	58,240	
Facility + misc.	33,786	
Amortization	15,324	$484,844
Net Loss		($41,969)

[a] (16 hours/week) x (52 weeks) x ($70/hour) = $58,240.

EXHIBIT 5

REVENUE AND FINANCIAL ANALYSIS OF EXPANDED HOURS AND GYNECOLOGIST OPTION

SERVICE REVENUE PER VISIT CALCULATION

Type of Visit	Projected Visits[a]	Prop. of Visits	Avg. Chg.[b]	Wtd. Avg. Chg (Col. 2 x Col. 3)
Personal Illness/Exam	2,480	.35	$ 54.00	$18.90
Worker's Compensation	975	.14	$ 84.24	11.79
Employment/Insurance Exams	1,380	.20	$101.52	20.30
Emergency	117	.02	$144.72	2.89
Gynecology	2,000	.29	$104.00	30.16
	6,952	1.00		$84.04

[a] Projections made by Ms. Worth.

[b] Assumes 8% price increase in charges; gynecology visit charge given.

PROJECTED INCOME STATEMENT (May 1, 2000 - April 30, 2001)

Gross Revenue (6,952 visits x $84.04)		$584,246
Less: Variable Costs (14.5%)		84,716
Contribution (85.5%)		$499,530
Less Fixed Expenses:		
Personnel (5% increase + 1/3 more hours)	$252,208	
Professional Services (Two Physicians)	288,288	
Professional Fees	43,720	
Gynecologist	58,240	
Facility + Misc.	33,786	
Amortization	15,324	691,566
Net Loss		($192,036)

6. On balance, it would seem that DHC seriously entertain the alternative of **adding gynecology services.** This move appears to bring about the changes necessary at DHC for it to meet its objectives of expanding the hospital's referral base, increase the referrals of privately insured patients and becoming self-supporting three years after opening. However, adding gynecology services does not contribute to meeting employers' specific health needs.

F. Epilogue

Ms. Worth advocated expending the DHC's operating hours and adding gynecology services. She reasoned that even though the risks were great, such action was necessary. Dr. Mahon disagreed and felt the gynecology option only warranted attention. He recommended this option to the Board in May. The Board agreed with his proposal and this service was offered. In June, 2000, 500 gynecology related visits were recorded. This figure was one-fourth of the forecast for the entire year! Dr. Mahon believed this change in the service mix will help the DHC to break-even in the 2001 operating year.

G. Summary Points

1. Marketing concepts, tools, and practices have direct bearing on the management of service operations, and in this case, health care. Even physicians and hospitals are not immune from the vagaries of the marketplace.

2. Managers of service organizations must deal with uneven demand, and a fixed service capacity as well as high operating leverage (e.g., high fixed cost as a percent of total cost). Other examples include airlines, hotel/motels, etc.

3. A critical issue in service marketing is the management of a service mix (portfolio) which in turn affects contribution and profitability.

Service marketing differs from product marketing in terms of the four I's:

Inconsistency - Quality of a service can be inconsistent depending who performs the service and when it is performed (e.g., day part).

Inseparability - It is difficult, if not impossible in many cases, to separate a service from the deliverer of the service or the setting in which it occurs.

Intangibility - Services are intangible, that is, they can't be held, touched, or seen before the purchase decision.

Inventory - It is difficult, if not impossible in most cases, to inventory services. The inventory cost of a service is the cost of the person used to provide the service along with any needed equipment.

PROCTER AND GAMBLE, INC.: SCOPE

Synopsis

Gwen Hearst, a Procter and Gamble brand manager responsible for Scope mouthwash in Canada, was in the process of preparing a three year marketing plan for the brand. Her assignment was particularly challenging since a new competitor, Plax, had entered the Canadian mouthwash market and quickly captured a 10 percent market share. Plax differentiated itself from competitors in the mouthwash market along two dimensions: (1) usage occasion and (2) consumer benefit. As a "pre-brushing" rinse that fights plaque, Plax had redefined the market since existing competitors had typically positioned mouthwash as an "after brushing" rinse to fight "bad breath" and germs.

The case provides a description of the Plax introduction and a wide variety of views on how P&G and Scope might deal with this new competitor. Specific proposals include launching a new flanker brand, introducing a line extension, repositioning Scope, and maintaining the status quo, but with a possible modification in Scope's marketing mix. The case provides extensive market, competitive, and P&G company data useful for assessing the qualitative and quantitative aspects of each option.

Teaching Objectives

This case has four teaching objectives:

1. To demonstrate how an innovative new entrant (Plax) can quickly capture a respectable market share by redefining a market by use occasion and product benefit.

2. To illustrate some of the behavioral aspects of product/brand management as evident in the team approach to planning at P&G. Specifically, different viewpoints expressed by sales, market research, finance, advertising and other professionals require consideration.

3. To give students an opportunity to evaluate the merits of different proposals, some of which represent different "shades of gray," and consider strategic and executional issues related to these proposals.

This teaching note is based on an analysis plan prepared by Professor Gordon H. G. McDougall, Wilfred Laurier University.

4. To provide students with an opportunity to prepare a brand marketing plan, based on analysis and judgment, which incorporates both marketing strategy elements and a pro forma income statement.

Teaching Suggestions

This case can be assigned in that portion of the course when the instructor wishes to examine product mix and branding issues. In this context, the case provides an opportunity to consider product management and strategy issues in the face of a competitive challenge and possible market redefinition. Alternatively, some instructors might wish to assign the case later in a course when comprehensive marketing programs are addressed. In this setting, emphasis is placed on drafting a comprehensive brand plan including the link between strategy issues and profit-impact under a variety of scenarios.

Past experience with the case indicates that it is suitable for examination purposes and as a group presentation assignment. The case is appropriate for graduate and undergraduate classes.

The case has proven to be an excellent class discussion vehicle given student familiarity with the product class. Most students probably use one or more of the brands described in the case and have opinions about each. Nevertheless, students sometimes struggle with the financial analysis and particularly the calculation of unit contribution. Unit contribution must be calculated separately from gross margin per unit (case Exhibit 8) since P&G incorporates certain fixed costs into its determination of cost of goods sold. These fixed costs per unit are based on a volume of 440,000 units. If volume changes, which is likely under different options, use of the unit gross margin figure will distort the financial analysis. Students are also reluctant, at times, to exercise judgment and make realistic assumptions supported by case data. When this happens, students find themselves in a quandary as to how they can assess the different options. Instructors should be prepared to push students to make useful (i.e., supportable) assumptions and make judgment calls, otherwise they cannot make a decision.

An in-class discussion can be handled in one of two ways. The traditional approach is to pose the following questions (assignment) which provides the instructor with a framework to guide the class discussion. The questions that may be posed to students prior to or during a class discussion are:

1. What significant changes have occurred in the Canadian mouthwash market in the past three years?

2. How would you evaluate the performance of Scope over the past three years?

3. What are the pros and cons of the options available for Scope?

4. Prepare a marketing plan for the forthcoming year.

The advantage of this approach is that the first two questions "set up" the central issues which are dealt with in the second two questions.

The second approach is to begin the class discussion by asking a student to present the major alternatives. Class members can then be asked to vote or declare their support for each alternative. This approach, while less structured, gets students committed to an alternative and typically increases student involvement in the case issues and their resolution.

Areas for Discussion Analysis

A. What significant changes have occurred in the Canadian mouthwash market in the past three years?

1. Scope is competing in a competitive, mature market where total unit sales have increased by 8 percent and 5 percent respectively in the past two years (case Exhibit 2). However, two innovations have had a major impact on unit sales in prior years; (1) the introduction of new flavors in 1987 led to an overall increase of 26 percent, and (2) the introduction of Plax - a pre-brush rinse with a plaque-fighting benefit - led to a 10 percent increase in 1989. These two developments suggests that the Canadian mouthwash market responds to innovation and P&G should consider a very proactive stance to this business (i.e., there may be other possible innovations that P&G could introduce).

2. Major observations about the Canadian mouthwash market are:

- The dominant brand is Scope (32% share), with five brands holding 80 percent of the market (case Exhibit 4).

- With the introduction of Plax, major share losses where experienced by Listermint and Cepacol.

- The introduction of Plax may be redefining the mouthwash business which had been positioned around fresh breath (tastes good) and killing germs. A new segment is emerging that is positioned around a health benefit - fighting plaque - and use occasion (pre-brush rinse). However, the evidence to date suggests that this segment may not grow beyond 10 percent of the market.

- There are considerable variations in the prices of competing brands, with up to a 70 percent differential (Plax versus Scope) in the marketplace (case Exhibit 5).

- In spite of a lot of jockeying among competitors, no new brand, with the exception of Plax, has gained substantial market share.

3. Some comments are warranted on the product category from a consumer perspective. The basic reasons for use are habit and reducing/eliminating bad breath/germs. Mouthwash is a convenience product that may have some consumer brand loyalty (taste, image) but switching among an acceptable brand set is probably likely and would be stimulated by promotions. Consumers' perceptions of brand images (case Exhibit 3) are relatively strong for their own brand but, with two exceptions, most brands are seen as "average" on a number of attributes. The two exceptions are Listerine, which is seen as strong on the "kill germs" side and Plax which is strong on the plaque/better gums side.

B. How would you evaluate the performance of Scope in the past three years?

1. While Scope is the dominant brand (32% share), is profitable (gross margin of $6.7 million), has a strong "tastes great" image, and has the "best" advertising to sales ratio, there is some cause for concern, namely:

- no market share growth in the past two years for Scope,
- P&G appears to evidence a reactive stance in the market (i.e., no apparent anticipation or response to Plax),
- lower Scope penetration in drug versus food stores,
- lower Scope price may be a major reason for market share,
- consumer perception of Scope image is average to below average among all users and, on a relative basis, is weak even among brand users of Scope.

2. The implication of this review of current marketing activities for Scope may result in changes that improve both the market position and profitability for the brand. The position of Scope and the competing brands should be discussed. First, the two major dimensions, fresh breath (which includes "tastes great") and killing germs, can be used to position the major brands (as shown in Exhibit 1 in this note). Then, the new "health" benefit and killing germs can be used to position the brands (as shown in Exhibit 2 in this note). The positions are based on case Exhibit 3, the verbal comments about brands, and judgment. The implication for Scope is that it is strong in "fresh breath," but weak on the other two dimensions. If the market moves more to the health and killing germs area, Scope is very vulnerable.

3. There are some side issues that the instructor may want to introduce here. First, an instructor may wish to address the issue of the regulatory environment which creates some hurdles for P&G if they wish to pursue the plaque claims. A second issue is the team approach to preparing the direction for Scope. Gwen Hearst needs to build team consensus among the team members for the future course of action. If not, support for her plans may not be forthcoming from upper management. The pros and cons of the team approach might be debated for a short time. The obvious problem is that each group has a different view that

EXHIBIT 1

BRAND POSITIONING MAP (GERMS AND BREATH)

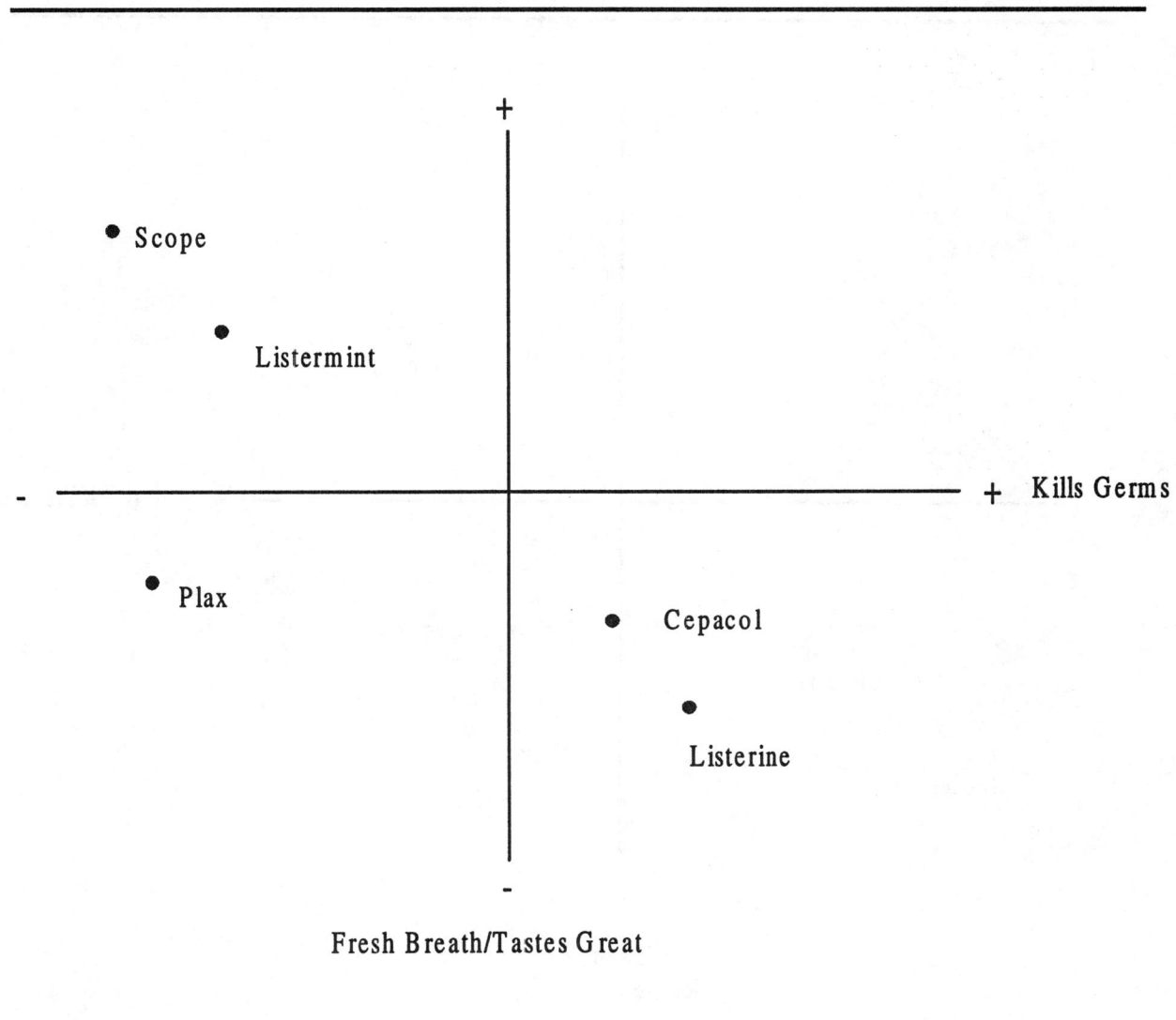

EXHIBIT 2

BRAND POSITIONING MAP (GERMS AND HEALTH)

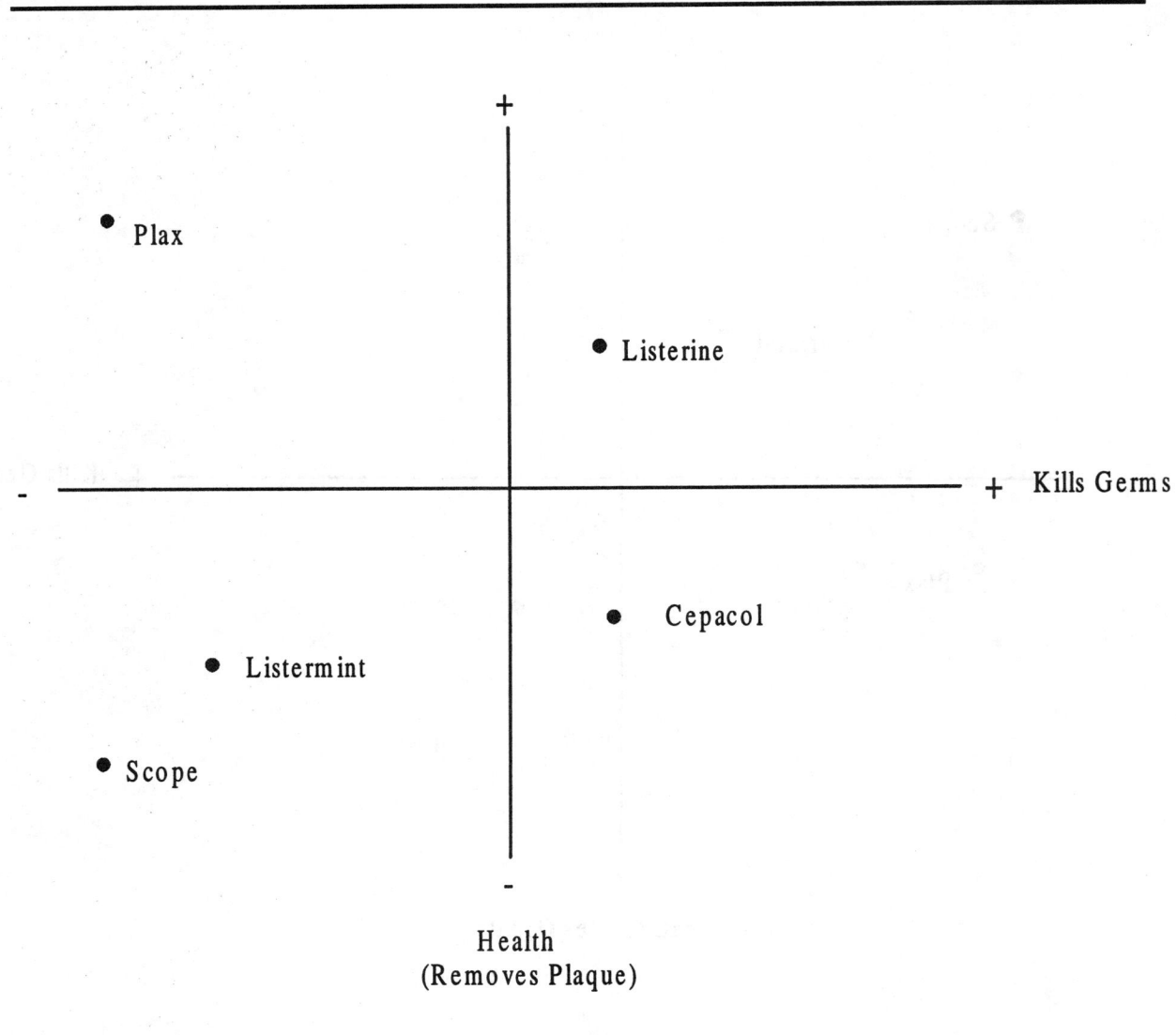

reflects their interests. Third is the issue of whether Plax is, in fact, beneficial. There is no evidence in the case that Plax or P&G's new product provides any meaningful value to the consumer.

C. What are the pros and cons of the options available for Scope?

1. The major alternatives are to maintain the status quo (which should include improving and increasing the marketing efforts for Scope), launch a line extension using the Scope name, introduce a (new) flanker brand, or relaunch Scope (with the plaque benefit). The pros and cons for each alternative are detailed in Exhibit 3 in this note.

2. The main criteria for evaluating each alternative are:

    - Consistent with P&G's mission statement and company philosophy,
    - Maximizes profits and market share in the long term,
    - Consistent with existing marketing strategy,
    - Achieves team/group consensus.

3. In considering the pros and cons against the criteria two key questions emerge:

    - Is the new "health" segment developed by Plax meeting a long-term consumer need that is likely to increase over time?

    - Has P&G developed a product with superior quality and value that best fills that need?

These questions should generate considerable debate as the alternatives are being evaluated. While arguments can be presented for both sides, the evidence (some very judgmental) would suggest that the "answer" to both questions is most likely to be "maybe" or "no".

4. Turning to the financial aspects of the analysis, the data provided in Exhibit 4 in this note provides the basis for examining various scenarios. Note that the "cost of goods sold" has been recast to reflect fixed and variable cost. Exhibit 5 in this note provides examples of likely scenarios that students might consider. Based on the pricing data provided in case Exhibit 5, Scope has an opportunity to increase prices relative to the other major brands. As shown in Exhibit 5 in this note, a 5 percent price increase will result in increased contribution of $906,400 at 1990 unit sales levels. The line extension analysis suggests that a price increase of 20 percent or more are probably required because of the increased costs (both fixed and variable) and that at an ongoing 5 percent market share, contributions of $490,000 to $775,000 might be expected (no cannibalization assumed).

5. Based on market share estimates provided in the case for a line extension (6.5%), assuming cannibalism of 5 percent (range between 2 and 9%), assuming a price increase of

EXHIBIT 3
PROS AND CONS OF ALTERNATIVES

---

1. **Status Quo** - (includes possibility of improved marketing and price increases)

    ☐ Pros
    - consistent with some managers' beliefs that no threat exists as Scope and Plax are in different markets
    - marketing and production remain focused
    - no interference/disruption of a solid performer (Scope)
    - no possible consumer confusion
    - does not compromise P&G mission or goals
    - may be most profitable (with price increase and more effective marketing)

    ☐ Cons
    - may lead to declining sales because of consumer move to new segment, "health benefits"
    - missing opportunity in growing, high margin segment
    - does not address consumer need for good tasting rinse that fights plaque
    - not recommended by sales and marketing
    - may not aid Gwen's career

2. **Line extension** (using Scope name)

    ☐ Pros
    - Scope's name enhances image, reduces marketing and listing costs
    - captures opportunity in a new segment
    - easier to market to trade (also incremental sales, increase sales $/foot)
    - higher price/unit may increase profits
    - competes directly with Plax

    ☐ Cons
    - cannibalization of Scope sales
    - possible damage to Scope name (dilution of brand image)
    - may confuse consumers
    - requires strategic shift in marketing/advertising

- not in line with P&G mission and goals - health benefits equal Plax whereas P&G looks for superior products
- possibly inconsistent brand positioning
- may reduce profits
- must adhere to health regulations which limits promotion flexibility

3. **Flanker brand** (similar to Alternative 2, only new or different pros/cons shown)

   ☐ Pros
   - avoids possible negative impact on Scope
   - reduces cannibalization
   - would not confuse consumers
   - no shift in strategy required

   ☐ Cons
   - requires considerable advertising and promotion expenditures just to build brand awareness
   - consumer acceptance is less likely with new brand name
   - may meet with some trade resistance
   - may be least profitable

4. **Relaunch Scope** (with the plaque benefit)

   ☐ Pros
   - reduces consumer switching to other brands
   - no major change to marketing strategy
   - potential for increasing price
   - minimal consumer confusion
   - penetration of a new market
   - Scope name aids acceptance
   - possibility for growth and profits

   ☐ Cons
   - potential damage to leading brand in market
   - may be somewhat inconsistent brand positioning
   - increases unit costs, requires price increase
   - major risk

EXHIBIT 4

FINANCIAL DATA

	Scope 1990 per unit	Scope 1990 per unit - variable	Proposed Line Extension
Ingredients	$8.16	$8.16	$10.71[5]
Packaging	5.10	5.10	5.40[6]
Manufacturing	7.00	3.50[1]	3.50
Delivery	3.12	3.12	3.12
Miscellaneous	2.55	.64[2]	.64
Cost of Goods Sold (case Exhibit 8)	$25.93		
Total Variable Cost		$20.52	$23.37
Fixed Costs			
• Manufacturing (000)[3]	—	1,540	
• Miscellaneous (000)[3]	—	842	
Total Fixed	—	2,382	
Total Cost of Goods Sold[3]	11,409	11,411	
General office overheads	1,366	1,366	
Advertising	1,700	1,700	
Promotion	1,460	1,460	
Total	4,526	4,526	
Total Costs	$15,935	$15,937	
Net Sales[4]	$18,150	$18,150	
Net Contribution[7]	$ 2,215	$ 2,213	

[1] 50% of manufacturing is fixed
[2] 75% of miscellaneous is fixed
[3] Based on 440,000 units sold
[4] Based on $41.25 per unit and 440,000 units sold
[5] $8.16 plus $2.55 (± 50%)(Assume $2.25)
[6] $5.10 plus $.30
[7] The difference in net contribution is due to rounding.

EXHIBIT 5

SENSITIVITY ANALYSIS FOR LIKELY SCENARIOS

1. **Status quo - improve current marketing, no change in costs**

    - Net sales per unit $41.25
    - Variable cost per unit $20.52
    - Contribution to fixed costs, profit, etc. $20.73

    - Market share increase/decrease of 1% equals 13,580 units (1990 market) or a contribution of $281,513 towards fixed cost, profit, etc.

    - A price increase of 5% per unit ($2.06) provides an increased contribution towards fixed cost profit, etc. of $906,400 at 1990 unit sales levels (440,000 units).

2. **Proposed line extension**

	Current Price	10% Price Increase	20% Price Increase	30% Price Increase
Net sales per unit	$41.25	$45.35	$49.50	$53.63
Variable cost per unit	23.37	23.37	23.37	23.37
Contribution to fixed, etc.	$17.88	$21.98	$26.13	$30.26
One percent market share (contribution)	$242,810	$298,488	$354,845	$410,931

    - Incremental increase in marketing expenditures - using Scope name - $1,000,000 (assumed)
    - Incremental increase in marketing expenditures - using new name - $3,000,000 to launch (assumed) and $1,000,000 thereafter (assumed)

    Examples:
    - 5% market share at a 10% price increase using Scope name provides a contribution of $492,440 ($298,488 x 5 minus $1,000,000)[1,2]

    - 5% market share at 30% price increase using new name provides a contribution of -$1,225,775 ($1,774,225 - $3,000,000) in first year and $774,225 ($1,774,225 - $1,000,000) thereafter.[1,2,3]

Notes: [1] Does not include any cannibalization. At current levels, a 1% share for Scope provides a contribution of $281,513.

[2] The estimates do not include testing fees ($50,000 per retail chain) or a product test ($20,000).

[3] Plax was launched with a promotion campaign estimated at $4 million.

20 percent over the current price of Scope (1.2 x $41.25 = $49.50), a cannibalism analysis is possible. Exhibit 6 in this note offers one perspective on the incremental profit (loss) from the line extension.

D. Prepare a marketing plan for the forthcoming year.

1. Student marketing plans will vary, depending on the alternative selected by the student. The plan should be based on a platform that incorporates segmentation, marketing mix strategy, and brand positioning. The financial analysis should be consistent with the plan.

2. As one example, the "Status Quo" alternative (i.e., no new product launch) with improved marketing of Scope could form the basis for a marketing program as follows:

Statement of Purpose and Strategy

We will continuously stay ahead of competition, while aggressively defending our established profitable businesses against major competitive challenges despite short-term profit consequences.

Segmentation

Scope will continue efforts to dominate the "breath freshener" segment which contains only one other competitor, Listermint. Forty percent of consumers purchase mouthwash products in order to receive the benefit of fresh breath. Scope will remain the market leader in this segment and will continue to benefit from sizable profit margins.

Product

Scope will remain the same high quality product that has enabled P&G to gain its 33 percent market share. The long run may require Scope to investigate new flavors or packaging in order to stimulate demand during its late maturity stage.

Price

Prices will be increased by 5 percent in 1991. This will still allow Scope to be positioned as a low price, high quality-value-product. Our focus is profit-oriented to maximize the financial benefit to the firm.

Distribution

Scope will continue to use its present intensive distribution strategy and system, but more time will be devoted to improving distribution and shelf facings in drugstores and wholesale clubs.

EXHIBIT 6

CANNIBALISM ASSESSMENT

PRODUCT ECONOMICS

	Scope (Regular)	Line Extension*
Unit Selling Price	$ 41.25	$ 49.50
Unit Variable Cost		
Ingredients	$ 8.16	$ 10.71
Packaging	5.10	5.40
Manufacturing	3.50	3.50
Delivery	3.12	3.12
Misc.	.64	.64
Total Unit Variable Cost	$ 20.52	$ 23.37
Unit Contribution	**$ 20.73**	**$ 26.13**

*The line extension unit contribution is calculated by increasing the Scope price by 20% to $49.50 and subtracting the $23.37 unit variable cost calculated in Exhibit 4 in this note.

CANNIBALISM ESTIMATION ILLUSTRATION**

Contribution of Line Extension (3rd yr.)		
$26.13 x 1,358,000 x 6.5%	=	$ 2,306,495
Contribution "Lost" from Scope (Regular):		
assuming 5% cannibalism:		
5% x 440,000 x $20.73	=	$ 456,060
Net Incremental Effect of Cannibalism on Contribution:		
$2,306,495 - $456,060	= +	$ 1,850,435
Less: Incremental Fixed Advertising + Promotion	= -	$ 2,000,000
Incremental Profit (Loss)		($ 149,565)

  **This illustration is based on the following inputs. Change any of these inputs and the results will change:
1.   1,358,000 is the 1990 Canadian market size in units from case Exhibit 2.
2.   6.5% is the estimated market share of the total mouthwash and "rinse" market on an ongoing basis from P&G's market research group.
3.   440,000 is the Scope (Regular) volume from case Exhibit 7.
4.   5% represents an approximate mid-point in Gwen Heart's 2% to 9% cannibalism range.
5.   Incremental fixed advertising & promotion of $2 million is an approximate expenditure.

Promotion

Scope will continue to emphasize a pull marketing strategy with an emphasis on consumer advertising. Advertising expenditures have been increased to $3.5 million to augment exposure of Scope. Selective-demand advertising and comparative advertising will be utilized to point out the key benefits of Scope versus its main competitors. Television advertising would be the most effective medium due to its ability to reach the largest number of people in the target market.

Promotional samples are being used in order to stimulate non-users to try our product and also to convince occasional users to try our product again. This will aid in obtaining market share from our competitors. Mailed couponing will be used to increase sales from our occasional users and to provide our loyal users with an incentive to continue to purchase Scope. In-store promotions include in-store couponing and point-of-sale displays to renew consumer awareness.

Budget Item	Expenditure
Advertising	$2,106,000
Samples	450,000
Couponing	455,000
In-Store Promotions	489,000
TOTAL	**$3,500,000**

The financial analysis of this plan is:

	1991	Comments
Total Market-units (000)	1,426	Assume a 5% increase
Scope share (%)	34	A 1-point share gain over 1990 through improved marketing - share taken from Listermint
Unit sales (000)	484.8	
Sales price (per unit)	$ 43.31	5% price increase over 1990
Variable cost (per unit)	20.52	Assume same as 1990 (Exhibit 4 in this note)
Contribution to fixed, etc.	$ 22.79	
Fixed cost (000)		
• Manufacturing	$ 1,540	Assume same as 1990
• Miscellaneous	842	Assume same as 1990
• Advertising	2,106	Revised - see budget
• Promotion	1,394	Revised - see budget
• General Overheads	1,366	Assume same as 1990
Total Fixed Cost	$ 7,248	
Total Contribution	$11,049	($22.79 x 484,800)
Less Fixed Cost	7,248	
Contribution to P&G	$ 3,801	

Compared to 1990, this increases the net contribution to P&G by $1,586,000 ($3,801 - $2,215 = $1,586,000).

E. **Summary Points**

1. The successful introduction of Plax illustrates how a new positioning can redefine a market. Compared with market incumbents which positioned their brands on the basis of a "post-brushing" rinse that prevents germs and provides a clean breath, Plax was positioned as a "pre-brush" rinse that prevents plaque - a new use occasion and a new attribute. Premium priced and supported by a $4 million introductory marketing campaign, Plax was able to capture 10 percent of the Canadian and 9.6 percent of the U.S. mouthwash market.

2. Effective marketing requires both a consumer orientation and a competitor orientation. P&G only launches superior performing products that focus on unmet consumer needs. However, the company also is alert to competitor actions which may undermine the market position of their brands.

3. This case illustrates the "management aspects" of product management by describing the team approach which brings together professionals from a variety of disciplines with different views and expertise. A product manager must "manage" these professionals without formal authority to do so, and move the team toward decision consensus on an action plan.

4. A thorough analysis behind developing a product/brand strategy often involves studying market/consumer information, competition, manufacturing, and financial data, in addition to considering market position(ing) of present products/brands and company objectives and policies.

5. Sensitivity analysis is often required in the development of product/brand strategy. Such analysis typically requires a cost-volume-profit analysis that involves making realistic assumptions and exercising judgment in the face of uncertainty.

FRITO-LAY COMPANY: CRACKER JACK

Synopsis

In mid-July 1997, Lynne Peissig, Vice President and General Manager for New Ventures at the Frito-Lay Company, assembled the business team responsible for studying the possible acquisition of the Cracker Jack caramel popcorn brand from Borden Foods Corporation. Cracker Jack had been owned by Borden since 1964 and was one of the oldest and best-known trademarks in the United States.

The purpose of the all-day meeting was to (1) consolidate the findings of the business team, (2) outline a plan for how Cracker Jack might be marketed as a Frito-Lay brand, and (3) estimate the "fair market value" of the Cracker Jack business. The valuation would be used to determine an acquisition price should a decision be made to bid on the Cracker Jack brand and related assets.

The case offers a unique, "behind-the-scenes" look at the sale of a brand from the perspective of a seller (Borden) and a prospective buyer (Frito-Lay). Central to the transaction is the seller's and buyer's assessment of the brand's marketing potential. Borden's and Frito-Lay's views on Cracker Jack's present situation, and future marketing strategy, resource requirements, and sales and profit opportunity are reflected in the brand's value which is based on the capitalization of Cracker Jack's forecasted net cash flows, discounted to a present value. Students will see that a brand's value is in the eye of the beholder and that the value of a brand will vary according to who owns it.

Teaching Objectives

This case has four teaching objectives:

1. To introduce students to strategic reasons why brands are bought and sold.

2. To illustrate that careful market and marketing analysis underlies the sale and purchase of brands.

3. To show that a brand's equity and financial value is based on the brand-building marketing practices of the brand's present and future owner.

4. To demonstrate how concepts from marketing and finance are reinforcing in the determination of a brand's economic value.

Teaching Suggestions

This case is best suited for that portion of the course that addresses product and brand strategy. Alternatively the case can be used as an integrative, comprehensive assignment toward the end of the course. The case has also proven to be popular for group presentations in both graduate and undergraduate classes. Graduate students tend to delve into the case more than undergraduates given the cross-functional elements of the decision-making process, including marketing, finance, and operations/manufacturing.

Some students will make a point of visiting a grocery store or vending machine to see if Frito-Lay bought the brand. In fact, they did in October 1997. This "market research" frustrates students because it means that they cannot simply make a go/no go decision. Rather, they will have to determine a "fair market value" and recommend a bid price. Fortunately, for teaching purposes, the purchase price is not publicly available.

The case is viewed as intimidating given its length and finance overtones by some students. However, the Appendix to the case, "Note on Valuing a Business," is clear and Exhibit A-1 essentially lays out what the student is ultimately expected to do and present. Instructors should resist saying what the "fair market value" or bid price for Cracker Jack should be. Rather, "value like beauty is in the eyes of the beholder." In this case, the student assessment of the market, Cracker Jack's present and future market position, assumptions about the future, and so forth should drive the analysis.

There are several possible ways to teach the case. As a class discussion case, Cracker Jack can be assigned over two days. On the first day, attention is placed on two topics. Discussion should first focus on preparing a SWOT analysis for Cracker Jack based on assessment of the Ready-To-Eat caramel popcorn category, Borden's experience with the brand, and Frito-Lay's own research. Once completed, the discussion should move toward articulating how Crack Jack might be marketed as a Frito-Lay brand. The topic for the second day is the financial valuation of Cracker Jack. Students should be expected to bring to class their financial analysis, including a recommendation for how much Frito-Lay should bid for Cracker Jack. Implicit in the student's recommendation is an evaluation of what they think Borden is expecting to get for the brand. The discussion can then focus on the assumptions underlying their financial analysis and differences in bid prices. The second day discussion can be heated since valuations and bid prices tend to vary greatly. Again, an instructor should let the students argue without rendering his/her opinion.

The case has proven to be an excellent group presentation assignment. When used in this manner, student teams are assigned responsibility for preparing the presentation that Lynne Peissig will deliver to senior PepsiCo executives. The written presentation should incorporate both a market and marketing analysis and a financial valuation, including a recommended bid price. A 15 to 20 minute oral presentation, based on the written report, should follow.

Specific questions that can be posed to students either before or during a class discussion/group presentation are:

1. Why has Borden Foods decided to sell Cracker Jack?

2. Why is Frito-Lay considering the purchase of Cracker Jack?

3. What might a SWOT analysis for Cracker Jack look like based on as assessment of the Ready-To-Eat caramel popcorn category, Borden's experience with the brand, and Frito-Lay's own research? What are the implications for Frito-Lay?

4. How should Cracker Jack be marketed as a Frito-Lay brand?

5. How much do you think Borden Foods wants for Cracker Jack?

6. What is the "fair market value" for Cracker Jack as a Frito-Lay brand?

7. How much should Frito-Lay bid for Cracker Jack?

Areas for Discussion/Analysis

A. Why has Borden Foods decided to sell Cracker Jack?

1. Borden Foods has stated two reasons why Cracker Jack is for sale:

   - A strategic assessment of the company's focus and resources indicated that Borden should focus on its pasta business and expand into grain-based meals that required a significant (financial) investment.

   - Borden believed that broadened distribution for Cracker Jack and a totally new sales and delivery infrastructure (direct-store-delivery) was needed to grow sales and product profitability. However, the company was not prepared to make the investment necessary to broaden distribution and implement a direct-store-delivery (DSD) system given the resource demands of other business (pasta, plus grain-based meals) opportunities.

2. Student will also conclude from case information that there may be additional reasons why Borden is selling Cracker Jack. For example, from Case Exhibit 5:

   ...Cracker Jack has evidenced "flat" dollar sales over the past four years.

   ...Cracker Jack has recorded a negative direct product contribution from 1994 to 1996 and only marginal profitability in 1993. Actual losses would have been larger had allocated selling costs and overhead been included in determining product profitability.

3. It is also reasonable to conclude that Cracker Jack's "brand equity" has eroded. The brand's price premium — historically 28 percent over major competitors, notably Crunch 'n Munch — has decreased. Frito-Lay's own research suggests the brand "... is a trademark living off residual heritage... that appears to have lost momentum (popularity) in recent years."

4. At this juncture, some instructors might refer students to the literature on brand equity, and particularly the seminal work of David Aaker. Aaker identifies five components of brand equity:

- Brand Awareness
- Brand Associations
- Perceived Quality
- Brand Loyalty
- Other Proprietary Brand Assets

Even though Cracker Jack has extremely high awareness — an important brand equity component — favorable associations and other components of brand equity are less apparent. In short, **Cracker Jack's brand equity is tarnished and may be in decline.**

B. Why is Frito-Lay considering the purchase of Cracker Jack?

There a variety of reasons why Frito–Lay is looking at Cracker Jack as an acquisition candidate.

1. The company is looking for growth opportunities outside its already successful snack business. Frito-Lay's New Venture Division was created in December 1996 with a defined mission:

> To drive significant Frito-Lay growth by seeking and creating new business platforms and platforms which combine the best of Frito-Lay's advantages with high-impact consumer food solutions.

This mission manifested itself in three broad growth opportunity avenues:

- Opportunities for building Frito-Lay's existing snack business by expanding into new eating occasions for current or new products. "Better-for-you" products for morning and all-day consumption fell into category.

- Opportunities to enter new product categories by capitalizing on Frito-Lay's store-door-delivery (also called direct-sales-delivery or DSD) sales force strengths, broad distribution coverage, and brand marketing skills.

- "Opportunistic acquisitions" made possible by related food companies offering products or entire businesses for sale as a result of corporate restructuring.

Cracker Jack initially appeared to fit all three growth opportunities. Subsequent research can be interpreted as casting some doubt on this initial appraisal, however, e.g., Cracker Jack's brand equity.

2. It is reasonable to conclude that a product development vs. acquisition trade-off was also considered. According to the case, the **financial investment** to internally develop and launch a new brand (trademark) in a consumer food category was $75 to $100 million, including the cost of product research and development, test marketing, and a national introduction. There was a **time cost** reflected in the two to three year time period from concept development to full-scale commercialization of a new brand. Finally, there was **significant risk** — the likelihood of a new product success was roughly one in ten.

C. **What might a SWOT analysis for Cracker Jack look like based on an assessment of the Ready-To-Eat caramel popcorn category, Borden's experience with the brand, and Frito-Lay's own research? What are the implications for Frito-Lay?**

1. The case contains an extensive description of the Ready-To-Eat caramel popcorn category, Borden's track record, and Frito-Lay's own brand research initiated under the code-name, Project Bingo. An illustrative SWOT analysis appears in Exhibit 1 in this note which is a useful way to summarize the case information.

2. **Cracker Jack Strengths**. Cracker Jack's principal strength is its almost universal awareness in the U.S. among people 15 to 60 years old (97%). The brand has distinct imagery among consumers reflecting favorable childhood experiences (the toy surprise) — nostalgia. Its a unique product, viewed as a good treat, and is popular with children. The brand occupies a strong, second place market share and enjoys a price premium relative to the category leader — Crunch 'n Munch.

Frito-Lay would benefit from these strengths. The high brand name awareness means that an investment in advertising/promotion to build awareness is unnecessary. The imagery too is favorable and can be presumed to be generally possible. Cracker Jack is a clearly differentiated product and an advertising opportunity exists for the brand (see Chapter 6). Furthermore, Cracker Jack commands a price premium which gives Frito-Lay flexibility in its pricing.

EXHIBIT 1

ILLUSTRATIVE CRACKER JACK SWOT ANALYSIS

Strengths

- 97% awareness among persons between the ages of 15 and 60; 95% awareness among heavy users of caramel popcorn.

- Ranked second in dollar (25%) and pound volume (14%) market share with a price premium relative to the category leader, Crunch 'n Munch.

- Distinct imagery and icons in consumer's minds (fond memories of growing up); toy surprise.

- Unique product, a good treat, popular with children.

Weaknesses

- Consumer awareness of Cracker Jack line extensions – Fat Free, Butter Toffee, Nutty Deluxe – less than 50%.

- Declining price premium relative to Crunch 'n Munch, appears to have lost momentum (dollar sales, unit volume). No meaningful advertising support; not effectively merchandised at the point-of-sale.

- Traditional/old-fashion associations, not contemporary and less contemporary than Crunch 'n Munch.

- Not perceived as "better-for-you," relative to other snacks; lacks flavor/type variety; not perceived to be easily extendible across eating occasions.

Opportunities

- "Under-marketed" product category compared to microwave popcorn, other snack categories.

- Only one major national brand competitor, International House Foods, Inc. (Crunch 'n Munch) - 32% market share.

- Sales appear sensitive to sales/delivery system and product placement – limited, controlled tests indicate direct-store-delivery system (DSD) with placement in DSD snack aisles can initially boost retail sales by 38%.

- International expansion possibilities – 98.9% of Cracker Jack sales occur in the U.S.

- Possible licensing possibilities (?)

Threats

- Decline in R-T-E caramel popcorn category sales and unit volume growth between 1995 and 1996.

- Seasonal, specialty, regional brands popular – represent about a third of R-T-E caramel popcorn category.

- Product gross margins are sensitive to agricultural commodity (corn, peanut) price fluctuations.

3. **Cracker Jack Weaknesses**. Cracker Jack's principal weaknesses lie in its past marketing by Borden and somewhat in the product itself. While the Cracker Jack brand evidences extremely high awareness, awareness of recent line (flavor) extensions is less than 50 percent. Borden has not advertised the brand nationally since 1993, relying instead on trade-related promotional spending. By comparison, Crunch 'n Munch is heavily advertised relative to Cracker Jack (see Case Exhibit 3). Furthermore, Case Exhibit 8 shows that 28 percent of Cracker purchasers do not buy the brand more often and 34 percent of Cracker Jack non-purchasers don't buy at all because they don't think about it or don't see it advertised. Case Exhibit 8 also shows that a lack of perceived availability is a problem which is symptomatic of Borden's retail merchandising or lack thereof. Frito-Lay's research suggests that Cracker Jack has lost momentum (popularity), has traditional/old-fashioned associations, and is not contemporary; and less contemporary than Crunch 'n Munch. Cracker Jack's historical price premium is also eroding. Cracker Jack, and probably caramel popcorn overall, is not viewed as "better-for-you" relative to other snacks, lacks flavor/type variety, and is not seen as easily extendible across eating occasions (80% of eating occasions are in the afternoon or evening hours).

Frito-Lay will have a challenge "remarketing" Cracker Jack. **Cracker Jack has become an orphan brand in Borden's line, that is, the brand has not been attended to nor has it been invested in**. In some respects, it can be inferred that **Cracker Jack has been "harvested" in recent years by Borden. It "is a trademark living off residual heritage ... " according to a Frito-Lay executive**. It is noteworthy, that Frito-Lay intends to reinvest in the brand — brand advertising — and has a sales/delivery system that should bolster the brand's retail presence. Brand and flavor extensions proposed by Frito-Lay address the flavor-type variety issue. However, a challenge might be overcoming the "better-for-you" snack perception and Cracker Jack's tarnished brand equity.

4. **Cracker Jack Opportunities**. The Ready-To-Eat caramel popcorn category is "under marketed" and only one major national competitor exists (International House Foods – Crunch 'n Munch). Further, sales appear sensitive to sales/delivery system (DSD) and product placement and international expansion is possible since 98.9 percent of Cracker Jack sales occur in the U.S.

It would seem that Frito-Lay unique capabilities and resources can energize the caramel popcorn category with added advertising and new flavor and form (bar) varieties. Frito-Lay's strong sales/delivery system and brand marketing skills suggest that Cracker Jack can replace Crunch 'n Munch as the dollar and volume share leader and promote category growth overall.

5. **Cracker Jack Threats**. The Ready-To-Eat caramel popcorn category registered a decline on sales and unit volume between 1995 and 1996. Is this decline symptomatic of the category's appeal and potentially the start of a trend, or a one-year dip? The decline followed steady annual increases since 1993. Cracker Jack, with popcorn and peanuts as the two ingredients, is subject to agricultural price fluctuations. The case suggests this happened to Cracker Jack in 1994 and 1995 and gross margins suffered. Finally, the apparent popularity

of seasonal, specialty, and regional brands, which account for about a third of category volume, is a threat to potential long-term sales growth.

Overall, none of these threats really cancel out the Cracker Jack opportunity for Frito-Lay. However, creating category growth and capturing market share are all the more difficult if Ready-To-Eat caramel popcorn primary demand is declining.

6. **Overall Qualitative Evaluation.** Students should conclude from a Cracker Jack SWOT analysis that a favorable opportunity does exist for Frito-Lay. The opportunity lies in what Frito-Lay can do for the brand: (1) advertise and promote the brand, (2) sell/deliver the brand through its DSD, and (3) build volume through line and flavor extensions. This conclusion leads to the next case discussion question.

D. **How should Cracker Jack be marketed as a Frito-Lay brand?**

1. The previous SWOT analysis suggests that Cracker Jack has considerable upside potential as a Frito-Lay brand. The potential lies in what Frito-Lay can do for the brand.

2. A marketing plan is needed to "relaunch" Cracker Jack. Reasonable objectives for a relaunch are identical to those outlined by Borden Foods; namely, (a) revitalize the base business, (b) improve operating efficiencies, and (c) extend the Cracker Jack trademark. These objectives translate to three strategy initiatives: (a) invest in advertising/promotion to build the base business, (b) improve operating efficiencies principally through Frito-Lay's store-door-delivery system and manufacturing capabilities, and (c) use brand and line (flavor) extensions to extend the Cracker Jack trademark.

3. The foundation for launching Cracker Jack as a Frito-Lay brand resides in the Simulated Test Market (STM) commissioned as part of Project Bingo and described in the case. Case Exhibit 10 displays 15 different combinations of advertising/promotion expenditure levels ($15 million, $22 million, $32 million), packaging type and size (bag-in-box, flex bag at 7 oz. and 8 oz. sizes), retail prices ($1.69, $1.99), and distribution/product placement (salty snack aisle, alternative snacks aisle). First-year pound volume and manufacturer net sales estimates are also given for each combination, subject to a $\pm$ 15 percent margin of error.

4. At the outset, the evaluation/recommendation of different marketing-mix combinations can be constrained by important observations from the case.

a. First, combinations that include the salty snack aisle product placement in stores are preferred over combinations that include placement in the alternative snack aisle. The reasoning is that Frito-Lay's direct-sales-delivery (DSD) system is best suited to merchandise this aisle.

b. Second, combinations that include consumer advertising expenditures are preferred over combinations that do not. The reasoning here is that Cracker Jack is in dire need of "visibility." Case Exhibit 8 shows that consumers do not buy Cracker Jack because they don't think about it or don't see it advertised.

c. Third, combinations that include the Flex Bag option are preferred over combinations that feature the Bag-in-Box option. The reasoning here is that Frito-Lay can realize cost reductions by building the flex bag volume.

These observations tend to simplify the class discussion. Four combinations emerge based on (a) package form (size) and retail price, and (b) advertising and promotion spending. These combinations are displayed below with pound/dollar sales showed for each from Case Exhibit 10:

Package Form (Size) And Retail Price:	Advertising/Promotion Spending	
	$22 mil.	$32 mil.
8-oz. Flex Bag @ $1.99	36.4 mil. lbs. $103.7 mil.	43.8 mil. lbs. $124.4 mil.
7-oz. Flex Bag @ $1.69	31.6 mil. lbs. $77.1 mil.	37.8 mil. lbs. $92.5 mil.

5. Instructors can expect students to favor the STM marketing-mix combination that yields the highest first-year pound and dollar sales volume. This combination consists of an 8-oz. flex bag sold for $1.99 in the salty-snack aisle and supported by a $32 million advertising/promotion budget that produces estimated volume sales of 43.8 million pounds and $124.4 million in sales. An important element of this initiative is the sizeable $32 million investment in advertising and promotion, including $15 million for consumer advertising.

    a. There are a variety of reasons why this initiative may be favored:

        ... It aggressively builds the base business by investing heavily in consumer advertising and promotion.

        ... A larger base business provides a foundation for larger incremental snack bar sales in the second year and a flavor extension in the third year.

        ... Heavy advertising/promotion is necessary to boost overall category volume and capture market share.

    b. However, there are also reasons why this initiative is questionable:

... Over one-in-five (22%) pounds of Cracker Jack sold is simply cannibalized from Frito-Lay snack chips at a cost of $1.05 per pound.

... The heavy advertising/promotion investment seems unnecessary given the almost universal awareness of Cracker Jack. A $15 million investment in consumer advertising alone is almost four times what was spent by Crunch 'n Munch in 1996.

... R-T-E caramel popcorn pound volume was 57 million pounds in 1996, according to the case. A 43.8 million pound projection translates to a 76.8 percent market share, assuming no category growth. Even with category growth, the market share seems overly optimistic and unlikely to be attainable.

... The $124.4 million volume estimate will require a capital investment of $10 million in the first year. [Note: Frito-Lay has an independent supplier that can produce the equivalent of $100 million in sales. Dollar sales above this amount will require Frito-Lay to make plant and equipment expenditures in increments of $10 million for every incremental $50 million in sales. The $124.4 million estimate suggests a first-year capital expenditure of $10 million. A lot depends on the confidence one has in the STM results.]

6. On a more general level, some students might properly question the wisdom of the $1.99 retail price. This price point clearly moves Cracker Jack to the price premium it previously had over Crunch 'n Munch and most likely exceeds it. Still, the STM pound volume results show higher volumes than what one might expect due to an additional one-ounce per package.

Students hesitant about the $1.99 price option might be asked how this price versus the $1.69 price option affects profitability across advertising/promotion expenditure levels. That is, assuming the pound volume/dollar sales estimates are taken as given, what might a pro forma income statement look like for each option? [Note: For students who do this, they will find that the only combination to show a first-year profit before tax is the $1.99 price, $22 million advertising/promotion expense combination, when cannibalism costs are accounted for.]

7. In a final analysis, the "best" combination seems to be a Cracker Jack marketing plan that merchandises the product in the salty snack aisle featuring a $1.99 retail price for an 8-ounce flex bag supported by a $22 million ($10 million consumer advertising) advertising/promotion budget.

8. However, it is unlikely that a class discussion will result in one marketing plan to relaunch Cracker Jack. What will be necessary is to look at several different first-year marketing-mix combinations and extrapolate each to include a brand extension (snack bar) in

the second year and a line (flavor) extension in the third year with corresponding estimates for incremental dollar sales volume (accounting for cannibalism) and incremental expenditures.

It is important for students to recognize that the more aggressive they are in projecting sales, the higher Cracker Jack's fair market value becomes. Ultimately, whatever marketing plan is proposed must be followed by a 5-year pro forma income statement and cash flow analysis.

E. How much do you think Borden Foods wants for Cracker Jack?

1. The purpose of this question is to serve as a benchmark for Frito-Lay's brand valuation based on its own projections. Case Exhibits 5 and 7, the case text, and the case Appendix provide the basis for responding to this question. The "mechanics" of the financial valuation are generally straightforward.

2. Exhibit 2 in this note shows the most common valuation analysis. This valuation uses the schedule shown in Case Exhibit A-1 from the Appendix, extracts figures from Case Exhibit 5 and 7, assumes a corporate income tax rate of 35.4 percent (Frito-Lay's 1997 tax rate), and applies discount rates from 12 percent to 18 percent (from Case Exhibit A-2) to arrive at a cumulative present value of cash flows. **The residual value is calculated using the income capitalization approach described in the Appendix. This approach assumes that fifth-year after-tax earnings or cash flow ($32.5 million) will be constant in subsequent years.** For example, the present value of the residual using a 15 percent discount rate is:

$$[\$32.5 \text{ million} / .15] \times .497 = \$107.68 \text{ million}$$

3. Some class discussion should be devoted to the (a) assumptions underlying Borden's sales forecast, expenses, and cash flow projection, (b) length of the projection period, (c) residual or terminal value at the end of the projection period, and (d) the appropriate discount rate.

Sales, expense, and cash flow projection assumptions. All of Borden's projections in Case Exhibit 7 are predicated on achieving three objectives. These objectives, stated in the case by Borden, were to (1) revitalize the base business, (b) improve operating efficiencies, and (c) extend the Cracker Jack trademark. These objectives would be realized by (a) expanded distribution within retail snack and food service marketing channels, (b) developing new packaging and flavors, (c) impactful product positioning, (d) enhanced gross margins via sustained price leadership, and (e) additional resources being allotted to

EXHIBIT 2

ILLUSTRATIVE CRACKER JACK BRAND VALUATION: BORDEN FOODS PROJECTION

(All Figures in Millions of Dollars and Rounded)

	1997 (Yr. 1)	1998 (Yr. 2)	1999 (Yr. 3)	2000 (Yr. 4)	2001 (Yr. 5)	Source
Revenues	50.5	78.5	191.4	209.1	258.9	Exhibit 7
Cost of Goods Sold	27.3	37.4	97.5	106.3	127.8	Exhibit 7
Gross Margin	23.2	41.1	93.9	100.8	131.1	Exhibit 7
Operating Expenses	19.9	31.3	61.8	62.8	72.9	Exhibit 7
Earnings Before Interest and Taxes (EBIT)	3.3	9.8	32.1	38.0	58.2	Exhibit 7
Income Tax Provision on EBIT (35.4% of EBIT)	1.2	3.4	11.2	13.3	20.4	(Assumes 35.4% Corporate Tax Rate given Frito-Lay's 35.4% tax rate)
After-tax Earnings Before Interest & Taxes on Interest	2.1	6.4	20.9	24.7	37.8	
Add non-Cash Items, including depreciation expense	1.4	1.9	3.7	4.2	4.7	Exhibit 7
Funds Provided	3.5	8.3	24.6	28.9	42.5	
Subtract:						
Increases to Working Capital	0.7	2.0	8.2	1.2	3.6	Exhibit 5 and 7
Capital Expenditures	0.4	4.0	19.3	4.3	6.4	Exhibit 7
Total Cash Flows Exclusive of Interest (Net of Tax)	2.4	2.3	(2.9)	23.4	32.5	

	1997 (Yr. 1)	1998 (Yr. 2)	1999 (Yr. 3)	2000 (Yr. 4)	2001 (Yr. 5)	Total PV of Cash Flow	+ PV of Residual*	= Fair Market Value
Present Value @ 12%	2.1	1.8	(2.1)	14.9	18.4	35.1	153.6	188.7
Present Value @ 13%	2.1	1.8	(2.0)	14.3	17.6	33.8	135.8	169.6
Present Value @ 14%	2.1	1.8	(2.0)	13.9	16.9	32.7	120.5	153.2
Present Value @ 15%	2.1	1.7	(1.9)	13.4	16.2	31.5	107.7	139.2
Present Value @ 16%	2.1	1.7	(1.9)	12.9	15.5	30.3	96.7	127.0
Present Value @ 17%	2.1	1.7	(1.8)	12.5	14.8	29.3	87.2	116.5
Present Value @ 18%	2.0	1.7	(1.8)	12.1	14.2	28.2	78.9	107.1

*Income Capitalization Method

consumer advertising. In addition, the projections assumed that Cracker Jack would be integrated into a national manufacturing, distribution, and sales infrastructure of a potential acquirer with an existing snack-related business (such as Frito-Lay?). It was also assumed that a Cracker Jack buyer would be willing and able to (a) fund trade promotion and consumer advertising to bolster sales of existing products and extend the product line, and (b) raise prices. Two other stated assumptions were that (a) projected 1998 sales (and presumably beyond 1998) reflected the impact of a fully operational direct-store-delivery (DSD) sales force, and (b) the projections only applied to the domestic (U.S.) opportunity for Cracker Jack. **It is reasonable to conclude that these assumptions and estimates represent a "best case" scenario for Cracker Jack.**

Length of the projection period and residual value. A five-year planning horizon is common for valuations, and probably appropriate for valuing a brand given a brand marketing program. The five-year horizon incorporates the major change in strategy; namely, the switch from a "broker/distributor" sales/delivery system to a DSD system. The effect of this switch is seen in 1999 with a 244 percent jump in sales.

As noted in the case Appendix, the shorter the projection period, the greater the reliance on the residual value when preparing a valuation. The residual value is based on the after-tax earnings or cash flow from the last year of the projection period. Borden shows a sizable cash flow ($32.5 million) in 2001 — the last year of the Cracker Jack projection period — based in part on a 23.8 percent projected sales increase in 2001 (see Case Exhibit 7) for which no rationale is given. The residual value estimate accounts for roughly 72 to 81 percent of the estimated Cracker Jack value shown in Exhibit 2 in this note (using the income capitalization approach). **It is reasonable to conclude that the Cracker Jack cash flow projection in 2001 is probably exaggerated for the purpose of increasing the brand's estimated value.**

Appropriate discount rate. Exhibit 2 in this note estimates the "fair market value" using seven different discount rates, ranging from 12% to 18%. Other things being equal, the fair market value ranges from $188.7 million to $107.1 million. An instructor might ask students: "What discount rate do you think Borden believes is reasonable?" A follow-up question is: "What discount rate might a potential acquirer apply to Cracker Jack?" **It is reasonable to conclude that Borden believes that Cracker Jack will have a lower discount rate than will potential acquirers.** Therefore, other things equal, Borden's valuation may be higher than an acquirer's valuation. The difference is what will determine a buyer's interest and possibly a bid being accepted.

4. Looking at Exhibit 2 in this note, assuming that Frito-Lay agrees with the financial projections, and given that Frito-Lay represents an "average risk," which translates to a 15 percent discount rate per case information, the fair market value for Cracker Jack from Frito-Lay's perspective is $139.2 million.

An instructor might ask: "Do you think Frito-Lay should submit a bid of roughly $139 million for Cracker Jack?" If students say "yes," an instructor may note:

Diane Tousley, the New Ventures Division finance director, says that recent acquisitions in the consumer foods industry indicate that transaction prices represented one to three times net revenues and 10 to 12 times after-tax earnings of the acquired companies. The higher multiples were associated with businesses that had strong brand names or trademarks, established distribution channels and trade relations, and a positive earnings history. Cracker Jack has a negative earnings history. The $139.2 million figure represents a net revenue multiple of almost three (2.88). Does our previous analysis justify this?

If students say "no," ask: "How much do you think Cracker Jack is worth to Frito-Lay?"

F. What is a "fair market value" for Cracker Jack as a Frito-Lay brand?

1. The class discussion logically leads to a Cracker Jack valuation from Frito-Lay's perspective using the relaunch marketing plan addressed earlier as a guide.

2. Students should be given latitude in performing a valuation provided they can constructively argue their point of view and demonstrate logic and thoroughness in their approach. The fair market valuation described in this section parallels the approach taken by Frito-Lay and the dollar value is very close to the actual "number" assigned to Cracker Jack.

3. Exhibit 3 in this note illustrates the Cracker Jack valuation from Frito-Lay's perspective. Exhibit 4 in this note details how each item in the valuation was determined and calculated, including the source(s) used. Undergraduate students often struggle with the valuation, as do some graduate students. The principal problem for students is linking together information in the text and case exhibits. Case Exhibits 5, 7, and 10 are the major sources used and the valuation format is identical to Exhibit A-1: Business Valuation Discounted Cash Flow Illustration in the case Appendix.

Comments and caveats on each item in the valuation follow:

Revenue Projection	Revenue projections begin with a first-year sales projection of $103.7 million and 36.4 million pounds. These figures correspond to a brand-marketing plan from Case Exhibit 10 consisting of an 8-oz. flex bag sold for $1.99 in the salty-snack aisle of grocery stores and supported by a $22 million advertising/promotion budget. Second and third-year sales include a snack bar and flavor extension, respectively. Year 4 and Year five sales stabilize at a 2% - 3% annual growth as described in the case; 3% in Year 4, 2% in Year 5.

EXHIBIT 3

ILLUSTRATIVE CRACKER JACK BRAND VALUATION: FRITO-LAY PERSPECTIVE

(All Figures in Millions of Dollars and Rounded)

	Year 1	Year 2	Year 3	Year 4	Year 5
Revenue	103.7	178.7	192.1	197.9	201.9
Cost of Goods Sold (46% of revenues)	47.7	82.2	88.4	91.0	92.9
Gross Margin	56.0	96.5	103.7	106.9	109.0
Cannibalism Cost (13% of pound Volume x $1.05 per pound)	5.0	8.7	9.3	9.6	9.8
Gross Margin, net of cannibalism	51.0	87.8	94.4	97.3	99.2
Operating Expenses					
Distribution and Sales (15% of revenue)	15.6	26.8	28.8	29.7	30.3
Advertising and Promotion	22.0	32.0	29.5	11.9	12.1
Other (R&D, Gen. Admin.) (5.5% of revenue)	5.7	9.8	10.6	10.9	11.1
Total Operating Expense	43.3	68.6	68.9	52.5	53.5
Earnings Before Interest and Taxes (EBIT)	7.7	19.2	25.5	44.8	45.7
Income Tax (35.4% of EBIT)	2.7	6.8	9.0	15.9	16.2
After-tax Earnings Before Interest and Taxes on Interest	5.0	12.4	16.5	28.9	29.5
Add Non-Cash Items, Including Depreciation Expense	0.0	1.3	1.3	1.3	1.4
Funds Provided	5.0	13.7	17.8	30.2	30.9
Subtract:					
Increases to Working Capital	4.5	5.0	.8	.5	.2
Capital Expenditures	0.0	20.0	0.0	0.0	0.0
Total Cash Flows Exclusive of Interest, Net of Tax	.5	(11.3)	17.0	29.7	30.7
Percent Value @ 15%	.45	(8.54)	11.19	16.99	15.26

	Perpetuity Method (2% Constant Growth)	Income Capitalization Method
Present Value of Projected Cash Flows	$ 35.35	$35.35
Present Value of the Residual Value	$117.37	101.72
Estimated Fair Market Value	$152.72	$137.07

EXHIBIT 4

SOURCES FOR CRACKER JACK VALUATION

Item	Explanation
Revenue	• Assume STM first-year sales of $103.7 million (STM result for 8-oz. flex bag at $1.99 with $2.2 million advertising and promotion from Case Exhibit 10. • Second-year sales ($103.7 million + $75 million) includes snack bar introduction at mid-range between estimated $50-$100 million incremental sales • Third-year sales ($178.7 million x 1.075) includes incremental sales of 7.5% due to flavor of extension which is the mid-range of a 5% to 10% increase • Fourth-year (3% growth), Fifth-year (2% growth) given statement that "sales will stabilize at a rate of two or three percent in the fourth and fifth year."
Cost of Goods Sold	• 46% of revenues. Reflects Frito-Lays belief that "Cracker Jack cost of goods sold could be 10 percent less than Borden management's projection." Case Exhibit 7 indicates that Borden projects cost of goods sold over the 5-year planning horizon to be 50.5%. At 10% less, costs of goods sold are about 46% when rounded up.
Cannibalism Cost	• 13% of Pound volume x $1.05 per pound. The 13% figure is for a $22 million advertising and promotion budget and is interpolated from the cannibalization estimate of 7% (for $15 million advertising and promotion) and 22% (for $32 million advertising and promotion). Estimated pound volume for first-year sales at $22 million with 8-oz. flex bag at $1.99 is 36.4 million pounds (Case Exhibit 10). Therefore, cannibalism cost in Year 1 is 36.4 mm x .13 x $1.05 = $4,968,600, or simply $5.0 million. • The $1.05 figure is the gross profit on Frito-Lay snack chip brands that will be cannibalized referred to in the text and footnote 4. • Pound volume estimates in Years 2-5 were determined from first-year data shown in Case Exhibit 10. For example, projected sales of $103.7 million ÷ 36.4 million pounds = $2.81/pound. Dollar sales revenue in subsequent years ÷ $2.81 = pound volume estimates. A 13% cannibalism rate is assumed over the 5-year planning horizon.
Distribution and Sales	• 15% of Revenue. Reflects Frito-Lay and industry analysts' view that Borden's estimates for sales and distribution expense for a direct-store-delivery (DSD) system are "understated by a factor of one-half, when stated as a percent of net sales." The Distribution Expense plus Variable Expense items, when computed as a percent of sales for 1998-2001 (DSD was not in place in 1997), shown in Case Exhibit 7 average 7.44%. Therefore, the appropriate cost if 14.88%, or 15% when rounded.

Item	Explanation
Advertising and Promotion	• Years 1 through 3 represent "focused brand development efforts supported by promotion and advertising spending... to rebuild and grow the business," according to Lynne Peissig. • Year 1: assumes $22 million advertising and promotion expenditure as described in Case Exhibit 10. • Year 2: assumes $10 million expenditure to support the snack bar extension and continued $22 million in brand-related advertising. • Year 3: assumes $7.5 million expenditure to support the flavor extension and continued $22 million in brand-related advertising. • Years 4 and 5: Sustaining advertising and promotion budget representing 4% to 8% of net sales, say 6%.
Other Costs (R&D, Gen. Adm.)	• 5.5% of revenues. Frito-Lay estimates for these costs range from 4% to 7%; say 5.5% on average.
Income Tax	• 35.4% of Earnings Before Interest and Taxes. Frito-Lay's corporate income tax rate in 1997, given in case.
Capital Expenditure and Depreciation Expense	• A $20 million capital investment is required in Year 2 since a $10 capital investment will be required to manufacture the equivalent of $50 million in sales. Sales of $178.7 million is $78.7 over the $100 million sales capacity of the independent supplier and sales of $192.1 million are projected for Year 3. • The $20 million in capital equipment is depreciated over 15 years – straight-line method as given in the case. Therefore, depreciation expense per year is $1.3 million ($20 million ÷ 15 = $1.33 million.)
Increases to Net Working Capital	• Net working capital represents 6.6% of revenue for Cracker Jack based on Borden's projections (Case Exhibit 7). • Assuming the same relationship applies to Cracker Jack as a Frito-Lay brand, working capital can be calculated as 6.6% x revenue for each year. Net change in working capital is the difference in dollar amounts between years. • Cracker Jack working capital in 1996 was $2.3 million (Case Exhibit 5). Projected Cracker Jack sales in Year 1 are $103.7 million. Therefore, the increase in net working capital for Year 1 is 6.6% x $103.7 million = $4.5 million. For Year 2, the increase in net working capital is 6.6% x $178.7 = $11.8 million minus $6.8 = $5.0 million, and so forth.
Risk-adjusted Discount Rate	• 15%. Frito-Lay considered an investment in Cracker Jack as an "average risk" between 12% and 18%, therefore 15%.

Cost of Goods Sold

Cost of goods sold (46% of sales) reflects Frito-Lay's belief that its cost is 10% less than Borden's projection. Students sometimes struggle to get this number because they overlook Case Exhibit 7.

Cannibalism Cost

The cannibalism rate (13%) is an interpolation. Students often overlook cannibalism as a cost and have difficulty accounting for it. Cannibalism cost is subtracted from gross margin since Cracker Jack is cannibalizing other Frito-Lay snack chips that have a $1.05 gross profit per pound.

Distribution and Sales

Here students should determine what Borden is projecting for Cracker Jack distribution and sales as a percentage of sales (Case Exhibit 7) and double this figure. Some students do not equate Borden's Distribution Expense and Variable Sales with Frito-Lay's DSD, or direct-store-delivery sales force.

Advertising and Promotion

The figures used reflect the first-year advertising and promotion figure ($22 million) given in Case Exhibit 10 and incremental expenditures for the snack bar and the flavor extension in Years 2 and 3. The advertising and promotion expenditure reflects Frito-Lay's "focused brand development efforts supported by promotion and advertising spending... to rebuild and grow the business."

Other Costs (R&D, Gen. Adm.)

These costs are given in the case and range from 4% to 7%.

Income Tax

Frito-Lay's corporate tax rate (35.4%) is given in the case.

Capital Expenditure and Depreciation Expense

These two items go hand-and-hand. An investment of $20 million is necessary in Year 2 at which time a depreciation expense is incurred and carried forward through Year 5, up to 15 years.

Increases to Net Working Capital

Students have difficulty with the determination of net working capital and its change. The major stumbling block is calculating the Year 1 figure.

Risk-adjusted Discount Rate

This figure (15%) is given in the case and represents an "average risk" for Frito-Lay.

4. The calculation of fair market value involves adding the present value of projected cash flows to the present value of the residual (terminal value). Two approaches are commonly employed for valuing the residual and described in the Case Appendix: (a) the

income capitalization method, and (b) the perpetuity method. The results of both approaches are shown in Exhibit 3 in this note.

- **Present value of projected cash flows.** Exhibit 3 shows the total cash flows, exclusive of interest, net of tax for Cracker Jack. Students should immediately see the similarity between the Year 5 cash flow in Exhibit 3 in this note using Frito-Lay's projections and Borden's projections in Exhibit 2 in this note. These cash flows are discounted at 15 percent and yield a present value of projected cash flow of $35.35 million.

- **Valuing the residual: perpetuity method.** The perpetuity method assumes a constant annual growth in after-tax earnings (cash flow) in the future. The assumption used for Cracker Jack assumes a 2 percent annual growth which is consistent with Year 4 and Year 5 projections. The perpetuity method applies the formula, E/k-g, to the Year 5 cash flow, where

    E = after tax earnings (cash flow) in the last year of the projection period ($30.7 million),
    k = the discount rate (15%), and
    g = the growth rate (2%) in perpetuity

    Applying the perpetuity method, the residual value is $236.15 ($30.7 million/[.15-.02]). The present value of this amount is $117.37 million ($117.37 million x .497) using a 15 percent discount rate. By adding the present value of the residual to the present value of projected cash flows, the estimated fair market value for Cracker Jack as a Frito-Lay brand is $152.72 million ($35.35 million + $117.37 million) as shown in Exhibit 3 in this note.

- **Valuing the residual: income capitalization method.** Some students might take issue with employing the perpetuity method to determine the residual value for Frito-Lay when the income capitalization method was used to determine the residual value for Cracker Jack from Borden's perspective (Exhibit 2 in this note). If this happens, the valuation can be easily recast to reflect their views. The residual value for Cracker Jack as a Frito-Lay brand using the income capitalization approach is simply:

    [$30.7 million/.15] x .497 = $101.7 million

    The fair market value for Cracker Jack using the income capitalization approach is therefore:

Present Value of Projected Cash Flows	$ 35.35
+ Present Value of the Residual Value	101.72
Estimated Fair Market Value	$137.07

Students should immediately recognize the similarity between Frito-Lay's valuation of Cracker Jack and Borden's valuation in Exhibit 2 in this note using the income capitalization approach:

Frito-Lay's valuation	=	$137.07
Borden's valuation	=	$139.20
(at a 15% discount rate)		

G. How much should Frito-Lay bid for Cracker Jack?

1. The previous analysis demonstrates the similarity in the fair market value for Cracker Jack from both Frito-Lay's and Borden's perspectives. The difference lies principally in the approach used to determine the residual value. Instructors might devote some class time to discussing this observation.

2. **The fair market value estimation sets the upper limit on how much Frito-Lay should bid for Cracker Jack.** Other estimates are also possible to determine a bid range. The case offers several useful benchmarks.

- **Net Revenue Multiples.** Diane Tousley, the New Venture Division finance director, reports that "...the transaction prices for these types of acquisitions represent one to three times net revenues..." Given Cracker Jack's Net Trade Sales of $48.4 million in 1996 (Case Exhibit 5), prices range from $48.4 million to $145.2 million:

  1 x $48.4 million = $48.4 million
  2 x $48.4 million = $96.8 million
  3 x $48.4 million = $145.2 million

- **Cost of Product Development.** A second estimate arises from the cost to internally develop and commercialize a new consumer food brand. The case refers to "industry sources" that report "...the financial investment to internally develop and launch a new brand (trademark) in a consumer food category was $75 million to $100 million, including the cost of product research and development, test marketing, and national introduction. The time interval from concept development to full-scale commercialization ranged from two to three years. The likelihood of a new product success was roughly one in ten."

3. It is reasonable to conclude that a bid of approximately $100 million is in the ballpark, given that Frito-Lay executives have yet to physically examine Borden's facilities and met with Cracker Jack management. In fact, a non-binding bid of say, $80 to $90 million, should get Frito-Lay in the door to take a look.

H. Epilogue

Lynne Peissig (disguised name) and the Project Bingo team completed its deliberations on the Cracker Jack brand in late July, 1997, and delivered their presentation and recommendation on acquiring Cracker Jack to senior management on August 1. The presentation included (1) an analysis of the Cracker Jack business, (b) its fit with Frito-Lay's new venture and marketing strategy, (3) a preliminary Cracker Jack business/marketing plan, and (4) the financial valuation and bid strategy.

The presentation included a SWOT analysis and identified specific areas where Frito-Lay's strengths would benefit the Cracker Jack brand. The preliminary business/marketing plan focused on (1) revitalizing Cracker Jack's base business, (2) improving manufacturing and sales/delivery efficiencies, and (3) Cracker brand (snack bar) extensions and line (flavor) extensions. The Simulated Test Market results (described in case Exhibit 10) provided the basis for projecting sales and expenses. The proposed advertising and promotion budget for the Year 1 relaunch was $20 million, allocated as follows:

Consumer Advertising	$10
Consumer Promotion	4
Trade Promotion	6
	$20

The preliminary plan placed Cracker Jack in the salty snack aisle in stores by Frito-Lay's store-door-delivery sales force and featured the $1.99 8-ounce Flex Bag. The number of Cracker Jack SKUs was pared to ten from the existing 32 sold by Borden. The plan also proposed that production would be assigned to Frito-Lay's independent supplier, thus avoiding the purchase of Cracker Jack production, box, and bag lines, and equipment.

First-year sales were projected to be $99 million, 90 percent of which was deemed incremental. That is, 10 percent of Cracker Jack sales (pound volume) would come from cannibalizing existing Frito-Lay snack foods. A snack bar brand extension was proposed for Year 2 and a line (flavor) extension was recommended for Year 3. Sales in Years 4 and 5 were projected to increase two to three percent.

Cost projections were identical to those described in the case. Manufacturing cost of goods sold was estimated to be 10 percent less than Borden's projected costs. The direct-store-delivery expense was estimated to be twice the figure projected by Borden. The capital expenditure estimate was $20 million in the second year and depreciation was $1.33 million per year.

Frito-Lay's valuation used the net revenue multiple approach and discounted cash flow analysis with consideration given to the cost and risk of internal development of a new brand. They concluded that the multiple approach yielded a bid range between $85 and $105 million. Their own discounted cash flow analysis indicated an average fair market value of about $138 million for Cracker Jack. The Project Bingo team recommended a non-binding bid range of $75 million to $85 million, with authorization to bid up to $100 million for Cracker Jack. Authorization was given to bid $60 million to $80 million, and the non-binding bid was submitted.

Frito-Lay's bid made the first cut, as did a bid from Nabisco. A third bid was thought to be from General Mills or Procter & Gamble. Frito-Lay believed its initial bid was at the lower end of the bid range. After conducting its due diligence, authorization was sought to bid as much as $100 million. The authorization was given.

The actual transaction price is not publicly available. However, non-Frito-Lay sources close to the situation indicated that the bid price was between $95 million and $100 million. In addition, Frito-Lay included a $5 million incentive for Borden if the company accepted its bid within 24 hours. Borden did and the transaction was consummated.

The transition of Cracker Jack to a Frito-Lay occurred during early 1998. Production was transferred to Frito-Lay's independent supplier and product quality assurance measures were put in place. Sales during the first twelve months of marketing Cracker Jack as a Frito-Lay brand produced sales of about $100 million. The Cracker Jack snack bar was put into test market in mid-1999 and plans for a peanut butter flavor extension were being developed. By early 2000, Cracker Jack was the market share leader in the R-T-E caramel popcorn category.

I. Summary Points

1. Brands represent a source of competitive advantage and future earnings streams provided they are managed properly and nurtured.

2. Brands have a financial value. Brand valuation is growing in importance for a variety of reasons:

- There is a growing interest in brand acquisition as an avenue for corporate sales and profit growth. Buying brands is often cheaper and less risky than creating and building brands.

- There is a growing interest in building "core business" leading to the sales of "orphan products/brands" by companies. Brand sales represent a source of capital to fund other alternatives.

- There is a growing recognition that "brand equity" is as much a financial concept as it is a marketing concept.

3. The financial value of a brand lies in the eyes of the beholder.

4. Careful market and marketing analysis underlies the sale and purchase of brands and often drives the financial analysis. Frito-Lay's assessment of Cracker Jack illustrates the importance of "marketing factors" in valuing a brand.

SWISHER MOWER AND MACHINE COMPANY: EVALUATING A PRIVATE BRAND OPPORTUNITY

Synopsis

In early 1996, Wayne Swisher, President and CEO of Swisher Mower and Machine Company (SMC), received an inquiry from a major national retail merchandise chain (such as JC Penney or Montgomery Ward). The inquiry concerned the chain's private branding proposal for SMC's line of riding lawn mowers. Mr. Swisher must assess whether this opportunity should be pursued by SMC.

Private label riding mower sales presently account for 40 percent of SMC sales. Therefore, the issue in the case is not whether private branding, per se, is an appropriate aspect of SMC product policy. Rather, if the present proposal is accepted, the majority of SMC sales would be private label. Therefore, the strategic issue faced by Max Swisher is whether private branding should be the dominant SMC product policy which it would be if the proposal is accepted.

Specific considerations related to this private branding proposal warrant attention. On the one hand, further private branding provides an opportunity to increase SMC sales volume and utilize excess production capacity. On the other hand, matters related to lost sales for the company's branded riding lawn mower line (Ride King), trade relations with present dealers and incremental costs must be considered. Furthermore, the economics of the private branding proposal must be assessed. The situation gives students an opportunity to construct an income statement, including revenue and costs, associated with the private brand proposal.

Teaching Objectives

This case has three teaching objectives.

1. To give students an opportunity to consider the generic advantages and disadvantages of private branding from a manufacturer's perspective.

2. To assess the merits of private branding as a matter of product policy when private label manufacturing exceeds manufacturer brand production for a small company.

3. To examine the details of a private brand proposal and particularly the profitability of a company's sales to a specific customer - a major national retail merchandise chain.

Teaching Suggestions

This case is particularly suited for that portion of the course when the instructor wishes to introduce students to brand strategy as an element of product policy. The issue posed is commonly faced by small companies, and for that matter, larger companies as well.

The case is suitable for both undergraduate and graduate classes. Specific questions that may be posed to students either prior to or during a class discussion are:

1. How would you characterize the riding lawn mower industry in 1995?

2. How would you characterize Swisher Mower and Machine Company's competitive position in this industry?

3. What are the pros and cons of private branding for a manufacturer in general and specifically for Swisher Mower and Machine Company?

4. What are the likely advantages and disadvantages of the specific private branding proposal made to Swisher Mower and Machine Company apart from the economics of the proposal?

5. What is the economic advantage of the private brand proposal to Swisher Mower and Machine Company?

6. Should Swisher Mower and Machine Company pursue this private branding opportunity? Why or why not?

This case has been taught at two levels of rigor with equal success. The least rigorous approach is to limit attention to the qualitative aspects of the private branding proposal. An instructor might simply describe and present what a financial analysis might look like. This approach is suitable for undergraduate classes. A more rigorous approach would include the financial dimensions and be suitable for graduate students. Instructors wishing to apply this more rigorous approach should be prepared to deal with aspects of cost analysis: relevant costs, opportunity costs, and financing costs.

Areas for Discussion/Analysis

A. How would you characterize the riding lawn mower industry in 1995?

1. The riding lawn mower industry is cyclical and seasonal. At the present time (1995), industry sales are growing reflecting economic conditions in general. Continued growth for 1995 and 1996 is projected. Over one-half of manufacturer shipments of riding lawn mowers occur in the period, January through April.

2. Ten firms comprise the major competitors in this industry. All firms sell their brand of riding lawn mowers (e.g., Toro, Honda, John Deere) and engage in private brand production.

3. Private brands (e.g., Sears Craftsman and J. C. Penney Grass Handler) account for an estimated 65-75 percent of riding lawn mower sales in the United States.

4. The principal distribution of outdoor power equipment (including riding lawn mowers) is through national merchandisers (e.g., Sears, Wal-Mart, Home Depot), lawn/garden stores, discount department stores, hardware stores, and farm equipment/farm supply stores. These retailers accounted for 90 percent of outdoor power equipment sales in 1995 (see case Exhibit 8).

5. Riding lawn mowers range in retail price from $800 to $5000. Although not discussed in the case, it may be assumed that riding lawn mowers are an infrequently purchased piece of home equipment, buyers probably rely upon store/brand name to infer product quality/reliability, store personnel are major sources of product information, and a consumer's decision to buy involves comparison of different types (front engine, mid engine, and rear engine), brands (national vs. private label), and prices.

B. How would you characterize Swisher Mower and Machine Company's competitive position in this industry?

1. SMC is a small player in the riding lawn mower industry with annual sales revenue of almost $4.3 million. Even though unit sales have been largely "flat" since 1989, SMC has remained profitable. Selected financial and operating data based on case Exhibit 6 and reported in the case text are shown in Exhibit 1 in this note. It is noteworthy that SMC is "debt free."

2. SMC has carved out a niche in the riding lawn mower industry due to (a) a unique and reliable product - zero turning radius, mid-engine placement vs. rear engine riding mower and (b) established distribution with farm supply, lawn and garden, home center and hardware stores, mostly outside (75% of sales) major metropolitan areas. Exhibit 2 in this note shows SMC's marketing channels and illustrate the strategy of dual distribution used by the company.

3. A major issue, however, is the sustainability of SMC's competitive niche as a small branded riding lawn mower producer given that:

   a. private label riding mowers are capturing a growing percentage of industry unit sales (currently 65-75% of industry sales);

   b. other costs of doing business are high, e.g., financing costs for inventories; and

EXHIBIT 1

SELECTED FINANCIAL AND OPERATING DATA FOR SMC

Profitability Data

Gross Profit Margin	Gross Profit/Sales	16.4%
Return on Sales	Net Income/Sales	10.0%
Return on Total Assets	Net Income/Total Assets	36.3%
Return on Owner's Equity	Net Income/Owner's Equity	44.2%

Operating Data

Asset Turnover	Sales/Total Assets	3.6x
Inventory Turnover	Cost of Goods Sold/Average Inventory	5.8x*
Accounts Receivable Turnover	Sales/Average Accounts Receivable	8.1x*
Working Capital	Current Assets - Current Liabilities	$920,200

*Turnover figures given in the text.

EXHIBIT 2

SMC MARKETING CHANNELS

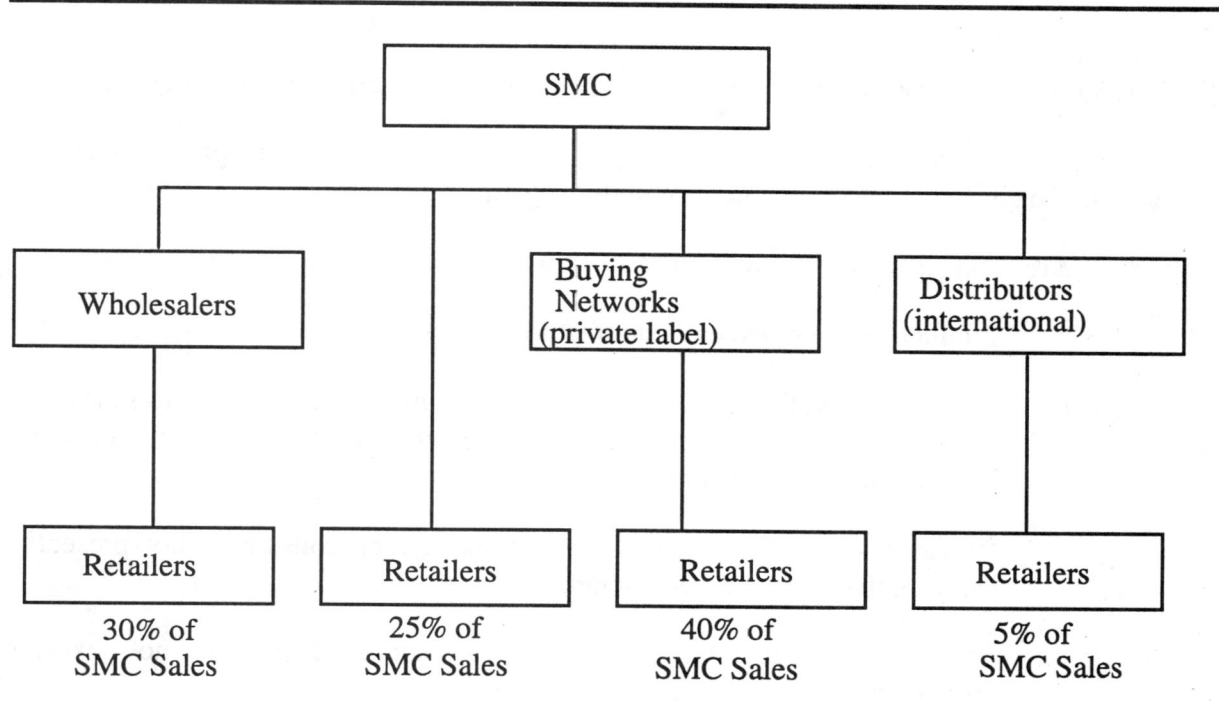

Principal Retailers: Farm supply stores, lawn and garden stores, home centers and hardware stores.

c. SMC is fundamentally a single product company (riding mowers) whereas most other competitors are multi-product/multi-business firms. The significance of being essentially a one-product company is illustrated in Exhibit 3 in this note. Riding mowers and replacement parts account for 83.6 percent of SMC sales and 86.8 percent of SMC gross profit.

C. What are the pros and cons of private branding for a manufacturer in general?

1. Students should be asked to first articulate the pros and cons of private branding in general. Chapter 5 offers some guidance in this regard.

2. **Advantages of private branding in general:**

   a. Productive use of excess manufacturing capacity.

   b. Minimal marketing expenses (e.g., advertising, promotion, selling) incurred by the manufacturer since these expenses are incurred by the intermediary (e.g., retailer or wholesaler).

   c. Provides access to distribution channels and/or consumers not presently carrying the manufacturer's brand.

   d. Enhanced profitability, assuming incremental costs do not exceed incremental revenues from private branding.

   e. Increased overall sales if the private brand does not cannibalize or replace the manufacturer's own brand.

3. **Disadvantages of private branding in general:**

   a. Gross profit margins on private brands are often lower than gross profit margins on a manufacturer's brand because of the lower price at which these brands are sold to intermediaries.

   b. A private brand manufacturer runs the risk of becoming "captive" to an intermediary **if** the sales of private brands become too large.

   c. An opportunity for a loss in "customer franchise" arises if a private brand manufacturer merely becomes one of several suppliers to an intermediary which buys only on specification.

   d. Private branding by a manufacturer may bring a loss of "market strength" and bargaining power with an intermediary **if** private brand sales become excessively large and alternative suppliers are available to the intermediary.

EXHIBIT 3

SMC PRODUCT LINE SALES AND GROSS PROFIT MARGIN

SMC Products	% of SMC Sales Revenue	% of SMC Gross Margin
Riding Mowers	63.6%	57.8%
Replacement Parts	20.0	29.0
Trailmower (T-44)	8.2	13.2
Push Mower	8.2	-0-
	100.0%	100.0%

4. If time permits, students might also discuss private branding from the perspective of a retailer or wholesaler.

D. What are the likely advantages and disadvantages of the specific private branding proposal made to Swisher Mower and Machine Company apart from the economics of the proposal?

1. Once students have addressed private branding in general, they should be asked to consider the merits of the specific proposal made to SMC by first describing the terms of the proposal. Exhibit 4 in this note shows specific terms of the proposal based on information given in the case. (Note: The terms of the contract are "typical" in the outdoor power equipment industry should students ask.)

2. **Advantages of the proposal to SMC:**

    a. The opportunity to almost triple SMC riding mower unit volume from 4,200 units annually to 12,400 units since the annual order could be 8,200 units.

    b. Ability to operate at full capacity; indeed another work shift required.

    c. Further access to metropolitan (urban) markets without incurring marketing costs, e.g., advertising and promotion. (Note: Only 25% of SMC sales are in metropolitan areas.)

    d. Access to a national retail merchandise chain since SMC does not presently sell through this channel.

    e. Duration of the contract (2-years with subsequent negotiation) allows for a trial period for both parties.

    f. Opportunity to increase complementary sales of the Trailmower and increased derived demand for replacement parts.

3. **Disadvantages of the proposal to SMC:**

    a. SMC could become a "captive supplier" to the national retail merchandise chain since almost two-thirds of riding mower unit volume (8200/12,400) would be sold to this single customer. As a captive supplier to a much larger customer, SMC's negotiation position on price and other terms might be eroded.

    b. A tripling of volume increases SMC's product liability exposure.

    c. Possible loss of some dealers in metropolitan areas and cannibalization of SMC riding mower sales (Wayne Swisher estimates that this figure will be small - 300 units per year).

EXHIBIT 4

TERMS OF THE PRIVATE BRAND PROPOSAL MADE TO SWISHER MOWER AND MACHINE COMPANY

1.	CONTRACT SIZE & DURATION	Initial order of 700 riding lawn mowers. Annual order of 8,200 riding lawn mowers. Two-year contract with extension on a year-to-year basis. Either party may terminate contract with a six month notice.
2.	PRICING	5% lower than SMC's list price for its standard model. Price negotiated again at end of two-year contract; annually thereafter.
3.	TITLE TRANSFER & PAYMENT	SMC to ship units to the chain's regional warehouses. Title transfer to occur when units shipped to chain's stores, after which payment made in 45 days. If units held in warehouses for two months, title would transfer and payment made 45 days after title transfer.
4.	PRODUCT MODIFICATIONS	Modified seat, a particular color and type of paint.
5.	REPLACEMENT PARTS	Parts purchased at present prices.
6.	WARRANTY	Standard SMC warranty (one-year). SMC to pay chain $22.00/hr. for labor on warranty work.
7.	MARKETING PRACTICES	No selling to chain desired. SMC prohibited from mentioning private label relationship in its advertising or promotion.
8.	PRODUCT LIABILITY	SMC would assume personal injury liability if injury caused in the use and maintenance of mowers.

d. Slight reduction in riding lawn mower gross profit on this contract since riding mowers will be sold at a price 5 percent less than the standard model.

e. Increased inventory requirements. The case notes that SMC will carry higher average inventory directly related to this proposal.

f. Some incremental costs will be incurred:

- Overtime to produce additional unit volume
- Some one-time expenses related to contract terms - $10,000 to $12,000
- Additional overhead costs, direct materials costs, and other production costs.

E. **What is the economic advantage of the private brand proposal to Swisher Mower and Machine Company?**

1. The economics of the private brand proposal involve an analysis of incremental revenues and costs. In this instance, **relevant** costs include:

   a. Incremental manufacturing costs arising from the special order

   b. Incremental asset costs, specifically inventory and accounts receivable carrying costs

   c. Gross margin lost due lost sales of present riding mowers

   d. One-time set-up costs associated with the proposal.

2. The case describes how the proposal will affect SMC costs in the section titled, "Evaluating the Proposal." Exhibit 5 in this note details relevant revenue and cost estimates useful in assessing the merits of the private brand proposal. It is important that instructors familiarize themselves with Exhibit 5 since the estimates contain calculations based on certain assumptions. Note particularly the discussion related to financing costs.

3. Exhibit 6 in this note provides an illustration of what a **pro forma income statement** might look like given the information given in Exhibit 5 in this note. Important elements of this statement are highlighted below:

   a. **Revenues** are based on unit sales of 8,200 at a selling price 5 percent below SMC's standard riding mower price.

   b. **Cost of Goods Sold** includes the current cost of goods sold ($553.00) plus the incremental costs identified by Wayne Swisher expressed as a percent of the standard price of $650 per unit.

EXHIBIT 5

REVENUE AND COST ESTIMATES RELATED TO THE PRIVATE BRAND

Proposal Price:	$617.50/Unit	(5% less than $650 price on SMC's standard model)
Current Cost of Goods Sold:	$553.00/Unit	(Currently $100 for labor and $453 for parts. Note that no direct overhead is included in this figure).
Incremental Costs		
Direct Materials:	$6.50/Unit	(Estimated at 1% of current price of $650)
Overhead Costs:	$6.50/Unit	(Estimated at 1% of current price of $650)
Other Incremental Costs:	$9.75/Unit	(Includes additional inventory insurance, pilferage and breakage, wear and maintenance on machines, and county property tax based on inventory. 1.5% of current price of $650)
Direct Labor:	$7.61/Unit	(Overtime will be paid on volume exceeding 10,000 units. Overtime is computed at 4% of the current price of $650, or $26.00 for each of 2,400 units produced. Total overtime cost is therefore, $26 x 2,400 = $62,400. $62,400 ÷ 8,200 = $7.61 which is the average incremental direct labor charge for the contract at 8,200 units)
Added Asset Carrying Costs		
Accounts Receivable:	$59,386.73	(Payment schedule indicates that chain will pay in 45 days, the sales price is $617.50, and the carrying cost is 9.5%. The 45 day payment is identical to that currently experienced by SMC since accounts receivable turnover is 8.1 times [365 days ÷ 8.1 = 45 days]. Therefore, the carrying cost is [8,200 units x $617.50 ÷ 8.1] x .095 = $59,386.73.)
Inventory:	$116,380.32	(The case states that the "incremental average inventory carried with this proposal would be 2,100 units." The estimated unit cost of goods sold with incremental costs is $583.36 and the carrying cost is 9.5%. Therefore, the carrying cost is 2,100 units x $583.36 x .095 = $116,380.32.)
One-Time Costs:	$10,000 - $12,000	(Rearrangement of production facilities, arranging material sources, etc.)

c. **Lost Gross Profit** reflects the expected loss of 200 Ride King unit sales times the gross profit on the standard model ($650.00 - $553.00 = $97.00).

d. **Incremental Asset Carrying Costs** reflect the carrying costs caused by larger accounts receivables and inventories related to the order, their expected turnover, and short-term financing cost of 9.5 percent.

4. Exhibit 6 in this note shows that the private brand proposal produces incremental revenues of $5,063,500, incremental costs of $4,783,552, and a net incremental profit of $63,080.95. In short, the economic advantage of the private brand proposal to SMC is promising.

5. This analysis does not include the need for possible insurance coverage to handle product liability resulting from personal injury using or maintaining the riding mower. Nor does this analysis include incremental revenue/profit from replacement parts (which will be negligible in the short-run) and incremental revenue/profit from selling the T-44 Trailmower. Furthermore, this analysis does not consider the potential increase in inventory and accounts receivable carrying costs if the 45-day payment period is stretched out. This latter factor alone could make the proposal a losing proposition.

F. **Should Swisher Mower and Machine Company pursue this private branding opportunity? Why or why not?**

1. A qualitative and financial analysis of the opportunity suggests that the private branding proposal warrants a close look. Depending on how the merits of further private branding by SMC are assessed and the pros and cons of the proposal are weighted, SMC might consider accepting the proposal.

2. On the other hand, the estimated annual incremental profit of $63,080.95 represents a return on sales of 1.25 percent. This return is far less than the 10 percent return on sales that SMC is currently achieving on its "branded" business and other "private brand" business. When the SMC branded and new private brand businesses are consolidated, and assuming SMC achieves sales and profit levels in 1990 as it did in 1989 (case Exhibit 6), SMC will

- More than double its sales: $4,292,000 to $9,355,500, but only

- Increase its net income by 14.7%: $430,200 to $493,280.95.

Furthermore, the company's return on sales will decrease dramatically.

EXHIBIT 6

ILLUSTRATIVE ECONOMICS OF THE PRIVATE BRAND PROPOSAL

(at 8,200 Unit Volume)

Revenue ($617.50 x 8,200 units)		$5,063,500.00
Cost of Goods Sold		
Current CGS		
($553.00 x 8,200)	$4,534,600.00	
Incremental:		
Direct Materials		
($6.50 x 8,200)	53,300.00	
Direct Labor		
($7.61 x 8,200)	62,402.00	
Overhead ($6.50 x 8,200)	53,300.00	
Other ($9.75 x 8,200)	<u>79,950.00</u>	<u>4,783,552.00</u>
Gross Profit/Margin		$ 279,948.00
Lost Gross Profit ($97.00 x 300)		29,100.00
Incremental Asset Carrying Costs		
Accounts Receivable	$ 59,386.73	
([8,200 x $617.50 / 8.1] x .095)		
Inventory	<u>116,380.32</u>	175,767.05
(2,100 x $583.36 x .095)		
One-time Added Costs ($10,000-$12,000)		<u>12,000.00</u>
Incremental Profit of Private Brand Proposal		<u>$ 63,080.95</u>

G. Epilogue

The private brand proposal was seriously considered by Wayne Swisher. However, Swisher decided not to accept the proposal. His reasoning was based on the concern about being a captive supplier to a large national mass merchandiser, the belief that SMC's dealers might be harmed, the view that other private brand arrangements might be put in jeopardy, and the financial reward was not that great. Furthermore, he was confident that the new "Trim-Max" trimmer, mower, edger unit would be a winner.

Swisher proved to be correct in his assessment of "Trim-Max." The product was an immediate success, both in terms of sales and profitability. By fiscal year end 1999, "Trim-Max" had replaced Ride King as the principal product sold by SMC. In early 2000, Swisher was again approached by a large mass merchandise chain, this time to private label "Trim-Max." He declined the proposal.

H. Summary Points

1. Branding is an important element of a firm's product strategy. Firms often employ a "mixed branding strategy" which includes both manufacturer brands and private (store) brands.

2. There are numerous advantages to private branding:

   - Productive use of excess manufacturing capacity

   - Minimal marketing investment (advertising, promotion, selling)

   - Access to marketing channels and different consumer segments

   - Increased sales revenue providing private brands do not cannibalize the manufacturer brand and increased profitability providing incremental sales revenue exceeds incremental costs.

3. However, there are also possible disadvantages related to private branding:

   - Usually lower unit gross profit margins

   - The potential for becoming a "captive supplier" to a large intermediary if private brand volume accounts for a sizable percentage of volume.

   - Little or no opportunity to build a customer franchise

4. Assessment of a private brand proposal requires an integrative analysis involving manufacturing capability, marketing implications and financial outcomes. Overlooking any one of these factors will result in an incomplete assessment of the merits of private branding.

THROCKMORTEN FURNITURE, INC. (A)

Synopsis

The apparent issue raised in this case is whether Throckmorten Furniture should accept the tentative proposal to increase consumer advertising of its product line in 2000. Acceptance of the proposal would increase the firm's promotion-to-sales ratio which is contrary to company policy. Alternatively, the firm can reduce funds allocated to other types of promotion and remain within the 5 percent promotion-to-sales ratio. An important point here is defining the company's communication objective(s) and the merits of alternative budgeting approaches.

A more subtle issue is the role of different kinds of promotion in stimulating demand at the retail and consumer level. The importance of "push" versus "pull" promotional strategies is important in this context. Furthermore, an opportunity exists for the student to view promotion as "integrated marketing communications" at different stages of the furniture shopping process and recognize the importance of personal selling, trade promotion, and advertising at each stage. Considerable data on buyer behavior is reproduced from *The Better Homes and Gardens Consumer Panel* to assist, and possibly overwhelm, the student.

Teaching Objectives

This case has three multi-faceted teaching objectives.

1. **Analysis of Furniture Industry and Furniture Buying Behavior.** What is the competitive environment in the industry? What does the number of firms in the industry indicate? What is Throckmorten's position in the industry?

What attributes do consumers look for in furniture? How do consumers shop for furniture and how do they utilize information about furniture? How would one classify furniture -- convenience, shopping, specialty good?

2. **Importance of Communication Program Objective Setting.** Does Throckmorten Furniture have a communication objective? What should it be? How will communication objectives assist in prioritizing promotion tools and budget setting?

3. **Evaluation of the Total and Individual Components of Throckmorten's Communication Budget.** In light of teaching objectives 1 and 2, which components are most important? Least important? Is the 5 percent promotion-to-sales policy appropriate?

Teaching Suggestions

This case is best suited for discussion early in that portion of the course focusing on integrated marketing communications strategy and management. When taught with the Throckmorten Furniture (B) case, students are exposed to a relatively thorough examination of advertising, trade promotion, and sales management issues. Accordingly, use of both cases is suggested.

Previous experience teaching this case suggests that students have a tendency to focus on recommendations for Throckmorten. When (if) this occurs instructors should ask students what they consider to be the purpose of advertising, promotion, and sales in this industry in general and for Throckmorten in particular. This question should communicate the need to focus on the industry setting, furniture buying behavior, and Throckmorten's communication objectives. In this regard, instructors should push students to examine and interpret the *Better Homes and Gardens Consumer Panel* data shown in the Appendix to the case.

Specific questions that might be posed to students prior to or during a class discussion are:

1. How would you characterize the household wood furniture industry and Throckmorten's relative position in this industry?

2. How do consumers buy furniture?

3. What is the purpose and role of advertising, promotion, and personal selling in the household furniture industry?

4. What should be the objective(s) for Throckmorten's communication program in 2000?

5. How might objectives be translated into an overall budget and spending for specific elements of Throckmorten's communication's program?

Areas for Discussion/Analysis

A. How would you characterize the household wood furniture industry and Throckmorten's relative position in this industry?

1. Household wood furniture sales accounted for 48 percent of total household furniture in 1999, or $11.8 billion. Wood furniture sales rose only 2.1 percent in 1999, but are expected to rise 4.2 percent in 2000 according to the American Furniture Manufacturer Association.

2. Industry sales are cyclical and affected by the incidence of new housing starts, consumer confidence, and disposable personal income. About 1 percent of household disposable income is spent for furniture. Since 1990, the Home Furnishings Council has conducted an advertising campaign to stimulate **primary demand** for home furnishings in general.

3. Even though there are 1000 furniture manufacturers, the household furniture industry is highly concentrated. The top 3 manufacturers account for 20 percent of industry sales; the top 25 manufacturers capture 52 percent of total industry sales. Imports are not a factor in the industry.

4. Over 100,000 specialty furniture and home furnishings stores, department stores, mass-merchandisers and Internet companies, sell furniture in the U.S. Independently-owned furniture stores are declining while furniture store chains are growing. The "Gallery" concept is popular whereby a space or entire store is dedicated to one furniture manufacturer.

The 25 largest furniture retailers capture 27 percent of total furniture retail sales. Heilig-Meyers is the largest furniture store retailer and accounts for 5 percent of total retail sales.

The buying and selling of furniture to retail outlets centers around manufacturers' expositions called "marts." A majority of manufacturer sales are made at these marts; however, retailers will buy throughout the year from manufacturer's salespeople and representatives.

5. Throckmorten is a small player in the household wood furniture industry. With net sales of $75 million in 1999, its estimated market share is .6 percent ($75 million/$11.8 billion).

6. Throckmorten specializes in medium-to-high-priced wood bedroom, living room, and dining room furniture (It **does not** sell upholstered furniture such as sofas and chairs). The company sells its furniture through 1,000 "high-quality" department stores and independent furniture stores suggesting a **selective distribution channel** strategy. As a matter of policy, Throckmorten does not sell to furniture chain stores and discount stores. Nevertheless, all Throckmorten retailers **do not** carry the company's full line.

7. Throckmorten is unique among furniture manufacturers because the company employs its own 10-person sales force. Typically, manufacturers use sales agents or manufacturer's representatives.

B. How do consumers buy furniture?

1. The purpose of this question is to get students to consider the (a) attributes examined in (wood) furniture (b) the buying process itself, and (c) the role and source of information about furniture. Students will find the *Better Homes and Gardens Consumer Panel* data useful in this regard.

2. **Attributes sought.** It would seem that the brand of furniture is of little importance in furniture selection. What is? The instructor should have students develop a ranking as follows:

Furniture Attribute List	Rank	Possible Ranking
Styling/Design		1
Brand Name/Image		5
Price		4
Construction/Quality Workmanship		2
Store Quality/Image*		3

*Store quality or image may have to be prompted from students. *BH&G* data indicate that respondents typically gave low importance ratings to "store reputation." However, several pieces of case data suggest that store quality and buyer confidence in the store and retail salespeople do impact the decision:

- 63% of subscribers say they need decorating advice "putting is all together."

- 60% of subscribers used furniture specialty and gallery stores.

- 56% of subscribers say that store displays were "most important" or "second most important" as influences on their choice of furnishings.

- 85% of subscribers say that "a highly dependable store" is very important" in store choice.

In addition, if students still have problems with the store quality/image attribute, the instructor might ask the question: "What do friends ask the recent furniture buyer?" The typical response is "Where did you buy the furniture?"

3. **Furniture Buying Behavior and Information Acquisition**

   a. **Furniture Buying is a Joint Decision.** The wife probably emphasizes aesthetics (Style, Color, Workmanship); the husband emphasizes economics (Price).

   b. **Furniture Buying is a Difficult Decision.** Furniture is a major purchase (particularly for Throckmorten -- high quality, middle to higher price), wide variety, compatibility with existing home furnishings, etc. A great deal of perceived financial and social risk exists. Note the quote from Standard & Poor's Industry Surveys in this case which focuses on purchase difficulty.

   c. **Consumers Have Little Real Knowledge of Product Quality.** Indeed, 84% of *BH&G* subscribers feel, "the higher the price, the higher the quality." It would seem that price and retail salespeople define quality construction, workmanship, etc.

d. It is important that students develop some type of model of buying behavior and information acquisition. This model will highlight, in particular, how various components of the promotion program come into play and the importance of each. Due to the importance of making a right purchase decision and little knowledge of furniture generally, it would be expected that a high involvement, extended purchase/shopping behavior will occur -- this implies **furniture is a shopping good**. The wife will probably initiate the product/information search with the husband acting in the later stages of product selection. A possible model of this phenomenon is described in Exhibit 1 in this note with various types of information shown.

D. What is the purpose and role of advertising, promotion, and personal selling in the household furniture industry?

This analysis should indicate to students that each component serves a distinct purpose:

1. **Consumer Advertising**: informs consumers of new styles, room arrangements, emphasizes "quality," develops some "share-of-mind," etc. It will assist in generating **selective (brand) demand**. Note that The Home Furnishings Council's advertising campaign is designed to stimulate **primary (product class) demand**.

2. **Company Salesperson**: trains retail salespeople, makes them knowledgeable of Throckmorten, develops rapport, emphasizes quality differences (workmanship), keeps retail salespeople thinking of Throckmorten, builds enthusiasm of retail salespeople, sells product, etc.

3. **Trade Advertising**: point-of-purchase displays to direct consumers' attention, ease salesmen's selling responsibility, "reminder" or take-along "brochure" to inhibit consumer forgetting -- useful in husband/wife deliberation, alternative evaluation. Note the reference made to **Living with Drexel Heritage** in the case which authorized Drexel retailers give to consumers.

4. **Cooperative Advertising**: directs consumers to those stores carrying furniture style, establish store image --imputed brand image. That is, high quality store; therefore, high quality furniture merchandise.

EXHIBIT 1

A MODEL OF FURNITURE BUYING BEHAVIOR

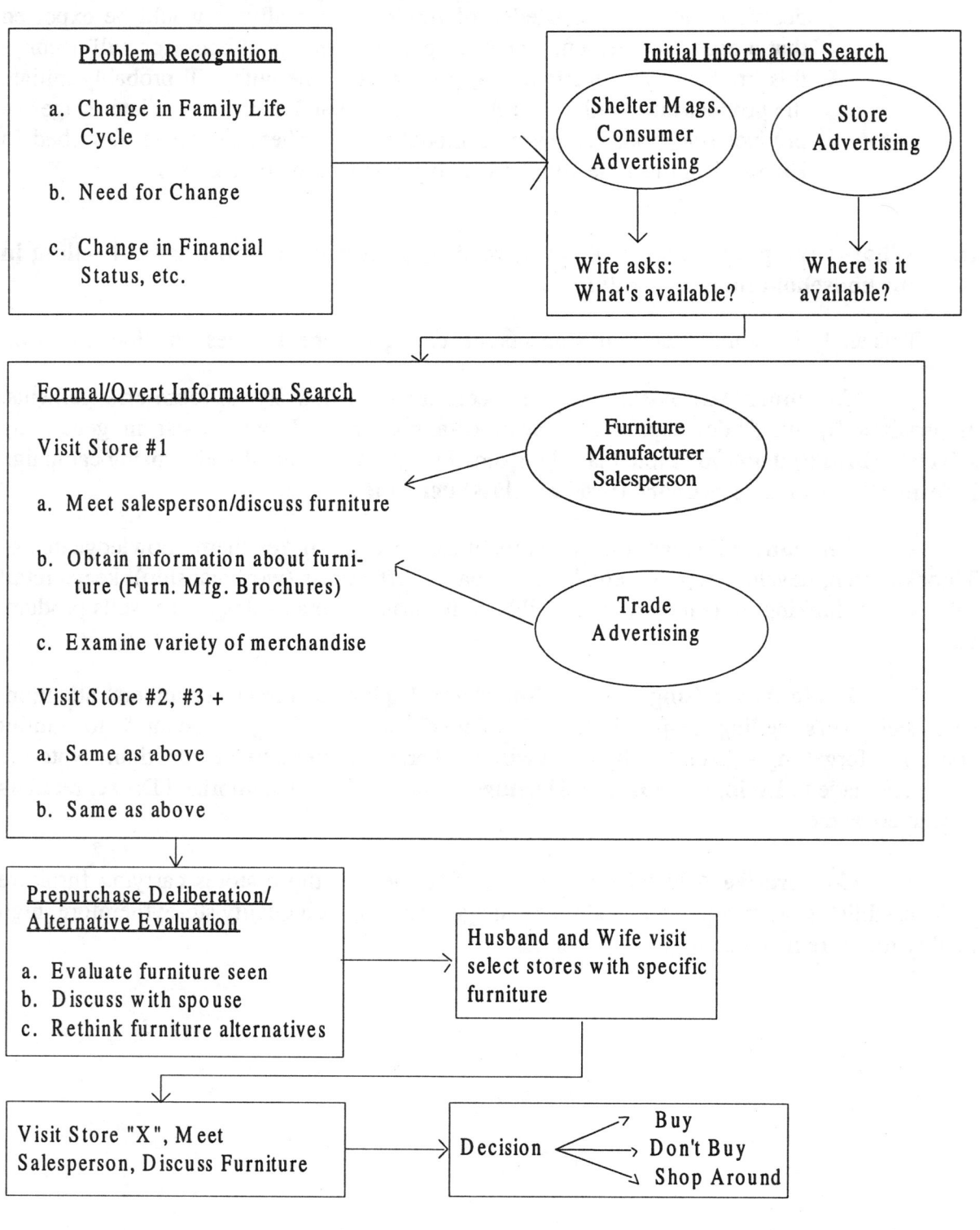

E. **What should be the objective(s) for Throckmorten's communication program in 2000?**

1. Students should be asked to state the objectives for Throckmorten's communication program. By doing so, they come to appreciate the **objective-task** approach to promotion planning and budgeting which is described to in Chapter 6.

2. At least four communication objectives are possible:

   a. **Maintain retail support**

   b. **Improve company brand image and brand awareness**

   c. **Penetrate existing outlets with Throckmorten's full line**

   d. **Reach consumer at critical points in furniture buying process**

3. A priority ranking (a hierarchy) of objectives would probably place "c" first, "a" second, "d" third and "b" fourth. Penetration is considered most important since Throckmorten's retailers do not carry its full line. It is difficult to make a sale when the product is not available. Brand image/awareness is cited last since they are not considered that important; rather store image/awareness is crucial.

4. The need to get Throckmorten's full line (and new styles) of furniture displayed by its retailers and the need to maintain retailer support suggests that these elements of the communication process should be emphasized. They are personal selling, trade advertising, and cooperative advertising. Consumer advertising is not critical given the challenges facing Throckmorten. In other words, a **push strategy** is more defensible than a **pull strategy** with an emphasis on consumer advertising.

5. What about the 5% policy? This policy called the **percent of sales** promotion budgeting procedure has no rationale other than it is easy to apply. Moreover, the reasoning is backward: Sales $\rightarrow$ Advertising/Promotion rather than Advertising/Promotion $\rightarrow$ Sales. In this particular case, the 5% policy acts as a constraint.

F. **How might objectives be translated into an overall budget and spending for specific elements of Throckmorten's communications program?**

1. Several issues deserve consideration. These include, of course, communication objectives, and the various spending proposals voiced by the company's advertising agency and Throckmorten's Vice President of Sales.

2. As pointed out by John Bott, Throckmorten's Vice President of Sales, a projected 4.2 percent increase in sales assuming a 5 percent percent-of-sales promotional budget

allocation, translates into an overall promotion budget of $3,907,500 million [1.042 x $75 million (1999 sales) = $78,150,000 x .05 = $3,907,500].

3. Bott's argument for an additional sales person at $70,000 per year given the addition of 50 new retail accounts and added sales management overhead costs ($50,000) has merit. The objectives of getting the full line into stores and maintaining retailer support favor his proposal.

4. The advertising agency's argument that since the National Home Furnishings Foundation recommends that furniture manufacturers spend 1-percent of sales exclusively on consumer advertising does have some merit (Furniture manufacturers spend 3.5% of sales for advertising of all types – consumer, trade, coop). This view emanates from a **competitive parity** approach to budgeting.

5. Cooperative advertising and trade advertising will likely need to increase given new retail outlets and new styles of living and dining room furniture being added in 2000.

G. Epilogue

Mr. Bates of Throckmorten Furniture (disguised name) decided that the sales effort, trade advertising, and cooperative advertising was in most need of attention. The final budget allocated was $3.9 million as follows:

Sales Expense and Administration	$1,115,500	28.6%
Cooperative Advertising	1,750,000	44.9
Trade Advertising	508,000	13.0
Consumer Advertising	526,500	13.5
	$3,900,000	100.0%

Mr. Bott added another sales representative. The bulk of the trade advertising and consumer advertising was devoted to the new styles of living room and dining room furniture. Consumer advertising actually decreased from the prior year's spending ($562,500 in 1999), and represented .6 percent of budgeted 2000 sales.

Mr. Bates continued to use the percent-of-sales method for budgeting purposes. Indeed, the overall budget was about 5 percent of projected 2000 sales. Budgeted expenditures for consumer, trade, and cooperative was slightly over the industry average of 3.5 percent of sales. Some instructors might wish to comment on this fact in light of Throckmorten's introduction of several new lines.

H. Summary Points

1. Understanding consumer information needs as they move through the buying process is critical because the impact and importance of different elements of the promotion mix will differ at each stage of the process.

2. Each element of the promotion mix has an important role in the communication process:

- **Consumer Advertising**: "Emphasizes Quality"... "Informs consumers of new styles"... "Increases share-of-mind."

- **Personal Selling**: "Train retail salespeople"... "Builds enthusiasm for the line"..."Emphasizes quality differences (workmanship)"

- **Trade Advertising**: "P-O-P materials and brochures ease the selling task at the retail level"

- **Cooperative Advertising**: "Directs consumers to stores"..."Establishes store image-brand image link"

3. The Percent-of-Sales budgeting method, which is administratively simple to apply, is based on the rationale that projected sales determine promotional dollars to be spent when, in fact, promotional dollars → sales. In this instance, the Percent-of-Sales method might not be appropriate this year given that new styles are being introduced.

4. The Objective-Task Method is the most effective means for aligning objectives with effort and allocating scarce promotional funds. Some objectives in this case might be:

- Maintain/Improve Retailer Support

- Penetrate Existing Stores with Throckmorten's Full Line

- Improve Brand Image, Brand Awareness

- Reach Buyers at Critical Stages in the Furniture Buying Process

5. Finally, this case raises the issue of a push vs. a pull communication strategy. Given the firm's situation, a heavier push strategy is called for with an emphasis on building the store network, educating retail sales people, gaining space for the company's full line, and so forth.

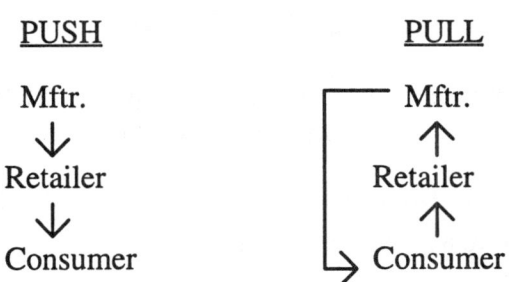

THROCKMORTEN FURNITURE, INC. (B)

Synopsis

The April, 2000 merger between Throckmorten Furniture, Inc. and Lea-Meadows, Inc. has prompted a question of how to sell the Lea-Meadows product line. Throckmorten has used its own sales force to represent its line of wood furniture for bedrooms and living and dining rooms. However, Lea-Meadows has relied upon sales agents to represent its line of upholstery furniture for living and family rooms. The question facing Throckmorten is whether to "give the upholstery line of chairs and sofas to its sales force or continue to use sales agents."

Several issues are raised by this question: What is the role of personal selling and who owns the customer franchise? If the line is taken on, what will be the impact on selling Throckmorten's line? How many, if any, new sales reps will be needed? A formula for computing the number of salespeople needed is described in Chapter 6. Other issues relate to Throckmorten's apparent desire to increase call frequency and the impact on call time, its past policy of using its own sales force, and the difference in gross margins between Throckmorten and Lea-Meadows furniture.

A behavioral aspect of sales management is also raised for consideration. A decision to drop sales agents would mean that the position held by Martin Moorman, the national sales manager of Lea-Meadows, Inc., would be eliminated. Moorman, who was 55 years old and had worked by Lea-Meadows for 25 years, was a family friend of Throckmorten's President and godfather to his youngest child. It is always interesting to observe how students incorporate this consideration into their analysis of the case.

Teaching Objectives

Class discussion should bring out the following points:

1. Understanding the role and importance of personal selling in developing sustained and profitable trade relations for high-ticket consumer durables.

2. The advantages and disadvantages of a company sales force and independent sales agents including the economic aspects of such decisions.

3. Determining the impact on call time, call frequency, and sales force size if the Lea-Meadows line is represented by Throckmorten's sales force.

Teaching Suggestions

This case is best suited for the portion of the course that emphasizes personal selling and sales management. The case can be taught without having discussed the Throckmorten (A) case. However, some instructors might assign the (A) case as background reading.

If the (A) case is used, students should have a basic understanding of the home furnishings industry and it is best to move directly to the decision at hand. However, if only the (B) case is taught, then the instructor might spend some discussion time (say 10 minutes) on examining the relative position of Throckmorten and Lea-Meadows and the importance of the "push" promotional strategy in the home furnishings industry. Best results with this case are achieved when the instructor encourages students to conduct a sensitivity analysis by manipulating call time and call frequency, sales force size, and sales costs. A useful means of stimulating discussion is to ask students to vote for or against giving the line to Throckmorten's sales force. Pros and cons of each side can then be developed by those students with opposing viewpoints.

Specific questions that might be posed to student either before or during the in-class case analysis are:

1. What is the role of personal selling in developing sustained and profitable trade relations?

2. What are the pros and cons of giving the Lea-Meadows line to the Throckmorten sales force?

3. What will be the impact on the sales effort if the Lea-Meadows line is given to the Throckmorten sales force with no increase in sales force size?

4. What are the costs and benefits of adding additional sales reps versus using sales agents?

5. Under what conditions, if any, should Throckmorten give the upholstery line to its sales force?

Areas for Discussion/Analysis

A. What is the Role of Personal Selling in Developing Sustained and Profitable Trade Relations?

1. A major question here is: Who "owns" the customer franchise? Is it the sales rep/agent or the company? The case makes frequent reference to the personal relationships between sales rep/agents and store buyers/sales people. It may be that a company owns the

franchise with its own sales force; however the sales agent may own the franchise when representing a number of different companies. This distinction is important.

2. **The role of personal selling in this industry is primarily <u>servicing</u> before and after the sale.** Note the case's frequent reference to information dissemination, display assistance, sales rep/agent knowledge, etc. **Selling, in the conventional sense, plays a less significant role than what one might expect.** This point is particularly important because, in the larger accounts, different retail buyers will be purchasing wood and upholstered or different room furniture.

B. **What are the Pros and Cons of Giving the Lea-Meadows Line to the Throckmorten Sales Force?**

1. **Pros**

   a. Greater control and direction over selling efforts.
   b. Possibility of greater "push" of Lea-Meadows line.
   c. Smaller commission on sales (Throckmorten gives 1/2%; sales agents get 5%). Therefore, greater return to Throckmorten per sale dollar.
   d. Throckmorten sales representatives would have more lines to sell; thus greater opportunity to increase overall compensation.
   e. Consistent with the Throckmorten policy of using its own sales force.

2. **Cons**

   a. Impact on selling time for existing products given additional product line for current sales force (assumes no new sales reps). Bott estimates 15 percent of selling time; Moorman estimates 25 percent (see below).
   b. Potential need for additional sales reps (see below).
   c. Issue of learning the "upholstery business" and presenting and displaying it in a knowledgeable fashion.
   d. Potential lost or slowed sales <u>if</u> the customer franchise is held by the sales agent, not Lea-Meadows.
   e. Possibility of restructuring sales territories if new sales reps added.

C. **What will be the Impact on the Sales Effort if Lea-Meadows Line is Given to the Throckmorten Sales Force with No Increase in Sales Force?**

1. Case information indicates that Throckmorten's 10 sales reps are making "10 calls/week with the average sales call running 3 hours. Remaining time was used for travel/administration." Therefore 5000 calls are made per year, the average call frequency per account is 5 (5000 calls/1000 accounts) and available selling time per rep/year is 1500 hours:

$$10 \text{ Reps} = \frac{(1000 \text{ accts})(5 \text{ calls / year})(3 \text{ hours / call})}{X}$$

Solving for X = 1500 hours. Or, about 10 hours per week or 2 hours/day allocated to travel/administration.

2. Bates wishes to increase the call frequency to 7 calls/account/year or 7,000 total calls/year. Thus 14 calls/week/rep will be needed [7000 calls/(50 weeks x 10 sales reps] vs. the current 10 calls/week/rep. If this is done, then **average time per sales call must be reduced to 2.14 hours/call**, if not less given additional calls:

$$10 \text{ Reps} = \frac{(1000 \text{ accts})(7 \text{ calls / year})(\text{hours / call})}{1500 \text{ hours}}$$

Solving for **hours/call** equals **2.14** hours/call.

3. If the line is assigned to the existing sales force, then 15-25 percent of the sales time must be given to upholstery, say 20 percent. In other words, 80 percent of the sales time will be available for Throckmorten's line or about 45 minutes (.2 x 2.14 hours).

4. If sales call activity is **not** increased to 7 calls/day, then 3 hours remain available for each sales call. This will mean that about 2½ hours are available for Throckmorten and ½ hour is available for Lea-Meadows.

5. Note that if sales agent's call time is also 3 hours and they spend 15 percent of their time on Lea-Meadows, then they spend about ½ hour on Lea-Meadows line. Even if they spend, say 4 hours/call, then Lea-Meadows call time is still only 36 minutes.

6. The principal point of this analysis is that the Lea-Meadows line will be relatively unaffected by the changeover to Throckmorten's sales force in terms of time; however Throckmorten's line will face a dramatic decrease in attention. Is this wise when Throckmorten's line produces a 5 percent higher gross margin than Lea-Meadows and the sales volume is 16 times larger?

D. What are the Costs and Benefits of Adding Additional Sales Reps Versus Using Sales Agents?

1. Assuming that the time given to Lea-Meadows is 30 minutes/call and Throckmorten wishes to maintain a 3 hour call time for its line, then the number of additional reps needed can be calculated under both a 5 call/account and a 7 call/account frequency.

2. Number of reps needed at 5 calls/account is 12:

$$NS = \frac{1000 \times 5 \text{ calls / acct.} \times 3.5 \text{ hours / call}}{1500 \text{ available hours}} = 11.6$$

3. Number of reps needed at 7 calls/account is 16:

$$NS = \frac{1000 \times 7 \text{ calls / acct.} \times 3.5 \text{ hours / call}}{1500 \text{ available hours}} = 16.3$$

4. Assuming new sales reps are paid $70,000/year (same as existing reps), then incremental costs for
   2 reps = $140,000
   6 reps = $420,000 (plus additional costs of sales administration since the possibility exists of added supervisory cost. This may include Moorman's salary which already exists, however.)

5. Lea-Meadows' sales agents currently receive a 5 percent commission. This amounts to $250,000 at the current $5 million sales level. At the same sales level, Throckmorten would pay $25,000 in commission at a ½% commission rate; a saving of $225,000.

6. From an incremental selling cost perspective, the cost of adding two sales reps when the call frequency is 5 calls/account and the average call is 3½ hours vs. the commission costs of sales agents is $85,000 less than sales agents at the $5 million sales level:

	Sales Agents	Sales Force
Commission	$250,000	$ 25,000
Salary	---	140,000
	$250,000	$165,000

As sales volume increases, the sales force alternative becomes even more attractive because the cost of the sales force is mostly fixed (see Exhibit 1 in this note). However, if Throckmorten **also** wishes to increase its call/account frequency, the $420,000 additional cost is prohibitive.

E. **Under What Conditions, if any, should Throckmorten give the Upholstery Line to its Sales Force?**

1. **The decision will not have a deleterious effect on trade relations.** The case suggests that this might happen. Furthermore, the possibility exists that Throckmorten's sales force, and particularly new sales reps, might not be able to service the Lea-Meadows products in the short-run. If the customer franchise is held by sales agents, then the possibility of lost sales looms, particularly if sales agents represent competitor lines.

EXHIBIT 1

GRAPHICAL DEPICTION OF SALES AGENT VS. COMPANY SALES FORCE COST

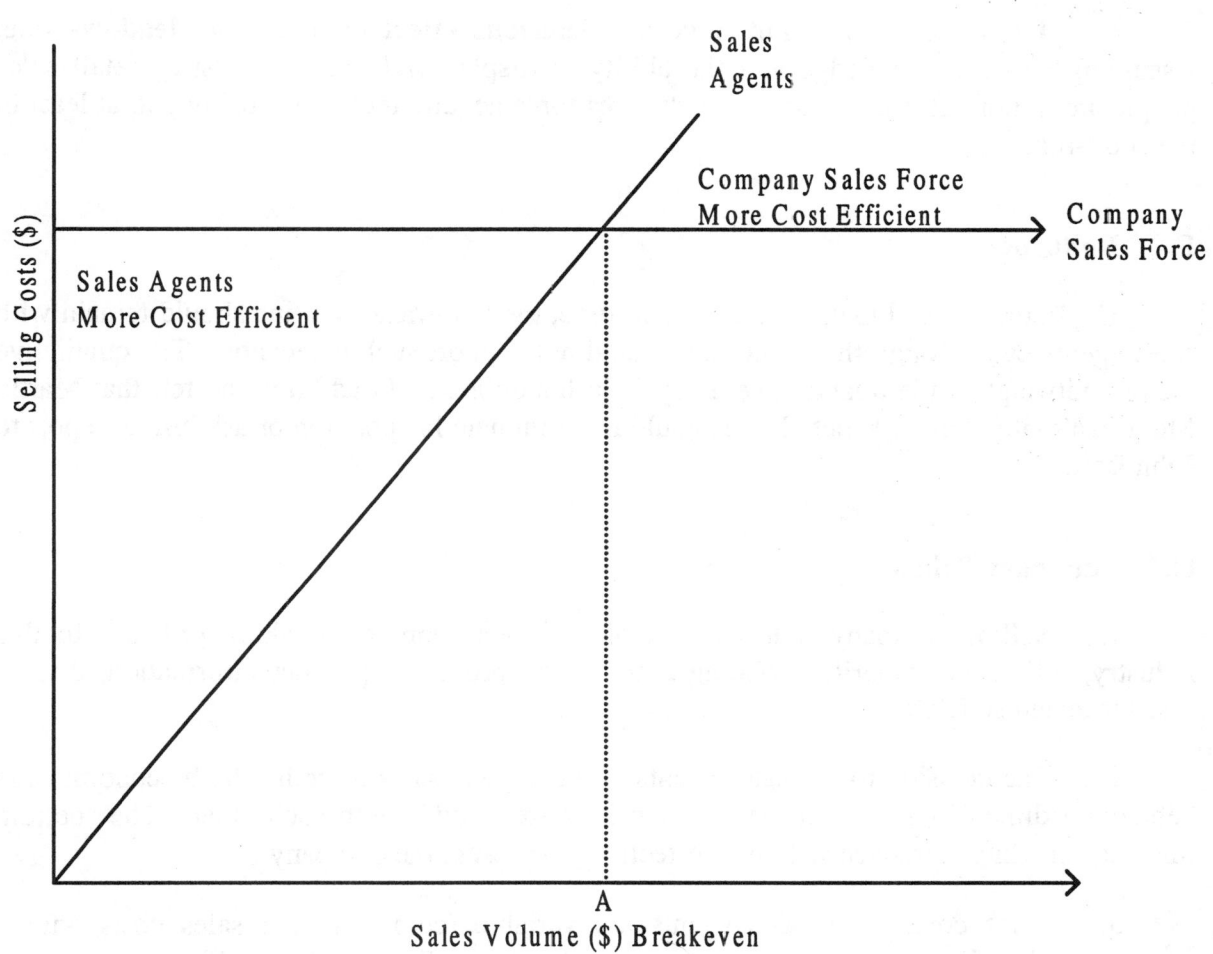

Sales agents are typically more cost efficient at lower sales levels, since most of the costs associated with agents are variable. However, at higher sales levels (beyond point A) a company sales force becomes more cost efficient since more costs are fixed.

2. **The decision will not have a deleterious effect on Throckmorten's own line.** Previous analysis suggests that to sell Lea-Meadows furniture, the sales force must either decrease time given to Throckmorten or increase the sales force size. Decreasing time spent on accounts seems unwise given the higher volume and gross margins associated with Throckmorten furniture. Increasing sales force size is not justified economically and operational problems of restructuring sales territories is indicated.

3. **The decision will not have a deleterious effect on the Lea-Meadows line.** Assuming product knowledge and the ability to display and teach upholstery retail sales people are important, can Throckmorten's sales force acquire them? Probably not, at least in the short-run.

F. Epilogue

Mr. Bates decided that, for the present time, the Lea-Meadows line should remain with sales agents even though the economics would not support such a decision. The qualitative factors outweighed the quantitative analysis in his opinion. In addition, he felt that Martin Moorman's situation was such that he could not eliminate his position or ask him to report to John Bott.

G. Summary Points

1. Selling in many industries involves much more than taking orders. In this industry, selling is primarily servicing accounts by providing product information, display assistance and so forth.

2. The decision to use sales agents or a company sales force has both economic and behavioral dimensions. Often these dimensions are at odds with each other. The "bottom line" lies in which approach will most effectively represent the company.

3. Sales costs with sales agents are variable (commissions); sales costs with a company sales force contain both a fixed (salary, benefits, administration) and variable (commission) costs. Understanding cost behavior is important in the decision to use sales agents versus a company sales force.

CADBURY BEVERAGES, INC.: CRUSH BRAND

Synopsis

In January 1990, marketing executives at Cadbury Beverages, Inc. began the task of relaunching CRUSH, HIRES, and SUN-DROP soft drink brands. These brands had been purchased from Procter & Gamble in October 1989, at a cost of $220 million. Kim Feil, who only recently joined Cadbury Beverages, Inc. as a Senior Product Manager, was assigned responsibility for the relaunch of the CRUSH brand.

The case raises a variety of issues. The two principal issues involve CRUSH positioning and the preparation of an advertising and promotion program for CRUSH, including determination of objectives, strategies, and expenditures.

The positioning question is made interesting because CRUSH must be positioned vis-a-vis PepsiCo's Mandarin Orange Slice, Coca-Cola's Minute Maid Orange, and Cadbury Beverages' own SUNKIST brand. The advertising and promotion program makes for a challenging assignment since students must (1) set objectives, (2) assess the merits of push (trade-oriented promotion) and pull (consumer-oriented advertising) strategies, and prepare a pro forma income statement. Related issues for student consideration concern the emphasis on diet versus regular soft drinks, assessing market/category dynamics (size, growth, served market), marketing channel (bottler) relationships, and case volume and revenue forecasts.

Teaching Objectives

This case has four teaching objectives:

1. To introduce marketing practices in what is the largest consumer package good category in the United States; namely, soft drinks.

2. To consider the U.S. soft drink industry structure and economics, marketing implications related to aspects of channel power and influence (i.e., the role of the bottler), and matters of profitability for concentrate producers and bottlers and type of beverage--diet versus regular carbonated beverages.

3. To expose students to two common assignments involved in product management: (a) product positioning and (b) planning advertising and promotion programs, including objective setting and strategy determination.

4. To force students to engage in sales forecasting and budget determination related to an articulated strategy and rationale for that strategy.

Teaching Suggestions

This case is suitable for that portion of the course when the instructor wishes students to integrate product and promotion issues. Some instructors have assigned the case as a comprehensive examination case at the end of the course.

Specific questions that can be posed to students prior to or during a class discussion are:

1. How would you characterize the carbonated soft drink industry in the United States?

2. How would you describe changes in the orange category during the period 1985 to 1989? What can be learned from these changes?

3. What is Cadbury Beverages relative competitive position in the U.S. soft drink industry? In the orange category?

4. Based on your assessment of the soft drink industry, the orange-flavored category, and the competitive situation of Cadbury Beverages and orange CRUSH, what is your recommendation for positioning orange CRUSH?

5. What objectives should be set for the CRUSH advertising and promotion program? What strategy(ies) should be pursued?

6. How much should be spent for advertising and promotion to relaunch orange CRUSH?

7. Prepare a pro forma income statement similar in form to that shown in Exhibit 3 in the case including a forecast of total dollar sales, total expenses, and finally, a pretax cash profit for orange CRUSH.

Previous experience teaching the case indicates that instructors should be prepared to assist students in the following areas. First, students occasionally overlook the actual size of the orange category. That is, they focus on supermarket case volume and do not consider that the total market is 2.5 times supermarket volume. Second, the notion of a **served market** is also overlooked by some students. This issue is important because orange CRUSH has the lowest market (bottler) coverage of the major competitors. Third, students are sometimes reluctant to project sales by beverage type (regular vs. diet) which in turn detracts from the preparation of a pro forma income statement. Relatedly, undergraduate students sometimes struggle with the income statements shown in case Exhibit 3 since they are portrayed on a per unit (case) basis. Finally, some students are prone to give recommendations related to positioning and the advertising and promotion program without providing the rationale based on a careful articulation of industry and product-market dynamics, competitive behavior, and the concentrate producer price-cost structure.

Areas for Discussion/Analysis

A. **How would you characterize the carbonated soft drink industry in the United States?**

Discussion related to this question would include reference to industry structure, industry economics, competitors/brands, product categories, and buyer behavior. Relevant observations from the case appear below.

1. **Industry Structure**

    a. Three major participants make up the industry. They are concentrate producers, bottlers, and retailers. Each is described below.

    b. There are 40 concentrate producers in the U.S. They manufacture the basic flavors (e.g., cola) for sale to bottlers. In addition to production, concentrate producers assumed responsibility for developing national consumer advertising and promotion programs, product development and planning, and marketing research.

    c. The soft drink industry is dominated by three major concentrate producers: (a) Coca-Cola, (b) PepsiCo, and (c) Dr Pepper/7 Up. These three firms capture about 82 percent of U.S. soft drink sales.

    d. There are some 1000 bottling plants in the U.S. They purchase the basic flavors from concentrate producers, add a sweetener (sugar or artificial sweetener) to carbonated water to create a carbonated beverage, and package the beverage in bottles and cans.

    e. In addition, bottlers take the lead in developing trade promotions to retail outlets and local consumer advertising. They are also responsible for selling and servicing retail accounts, including the placement and maintenance of in-store displays and stocking supermarket and convenience store shelves with their brands. **A bottling network is considered central to a successful marketing effort**.

    f. Bottlers are either owned by concentrate producers ("forward vertical integration"), or franchised to sell the brands of concentrate producers in a defined territory. Franchised bottlers are prohibited from marketing a directly competitive brand (e.g., Coca-Cola and Pepsi-Cola), but are allowed to represent non-competitive brands.

    g. The principal retail channels for soft drinks are supermarkets, convenience stores, vending machines, fountain service (e.g., McDoanld's) and thousands of small retail outlets. **Supermarkets account for 40 percent of**

carbonated soft drink sales and supermarket sales are considered the key to a successful marketing effort.

2. **Industry Economics**

   a. Case Exhibit 3 shows the economics of the industry from the perspective of concentrate producers and bottlers. Students should pay particular attention to the price/cost/margin structure. The case states that concentrate producer pricing was similar across competitors within flavor categories.

   b. In the domain of pricing,

   - concentrate producers sell diet beverages for a higher price than regular beverages.

   - bottlers sell diet and regular beverages at the same price.

   c. In the cost domain,

   - Since the cost of goods sold for diet beverages is only one cent higher for diet than regular beverages, and other costs are identical, **concentrate producers have a higher gross profit/case and a higher pretax cash profit per case for diet beverages than regular beverages.**

   - Since concentrate producers sell diet beverages to bottlers at a higher price/case, **bottler gross profit/case on diet drinks is less than that for regular drinks. Since all other costs are identical, bottlers record a lower pretax cash profit/case on diet beverages than regular beverages.**

   d. An assessment of industry economics suggests that it is in the best interest of concentrate producers to promote diet beverage consumption while bottlers benefit more from selling regular beverages! This observation raises some interesting questions concerning producer-bottler goal congruence at least from a cash profit/case standpoint. It may very well be that concentrate producers have to "sweeten" the diet beverage business for bottlers.

3. **Brands and Product Categories**

   a. There are more than 900 registered soft drink brands in the U.S. and most are sold regionally. Ten brands capture 71.4 percent of total U.S. soft drink sales (see case Exhibit 4). All ten brands are sold by Coca-Cola, PepsiCo, and Dr Pepper/7 Up, and none are orange-flavored. These observations suggest that gaining shelf space/facings in retail outlets will be challenging if a brand is not a major player.

b. Soft drinks divide into several **categories**: (a) Diet vs. Regular, and (b) flavors (Cola, lemon-lime, etc.). Regular drinks account for 69 percent of the market while diet drinks account for 31 percent. Colas capture 65.7 percent of the market followed by lemon-lime with 12.9 percent and orange with 3.9 percent. In short, there appears to be clear preferences for regular drinks and colas.

4. **Buyer Behavior**

   a. Regionality and seasonality exists in the industry. East South Central states record the highest level of per capita consumption (54.9 gallons); consumers in Mountain states consume the least (37.1 gallons per capita). Soft drink consumption is slightly higher during summer months than winter months.

   b. Supermarket purchases of soft drinks are typically married women with children under 18 living at home. The purchase itself is often unplanned. This suggests that in-store merchandising is important in the soft drink industry. Indeed, the case quotes an industry analyst as saying that a brand is "locked out of 60 percent of the [supermarket soft-drink] volume if it can't get end-aisle displays."

B. How would you describe changes in the orange category during the period 1985 to 1989? What can be learned from these changes?

1. The orange category is the third largest flavor category behind cola and lemon-lime with 3.9 percent share of the soft drink market.

2. A large percentage of orange category sales occur in supermarkets - 40 percent. Even so, it is important that students recognize that total orange category sales are 2.5 times supermarket case sales. **This means that total orange category sales in 1989 were 315 million cases** (126 million in supermarket case sales x 2.5). Furthermore, **orange CRUSH sales with an 8 percent market share would be equivalent to 25.2 million cases** (315 million case x .08), of which 10,080,000 cases or 40 percent would come from supermarkets.

3. The orange category was dominated by SUNKIST and CRUSH prior to 1986 when these two brands captured 32 percent and 22 percent of category sales, respectively (see case Exhibit 5). During that time, the annual category sales volume in supermarkets hovered in the range of 100 to 102 million cases.

4. In 1986, Minute Maid Orange (Coca-Cola) and Mandarin Orange Slice (PepsiCo) were introduced supported by widespread distribution and heavy advertising and promotion. These entries:

   • Increased category sales to 126 million cases in 1986 and 131 million cases in 1987 and 1988. Case sales fell to 126 million in 1989.

- Caused SUNKIST and CRUSH to experience rapid and sizable declines in market shares (SUNKIST from 32% in 1985 to 14% in 1989; CRUSH from 22% in 1985 to 8% in 1989).

5. It would appear that orange brand sales (market share) are sensitive to bottler market coverage and media advertising. Exhibit 1 in this note plots market coverage (case Exhibit 7) against market share (case Exhibit 5) and shows a positive relationship. Similarly, Exhibit 2 in this note suggests a positive, although less direct, relationship between the media advertising dollar share (from case Exhibit 9) of the four brands and brand market share shown in case Exhibit 5 (although this relationship is obviously affected by market coverage). Therefore,

- market (bottler) coverage is critical for success (a success requirement).

- dollar media advertising is important in gaining/holding market share, although there appears to be threshold effect operating. That is, for Mandarin Orange Slice, the market leader and heaviest advertiser, increasing its **share of voice** (advertising share of major brands) does not further improve market share. However, the steeper positive slopes for SUNKIST, CRUSH, and to some extent Minute Maid Orange, suggest that share gains are more likely with an increasing share of media advertising. This topic is addressed again later in the discussion related to advertising budgeting.

6. **Targeting and positioning influence the relative competitive standing of individual brands**. The case text discussion on brand positioning and case Exhibit 8 suggest that brands are typically positioned along an attribute dimension (taste) and an end user dimension (teens, young adults, family with children at home). Exhibit 3 in this note shows one possible brand positioning plot given case information:

- Mandarin Orange Slice: Teen focus, "Who's got the juice?"

- Minute Maid Orange :   Teen/Young Adult focus, "The orange, orange, orange, flavor, taste of real orange."

- SUNKIST: Teen/Young Adult focus, "Teens on the beach. Drink in the sun."

- CRUSH: Teens, Young Adults -households with children at home, "Don't just quench it, CRUSH it!"

This analysis suggests that Mandarin Orange Slice and Minute Maid have occupied the teens/young adults-orange taste position. SUNKIST is decidedly "non-taste" with a teen/young adult emphasis. CRUSH is in the "middle," but closer to SUNKIST than

EXHIBIT 1

RELATIONSHIP BETWEEN MARKET SHARE AND MARKET COVERAGE
FOR ORANGE CARBONATED SOFT DRINK BRANDS

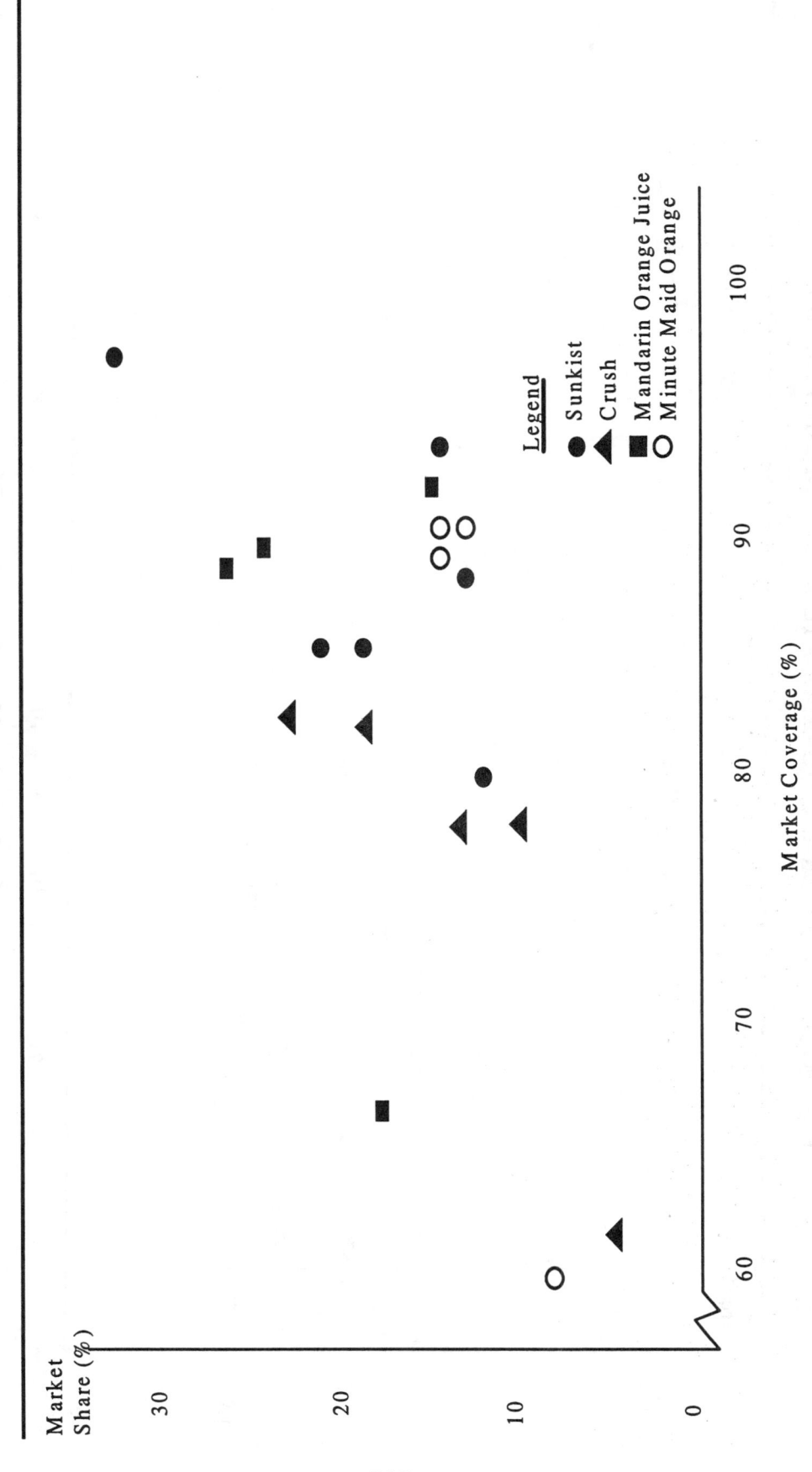

Source: Case Exhibits 5 and 7

EXHIBIT 2

RELATIONSHIP BETWEEN MARKET SHARE AND ADVERTISING SHARE
FOR FOUR MAJOR ORANGE CARBONATED SOFT DRINK BRANDS

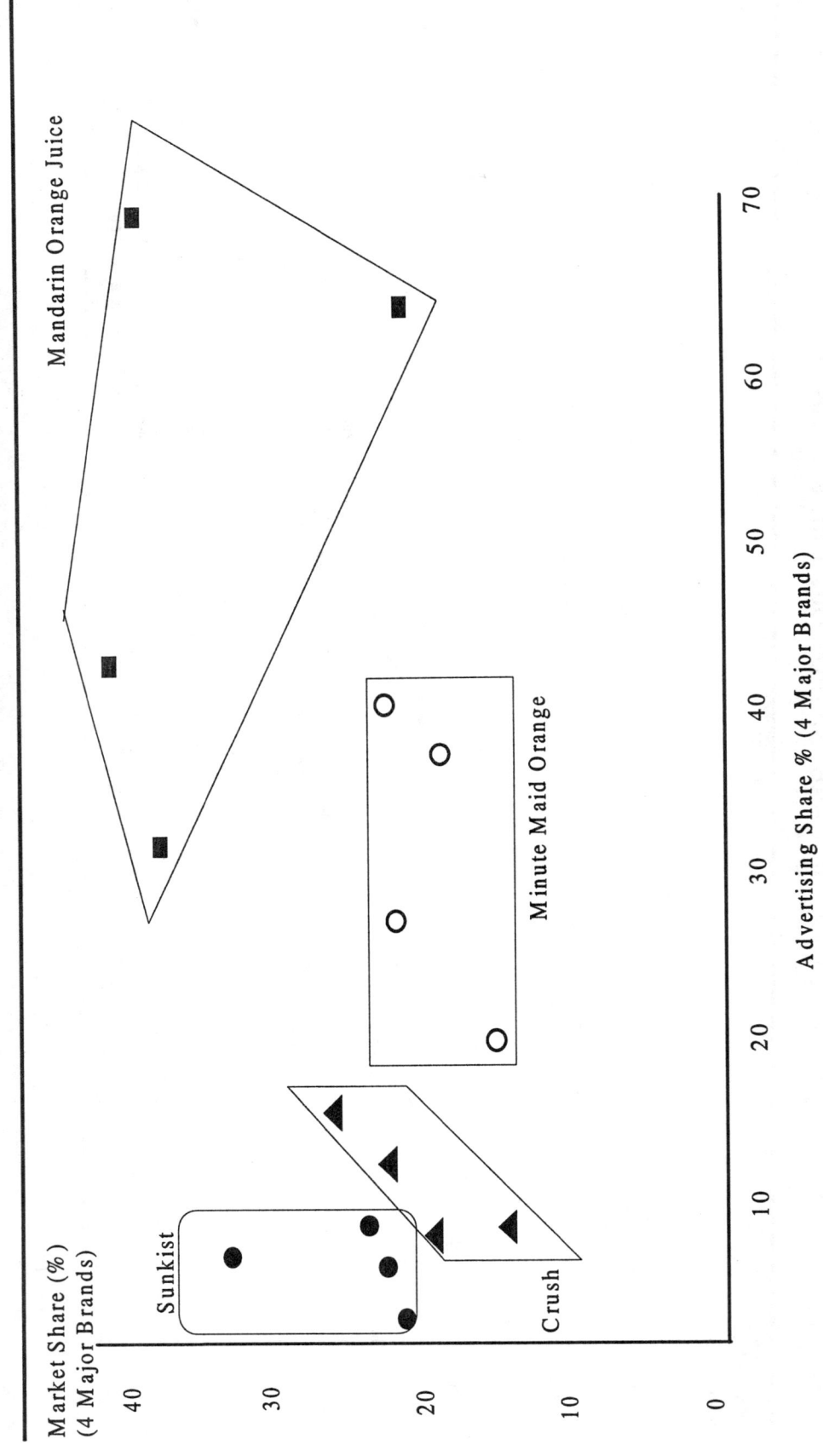

Source: Case Exhibits 5 and 9

EXHIBIT 3

APPARENT BRAND POSITIONINGS: 1989

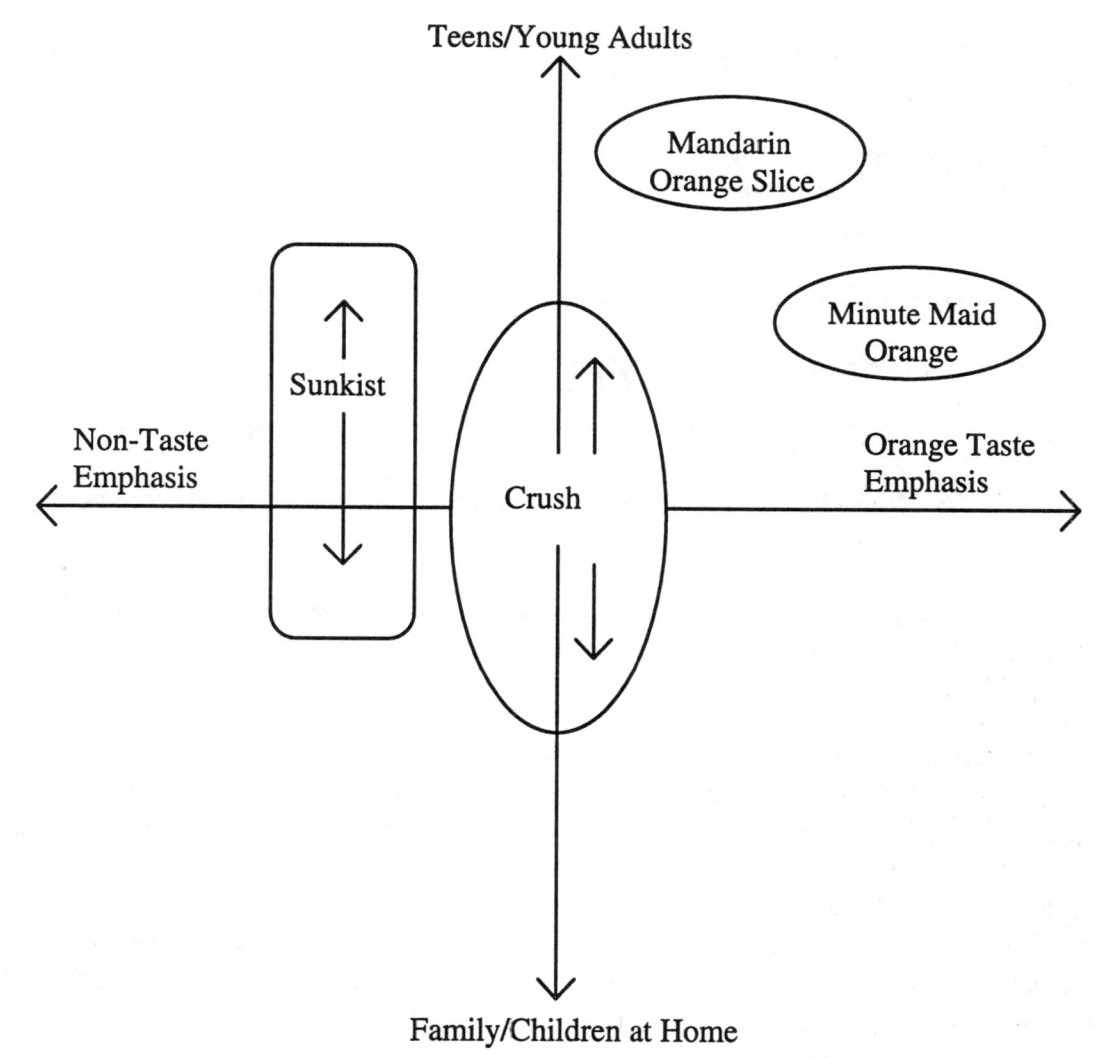

Mandarin Orange Slice and Minute Maid Orange. This positioning could present a cannibalization problem for Cadbury's SUNKIST and CRUSH brands.

C. What is Cadbury Beverages relative competitive position in the U.S. soft drink industry? In the orange category?

1. Cadbury Beverages is the fourth largest soft drink firm in the US. (It ranks third behind Coca-Cola and PepsiCo in world-wide sales.)

2. The company captured 3.4 percent of U.S. soft drink sales in 1989.

3. Cadbury Beverages is a niche marketer, avoiding the cola category. Its

   - CANADA DRY is the top-selling Ginger Ale in the U.S.

   - SCHWEPPES is the leading tonic water in the U.S.

   - CANADA DRY seltzers top the club soda/seltzer category in the U.S.

   - SUNKIST and CRUSH brands combined lead the orange-flavored category in the U.S.

4. The company appears to have considerable **brand equity** in CANADA DRY, SCHWEPPES, and SUNKIST in the U.S. A question, however, relates to the **brand equity** of the CRUSH brand.

5. A cursory examination of case Exhibit 5 would suggest that CRUSH is a weak brand. However, students should also consider that CRUSH has the lowest market coverage of the four major brands with 62 percent coverage (see case Exhibit 7). Lack of market coverage would affect case sales and ultimately market share. With an 8 percent market share, CRUSH sells some 25.2 million cases in total (total market = 315 million cases in 1989 x .08 market share). With a market coverage of 62 percent, its **served market** can be estimated as 195.3 million cases (315 million cases x .62). Therefore, CRUSH market share in served markets is 12.9 percent (25.2 million cases/195.3 million cases). **CRUSH is a major player where it is sold!**

6. Cadbury Beverages' apparent competitive strategy is growth through acquisition of brands with an established customer franchise. These brands are further developed through line extensions.

D. Based on your assessment of the soft drink industry, the orange-flavored category, and the competitive situation of Cadbury Beverages and orange CRUSH, what is your recommendation for positioning orange CRUSH?

1. Students should make note of specific issues related to CRUSH positioning raised in the case. First, there was a need to define a clearly differentiated position for orange CRUSH vis-a-vis SUNKIST. Second, the relative emphasis on regular versus diet CRUSH had to be considered. Third, the positioning could not run counter to previous positionings and should build on the customer franchise or **brand equity** held by orange CRUSH. Students also should be expected to translate their previous analyses into the rationale for the positioning approach they recommend.

2. As noted in Chapter 5, there are numerous ways to position a product/service as well as combinations of approaches. Exhibit 4 in this note gives possible positionings. Based on the earlier discussion, attribute (taste) and end-user (teens/young adults/family) appear to be the principal emphasis in positioning to date.

3. It would seem that orange CRUSH might be more actively positioned as an **all family/children at home** soft drink with **exceptional orange flavor**. This positioning approach is defensible on the grounds that:

- This approach moves CRUSH away from SUNKIST (this would move CRUSH into the taste, and Family/Children at Home quadrant in Exhibit 3 in this note. This quadrant is not presently occupied by any of these major competitor brands.

- Taste and flavor would seem to be a determinant attribute in brand choice.

- By also emphasizing the all family with children at home end user, there is a good likelihood that the diet beverage drinker might be attracted to CRUSH. The case states that "Consumption of diet beverages was more pronounced among consumers over 25 years of age."

- This approach does not run counter to previous orange CRUSH positionings (see case Exhibit 13). That is, taste has been a prominent factor in positioning CRUSH and the CRUSH brand has historically (at least prior to 1985) focused on the 13-39 age segment.

Students might offer different recommendations. However, their recommendations should be defensible based on the points raised in #1 above and developed in a manner similar to the previous discussion.

EXHIBIT 4

POSSIBLE POSITIONING APPROACHES FOR ORANGE CRUSH

Approach	Example
1. By Attribute	Orange flavor; refreshing taste; orange color
2. By Use	For parties, weekends. A "change of pace."
3. By User	For teens, young adults, older adults, families. "Orange Lovers."
4. By Product Class	The "un-cola." The fruit alternative (against lemon-lime). The real orange orange.
5. By Competitor	Against Minute Maid Orange or Mandarin Orange Slice; Move away from SUNKIST

E. What objectives should be set for the CRUSH advertising and promotion program? What strategy(ies) should be pursued?

1. Students should be expected to identify specific objectives for the advertising and promotion program. These objectives should be based on the previous industry, category, company, and CRUSH brand analysis. Ideally, students should think in terms of the **objective-task** in approaching this question and the subsequent development of strategy and budgeting.

2. At least three objectives should be set for the advertising and promotion program. These three objectives might be:

   a. To build a cooperative relationship with CRUSH bottlers that will assure that adequate attention is given the brand.

   b. To capitalize on previous positionings and communicate the new positioning of orange CRUSH as a flavorful orange drink for the family with children at home.

   c. To build sales volume of diet beverages for orange CRUSH.

Students can be expected to mention other objectives, e.g., increase sales, improve market share, etc. However, reference to creating brand awareness and recognition is not necessarily valid. The case text notes that CRUSH marketing executives "were pleasantly surprised to learn that the CRUSH brand had high name awareness in the markets served by existing and new bottlers." Furthermore, reference to increasing sales/market share is probably as much a result of expanded bottler market coverage as it is advertising or promotion.

3. CRUSH executives have the option of emphasizing either a **push strategy** with principal attention placed on bottler incentives, merchandising programs, and local event activities, or a **pull strategy** with a focus on consumer advertising (electronic and print media).

4. It is noteworthy that the objective related to the bottlers suggests a "push" strategy emphasis. The objective to communicate the new positioning suggests a "pull" strategy emphasis. The objective of building the diet CRUSH business has both "push" and "pull" implications. For example, since bottlers have traditionally sold more regular than diet CRUSH (see case Exhibit 6), they may have to be given incentives to promote diet CRUSH. On the other hand, effective communication through advertising of the new positioning should increase diet sales volume.

F. How much should be spent for advertising and promotion to relaunch orange CRUSH?

   1. The response to this question should elicit numerous proposals. However, students should be prepared to provide a rationale for their spending proposals both for advertising and for promotion.

   2. A wide variety of perspectives can be brought to bear on this assignment. For example,

   a. According to case Exhibit 3, concentrate producers spend a total of $.38 per case for advertising <u>and</u> promotion.

   b. Media advertising per case spent on each of the four major brands can be calculated. Exhibit 5 in this note shows these calculations. It is noteworthy that SUNKIST, the only Cadbury Beverage brand, spends the least on media advertising. (Can orange CRUSH be budgeted to spend more than SUNKIST?)

   c. Numerous bottler and consumer-related promotions are possible:

   5¢/case = for cups, caps, glasses
   10¢/case = for T-shirts
   20¢/case = for displays (end-aisle, display loader) 25¢/case = for local event marketing
   15¢ to 25¢/case = for distribution incentives (price promotions)

   d. **Total dollar media expense** can be budgeted. Also, a breakdown by regular, diet, and regular + diet expenditures is possible as shown in case Exhibit 9.

   e. Consideration of cooperative promotions and advertising with bottlers is also necessary since concentrate producers and bottlers split the cost 50-50.

   f. Students should give consideration to an advertising-sales response function. That is, they should consider incremental sales to advertising expenditures like that shown in Exhibit 6 in this note. As indicated, and based in part on Exhibit 2 in this note, Mandarin Orange Slice and Minute Maid Orange are already spending at high levels and **sizable** incremental sales due to more advertising is unlikely. However, for SUNKIST, and particularly orange CRUSH, their spending is so low that increases in dollars spend **could** produce increases in sales (market share).

   g. Students should recognize that bottler coverage of the orange category has been expanded from 62 percent (case Exhibit 7) to 75 percent as stated in the case. Expanded coverage will mean that media advertising should

EXHIBIT 5

MEDIA ADVERTISING $/CASE FOR MAJOR BRANDS: 1985-1989*

Brand	1985	1986	1987	1988	1989
SUNKIST	$.09	$.06	$.02	$.04	$.05
Mandarin Orange Slice	--	$.64	$.41	$.22	$.17
Minute Maid Orange	--	$.32	$.20	$.30	$.24
CRUSH	$.08	$.13	$.09	$.19	$.07

Note: Media advertising $/case is calculated as follows.

Numerator: Advertising expenditures per brand per year (from case Exhibit 9)

Denominator: Supermarket case volume x 2.5 (from case footnote 4) x brand market share/year (from case Exhibit 5)

For example: SUNKIST Media Advertising $/case in 1985 =

$$\frac{\$7{,}176{,}200}{100{,}000{,}000 \times 2.5 \times 32\%} = \$.0897$$

EXHIBIT 6

ADVERTISING-SALES RESPONSE CURVE AND BRAND PLACEMENTS

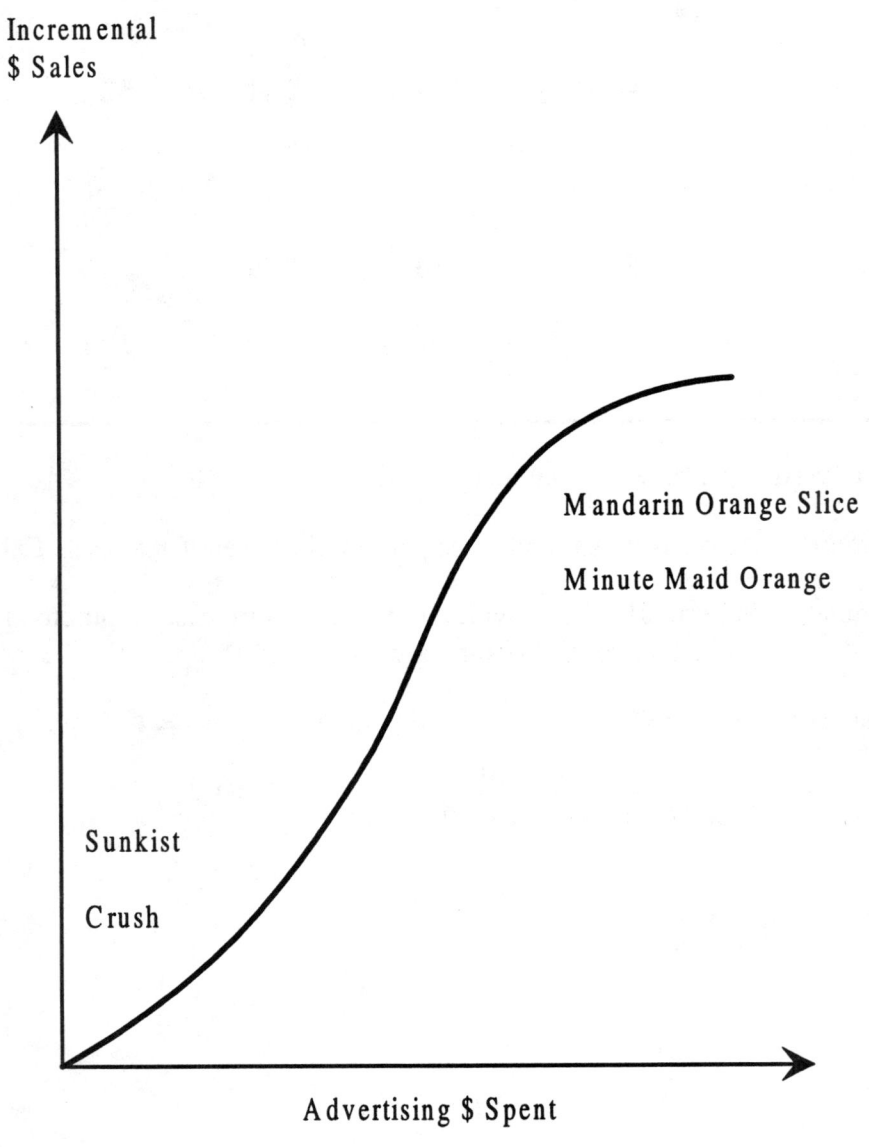

increase. If media remains unchanged, fewer dollars will be spent in markets served than previously.

3. These numerous perspectives argue for an increase in media advertising (a "pull" strategy). However, CRUSH executives are also involved in rebuilding possibly strained relationships with bottlers. As Kim Feil notes:

> "We knew that reestablishing trade relations was an important first step. However, we also knew that new and existing bottlers would be gauging the kind and amount of advertising and promotional support we would provide when we relaunched CRUSH."

Therefore, CRUSH might find it advantageous to also provide promotional support in the form of cooperative advertising and merchandising programs (a "push" strategy). Moreover, bottlers will need an incentive to push diet CRUSH.

4. Ultimately, students should be expected to prepare an advertising and promotion budget. This budget should include media advertising expenditures and, ideally, an itemized promotion budget.

    a. **Media advertising**. Advertising will need to be increased given broadened market (bottler) coverage. The 21 percent increase in coverage (from 62% to 75%) would suggest an expenditure level of $2,242,856 (1989 expenditure of $1,853,600 from case Exhibit 9 x 1.21).

    It should be noted, however, that this expenditure approaches SUNKIST's advertising expenditure with SUNKIST's 91 percent market coverage.

    b. **Promotions**. The choice of promotions and accompanying expenditure level should be based on the previous analysis related to the industry, CRUSH's relaunch through bottlers, and the need to build the bottling network. At a minimum, end-aisle displays should be used at an allocated cost of $.20/case. The case states that a brand is "locked out of 60 percent of the [supermarket soft-drink] volume if it can't get end-aisle displays."

    In addition, a price promotion in the form of a distribution incentive is probably necessary. Ranging in cost from $.15 to $.20 per case, these incentives will likely be needed to stimulate bottler "push." A reasonable figure is $.15 per case.

    c. Therefore, an advertising and promotion budget for orange CRUSH might like that below:

	Media Advertising	$2,242,856
	Promotions:	
	End-aisle displays	$.20/case
	Price/bottler incentive	$.15/case

This budget is likely to exceed the "norm" of $.38/case for advertising and promotion shown in case Exhibit 3. However, the additional spending might warrant this "investment" under the circumstances.

G. **Prepare a pro forma income statement similar in form to that shown in Exhibit 3 in the case including a forecast of total dollar sales, total expenses, and finally, a pretax cash profit for orange CRUSH.**

1. A central issue in preparing a pro forma income statement is the determination of a case and dollar sales forecast. Also, students should be prepared to also forecast regular and diet beverage sales since price, cost, and gross profit differs between regular and diet beverages.

2. **Sales Mix: Regular and Diet.** Presently, CRUSH's sales mix is 71.3 percent regular and 28.7 percent diet (see case Exhibit 6). Therefore, given the price/cost structure in case Exhibit 3, CRUSH has a **weighted average gross profit/case of $.69**:

	% of Sales		Price/Case	% of Sales		Cost of Goods Sold/Case
Regular	.713	x	$.76	.713	x	$.11
Diet	.287	x	$.92	.287	x	$.12

Weighted Avg. Price = $.80/case Weighted Avg. Cost = $.11/case

Weighted Avg. Gross Profit: $.80/case - $.11/case = $.69/case

Alternatively, students might simply multiply the sales mix figures by gross profit as follows:

Regular	Diet

$$[(.713)(\$.65)] \quad + \quad [(.287)(\$.80)] = \$.693$$

Students should recognize that by altering the sales mix to increase diet beverages relative to regular beverages, a gross profit per case improvement will result. For instance, if the new positioning, advertising, and bottler programs can produce a sales mix of 60 percent regular beverages and 40 percent diet beverages, gross profit per case increases to $.71 per case:

Regular	Diet

$$[(.60)(\$.65)] + [(.40)(\$.80)] = \$.71$$

A 50-50 split of regular and diet, similar to Mandarin Orange Slice and Minute Maid Orange, will produce a gross profit per case of $.725:

Regular	Diet

$$[(.50)(\$.65)] + [(.50)(\$.80)] = \$.725$$

While seemingly minor, a two to three cent increase in case gross profit can be used to pay for advertising and promotion or improve brand profitability. For example, if orange CRUSH had a gross profit of $.71 per case in 1989 rather than the $.69/case, an additional $504,000 would have been available for promotion and profit! [Note: 1989 CRUSH case unit sales = 126 million case x 2.5 (per footnote 4) x .08 (market share per Exhibit 5) x $.02 = $504,000]

3. **Volume Projections**. Volume projections can be slippery in this case. However, student projections should incorporate several different perspectives into any sales projections.

    a. **Broadened market (bottler) coverage**. Broadened market coverage should lead to an increase in case volume. By increasing bottler coverage of the orange category by 21 percent (62% in 1989 to 75% when orange CRUSH is relaunched), it is possible to project case sales of 30,492,000 (25,200,000 cases in 1989 x 1.21). This calculation assumes that

- CRUSH orange category market share remains at 8 percent.

- New bottler markets are similar to existing bottler markets.

    b. **Market share gains through expanded bottler coverage**. As discussed earlier, there appears to be positive relationship between market coverage and market share (see Exhibit 1 in this note). A rough visual estimate would suggest that a 75 percent market coverage is related to a 10-12 percent market share of the orange category. With a 75 percent market coverage and assuming a market share of 10 to 12 percent, projected case sales would be:

Total Orange Category Sales	x	CRUSH Mkt-Share	=	CRUSH Volume (cases)
315,000,000 cases	x	10%	=	31,500,000
315,000,000 cases	x	12%	=	37,800,000

This calculation assumes that:

- Category sales remain unchanged at 126 million cases sold through supermarkets and the total case volume is 2.5 times this figure per footnote 4 in the case.

c. **Advertising and promotion effects.** Assessing the sales volume effects of incremental advertising and promotion is very difficult. There would appear to be a positive relationship as discussed earlier and CRUSH is likely to reap incremental sales from incremental advertising and promotion. Acknowledging that advertising and promotion will increase case volume, a prudent assumption is to factor these effects into the market share gains considered above under market share gains through expanded bottler coverage. A major role of advertising and promotion is to covey the new positioning, hopefully improve the diet/regular sales mix, and build bottler relations and support of CRUSH. Sizable sales volume gains attributable directly to advertising and promotions are unlikely.

4. **Advertising and Promotion Budgeting.** Deciding how much to spend on advertising and promotion is also a challenge. The previous discussion (Question #6) addresses this issue.

5. **Other Costs.** Remaining costs to be considered in the budgeting process relate to (a) selling and delivery ($.02 per case) and (b) general and administrative expense ($.13 per case). For budgeting purposes, these might be treated as variable expenses; that is, they should be multiplied by case volume to obtain a dollar figure.

6. Exhibit 7 in this note shows an illustrative pro forma income statement for the relaunch of orange CRUSH. This illustration shows:

a. **Case sales** of 31 million; 65 percent of which are regular and 35 percent are diet. Total dollar net sales are $25,296,000.

b. **Advertising and promotion** totals $13,050,000, or $.42 per case. This figure is 4¢ higher than the "norm" (see case Exhibit 3).

c. **Pretax cash profit** is $4,077,500 after subtracting other expenses. This figure represents 16.2 percent of net sales.

7. **Reality Check.** The pro forma illustration "seems" to be in the ballpark.

a. Case sales of 31 million represents a market share of 9.8 percent (assuming no change in category volume, i.e., 126 million supermarket cases x 2.5 = 315 million cases: 31 MM cases/315 MM cases = 9.8%).

EXHIBIT 7

PRO FORMA INCOME STATEMENT FOR RELAUNCH OF ORANGE CRUSH
(FOR ILLUSTRATION PURPOSES)

			% of Sales
Net Sales*			
Regular	$15,314,000		65%
($.76/case x case units)			
Diet	9,982,000		35%
($.92/case x case units)			
Total Net Sales		25,296,000	100%
Cost of Goods Sold			
Regular	$ 2,216,500		
($.11/case x case units)			
Diet	1,302,000		
($.12/case x case units)			
Total Cost of Goods Sold		$ 3,518,500	13.9%
Gross Profit (Total Net Sales - Total CGS)		$21,777,500	86.1%
Selling & Delivery	$ 620,000		2.4%
($.02 x case units)			
Advertising & Promotion**			
Media Advertising	$ 2,200,000		8.7%
Promotion**	10,850,000		42.9%
($.35/case x case units)			
General & Admin. Expense	$ 4,030,000		15.9%
($.13/case x case units)			
Total Expenses		$17,700,000	69.9%
Pretax Cash Profit		$ 4,077,500	16.2%

*Volume Projection: 31,000,000 cases. Regular beverages = 65% of sales; Diet beverages = 35% of sales.

**Media advertising = $2,200,000; Promotion = $.35/case x 31 million cases.

Moreover, from a **served market** perspective, the 31 million cases projection represents a market share of 13.1 percent (assuming no change in category volume, i.e., 315 MM cases x 75% market coverage = 236,250,000 cases; 31 MM cases/236.25 MM cases = 13.1%).

These figures appear attainable and are consistent with CRUSH's market share in total and in terms of served market, **given** (1) effective positioning and (2) more aggressive advertising and promotion.

The 65%/35% split on regular/diet sales seems reasonable, although aggressive given past CRUSH sales history. Nevertheless, the relaunch strategy should alter the present 71.3%/28.7% split for regular and diet beverages.

b. Advertising and promotion also seem reasonable. An advertising expenditure of $2,200,000 translates to 7¢/case. ($2.2 million/31 million cases). This figure is identical to the expenditure in 1989 and compares favorably to SUNKIST, **given** the market development effort.

Most notably, the promotion expense of $10,850,000 represents a sizable investment and is indicative of a "push" strategy through bottlers. This is needed given the effort required to reestablish CRUSH in its current and new bottling network.

c. Pretax cash profit also seems reasonable at 16.2 percent of net sales. According to case Exhibit 3, and the typical split between regular and diet beverages being 68.9%/31.1% (see case Exhibit 6), the typical orange concentrate producer achieves a pretax cash profit of 19.75 percent computed as follows

$$\underline{(Regular\ \%)(Profit\ \%)} + \underline{(Diet\ \%)(Profit\ \%)}$$
$$(.732)(.16) + (.268)(.30) = 19.75\%$$

Therefore, profitability of the relaunch is slightly lower than the norm - not expected given the unique circumstances.

H. Epilogue

Kim Feil's presentation to Cadbury Beverages, Inc. senior management focused on the specific issues presented in the case. A synopsis of her presentation and the results are highlighted below.

Positioning: Orange CRUSH was positioned as a beverage for families with children at home. Also, taste was emphasized. Since orange CRUSH was part of a flavor-line (i.e., grape, strawberry), the positioning theme was "Bright

Colors, Powerful Taste." The tag line used in advertising was "Taste Buds, Fasten Your Seat Belts.

Advertising/Promotion Objectives/Strategy: Two objectives in priority order were set for the advertising/promotion effort

1. Solidify bottler relationships.
2. Communicate the new positioning.

The strategy emphasis was principally "push" with a heavy emphasis on bottler and retail promotions. Secondary emphasis was placed on consumer (media) advertising.

Budgeting: Consistent with objectives and strategy, spending for consumer (media) advertising and promotions were:

Consumer (Media) Advertising	$2,220,000
Promotion (bottler/retail)	35¢/case

Projected Volume: The projected volume for orange CRUSH was 30,000,000 cases.

Orange CRUSH achieved case sales of 27.6 million cases -- some 2.4 million cases short of projected volume. Orange CRUSH did not cannibalize SUNKIST; incremental volume came mostly from regional brands. No information on the breakdown between diet and regular beverages was available.

The relaunch of the CRUSH brand of fruit-flavored carbonated beverages was deemed a marketing and financial success by Cadbury Beverages. Since total orange category sales remained at about 315 million cases, orange CRUSH increased its overall share from 8 percent to 8.8 percent, which represented a 10 percent increase in market share. Efforts to sustain this share continue with marginal increases in consumer advertising as market (bottler) coverage grows and continued emphasis on the bottling network ("push" strategy).

The year following the successful relaunch of CRUSH, Kim Feil was given responsibility for the CRUSH line in Canada as well as the United States. In early 1992, her attention was directed toward rebuilding the HIRES and SUN-DROP soft drink brands which were also successful. In 1993, Kim Feil was promoted to Vice President, Orange and Citrus Beverages at Cadbury Beverages where she was responsible for more than a $150 million business.

In 1995, Cadbury Schweppes PLC acquired Dr. Pepper/7Up. Kim Feil was promoted to Senior Vice President at Cadbury Beverages and was responsible for all Cadbury soft drinks, except Dr. Pepper, in North America.

I. Summary Points

1. This case illustrates two major responsibilities of product managers in consumer goods firms:

   • Product (brand) positioning

   • Advertising and promotion planning

2. Developing an advertising and promotion program often involves a strategic assessment of a firm's competitive environment and current operations. This assessment can provide guidance in developing a positioning strategy which in turn can be conveyed through creative marketing communications.

3. Effective budgeting of advertising and promotion dollars begins with objective setting followed by strategy formulation. In other words, budgeting should be grounded in the **objective-task approach** to resource allocation.

4. "Push" and "Pull" advertising and promotion strategies are often integrated and coordinated when formulating an overall communications program:

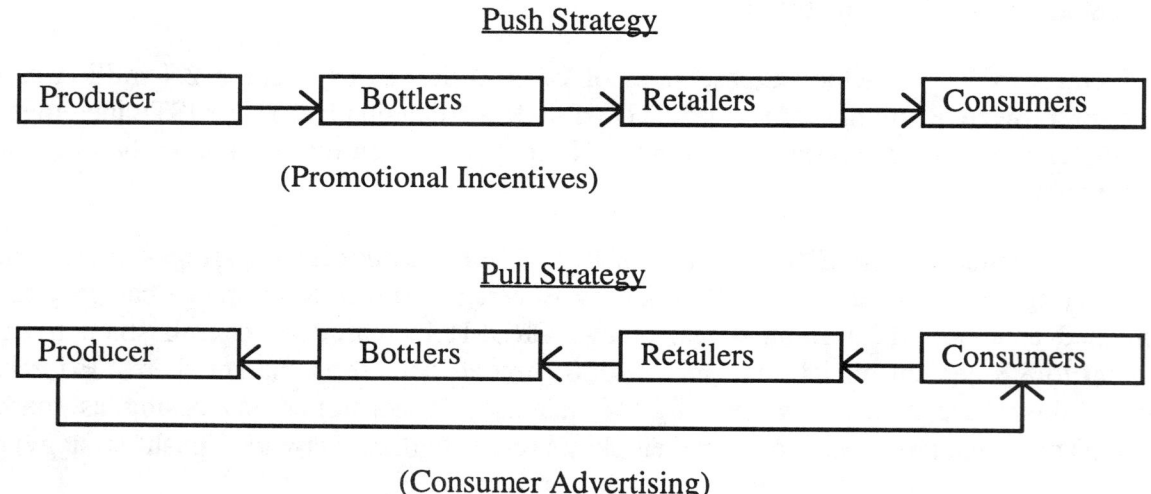

"Push" is more important than "Pull" in terms of dollars spent in the soft drink industry.

5. A pro forma income statement is a tangible representation of an intended strategy in action. It reflects a manager's expectation (sales) given certain inputs (expenses) and should be based on the strategic realities.

DRYPERS CORPORATION: NATIONAL TELEVISION ADVERTISING CAMPAIGN

Synopsis

In 1997, senior executives at Drypers Corporation were discussing the merits of spending upwards of $10 million on national television advertising in 1998 for its Drypers brand of disposable diapers and training pants. The national television advertising effort was significant for two reasons. First, the company had not used television advertising in its 10-year history. Second, a $10 million expenditure represented a 33 percent increase in the company's combined 1997 advertising and promotion budget and a tripling of advertising expenditures.

The case describes the U.S. disposable diaper and training pant market, Drypers Corporation competitive position in this market, and the company's rationale for investing $10 million in national television advertising, expressed in different ways. The students' task is to examine the pros and cons of the national television advertising campaign for Drypers Corporation in light of its competitive position and corporate objective: To achieve full U.S. distribution of Drypers brand diapers and training pants. In this context, students are expected to consider the short- and long-run sales and brand-building effect and profit impact of this strategic initiative.

A unique feature of this case is the follow-on case — **Drypers Corporation: 1998 Year-end Review** — which appears at the end of this note. The 1998 Year-end Review briefly describes the marketing and financial position of Drypers Corporation following the initiatives pursued in 1998. Students are expected to evaluate the success of the national television advertising campaign and make an advertising expenditure recommendation for 1999 given these results.

Teaching Objectives

This case has four teaching objectives:

1. To expose students to the challenges that face a small company when competing in a market dominated by giants.

2. To allow students to judge whether an advertising opportunity exists for Drypers-brand diapers and training pants and examine how a change in communications strategy emphasis will help a company achieve its corporate objective of achieving full U.S. distribution of its products.

3. To provide students an opportunity to discuss the short- and long-run term sales and brand-building effect and profit impact of a first-time national television advertising campaign.

4. To give students an opportunity to assess the results of a national television advertising campaign and make a subsequent recommendation for future investments.

Teaching Suggestions

This two-part case assignment is best suited for that portion of the course that focuses on marketing communications strategy and management. The case has been used in both graduate and undergraduate classes with equal success.

The case can be taught alone using the follow-on case an as Epilogue. However, best results are achieved when both cases are used. A recommended approach for using both cases in an 75-minute class period is to assign the text case for class discussion. The discussion should last about 40 minutes, during which the major student views and case issues can be fleshed out. Students will be initially in favor of the national television advertising idea, until a more in-depth analysis highlights short-run profitability concerns. The second case can then be distributed to the class. After about five to ten minutes, the instructor can ask students to judge the success of the national television advertising campaign and decide whether or not to continue the program and subsequent implications. The Epilogue at the end of this note describes events and financial results through 1999. The case can be taught over two days in a 50-minute class period.

Different approaches for beginning the case discussion are possible. A straightforward approach is to ask the class the following question: "Should Drypers Corporation invest $10 million in a national television campaign in 1998? All those in favor . . ." Most students favor spending the money. This questions can then be followed by another question: "What do you think is the short- and long-run sales and brand-building effect and profit impact of this initiative?"

Alternatively, an instructor might begin the class by asking a student to give an overview of the marketing environment and the company's competitive position in the context of a SWOT analysis (see Exhibit 1 in this note). With this approach, the following questions can be posed to the class either before or during a class discussion:

1. How would you characterize the U.S. disposable diaper and training your market?

2. How would you characterize the Drypers Corporation competitive position and marketing effort in the U.S. disposable diaper and training pant market? What might a SWOT analysis look like?

3. Is there an advertising opportunity for Drypers brand?

4. Is the $10 million expenditure for a national television advertising campaign too high, too low, or about right? Why?

5. What is your assessment of the short- and long-term sales and brand-building effect and profit impact of the national television advertising campaign?

Areas for Discussion/Analysis

A. How would you characterize the U.S. disposable diaper and training pant market?

1. The U.S. disposable diaper and training pant market has recorded modest dollar sales growth since 1994, with training (and youth) pants showing a higher growth rate than diapers (see case Exhibit 1). **Primary demand is not strong.** The number of infants (birth to 30 months) and children (18 months to 8 years) is not increasing.

2. Two major premium-priced branded manufacturers (P&G and Kimberly-Clark) account for a growing share of the disposable diaper and training pant market, reaching a combined dollar market share of 78.9 percent in 1997 (see case Exhibit 2). Private labels account for a dollar market share of 16.1 percent (see case Exhibit 3). Drypers Corporation — described as a value-priced branded manufacturer — captured about a 3.1 percent dollar market share.

3. Grocery stores, mass-merchant, and drug stores represent the principal distribution channels for disposable diapers and training pants. While grocery stores account for the majority of sales in 1997, their share has declined since 1994. Mass-merchants have increased their percent-of-sales shares since 1994. The percent-of-sales breakdown by channel for 1994 and 1997 is shown below:

Marketing Channel	Percent-of-Sales in:	
	1994	**1997**
Grocery store	60%	51.2%
Mass merchant	30%	39.4%
Drug store	10%	9.2%
"Other"	--%	.2%

4. Kimberly-Clark seems to have benefited from this sales change in distribution channels. It has a 41.8 percent share of the mass merchant-drug store channel compared with P&G's 39.4 percent. Kimberly-Clark is also the market share leader in grocery stores.

It would seem that distribution coverage is an important driver of sales and market share for disposable diapers and training pants. Kimberly-Clark and P&G presently sell their products in stores that account for over 90 percent of U.S. diaper and training pant sales.

5. Based on data given in case Exhibit 1, average retail prices in the disposable diaper market have been unchanged for the most part since 1994. The average retail prices for training pants has actually decreased from $.50/unit in 1994 to $.42/unit in 1997.

6. Training pants appear to be driving the modest sales growth that exists in the U.S. market. Kimberly-Clark pioneered this product-market and presently commands a 77 percent market share, on a unit volume basis.

B. How would you characterize Drypers Corporation competitive position and marketing effort in the U.S. disposable diaper and training pant market? What might a SWOT analysis look like?

1. At this juncture in the class discussion, an instructor might ask students to prepare a SWOT analysis for Drypers Corporation. An illustrative SWOT analysis is shown in Exhibit 1 in this note.

2. Drypers Corporation is the third largest marketer of brand-name disposable diapers in the U.S. Its Drypers brand is the fourth largest selling diaper brand. Drypers Corporation's dollar market share in the U.S. disposable diaper and training pant market is 3.1 percent.

3. The company markets branded and private-label products for both domestic (U.S.) and international use. Domestic sales accounted for two-thirds of company sales. However, total company sales growth is primarily due to a rise in international sales made possible by Wal-Mart. Drypers Corporation is the exclusive private-label supplier to Wal-Mart in Latin America and also sells its Drypers brand through Wal-Mart in Latin America.

4. The company sells its products almost exclusively in the grocery store channel. Its brands captured a 6.4 percent dollar market share and a 6.6 percent unit market share in the grocery channel in 1997. Moreover, it markets through grocery stores that represented 66 percent of the total U.S. grocery store market for disposable diapers and training pants. Three items are worth noting in this regard:

   a. Drypers Corporation has a respectable, though limited relative distribution coverage in a marketing channel that is declining as a retail source for disposable diapers and training pants; namely grocery stores.

EXHIBIT 1

DRYPERS CORPORATION: SWOT ANALYSIS

Strengths

- Proven product innovation/augmentation skills – Drypers offers a differentiated product.

- Close ties with Wal-Mart: exclusive private label supplier in Latin America.

- A strong customer value proposition: unique product benefits featuring skin care at price points 40% lower than major premium-priced branded manufacturers.

Weaknesses

- Limited distribution coverage in U.S. grocery stores, relative to P&G and Kimberly-Clark, where 51.2% of diaper sales occur.

- No meaningful presence in the mass-merchant channel where diapers and training pant sales are growing.

- Smaller and likely weaker financial position than major premium-priced diaper marketers.

Opportunities

- Capitalize on licensing agreement to use Sesame Street trademark and characters on Drypers' products, packaging, and advertising.

- Conversion of regional diaper brands to Drypers lable (1995-1996) provides opportunity to gain economies of scale in production, marketing and servicing large mass merchants.

Threats

- Grocery store channel, where Drypers principally markets its products, is declining as a retail source for diapers and training pants.

- Premium-priced manufacturers (P&G and Kimberly-Clark) are growing in market share dominance.

b. Drypers Corporation's 66 percent distribution coverage in grocery stores, which account for 51.2 percent of total U.S. diaper and training pant sales, means that the company only reaches about 33.8 percent of the total market (66% x 51.2% = 33.79%).

c. If Drypers Corporation is to grow sales, it must
   ... increase its market share in current grocery stores,
   ... achieve a higher penetration in the grocery store channel
       (i.e., add more grocery store chains), and /or
   ... broaden its distribution channels to include mass-merchants.

It is therefore understandable that Drypers Corporation has a stated corporate objective: "To achieve full U.S. distribution of diapers and training pants."

5. An instructor might ask the class how increased distribution coverage translates to higher market share (and sales) by posing the question:

> Let's say Drypers keeps the same market share, about 6.5%, it has in its current grocery stores, but increases its distribution coverage from 66 percent to 70 percent of the total grocery market for diapers and training pants. What will be its market share of the grocery store channel?

The answer can be arrived at using the following expression, and solving for "X:"

$$\frac{6.5\% \text{ (Current Share in Grocery Channel)}}{66.0\% \text{ (Current Distribution Coverage in Grocery Channel)}} = \frac{X}{70.0\%}$$

Solving for "X," Drypers Corporation's grocery store channel market share will be 6.89 percent:

$$(6.5)(70.0) = (66)(X)$$
$$6.89 = X, \text{ or } 6.89\%$$

Using the same approach, if Drypers Corporation achieves 90 percent distribution coverage of grocery stores, like P&G and Kimberly-Clark, and simply retains its current share within stores, its share of the grocery market channel will increase to 8.9 percent.

6. The company's marketing effort to date is sketched in Exhibit 2 in this note. Product differentiation has been the centerpiece of Drypers' market effort. Its focus on skin care vs. diaper absorbency, linkage control coupled with price points that are 40 percent lower than P&G and Kimberly Clark for comparable items, suggest a potentially powerful customer value proposition.

EXHIBIT 2

OVERVIEW OF DRYPERS CORPORATION MARKETING EFFORT

- Product — Emphasis on product development / augmentation. The focus on skin care vs. absorbency, etc. in diapers reflects this orientation.

- Pricing — "Value-priced" relative to premium-priced branded manufacturers (P&G, Kimberly-Clark). (Suggested) retail prices are often 40% lower than premium-priced brands.

- Distribution — Primarily in grocery stores; some placement in other channels. Growing international distribution, principally through exclusive private-label agreement with Wal-Mart.

- Advertising/Promotion — Advertising/promotion (A/P) is skewed toward in-store promotions, and consumer promotions (coupons, sampling). Of the $30 million spent for A/P, only 10.7% is spent on advertising, principally print (magazine, newspaper) and cooperative advertising.

This focus has resulted in the sales growth of the Drypers brand. Even though the Drypers brand has accounted for declining percentage of total company net sales (61.3% in 1995; 62.3% in 1996; 52.3% in 1997), absolute dollar sales has increased as shown below (given case information):

Year	Total Company Net Sales ($ Mil.)	Drypers Brand Percentage	Drypers Brand Dollar Sales ($ Mil.)
1995	$163.9	61.3%	$100.5
1996	$207.0	62.3%	$129.0
1997	$287.0	52.3%	$150.1

It should be noted, however, that sales attributed to the Drypers brand also reflects the conversion of regional diaper brands to the Drypers brand name. Therefore, a portion of the growth in Drypers brand sales, at least between 1995 and 1996 when the conversion was underway, simply reflects a relabeling of brands. This issue is addressed again later in this note. Furthermore, as shown in case Exhibit 5, the company's stock price has increased in 1996 and 1997, suggesting that the financial community believes the company's marketing efforts and results are creating value for shareholders (as well for customers).

Nevertheless, limited distribution coverage and limited advertising support, relative to P&G and Kimberly Clark, remain problematic for the company. It is therefore understandable why the company has chosen to invest in one element of its marketing program to improve another: invest in advertising to build distribution.

C. Is there an advertising opportunity for Drypers brand?

1. The purpose of this question is to focus student attention on what appears to be an emphasis shift toward a "pull" communication strategy for the Drypers brand. In fact, the quote on the first page of the case is a classic description of the reasoning behind a pull strategy to build distribution:

> [Television] advertising will build consumer awareness for Drypers as a national brand that stands for quality and innovation. Awareness will boost demand, and increased demand will yield three important results. One, we will increase our penetration of grocery outlets. Two, increased grocery penetration will help mass merchants see us in a new light and help us break into this all-important retail channel. And three, we will move away from higher-cost, promotion-driven sales to brand-driven sales.

2. The success of a pull communication strategy, depends in part, on whether or not an advertising opportunity exists for the Drypers brand. Chapter 6 identifies four criteria for judging whether or not an advertising opportunity exists:

Criteria	Assessment
• Favorable primary demand for a product (service) category.	• As noted earlier, primary demand is not strong.
• The offering advertised can be significantly differentiated from its competitors.	• Drypers has differentiated its products, with the addition of Aloe Vera and baking soda to its diapers.
• The offering has hidden qualities or benefits that can be portrayed effectively through advertising.	• Drypers focus on skin care is a distinct benefit.
• There are strong, emotional buying motives involved.	• Concern for an infant's comfort is a powerful buying motive.

    3.   Clearly, there is advertising opportunity for Drypers brand.

D. Is the $10 million expenditure for a national television campaign too high, too low, or about right? Why?

    1.   This question is designed to elicit a more fundamental question: Too high, low, or about right relative to what? Astute students will quickly recognize that the "correctness" of the $10 million expenditure can be viewed from two different budgeting perspectives outlined in Chapter 6: (a) the objective-task approach, and (b) the competitive-parity approach.

    2.   The **objective-task approach** focuses on (a) the objective(s) to be achieved with the national television advertising campaign, (b) the tasks needed to attain the objectives, and (c) the costs associated with the performance of the tasks. It is instructive to develop an objective-strategy hierarchy to organize the class discussion. As an example:

- **Corporate Objective:**   To achieve full U.S. distribution of Drypers diapers and training pants. [Note: This objective does not have a time frame, e.g., "in 1998," or "within __ years."]

- **Advertising Objective:**   Build [consumer/retailer] brand awareness / recognition to increase distribution of Drypers-branded products to increase sales in the second half of 1998.

- **Advertising Strategy:** Pull strategy with an emphasis on national television advertising to communicate Drypers-brand value proposition.

- **Media Strategy:** Blitz strategy, concentrating national television advertising in the first 6-months of 1998.

- **Budget:** An estimated $40 million with $30 million devoted to promotions, coupons, sampling, etc. and $10 million designated for national television advertising.

3. The **competitive-parity approach** seeks to achieve some parity in communication expenditures with competitors. P&G and Kimberly-Clark maintain parity in expenditures, spending $75.6 million and $69.6 million, respectively, for media advertising in 1997. More specifically, these two competitors spend almost identical amounts on a per-share point basis for media advertising:

Kimberly-Clark:

$$\frac{\$75.6 \text{ mil. for 1997 media advertising}}{41.2 \text{ market share pts. (Case Exh. 2)}} = \$1.835 \text{ mil. per share point}$$

P&G:

$$\frac{\$69.6 \text{ mil. for 1997 media advertising}}{37.7 \text{ market share pts. (Case Exh. 2)}} = \$1.846 \text{ mil. per share point}$$

By comparison, Drypers Corporation spent much less for advertising on a per-share point basis.

Drypers Corp.:

$$\frac{\$3.219 \text{ mil. for 1997 advertising}}{3.1 \text{ market share pts.}} = \$1.038 \text{ mil. per share point}$$

It is important to recognize that Kimberly-Clark and P&G media advertising is not necessarily focused on building brand awareness and distribution. Both companies sell their well-known brands and products in stores that account for over 90 percent of U.S. diaper and training pant sales. These competitors focus their advertising on building market share (brand preference) within marketing channels. The objective-task is very different for Drypers Corporation.

4. The challenge facing Drypers Corporation is building brand awareness and distribution coverage. It is obvious that Drypers Corporation cannot match P&G and Kimberly-Clark media advertising expenditures in absolute dollar terms. However, it is reasonable to consider an equivalent spending level on a per-share basis (see above). As described earlier, increased distribution coverage will increase market share. If Drypers Corporation spends, say $1.84 million per share point, it is possible to calculate what this means in terms of needed share. Using the $10 million expenditure, Drypers Corporation projected overall market share in the U.S. diaper and training pant market will be 5.43 percent:

$$\frac{\$10 \text{ Million Advertising Expenditure}}{X} = \$1.84 \text{ mil. per share point}$$

Where X = total U.S. diaper and training pant market share point.

Solving for X, Drypers Corporation market share will be 5.43 percent (compared to an overall market share of 3.1 percent in 1997). This overall market share translates to a grocery store market share of 10.6 percent, as calculated below since grocery stores account for 51.2 percent of total industry sales:

$$\frac{5.43 \ (\% \text{ total U.S. market share})}{51.2 \ (\% \text{ of diaper/training pant sales sold in U.S. grocery stores})} = 10.6 \text{ percent}$$

For comparison, Drypers Corporation currently commands 6.4% to 6.6% of diaper and training pant sales in the U.S. grocery store channel.

5. In short, equivalent spending by Drypers Corporation translates to an increase in total market share and an increase in the grocery market share. A major issue is the speed at which awareness will boost demand and demand will increase penetration of grocery outlets — the announced expectation for the $10 million television advertising program.

6. Another perspective is that Drypers Corporation will have to spend more for market share than competitors and probably get slightly less in return, at least in the short-run. That is, some multiple of $1.84 million per share point will be necessary. As an example, Drypers Corporation might have to spend the equivalent of 1-1/2 times what P&G and Kimberly-Clark are spending, or $2.76 million per share point. Using the previous calculation, this means if Drypers Corporation spends $10 million, it can project an overall market share of 3.62 percent ($10 million / x = $2.76 million per share point; x = 3.62%). This converts to a market share in the grocery store channel of 7 percent (3.62 / 51.2 = 7%). The 7 percent market share seems more attainable than 10.6 percent.

7. In summary, the $10 million advertising expenditure seems "about right." More might be better. However, $10 million could be all that Drypers Corporation can afford. Without having any previous experience to determine what the sales response function might be, $10 million is probably a good number.

E. What is your assessment of the short- and long-term sales and brand-building effect and profit impact of the national television advertising campaign?

1. At this juncture in the class discussion, there is a general sentiment that the national television advertising campaign has merit and the $10 million expenditure is reasonable from a marketing perspective.

2. It is suggested that a student be called upon to summarize the argument for the initiative. Important points to touch upon include the following:

   a. Drypers Corporation needs to increase its distribution coverage in order to build market share.

   b. There appears to be an advertising opportunity for the Drypers brand.

   c. Television advertising should improve Drypers brand awareness, particularly in areas where regional brands were converted to the Drypers labels.

   d. Commitment to a $10 million national television advertising campaign by Drypers Corporation is likely to be welcome by existing distributors (grocery stores) and be viewed favorably by new grocery store chains that are considering stocking the Drypers brand.

   e. Drypers Corporation's prior marketing efforts have generated favorable marketing and financial results in 1997. The time is right to act given the momentum.

   f. A reasonable projection of market share for the total U.S. diaper and training pant with a $10 million expenditure for a national advertising campaign lies between 3.62 percent and 5.43 percent. This share is equivalent to a market share projection of 7 percent to 10.6 percent of the grocery store market.

3. A national television advertising campaign is certainly likely to create consumer awareness and trial. This **blitz media strategy** — television advertising is in the first six months of 1998 — is consistent with short-run sales growth.

4. Long-term sales growth and brand-building effects arising from the national television advertising campaign are less apparent. Both are more to occur *if* distribution coverage increases. In this regard, the $10 million expenditure is truly an investment. However, the matter of continuousness or sustainability of advertising needs to be addressed. Is a one-time investment sufficient?

5. The profit-impact of investing $10 million in a national television advertising campaign over and above ongoing promotional programs is likely to have a short-term negative effect on company profitability, particularly in the first two quarters of 1998. Since, the $10 million expense represents an incremental cost, it is possible to calculate how much

Drypers brand sales need to increase to recoup the expense in 1998. An approximate sales increase can be calculated by dividing the incremental $10 million expenditure by Drypers Corporation's 1997 gross profit margin of 38.8 percent (from Case Exhibit 4):

$$\text{Incremental Drypers Brand Sales To Recoup Advertising Expense} = \frac{\$10,000,000}{.388} = \$25,773,195$$

Since Drypers brand sales were $150.1 million in 1997, sales will need to increase 17.17 percent ($25.78 mil. ÷ $150.1 mil. = .17168) to recoup the expense. If sales do not increase by this amount, then Drypers Corporation's operating income will decrease, other things being equal. Note that Drypers brand sales increased 16.3 percent between 1996 and 1997.

6. It is reasonable to speculate that Drypers Corporation could incur a short-run decline in profit, compared to 1997, if the national television advertising campaign is implemented. An instructor may wish to point out that this is an immediate price to pay for expanded distribution coverage which has long-term benefits.

F. Summary Points

1. Creative marketing is needed to successfully compete in a market dominated by giants. An impactful customer value proposition is a necessary, though not always a sufficient requirement for success.

2. Advertising can play an important role in communicating a customer value proposition, provided an advertising opportunity exists:

- Favorable primary demand for a product (service) category.
- The offering advertised can be significantly differentiated from competitors.
- The offering has hidden qualities or benefits that can be portrayed effectively through advertising.
- There are strong, emotional buying motives involved.

3. Advertising can also be used to build distribution and improve trade (channel) relations. For Drypers Corporation, advertising assumed strategic importance as a **means** toward an **end**: To achieve full U.S. distribution of Drypers brand diapers and training pants. In this regard, advertising can be viewed as an investment, not simply an expense.

4. Determination of a communications (advertising) budget is not easy. In this case, combining the objective-task approach and the competitive parity approach provided helpful guidance.

5. When judging the merits of an advertising campaign, consideration needs to be given the short-and long-run sales and brand-building effect and profit impact of the initiative. Short-run sales and profit impact are much easier to measure than long-run sales and brand-building effects.

DRYPERS CORPORATION: 1998 Year-end Review

Follow-on Case

The short follow-on case at the end of this note details the 1998 year-end marketing and financial results of the initiatives described in the text case. Drypers Corporation did spend an incremental $10,383,000 for a national television campaign in 1998.

The following questions can be posed to students after they have read the case and digested its contents:

1. How would you judge the impact of the national television advertising campaign?

2. Should Drypers Corporation again spend $10 million for national television advertising in 1999? Why or why not?

Areas for Discussion/Analysis

A. How would you judge the impact of the national television advertising campaign?

1. Students should immediately note that the national television advertising campaign yielded several favorable results:

   a. Domestic sales increased 11.7 percent from 1997 to 1998 — a growth rate that was more than triple the 3.4 percent market growth rate. This growth in domestic sales also compares favorably with the company's domestic sales increase of 6.8 percent between 1996 and 1997. However, company domestic sales increased 16 percent between 1995-1996.

   b. Drypers brand sales, while decreasing as a percent of overall company sales (52.3% in 1997; 47.6% in 1998), actually increased in dollar amount:

Year	Total Company Net Sales ($ Mil.)	Drypers Brand Percentage	Drypers Brand Dollar Sales ($ Mil.)
1997	$287.0	52.3%	$150.1
1998	$332.6	47.6%	$158.3

   However, the annual percentage increase of 5.5 percent was considerably lower than annual percentage increases since 1995.

   c. Drypers brand unaided awareness increased a reported 67 percent. The advertising campaign did increase brand awareness as intended. It is important to note however that the base brand awareness percentage upon which the increase is reported is not given in the case.

- d. Drypers Corporation distribution coverage in the grocery channel increased from 66 percent in 1997 to 71 percent in 1998, consistent with announced intention of the advertising campaign. Furthermore, Wal-Mart and K-Mart agreed to initiate distribution tests of the Drypers brand thus representing initial penetration of the mass merchant channel. Penetration of the mass merchant channel was an intended effect of the national television advertising program.

- e. The Drypers Corporation market share in the grocery store channel was estimated to be 7.7 percent by year-end 1988 — up from 6.4 to 6.6 percent in 1997. Again, the advertising campaign appears to have yielded positive results.

- f. Drypers Corporation gross margin also increased from 38.8 percent in 1997 to 40.8 percent in 1998.

2. Students should also acknowledge the unfavorable profit impact from the national television campaign. This profit impact could have been anticipated based on the previous case analysis. Specific financial results include the following:

- a. The domestic sales increase and the growth in sales of the Drypers brand were less than that required to "breakeven" on the incremental advertising expenditure.

- b. Therefore, it is not surprising that Drypers Corporation recorded an operating profit decline in 1998. Students might calculate the actual operating income from Exhibit 1A for 1997 and 1998. They will report a 1997 operating income of $21.52 million and a 1998 operating income of $11.97 million: a difference of $9.55 million.

- c. The quarterly stock price for Drypers Corporation has evidenced a downward trend during 1998. The 1998 fourth quarter high stock price was $3.00, compared with a 1997 fourth quarter stock price of $9.00. Clearly, the stock market has not looked favorably upon short-term Drypers Corporation performance (earnings). To the extent that stock valuation reflects the "market's" future expectations, the downward trend is even more troublesome. An instructor might ask students to give their interpretation of the decline in stock price.

B. Should Drypers Corporation again spend $10 million for national television advertising in 1999? Why or why not?

    1. An immediate and easy response to this question is no. The announced expectations for the advertising campaign were realized: increased brand awareness and increased distribution coverage in both the grocery and mass merchant channel.

    2. It may be appropriate to gather the fruits of the advertising effort, before again making another investment. Besides, Wal-Mart and K-Mart have agreed to initiate distribution tests of the Drypers brand in the U.S., thus further increasing distribution coverage in the mass merchant channel. In short, the reasoning behind the national television advertising campaign proved to have validity. As stated on p. 1 of the text case:

> [Television] advertising will build consumer awareness for Drypers as a national brand that stands for quality and innovation. Awareness will boost demand, and increased demand will yield three important results. One, we will increase our penetration of grocery outlets. Two, increased grocery penetration will help mass merchants see us in a new light and help us break into this all-important retail channel. And three, we will move away from higher-cost, promotion-driven sales to brand-driven sales.

Furthermore, Drypers Corporation recorded a decline in operating profit, which is not surprising given the previous analysis.

    3. On the other hand, an argument can be made for continuing the national television advertising. The quote from Terry Togrietti, Drypers Corporation co-CEO and President is applicable here:

> "What mass merchandisers want to see is that your product will move off the shelf on its own with little promotion, versus having them move it off the shelf for you."

This suggests that continuous advertising is important. Grocery stores and mass merchants can delist a brand/product just as easily as stocking it if product isn't moving off the shelf. Also, a one-shot advertising campaign is not necessarily consistent with a brand-building effort.

    4. As a practical matter, it is probably unlikely that Drypers Corporation can afford another investment of $10 million dollars in national television advertising given its financial condition at 1998 year-end.

C. Epilogue: 1999

Drypers Corporation did not again spend $10 million for a national television advertising campaign in 1999. Instead, advertising and promotion spending returned to "normal" levels (as a percent of sales) and normal channels (print, couponing, sampling, etc.), with no television advertising at all.

In November 1999, Drypers Corporation announced that it would discontinue its Drypers Supreme with Germ Guard baby diaper. This product was introduced in October 1998 as part of the 1998 Business Plan. Drypers Antibacterial Baby Wipes with Germ Guard is still sold.

Progress toward the company's announced objective of achieving full U.S. distribution for diapers and training pants was made in 1999. By 1999 year-end, the company had distribution in grocery stores representing 76 percent of all grocery channel diaper and training pant sales, compared with 71 percent at 1998 year-end. Furthermore, K-Mart and Wal-Mart elected to stock the Drypers brand in their U.S. stores in 1999. This meant that the company had distribution coverage that represented 43 percent of all mass merchant diaper and training pant sales in 1999.

DRYPERS CORPORATION: 1998 YEAR-END REVIEW

In early 1999, Drypers Corporation executives convened to review the year-end marketing and financial results of the initiatives pursued in 1998. A top-line marketing item on the agenda was the national television advertising campaign. The company spent $10,383,000 for advertising in 1998 versus $3,219,000 in 1997.

Performance Overview

Drypers Corporation reported record net sales for the year-ended December 31, 1998. Net sales increased 15.9 percent to $332.6 million from net sales of $287.0 million for the year-ended December 31, 1997. Domestic sales increased 11.7 percent; international sales increased 24.2 percent over the previous year. The company's domestic and international net sales for each of the past three years is shown below:

	1996		1997		1998	
			(dollars in millions)			
Domestic*	$179.2	86.6%	$191.3	66.7%	$213.7	64.3%
International	27.8	13.4	95.7	33.3	118.9	35.7
Total Net Sales	$207.0	100.0%	$287.0	100.0%	$332.6	100.0%

*Domestic sales include the United States, Puerto Rico, and exports from these manufacturing operations.

This case was prepared by Professor Roger A. Kerin, Southern Methodist University, as a basis for class discussion and is not designed to illustrate effective or ineffective handling of an administrative situation. This case is based on published sources, including the Drypers Corporation annual reports, U.S. Securities and Exchange Commission Form 10-K and 10-Q reports, and company news releases. The information presented in the case does not necessarily depict the explicit situation faced by Drypers Corporation, but is introduced only for class discussion purposes. Where appropriate quotes, statistics, and published information are footnoted for reference purposes. Copyright © 1999 Roger A. Kerin. No part of this case may be reproduced without written permission of the copyright holder.

Marketing and Distribution Performance

The company attributed the record net sales to the initiatives outlined in its 1998 business plan.[1] For example, in October, 1998, Drypers Corporation introduced two new product innovations, Drypers Supreme with Germ Guard and Drypers Antibacterial Baby Wipes with Germ Guard. The national television advertising campaign was credited with increasing Drypers brand unaided brand awareness by 67 percent and increasing the company's distribution coverage in the grocery store channel. By year-end 1998, the company's distribution coverage had increased to 71 percent of the total grocery store market for disposable diapers and training pants, from 66 percent in 1997. Expanded grocery store distribution included two East Coast chains, Giant and Hannaford Bros.; Drypers was also being tested in Food Lion, a major southeastern grocery store chain. At year-end 1998, Drypers Corporation market share in the grocery store channel was estimated to be 7.7 percent compared with 6.4 percent to 6.6 percent in 1997. The company's Drypers premium brand diapers and training pants represented 47.6 percent of total net sales in 1998, compared with 52.3 percent in 1997.

The company's sales results were achieved despite a low 3.4 percent overall growth in retail dollar sales in the U.S. disposable diaper and training and youth pant market. Disposable diaper retail sales in 1998 increased 2.17 percent over 1997 levels; training and youth pant retail dollar sales increased almost 16 percent between 1997 and 1998.

Progress was made toward obtaining distribution through mass-merchants, both domestically and internationally. Wal-Mart and K-Mart agreed to initiate distribution tests of the Drypers brand in the United States. Also, Wal-Mart has expanded distribution of Drypers

---

[1] "Drypers Reports Record Net Sales for Fourth Quarter and Year," Company News Release, February 19, 1999; "Drypers Expands International Distribution with Wal-Mart," Company News Release, February 19, 1999.

branded and private label products in Canada, Germany, and China in addition to Argentina, Brazil, Mexico, Puerto Rico and Asia. Finally, Drypers Corporation announced it had acquired Primosoft Sdn Bhd, a Malaysian manufacturer of diapers in September, 1998.

Less promising results were registered from the new line of detergent products. Drypers Corporation reconsidered its plans for these operations following an operating loss of $1.2 million and the operation was discontinued. Nevertheless, in summing up the year, Walter V. Klemp, Drypers Corporation Chairman and co-CEO said, "We are beginning to see the payoff from the strategic actions we took in 1998."

Financial Performance

Drypers Corporation operating income decreased $9.6 million to $11.9 million for the year-ended December 31, 1998 from $21.5 million for 1997. Operating income, as a percent of net sales was 3.6 percent in 1998, compared with 7.5 percent in 1997. Income from continuing operations, as a percentage of net sales, decreased from 4.1 percent in 1997 as well. The company's investment in the laundry detergent business, along with the 1998 operating loss, is presented as a discontinued operation in the consolidated statement of earnings for the year-ended December 31, 1998 (see Exhibit 1-A). Drypers Corporation recorded a consolidated net loss from continuing operations of $8,125,000 in 1998, compared with a net profit of $1,675,000 in 1997.

Exhibit 1-B and 1-C shows Drypers Corporation unaudited quarterly financial data and stock prices for 1997 and 1998. According to Walter Klemp, "As we continue to build domestic distribution and international market penetration, we expect to see substantial earnings improvements for 1999."

Drypers Corporation Year End and Quarterly Financial Data: 1997 and 1998

A: Abbreviated Income Statements: 1997-1998
(Expressed as a percentage of net sales)

	Year Ended December 31	
	1997	1998
Net sales	100.0%	100.0%
Cost of goods sold	61.2	59.2
Gross profit	38.8	40.8
Selling, general and administrative expenses	31.3	37.2
Operating income	7.5	3.6
Interest expense, net	3.5	5.0
Other income	0.1	1.3
Income (loss) from continuing operations before income tax Provision and extraordinary item	4.1	(0.1)
Income tax provision	0.8	0.4
Extraordinary item	(2.7)	-
Income (loss) from continuing operations	0.6	(0.5)
Discontinued operations	-	(1.9)
Net income (loss)	0.6%	(2.4)%

B: Quarterly Financial Data (Unaudited): 1997-1998
($ thousands)

	First Quarter	Second Quarter	Third Quarter	Fourth Quarter	Total
1997					
Net sales	$ 60,161	$ 72,551	$ 80,086	$ 74,212	$ 287,010
Gross profit	23,405	27,568	31,701	28,791	111,465
Income before extraordinary item	1,973	2,183	2,750	2,538	9,444
Net income (loss)	1,973	(5,586)[a]	2,750	2,538	1,675
1998[b]					
Net sales	$ 78,592	$80,302	$ 85,841	$ 87,905	$ 332,640
Gross profit	31,343	33,003	33,473	37,836	135,655
Income (loss) from continuing operations	(5,455)	1,259	1,519	1,023	(1,654)
Net income (loss)	(5,669)	1,099	701	(4,256)	(8,125)

[a] Includes a noncash extraordinary expense of $3,745,000 for the write-off of capitalized debt issuance costs and a cash extraordinary expense of $4,024,000 for prepayment and other fees in connection with the early extinguishment of debt.

[b] Net sales, gross profit, income (loss) and earnings (loss) per share from continuing operations for the first, second and third quarters of 1998 have been restated to reflect the discontinued operations of the Company's laundry detergent business. This resulted in a one-time charge of $6,471,000 in 1998.

C: Quarterly Common Stock Price: 1997-1998

	1997		1998	
	High	Low	High	Low
Quarter -				
First	$4.75	$3.63	$6.64	$6.29
Second	7.75	3.88	7.13	6.82
Third	7.94	6.13	4.58	4.25
Fourth	9.00	5.13	3.03	2.83

Source: Drypers Corporation, U.S. Securities and Exchange Commission, Form 10-K, 1998, at pp. 15, 50

PRICE WATERHOUSE

Synopsis

Price Waterhouse (PW) is the sixth largest public accounting firm in the United States and is considered to be the most prestigious. PW has the distinction of listing more *Fortune 100* firms among its clients than any other U.S. public accounting firm. In 1990, PW operated 100 offices in the U.S. and had a total of 400 offices in 13 countries and territories worldwide.

Like other public accounting firms in the 1980s, PW expanded its service mix to position itself as a full-service financial counselor for its clients. In early 1990, PW created the Corporate Finance Group (CFG). CFG, composed mostly of corporate finance specialists, was formed to provide investment banking-related services to "middle market companies" or those with annual sales in the range of $10 million to $150 million. A year later in early 1991, senior management at PW felt it was necessary to focus attention on making this service achieve its potential and relating it to existing services offered by the firm.

This case is rich in issues and provides insight into the challenges of introducing a new professional service. Students must address not only traditional issues in marketing a service to present and potential customers, but also **internal marketing** to PW accounting professionals. Subtleties related to organizational culture are raised and should be considered. The "buying process" involved in engaging a firm to perform a professional service, **relationship marketing**, cross-selling services, and professional synergies also might be considered in the case discussion.

Teaching Objectives

This case has four multi-faceted teaching objectives:

1. To introduce marketing students to the public accounting industry, the investment banking industry, and the subtleties involved in providing services to both.

2. To expose students to the nature and importance of **internal marketing** and **relational marketing** in delivering a high-level and complex professional financial service.

3. To demonstrate that marketing concepts and perspectives play an important role in companies and industries traditionally thought to be "immune" from marketing.

4. To illustrate to students how professional financial service organizations operate, including matters of organizational culture and innovation.

Teaching Suggestions

This case is best suited for that portion of the course when an instructor wishes to examine issues related to the marketing of services. Some instructors have also used the case in the communications strategy and management portion of the course since issues related to sales and sales management are important in the case analysis.

The case has proven to be an exceptional discussion device when students have had work experience in general, and particularly in either the public accounting or brokerage (investment banking) industries. They will quickly recognize the nuances present in the case. Students with little or no work experience come to recognize and appreciate these subtleties.

This case is different from most other cases in the book. Most notably, there are no numbers, although students can make some judgments regarding the opportunity for and profitability of the corporate finance initiative at PW. Also, there is no neat outcome. The outcome will depend on how students view the issues. Some instructors have found that referring to "critical incidents" helps students deal with the issues of the case.

Questions that might be posed to students either prior to or during a class discussion are:

1. What has prompted the Big Six public accounting firms to offer investment banking-related services?

2. How would you describe the Corporate Finance Group initiative at Price Waterhouse?

3. How will the successful implementation of the Corporate Finance Group initiative at Price Waterhouse be affected by the buying and selling process for this service?

4. What is your assessment of the Corporate Finance Group's progress as of early 1991? What recommendations would you suggest for 1991?

Areas for Discussion/Analysis

A. **What has prompted the Big Six public accounting firms to offer investment banking-related services.**

   1. The purpose of this question is to get students thinking about trends in the public accounting industry.

   2. There are numerous reasons why the addition of investment banking-related service makes sense for public accounting firms:

   - The traditional auditing business, which has been the mainstay of public accounting firms, has become an undifferentiated (commodity-type) service whereby the lowest bid often wins a client. Therefore, public accounting firm profit margins for auditing services have dwindled.

   - The client pool, at least among larger clients, has declined due to mergers and acquisitions in the 1980s. Therefore, there was a need to "sell" more services to existing clients to maintain/increase revenue. Almost 50 percent of public accounting firm revenue now comes from non-auditing services (see case Exhibit 1).

   - The addition of new services (e.g., management consulting) provides more opportunities for **cross-selling** services and building incremental revenue from existing clients.

   - Public accounting firms have some prior experience with mergers and acquisitions and related investment banking services. Therefore, it makes sense to broaden this capability.

   - Investment banking-related services provide an additional justification for the claim of a "one-stop source of business expertise" by public accounting firms for present and prospective clients.

B. **How would you describe the Corporate Finance Group initiative at Price Waterhouse.**

   1. This question is designed to force students to verbalize this service offering. This offering is sketched below:

   - **Target Marketing:** "Middle-market companies with sales revenue in the range of $10 million to $150 million

- **Service Offering:** This service offering is described in case Exhibit 5 and includes:
  - **Exclusive Sales Assignments**
  - **Acquisitions**
  - **Recapitalization**
  - **Financial Restructuring**

- **Implementation:** Services will be offered out of six PW offices in New York City, Chicago, Dallas, Los Angeles, San Francisco, and Atlanta.

2. Exhibit 1 in this note shows the offering-market matrix for the Corporate Finance Group initiative at Price Waterhouse.

3. Two questions can be posed to students at this phase in the class discussion:

- How consistent are these new services with present services offered by PW?

- Is there a viable market niche for these services?

C. **How will the successful implementation of the Corporate Finance Group initiative at Price Waterhouse be affected by the buying and selling process for its services?**

1. This multi-faceted question addresses the central issue posed in the case:

> In early 1991, senior firm management was focusing attention on making this service achieve its potential and relating it to existing services offered by Price Waterhouse.

This question also serves as a bridge between the promise and reality of marketing investment banking services by public accounting firms. It also forces students to think internally as well as externally from a buying-selling perspective. Exhibit 2 in this note displays one approach for looking at the implementation issues for PW.

2. The buying-selling process for investment banking services can be characterized as follows:

- Often **lengthy**

- Based on **established relationships, trust**

- Requires **creditability** (history of success)

- Involves **referrals, "word-of mouth"**

EXHIBIT 1

PRICE WATERHOUSE CORPORATE FINANCE OFFERING-MARKET MATRIX

Market Scope
("middle-market companies")

Service Offering	Existing Clients	New Clients
Exclusive Sale Assignments		
Financial Restructing		
Recapitalization		
Acquisitions (general financial advisory service)		

EXHIBIT 2

IMPLEMENTING THE INVESTMENT BANKING INITIATIVE AT
PRICE WATERHOUSE

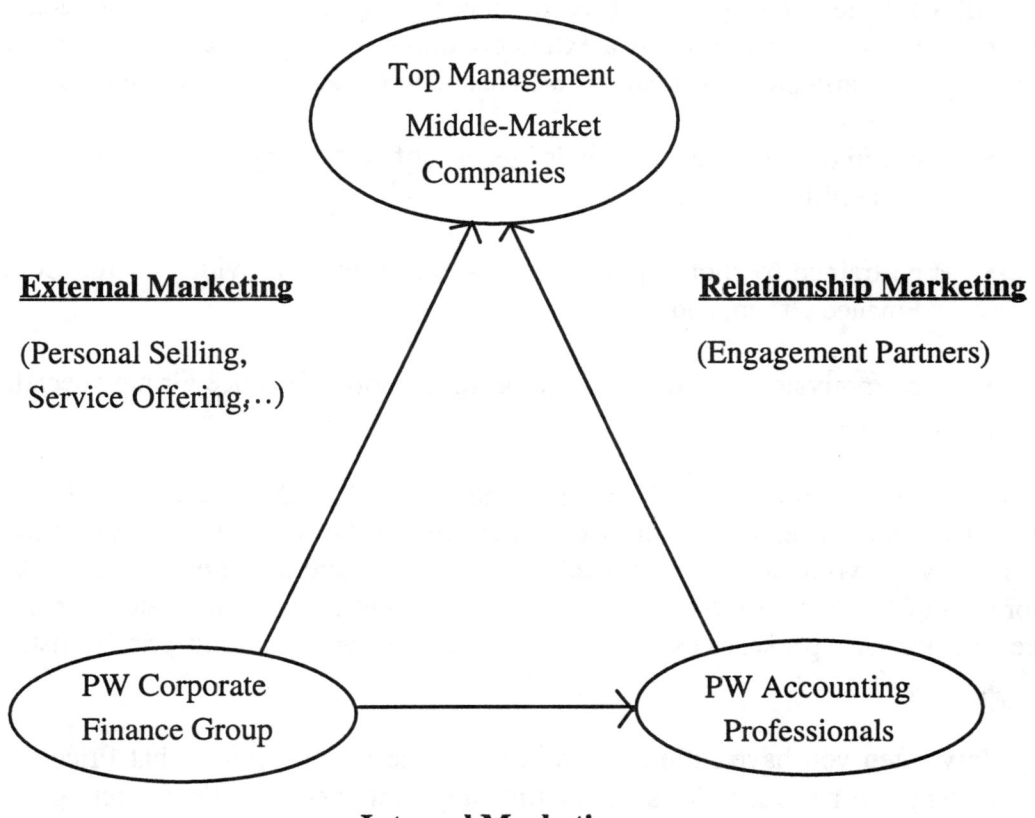

259

- Involves **networking** across professionals (law firms, financial institutions, private investors to identify opportunities)

In short, these services are not "sold or bought" in a traditional sense. To some extent, the notions of **external marketing** (the "4Ps") are less important than **internal marketing** and **relationship marketing**, at least at this stage in the development of the PW Corporate Finance Group.

3. **Internal marketing** - the task of successfully training and motivating able employees to serve customer needs – is a extremely important. Specifically, PW accounting professionals, particularly partners, many of who reside in the auditing function must...

- become aware and knowledgeable of the Corporate Finance Group's capabilities,

- be trained to spot opportunities for the services provided by the Corporate Finance Group, and

- be motivated to introduce and bring Corporate Finance Group specialists to clients.

Initial efforts evidence progress. The case notes that "... about 20 percent of Price Waterhouse partners had embraced the Corporate Finance Group and its services by early 1991..." However, two incidents mentioned in the case indicate that much more needs to be done. For example, one auditing partner said that if a client does not indicate interest in the Corporate Finance Group's services, these services are put on a "second priority list." The partner said:

> Very often you have little time to describe the many services that Price Waterhouse provides. Most of the time a typical one-hour client meeting is spent listening to the client. If CFG service opportunities are not indicated, they like some other services are put on a "second priority list" to be raised at a later time.

An interesting question to pose to the students in reference to this incident is:

> Did the client not mention anything, or did the engagement partner not recognize an opportunity?

The other incident related to the Corporate Finance Group finding out about a client's private placement after it was completed suggests a lack of communication. According to a Corporate Finance Group specialist:

> A few weeks ago our group read about a private placement by one of our blue chip clients after the placement happened. It seemed that the

engagement partner was either not aware of the opportunity or did not bring it to our attention.

Internal marketing becomes all the more important given that the PW Corporate Finance Group is populated by MBAs. This issue is highlighted in the case noting that "... these corporate finance professionals may be looked at as outsiders and not easily accepted into the public accounting culture."

4. **Relationship Marketing** - building trust and positive, long-term associations with clients – is a central practice in the marketing of professional services. Good relationships with clients provide opportunities to better service clients and provide access to client decision makers.

In the context of investment banking services at PW, the **relationship exists between engagement partners and the client.** Furthermore, the relationship is often built upon the auditing function and related services, e.g., tax consulting. The engagement partner can serve as a **gatekeeper** and not allow corporate finance specialists access to his/her clients.

The central role of the engagement partner is evident in the incident recalled dealing with advice given a client.

> People in the CFG had been talking to my client about their business and had recommended that my client buy another company. However, our auditors had identified an under performing division and recommended to the company president that they sell it. What started out as acquisition mindset in company ended up as a program for a divestiture.

Aspects of relationship marketing became important in targeting existing PW clients and non-PW clients. **The engagement partner is the key player in gaining access to existing PW clients**; therefore, internal marketing plays an important role.

At the same time, relationships play a less significant role for non-PW clients. "Cold-calling" by the Corporate Finance Group makes more sense for non-PW clients.

5. **Goal Congruence.** An interesting issue for consideration relates to goal congruence. PW is committed to delivering professional services to its clients (see the PW Client Bill of Rights in case Exhibit 2). At the same time, there is a subtle issue related to profitability of services provided by the Corporate Finance Group.

Most notably, the most profitable service to PW of the Corporate Finance Group is exclusive sale assignments – the sale of all or a portion of a client's business. However, the sale of a business or portion of a business has the potential to eliminate or reduce an auditing engagement partner's revenue. Why would this engagement partner recommend a sale? The quote by one engagement at the very end of the case is very telling in this regard. The partner said: "A client can buy and buy again, but it can only sell itself once."

D. **What is your assessment of the Corporate Finance Group's progress as of early 1991? What recommendations would you suggest for 1991?**

1. The purpose of this question is to focus attention on the fact that the Corporate Finance Group was formed in early 1990 (one year previously). Much of 1990 was devoted to recruiting 35 corporate finance professionals for six PW offices.

2. On the positive side of the ledger:

   - Internal marketing efforts have resulted in about 20 percent of PW partners seeing the potential contribution of the Corporate Finance Group's service.

   - The Corporate Finance Group has been termed "moderately successful" in that "both external and internal relationships were being built and service proposals and engagements were being produced."

3. On the other side of the ledger:

   - There is a feeling from reading the case that initial expectations which were never articulated have not been met. The reference to the Persian Gulf conflict in August 1990 provides an external cause for limited business being generated by the Corporate Finance Group.

   - Some 80 percent of PW partners have not (presumably) seen the potential contribution of the services provided by the Corporate Finance Group. It is not clear that the Corporate Finance Group is accepted as yet (an organization culture issue).

   - The services provided by the Corporate Finance Group are not quickly or easily "adopted" by clients. Hence, the labors of the Corporate Finance Group will take time to bear fruit. Several questions exist in this regard.

     ...What is the **relative advantage** of PW's Corporate Finance Group's services over, say, investment bankers?

     ...Can the tradition of using investment bankers for many of the services provided be broken or circumvented?

     ...How can PW build **credibility** quickly?

4. On balance, it may be too early to fairly assess the progress of the Corporate Finance Group's efforts. Nevertheless, the previous analysis offers some insights for recommendations:

- **Market Targeting/External Marketing** Primary emphasis should be on existing PW clients.

    Existing PW Clients: Work through engagement partners to gain access to clients. Refrain from "cold-calling" on existing PW clients without checking with the PW engagement partner.

    Non-PW Clients: "Cold-calling" is possible but unlikely to be immediately successful. Networking through other professionals (lawyers, brokers, etc.) for referrals is preferred.

- **Internal Marketing** Continue educational efforts, relationship building with PW engagement partners.

- **Relationship Marketing:** Corporate Finance Group professionals need to build their own relationships with present and prospective PW clients through engagement partners and professional networks, respectively.

- **Service Emphasis:** The Corporate Finance Group will need to recognize that large and profitable assignments (e.g., exclusive sale assignments, private placements) are likely to come only after smaller, less risky assignments have been performed on behalf of clients. This might suggest that the Corporate Finance Group should not try to hit a "home run" exclusively. Rather, general financial advisory services and less risky assignments might be pursued. Note that this view is somewhat at odds with a corporate finance specialist who said: "What will be needed are a few large engagements" (in order to be accepted).

E. Epilogue

By early 1992, one year after the date of the case, PW continued to offer investment banking services through six offices. The Corporate Finance Group saw its revenues increase 80 percent over the first full year of its existence; however, "success" varied greatly between offices. The principal revenue source was general financial advisory services (acquisitions).

Throughout 1992, an important issue remained unresolved. That was, whether the Corporate Finance Group should place greater emphasis on existing PW clients or non-PW clients. Senior management at PW wanted to see more emphasis on non-PW clients. The Corporate Finance Group preferred to focus on existing PW clients and continue the internal marketing and relationship-building efforts with PW engagement partners. An estimated 98 percent of the business generated by the Corporate Finance Group had come from existing PW clients.

In 1993, PW experienced considerable turnover in the Corporate Finance Group. Turnover affected the internal and relationship marketing efforts begun in 1992. By late

1993, the Corporate Finance "initiative" was folded into the broader Merger & Acquisition activity at PW and investment banking-type effort was minimized. Few corporate finance professionals remained at PW by early 1994.

F.   Summary Points

1. Marketing issues and questions play an important role in organizations and industries traditionally thought to be "immune" from marketing. For example:

- In the domain of product/service management...

    ... How consistent are investment banking services with present services offered by Price Waterhouse?

    ... Is there a viable market niche for these services?

- In the domain of marketing communications (personnel selling)...

    ... Are there opportunities for "cross-selling" services?

    ... Are there better opportunities for "team-selling" with engagement partners or "cold-calling?"

- In the domain of market selection...

    ... Should existing clients be pursued more aggressively than new clients?

2. Understanding the "buying and selling process" for professional services is a prerequisite for effective marketing. In this case, the role of an engagement partner as a "gatekeeper" or "facilitator" in marketing investment banking services is underscored.

3. Successful introduction of new services by professional organizations often involves external marketing, internal marketing, and relationship marketing.

- **External Marketing** requires the identification of market targets and service mixes, the means for communicating and delivery services, and the determination of fees.

- **Internal Marketing** involves training and motivating able employees to serve customer needs. Ineffective internal marketing can limit the success of external marketing initiatives.

- **Relationship Marketing** is fundamental to the successful marketing of professional services. Relationships are based on trust and take time to build. Networking is a critical aspect of relationship marketing.

GODIVA EUROPE

Synopsis

Charles van der Veken, President of Godiva Europe, is presented with an opportunity to shape the worldwide advertising program for Godiva chocolate as Godiva Europe examines its advertising strategy for Europe and Belgium. Godiva USA has sent van der Veken an outline for an international advertising campaign which seems to fit the United States but not Europe and specifically Belgium--the birthplace of chocolates and Godiva Europe's largest single market.

There are three subtle issues present in the case setting. First, Godiva International, composed of Godiva Europe, Godiva USA, and Godiva Japan, is concerned with conveying a single global message about Godiva chocolates across the world. That message consists of a luxury chocolate that is typically Belgian. Second, Godiva Europe is concerned with conveying an advertising message targeted at Europe, the USA, and Japan while taking into consideration the cultural differences among countries. Third, Belgium is viewed as the centerpiece of the European strategy for Godiva Europe, but Godiva's Belgian competitive position is fragile and may require a unique approach. In short, van der Veken is faced with the challenge of thinking about the merits of a global advertising campaign for Godiva chocolate while "globalizing" Europe and "localizing" Belgium.

The case provides extensive background information on the worldwide chocolate industry, including competitors in Europe, cross-cultural consumer purchase behavior, and Godiva's European marketing strategy, with particular emphasis placed on the marketing strategy for and the situation in Belgium. While the focus of the case is on Godiva's advertising strategy and message, important issues related to product policy, pricing strategy, and distribution practices need to be addressed in the context of the EC92 initiatives to create a borderless Europe.

Teaching Objectives

This case has four teaching objectives:

1. To introduce students to the worldwide chocolate market and particularly the nuances of chocolate purchase behavior and consumption in Europe, Japan, and the USA.

This note is based in part on an analysis plan prepared by Professor J. J. Lambin, Louvain University, Louvain-la-Neuve, Belgium.

2. To raise for consideration the question of whether Godiva is a global brand and whether Godiva is ready for a single global advertising message/campaign in 1991/1992.

3. To illustrate that advertising strategy is part of a broader marketing effort that must be consistent with the needs of the markets served and be internally consistent.

4. To give students an opportunity to consider what kind of message, if any, is universal for Godiva chocolates.

Teaching Suggestions

This case is best taught in that portion of the course which focuses on communications strategy and management and specifically global marketing. The case works well with both undergraduate and graduate classes and is particularly suited for a group presentation.

Previous experience teaching the case suggests that students sometimes overlook the subtle issues present in the case, i.e., those indicated in the synopsis. Accordingly, it is useful for instructors to briefly "set-up" the case by linking together Godiva International's view, Godiva Europe's view, and Godiva's specific situation in Belgium. Also, students often tend to overlook the differences and emphasize the similarities among the different competitive and societal environments in which Godiva competes.

Specific questions that can be posed to students prior to or during a class discussion are:

1. How would you characterize consumer purchasing behavior and consumption in the chocolate praline market and the major differences observed among countries?

2. How would you characterize the strengths and weaknesses of Godiva in Europe and particularly Belgium?

3. How might you characterize Godiva's existing marketing strategy on a "standardization--customization" continuum? Does a single global advertising campaign make sense?

4. What is your assessment of Charles van der Veken's views on Godiva's advertising objectives and strategy?

5. Are the economics of the proposed incremental expenditure for advertising sound? Why or why not?

Areas for Discussion/Analysis

A. **How would you characterize consumer purchasing behavior and consumption in the chocolate praline market and the major differences observed among countries?**

1. General observations include the following:

    - Chocolate pralines are a food item which belongs to the category of luxury product but which is accessible to everyone.

    - The two use occasions are "gift" and "self consumption".

    - The purchasing behavior is "involved" because chocolate are purchased for special occasions (gift or self-indulgence) and because the retail price is relatively high.

    - The purchase process is more "emotional" than rational since consumption of chocolate is associated with pleasure and gift-giving.

    - The demand is highly seasonal. Deseasonality of demand depends on self consumption development which is a more expansible use occasion than giftable products.

    - Many substitute products exist for gifts (flowers, wines, perfumes, ...) and for self-indulgence (chocolate bars, snacks, candies, ...)

    - The distinctive qualities of chocolates are refinement, decoration, gourmet, hand-made fabrication and decoration, freshness, ...)

    - Brands are important for the consumer.

    - The chocolate pralines market is highly fragmented and there are few competitors having an international market coverage, with the exception of Léonidas and to a lesser extent, Neuhaus.

2. Major differences among countries can be summarized as follows:

    - Chocolate consumption is common practice throughout the world and therefore there is a potential for chocolate pralines as a global product.

    - Belgian consumers are probably "blasés" because they are exposed to many brands of chocolates which tend to be perceived more as a food item than as a luxury product.

- Mediterranean countries seem to be more receptive to the chocolate concept than Nordic countries.

- The pattern of seasonality also differs from one country to the other.

- The image of chocolate praline as a luxury item is well accepted in Spain, Portugal, France, USA and Japan. Thus, the price sensitivity is probably lower than the one observed in Belgium where it is more of a food item.

- Packaging practices also differ. In several countries, chocolates are pre-wrapped, while in Belgium, France and Spain the assortment is made at the request of the consumer.

B. **How would you characterize the strengths and weaknesses of Godiva in Europe and particularly in Belgium?**

1. **Godiva Strengths in Europe**

    - Godiva has a board international coverage and its brand name is known around the world. It has a strong position in three countries: Belgium, USA and Japan.

    - Godiva has a strong image as a luxury product in several markets.

    - Godiva is part of a large international group, Campbell Soup.

    - Godiva Europe has a 3,000 tons production capacity which is not fully exploited.

    - Godiva has a strong know-how in the development and fabrication of hand-made and fine chocolate pralines.

    - The markets in which Godiva operates have strong growth potential.

    - Godiva has a strong foothold in the duty-free segment which caters to the air travelers - a wealthy segment.

2. **Godiva Weaknesses in Europe (Belgium)**

    - An aging image in Belgium, the home market of Godiva chocolates.

    - A small unit market share in Belgium and small shares throughout Western Europe.

    - An aging distribution network recently revitalized in Belgium.

- A thin (or weak) distribution coverage in Europe with the exception of Belgium.

- The price differential between Godiva and its main competitor (Léonidas) is very high: (a 3 to 1 ratio).

?
- Evidence of inelastic demand for Godiva. A recent price increase of 10 percent in Belgium resulted in a 7 percent decline in volume (E = -7%/+10% = -0.7%.

3. **Godiva Europe's Competitive Position in Europe (Belgium)**

    - Total sales for Godiva Europe in 1990 were 926 million Belgian francs (bf) broken down as follows: 65 percent of sales were of Godiva-brand chocolates in Europe and 35 percent were sales at a transfer price to Godiva USA and Japan, Corné Tolson d´Or and private brands. **Godiva brand sales in Europe are therefore 601.9 million bf (.65 x 926 million bf).**

    - **Godiva is the highest priced brand in Europe**. Godiva's market share cannot be determined for each European country; however case Exhibit 11 indicates that Godiva's sales market share is 10.3 percent in Belgium, 3 percent in France, and 2.6 percent (roughly) in the United Kingdom. Léonidas, a Belgian competitor, is the market share leader **and** is the lowest priced brand in Belgium and France.

    - **Godiva's competitive position in Europe is fragile**. To illustrate this point, it is instructive to note that Godiva Europe's sales of the Godiva brand rests on its performance in Belgium. As estimated in Exhibit 1 in this note, over one-third of Godiva Europe's total sales come from Belgium alone. Furthermore, even though Godiva captures 10.3 percent of the Belgian market in terms of sales volume (case Exhibit 11), Godiva captures only 4.3 percent of unit (ton) volume in Belgium (see Exhibit 1 in this note). In short, Belgium as a market is very important to Godiva Europe and it is understandable why its president, Charles van der Veken, has focused so much of his attention on Belgium.

    - **Efforts to bolster Godiva's competitive position in Belgium and Europe are therefore warranted**. However, important issues remain. For example,

    ... The case points out that the chairman of Godiva International has frequently questioned the costly exclusive boutique distribution system implemented by

EXHIBIT 1

GODIVA EUROPE'S COMPETITIVE POSITION IN EUROPE (BELGIUM)

A. **Godiva-Brand Belgian Sales as a Percent of Godiva Europe Sales**

	Belgian Retail Market Size	3.6 billion bf (given in case)
x	Godiva's Retail Market Share	10.3% (case Exhibit 11)
=	Godiva's Belgium Retail Sales	370.80 million bf
x	Franchise Price/Retail Price - VAT incl. (640 bf/1080 bf)	.593 (case Exhibit 8)
=	Godiva's Belgian Sales @ Manufacturer Prices	219.88 million bf
	Godiva-Brand Sales in Europe (65% x 926 million bf):	601.9 million bf
	Godiva-Brand Belgian Sales as a % of Godiva Europe Sales:	36.6% (219.88 ÷ 601.9)

B. **Godiva-Brand Volume Share of Chocolate in Belgium**

	Godiva Belgium Sales @ Manufacturer Prices	219.88 million bf
÷	Kilogram Price to Franchise	640 (case Exhibit 11)
=	Godiva Volume in Kilograms	343,563 kilograms
x	Conversion to Pound Volume (1 kilogram = 2.205 lbs)	2.205 lbs
=	Godiva Pound Volume	737,556 lbs
÷	Pounds per Ton	2,000
=	Godiva volume (Tons)	378.8 tons
	Belgium Market (Tons):	8,800 (given in case)
	Godiva Share of Belgian Volume:	4.3% (378.8 ÷ 8,800)

Godiva Europe in Belgium. **Mr. van der Veken is convinced, however, that the Godiva boutique is a key component of the Godiva image as a luxury good. But is it?** Belgian consumers are favorably disposed toward the boutique concept although the stores are sometimes viewed as being too beautiful.

... **Godiva has an "old" image in Belgium and is not viewed as a luxury good or anything specifically special in Belgium.** Obviously, this presents a problem given the premium price for Godiva in Belgium (and elsewhere in Europe). In some respects, chocolate as a product class is viewed as a commodity, not a specialty item, in Belgium.

... **The competitive advantage of Godiva Europe as a chocolatier may require that Godiva Europe succeeds in Belgium first before success in Europe can be achieved.** Following Porter (Competitive Advantage of Nations, The Free Press, 1990), a necessary condition for a firm to be successful in global markets is that it first succeeds in intense domestic (Belgium) competition. An instructor might introduce this idea for consideration by the class. Godiva has not succeeded in Belgium if market share and brand image are success measures.

C. **How might we characterize Godiva's existing marketing strategy on a "standardization-customization" continuum? Does a single global advertising campaign make sense?**

1. We have found it useful to refer to Exhibit 2 in this note when the discussion moves to this topic. Students can evaluate Godiva on each of the six dimensions shown.

2. **Tangible product:** The rating is "high". Godiva chocolates are identical for all countries, only sales by item slightly differ by country according to local preferences. The output of the USA and Belgian factories will become more and more similar.

3. **Product concept:** The rating is "moderate". The concept of a luxury, prestigious and refined product is well accepted in the USA, Japan, and in most European countries with the exception of Belgium, where the product tends to be perceived as a commodity. The chocolate praline has, however, the characteristics of a universal product. The benefits provided, such as unique taste experience, exceptional look, gift, self-indulgence, ... are universal. To the extent that the product is a proven success in meeting these universal needs in a particular country, it is logical to expect a similar success in other countries, provided adaptations to local habits.

4. **Packaging:** The rating is "low". Significant differences exist between Europe, USA, and Japan. Pre-wrapped assortments of chocolates dominate in the USA, whereas custom-made assortments dominate in Europe and in Japan. Also the average quantity purchased differs.

EXHIBIT 2

STANDARDIZATION OF GODIVA MARKETING VARIABLES

Market Variables	Degree of Standardization		
	Low	Medium	High
Tangible Product	_____	_____	_____
Product Concept	_____	_____	_____
Packaging	_____	_____	_____
Distribution	_____	_____	_____
Pricing	_____	_____	_____
Advertising	_____	_____	_____

5. **Distribution:** The rating is "moderate". In Europe, the typical outlet is the Godiva boutique selling exclusively chocolates. These boutiques do not have as yet a uniform look, but the renovation program is well under way, particularly in Belgium. In the USA, the distribution network is broader and more diversified; namely through luxurious department stores located in suburban shopping malls. The market coverage of European countries like Italy, Germany, Holland, even France, is very thin and increasing the number of outlets is certainly a priority objective. Should Godiva maintain its exclusive (and costly) distribution system or try to extend its distribution through other outlet categories? Remember, this question was posed by the Godiva International Chairman.

6. **Pricing:** The rating is "low". Prices are very different not only between Europe, the United States and Japan, but also between European countries. Are these price differences within Europe a major issue? The upward price alignment policy is particularly difficult in Belgium where the price gap between the high and the low end of the market is already very large.

7. **Advertising:** The rating is "low". Godiva has advertised only in Belgium and on a very modest scale. The US advertising has adopted a communication style similar to the one adopted by Cartier or Gucci. The perceived brand images are very different between Belgium and the other European countries and between Europe, the United States and Japan. Is Godiva ready for a common advertising message targeted at the three main markets.

8. The previous analysis would suggest that Godiva is not particularly suited for a single, global advertising campaign that will play well in Western Europe (Belgium), the USA, and Japan simultaneously.

... While the current concern of Godiva International (and possibly Godiva USA and Godiva Japan) is to convey a global image of Godiva chocolates as

"... a luxury chocolate that is typically Belgian." This view may not be believable by Belgians and Western Europeans. It may be believable in the USA and Japan, however.

... The message of Godiva International's proposed campaign (see case Exhibit 13) to convey Godiva chocolates as "expertly crafted to provide an unparalleled sensory experience" with a tone emphasizing "luxurious, energetic, modern, upscale, and emotionally involving" may not be believable by Western Europeans and Belgians. It may be believable in the USA and Japan, however.

D. How would you assess Charles van der Veken's views on Godiva's advertising objectives and strategy?

1. Mr. van der Veken expressed two views on Godiva's advertising and strategy. Reflecting on the USA vs. Europe, he noted

> "The least one can say is that differences of mentality exist between our two continents. We certainly need to wake up our old-fashioned Godiva, but we should also be careful of overly racial changes..."

Reflecting on the advertising objective(s) appearing in case Exhibit 13, he said:

> "The objective of Godiva USA is to increase the frequency of the purchase of chocolates for gifts as well as for self consumption, whereas Belgium wants to make its brand image more youthful. Thus, the United States should adjust its advertising slightly "downward", in making the product more accessible through convivial advertising and less "plastic beauty". While Belgium should strive jointly with other marketing efforts (redesign of boutiques, increased quality of service, creation of "collections"), to adjust its advertising slightly "upward", in affirming itself as a prestigious luxury product, only younger".

2. His objectives were:

Qualitative Objectives:
- Rapidly reinforce the luxury image of Godiva
- Make visibility a priority

Quantitative Objectives:
- Increase the frequency of purchase

Other Objectives:
- Concentrate all efforts on Belgium during several months (months of peak sales)

- Synergy of all methods of promotion and advertising

3. Students might be asked to evaluate the merits of his views in light of the previous analysis. Most notably, students might conclude that Godiva's marketing challenge is to increase its penetration of the Belgian market (market penetration) and better differentiate its (total) offering from competitors (particularly Léonidas). Also, students can draw on the research shown in Appendix A to define communication objectives that are quantitative, and measurable, e.g.,

> increase by x% consumer acceptance of the belief that Godiva is ideal for "self-indulgence."

4. In addition, it is not altogether evident that Mr. van der Veken's proposed advertising objectives and strategy necessarily make sense as a Pan-European effort for several reasons:

- The competitive/cultural settings and Godiva's situation across Europe are such that a single, Pan-European approach might be premature. Attention might be first placed on matters of distribution.

- The exchange rate data given in the case support, for instance, that the cost might be prohibitive. As an example, in terms of media costs and for the same impact, 1 bf in Belgium is equivalent to 1.6 bf in France, and 1.9 bf in the UK. It will cost 1½ times as much in France and almost twice as much in the UK to get the same impact.

- The advertising objectives outlined by Mr. van der Veken themselves are sufficiently vague that the purpose of the advertising is not clear.

E. **Are the economics of the proposed incremental expenditure for advertising sound? Why or why not?**

1. A rough break-even analysis will shed light on the merits of the proposed 13 million bf incremental expenditure for advertising referenced in the case:

Incremental advertising expenditure:	13 million bf
Godiva price to franchises:	640 bf/kilogram
Estimated gross profit margin: (case states that gross margin ranges from 35% to 40%)	37.5% or 240 bf/kilogram (37.5% x 640)

$$\text{Break-even (in kilograms)} = \frac{13 \text{ million bf}}{240 \text{ bf}} = 54{,}167 \text{ kilograms}$$

A 54,167 kilogram increase to recoup the 13 million bf increase in advertising suggests a 15.8 percent increase in kilogram volume [54,167 ÷ 343,563 (from Exhibit 1 in this note] or a 54.8 ton increase. This increase in tonnage would mean that Godiva's volume market share in Belgium must increase from an estimated 4.3 percent to 4.9 percent given that Belgian market growth is relatively flat. [Note: Break-even can be calculated in Belgian francs as well: 13 million bf ÷ .375 = 34,666,666 bf. The same 15.8 percent increase results.]

2. Given that the break-even calculation suggests a 15.8 percent in sales (volume), students might calculate a rough advertising-sales elasticity; that is, dividing the sales (volume) increase of 15.8 percent by the incremental advertising in percentage terms, 42 percent (13 million bf ÷ 31 million bf = 42%). The elasticity is .376 (15.8% ÷ 42% = .376). If the actual advertising-sales elasticity is less than .376, Godiva will not recoup its incremental investment in advertising.

E. Summary Points

1. Global marketing is a challenging assignment requiring attention to unique and often subtle differences in the consumer and competitive environments around the world.

2. An important question in designing a global communications program is designing a program along the continuum from a single, universal message for all to many, individual messages for each country/society. Frequently, global marketers adopt a "glocalization" approach where both uniform and custom messages are employed depending upon similar/unique circumstances.

3. Advertising is only one part of a global marketing strategy. Advertising efforts must be consistent with other elements of the marketing mix otherwise such efforts are doomed to failure.

4. The case raises a subtle strategic issue: Can Godiva achieve a global competitive advantage without first establishing itself as the premier Belgian chocolate in Belgium?

DELL COMPUTER CORPORATION: THE HIGHER EDUCATION MARKET

Synopsis

In early 1996 Diane Jeni, a marketing manager for Dell Computer Corporation's Education, State & Local Government (ESL) Business Unit, was faced with a decision regarding the company's marketing strategy for the higher education (college and university) market. She had been tasked with developing the 1996/97 marketing plan for higher education and, as such, created a planning team to assist her. In a brainstorming session, the team came up with four preliminary strategic alternatives: do nothing different (status quo), aggressively pursue campus microcenters (retail outlets on college and university campuses that sell computers and related hardware and software exclusively to the campus community), develop a student purchase program, or reduce the emphasis on microcenters and instead focus on direct marketing to colleges and universities.

The decision was complicated by three factors. One was the fact that Dell Computer Corporation used a special channel—the microcenter—to reach the higher education market. Dell Computer pioneered direct marketing of computers through telemarketing and direct response advertising in the 1980s, and virtually all of it revenues were derived from the direct channel (even those emanating from large corporations). The microcenter represented the only indirect channel that Dell used (an earlier attempt to enter indirect [retail] channels in the early 1990s was not profitable), and hence was an exception to its standard way of doing business.

The second factor was the current uncertainty regarding the higher education market. The microcenter channel has been traditionally supported by Apple Computer through its generous pricing programs and large promotional budgets; this support had allowed Apple to dominate the channel. Now, however, Apple was in financial disarray, and no one in the industry knew whether it would continue to support the channel. At the same time, other computer manufacturers, such as Compaq Computer, were rumored to be entering the channel, and mass merchandisers including CompUSA were increasingly encroaching on the channel.

Finally, there was considerable uncertainty regarding the future size and growth of the higher education market. Although student enrollment was projected to increase, college and university budgets were stagnant and computer purchasing and ownership behaviors were in flux.

Teaching Objectives

This case has four general teaching objectives:

1. To familiarize students with the intricacies of marketing computers to well-defined segments within a particular target market.

2. To expose students to the implications of using a distribution channel that is unique within a firm's distribution strategy.

3. To illustrate analyses required when attempting to forecast market growth and size.

4. To reinforce the notion that strategic marketing decision making must integrate and accommodate seemingly disparate marketing activities and must continually be monitored and re-evaluated.

Teaching Suggestions

Students find this case to be relatively enjoyable for several reasons. The company featured in the case, Dell Computer Corporation, is well-known, and many students identify with Michael Dell because of his age and background. (At the time this case was written, Michael Dell was one of the youngest self-made billionaires of all time, as well as one who made his money in the shortest period of time.) Likewise, the product featured in the case, computers, is very familiar to students and a frequent topic of conversation. Finally, a significant portion of the case focuses on college students as a target market. Many of the students may own a Dell computer or may have even purchased a computer through a campus microcenter. As a result, students usually become very involved in the issues in the case and class discussions are typically lively.

Because the decision alternatives are explicitly set out in the case, students sometimes try to address them before performing a background analysis and establishing an appropriate decision context. An instructor should not encourage such an approach because it does not permit the richness of broader issues to emerge. It is suggested that class discussion begin with a general directive such as "Let's begin by talking about the characteristics of Dell Computer Corporation." This allows a discussion of the Dell corporate culture and the company's strengths and weaknesses; it also results in a solid foundation for analyzing the decision to be made.

Successful resolution of the issues in the case requires a combination of qualitative and quantitative analytical skills. Although positioned as a marketing channels case, it can be used to illustrate a variety of other marketing issues and decisions, including segmentation and the need to integrate marketing mix strategies into an internally consistent and comprehensive marketing program. The case issues are straightforward and relatively well-defined. Consequently, the case is more appropriate for undergraduate than graduate students and can be used as an examination or assigned as a group presentation.

Specific questions that might be used to guide an analysis and discussion include the following:

1. How would one characterize Dell Computer Corporation?

2. From where does the ESL Business Unit obtain its revenues?

3. How would one describe the higher education market for computers?

4. How well does Dell Computer's marketing approach "fit" the higher education market?

5. What should Dell Computer do, and why?

Areas for Discussion/Analysis

A. How would one characterize Dell Computer Corporation?

1. Dell Computer Corporation's distinctive competency obviously lies in its marketing skills. Oversimplifying a bit, Dell Computer appears to be a marketing machine. For fiscal years 1991 through 1996 revenues increased nearly tenfold, which represents an average annual increase of about 57%.

2. Dell Computer has achieved its impressive revenue and revenue growth by being a marketing innovator and by constantly focusing on the customer:

- The cornerstone of its marketing effort has been the high value that it offers customers by combining high quality with reasonable prices and "mass customizing" computers to meet each customer's specific needs.

- Dell Computer pioneered the direct marketing channel for computers and was the first to offer its customers telephone-based technical support 24 hours a day and guaranteed next-day on-site service.

3. Dell Computer's rapid revenue growth, however, has not resulted in continuous profitability. Case Exhibit 2 reveals relatively large variations in its operating statistics. In fiscal year 1994 the company actually lost money. This exhibit also reveals that the company spends relatively little on research, development, and engineering (1.8% of revenues in FY 1996). Compare this with 3M (Chapter 10), which spent 6.6% of its revenues over roughly

the same time period. This reinforces the idea that Dell Computer's strength lies in marketing computers, not creating or developing new ones.

4. Dell Computer's marketing strategy can be somewhat facetiously termed "ear-to-ear" because of its reliance on the telephone. Even though the company now has field representatives personally working with large corporate and government customers, virtually all orders enter Dell Computer through the telephone. The direct manufacturer-to-customer relationship offers many benefits to both parties. For example, it allows the company to centralize most business functions. At the same time, though, it may be incompatible with marketing through university microcenters (an indirect channel).

5. Dell Computer is organized around three customer groups: (a) major accounts (large firms, government agencies, and educational and medical institutions), (b) small and medium-sized businesses, and (c) individuals (consumers). Major accounts are served by the Major Accounts Division, whereas the latter two customer groups are served by the Dell Direct Division. The vast majority of Dell Computer's customers, more than 90 percent, are businesses and organizations. According to the case, Dell Computer Corporation does not have a marketing program specifically for individuals.

6. Given the corporate structure it is not surprising that Dell Computer focuses its marketing efforts on sophisticated computer buyers and users (since they typically are found in large corporations and government agencies). By definition, these buyers and users are not first-time buyers and users. Additionally, these buyers and users tend to want high performance computers and not be as price-sensitive as first-time buyers.

7. Dell Computer markets four major product lines. Two of the lines are personal computers. One is the Optiplex line, which is designed for large customers with networking needs; the other is the Dimension line, which is designed for smaller, independent users, such as small businesses and consumers. The Optiplex line is marketed through the Major Accounts Division; the Dimension line is marketed through the Dell Direct Division. The other two lines are the Latitude line of high-end notebook computers and the PowerEdge line of servers. The focus of both of these lines is the major account (large customer).

B. From where does the ESL Business Unit obtain its revenues?

1. The Education, State & Local Government (ESL) Business Unit is one of five business units in Dell Americas that collectively comprise the Major Accounts Division. The unit seems to possess the typical Dell Computer sales organization with one exception. There is a marketing program manager and several marketing support personnel dedicated to the higher education market.

2. In 1995 the higher education market accounted for about 40% of the ESL Business Unit's revenue. Of this revenue, 35-40% in turn was derived from the microcenter channel. Hence microcenters appear to be important contributors to unit revenue. At the

same time, 60-65% of the revenue derived from the higher education market resulted from Dell Computer's direct marketing approach.

3. Simultaneously, in 1995 80% of the ESL Business Unit's higher education revenue came from college and university departments and other organizational units (the "institutional" segment); 20% was derived from the FSS—faculty, staff, and student—segment. When considered in the context of the microcenter channel, this 80% suggests that 15-20% of higher education institutional revenue (80% minus the 60-65% not emanating from microcenters) flows through microcenters. Thus microcenter revenue comes from both of the higher education segments (institutional as well as FSS).

4. Examination of the gross margins of the computer systems (that is, the hardware and bundled software) sold in the higher education market suggests the speculation that the Optiplex (gross margin of 24%) and Latitude (gross margin of 21%) lines contribute significantly to corporate profits, whereas the Dimension line (gross margin of 15%) may not be contributing as significantly. This speculation is based on a comparison of the product line gross margins with the corporate gross profit margin for FY 1996 given in case Exhibit 1 (20.2%). The comparison is a bit suspect because of channel differences and the manner in which variables are defined, but the point is often useful in class discussions.

5. The 1996/97 planning year goal of $150MM in revenue and 69,000 units results in an average price of $2,174 per computer. This is somewhat less than the average prices currently obtained in the higher education market. The implicit assumption underlying the goal is that computer prices will be declining; it is consistent with the statement in the case that computer component costs are constantly decreasing (leading to price declines).

6. Finally, note that the revenue goal of $150 million is but a small percentage (2.5-3%) of the higher education market potential. Note further that since 80% of ESL Business Unit revenues come from the institutional segment, which represents 20% of the higher education market potential, Dell Computer's revenue goal reflects an anticipated penetration of 10-12% of the institutional segment ($150MM x .8/($5B or $6B x .2)) but only a .5-.6% penetration of the FSS segment ($150MM x .2/($5B or $6B x .8)). The latter is probably a function of the fact that the company only reaches about 9% of the FSS segment through its microcenter channel (see below).

C. **How would one describe the higher education market for computers?**

1. The higher education market, which has an annual sales potential of $5 to $6 billion, consists of two distinct user segments, institutions (college and university departments and organizational units) and faculty, staff, and students (FSS). These segments differ substantially in their computing and purchasing needs. Based on the case and exhibits, the institutional segment is essentially a type of major account that:

- requires many computers

- requires large scale computing capabilities
- needs computers that can be networked
- purchases computers in volume through long-term contracts
- probably consists of numerous subsegments or niches
- typically purchases and prefers to purchase directly from a manufacturer
- probably purchases through buying committees consisting of faculty and staff members

The FSS segment consists of individuals who:

- typically purchase one computer for their personal use
- tend to be price conscious
- usually purchase by personal check or credit card
- (by inference) are likely to be first-time buyers

2. The FSS segment is by far the larger segment. It is estimated to represent 75-80% of the higher education market potential (somewhere in the neighborhood of $4.26 billion if the $5-6 billion potential and the 75-80% figures are respectively averaged and multiplied).

3. An implicit and important (but unasked) question in the case relates to the expected demand for computers in the higher education market. The case contains rich data to address this question, and through a few simple analyses various estimates can be calculated. Even so, the data are limited to the FSS segment. Little information is available about institutional demand for computers. However, "in the long run" the FSS segment probably requires the most attention. This is so for three reasons. First, the majority of the institutional demand, about 78% (60-65%/80%), is satisfied through Dell Computer's traditional direct marketing approach and therefore "under control." Second, the case points out that the FSS segment represents a larger market potential than the institutional segment (80% versus 20%). Third, "saturation" is more likely to occur for the institutional segment than the FSS segment, which annually "renews" itself through the addition of entering freshmen. (It should be noted, however, that institutional demand is also likely to be at least partially a function of student enrollment.) The FSS segment is dominated by students. In 1995 there were nearly 14.4 million students enrolled in higher education institutions. (This number is expected to grow at an average annual rate of 1.9% through the year 2000, at which time there will be 15.5 million students enrolled in higher education institutions.) At the same time, there are approximately 1.4 million college and university administrators, staff, and faculty members (F/S), of which 800,000 (56%) are faculty. Thus there are 10 students for every administrator, staff, and faculty member.

4. If one assumes that (a) faculty are reasonably representative of the F/S subsegment and (b the ownership percentages in case Exhibit 5 can be meaningfully weighted by the number of schools in each category, then F/S ownership of computers is approximately 53% and student ownership of computers is approximately 29%, 26% for students enrolled in community colleges and 31% for students enrolled in other institutions of higher education (14.4MM x .40 x .26 + 14.4MM x .60 x .31 = 4.21MM; 4.21MM/14.4MM = 29%).

Applying these percentages to the number of individuals in the two FSS subsegments suggests that at the beginning of 1996 the market potential for the F/S subsegment was 658,000 computers, whereas that for the student subsegment was 10.2 million computers (for a ratio of student potential to F/S potential of nearly 16-to-1). Note that the numbers are estimated with considerable error. Even so, the point of the calculation, and what should be transmitted to students, is that there is a major difference between the two subsegment market potentials.

5. Moreover, student demand is self-renewing. Consider AY 1996-1997. Exhibit 4 reveals that approximately 2.5 million individuals will graduate from high school in 1996. According to information in the case, 1.55 million (62%) will enroll in an institution of higher learning in the fall. Of the individuals who enroll, nearly half (say 50%), 775,000, will not have a computer and therefore will be added to the FSS segment market potential. Similar calculations can be made for future years. Although the percentage of students owning a computer when they enter a higher education institution may increase over time (and hence decrease the market potential), this will be compensated for by the increasing number of high school graduates (see case Exhibit 4).

6. Through the microcenter channel Dell Computer currently has access to 1.3 million students in 81 colleges and universities. (The average number of students per institution is about 16,000, as compared to the national average of about 3,900 students per institution (assuming 3,664 institutions).) This corresponds to about 9% of the total higher education student market and 15% of the noncommunity college higher education market. Ceteris paribus, the 81 colleges and universities will enroll nearly 140,000 incoming freshmen in 1996 since 1.3MM/14.4MM = .09; 1.55MM x .09 = 139,500. If half of these freshmen do not have a computer, their entry into higher education institutions will increase the FSS segment market potential for the microcenter channel by 70,000 computers. Likewise, if 31% of the students enrolled in other than community colleges own a computer, then the 1.3 million students represent a market potential of 897,000 computers (see assumptions and calculations above).

7. Assuming that there is a linear relationship between number of students and number of college and university administrators, staff, and faculty (F/S), then the microcenter channel also gives Dell Computer access to 126,000 (.09x1.4MM) administrators, staff, and faculty members at the 81 colleges and universities served by microcenters. Further, if F/S ownership of computers is 53%, then the F/S subsegment represents a market potential of more than 59,000 computers through the microcenter channel.

D. How well does Dell Computer's marketing approach "fit" the higher education market?

1. Dell Computer's marketing approach would seem to be a good fit with the institutional higher education market segment (that is, departments and organizational units). Currently this segment tends to purchase institutional computers directly from manufacturers;

the direct-from-manufacturer channel also is the most preferred channel. For example, case Exhibit 9 reveals that of the college and university senior administrators whose institution purchased computers (in the past 12 months, probably 1995), 61% (44%/ (100% - 28%)) did so directly from a manufacturer. Such purchasing is very compatible with Dell Computer's marketing approach. Indeed, the case notes that 80% of the ESL Business Unit's higher education revenues were derived from the institutional segment in 1995.

2. In brief (see C.1), the institutional higher education segment appears to be a typical major account segment for Dell Computer. Buyers are sophisticated, computers are purchased in volume (most likely Optiplex computers), and purchase contracts are used.

3. Dell Computer's marketing approach does not appear to fit the FSS segment as well as it does the institutional segment. This is so for several reasons:

- The case states that the typical FSS buyer is "consumer-like," hence he or she is likely to be a first-time (unsophisticated) buyer and therefore inconsistent with the company's typical (and preferred) buyer. Individuals who buy through microcenters tend to be students.

- Dell Computer has no specific marketing program for individuals.

- The typical FSS buyer is price sensitive and, given his or her characteristics, more likely to purchase a Dimension computer than an Optiplex or Latitude computer (with the contribution margin of the former being considerably less than those of the latter two lines).

- Microcenters require an inventory of computers. This means computers are standardized since they must be manufactured (and thus configured) before they are purchased. Among Dell Computer's distinctive competencies is its ability to mass customize computers once an order has been received. Are the two types of manufacturing compatible?

4. On the basis of a survey of its higher education marketing advisory council, one ESL Business Unit analyst concluded that Dell Computer faced some potential problems in its microcenter channel. These problems were in part due to (a) the manner in which information was provided to microcenters, (b) pricing inconsistencies, and (c) how support and service activities were provided for microcenter purchases.

5. The analyst's conclusions seem to be supported by other (independent) case information:

- The FSS segment in particular may be overlooked in the company's selling process. Case information suggests that the traditional "ear-to-ear" approach does not provide specific information to a segment member wishing to buy directly from the company. For example, it is likely that FSS segment members calling Dell Computer will be confused as to the proper option to pursue. The "dial 2" option is for major accounts (including higher education institutions), not for the FSS segment (even though it is an "education" option). The "dial 3" option is for small businesses and consumers. Neither option intuitively fits the FSS segment caller.

- Although the Optiplex line consists of computers that are in general more expensive than those in the Dimension line, the average price of a Dimension computer system (hardware plus bundled software) sold in the higher education market ($2,423) is greater than that of an Optiplex computer system sold in this market ($2,381). This in itself hints at pricing problems.

- Microcenters are full service retail stores. Dell Computer prefers to service computers itself, partially as a desire to build relationships with its customers through its traditional (telephone and onsite) service and support approach. The case notes that Dell Computer entered then exited the indirect channel previously in the decade (perhaps due in part to potential channel conflicts and in part due to the servicing problem). Is Dell Computer's traditional service and support approach inconsistent with the microcenter being a full-service operation?

- Moreover, is there a product line problem in the microcenter channel? The microcenter channel is managed by the ESL Business Unit, which is a component of the Major Accounts Division. The focus of the division and unit is the Optiplex computer line, whereas the computer of choice for the FSS segment is probably the Dimension. The question of which line microcenters should feature or emphasize is difficult to answer, especially when one considers that a sizable proportion of Dell Computer's microcenter sales are institutional and the Optiplex-Dimension price relationship in the higher education market is contrary to the company's experience elsewhere. In sum, is there a potential product line conflict in the channel?

6. In general, the fit between Dell Computer's marketing approach and the FSS segment would appear to be less than ideal.

7. In spite of the apparent lack of fit between Dell Computer's marketing approach and the major higher education marketing segments, there does not seem to be any inherent conflict between the company's direct and indirect channels. The two channels can co-exist in the higher education market.

E. **What should Dell Computer do, and why?**

1. The ESL Higher Education Planning Team came up with four strategic alternatives:

- Do nothing.
- Go all out with the microcenters.
- Develop a student purchase program.
- Scale back on microcenters.

2. The team was told to assume that the higher education marcom budget would be $1 million, that four Dell field representatives could be dedicated to the higher education market, and that eight additional sales representatives could possibly be hired. It was also informed that additional resources would be available if there was a possibility of a substantial revenue increase.

3. The first alternative, "do nothing," was essentially a status quo alternative. Under this alternative the ESL Business Unit would follow the current marketing approach. As such, it would be a "fall back" alternative.

4. The second alternative was for Dell Computer to aggressively pursue the microcenter channel. An argument in favor of this strategy is based on the assumptions that (a) Apple Computer will not continue to support the channel at its present level and (b) other major competitors such as Compaq Computer (the largest manufacturer and marketer of personal computers) would not enter and become a major force in the channel. If the assumptions prove to be correct, Dell Computer could become a dominant player in the channel. Both assumptions, though, appear questionable. Education has traditionally been a market where Apple Computer has done well. How likely is it to abandon or even decrease its emphasis in this channel?

5. To become dominant in the channel, Dell Computer would probably have to dedicate considerable dollar resources to the channel. Although sizable, $1 million would not go very far if allocated across the 81 colleges and universities having microcenters (equal allocation—for illustrative purposes only—would result in about $12,300 per institution) for advertising, direct mail, trade shows, computer fairs, and so forth. This hardly seems sufficient to accomplish the necessary tasks. Although the number of field representatives could be increased, it is not clear that they would add value to the Dell Computer-microcenter relationship. The case states that field representatives are charged with developing relationships with the company's major accounts and, through the relationships, building repeat sales. Given the characteristics of microcenter buyers (that is, the characteristics of the FSS segment), the field representatives' charge (and probable expertise) does not seem to be very appropriate for the microcenter channel.

6. The microcenter channel only reaches approximately 9% of all college and university students as well as college and university administrators, staff, and faculty

members (15% of all noncommunity college students and administrators, staff, and faculty members), and, given the state of college and university budgets, is not likely to expand. (If Apple Computer—with a 56% market share in the education market—could not entice more colleges and universities to establish microcenters, it is not likely that Dell Computer could.) Thus the growth potential of the channel, per se, is probably limited.

7. About 35-40% of the ESL Business Unit's revenues flow through the microcenter channel, but some of these revenues reflect institutional business.

8. In general, additional emphasis or investment in the microcenter channel does not appear warranted at the present time. This conclusion is reinforced by information in the case alluding to channel encroachment by mass merchandisers. How viable is the channel in the long run?

9. The third strategic alternative -- developing a student purchase program -- is primarily appealing because of the large number of students and the fact that students are self-renewing. At the same time, this strategy would likely possess many of the same drawbacks as the second alternative. The company currently does not possess a marketing program for individuals, and a student—probably a relatively unsophisticated first-time buyer of a single unit with little likelihood of a quick repeat purchase—would likely be the antithesis of the company's preferred customer. Moreover, the distribution of students (in 3600+ institutions) in combination with the available Dell Computer resources do not bode well for reaching them through a means other than the microcenter channel. For example, how would field representatives be used?

10. Thus, although the higher education student market may be superficially appealing because of its magnitude, targeting individuals in it (not to mention servicing them after a sale) probably could not be accomplished in a cost-effective manner.

11. The final alternative, scaling back on microcenters, might initially appear viable, especially given prior arguments against this channel. However, it is not that their future is "too risky." Rather, the issue is whether they are producing revenue for the company in a cost-effective manner. The microcenters do make a positive contribution (recall the margin discussion in C.4) with apparently only a minimal cost (only a few Dell Computer employees are dedicated to the channel). Moreover, both of the higher education market segments, institutional and FSS, purchase through microcenters, and the microcenters account for 35-40% of the ESL Business Unit's sales to the higher education market.

12. All things considered, Dell Computer should not exit the microcenter channel or even scale back its involvement in microcenters.

13. Through a process of elimination only the status quo option remains. Dell Computer Corporation should probably continue following its current marketing strategy. Given the current uncertainty in the higher education market and Dell Computer's

performance, all signals suggest that the company not attempt any radical changes in its strategy.

F. Epilogue

After considerable debate, the Higher Education Planning Team members agreed that no major changes should be made in the unit's higher education marketing strategy at the present time. Rather, a wait-and-see approach was recommended. Shortly after the team decided to continue the present strategy, the College Reseller Association decided to endorse Dell computers. As a consequence, microcenter sales increased dramatically. Corporate revenues as a whole increased in FY 1997 to more than $7 billion.

G. Summary Points

1. Marketing strategies must be periodically evaluated and, when necessary, changes made. However, changes should not be made simply for the sake of change. If a marketing strategy appears to be "working" and no alternative exists that is unequivocally superior, the strategy should be continued.

2. Making a correct distribution channel decision requires detailed knowledge of market segments being served. Careful analysis of segment members' purchasing and ownership behavior is necessary prior to adding, deleting, or modifying a distribution channel.

3. When there is considerable uncertainty in the marketplace, a firm is usually well-advised to pursue a conservative strategy unless a compelling reason exists for doing otherwise. Reacting too quickly to some environmental event (whether actual or perceived), without carefully taking into consideration all of its aspects and implications, may result in poor decisions.

AMWAY JAPAN LIMITED

Synopsis

In April 1997, Bruce Stephens, President of Amway Japan Limited (AJL, Tokyo, Japan), pondered how to reverse the first performance decline the company has experienced since entering the Japanese direct selling market in 1979. Founded as the tenth overseas subsidiary of Amway Corporation of Ada, Michigan, AJL had grown to become a successful company with Fiscal Year 1996 sales of ¥212 billion ($1.9 billion), accounting for 30% of Amway's worldwide sales. Having succeeded in doubling AJL's sales during the five years of his presidency, Bruce Stephens now needed to develop a strategy not only for rebuilding growth in the second half of FY 1997, but also for achieving AJL's long-term sales goal of ¥300 billion by FY2000.

This data-rich case provides a vehicle whereby students can dig deep into the details of a distinctive distribution business model, that of direct selling. In analyzing the business, students are learning about the economics of this growing sector of distribution, and in particular gain an understanding of the dual importance of the products carried (as in any distribution business) and the career opportunities offered to distributors in the network, a unique feature of network-based direct selling businesses. It is vital that the instructor establishes early in the class that the core business of Amway (as expounded by its senior managers) is the career opportunity, rather than the product line it sells.

At a more general level, the case also serves as an immersion into the mechanics of running a distribution operation, because of its rich detail. The analysis required by the case consists of issues generic to distribution businesses, such as the trade-off between penetration and productivity at the distributor and product level, and the issue of distributor motivation and incentives, and the relationship between tiers of distributors (measured by sales volumes).

Finally, the case provides an opportunity to discuss Japanese culture and business practice and ethical issues relative to "network marketing" or "pyramid selling." Ample case information is provided so that an informed discussion of these topics is possible.

Doctoral Candidate Yashinori Fujikawa and Professor David Arnold prepared this teaching note as the basis for class discussion rather than to illustrate either effective or ineffective handling of an administrative situation. Copyright © 2000 by the President and Fellows of Harvard College. Used with permission.

Teaching Objectives

This case has four teaching objectives:

1. To expose students to the direct selling industry in general, and specifically its development in Japan.

2. To introduce students to the sales and marketing practices of one of the largest direct selling companies in the world.

3. To illustrate the challenges and opportunities facing a successful company as it seeks to build its business.

4. To give students an opportunity to assess the feasibility of strategic options in operational and financial terms.

Teaching Suggestions

This case has several possible uses. It can be assigned as a case on international marketing, as a case on direct selling, or a distribution case. The case is suitable for both undergraduate and graduate courses.

In teaching the case, instructors should be sure that significant time is spent early in the class analyzing the case data on the current situation facing AJL. If students are allowed to debate the strategic options or an action plan too early, the depth of analysis to support the arguments is likely to be missing. The opening analysis should be positioned as putting students in the shoes of an executive in charge of a distribution business – the level of detail, and the combination of minutiae and strategic trends, goes a considerable way towards capturing the feeling of such a job.

The opening analysis should focus on three major areas. First, students should be pressed on the Amway business model, and in particular be made to understand that the driver of the model is the entrepreneurial opportunity offered ("the career", as it is known in some direct selling organizations) rather than the more conventional distribution drivers such as location or assortment. This is reflected in the economics of the AJL business, e.g. huge variance in distributor commitment to growing their business, despite approximately equal cost-to-serve. It is likely that this portion of class discussion will include some pejorative comments about "network marketing" or "pyramid selling" as unethical business models, especially if the class includes Asian students. The data in the case enables informed discussion of these issues, both in terms of the general business model and the topical public debate in Japan, and instructors are well advised to refer students back to case data to justify their positions.

Secondly, students should be pressed on problem diagnosis. Given the wealth of data in the case, it is no easy task to sort out the indicators of the strategic health of the business. On occasion, it has proven useful for the instructor to stand back from the case and ask students to discuss their opinions of the key indicators for a distribution business. Thirdly, students should be pressed on possible solutions to the issues diagnosed as responsible for the recent sales downturn. It is useful to distinguish between those aimed at short-term sales growth resumption, and those at a more strategic level. In general, detailed analysis leads students to incline toward the view that AJL's era of heady growth is over, and that it is nearing saturation in the Japanese market. To discuss this, it is useful to assess the feasibility of the strategic options in terms of required increases in sales in different distribution tiers (see Exhibit 1 in this note).

Finally, extensive information is available (at the end of this note) on the plan adopted by AJL in response to the situation described in the case. It is useful to allow sufficient time at the end of the class for the instructor to run through the key points of the plan, evaluating them against the class analysis and recommendations.

Experience teaching the case indicates that students will rush toward the "strategic options" and express their views. Therefore, instructors might assign the following questions prior to the class meeting to provide context for evaluating the options presented in the case.

1. How would you characterize the performance of Amway Japan Limited to date?

2. What internal (strategic) and external (environmental) factors have contributed to the performance of Amway Japan Limited?

3. What explains the recent sales downturn?

4. What are the pros and cons of AJL's strategic options—penetration or productivity? Describe the feasibility of each in achieving AJL's revenue goal in FY2000.

Areas for Discussion/Analysis

A. **How would you characterize the performance of Amway Japan Limited to date?**

Since its entry into the Japanese market, AJL has been very successful in various ways. The following case facts indicate AJL's success:

- **Financial Performance**. AJL's sales, income, and EPS had all grown at a compounded annual growth rate of 14% for the last five years. ROA and ROE grew at 6.4% and 9.8% respectively (case Exhibit 1).

- **Distributor Network.** The AJL distributor network had grown at about 10% annually to reach the all-time record of over 1.1 million, accounting for 44% of the Amway's worldwide distributorships (case Exhibit 1).

- **Ranking within Amway Group.** AJL's FY 1996 sales was $1.9 billion, the largest among the entire Amway Group (about 30% of worldwide sales of $6.8 billion) (p. 1).

- **Ranking in Japanese Direct Selling Industry.** AJL ranked first among all the direct selling companies in Japan in 1995-1996 (case Exhibit 5).

- **Ranking in Japanese Industry.** AJL ranked third among all the foreign firms in Japan, after IBM and Coca-Cola (case Exhibit 5).

B. **What internal (strategic) and external (environmental) factors have contributed to the performance of Amway Japan Limited?**

1. Key factors that have contributed to AJL's success to date can be attributed to both internal (strategic) and external (environmental) factors.

2. **Internal (Strategic) Factors.** AJL had been pursuing a "penetration" strategy, which emphasized the expansion behind distributor network through recruiting new distributors. The formula behind AJL's current success include: (1) growth in distributorship, (2) a small number of best selling products, especially big ticketed items, and (3) heavy reliance on a limited number of up-line distributors:

- **Growth in Distributorships.** As explained earlier, the AJL's distributor network expanded at annual growth rate of about 10% for the past 5 years to exceed 1 million (case Exhibit 1). Note that Japan's population was about 120 million.

- **Focus on Core Product Range.** The top 5 selling products accounted for 47% of total sales in FY1996 (case Exhibit 6). Especially, the new distributors tended to buy "big ticket items" such as Amway Water Treatment System and Amway Queen Cookware, which sold at over $1,400. Since they could receive a 30% discount on all the Amway products, their benefit of joining the distributor network would be over $400 whereas the membership cost only $77 for a starter kit. Many of these "consumer-type" distributors did not have any intention to stay with AJL to build their business.

- **Reliance on Up-line Distributors.** Students should note that AJL's financial success has been a function of the performance of a relatively small number of top-performing distributors. Up-line distributors (DDs and above, in particular) generated revenue about 58 times more than down-line distributors:

	a. % of sales	b. # of distributors	c. Annual Sales per Distributor = a/b
DDs and Above	30% = $ 600 mil.	8,500	$70,000 (¥ 7.5 mil.)
Below DD and Consumer-Type	70% = $1,400 mil.	1,091,500	$ 1,200 (¥ 135,000)
Total	100% = $2,000 mil.	1,100,000	$ 1,818 (¥ 198,000)

3. **External (Environmental) Factors.** AJL's success could also be explained by the factors unique to the Japanese market during the 1970s and 1980s, including (1) a complex and costly distribution sector, (2) Japanese consumers' preference for high value propositions, (3) Japanese women as an untapped labor force, and (4) a lack of direct competition.

- **Complex and costly distributor channel system in Japan.** The Japanese distribution channel industry was known for its arcane nature with multiple-layers of wholesalers, a large number of small "mom-and-pop" retailers, a wide range of government regulations, and a lot of culturally-rooted business practices, which had prevented foreign firms from succeeding in Japan. Amway's direct selling method could bypass all these obstacles by not relying on the existing local distribution channel.

- **Japanese consumers' preference for high value propositions.** Japanese consumers were well known for their faith in high-priced, high quality products, especially the imported goods. Case Exhibit 8-a shows 33% of consumers associated Amway with "high quality" and 35% with its image of an "American company." Case Exhibit 8-d indicates that the majority of distributors were satisfied with the quality of Amway products.

- **Japanese women entrepreneurs as an untapped labor force.** Women had been ignored by corporate Japan as potential employees; equal employment opportunity was not enacted as legislation until the mid 1980s, and women in the workforce remained disadvantaged relative to their male counterparts. AJL's business model provided the perfect opportunity for those women of an entrepreneurial bent seeking gainful employment. Case Exhibit 2 shows that 85% of the salespeople in direct selling industry were female. In addition, Case Exhibit 8 shows that more than 80-90% of young female recognized Amway as a brand (whereas only 50-60% of male counterparts) and more than 50% of them have ever purchased Amway products (as opposed to less than 20% of males).

- **Lack of direct competitors.** There were no direct competitors who employed the direct selling method and sold products similar to Amway's (i.e., "person-to-person" method). Most of the local direct selling companies such as Pola and Noevir used traditional "door-to-door" approach. It was not until the 1990s that direct competitors such as Nu Skin and Tupperware entered the market. Case Exhibit 8-c shows Amway's high awareness (65% in 1996) and highest purchase experience (16%) vis-à-vis competitors.

C. **What explains the recent sales downturn?**

1. AJL's successes created new challenges as market conditions evolved in the 1990s. Just as with AJL's previous growth, the downturn in sales was a function of both external/market factors and a number of AJL policies, designed to achieve AJL's initial goal of market penetration but the source of new problems as the distribution network grew.

2. **Internal Factors:**

   - **Vulnerability to changing distributor motivation.** AJL's heavy reliance on a small number of up-line distributors and a narrow range of heavy-selling high-ticket items made it vulnerable to changes in distributor motivation.

   - **Increasing difficulty in controlling distributor network.** The rapid expansion of the distributor network to almost 1% of the entire Japanese population made it increasingly difficult to monitor instances of distributor misconduct, such as coercive recruiting and selling to down-lines. As a result, the increasing number of AJL-related complaints to consumer organizations had tarnished AJL's reputation, and the company was starting to be tarnished with the "pyramid-selling" brush (Case Exhibit 12b). This is particularly challenging given that distributors are not AJL employees but contract-based entrepreneurs (one of the factors which enabled such growth of the network).

     However, the challenge is that AJL could not easily impose any formal constraint on distributors' activities since distributors are not AJL's employees but theoretically contract-based entrepreneurs.

   - **Untapped distributor database.** A distributor database had been recently built and started to be utilized for "targeted marketing initiatives." However, there still remain issues to be solved:

     ... database was not shared effectively across departments;

     ... distributors' purchase data were discarded annually;

... no follow-up effort was made for those who did not renew their membership;

... 50% of consumer-type distributors' orders were made directly to AJL, whereas the other half were through their up-line distributors, indicating that AJL was not necessarily collecting the purchase data at the level of individual distributors.

3. **External Factors:**

- **Increasing price sensitivity among consumers.** All the changes in Japanese market in the 1990s, including continuing economic recession, increasing government deregulation, changing life styles, and expanding access to information on overseas markets (through Internet and travel) raised consumers' price sensitivity.

    Case Exhibit 8-d indicates that less people were satisfied with the price of Amway products than with quality, and less and less people were satisfied with prices over time: only 62% of current Amway users and 41% of non-users were satisfied with price.

- **Increasing openness of the labor market.** AJL no longer enjoyed the privileged position of being one of only a few opportunities for entrepreneurial women. A number of social changes were creating greater flexibility and opportunity in the labor market for entrepreneurially-inclined Japanese, including the new equal opportunity legislation, corporate restructuring, and diminishing lifetime employment. As AJL's business model relied on career opportunities, changes in the labor marker could have as much influence on its business as product policy or price sensitivity.

D. **What are the pros and cons of AJL's strategic options—penetration or productivity? Describe the feasibility of each in achieving AJL's revenue goal in FY 2000.**

1. AJL could enhance its sales growth through boosting sponsoring, retention, and/or productivity of its distributor membership. Strategic options for AJL included: (1) Penetration Growth, (2) Productivity Growth, or (3) Both. The pros and cons on these options are shown below:

Strategic Option	Pros	Cons
Penetration	• Proven strategy. • Large potential for new distributorship due to oversupply in the labor market (e.g., older people, women).	• Difficulty in controlling ever-expanding network; may deteriorate corporate image. • May not be sustainable: saturation may occur at some point.
Productivity	• Distribution of orders indicate untapped opportunities in different segments of the distributors (Case Exhibit 10).	• Difficulty in collecting individual distributor data because 50% of the order through uplines.
Both	• Revenue Growth	• More difficulty in controlling distributors

2. The feasibility of each option in achieving AJL's revenue goal in FY 2000 is addressed in Exhibit 1 in this note.

E. Epilogue

Short-term responses to sales downturn. The specific steps AJL took to rebuild growth in the second half of FY 1997 fell primarily into the following three areas — (1) boosting distributor motivation, (2) redesigning product promotion strategy, (3) target marketing for improving distributor productivity, and (4) rolling out new products and alliances.

1. **Boosting Distributor Motivation.** In order to boost and sustain distributor motivation at the highest possible levels, AJL launched distributor relations programs. In FY1997, 62% of the operating expenses were spent for such programs that provide incentives and activities designed to train, reward and support the distributors.

To cope with the negative impact of the revisions to Japan's Door-to-Door Sales Law, AJL used the nationwide programs to educate them on the revised law's provisions. The challenge AJL faced was to spread the word efficiently and effectively to more than one million individuals throughout Japan. AJL conducted seminars nationwide, using the network of eight customer service centers available to the distributors around the country.

EXHIBIT 1

FEASIBILITY OF STRATEGIC OPTIONS

Strategic Option	**Implications**
Penetration	• In order to achieve the ¥300 bil. revenue goal in FY2000, AJL will need to: – (a) recruit 450,000 more distributors to reach a network of 1.55 mil. (assuming average sales of ¥ 200,000, which is aggressive) or – (b) increase retention rate substantially from 73% to 97% (assuming current rate of core distributors to total)
Productivity	• In order to achieve the ¥300 bil. revenue goal in FY2000, AJL will need to increase its sales by ¥85 bil. Assuming 30% (¥25.5 bil.) from DDs and above and 70% (¥59.5 bil.) from below, AJL will need to: – (a) improve DD and above's average sales by ¥3M (= ¥25.5 bil./8,500), which is 40% of FY1996 level and 9% CAGR until FY2000; and – (b) increase other down-line's sales by ¥55,000 (= ¥59.5 bil./1,091,000), which is 40% of FY1996 level and 9% CAGR; • Assuming 100% (¥85 bil.) from DDs and above, AJL will need to improve their sales by ¥10 mil. (= ¥85 bil./8,500), equivalent to 133% of FY1996 level and 24% CAGR. • Assuming 100% (¥85 bil.) from down-lines, AJL need to increase their sales by ¥75,000 (= ¥85 bil./1,091,000), which equals to 58% of FY1996 and 12% CAGR.

AJL also prepared fact sheets and other literature describing the new law's implication to Amway business so that they need to be reassured of their freedom to continue business as usual.

2. **Flexible Mix of Product Promotion**. The second core element in AJL's strategy for rebuilding near-term growth was to redesign category-by-category promotion for Amway products. AJL had a diverse product line comprising over 140 consumer products ranging from expensive durable products such as the Amway Water Treatment System to a broad range of inexpensive consumable items. The breadth and depth of the product range gave AJL flexibility to manage growth across product categories.

For example, AJL delayed planned promotions of expensive durable products in the Houseware category until the first half of FY 1998, when AJL expected them to have the greatest impact of the direct sales law revision. Accordingly, AJL has developed an aggressive promotion programs for selected consumable products in the Personal Care and Nutrition categories to make up for lost sales of high-priced durables.

According to Stephens, AJL has "the ability through promotions to powerfully re-invigorate interests in selected products when we need to. We are confident our aggressive promotion schedule will play a major role in allowing us to rebuild growth in the second half of the year."

3. **Target Marketing for Improving Distributor Productivity**. AJL was determined to achieve growth based not only on expansion of its core distributor force, but also on increased distributor productivity. AJL has embarked on an ambitious program of targeted marketing initiatives designed to further raise distributor productivity. These initiatives were based on intensive studies on distributors' buying habits and motivations.

Following the success of these first initiatives, AJL was implementing a new series of targeted marketing programs in the second half of FY 1997, including a reopening of membership of Club Artistry. This is a frequent buyer's club that made an immediate success when launched in FY 1996. "We have every reason to be confident that our targeted marketing techniques will lead to a significant improvement in distributor productivity over time," according to Stephens.

4. **Rolling Out New Products and Alliances**. AJL also expected new product introductions to play a very strong role in boosting FY1997 second half sales. One of the examples was the Amway Air Treatment System, a big-ticket item in the Housewares category which was scheduled to be introduced during the fourth quarter of FY1997. Others include Artistry Body Gel and Swiss Serum anti-aging treatment in the Personal Care category; Premier Breed Dogfood and revised swallowable food supplement tablets in Nutrition; and performance-enhanced SA8 laundry detergent in Home Care.

Furthermore, AJL pursued strategic alliances with other companies. Jointly with Rubbermaid, AJL also developed a new line of co-branded storage containers in Spring 1997.

The alliance with Playtex Apparel Division of Sara Lee Corporation provided a line of premium, co-branded apparel in Fall 1997. In both cases, the products were developed exclusively for AJL.

Long-Term Strategic Plan Toward Year 2000. Stephens also devised the long-term strategic plan to reinforce AJL's core strengths. The plan included: (1) further investments in distributor partnerships, (2) investments in corporate visibility and image, and (3) investments in future new product line-up.

1. **Further Investments in Distributor Partnership.** The first investment AJL was making in distributor partnership took the form of not passing on to distributors the 21% rise in Amway Corporation's export prices. Stephens was confident that AJL could minimize the impact of the price increase on operating margin to approximately three percentage points in FY1997. AJL's ability to do this was in the exceptionally low cost of sales ratio. AJL's cost of goods sold, which was consistently in the 26 to 30% of sales, was counted for much less than it did for traditional consumer products companies and most other direct selling companies. Also mitigating the effect of the price increase was the fact that 35% of the products were locally sourced and therefore unaffected.

A second major investment in distributor partnership was to strengthen the organizational infrastructure on which distributors could rely to build their businesses. The most visible sign of this commitment was the recent completion of sixth Regional Distribution Center in suburban Tokyo. As the largest Amway distribution center in the world, it was expected to give AJL the capacity to support sales of 50% more than at present.

A third investment took the form of a new program, called distributor interface reengineering program, aimed at enhancing the efficiency of each and every point of contact with distributors. The program was based on the results of a recently conducted in-depth study of all points of distributor interface. Among other things, it involved stationing more AJL staff in the field working alongside distributors with improved telecommunications services. It also meant further expansion and refinement of the Internet homepage, providing distributors with a new source of information.

2. **Raising AJL Visibility.** Another very important action AJL took for the future growth was through measures to raise the visibility and positive image of the company. By far the most prominent investment in this regard in FY 1997 was Gold Sponsorship of the 1998 Nagano Winter Olympic Game. As a Gold Sponsor for the food supplements, cosmetics and toiletries and kitchen-care and laundry-care product categories, AJL was working with its distributors to contribute to the success of the Nagano Olympics as well as the Japanese Olympic team. This sponsorship was believed to send a positive signal of the strength and depth of AJL's commitment to the Japanese market. Stephens was confident that the investment AJL was making would be more than justified by the benefits that would follow from heightened visibility and prestige, and enhanced distributor motivation.

3. **Investing in New Product Development**. AJL increased its commitment to introducing a flow of successful new products while continuing to improve existing products by intensifying the interaction with distributors who after all were AJL's customers as well. With their help, new product introductions were carefully differentiated from competing products through demonstrably unique features which have in effect been pre-tested by distributors for success.

In addition to the first two alliances with Sara Lee and Rubbermaid; AJL was committed to reaching further alliances in the future, and these could be with either Japanese or foreign companies. AJL has now become a major Japanese distribution chain in its own right. As such, it can offer prospective strategic alliance partners a unique and powerful alternative to the traditional Japanese distribution system.

Stephens concluded his Interim 1997 Investor Presentation as follows:

"We are successfully managing a difficult year while continuing to invest and build for our future. We are committed to reinforcing, exploiting and leveraging our core strengths, which lie in our direct selling system, our distributor network and our broad and diverse range of products.

Above all, we are committed to preserving the full power of our most important single asset, which is the partnership we have built with our distributors. It is through the power of that partnership that we shall continue to meet our enduring commitment to serving the interests of all the shareholders of AJL."

GOODYEAR TIRE AND RUBBER COMPANY

Synopsis

In early 1992, Goodyear Tire and Rubber Company executives were reconsidering a proposal from Sears, Roebuck & Company that was originally made in 1989. The proposal from Sears was for Goodyear to sell its popular Eagle brand tire through 850 Sears Auto Centers in the U.S. This proposal was declined in 1989 because Goodyear management felt that selling through a mass merchandiser such as Sears would undermine the tire sales of company-owned Goodyear Auto Service Centers and franchised Goodyear Tire Dealers. However, following a $38 million loss in 1990 and a change in Goodyear top management in 1991, the Sears proposal resurfaced.

Two factors apparently prompted Goodyear's renewed interest in the Sears proposal. First, the Goodyear-brand passenger-car replacement tire market share had slipped in the U.S. Second, Goodyear executives believed that nearly 2 million Goodyear original equipment tires were being replaced annually at some 850 Sears Auto Centers. According to a Goodyear executive, the failure to repurchase Goodyear-brand tires happened by default "because the remarkable loyalty of Sears customers led them to buy the best tire available from those offered by Sears," which did not include Goodyear-brand tires.

The case links two strategic marketing decisions. First, broadened distribution through Sears would change a long-standing Goodyear marketing channel policy of selling primarily through company or franchised Goodyear dealers and not mass merchandisers. Second, a product policy decision exists. That is, should Goodyear sell all, some, or one (e.g.. Eagle) brand(s) through Sears? Related issues include trade relations in marketing channels, assessing market evolution in the replacement tire segment, the merits of dual distribution and the potential for product cannibalization of Goodyear retailer tire sales. Sufficient case information is provided for students to perform an in-depth qualitative analysis and a limited quantitative assessment of the Sears proposal.

Teaching Objectives

This case has five teaching objectives:

1. To introduce students to the U.S. passenger car tire industry and particularly the challenge of retail marketing in this highly competitive industry setting.

2. To explore environmental conditions that promote consideration of a change in marketing channel strategy, such as market evolution.

3. To give students an opportunity to assume the roles and perspectives of Goodyear Tire and Rubber Company executives, Sears, Roebuck & Company executives, and franchise Goodyear Tire Dealer owners for the purpose of assessing the upside potential, downside risk and potential channel conflict arising from Goodyear's consideration of Sears as a channel for the company's replacement tires.

4. To illustrate to students the importance of market segmentation, buyer requirements, and profitability when making channel choice decisions.

5. To demonstrate that marketing channel strategy and product strategy decisions are often linked together, particularly if dual distribution is employed.

Teaching Suggestions

This case is best suited for use in the course when the instructor wishes to examine strategic issues in channel selection and management. This case has been taught in both undergraduate and graduate courses with favorable results.

Previous experience teaching the case indicates that the marketing channel issue be addressed initially. Subsequent attention can then be given the product policy issue(s). One way to begin the class discussion is to break-out the class into three groups representing the Goodyear Tire and Rubber Company, Sears, Roebuck & Company, and franchised Goodyear Tire Dealers. Once done, a general question can be posed:

How might the Goodyear Company, Sears, and franchise Goodyear Tire Dealers view broadened distribution of Goodyear-brand tires through Sears Auto Centers?

Specific questions that might be posed to students prior to or during a class discussion are:

1. How would you characterize the competitive environment in the tire industry in 1991?

2. What is Goodyear's relative competitive position within the tire industry?

3. Does it make strategic sense for Goodyear to broaden its distribution beyond company-owned and franchised Goodyear tire retailers as a matter of channel policy? Why?

4. What are the strategic implications of broadened distribution of Goodyear-brand passenger tires through Sears Auto Centers?

5. What effect, if any, does the number of brands and specific brands sold through Sears have on the distribution decision? Why?

6. Should Goodyear broaden its distribution through Sears Auto Centers? If yes, what brands or models should it sell through Sears?

Areas for Discussion/Analysis

A. How would you characterize the competitive environment in the tire industry in 1991?

1. The tire industry divides into two segments: original equipment (OE) tires and replacement tires. The OE segment accounts for 20-25 percent of tires sold annually; unit sales are trending downward. The replacement tire segment accounts for 70-75 percent of tires sold each year; the unit sales trend is "flat". Passenger car tires account for 75 percent of annual sales.

2. Although 10 tire manufacturers account for 75 percent of worldwide production, three firms account for 60 percent of all tire sales sold. They are in order: Groupe Michelin, Goodyear, and Bridgestone. These firms compete in both the OE and replacement tire segments. Although Goodyear is second to Groupe Michelin in worldwide production, it is the perennial U.S. market leader in both the OE and replacement segments.

3. Even though the OE segment is smaller, it is viewed as strategically important by tire manufacturers for two reasons. First, prominence in the OE segment provides volume-related scale economics in the production of tires. Second, it is believed that car/truck owners satisfied with their OE tires on new vehicles will buy the same brand when they replace their worn tires. However, the case also states that passenger replacement tire buyers are becoming more price-sensitive and less likely to simply replace their branded OE tire with the same brand of replacement tire. This point is significant for two reasons:

- It relates to "store loyalty" evident with Sears buyers mentioned earlier

- Tire retailers can influence the replacement brand chosen from among those carried in their store. Disgruntled franchise Goodyear Tire Dealers might actually be able to switch replacement tire buyers over to other (private-label) brands as some have threatened.

4. Exhibits 1 and 2 in this note shows the relationship between passenger-car replacement tire market share and OE passenger tire market share and share of "retail points of sale". As can be seen, there is a positive relationship. Moreover, the relationship between passenger-car replacement market share and "retail points of sale" is more pronounced. Some observations worth noting by the instructor or mentioning by students are:

- Bridgestone is an obvious "outlier" in the relationship between replacement market share and "retail points of sale". One explanation is that Bridgestone has so little share (1.25%) of the OE tire segment.

EXHIBIT 1

BRAND SHARES OF PASSENGER OE AND REPLACEMENT TIRE SALES AND "SHARE OF RETAIL POINTS OF SALE": 1991

Brand	Percentage Share of...		
	Passenger OE Tire Market	Retail Pts. of Sale	Passenger-car Replacement Tire Market
Goodyear	38.0%	18.0%	15.0%
Michelin	16.0%	16.7%	8.5%
Firestone	16.0%	9.8%	7.5%
Uniroyal/Goodrich	14.0%	15.2%	14.0%
General	11.5%	4.9%	4.5%
Bridgestone	1.25%	13.8%	3.5%
Sears	-	2.0%(est.)	5.5%

Source: Based on case Exhibits 2, 5, and 6

- Sears is unique as it does not produce tires for the OE tire segment; yet it captures 5.5 percent of the passenger-car replacement tire segment with its mostly private (store) brands.

- Yes, retail coverage, as measured by "retail points of sale", is related to replacement tire market share. However, the nature of the relationship may not be perfectly linear. That is, a certain proportional increase in "retail points of sale" may not result in the same proportional increase in passenger-car replacement tire market share.

5. Competition is intense in both the passenger OE and replacement tire segments. The nature and scope of competition differs, however. Competition in the OE segment revolves around the major vehicle manufacturers and supplying some or all of the tire needs for their new model year cars and trucks. Vehicle manufacturers typically use multiple sources for their tires and appear to be highly price sensitive. OE tires are essentially "produced to order" and may be viewed as a "commodity" by vehicle manufacturers. Competition in the replacement tire segment occurs across the marketing mix. Major tire manufacturers compete on the basis of "retail points of sale," product variety and innovation, price, and promotion (advertising, retail promotions, and event sponsorship).

EXHIBIT 2

RELATIONSHIP BETWEEN REPLACEMENT MARKET SHARE AND OE TIRE MARKET SHARE AND SHARE OF "RETAIL POINTS OF SALE"

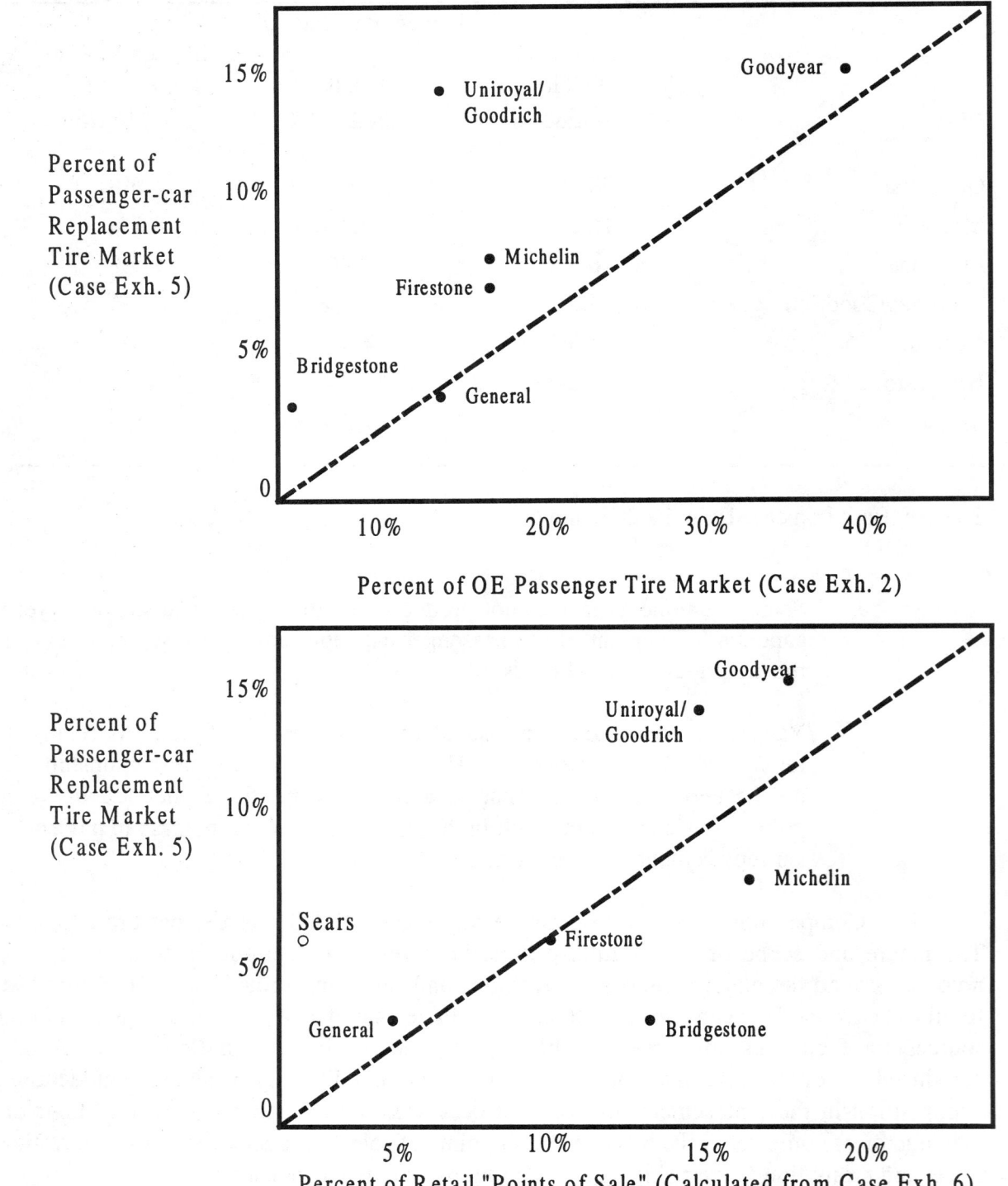

B. What is Goodyear's relative competitive position within the tire industry?

1. Goodyear is the second largest tire manufacturer in the world, behind Groupe Michelin which manufacturers and markets the Michelin and Uniroyal/Goodrich brands.

2. The Goodyear brand is the single largest brand, in terms of sales to the OE tire segment. Its share of this segment is 38 percent (case Exhibit 2). It is noteworthy, however, that Groupe Michelin with its Michelin and Uniroyal/Goodrich brands combined capture 30 percent of the OE tire segment (case Exhibit 2).

3. Goodyear-brand tires capture the largest portion of sales in the U.S. replacement tire market: 15 percent of passenger-car tires, 11 percent of light-truck tires, and 23 percent of highway truck tires. Company-wide share increases in each category when sales of its Kelly-Springfield brand is included (see case Exhibit 5).

4. Students might also note that Goodyear's relative competitive positive is due, in part, to the following:

- The broadest line of tire products of any tire manufacturer: product line width and depth.

- The largest number of "points of sale" for any branded tire with controlled distribution; that is, company-owned and franchised dealers.

- Price-Performance Positioning: Premium pricing supported by product innovation and umbrella brand advertising that emphasizes, "The best tires in world have Goodyear written all over them."

5. Nevertheless, there is evidence that Goodyear has encountered some problems which might be categorized as follows:

- **Flat or downward trend in OE tire volume.** Goodyear has likely felt the effect of plateaued unit volume in the OE segment (see case Exhibit 3). Unit volume growth is possible through market share gains; however, market share is increasingly "purchased" through lower prices to vehicle manufacturers. Lower prices serve to squeeze already slim profit margins in the OE segment as indicated in the case text.

- **Changing retail distribution.** Exhibit 1 in the case shows that tire company stores share of replacement tire sales declined somewhat from 10 percent in 1982 to an estimated 9 percent in 1992. The market share for replacement tire sales captured by retailers not serviced by Goodyear (discount multi-brand independent dealers, chain/department stores, and warehouse clubs) has grown from 17 percent in 1982 to 35 percent in 1992. Given Goodyear's primary distribution through company-owned Goodyear

Auto Service Centers and company-franchised Goodyear Tire Dealers, which represent tire company stores, the company is effectively "closed out" of retail outlets that are capturing a larger percentage of the replacement tire segment.

- **Decline in replacement tire market share in the U.S..** Goodyear recorded a 3.2 percent decline in the U.S. passenger-car replacement tire market between 1987 and 1991. This decline represented a loss of about 4.9 million units according to a company spokesperson. Moreover, the case notes that the replacement tire market, which accounts for some 60 percent of Goodyear worldwide sales is more profitable than the OE market.

C. Does it make strategic sense for Goodyear to broaden its distribution beyond company-owned and franchised Goodyear tire retailers as matter of channel policy? Why?

1. As indicated earlier, the changing retail environment would strongly suggest that non-company-owned or franchised tire company stores are capturing a larger percentage of replacement tire volume (see case Exhibit 1). The principal retailers gaining share are discount multi-brand independent dealers. These dealers more than doubled their market share (7% to 15%) from 1982 to 1992. During the same time frame, warehouse clubs went from 0 percent to 6 percent. Tire company stores recorded a modest decline in market share from 10 percent in 1982 to 9 percent in 1992. Students should recognize that retail channel change is a form of **market evolution** (see Chapter 10 in the text).

2. It is also worth noting that chain and, department stores actually experienced a decline in market share (20% to 14%) from 1982 to 1992. This change has direct implications for a decision to sell through Sears as discussed in part D. below.

3. Broadened distribution through Sears represents a change in distribution policy in two ways. First, Goodyear is moving beyond a form of exclusive distribution evident in company-owned and company franchised Goodyear tire retailers. As such, Goodyear will (a) increase its retail density/coverage, (b) but possibly decrease its control over retail marketing practices and (c) reduce the "exclusivity" of the brand. Second, distribution through Sears suggests that Goodyear is exploring a **dual distribution** strategy. A critical issue with dual distribution is that different channels reach different customers - an issue discussed in part D. below.

4. Broadened distribution through Sears is bound to create channel conflict and affect trade relations with franchised Goodyear Tire Dealers. The extent and severity, however, is not known, nor is franchise retailer reaction, i.e. incidence of carrying more private labels and switching tire buyers to competing brands. Is this the time to create channel conflict when replacement tire unit volume is "flat?"

D. What are the strategic implications of broadened distribution of Goodyear-brand passengers tires through Sears Auto Centers?

1. Based on the case information, reconsideration of the Sears proposal is a **defensive strategic move**. Declining market share in the replacement tire segment, changing retail structure, and "flat" OE tire volume resurrected the Sears proposal. It is also noteworthy that a new management team is now looking at the Sears proposal. It may be that they are less tied to past Goodyear distribution/channel policies or strategies.

2. From a strategic perspective and for class discussion, students may be directed toward the three criteria for choosing a marketing channel which are described in Chapter 7:

- Provide the best coverage of the target market sought.

- Satisfy the buying requirements of the target market sought.

- Maximize potential revenues and minimize cost.

Target Market Sought. What is the target market? Is it...

...Loyal Sears customers with worn-out-out Goodyear or competitor tires?

...Vehicle owners in general with worn-out Goodyear-brand or competitor tires?

If it is the **loyal** Sears customer, then this segment is separate and distinct from Goodyear dealers and represents a previously untapped segment **and** incremental tire unit sales, or a portion thereof. This segment represents 2 million tires according to Goodyear executives.

If the target segment is vehicle owners in general with worn-out tires, then cannibalization of Goodyear dealers' tire sales is more likely.

Interesting issues to explore include the distinction between store and brand loyalty and preference for different kinds of retail (replacement) tire outlets (e.g. tire company stores vs. department stores, vs. multi-brand tire stores, etc.)

Buying Requirements. What do replacement tire buyers want and how well do retailers satisfy these wants? Instructors might ask students who have purchased replacement tires about their buying experience.

It is reasonable to conclude from the case text that replacement tire buyers are highly price conscious, and prefer choices (some "price-quality" ranges). It is also reasonable to believe that prompt and proper installation, a "pleasant" tire store environment, and credible salespeople are important since tire buyers appear to know little about tire quality.

Can Sears satisfy these wants? Sears currently captures 5.5 percent of the passenger-car replacement tire segment. It is also noteworthy, however, that Sears' share has declined from 6.5 percent in 1989 to 5.5 percent in 1991. Is this decline in market share indicative of Sears' ability to satisfy buyer requirements?

Maximize Revenues/Minimize Cost. Will broadened distribution through Sears generate incremental revenue? As stated earlier, yes it could provided the **loyal Sears customer** is the target segment reached **and** the draw from Goodyear dealers is minimized. Unfortunately, there is no specific cost data in the case to assess the profit impact.

Potentially useful calculations for students to make concerns the average number of tire units sold by Sears Auto Centers and Goodyear tire dealers. As shown in Exhibit 3 in this note, on average, a Sears outlet sold some 10,055 replacement tires in 1991 compared with 2,927 replacement tires sold through Goodyear tire dealers.

EXHIBIT 3

ESTIMATES OF PASSENGER REPLACEMENT TIRE SALES SOLD BY
SEARS AUTO CENTERS AND GOODYEAR RETAIL OUTLETS IN 1991

Given:
1. Sears Replacement Tire Market Share: 5.5% (case Exhibit 5)
2. Goodyear Replacement Tire Market Share: 15.0% (case Exhibit 5)
3. Sears Auto Centers: 850 (stated in the case)
4. Goodyear "Retail Points of Sale": 7,964 (case Exhibit 6)
5. Replacement Tire Unit Volume: 155.4 million (case Exhibit 3)

Average Replacement Tire Volume Through Sears Auto Centers:

[155.4 million tires x .055] ÷ 850 = 10,055 tires

Average Replacement Tire Volume Through Goodyear Outlets:

[155.4 million tires x .15] ÷ 7,964 = 2,927 tires

---

3. It is also important that students give attention to how the Goodyear Company, Sears, and Goodyear dealers might view the strategic implications of broadened distribution. Selected viewpoints are outlined in Exhibit 4 in this note in terms of upside potential and downside risk. We have found that breaking-out students into three groups representing the Goodyear Company, Sears, and franchised Goodyear Tire Stores helps stimulate class discussion and, at times, argument!

EXHIBIT 4

SELECTED VIEWPOINTS ON BROADENED DISTRIBUTION THROUGH SEARS

Goodyear Tire & Rubber Company Perspective	Sears Roebuck & Company Perspective	Franchised Goodyear Tire Dealer Perspective
<u>Upside Potential</u> 1. Provides access to tire buyers who are loyal to Sears and capture some of the 2 million worn-out Goodyear tires being replaced at Sears. 2. Provide access to 5.5% of annual replacement tire volume captured by Sears.	<u>Upside Potential</u> 1. Will carry the No. 1 tire brand in the U.S. thus enhancing the "image" of Sears Auto Centers. 2. May allow for incremental tire volume from vehicle owners with Goodyear-brand OE tires who need replacements (Goodyear already believes that 2 million worn-out Goodyear tires are being replaced at Sears) <u>and</u> who are Goodyear brand-loyal.	<u>Upside Potential</u>
<u>Downside Risk</u> 1. Could lead to strained trade reductions with franchised Goodyear Tire Dealers. They might: (a) Begin carrying more private labels (b) Withdraw from the franchise and become multi-brand independent dealers. 2. Sears replacement tire market share decreased from 6.5% in 1989 to 5.5% in 1991. In fact, the chain/department store tire share has also declined (see case Exhibit 1). Is this the channel (store) to be in?	<u>Downside Risk</u> 1. Goodyear-brand tires could cut into Sears private label tires (i.e., Weather Beater). This is an issue to the extent profit margins are better on private label tires (which they generally are).	<u>Downside Risk</u> 1. Broadened distribution through Sears eliminates franchised dealer "exclusivity". It also allows for the potential of further price competition. 2. Potential for lost sales is very real, particularly where Sears has a strong market presence.

E. What effect, if any, does the number of brands and specific brands sold through Sears have on the distribution decision? Why?

1. The number of brands and specific brands sold through Sears has a very important effect on the distribution decision. The brand (product) policy decision can be again viewed from the three parties: Goodyear Company, Sears, and franchised Goodyear Tire Dealers.

- The Goodyear Company and Sears might benefit more from having Sears carry the full line of Goodyear-brand tires.

- Franchised Goodyear Tire Dealers would benefit from fewer brands being sold through Sears.

2. In general, there are four brand (product) policy choices available to the Goodyear Company. They are:

   a) Distribute only the Eagle brand through Sears since this brand was part of the original proposal made by Sears in 1989. **Note**: Based on case Exhibit 9, the Eagle brand represents 12 of the 30 (60%) of Goodyear brand models.

   b) Distribute the complete brand (product) line through Sears.

   c) Sell certain brands through Sears and others through dealers, i.e., Sears gets exclusive rights to Goodyear Eagle and Arriva brands. Goodyear Tire Dealers retain exclusive right to all others.

   d) Provide some brand **model** exclusivity for both Sears and franchised Goodyear Tire Dealers and let both retailers carry the other brands, i.e., Sears gets only selected Eagle brand models; Goodyear Tire Dealers has the Aquatred on an exclusive basis and top quality brand models (e.g. Eagle GT II) and other brands, except designated Eagle brand models..

The pros and cons of each policy or possible variation can again be discussed by students representing the Goodyear Company, Sears, and franchised Goodyear Tire Dealers. Student attention should be directed toward case Exhibit 9 which describes the brands and models and their tread wear, traction, and temperature ratings which correspond to both quality and price. As a quick point of reference, the following categorization can be derived from case Exhibit 9:

Higher Quality/Price:	Lower Quality/Price:
1. Aquatred	1. Decathlon
2. Eagle GT II	2. T-Metric

When making brand (model) decisions, students should be sensitive to the fact that franchised Goodyear Tire Dealers would like to have a full range on the price-quality continuum. Also, given Aquatred recent introduction, should this brand retain some exclusivity?

F. Epilogue

Goodyear elected to broaden its distribution coverage by selling Goodyear-brand tires through Sears in March, 1992. Goodyear also elected to supply Sears with the Arriva brand on an exclusive basis and the following brands and models: Corsa GT, four high-performance Eagle models (Eagle GT+4, Eagle GA, Eagle VR, and Eagle ZR), and two Wrangler models for light trucks (Wrangler AT and HT). Goodyear dealers would sell the Aquatred brand on an exclusive basis as well as the brands/models sold by Sears, except the Arriva. All other brands/models would be retained exclusively by Goodyear retailers. Commenting on the decision, Stanley Gault, the Goodyear chairman and CEO, said the decision to move toward mass merchandising channels "can only further strengthen the Goodyear brand and Goodyear itself."

On June 11, 1992, the California Department of Consumer Affairs accused Sears of systematically overcharging automobile repair customers at its 72 Sears Auto Centers in the state. Four days later similar accusations appeared in New Jersey and several other states. On September 2, 1992, Sears agreed to pay an estimated $15 million to settle charges in California and 41 other states, as well as settle 19 related class-action suits. Denying any charges, it was estimated that Sears would pay over $46 million in damages. The damage to Sear's reputation and the effect on Goodyear tire sales was modest.

In early 1995, Goodyear executives and the tire industry analysts were still debating what effect, if any, Goodyear's decision to broaden its distribution through Sears had on Goodyear's market share. According to Modern Tire Dealer, an industry trade publication that collects and reports market statistics, Goodyear's share of the U.S. passenger-car replacement tire market rose 1% in 1992 to 16%. This 16% figure remained unchanged in 1993 and 1994 according to Modern Tire Dealer. Goodyear executives dispute this figure saying its market share rose 2% by 1994. Either way, the 1% to 2% market share gain is less than Goodyear had probably hoped for from broadened distribution through Sears. (Source: Based on "Goodyear Plans To Sell It's Tires at Sears Stores," *The Wall Street Journal*, March 3, 1992; "Goodyear Brand Tires To Be Sold By Sears," *Modern Tire Dealer - Newsfocus*, March 1992; "Sears Will Pay $15 Million Settling Charges," *The Wall Street Journal*, September 3, 1992, "And Fix That Flat Before You Go, Stanley," *Business Week*, January 16, 1995.)

G. **Summary Points**

1. To the extent that a marketing manager has alternative channels to reach prospective buyers, the decision facing the manager is one of selecting the channel that

- Provides the best coverage of the target market sought.

- Satisfies the buyer requirements of the target market.

- Maximizes revenues and minimizes cost of distribution.

2. Dual distribution is a means to reach different market segments. However, dual distribution can affect trade relations with channel members and lead to channel conflict.

3. Market evolution evident in changing retail distribution structure often requires modification in a firm's marketing channel policy.

4. Marketing channel decisions often involve product policy decisions as well. When using different channels, a major product policy question is "who gets what?"

HENDISON ELECTRONICS CORPORATION

Synopsis

Hendison Electronics Corporation is a small ($67.5 million in sales) assembler and marketer of home entertainment equipment. In 1996, the corporate plan established a sales objective of $92.5 million for 1997. Mr. Richard Hawly, the Vice President of Marketing, was charged with the responsibility for assessing the company's existing distribution program and developing, within a short time, a complete distribution program consistent with the corporate policy and sales objective.

This case illustrates a situation where the distribution system must mirror elements of the marketing strategy, the environment, and consumer and dealer purchasing requirements. Even though Hendison has limited market coverage in eleven Western and Rocky Mountain states, coverage within some markets reflects an intensive distribution strategy while in other markets coverage reflects an exclusive distribution strategy. Sales per outlet demonstrate this disparity in strategy. Company executives are not in agreement as to whether this "mixed" strategy should be continued or modified.

Teaching Objectives

The principal objective of this case is to introduce students to the problem of devising a complete distribution strategy. In doing so, students should learn to appreciate the impact of the marketing environment, buyer and dealer requirements, and other marketing mix elements on distribution strategy. A second objective is for students to gain practice in diagnosing or "auditing" an existing distribution strategy to determine its strengths and weaknesses. An important point to emphasize here is the "80-20 rule" concept (actually 80-10 in this instance), i.e., most sales volume arises from a minority of dealers. A third objective is to develop the link between distribution strategy and sales effort. Finally, students should be made aware of the necessity to consider both the qualitative and quantitative aspects of marketing channel strategy.

Teaching Suggestions

This case should be used in that portion of the course where the instructor wishes to examine marketing channel issues and the appropriateness of different distribution strategies at the retail level. The case can be taught as a marketing channels case or as a marketing control case. The case is also suitable for examination purposes later in the course.

As with those cases that outline potential options, students have a tendency to focus on picking one from among the alternatives. However, debate on the alternatives should be deferred at least until the existing system has been diagnosed thoroughly. The following questions will get students on the right track:

1. What is the marketing environment for Hendison Electronics Corporation?

2. What are buyer requirements in purchasing home entertainment equipment?

3. What are outlet requirements for carrying and promoting home entertainment equipment?

4. How well does the current system fit the environment, buyer and outlet requirements?

5. What is the 1997 marketing thrust of Hendison Electronics Corporation?

6. What are the "pros" and "cons" of the alternative distribution systems under consideration?

7. Which alternative would you select and why?

Areas for Discussion and Analysis

A. **What is the marketing environment for Hendison Electronics Corporation?**

1. Five firms account for "the bulk" of total dollar and unit sales volume in the industry. These firms are Thomason (GE and RCA brands), Zenith, Matsushita (Panasonic and Quasar brands), Sony, and North American Philips (Magnavox, Sylvania, and Philco brands. Private brands also account for a sizable amount of industry sales of $20.5 billion in 1996.

2. The product mix in the home entertainment industry consists of five major categories: television, compact disc players, videocassette players, audio systems, and tape players and recorders. Market dollar sales growth for "home entertainment" products was 2.4 percent between 1995 and 1996. However, individual product categories vary in saturation levels, hence rate of growth. TVs are highly saturated (99% of U.S. households own a TV). VCRs, audio systems, tape players, and compact disc players are probably growth products -- early in product life cycle.

3. Product innovation is important in this industry.

4. How might one classify home entertainment products? Some shopping goods, others specialty products? The median number of shopping trips made before purchasing these products was 2.4.

5. The most frequently shopped retail outlets for home entertainment products were radio/TV stores.

6. TV purchases are probably mostly replacement due to the high penetration of U.S. households -- buyers have some product knowledge. Buyers of VCRs are probably first-time buyers -- buyers have limited product knowledge. Buyers are probably "trading up." This is probably so for replacement buyers as opposed to those buying in addition to the product now owned.

7. Home entertainment equipment is sold through a variety of outlets including (a) home furnishings/furniture stores, (b) housewares/hardware stores, (c) auto supply stores, (d) department stores/mass merchandisers, and (e) radio/TV stores. For Radio/TV outlets (the stores that sell Hendison Electronics' products), the following analysis indicates that manufacturer volume through an average outlet was $1,050,478 based on case Exhibit 2 and case information:

Radio/TV Outlets	Retail Sales ($ thou.)	Average Sales/ Outlet	Retail Gross Margin %*	Est. Wholesale Sales/Outlet**
4,289	$6,214,483	$1,448,935	27.5	$1,050,478

*Retail gross margin given in the case.

**Wholesale sales/outlet is the dollar value of manufacturer sales to Radio/TV stores calculated by multiplying $1,448,935 by .725.

The $1,050,478 wholesale sales figure is useful in the subsequent analysis related to Hendison Electronics' distribution strategy.

B. What are buyer requirements in purchasing home entertainment equipment?

From the previous discussion it appears that buyers require:

1. **Product Information**--particularly for first time purchases and innovations.

2. **Service**--delivery, credit, maintenance, etc.

3. **Depth/Breadth of Assortment**--"shop for best buy" **within** and **between** stores.

C. **What are outlet requirements for carrying and promoting home entertainment equipment?**

  1. Stores desire to attract customers with an assortment of home entertainment equipment competitive in quality and price **and** available only from that outlet.

  2. Earn highest margins possible and achieve adequate turnover on items with brand acceptance.

  3. Obtain from the manufacturer assistance in merchandising, display, and training of retail sales personnel.

  4. Obtain from the manufacturer assistance in post-sale activities, e.g., maintenance equipment/parts.

D. **How well does the current distribution system fit the environment, buyer and outlet requirements?**

  1. In order for students to respond to this question, they will need to recognize that Hendison serves 150 markets with 475 dealers in an eleven state area. Of these, 50 markets are served by 50 outlets **exclusively**; therefore, 100 markets contain the 425 remaining dealers.

  2. Currently Hendison appears to be employing an **intensive distribution** strategy for this type of product with 425 outlets in 100 markets or **4.25 per market**. Again, note that 50 outlets have exclusive arrangements; therefore 150 markets are covered.

  3. Hendison's markets are situated in markets with populations of 100,000 or less. Major producers, by comparison, serve markets with 1 million or more inhabitants.

  4. Present concentration of Hendison's sales implies great variability at the retail level since 80 percent of Hendison's sales volume comes from 10.5 percent of its (exclusive) retail outlets:

Exclusive Dealers: $\dfrac{80\% \text{ of } \$67.5 \text{ million}}{10.5\% \text{ of } 475 \text{ outlets}} = \dfrac{\$54 \text{ million}}{50} = \$1{,}080{,}000/\text{outlet}$

Nonexclusive Dealers: $\dfrac{20\% \text{ of } \$67.5 \text{ million}}{89.5\% \text{ of } 475 \text{ outlets}} = \dfrac{\$13.5 \text{ million}}{425} = \$31{,}765/\text{outlet}$

Calculating average sales per outlet in this manner indicates that Hendison Electronics is a minor source for about 90 percent of its outlets. In some 10 percent of its outlets, where Hendison Electronics is the exclusive source, volume is slightly above the calculated industry average of $1,050,478/outlet (wholesale). These calculations assume additional importance later when determining the likelihood of achieving the $92.5 million sales goal.

5. Is there an explanation for the low sales in independent outlets? Yes. It would seem that:

- Hendison has not been very aggressive in promotion in past years.

- Hendison has not adequately satisfied outlet requirements which in turn satisfy buyer requirements.

- Sales force activity has been inadequate.

Each of these factors probably contributes to overall performance. An analysis of sales force activity is particularly noteworthy.

- Call rate on 425 independent dealers is seemingly inadequate both in time and probably quality. Given that these dealers are called on twice a month:

  425 dealers x 24 calls/yr = 10,200 calls/yr ÷ 10 salesperson = 1,020 calls/yr/salesperson.

  1,020 calls/yr/salesperson ÷ 50 wks = 20.4 calls/wk or 4 calls/day

Given travel time, etc., this would amount to 2 hours per outlet per month. Given answers to Questions B and C above, it can be questioned whether this call activity is appropriate.

E. What is the 1997 marketing thrust of Hendison Electronics Corporation?

The thrust of the company can be categorized into six major areas.

1. **Sales Objectives**: $92.5 million; a 37 percent increase over 1996 dollar volume.

2. **Market/Consumer**: Urban areas of 100,000 population or less in eleven Western and Rocky Mountain states. Company wishes to attract the discriminating purchaser of home entertainment equipment who approach their purchases as an "investment." Sales objective states further that the company should gain $16.25 sales per capita in markets served.

3. **Product**: Home entertainment products exhibiting superior performance, styling, reliability which require display, demonstration and product education.

4. **Price**: Higher priced products selling for more than $500 at retail.

5. **Promotion**: Major change from previous years where emphasis was on promotionally priced items. Major change this year by using television advertising; $7.5 million in expenditures for TV advertising in 100 markets. Formerly, heavy reliance on newspaper advertising.

6. **Distribution**: Emphasis on specialty home entertainment dealers (radio and TV stores) who will provide professional selling and service and delivery.

F. **What are the pros and cons of alternative distribution systems under consideration?**

1. Four principal alternatives are described in the case:

   a. Status Quo

   b. Increase the number of dealerships: add 100 independent stores (more intensive distribution)

   c. Reduction in dealerships: 475 to 150 (more selective distribution)

   d. Exclusive distribution with "franchise-type" arrangement: 100 dealers in 100 markets.

2. **Status Quo**

   Pros: Based on Question D, there aren't any!
   Cons: See Question D

3. **Increase in Dealerships**: Increase dealers from 475 to 575 in 150 markets. This strategy would assume that Hendison keeps its 50 exclusive dealership markets and add 100 dealers in the 100 non-exclusive dealer markets. In effect, this would mean that Hendison Electronics would sell to 525 independents in 100 markets, or **5.25** (on average) dealers per market. Remember, Hendison currently has 4.25 dealers in these markets - a 24 percent increase. This is an even more intensive distribution strategy than currently exists.

   a. **Pros:**
   - Hendison "might" pick up additional volume due to more intensive coverage
   - Places less pressure on existing dealers to expand sales.

   b. **Cons:**
   - Hendison will likely need to expand its sales force which represents an incremental direct cost of $80,000 per salesperson.

     If Hendison Electronics maintains its call frequency per dealer (twice per month), then two additional salesperson will be needed:

     525 dealers x 24 calls/yr = 12,600 calls/yr.

     Each salesperson makes 1,020 calls/yr. Therefore, a total of 12 (12,600 calls/yr ÷ 1,020 calls/yr/salesperson = 12.3 salespeople) salespeople will be needed or two more. At a cost of $80,000/yr., a

$160,000 incremental cost results. Probably more salespeople are needed given the previous analysis indicating that present call activity is inappropriate. Indeed, if total salesperson costs are $800,000 annually (10 salespeople x $80,000/yr), this would mean a minimum 20 percent increase in sales cost to achieve a 37 percent increase in sales. More likely there would be a 30 percent increase in cost with three new salespeople.

- Increasing dealers may result in <u>fewer sales</u> per individual dealer due to cannibalism which might negatively affect trade relations.

- It is not consistent with advertising program/target market strategy to focus on 100 markets.

4. **Reduction in Dealerships**: This option would mean that dealers would be reduced from 475 to 250 in 150 markets. This strategy would assume that 100 markets would include 200 dealership markets plus 50 dealers in exclusive other markets. In effect, this would lead to 200 independent dealers in 100 markets, or <u>2</u> independent dealers per market: a **selective distribution** strategy.

    a. **Pros:** • Focuses on 100 TV advertising program markets.

- Reduces call frequency substantially, thus the possibility of better satisfying dealer requirements increases. Might this increase revenue?

- Dealers may be more inclined to emphasize Hendison's products because of less competition.

    b. **Cons:** • Dealer emphasis must be **extremely** heavy. Is this possible or reasonable to assume given the variety of brands carried?

In order for Hendison to achieve its $92.5 million objective, the 200 independent dealers must increase their Hendison average sales volume to $186,020 annually. This figure is determined as follows:

- Given that each of the 50 exclusive dealers produced average sales of $1,080,000 in 1996, then it can be estimated that their 1997 sales will be $1,105,920 ($1,080,000 + 2.4% growth in 1997 becomes $1,105,920).

- Exclusive dealer sales in total will be $55,296,000 ($1,105,920 x 50 = $55,296,000)

- The "shortfall" to be met by independent dealers will be $37,204,000 ($92.5 million − $55,296,000)

- Each of the 200 independent dealers must therefore sell $186,020 for the $92.5 million objective to be met ($37,204,000 ÷ 200 = $186,020)

- **The $186,020 figure represents a 5.86-fold increase!**

5. **Exclusive-franchise Approach**: This approach would result in 100 exclusive dealers in 100 markets that were previously served by independent dealers. The other 50 exclusive dealer (markets) would not be affected. This strategy represents an **exclusive distribution** strategy for Hendison Electronics.

    a. **Pros:**
- Strong incentive for dealers to sell and service Hendison products since only one brand is sold.

- Satisfy dealer requirements providing proposed plan is adequately implemented.

- Twenty-seven dealers in separate markets requesting this approach. But are they of sufficient quality?

- If 50 exclusive dealers + 27 new dealers that have expressed interest can each generate $1,105,920 in sales volume in 1997, then these 77 dealer/markets will produce $85,155,840 in sales. Hendison Electronics will only need to attract seven more to exceed the $92.5 million objective. How likely are the new dealers to do this? Again assuming the 50 existing dealers can produce $55,296,000, then 50 new exclusives must make up the $37,204,000 shortfall. This means each must achieve an average of $744,080 in sales. This is slightly over 67 percent of projected average volume through existing exclusive dealers in 1997. **It could happen!**

    b. **Cons:**
- If Hendison selects this strategy, can they attract the proper outlets?

- Will existing dealers fight it? This will depend upon Hendison Electronics' contribution to each outlet and will vary by market.

- Is this level of exposure **too limited**?

- Hendison may not have to incur possible dealer conflict arising from the adoption of an exclusive-franchise approach <u>and</u> it can still achieve its $92.5 million sales objective. How? Assume first that each current (50) and new (27) exclusive dealer will produce 1997 sales of $1,105,920. Assume further that the remaining 73 dealer markets keep their average of 4.25 outlets and each outlet sales (currently $31,765) grows at the industry rate of 2.4 percent.

Then, Hendison can achieve sales of $95,247,453 in 1997! This calculation is shown below:

50 existing exclusive dealer 1995 sales ($1,105,920 x 50)	$55,296,000
27 new exclusive dealer 1995 sales ($1,105,920 x 27)	29,859,840
73 dealer markets x 4.25 dealers/market x ($31,765 x 1.024)	10,091,613
	$95,247,453

- The possibility that Hendison can achieve its $92.5 million sales objective with or without franchising raises an interesting issue for students to consider. Instructors should "play up" this point in a class discussion and ask students to again consider the merits of a franchising approach and the "believability" of the calculated numbers.

G. Epilogue

Hendison Electronics Corporation (disguised name) elected to pursue the exclusive-franchise distribution strategy after a lengthy debate. Dealer reaction was mixed. Although the necessary number of exclusive dealers were recruiting in the 100 markets, some dealer discontent arose among those not carrying the Hendison line. Hendison resolved these problems. The sales volume objective of $92.5 million for 1997 was achieved.

Richard Hawly acknowledged that the exclusive-franchise distribution strategy was risky. He added, "At least it represented a coherent distribution strategy which was something which was something this company had lacked. It also provided the basis upon which to 'rationalize' our distribution and achieve marketing impact. The company's commitment to an aggressive advertising and promotion program and the need to more effectively serve and service dealers were important considerations."

For 1998, five additional markets were converted to exclusive-franchise markets and sales volume for the company as a whole exceeded the industry growth rate.

H. Summary Points

1. Corporate strategy often dictates a change in marketing strategy.

2. The "80-20 Rule" applies in many marketing situations. In this particular case, a small number of outlets accounted for a sizable percentage of total company sales. The same phenomenon exists in a firm's product mix.

3. Marketing channel control involves assessing the profitability of different marketing channel strategies. In this case, the profitability of exclusive, selective, and intensive distribution strategies was assessed.

4. Channel strategy decisions must include an evaluation of buyer requirements and outlet requirements.

5. Channel strategy is closely linked to a firm's sales and advertising strategy as this case illustrates.

6. The three levels of market coverage (channel strategies) are:

- Intensive Distribution
- Selective Distribution
- Exclusive Distribution

CHESTERTON CARPET MILLS, INC.

Synopsis

Suzanne Goldman, assistant to the president of Chesterton Carpet Mills, Inc., has been given the assignment of exploring the possibility of replacing floorcovering wholesalers with company-owned warehouses and a direct sales program. Ms. Goldman must prepare a position paper on the direct sales and distribution question including an economic justification and plan of action. Soon after she begins her investigation, a Chesterton Carpet Mills wholesaler informs her that the company's present floorcovering wholesalers will likely drop the company's carpet line soon after the first Chesterton Carpet Mills warehouse is opened.

The case provides an overview of the U.S. carpet and rug industry. This industry is experiencing modest sales growth, increasing concentration at the manufacturing level, and marginal profitability. Numerous changes have and are presently occurring in the industry's channel of distribution. Large carpet and rug manufacturers vertically integrated by first opening their own distribution centers in the 1980s. By the early 1990s, floorcovering wholesalers were declining in significance due to direct distribution by manufacturers and the creation of buying groups by retailers. Larger mass merchandisers such as Kmart, Wal-Mart, and Home Depot were replacing department stores, furniture outlets, and independent floorcovering specialty stores, the traditional outlets for carpets and rugs. In 1996, Shaw Industries, the industry's largest manufacturer, announced that it would begin operating its own retailers, only to reverse itself in 1998. Depressed manufacturing profit margins and trade margins among wholesalers and retailers has produced strained relations among all channel members.

As a profitable medium-size, privately-held producer of a full line of medium-to high-priced carpets, Chesterton Carpet Mills faces pressure from its floorcovering wholesalers to shave profit margins to accommodate demands of retailer buying groups desiring quantity (price) discounts. At the same time, Chesterton Carpet Mill's wholesalers are carrying less inventory and expecting more frequent deliveries. Wholesalers are complaining about slow payments from retailers which has slowed their payments to Chesterton Carpet Mills.

As the case unfolds, it becomes clear that Chesterton Carpet Mills must address a classic strategic marketing channel issue: to sell direct to retailers or use intermediaries. For students, the case illustrates a classic marketing proposition: "you can eliminate the middleman, but not its function."

This teaching note benefited from the insights and calculations provided by Professor Michael Levy, Babson College.

Teaching Objectives

This case has five teaching objectives:

1. To challenge students to weigh the qualitative advantages and disadvantages of indirect vs. direct distribution in general, and later with specific reference to Chesterton Carpet Mills.

2. To have students realize that intermediaries have "costs" reflected in margins and services provided. These costs arise from functions being performed and possibly not being performed by intermediaries. These costs must be absorbed by a manufacturer contemplating direct distribution.

3. To illustrate how marketing channel functions can and should be monetized.

4. To sensitize students to the fact that manufacturers contemplating direct distribution must perform channel functions.

5. The impact on trade relations must be considered when making channel modification decisions.

Teaching Suggestions

This case is suitable for use when an instructor chooses to examine channel modification considerations, direct versus indirect distribution, and trade relations. This case also has been used as an in-class examination (75 minutes) or part of a final examination.

Experience with the case indicates that the calculations of most direct vs. indirect distribution "costs" is not difficult for the better student. However, the instructor should encourage students to go beyond this point to (1) consider the costs of implementation from a working capital perspective and (2) consider the impact of a sales volume loss if wholesalers do drop Chesterton's line.

A useful way to begin a class discussion is to ask: "If you were Suzanne Goldman, what recommendation would you give to Robert Meadows?" This opening question can be followed by the following questions:

1. How might we characterize the carpet and rug industry and Chesterton Carpet Mill's position in the industry?

2. What are the pros and cons of a wholesale vs. a company distribution system from a qualitative perspective?

3. What are the economies of the wholesale vs. company distribution system? Can Chesterton Carpet Mills afford "going direct?"

Areas for Discussion/Analysis

A. **How might one characterize the carpet and rug industry and Chesterton Carpet's position in the industry?**

1. **Industry Sales Trends**

    a. The U.S. carpet and rug industry recorded sales of $10.3 billion at manufacturer's prices in 1998. Industry sales actually increased 6.6 percent between 1997 and 1998.

    b. The U.S. carpet and rug industry accounted for 70.8 percent of total U.S. floorcovering sales in 1998. This share has been declining at least since 1985 when carpet and rugs represented 82 percent of total U.S. floorcovering sales.

    c. U.S. exports of carpets and rugs has also declined. In 1970, U.S. companies supplied 51 percent of the world's carpets; by 1997 this percentage had declined to 45 percent.

    d. Industry sales are divided between "contract," or commercial, sales for institutions and businesses and residential sales for household replacement carpets. The residential segment accounts for 57 percent of sales based on yards of carpet sold; the contract segment accounts for 43 percent of sales in 1998. The percentages reflected a 5 percentage point decline in residential sales since 1985.

2. **Industry Competitors**

    a. The U.S. carpet and rug industry is consolidating. There were 300 manufacturers in the mid-1980s, but only about 100 manufacturers remain in 1998.

    b. Three manufacturers - Shaw Industries, Mohawk Industries, and Beaulieu of North America - account for 85 percent of U.S. residential carpet and rug sales. The top 10 manufacturers accounted for 91 percent of sales; the remaining 90 manufacturers accounted for just 9 percent of industry sales.

    c. Shaw Industries is the industry leader with 1998 sales of $3.5 billion. Shaw Industries sales are more than 34 percent higher than its next largest competitor - Mohawk Industries (see case exhibit 2).

d. Carpet and rug industry competitors compete primarily on price and manufacturers appear to be focusing on cost reduction and economies of scale with little emphasis on marketing according to industry critics. All in all, the industry exhibits marginal profitability.

3. **Carpet and Rug Distribution**

a. Distribution in the U.S. carpet and rug industry has been evolving since the mid-1980s. Beginning in the mid-1980s, the largest manufacturers began bypassing floorcovering wholesalers and selling direct to retailers through manufacturer-owned distribution centers. The intent was to capture floorcovering wholesaler margins and offset small or negative manufacturer profit margins. By 1990, the majority of carpet and rug sales for residential use were distributed directly to retailers. However, the majority of manufacturers still distributed through floorcovering wholesalers.

b. The early 1990s witnessed increasing wholesale and retail consolidation. The number of floorcovering wholesalers declined as did their share of industry sales. The share of wholesaler floorcovering sales was projected to decline from 26 percent in 1995 to less than 23 percent in 2000. Retail consolidation was also apparent. Carpet and rug retailers were forming "buying groups" - an organization of similar retailers which combine their purchases to obtain price (quantity) discounts. These buying groups were exercising a greater influence in the marketing channel and include well-known stores - CarpetMax, Carpet One, and Abby Carpets. Almost one-half of all U.S. residential carpet and rug sales volume was accounted for when buying group purchases were combined with those of carpet store chains (e.g. Carpet Exchange), mass merchandisers and discount stores (Kmart, Wal-Mart), and home centers (Home Depot). About 40 percent of the roughly 23,000 U.S. carpet and rug retailers were members of buying groups, mass merchandise, discount or home center chains. By 1998, CarpetMax, Carpet One, and Home Depot accounted for 45 percent of total U.S. floorcovering sales.

c. In December 1995, Shaw Industries announced it would vertically integrate further and begin operating retailers. This action prompted an immediate negative response from large retailers. For example, Home Depot dropped Shaw as a supplier and switched to Mohawk. Two buying groups - Carpet One and Abby Carpets - asked member stores not to do business with Shaw. Shaw Industries reversed its course in June 1998 when it announced it would sell-off its retail stores to the Maxim Group, the owner of CarpetMax stores.

4. **Chesterton Carpet Mills' Competitive Position**

   a. Chesterton Carpet Mills is a profitable medium-size, privately held producer of a full-line of medium-to high-priced carpets. It sells primarily to the residential segment (72% of sales). With fiscal 1999 sales of $75 million, Chesterton captured about 0.73 percent of industry carpet and rug sales ($75 million ÷ $10.3 billion). Although apparently small, Chesterton would be viewed as a major manufacturer outside of the industry's top twenty firms.

   b. Chesterton Carpet's estimated market share in residential carpets is about 0.9 percent [About 57% of industry carpet sales is residential or $5.87 billion; 72% of Chesterton sales are residential, or $54 million. Therefore, $54 million ÷ $5.871 billion = 0.9%].

   c. Chesterton has the distinction of being one of the few U.S. carpet and rug manufacturers to turn a profit.

   d. Chesterton marketed its residential carpet through seven floorcovering wholesalers which supplied 4,000 retail accounts. Company records indicated that 80 percent of its residential carpet sales, or $43.2 million (.8 x $54 million) was distributed through 50 percent, or 2,000, of its retail accounts. With sales through department, furniture, and floorcovering specialty stores, Chesterton clearly does not market through mass merchandise, discount, or home center stores.

   e. Chesterton is beginning to feel pressure from its wholesalers to grant price breaks to accommodate retailer buying group pricing demands. It appears that 30 percent (1,200 retailers/4,000 retailers total) of its current retailers, which account for about one-third of Chesterton's residential sales, were members of buying groups and seeking price discounts.

B. **What are the pros and cons of a wholesaler vs. a company distribution system?**

In general, the advantages of a wholesaler system might be viewed as disadvantages of a company distribution system and vice versa. Further, the distinction between short-run and long-run implications should be identified.

   1. **Advantages of Direct Distribution and Sales Effort:**

      a. Chesterton can work more closely with selected (larger) retailers and buying groups

      b. Better Chesterton service (inventory) for retailers

      c. Better Chesterton sales/support time spent with retailers

d. More Chesterton monitoring of and control over retailer sales efforts

e. Chesterton will "capture" wholesaler margins on sales to retailers

f. Appears to be "cheaper" than marketing through wholesalers (see discussion in C below)

2. **Disadvantages of Direct Distribution and Sales Effort:**

a. Must find capital for inventory, receivables, and warehouse system

b. Must develop and manage a field sales force and pay for it

c. Potential for inventory losses is increased given cyclical nature of carpet sales

d. Potential lost sales during transition

e. Direct distribution/sales cost have a higher **fixed** component (as opposed to higher variable component with a wholesale distribution system)

C. **What are the economics of the wholesale vs. company distribution system?**

1. **Costs of Wholesale Distribution:**

a. According to the case, wholesalers' margins are 20% of sales billed at the price to retailers. This represents 25% of manufacturer's prices:

(.20/.80 = .25) or .25 x $54 million = $13,500,000.

Sometimes students fail to see the rationale behind this calculation. The following description should be helpful and useful in subsequent calculations.

Margins represent how much money Chesterton gives to its wholesalers. This figure is 20% of the retail cost which is 100%. Therefore, the wholesaler cost of Chesterton's selling price is 80 percent of the retail cost. The $54 million in sales represents residential sales to wholesalers. If Chesterton eliminates wholesalers, it would capture the wholesaler margin of 20 percent. Therefore, Chesterton's residential dollar sales would increase to $67,500,000 by eliminating wholesalers and selling direct to retailers ($54 million/.80 = $67,500,000). If one subtracts $54 million from $67,500,000, then $13,500,000 results which is the estimate of wholesaler margin.

b. Chesterton's **costs of servicing** wholesalers is 6 percent of its present sales, or .06 x $54 million = $3,240,000.

c. A third "hidden cost" is the cost of financing wholesalers' **accounts receivable**. The case states that a 90-day collection period exists, therefore accounts receivable turnover is 4.06 (i.e., 365 days/90 days). Average accounts receivables are therefore $54 million/4.06 = $13,300,492. Since the case states that accounts receivable carrying costs are 10%, the accounts receivable carrying costs are $1,330,049 ($13,300,492 x .10 = $1,330,049).

d. The total estimated cost of wholesale distribution is:

Margins Provided	$13,500,000
Service Cost	3,240,000
Accounts Receivable Carrying Cost	1,330,049
Total Estimated Cost	$18,070,049

2. **Costs of Direct Distribution:**

   a. **Warehouse Expense.** Annual fixed cost of operating a warehouse is $700,000: 7 warehouses x $700,000 = $4,900,000.

   b. **Sales Representatives.** Assuming that Chesterton wishes to service all of its 4,000 accounts, salespeople make one call per month of 1 hour each, and 25 percent of sales representative's time is non-sales (50 weeks x 40 hours/wk x .75 = 1500 hours of selling time). Then,

   $$\frac{4{,}000 \text{ accts.} \times 12 \text{ calls/yr.} \times 1 \text{ hr.}}{1500 \text{ hrs. of available selling time}} = 32 \text{ reps. needed.}$$

   32 reps. at an average cost/rep. of $70,000 = $2,240,000.

   c. **Sales Managers.** One sales manager is needed per 8 sales reps; therefore, with 32 new sales reps, 4 managers are needed at $80,000 per year each = $320,000.

   d. **Sales Administration.** Estimated to be 40 percent of total sales force/management cost: .40 x [$2,240,000 + $320,000] = $1,024,000.

   e. **Inventory.** Chesterton Carpet will likely assume some additional inventory carrying costs at the warehouses which it did not incur when it simply "sold" inventory to wholesalers. These inventory costs are also "hidden." There are at least two ways of thinking about handling inventory and its carrying cost.

- If Chesterton treats its warehouses as "profit centers" it might conclude that they are simply wholesalers and price the inventory the same way that it sold to these wholesalers. Since Chesterton says that 4 inventory turns are necessary, then $54 million/4 = $13,500,000 of average inventory at a carrying cost of 10 percent equals $1,350,000 ($13,500,000 x .10).

- Alternatively, Chesterton might simply transport the inventory at cost without a mark-up to its warehouses. This calculation would involve taking the cost of goods sold figure from Exhibit 3 in the case, multiplying it by 72 percent to reflect the percent of total sales sold for residential use, divide by 4 turns, and then multiplying this figure by the carrying cost of 10%.

    [$56,250,000 mm x .72]/4 = $10,125,000;

    $10,125,000 x .10 (carrying costs) = $1,012,500

    Note that the difference between the two inventory carrying costs is $1,350,000 - $1,012,500 = $337,500. Either figure can be used since neither materially affects the decision.

f. **Accounts Receivable.** Accounts receivable costs are calculated as before. Note however that the dollar value of accounts receivable is $67,500,000 instead of $54 million because accounts receivables are based on sales to retailers, not wholesalers. This calculation is as follows:

    $67,500,000/4.06 (turns) = $16,625,615 (average A/R)

    $16,625,615 x .10 (carrying cost) = $1,662,562.

g. **Transportation.** An additional cost of transportation must be considered. This was estimated to be 4 percent of sales. Therefore, .04 x $67,500,000 = $2,700,000.

h. The total estimated cost of going direct is:

Warehouse Expenses	$ 4,900,000
Sales Representatives	2,240,000
Sales Managers	320,000
Sales Administration	1,024,000
Inventory Carrying Cost (higher number)	1,350,000
Accounts Receivable Carrying Cost	1,662,562
Transportation	2,700,000
Total Estimated Cost	$14,196,562

Chesterton will likely "save" money by using direct distribution rather than wholesale distribution since the estimated cost of floorcovering wholesaler distribution is $18,070,049.

D. Can Chesterton "afford" the conversion?

1. The case states that Chesterton would have to finance the conversion from internal funds. Case Exhibit 3 indicates that the company's working capital is:

Current Assets	$26,937,500
- Current Liabilities	10,312,500
Working Capital	$16,625,000

2. In short, Chesterton could finance the conversion from internal funds. However, it could be tight if the estimated costs are understated.

E. Epilogue

Ms. Goldman's report recommended against direct distribution. She argued that cash flow considerations, the time necessary to recruit and train a sales force, and "unrest" in the channel, mitigated against a structural change in distribution at the present time despite potential savings. Her recommendation was followed. She contacted the disgruntled wholesaler and said that the direct distribution idea was simply a rumor.

In mid-2000, the matter of direct distribution was again raised when two of Chesterton's floorcovering wholesalers approached the company about becoming exclusive distributors for Chesterton carpet and rugs. The inquiries also included an offer for Chesterton to acquire an equity interest in each. A final decision was pending as of the writing of this note.

F. Summary Points

1. This case illustrates the truism that "you can eliminate the middleman, but not its function." If the company decided to go direct to retailers then it has to perform such functions as inventory management, collecting accounts receivable, warehousing, and selling.

2. Marketing channel functions can and should be monetized.

3. The capacity of a producer to perform channel functions must be addressed from both a qualitative and quantitative or financial perspective.

4. The impact on trade relations is an important consideration when making channel modification decisions.

SOUTHWEST AIRLINES

Synopsis

In October 1994, United Airlines (the world's largest airline) launched "Shuttle By United" to compete directly with Southwest Airlines in nine markets in California and adjacent states. When "Shuttle By United" was announced, United's CEO predicted: "We're going to match them (Southwest) on price and exceed them on service." In response to United's initiative, Southwest's chairman Herb Kelleher said, the "United Shuttle is like an intercontinental ballistic missile targeted directly at Southwest."

"Shuttle By United" represented United's effort to operate on airline-within-an-airline alongside its hub-and-spoke route system to compete with Southwest Airlines (SWA). SWA had established itself in the U.S. passenger airline industry as a low cost, short-haul, point-to-point carrier with minimal passenger amenities that focused on fast turnaround of aircraft between flights. Its low operating costs were passed on to customers in the form of consistently low fares. "Shuttle by United" was created to be a clone of SWA in both service and price.

In late January 1995, after three months of head-to-head competition, United announced that its "Shuttle By United" service for the Oakland-Ontario, California market would be discontinued effective April 2, 1995. United also announced that its one-way walk up first and coach class fares on all "Shuttle By United" routes would increase by $10.00.

The United announcement caught SWA executives by surprise. SWA executives had to determine (1) what to make of these developments, and (2) how SWA might respond, if at all, to United's actions.

The case is rich in both tactical and strategic issues. On a tactical level, students are expected to consider whether SWA should follow "Shuttle By United" and raise its one-way walk-up fare by $10 (or some fraction of this amount) or keep its present fare and assess the profit impact of such actions. On a strategic level, SWA executives must consider the broader implications of an expanded United airline-within-an-airline strategy for SWA, not only in California, but also in other markets where United and SWA have a mutual presence. One such area is the midwest where United operates a large hub-and-spoke system out of Chicago's O'Hare Airport and SWA flys out of Chicago's Midway Airport. When couched in this context, the immediate short-run, tactical pricing issues take on more significant proportions and becomes a strategic marketing problem needing SWA attention.

Teaching Objectives

This case has four teaching objectives:

1. To introduce students to the economics of the U.S. passenger airline industry and developments in this industry since it was deregulated in 1978.

2. To expose students to Southwest Airlines' operations, marketing, and customer service philosophy and practice which is considered to be a model for the U.S. passenger airline industry.

3. To engage students in a marketing strategy competitive game setting that forces them to consider short- and long-run actions and reactions of competitors.

4. To give students an opportunity to examine airline service and price strategy and tactics and assess the profit impact of both.

Teaching Suggestions

This case has multiple uses and has been assigned in both graduate and undergraduate courses. Instructors may assign the case when they wish to emphasize (1) the marketing of services, (2) competitive marketing strategy, or (3) pricing issues. The case is best used later in a course after students have become comfortable with case analysis. The case has been successfully assigned as an examination case and as a group presentation case.

This case has proven to be a challenging assignment for students. A major challenge for students resides in the financial analysis and particularly the calculation of route profitability even though the case devotes considerable attention to "Industry Economics and Carrier Performance." The text describes how airline yield, load factor, and cost combine to determine the profitability of passenger operations for individual carriers (and routes). The calculation of <u>yield</u> is particularly problematic for some students. Accordingly, this note provides extensive treatment of this topic. A second challenge resides in the failure of some students to consider the broader strategic issues present in the case. Instructors should be prepared to introduce these issues if necessary.

Prior use of the case suggests that a stimulating discussion arises when attention is placed on competitive/competitor analysis. Some instructors have suggested using Michael Porter's competitor analysis framework to organize a class discussion. This framework is adapted for use with this case and shown in Exhibit A in this note.

EXHIBIT A

ELEMENTS OF A COMPETITOR ANALYSIS

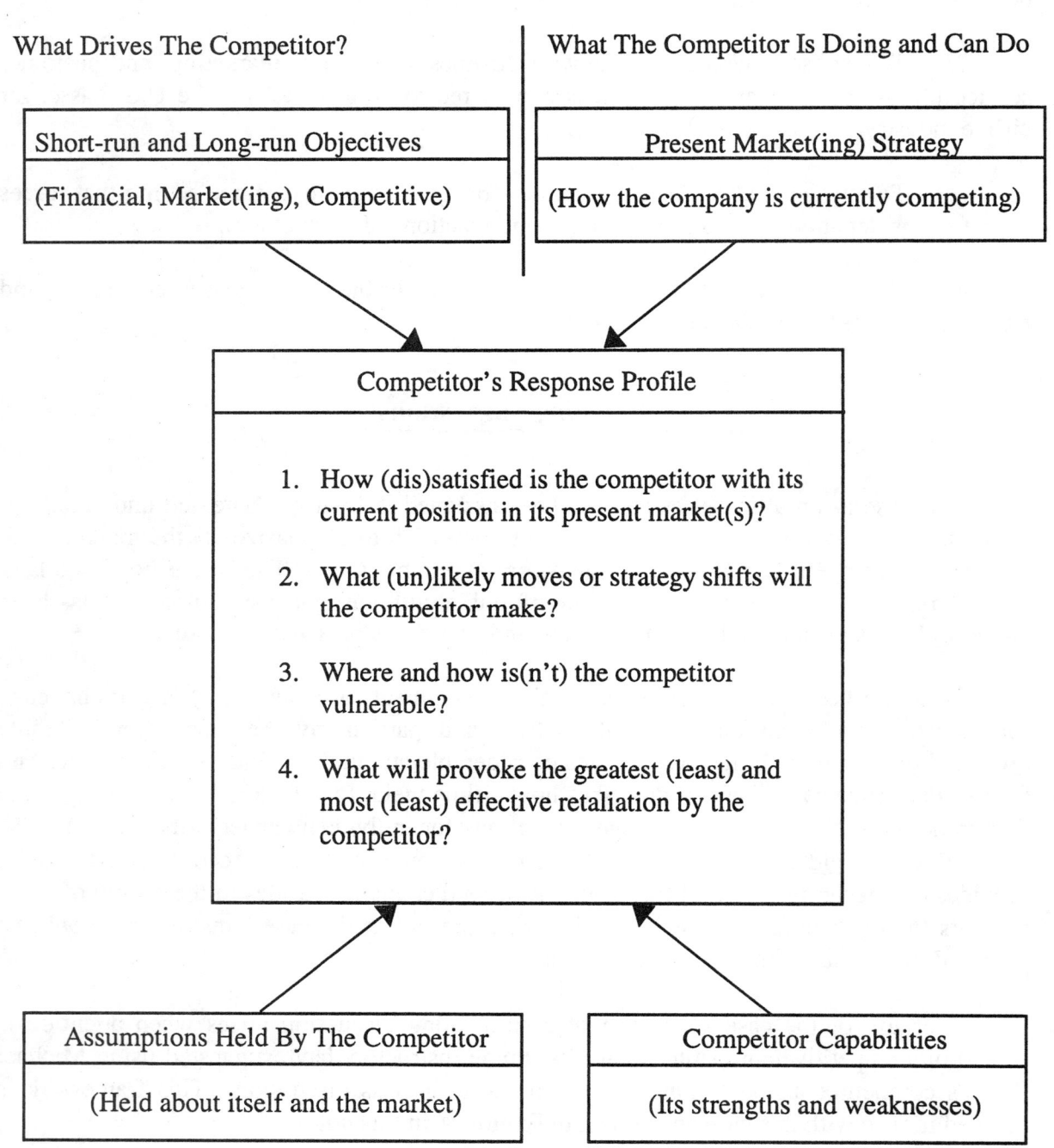

Questions that can be assigned to students prior to or during a class discussion are:

1. How would you characterize the U.S. airline industry in the early 1990's?

2. How can the "economics" of the airline industry be used to explain the performance of individual airlines and the industry as a whole?

3. How is it that Southwest Airlines has been able to consistently grow and prosper in the U.S. passenger airline industry?

4. How would you describe United's goals, objectives and strategy for "Shuttle By United?"

5. How has Southwest Airlines responded to the "Shuttle By United" initiative? What assessments can be made about Southwest's market and financial position on competitive routes based on 1994 Fourth Quarter results?

6. What assessments can be made about the "Shuttle By United" market and financial position based on 1994 Fourth Quarter results?

7. Based on your assessments, how would you interpret United's decision to (a) discontinue "Shuttle By United" service for the Oakland-Ontario market and (b) raise the one-way walk-up first class and coach fare on all 14 "Shuttle By United" routes by $10.00?

8. How should Southwest Airlines respond, if at all, to the "Shuttle By United" decision to change its service and price? Why?

Areas for Discussion/Analysis

A. How would you characterize the U.S. airline industry in the early 1990's?

1. Airline bankruptcy and collapse marked the early 1990's due to a recession, a doubling of fuel prices during the Gulf War in 1991, and excess airline capacity. Between 1989 and 1992, Pan Am, Continental, America West, Midway, Eastern and TWA filed for bankruptcy. Eastern, Pan Am, and Midway ceased operations in 1991. Continental and TWA emerged from bankruptcy in 1993 as did America West in late 1994.

2. The airline industry as a whole recorded a cumulative deficit of $12 billion from 1990 through 1993. (Although not mentioned in the case, the $12 billion industry deficit wiped out the cumulative profit earned by the U.S. airline industry since its inception!). The industry recorded a modest operating profit in 1994.

3. Still, only four of the nine major U.S. carriers recorded a profit in 1994. They were America West, Northwest, Southwest, and United (see case Exhibit 3).

4.   Only Southwest Airlines appeared able to prosper during the 1990's. Operating as a short-haul, point-to-point, low fare, high frequency airline committed to exceptional customer service, Southwest had more than doubled its operating revenues and almost quadrupled its operating income from 1990 through 1994.

5.   Financial calamity in the airlines industry had numerous effects. First, carrier collapse meant their was further consolidation in the industry. In the late 1980's, eight airlines controlled 91 percent of U.S. traffic. In 1994, nine carriers accounted for 95 percent of domestic passengers carried. Five carriers - American, Continental, Northwest, and United - accounted for over 80 percent of all major carrier domestic traffic.

Second, new "low fare, low frill" airlines were being formed from the carnage of the older, now bankrupt airlines. Benefiting from a cheap supply of aircraft grounded by major carriers from 1989 to 1993, the availability of furloughed airline personnel, and cost economics of point-to-point route systems, new airlines (e.g. ValuJet, Reno Air, Kiwi International) had cost structures (and prices) that were significantly below most major carriers.

Third, the effect of "low fare, low frill" airlines was to depress fares for the industry as a whole and for major carriers in particular. In 1994, 92 percent of airline passengers bought their tickets at a discount, paying an average just 35 percent of the posted full fare.

Fourth, major carriers found themselves scrambling for ways to reduce operating costs. The largest single cost to an airline is people (salaries, wages, and benefits), followed by fuel. Airlines attempted to reduce labor costs by seeking labor concessions and furloughing more airline workers. Between 1989 and 1994, 100,000 airline workers lost their jobs.

Finally, major airlines began looking for ways to reorganize their operating procedures. An innovation, pioneered by Continental in October 1993, was to establish an "airline-within-an airline." This innovation involved operating a point-to-point, low fare, short-haul, route system alongside a major carrier's hub-and-spoke route system. United launched its version of an "airline-within-an-airline" in October, 1994. Both efforts were designed to emulate Southwest's operating practices. Continental's effort, dubbed "Continental Lite," had expanded rapidly only to be cut back in January 1995 due to operating difficulties resulting in a sizable financial loss. United's effort, called "Shuttle By United," continued operations primarily in California and in adjacent states.

B.   How can the "economics" of the airline industry be used to explain the performance of individual airlines and the industry as a whole?

1.   The "economics" of the airline industry play a pivotal role in the performance of each and every carrier. These "economics" have much to do with airline costs and revenue which in turn depend on airline capacity, asset utilization and productivity. It is important

that these "economics" are brought out early in the case discussion. Instructors should familiarize themselves with how airline calculate operating income for passenger operations. This is done in Exhibit 1 in this note using the information provided in the case. Exhibit 2 in this note shows the primary determinants of yield, load factor, and operating cost for airlines.

2. Labor and fuel costs represent one-half of an airline's costs. Both costs are relatively fixed at a particular level of operating capacity regardless of the number of passengers carried. With one-half of costs being fixed, airlines have **high operating leverage**. As discussed in Chapter 2, firms with high operating leverage incur losses at a faster rate once volume falls below break-even and generate profits at a faster rate once volume increases above break-down (This is one reason why the airline business seems to have a boom and bust cycle). It is understandable, therefore, why firms continually monitor their break-even points as mentioned in the case.

3. Revenue in the airline industry is determined by "yield" and "load factor." As noted in the case, yield has been trending downward for 25 years: "In terms of real yield (discounting for inflation), fares in the years 1969 to 1971 produced an average yield of 21.4 cents in 1994. By 1994, the average industry yield was 12.73 cents." Load factors (or simply occupied seats) have fluctuated due to periodic imbalances between industry (carrier) capacity and passenger demand. An important challenge facing individual airlines is uncovering ways to lower costs and finding the optimum balance between yield and load factor.

C. How is it that Southwest Airlines has been able to consistently grow and prosper in the U. S. passenger airline industry?

1. In 1994, Southwest (SWA) marked its 22nd consecutive year of profitable operations. This feat was unmatched in the U.S. airline industry over the past two decades. Students should be expected to explain why they think SWA has been so successful.

2. Students will undoubtedly refer to SWA's "culture" as having a bearing on its success. This is fine providing students recognize that "culture" or the "Southwest Model" has a positive impact on the economics of running the airline. We have found it useful for instructors to make a transparency of Exhibit 2 in this note and bring it to class. Students should be expected to articulate how SWA has masterfully managed the determinants of yield, load factor, and operating cost to make it successful. Exhibit 3 in this note provides a summary of how SWA has leveraged the determinants of yield, load factor, and operating costs in its favor.

3. SWA's success had not gone unnoticed by major carriers in the U.S. airline industry and the U.S. Department of Transportation (DOT). As noted in the case, a 1993 DOT study concluded:

EXHIBIT 1

CALCULATION OF AIRLINE OPERATING INCOME
FOR PASSENGER OPERATIONS

---

1. The case notes that an airline's operating income for passenger operations is determined as follows:

   Operating Income = (Yield × Load Factor) − Operating Cost, or

   $$\frac{\text{Operating Income}}{\text{ASM}} = \left(\frac{\text{Passenger Revenue}}{\text{RPM}} \times \frac{\text{RPM}}{\text{ASM}}\right) - \frac{\text{Operating Cost}}{\text{ASM}}$$

   where... <u>Yield</u> is an average dollar amount received for flying one passenger one mile, or revenue passenger mile.

   <u>RPM</u> (revenue passenger mile) is one seat flown one mile with a passenger in it.

   <u>ASM</u> (available seat mile) is one seat flown one mile whether the seat is occupied by a passenger or is empty.

   <u>Load Factor</u> is determined by the number of seats flown one mile with a passenger in it (RPM) divided by the number of seats flown one mile whether the seat is occupied or not (ASM).

   <u>Operating Cost</u> is the cost of operating the airline, and is typically expressed as "the cost per available seat mile."

2. Operating income can be easily simplified by canceling the RPM terms in the expression shown in #1 above. That is,

   $$\frac{\text{Operating Income}}{\text{ASM}} = \frac{\text{Passenger Revenue}}{\text{ASM}} - \frac{\text{Operating Cost}}{\text{ASM}}$$

   In words, yield times load factor equals passenger revenue per available seat mile.

EXHIBIT 2

PRIMARY DETERMINANTS OF YIELD, LOAD FACTOR, AND OPERATING COST

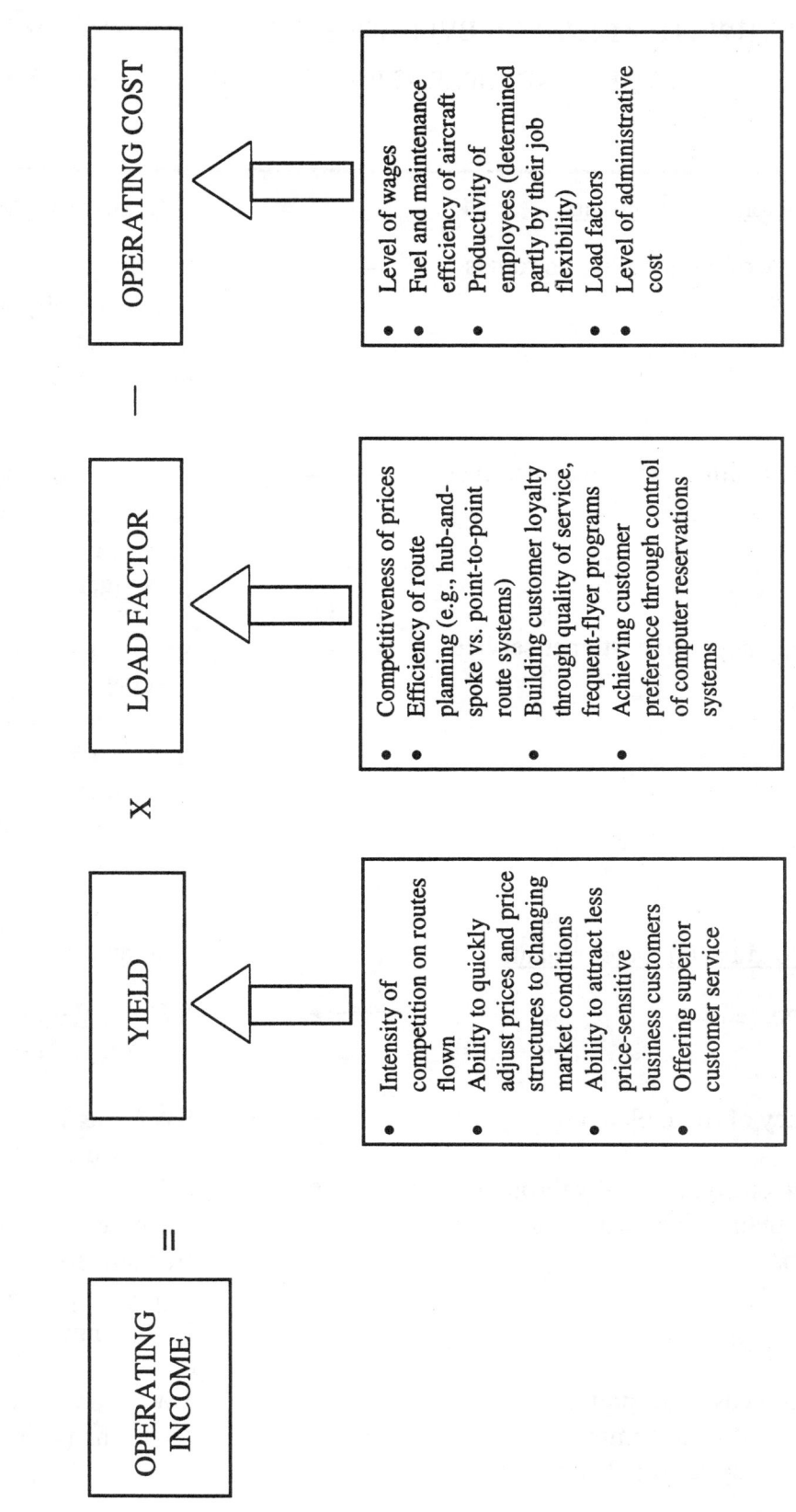

EXHIBIT 3

HOW SOUTHWEST AIRLINES LEVERAGES DETERMINANTS OF YIELD, LOAD FACTOR, AND OPERATING COST IN ITS FAVOR

Yield Determinants	Southwest "Model"
Intensity of competition on routes flown	SWA typically flys between secondary airports in large cities and smaller communities that are not serviced by major carriers
Ability to attract business customers	SWA provides convenient schedules and flight frequencies between city-pairs 80% of passengers fly non-stop.
Offering superior customer service	SWA has won the "triple crown" in the airlines industry for three consecutive years in the areas of on-time performances, baggage handling, and overall customer satisfaction.

Load Factor Determinants	Southwest "Model"
Price competition	SWA is the low fare airline with an average fare of $58.44
Efficiency of route planning	SWA has mastered the point-to-point route system
Building customer loyalty through service quality, frequent-flyer programs	SWA has lead the industry on customer service and its frequent-flyer program promotes flight frequency (# of trips) vs. flight length
Achieving customer preference through control of computer reservation systems (CRS's)	SWA books its own reservations rather than using CRS's

Operating Cost Determinants	Southwest "Model"
• Level of wages	• (Nothing mentioned in the case)
• Fuel and maintenance efficiency of aircraft	• SWA flys a single type of plane (Boeing 737) which reduced maintenance costs; SWA airplane fleet is among the youngest of major airlines
• Productivity of employees (determined partly by their job flexibility)	• SWA is second only to United in terms of the thousands of seat miles flown per employee (see case Exhibit 3); SWA emphasizes job flexibility as noted by ticket agents handling baggage and pilots assisting at the boarding gate
• Load factors	• see above
• Level of administrative cost	• Even though no case information mention this, SWA's operating cost per ASM of 7.08¢ in 1994 suggests this cost is low

The dramatic growth of Southwest has become the principle driving force in changes occurring in the airline industry...As Southwest continues to expand, other airlines will be forced to develop low-cost service in short-haul markets.

D. **How would you describe United's goals, objectives and strategy for "Shuttle By United"?**

1. It is important for students to articulate what they believe United's goals and objectives are for its "Shuttle By United." It can be inferred from the case that United has both short-run and long-run goals and objectives for the "Shuttle." Exhibit 4 in this note lists possible market, financial, competitive, and operational goals and objectives.

2. The "Shuttle' strategy is a "clone" of SWA's strategy in many, but not all, respects. Exhibit 5 in this note summarizes the "Shuttle' strategy. Some noteworthy differences between "Shuttle' and SWA are:

- "Shuttle" offers first and coach class; SWA offers only coach class. Business class charges a small $20 fare premium.

- "Shuttle" boarding groups passengers by seat assignment, window, middle, aisle, a practice called WILMA; SWA boards in groups of 30 in a first-come, first-serve basis.

- "Shuttle" operates a portion of its business out of a hub airport; SWA avoids hub airports for the most part.

- "Shuttle" will arrange for through-passenger ticketing and baggage transfers and offers frequent flyer miles in the United system. SWA does not provide these services. "Shuttle" and SWA provide frequent trip coupons.

E. **How has Southwest Airlines responded to the "Shuttle By United" initiative? What assessments can be made about Southwest's market and financial position on competitive routes based on 1994 Fourth Quarter results?**

1. SWA's response to the "Shuttle" initiative was expressed by a SWA spokesperson in the case. SWA would "vigorously fight to maintain our stronghold in California." SWA's specific response to "Shuttle" included:

- SWA committed additional aircraft to California to boost flight frequencies on competitive routes.

- SWA kept its "California State Fare" (one-way walk-up fare) at $69, but actively promoted its 21-day advance fares and other discount fares.

EXHIBIT 4

POSSIBLE GOALS AND OBJECTIVES FOR SHUTTLE BY UNITED

OBJECTIVE/GOAL	TIME FRAME	
	Short-Run	Long-Run
Marketing	• Recapture market pressure in California and adjacent states • Signal to SWA that United intends to match SWA on price and exceed SWA on service.	• Expand "shuttle" to 20 percent of United's domestic operations, and particularly to areas where United has a significant presence.
Financial	• Achieve a financial break-even point for "Shuttle" routes <u>both</u> out of United's San Francisco hub and from satellite airports	• Achieve profitability (operating income per available seat mile) comparable to other domestic long-haul routes
Competitive	• Reclaim Oakland Airport lost to SWA in the early 1990's	• Expand "Shuttle" to the midwest region. Operate "Shuttle" out of United's Chicago O'Hare Hub <u>and</u> Chicago's Midway Airport (where SWA has established a significant presence.)
Operational	• Install a high frequency, low fare, minimal amenity, short-haul flight operation initially serving destinations in California and adjacent states. • Lower operating cost for shorter domestic routes (under 750 miles) from 10.5 cents per available seat mile to 7.5 cents.	• Expand airline-within-an-airline concept, by operating the "Shuttle" out of other United's hubs and satellite airports. • Replicate and refine "Shuttle" operations to achieve these economies on a large scale.

EXHIBIT 5

SHUTTLE BY UNITED STRATEGY AT A GLANCE

<u>Target Markets</u>	14 city-pairs (routes) in California and adjacent states... • 6 routes involved United's San Francisco hub • 8 routes involved point-to-point routes separate and apart from United's San Francisco hub • 9 of the 14 routes competed directly with SWA
<u>Fare Classes and Fares</u>	Offer first and coach class service. "Shuttle" coach fares were identical to SWA's in the 9 routes served by both airlines. Business class fares were typically $20 higher than coach class. "Shuttle" fares in noncompetitive markets were 5 to 10 percent higher.
<u>Flight Service and Aircraft</u>	Frequent "Shuttle" service between city-pairs, featuring Boeing 737 jets (same as SWA). Focus on achieving 20 minute aircraft turns. Only beverage and snack service. Use of WILMA boarding practice featuring boarding by window seats first, then middle seats, and finally aisle seats.
<u>Reservation System and Frequent Flyer Program</u>	"Shuttle" uses United's reservation system and allows for continuing flights (ticketing, baggage handling) on United or other airlines out of San Francisco hub. "Shuttle" flight miles apply to United's frequent flyer program. Also, "Shuttle" offers free trips based on flight frequency as does SWA

- SWA boosted its advertising and promotion on competitive routes and emphasized its "The Low Fare Airline" advertising campaign.

2. The outcomes of "Shuttle's" action and SWA's response can be summarized as follows, as regards SWA's market and financial position on competitive routes:

- SWA's average fare on competitive routes has declined somewhat. The SWA fare in markets also served by the "Shuttle" (excluding Oakland-Seattle) declined from $45 to $44. The average Oakland-Seattle fare declined from $60 to $51.

- SWA's load factors declined in some markets and increased in others. SWA's load factors were hit hardest on flights into and out of the Oakland airport (see case Exhibit 11). The Oakland airport was the main base of SWA's Northern California's operation and was the fastest growing of California's ten major airports in terms of air traffic.

3. More broadly, the "Shuttle" initiative can partially account for SWA's systemwide performance during the 1994 Fourth Quarter. SWA consolidated net income in this quarter fell 47 percent compound to the 1993 Fourth Quarter. 1994 Fourth Quarter operating revenues were up only three percent compared to the same period in 1993. These results sent SWA's stock price reeling to close at a 52-week low of $15.75 in December 1994, down from a record $39.00 in February 1994. In addition, SWA's consolidated yield and load factor for January 1995 were tracking lower than the consolidated yield and load factor for January 1994. According to the case, SWA's consolidated load factor would be about 5 points lower in January 1995 as compared to January 1994 if present traffic patterns continued.

4. It is important that students compute and analyze the 1994 Fourth Quarter profitability of SWA on contested routes with "Shuttle". This is done in Exhibit 6 in this note along with an explanation for the calculations. As mentioned earlier, students often have trouble computing "yield." This is done in Exhibit 7 in this note. Two conclusions can be drawn from these computations:

- SWA does make a consolidated daily operating profit on the nine "Shuttle" routes. It is reasonable to assume that this profit is less than SWA achieved prior to "Shuttle's" entry since SWA's yield and load factors have declined.

- However, SWA loses money on 4 of the 9 routes. It incurs a loss on the San Francisco-San Diego route where "Shuttle" operates its San Francisco hub. SWA also loses money on the following routes:

Oakland-Ontario
Oakland-Seattle
San Diego-Sacramento

EXHIBIT 6

SOUTHWEST AIRLINES 1994 FOURTH QUARTER OPERATING RESULTS IN SHUTTLE BY UNITED COMPETITIVE MARKETS

Market (City - Pair)	Avg. Fare	÷ Air Miles	= Route Yield	x Load Factor	= Pass. Rev. per ASM	- Cost per ASM	= Op. Profit per ASM	x Avail. Seat Mi	= Daily Op. Profit	
San Fran. - San Diego	$44	417	10.55¢	61%	6.44¢	7.08¢	(.64¢)	1,371,096	($8,775)	($8,775)
Oak. - L. Angeles	$44	338	13.02¢	59%	7.68¢	7.08¢	.60¢	1,759,628	$10,558	
Oak. - Burbank	$44	326	13.50¢	63%	8.51¢	7.08¢	1.43¢	1,161,212	$17,021	
Oak. - Ontario	$44	362	12.15¢	57%	6.93¢	7.08¢	(.15¢)	1,190,256	($1,785)	
Oak. - Seattle	$51	671	7.60¢	66%	5.02¢	7.08¢	(2.06¢)	735,416	($15,150)	$10,644
L. Angeles - Sacramento	$44	374	11.76¢	65%	7.64¢	7.08¢	.56¢	512,380	$2,869	
L. Angeles - Phoenix	$44	366	12.02¢	61%	7.33¢	7.08¢	.25¢	2,507,100	$6,268	
L. Angeles - L. Vegas	$44	241	18.26¢	65%	11.87¢	7.08¢	4.79¢	858,442	$41,119	$50,256
San Diego - Sacramento	$44	481	9.15¢	68%	6.22¢	7.08¢	(.86¢)	1,186,146	($10,201)	($10,201)

Southwest Total Daily Operating Profit $41,924

Note:
1. Air miles given in case Exhibit 11
2. Given in case as SWA average fares on each route
3. Yield = Average Fare/Air miles
4. Load Factor given in Exhibit 11
5. Passenger Revenue per ASM = Yield x Load Factor
6. Cost per ASM given in case Exhibit 11 and in the text.
7. Operating Profit per ASM = Passenger Revenue per ASM - Cost per ASM
8. Available Seat Miles = Air miles x 137 seats x 2 (round trips) x Number of Daily Round-trips (given in case Exhibit 11)

EXHIBIT 7

YIELD CALCULATION

$$\text{YIELD} = \frac{\text{Passenger Revenue}}{\text{Revenue Passenger Miles}},$$

Computed as follows:

$$\frac{\text{Passenger Revenue}}{\text{Revenue Passenger Miles}} = \frac{\left(\begin{array}{c}\text{Average}\\ \text{Fare}\end{array}\right) \times \left(\begin{array}{c}\text{Airplane Seating}\\ \text{Capacity}\end{array}\right) \times \left(\begin{array}{c}\text{Number of}\\ \text{Roundtrips}\end{array}\right) \times 2 \times \left(\begin{array}{c}\text{Proportion of}\\ \text{Seats Occupied}\end{array}\right)}{\left(\begin{array}{c}\text{Air}\\ \text{Miles}\end{array}\right) \times \left(\begin{array}{c}\text{Airplane Seating}\\ \text{Capacity}\end{array}\right) \times \left(\begin{array}{c}\text{Number of}\\ \text{Roundtrips}\end{array}\right) \times 2 \times \left(\begin{array}{c}\text{Proportion of}\\ \text{Seats Occupied}\end{array}\right)}$$

By canceling terms,

$$\text{YIELD} = \frac{\text{Average Fare}}{\text{Air Miles}}$$

F. **What assessments can be made about the "Shuttle By United" market and financial position based on 1994 Fourth Quarter results?**

1. "Shuttle" president, A. B. "Sky" Magary, is quoted in the case as saying: "The Shuttle is working well." The case also states the United executives reported that the "Shuttle" was exceeding expectations and some routes were profitable. Students should be asked to evaluate these comments in the context of what they view are United's goals and objectives for the "Shuttle" (see Exhibit 4 in this note).

2. Exhibit 11 in the case provides additional data for assessing "Shuttle's" performance during the 1994 Fourth Quarter:

- "Shuttle's" load factors for four out of the five routes out of its San Francisco hub were lower in the 1994 Fourth Quarter than the 1993 Fourth Quarter. Only the San Francisco-San Diego routes evidenced a higher load factor. The load factor for the Los Angeles-Sacramento route also increased over the 1993 Fourth Quarter. It is reasonable to conclude that the "Shuttle's" Oakland Airport operations have cannibalized some of United's San Francisco hub traffic.

- The "Shuttle" has expanded its flight frequency out of San Francisco. Flight frequencies also have increased out of Oakland and Los Angeles.

3. The "Shuttle's" operating cost per available seat mile is apparently lower than United's past 10.5 cents for short-haul (under 750 miles) flights which is mentioned in the case. The "Shuttle's" goal was to operate at cost of 7.5 cents per available seat mile. In December, 1994, A. B. "Sky" Magary, the "Shuttle" president, is quoted as saying: "We're vaguely better than halfway there." A reasonable cost per ASM estimate is that the "Shuttle" has a 9-cent cost per available seat mile which is exactly the mid-point between 10.5 cents and the targeted 7.5 cents.

4. As with SWA, students should be expected to compute and analyze the 1994 Fourth Quarter profitability for the "Shuttle." This is done in Exhibit 8 in this note along with the accompanying explanations for the calculations. Several conclusions can be drawn from these computations:

- United executives accurately portrayed "Shuttle" profitability; that is, some "Shuttle" routes were profitable. Actually, 6 or the 14 routes were profitable in the 1994 Fourth Quarter.

EXHIBIT 8

SHUTTLE BY UNITED: ESTIMATED 1994 FOURTH QUARTER OPERATING RESULTS

Market (City - Pair)	Avg. Fare	÷ Air Miles	= Route Yield	x Load Factor	= Pass. Rev. per ASM	– Cost per ASM	= Op. Profit per ASM	x Avail. Seat Mi	= Daily Op. Profit	
San Fran. - L. Angeles	$64	338	18.93¢	66%	12.49¢	9.0¢	3.49¢	2,870,972	$100,197	
San Fran. - Burbank	$64	359	17.83¢	60%	10.70¢	9.0¢	1.70¢	1,082,026	$18,394	
San Fran. - Ontario	$64	364	17.58¢	47%	8.26¢	9.0¢	(.74¢)	1,097,096	($8,119)	
San Fran. - L. Vegas	$64	417	15.35¢	73%	11.21¢	9.0¢	2.21¢	1,028,322	$22,726	
San Fran. - Seattle	$71	678	10.47¢	74%	7.75¢	9.0¢	1.25¢	2,415,036	$30,188	
*San Fran. - San Diego	$47	417	11.27¢	77%	8.67¢	9.0¢	(.33¢)	1,142,580	($3,771)	$99,239
*Oak. - L. Angeles	$47	338	13.90¢	62%	8.62¢	9.0¢	(.38¢)	926,120	($3,519)	
*Oak. - Burbank	$47	326	14.42¢	40%	5.77¢	9.0¢	(3.23¢)	625,268	($20,196)	
*Oak. - Ontario	$47	362	12.98¢	32%	4.15¢	9.0¢	(4.85¢)	694,316	($33,674)	
*Oak. - Seattle	$54	671	8.05¢	52%	4.19¢	9.0¢	(4.81¢)	735,416	($35,374)	($92,763)
*L. Angeles - Sac.	$47	374	12.56¢	81%	10.17¢	9.0¢	1.17¢	512,380	$5,995	
*L. Angeles - Phoenix	$47	366	12.84¢	48%	6.16¢	9.0¢	(2.84¢)	902,556	($25,633)	
*L. Angeles - L. Vegas	$47	241	19.50¢	61%	11.90¢	9.0¢	2.90¢	660,340	$19,150	($488)
*San Diego - Sac.	$47	481	9.77¢	50%	4.89¢	9.0¢	(4.11¢)	658,970	($27,084)	($27,084)

Shuttle Total Daily Operating Profit	($21,096)
*Shuttle Total Daily Operating Loss in Markets with Southwest	($124,106)
Shuttle Total Daily Operating Profit in Markets without Southwest	$103,010

Note: 1. Shuttle fares are 5 to 10% higher than SWA's average fare in competitive markets according to the case. SWA's average fare is $44. A reasonable approximation for shuttle is $47, except for Oakland-Seattle route with its higher fare. Shuttle fares out of San Francisco (excluding San Fran.-Seattle) were $20 higher than SWA in five markets not served by SWA, or $64. The San Francisco-Seattle is $71.

2. All other calculations follow the notes detailed in Exhibit 6 in this note.

3. Cost per available seat mile is 9¢ which is midway between 10.5¢ for United's short-haul flights and the targeted 7.5¢ for the Shuttle

- The "Shuttle" is unprofitable overall with an estimated daily operating loss of $21,096. However, it is important for students to recognize that...

    ... "Shuttle" loses $124,106 daily on routes where it competes head-to-head with SWA. Its losses are greatest on Oakland routes ($92,763). Los Angeles routes roughly break-even. "Shuttle" incurs a loss on 7 out of 9 routes where it competes with SWA.

    ... "Shuttle's" profit is generated mostly from its San Francisco hub. This profit comes from the San Francisco-Los Angeles, San Francisco-Seattle, San Francisco-Las Vegas, and San Francisco-Burbank routes.

    ... The "Shuttle" is profitable on routes where it does not compete head-to-head with SWA and where it has higher yields and higher load factors.

G. **Based on your assessments, how would you interpret United's decision to (a) discontinue "Shuttle By United" service for the Oakland-Ontario market and (b) raise the one-way walk-up first class and coach fare on all 14 "Shuttle By United" routes by $10.00?**

1. Exhibit 9 in this note summarizes the profitability analysis detailed in Exhibit 6 and 8 in this note. As indicated,

    ... Both SWA and Shuttle incur a profit in the Los Angeles-Las Vegas and the Los Angeles-Sacramento routes.

    ... SWA records a loss on four routes.

    ... Shuttle is incurring losses on the remaining 7 routes where they compete head-to-head.

2. This and the previous analysis indicates that **"Shuttle" incurs a loss on its Ontario, California service both out of San Francisco and Oakland.** The combined dollar loss is $41,793 per day. The Oakland-Ontario route suffers from a lower load factor (32%) and a lower yield than the San Francisco-Ontario route. It makes sense for United to service Ontario out of San Francisco with its higher yield due to a lack of competitors from SWA. It could very well be that the San Francisco-Ontario load factor could increase to at least break-even when the Oakland service is terminated.

At what load factor would the San Francisco-Oakland route break-even given the current yield (17.58¢) and current estimated cost? As described in the case, a break-even load factor can be computed by setting operating income to zero, inserting the yield and cost per ASM, and solving for the load factor, or "x." This is shown below:

EXHIBIT 9

SHUTTLE BY UNITED AND SOUTHWEST AIRLINES FINANCIAL PERFORMANCE FOR THE 1994 FOURTH QUARTER

Airline Performance in Competitive Markets

Southwest Airlines

	Profit	Loss
United Shuttle — Profit	L. Angeles - L. Vegas L. Angeles - Sacramento	
United Shuttle — Loss	Oakland - L. Angeles Oakland - Burbank L. Angeles - Phoenix	San. Fran. - San Diego Oakland - Ontario Oakland - Seattle S. Diego - Sacramento

Shuttle Performance in Non-competitive Markets

United Shuttle	
Profit	San Francisco - L. Angeles San Francisco - Burbank San Francisco - Seattle San Francisco - Las Vegas
Loss	San Francisco - Ontario

Calculating the Break-even Load Factor for
"Shuttle's" San Francisco-Oakland Route

Income	=	Yield	x	Load Factor	-	Cost
0		17.58¢		x		9¢ per ASM
.09	=	.1758 x				
.512	=	x , or 51.2% load factor				

Of course, should Shuttle raise its price on one-way, walk fares or first and coach classes, the yield increases and the break-even load factor declines.

3. The "Shuttle" $10.00 fare increase can be viewed in a number of different ways.

- First, SWA might view this as a signal that United believes there is no longer a need for both carriers to incur losses. A fare increase will increase yield (see below), and assuming no change in load factors, both carriers will improve their profitability in competitive markets. Call this a "win-win" proposition.

- Second, SWA might view this as a signal that "Shuttle" has "blinked." That is, "Shuttle's" yields cannot sustain its service outside of its hub system and its costs are still too high. This view is plausible given the previous profitability analysis. Perhaps, the fare increase means "Shuttle" is prepared to suffer lower load factors (with a fare increase) on non-hub routes which will be offset with higher yields and only slightly lower load factors on say, San Francisco routes.

4. The joint effort of a fare increase and service reduction also deserves attention. SWA might view this as a systematic approach to prune unprofitable routes while building profit or breaking even on other routes.

5. The effect of a $10.00 fare increase on yield can be estimated by looking at the ratio of the one-way, walk-up fare and the average fare for "Shuttle." This is shown below:

$$\text{New Fare} \rightarrow \frac{\$79}{\$69} = \frac{x}{\$47} \quad \begin{matrix}\leftarrow \text{New Avg. Fare} \\ \leftarrow \text{Current Avg. Fare} \\ \text{(see Exh. 8 in this note)}\end{matrix}$$

$$\text{Current Fare} \rightarrow$$

Solving for x, the new avg. Shuttle fare is $53.81 or $54.

6. An increased yield will allow the "Shuttle" load factor to decrease. An interesting question to ask students is: "What load factor will "Shuttle" need to break-even given a higher yield, on say the San Francisco-San Diego route?" An answer can be computed as follows:

$$\frac{\text{Income}}{0} = \frac{\text{Yield}}{\$54 / 417 \text{ mi}} \quad x \quad \frac{\text{Load Factor}}{x} \quad - \quad \frac{\text{Cost}}{9¢ \text{ per ASM}}$$

```
     0    =   $ .1295    (x)   -    $ .09
    .09   =     .1295 (x)
   .695   =        x  ,  or 69.5%
```

Other route analyses of this type are also possible.

H. How should Southwest Airlines respond, if at all, to the "Shuttle By United" decision to change its service and price? Why?

1. The case states: Should Southwest follow with a $10.00 fare increase of its own or continue with its present price and service strategy? Exhibit 10 in this note identifies some pros and cons of SWA increasing its fare.

2. On balance, it would seem that SWA should hold to its present one-way, walk-up $69 California State Fare and not increase this fare. Reasons favoring this course of action are:

- Based on the previous analysis, "Shuttle" has "blinked"; that is, its point-to-point service outside of its hub system has not met short-run expectations.

- Even with higher yields and sometimes comparable load factors, "Shuttle" has not reduced its cost to produce a profit.

- It is reasonable to assume that "Shuttle" has or is about to concede the Oakland airport to SWA. This was the "prize" to be won or lost in the competitive game in California.

- SWA has been able to withstand "Shuttle's" assault, but not without some injury. The injury, however, is better localized in California. To give "Shuttle" breathing room is not a prudent act. Matching the $10 fare increase does provide some breathing room for "Shuttle."

- "Shuttle's" departure from the Oakland-Ontario route is bound to increase SWA's load factor, hence profitability, even without a fare increase. [Note: Students may be asked to compute SWA's profitability by multiplying the 1993 Fourth Quarter load factor (65%) by yield (12.15¢) and subtracting the 7.08¢ per ASM followed by multiplying this positive amount by the Oakland-Ontario ASM (1,190,256) for the 1994 Fourth Quarter. This route will produce a daily operating profit of $9,730.]

EXHIBIT 10

PROS AND CONS OF SOUTHWEST INCREASING ITS FARE TO MATCH "SHUTTLE'S" FARE INCREASE

Pros	Cons
1. A fare increase will increase SWA's yield. Assuming no change in load factor, SWA's profit should increase on all routes. A $10.00 fare increase could increase the SWA average fare to $50.00 as shown below: $$\frac{\text{New fare } \$79}{\text{Old fare } \$69} = \frac{x \text{ (New avg. fare)}}{\$44 \text{ current avg. fare}}$$ x = $50.37, say $50.00 This average fare, assuming no change in load factor, will make all routes, except Oakland-Seattle and San Diego-Sacramento profitable. 2. SWA can compete on flight frequency, quality of service, and lower cost per ASM. What is the merit of prolonging what seems to be a stalemate? Raise the price! 3. Assuming that profits will increase, SWA can report higher earnings during the 1995 First Quarter and possibly pump up stock analysts' perceptions of SWA.	1. A fare increase would increase "Shuttle's" yield. Assuming no change in load factors, "Shuttle's" profit should increase A $10.00 fare increase could increase "Shuttle's" average fare to $54.00 as described earlier. A fare increase will make the San Francisco-San Diego and Oakland-Los Angeles routes profitable; however, other unprofitable routes remain unprofitable, only less so. 2. When "Shuttle" stops its Oakland - Ontario service, its Oakland operation (with flights to Los Angeles, Burbank, and Seattle) approaches break-even. This is not in SWA's best interest, since Oakland is presently losing $92,763 per day. Oakland is a major "prize" in the "Shuttle"- SWA battle. 3. By making "Shuttle" more profitable, SWA runs the risk of giving United some incentive to continue operating its point-to-point route system outside its hub. More importantly, United might view this situation as positive enough to expand the "Shuttle" operation. 4. The longer United is able to operate "Shuttle," the more time it has to hone its point-to-point route system and decrease its cost per ASM. Giving United this opportunity has negative long-term implications for SWA. Again, United expands its "Shuttle" operation.

I. **Epilogue**

How did Southwest Airlines respond to the "Shuttle By United" $10.00 fare increase and decision to discontinue service for the Oakland-Ontario market? Southwest Airlines retained its $69.00 one-way, walk-up fare and maintained its daily round-trip flight frequency on the Oakland-Ontario route at 14 flights per day. According to Dave Ridley, the rationale for this decision was as follows:

> First of all, we were profitable in California at a $69 one-way, walk-up fare. Second, given the public's focus on our battle with the Shuttle and our commitment to "THE Low Fare Airline," we didn't want to send mixed messages to our customers by raising fares. Lastly, and perhaps most importantly, we viewed the attempt to raise fares by United as a possible indication that they were not being as successful as they wanted (and needed) to be in getting their costs down. If, in fact, they were not hitting their cost targets, then it called into question what their long term commitment to the Shuttle would be in their non-hub Shuttle markets, particularly in Oakland. We certainly did not want to give them relief from their cost problem by allowing them to achieve their desired margins through fare increases. Holding our fares in check allowed us to leverage our greatest strategic advantage: our superior (lower) operating costs.

What was United's response? When Southwest Airlines did not match the fare increase, United retracted their proposed increase for "Shuttle By United."

The longer-term outcome of the Southwest Airlines - "Shuttle By United" rivalry on the West Coast is also worth noting. By late January 1996, "Shuttle By United" had all but conceded markets that did not fly out of or into San Francisco and Los Angeles to Southwest. This meant that the Southwest-Shuttle route overlap was substantially reduced. "Shuttle" had competed on 13 percent of Southwest's total available seat miles in January 1995. By January 1996, this percentage had shrunk to 7 percent. Furthermore, by January 1998, Southwest and the "Shuttle" directly competed on only five routes. Southwest's share of the intra-California market was 50% in January 1998 - down from 56.4% in mid-1995.

United did not achieve its targeted 7.5 cent per available seat rule for "Shuttle." In January 1996, United reported that the "Shuttle" was able to operate with an 8-cent per available seat mile cost. While the 7.5 cent per ASM was still a target, Ronno Dutta, United's senior vice president of planning, acknowledged that, "It'll be tough," (to reach this target). According to Mr. Dutta, the "Shuttle" was operating essentially on a break-even basis. "Some months it makes money," Mr. Dutta says, "Some months it doesn't." In January 1996, Southwest continued to offer its one-way, walk-up fare of $69.00 from Oakland to Southern California markets (Ontario, Burbank, and Los Angeles). However, "Shuttle's" one-way, walk-up coach fare to these markets was a much as $30.00 higher than Southwest Airlines from United's San Francisco hub.

United officials believe the "Shuttle" initiative has been successful in California. Says United's Ronno Dutta, "We finally profitably stopped the Southwest machine." It is worth noting, however, that United has not expanded "Shuttle" outside the Western U.S. (as of 2000).

Did "Shuttle's" effort and outcome mean that the "airline-within-an-airline" concept for major carriers has been abandoned? In a word, no. In August 1996, Delta Airlines began operating a low-fare, semi-point-to-point route system in the southeastern U.S. Why the southeast? Southwest began point-to-point service in Florida in January 1996. Southwest inaugurated point-to-point service in the northeast in the fall of 1996 with 16 flights between Providence, Rhode Island and Baltimore, Maryland. The fare? $118 for a round-trip. Existing fares by competing carriers ranged from $518 to $538.

Sources: Based on an interview with Dave Ridley, VP-Marketing and Sales, Southwest Airlines and "Southwest Flies Circles Around United's Shuttle," <u>Wall Street Journal</u> (February 20, 1996), pp. B1, B8, and "Delta The Latest to Attempt Low-Fare Approach," <u>Dallas Morning News</u> (August 10, 1996), pp. 1F, 11F; "Competitors Quake As Southwest Air Is Set To Invade Northwest," <u>Wall Street Journal</u> (October 23, 1996), pp. A1, A10; "Aided By Its Shuttle, United is Taking Los Angeles By Storm," <u>Wall Street Journal</u> (January 16, 1998), pp. A1, A9.

J. Summary Points

1. Price is the easiest marketing mix element to imitate. Shuttle by United matched Southwest on price; however, other elements of the marketing mix were not so easily imitated including Southwest's "offering" and how it is delivered.

2. The profit equation states that Profit = Total Revenue - Total Cost. This relationship also applies to the airline industry even though the terminology differs.

$$\frac{\text{Operating Income}}{\text{ASM}} = \left(\frac{\text{Passenger Revenue}}{\text{RPM}} \times \frac{\text{RPM}}{\text{ASM}}\right) - \frac{\text{Operating Cost}}{\text{ASM}}$$

By canceling the RPM term, the profit equation remains:

$$\frac{\text{Operating Income}}{\text{ASM}} = \frac{\text{Passenger Revenue}}{\text{ASM}} - \frac{\text{Operating Cost}}{\text{ASM}}$$

3. The Southwest - United Shuttle battle in California can be viewed as a competitive game reflecting moves and countermoves by the players. The game is played by considering both short-run and long-run implications of these moves and countermoves, the objectives/goals of players, and the measures players use to score the game, e.g., market share, profit, etc.

BURROUGHS WELLCOME COMPANY: RETROVIR

Synopsis

In January 1990, Burroughs Wellcome executives were under continued pressure to reduce the price of Retrovir. Retrovir is the trade name for a drug called azidothymidine (AZT) which has been found to be effective in the treatment of immune deficiency syndrome (AIDS) and AIDS-related complex (ARC).

Burroughs Wellcome introduced Retrovir in March 1987. The company was immediately criticized by AIDS patient advocacy groups, members of the U.S. Congress, and the media for charging a high price for the drug. In December 1987, Burroughs Wellcome reduced the price by 20 percent and again reduced the price by 20 percent in September 1989. These reductions continued to be met with harsh and vocal criticism. The company was still being charged with "inappropriate" pricing of the drug and renewed pressure for another price reduction was evident in January 1990. Burroughs Wellcome executives must decide whether the price for Retrovir should be reduced again.

This case describes the history of AIDS in the United States, the development of Retrovir, criticisms of Burroughs Wellcome, and the background for the pricing situation, including the economics of Retrovir, market demand, and public concern. Students are expected to grapple with the economic and ethical/social responsibility issues and propose a course of action with an accompanying rationale.

Instructors have found that this case can be easily generalized to the continuing controversy related to drug pricing. The end-of-case Summary Points also apply in this broader context.

Teaching Objectives

This case has four teaching objectives:

1. To familiarize students with a significant public health concern and the manner in which pharmaceutical firms develop and market drugs.

2. To introduce matters of ethics and social responsibility under the guise of a strategic marketing issue; namely, the pricing of Retrovir, the only drug available for the effective treatment of AIDS.

3. To raise for consideration alternative pricing objectives such as return on investment given that Burroughs Wellcome has a monopoly status with Retrovir until 1994.

4. To force students to evaluate pricing strategies (e.g. skimming) in the pharmaceutical industry, including the role of demand, cost, and competition, and the economic and social effects of price changes for a specific drug - Retrovir.

Teaching Suggestions

This case is best suited for use when the instructor wishes to examine pricing issues and matters of ethics and social responsibility. The case is most appropriate for use later in the course.

Past experience with the case suggests that students find the background on AIDS and Burroughs Wellcome's product development efforts very interesting. A challenge teaching the case is to focus student attention on Burroughs Wellcome executives who, at times, appear to be naive both in their handling of the "public's" indignation concerning the pricing issue and how they arrived at their pricing decisions. We have found that students sometimes are quick to criticize Burroughs Wellcome without objectively placing themselves in the role of company executives.

A good way to start the case is to poll students with the question:

Should Burroughs Wellcome reduce the price of Retrovir in 1990?

Instructors might ask for a show of hands or ask students to write yes or no on a slip of paper to be forwarded to the instructor. If instructors simply ask for a "hand vote," then the class discussion can quickly move to: "Why should they cut the price and why shouldn't Burroughs Welcome cut the price? If a ballot approach is used, a student can tally the votes while the instructor asks the class to comment on the AIDS epidemic in the United States.

After the class discussion, a second vote can be taken as to whether the Retrovir price should be reduced again. The following questions might be posed to students prior to or during a case discussion:

1. How would you describe the situation related to the AIDS epidemic in the United States?

2. How would you characterize the R&D efforts undertaken by Burroughs Wellcome to develop Retrovir?

3. What arguments can be made on the basis of demand, cost, and competitive conditions to justify the pricing of Retrovir?

4. What arguments can be made on the basis of ethical grounds and a social responsibility perspective for the pricing of Retrovir?

5. How profitable has Retrovir been for Burroughs Wellcome?

6. Should Burroughs Wellcome reduce the price of Retrovir below $120 for 100 capsules? If yes, why and when? If no, why not?

Areas for Discussion/Analysis

A. **How would you describe the situation related to the AIDS epidemic in the United States?**

1. **Incidence of AIDS and HIV**

    a. Centers for Disease Control reports that the number of AIDS cases in the U.S. increased almost six-fold from 1984 to 1989.

    b. Incidence of HIV infections ranged between 800,000 and 1.3 million in 1990.

    c. Incidence of AIDS was most pronounced among homosexual men and intravenous drug users.

    d. One-half of all AIDS cases were in San Francisco, Miami, New York City, Los Angeles, and Houston.

    e. The AIDS fatality rate is declining - the fatality rate was 91 percent in 1981, but 46 percent in 1989.

2. **Economic Consequences**

    a. Lifetime medical cost of an AIDS patient ranged between $70,000 and $141,000, or two to three times the cost of cancer treatment.

    b. Estimated Medicaid costs for AIDS in 1988 ranged between $700 and $750 million. Medicaid spending could reach $2.4 billion in 1992.

3. **Treatment**

    a. There is no cure for AIDS.

    b. AZT (Retrovir) supplied by Burroughs Wellcome is the only commercial treatment for AIDS approved by the Federal Drug Administration. AZT interferes with HIV, but does not cure it.

c. Burroughs Wellcome has an exclusive seven-year marketing right to AZT (Retrovir) under provisions of the Orphan Drug Act. Exclusivity will be in effect until 1994 - seven years from its 1987 introduction date - or for four more years from the date of the case (1990).

d. Several other pharmaceutical firms are testing treatments:

- DDI by Bristol Myers
- DDC by Hoffman-LaRoche
- Other drugs by Glaxo and Triton Biosciences

None of these drugs are cures, but only treatments.

4. **Social and Political Mileau**

a. The AIDS epidemic has created a social and political storm with Burroughs Wellcome at the epicenter. The personal and economic costs of AIDS have produced vocal social and political unrest. While the issue of pricing is emphasized in the case, issues related to the process of drug approval and testing, the roles played by the U.S. government in granting exclusive marketing rights and patents, and the various political, governmental, institutional (National Cancer Institute) groups, other advocacy groups (AIDS Patient Advocacy Groups, ACLU), and the media need to be emphasized.

b. Exhibit 1 in this note displays these various constituencies with Burroughs Wellcome at the center. Note that Burroughs Wellcome has its "proximate constituencies;" namely, its customers (AIDS patients), Wellcome PLC (parent company), company shareholders, and competitors, which are actively testing alternative treatments. It is noteworthy that students recognize that this "proximate environment" played an important role in the company's price decision-making as evidenced by the statement in its 1989 Annual Report:

> In arriving at our decision to reduce the price, we carefully weighed a number of factors. These included our responsibility to patients and shareholders, the very real remaining uncertainties in the marketplace and the vital need to fund our continuing research and development programs.

Other constituencies in the external environment were not explicitly mentioned as having an influence on Burroughs Wellcome decision-making. Students might be asked to comment on this point:

EXHIBIT 1

CONSTITUENCIES IN BURROUGHS WELLCOME PROXIMATE AND EXTERNAL ENVIRONMENT

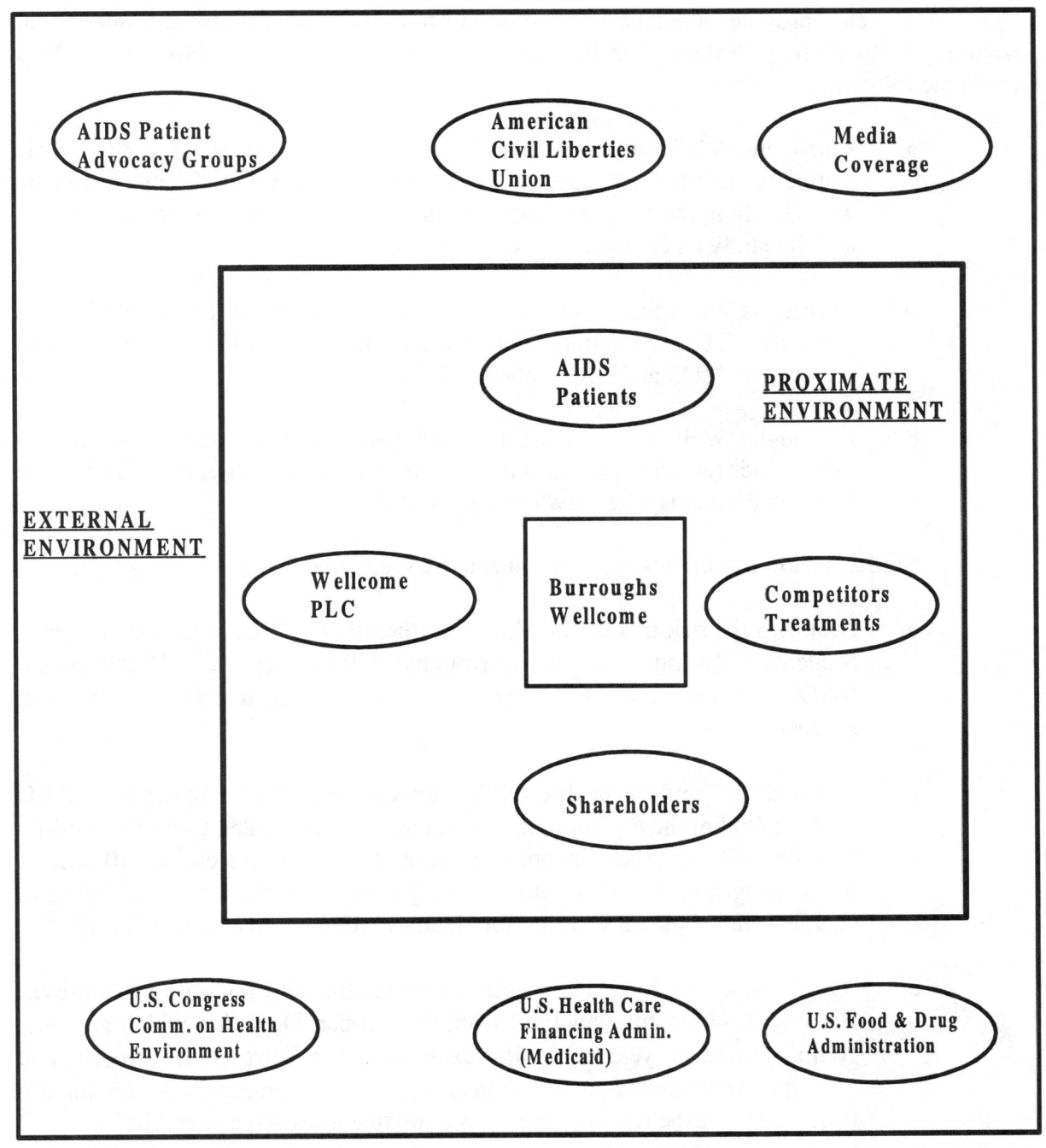

What consideration, if any, should Burroughs Wellcome give to the views expressed by the various advocacy and political groups on its handling of Retrovir?

B. How would you characterize the R & D efforts undertaken by Burroughs Wellcome to develop Retrovir?

1. The case provides a detailed description of how Burroughs Wellcome went about developing Retrovir (e.g., Exhibit 5 in the case). Specific points that might be highlighted include the following:

    a. Burroughs Wellcome was not the original synthesizer of AZT. This distinction resides with a researcher at the Michigan Cancer Foundation who was searching for a cancer cure. Burroughs Wellcome did resynthesize AZT and did study its characteristics.

    b. Burroughs Wellcome apparently followed a rigorous regimen for testing the effect of AZT as a treatment for persons affected with HIV and as a useful therapy for AIDS and ARC patients.

    c. Burroughs Wellcome did identify and persuade a German subsidiary of Pfizer, Inc. (another pharmaceutical firm) to produce thymidine by the ton since thymidine is a key raw material in AZT.

2. Students should acknowledge that Burroughs Wellcome:

    a. Assumed the risk in studying AZT as a therapy for AIDS and ARC patients. Students might note also that Burroughs Wellcome spend $726 million for R&D over the past five years without producing a major commercial success.

    b. Invested $50 million in direct R&D expenditures for Retrovir; total R&D costs, including new plant and equipment, were estimated to be $80 million to $100 million. Also, the company provided the equivalent of $10 million of the drug free to AIDS patients and gave one metric ton of AZT free of charge to the National Institute for Health's AIDS Clinical Trials Group.

    c. Sought whatever legal and regulatory protection was possible for Retrovir. Burroughs Wellcome benefited from the Orphan Drug Act which gave the company a seven-year marketing exclusivity for Retrovir, tax credits, and government subsidization of clinical trials. The company also obtained a U.S. patent for the use of Retrovir as a treatment for AIDs and ARC.

C. **What arguments can be made on the basis of demand, cost and competitive conditions to justify the pricing of Retrovir?**

1. The purpose of this question is to direct student attention to fundamental considerations in pricing, the explicit (implicit) attention to these considerations by Burroughs Wellcome executives, and the consequences of the actions taken. In directing student attention, we have found it useful to refer to specific comments made by company officials and then asking students to draw upon pricing concepts to evaluate or interpret them.

2. It is noteworthy that one company official specifically made reference to uncertainties related to demand, cost and competition - three fundamental pricing considerations - with the statement by a company official given in the case:

> "We didn't know the demand, how to produce it in large quantities or what competing drugs would come out in the market. There was no way to find out."

3. **Uncertainties related to demand, cost, and competition coupled with patent protection and Burroughs Wellcome interest in reinvesting funds for further R&D dictate a skimming pricing strategy.** Instructors might direct student attention to the Chapter 8 discussion on pricing which mentions conditions favoring a skimming strategy:

   a. Demand is likely to be price inelastic;

   b. The offering is unique enough to be protected from competition by a patent, a copyright, or trade secrets;

   c. Production or marketing costs are unknown;

   d. A capacity constraint in producing a product or providing a service exists;

   e. An organization wants to generate funds quickly to recover its investment or finance other developmental efforts;

   f. There is a realistic perceived value in the product or service.

In short, Burroughs Wellcome literally followed an apparent "textbook" rationale for a skimming strategy for Retrovir!

4. Also, the **price inelasticity** of demand for Retrovir arising from its unique properties, consumer need, and lack of substitutes (competitive treatments), would argue for a high price. A low initial price, or lowering the price would not necessarily increase sales volume. A company official implicitly incorporates the view that consumer price insensitivity was considered with the statement:

> "I guess we assumed that the drug ... would be paid in some manner by the patient himself out of his own pocket or by third-party payers. We really didn't get into a lot of calculations along those lines."

In other words, if an AIDS patient wanted the drug, the patient would find the means to get it regardless of price.

D. What arguments can be made on the basis of ethical grounds and social responsibility perspective for the pricing of Retrovir?

1. Student attention should be directed to three quotes which introduce the case as a starting point for considering matters of ethical and social responsibility:

   a.) "I think that Burroughs Wellcome is very interested in getting all their money back as soon as possible, because the sun won't shine forever."

   Co-founder of Project Inform an AIDS treatment information agency (1987)

   b.) "Once the drug is out on the marketplace, the company controls the pricing."

   Dr. George Stanley, Food and Drug Administration (1987)

   c.) "To make AZT accessible to everyone who should be on it, Burroughs Wellcome has an obligation to give up a significant amount of money to allow people to get access."

   Executive Director, National Gay and Lesbian Task Force (1989)

Students should again be directed to the quote from the 1989 Wellcome PLC *Annual Report* which is illustrative of the company's point of view:

> In arriving at our decision to reduce the price, we carefully weighed a number of factors. These included our responsibility to patients and shareholders, the very real remaining uncertainties in the marketplace and the vital need to fund our continuing research and development programs.

2. These points of view represent two very different moral philosophies:

   Moral Idealism: Certain individual rights or duties are universal regardless of the outcome or consequences.

   Utilitarianism: Actions taken should focus on the "greatest good for the greatest number" after assessing the costs and benefits of the consequences of the behavior.

- a. **Moral Idealism** is evident in the views of AIDS patient advocacy groups. Note the reference to "obligation."

- b. **Utilitarianism** is apparent in the statements made by Burroughs Wellcome. Note the reference to multiple constituencies.

3. Matters of social responsibility are also apparent.

- a. **Stockholder/Profit Responsibility**. Burroughs Wellcome apparently views its social responsibility more narrowly than AIDS patient advocacy groups, the U.S. Congress, the media, and other constituencies. The focus on patients, shareholders, and the need to fund further R&D is indicative of this viewpoint. Instructors might quote Nobel Laureate Milton Friedman who espouses this view:

  There is one and only one social responsibility of business -- to use its resources and engage in activities designed to increase its profits so long as it stays within the rules of the game, which is to say, engages in open and free competition without deception or fraud (*New York Times Magazine* (September 13, 1970)).

- b. **Societal Responsibility**. Other constituencies view Burroughs Wellcome's social responsibility more broadly. They emphasize potential human suffering and economic hardships placed on individual and society as a whole as central issues.

4. These differing views on ethics and social responsibility are presented in the context of setting a specific price for Retrovir and the pricing policy of Burroughs Wellcome. Some of the issues that warrant attention include:

- a. What is Burroughs Wellcome's ethical obligation in setting a price for Retrovir?

- b. Who is Burroughs Wellcome responsible to in setting a price for Retrovir?

- c. What is a **fair** price and a **fair** profit? What does **fair** mean in this context?

E. How profitable has Retrovir been for Burroughs Wellcome?

1. The answer to this question is not easily determined. Nevertheless, it is possible to calculate profitability from two perspectives: (1) fully allocated costs which allow for estimates of rate of return measures (return on sales and return on investment) and (2) gross margin dollars or more broadly, contribution dollars.

The fully allocated cost perspective assumes that Retrovir "sits on its own bottom." That is, Retrovir self-funds further R&D on new applications and pays its own selling, general, and administrative (S,G&A) expenses. Furthermore, the amount allocated mirrors Burroughs Wellcome allocations (i.e. 13.4% of sales for R&D and 36.9% for S,G&A based on case Exhibit 3). The gross margin perspective simply looks at dollar sales volume less direct costs and focuses on gross margin contribution dollars to cover overhead, however allocated.

2. Exhibit 2 in this note provides an illustration of a fully allocated cost-profitability analysis for Retrovir in **fiscal 1989**. This analysis allocates R&D and S,G&A expenses to Retrovir based on company figures. If some students to not agree with this perspective, they might be asked, "Who pays for Retrovir's R&D efforts and who pays for overhead?"

Two important issues need to be resolved: What Retrovir price should be used - the original price of $188, the 20% reduction to $150, or the most recent 20 percent price of $120, - and what direct cost of marketing and production should be employed since the case gives a range of $.30 - $.50/capsule. It is important for students to recognize that Burroughs Wellcome financial data are reported on a fiscal year basis ending August 31 and the timing of pricing decisions:

Fiscal 1987: Sept. 1, 1986 - August 31, 1987
(Initial price set at $188/100 capsules in March, 1987. Therefore, 1987 sales data in case Exhibit 6 are for six months).

Fiscal 1988: Sept. 1, 1987 - August 31, 1988
(First price reduction of 20 percent to $150/100 capsules in December 1987. The $150 price was in effect until September, 1989.

Fiscal 1989: Sept. 1, 1988 - August 31, 1989
(The $150/100 capsules price was in effect through all of fiscal 1989).

Fiscal 1990: Sept. 1, 1989 - August 31, 1990
(Second price reduction of 20 percent to $120/100 capsules in September, 1989. Therefore, the $120 price relates to fiscal 1990, not to fiscal 1989).

Recognition of price data on a fiscal year basis means that the price of $150/100 capsules applies to 8 months of fiscal 1988 and all of fiscal 1989. Therefore, the $150 price is the appropriate price for profitability calculations, not $188 or $120. The $120 price, however, can be incorporated into the discussion.

A direct cost of $.40/capsule is used as it is the mid-point/average of the range given. However, as is discussed later, both the $.30 and $.50 figure can be used.

EXHIBIT 2

RETROVIR PROFITABILITY: FISCAL 1989
(For Illustration Purposes)

Case Data and Assumptions

1. Case Exhibit 3 shows that for Wellcome PLC as a whole in Fiscal 1989:

Gross Profit/Sales	=	70.6%
S,G&A/Sales	=	36.9%
R&D/Sales	=	13.4%
Net Income/Sales	=	20.0%

2. Case states that the direct cost of marketing and manufacturing for Retrovir is 30¢ to 50¢/capsule at the $1.50/ capsule ($150 for 100 capsules) wholesale price effective at the end of Fiscal 1989. Assume 40¢ per capsule.

3. **Assume** that Retrovir R&D Expenses/Sales percent and the S,G&A/Sales percent is the same as for the company as a whole.

Profitability (Fiscal 1989)

	Company Overall	Retrovir (capsule)	
Sales	100.0%	$1.50	Sale price
- Cost of Goods Sold	29.4% (plug fig.)	.40	(Direct Cost)
= Gross Margin	70.6%	1.10	= Gross Margin (73.3%)
- S,G&A	36.9% ————>	.55	
- R&D	13.4% ————>	.20	
- "Other"	.3% (plug fig.)		
Return on Sales	<u>20.0%</u>	<u>$ .35</u>	Return on Sales (23.3%)

Exhibit 2 in this note suggests:

    a. At a $150 price/capsule, Retrovir gross margin is above that for the overall company (73.3% vs. 70.6%).

    b. If Retrovir has S,G&A and R&D allocations identical to the overall company, Retrovir's return on sales is higher that the company average (23.3% vs. 20%).

However,

    c. If direct costs were $.50/capsule and cost allocations were identical to those in Exhibit 2 in this note, Retrovir gross margin decreases to $1.00 (66.7%) and return on sales decreases to 16.7 percent ($.25/capsule).

    d. If direct costs were $.30/capsule and cost allocations were identical to those in Exhibit 2 in this note, Retrovir gross margin increase to $1.20 (80%) and return on sales increase to 30 percent ($.45/capsule).

3. The profitability calculations allow for consideration of the return on investment for Retrovir. The case states that unconfirmed (but not denied) estimates of the investment in Retrovir was in the range of $90 million to $100+ million:

Total Research & Development Costs (includes plant and equipment and direct R&D costs of $50 million)	$80-$100 million
Free Distribution of Retrovir	$10 million
Free Supply of AZT to the National Institute of Health (one metric ton)	?
	$90-$110+million

Using a fully allocated cost analysis and assuming a Burroughs Wellcome investment of $100 million in Retrovir, a return on investment calculation for fiscal 1989 is possible. For example, if Retrovir's return on sales is 23.3 percent (see Exhibit 2 in this note), then net profit before taxes is $52.45 million (.233 x $225.1 million in sales). Return on investment for fiscal 1989 would be about 52.5 percent ($52.45/$100 million). Return on investment calculation using the highest direct cost figure ($.50/capsule) still produces an ROI of 37.6 percent (.167 x $225.1 million/$100 million).

4. Cost allocations are always problematic and subject to debate. Therefore, calculation of contribution alone provides another useful insight into Retrovir profitability. Assuming that the direct costs of marketing and manufacturing were $.50/capsule in fiscal 1987, $.40 in fiscal 1988, and $.30 in fiscal 1989, approximate margin percentages can be calculated. When these percentages are multiplied by Retrovir sales from case Exhibit 6, contributions for each fiscal year and in total can be determined as follows:

Fiscal Year	Contribution Margin x Sales =	Contribution $
1987	$1.88 - $.50 = $1.38 $24.8 million $1.38/1.88 = 73.4% contribution	$ 18.20 million
1988	$1.50 - $.40 = $1.10 $158.4 million $1.10/$1.50 = 73.3% contribution	$115.63 million
1989	$1.50 - $.30 = $1.20 $225.1 million $1.20/$1.50 = 80% contribution	$180.08 million
		$373.91 million

The $373.9 million contribution to overhead including R&D and S,G&A expenditure at Burroughs Wellcome, and profit. Note: Alterations in the margins do not materially affect the total. It's still very large!

5. **Summary Observations**. Retrovir is a highly profitable product for Burroughs Wellcome and the company has been in need of a commercial success from its R&D efforts. As stated in the case, the company had spent $726 million for R&D on dozens of drugs in the five years preceding the introduction of Retrovir without a commercial success. Retrovir profits help recoup some of these dollars.

The marketing exclusively awarded Burroughs Wellcome with the Orphan Drug Act expires in 1994 - seven years after the Retrovir's 1987 introduction. Retrovir is likely to remain highly profitable for the foreseeable future provided competitors do not successfully introduce alternative treatments. Even with the commercial success of Retrovir, financial performance indicators shown in case Exhibits 3 and 4 suggest that Wellcome PLC is an "average" performer. Given this situation, actions that would jeopardize the profit picture of Retrovir would jeopardize the company's financial standing. After students have performed a financial analysis, they might be asked one or more of the following questions which, in different ways, were posed earlier in the discussion of ethics and social responsibility:

a. What in your estimation, is a fair profit for Retrovir?

b. What is a fair rate of return for a product like Retrovir?

c. Indeed, what is meant by the term "fair" in this context?

F. Should Burroughs Wellcome reduce the price of Retrovir below $120 for 100 capsules? If yes, why and when? If no, why not?

1. At this juncture in the case analysis, students should have expected to consider the multitude of factors impinging on Burroughs Wellcome executives. The instructor might wish to highlight a few major points raised, including the (a) broader social and public health context in which the pricing decision exists, (b) economic considerations related to estimated profitability, (c) the unique posture Burroughs Wellcome finds itself (monopoly situation, history of price cuts and consumer and political response and so forth), and (d) ethical/social responsibility considerations.

2. Students should also consider the present situation with regard to (a) the recent price cut from $150 to $120, (b) the social and economic cost of treatment and market/governmental response with each successive price cut, (c) the fact that FDA dosage recommendations call for a 40% reduction, (d) the fast approaching end to its marketing exclusivity (1994) under the Orphan Drug Act, and (e) the likelihood of competitive treatments being commercially available, e.g., DDI produced by Bristol Myers and DDC developed by Hoffman-LaRoche.

3. **Possible arguments for keeping the price at $120**

   a. Chairman of Wellcome PLC, Sir Alfred Sheppard, has said: "There's no plan to make another price cut." Why go against the top company official?

   b. Burroughs Wellcome is damned if it reduces its price and damned if it doesn't! Keep the price, take the heat, and record better profit margins! Again, according to Sir Alfred, "If we wrapped the drug in a E10 note and gave it away, people would say it cost too much."

   c. A further price reduction would reduce funds available for further R&D on AIDS treatment for children and other HIV-infected populations.

   d. By reducing the price from $150 to $120 in September 1990, Burroughs Wellcome will give up $68.9 million in revenues for fiscal 1990. Assuming that demand is relatively insensitive to price (i.e. price inelastic), a 53 percent increase in Retrovir unit volume forecasted for fiscal 1990 at the $150 price would mean revenues of $344.4 million. [1.53 x $225.1 million (at $150 price) = $334.4 million]. At a $120 price, this unit volume increase would produce revenues of $275.5 million [1.53 x $225.1 million (at $150 price) x $120/$150 = $275.5 million]. Therefore $344.4 million $275.5 million = $68.9 million.

   e. The effective annual cost to AIDS patients has declined by 36 percent with price reductions from $188/100 capsules to $120/100 capsules (see Exhibit 3 in this note).

EXHIBIT 3

RETROVIR ECONOMICS: PATIENT PERSPECTIVE

March - December, 1987 (original pricing)

1. Recommended dosage: 1200 Milligrams per day administered in 12,100-milligram capsules, or 4,380 100-milligram capsules per year.

2. Retrovir price to wholesaler: $188 for 100, 100-milligram capsules, or $1.88 per 100-milligram capsule.

3. Annual cost to patient at Burroughs Wellcome price to wholesaler:* 4,380 capsules x $1.88/capsule = $8,234.40.

December 15, 1987 - August, 1989 (first price cut of 20% on December 15).

1. Recommended dosage: Unchanged

2. Retrovir price to wholesalers: .8 x $1.88/capsule = $1.504/capsule

3. Annual cost to patient at Burroughs Wellcome price to wholesaler: 4,380 capsules x $1.504/capsule = $6,587.52 (or simply, .8 x $8,234.40)

September, 1989 to December, 1990 (second price cut of 20% in September)

1. Recommended dosage: Unchanged

2. Retrovir price to wholesaler: .8 x $1.504 = $1.203/capsule

3. Annual cost to patient at Burroughs Wellcome price to wholesaler: 4,380 capsules x $1.203 = $5,269.14 (or simply, .8 x $6,587.52)

---

*The retail price would be higher since the case notes that the combined margins of wholesalers and pharmacies ranged from 5 to 20 percent.

f. If the FDA recommended dosage of 500 milligrams becomes the norm (vs. 1200 milligrams), the effective cost to patients is substantially reduced as are Retrovir revenues. In fiscal 1990, for example, an approximate calculation suggests Retrovir revenues would be $114.8 million! [1.53 x $225.1 million (at $150 price) x $120/$150 x 500/1200 = $114.8 million].

Even though the likelihood of **all** patients being treated at a lower dosage is small, it is still a possibility. Students might be asked to speculate on what percent of AIDS patients might safely be treated with a lower dosage. For example, if students believe 20 percent could be treated at a lower dosage, then 80 percent would still require 1200 milligrams/day. On average, this would mean that the average dosage would fall to 1060 milligrams/day [(.2)(500)+(.8)(1200) = 1060 capsules/day, or about 88% of the average present dosage.] This would mean that Retrovir revenue for fiscal 1990 would be: $275.5 million (at $120 price and 1200 milligram dosage with a 53% increase in unit volume) times .88, or $242.4 million.

4. **Possible arguments for cutting the price**

   a. Congressional pressure focusing on "inappropriate pricing" of Retrovir and Congressional lobbyists launching a campaign to curb "excessive profits earned by the drug industry as a whole" does not bode well for Burroughs Wellcome and the pharmaceutical industry as a whole. Also challenges to the patent on Retrovir and threats to nationalize the drug could all but eliminate a future revenue stream. Another price cut might relieve some pressure.

   b. Burroughs Wellcome is well on its way to recouping its investment of about $100 million in Retrovir. For example, at the $150 for 100 capsule price with fully allocated costs (see Exhibit 2 in this note), Retrovir is producing a 23.3 percent Return on Sales. Since this price was effective for most of fiscal 1988 and all of fiscal 1989, the Return on Sales percentage can be multiplied by total sales in 1988 and 1989 to arrive at and estimated profit of $89.36 million [(1988 Sales: $158.4 million + 1989 sales: $225.1 million) x .233 = $89.36 million]. A price reduction to say, $100, would still mean that Retrovir has recouped its investment while funding related R&D and covering S,G&A in the process.

   c. Burroughs Wellcome's public (media) image, which has probably been tarnished during the initial testing and subsequent introduction of Retrovir, might be improved with another price cut.

   d. There is also a moral argument for making Retrovir available to those in need at a price that does not cause economic hardship for individuals and society as a whole, even if the profit consequences are significant. This argument is consistent with the philosophy of Moral Idealism. In a similar vein, it might be argued that the social responsibility of Burroughs Wellcome is broader than to its patients and stockholders and includes societal welfare as well. The burden of AIDS on society as a whole is significant in both social and economic terms.

G. Epilogue

Burroughs Wellcome did not reduce the price of Retrovir in the 1990 calendar year nor did it reduce the price in the 1991 calendar year. Estimated dollar sales for Retrovir in fiscal 1990 ended September 1, 1990, were $287.3 million. Sales were $315 million in fiscal 1992. Industry analysts estimated that total worldwide Retrovir sales from 1987 through fiscal 1994 amount to nearly $2 billion.

None of the competitive treatments for AIDS were commercially introduced in 1990. However, in October 1991, Bristol-Myers received FDA approval to market DDI under the trade name Videx. The annual cost of Videx to an AIDS patient would be $1,745.00. Industry sources estimated that Videx would produce annual sales of $50 million in the U.S. Bristol-Myers was believed to have spent about $75 million developing Videx (*Wall Street Journal*, October 10, 1991, p. A1). Hoffman-LaRoche received FDA approval to market DDC in June, 1992. This approval required that DDC be used in combination with AZT.

In September 1991, the U.S. Government announced it had granted a conditional license to Barr Laboratories to make a generic form of AZT. This license was granted because the National Institutes of Health, whose staff argues that it did most of the initial testing and development of the drug, should share the patent. A generic form of AZT could be priced 40-50 percent less than the branded version (Retrovir). Burroughs Wellcome subsequently brought a patent-infringement suit against Barr Laboratories. Burroughs Wellcome won the suit in 1993 and held the U.S. patent through 1994 (*Wall Street Journal*, 1993, p. B1). However, Barr Labs presently sells the generic AZT in Canada for roughly one-half the price of Retrovir. It has been estimated that medical costs associated with AIDS in the United States totaled more than $6 billion in 1993.

The AIDs crisis continues for people living in Africa. In 2000, an estimated 23 million people were diagnosed with the HIV virus in Africa. In a landmark agreement in May 2000, makers of AZT and complementary drugs agreed to reduce their prices to only a few cents above manufacturing costs (*Wall Street Journal*, May 11, 2000, p A1, A12).

H. Summary Points

1. Price determination is a difficult process particularly when matters of a fair price and a fair profit are raised for consideration. This issue often arises in the health care industry in general and specifically in the pharmaceutical industry.

2. Demand, competition, and cost issues clearly were apparent in the pricing of Retrovir. Based purely on a marketing perspective, a **skimming price strategy** was appropriate:

- Demand was price inelastic
- Retrovir was unique and patented
- Production and marketing costs were uncertain
- A capacity constraint in producing AZT existed
- High perceived value of AZT

But was a skimming strategy ethical and socially responsible?

3. The case raises for consideration two very different moral philosophies:

Moral Idealism: Certain individual rights or duties are universal regardless of the outcome or consequences.

Utilitarianism: Actions taken should focus on the "greatest good for the greatest number" after assessing the costs and benefits of the consequences of the behavior.

Moral Idealism is evident in the views of AIDS patient advocacy groups who argue Burroughs Wellcome has an obligation to make AZT available at a price they can pay.

Utilitarianism is evident in the quote from the 1989 Wellcome PLC Annual Report:

> In arriving at our decision to reduce the price, we carefully weighed a number of factors. These included our responsibility to patients and shareholders, the very real remaining uncertainties in the marketplace and the vital need to fund our continuing research and development programs.

Which philosophy is morally right and just in this case?

AFTON INDUSTRIES

Synopsis

In January 1999, Bob Shearer, the Director of Sales, and Dan Egan, the Director of Planning and Administration for Afton Industries met to prepare a recommendation on the price per square of the company's asphalt shingle line. Afton had been a price leader in its regional market. However, in January 1998, when Afton raised its average price square to $44.50 from $40.50 per square, its two major competitors did not follow. Afton saw its shingle market share decline five-percentage points, from 49 percent in 1997 to 44 percent in 1998, as regional shingle market growth exceeded 11 percent. The decline in 1998 market share is further complicated by some industry forecasts that project a slowing or declining demand for asphalt shingles in 1999.

The issue posed in the case is whether Afton should maintain its average price per square at $44.50, or return the average price to $40.50. The case presents a rich context to simultaneously examine demand, cost and competitive factors when making a pricing decision in a business-to-business marketing setting. An opportunity also exists to apply decision analysis in the case setting.

Teaching Objectives

This case has three teaching objectives:

1. To highlight the importance, and difficulty, of simultaneously assessing demand, cost, and competitive factors when making a pricing decision.

2. To apply the concept of relevant cost in a pricing context.

3. To provide an opportunity to apply decision analysis in a pricing context.

Teaching Suggestions

This short case is best suited for that portion of the course that focuses on pricing issues in marketing management. The case has been used in both undergraduate and graduate courses. Experience indicates that the depth of student analysis is typically greater in graduate classes, however.

This case has been used as an in-class examination or part of a final examination given its length. It has been also used early in the course to illustrate an application of competitive marketing decision-making, decision analysis, and financial analysis.

The class discussion can be initiated by posing the question below, followed by a class vote:

> What pricing recommendation would you make to Afton's president? (1) keep the average price at $44.50 per square or (2) reduce the price to $40.50 per square?

Our experience indicates that a large majority, if not all students, vote to reduce the price to $40.50. This initial vote is fine and can be used in a novel way during the class discussion. After the initial vote, which should be recorded on the board, an instructor should ask a student to articulate his/her rationale. Typically, the student(s) will refer to the "higher predicted market shares" with dropping the price. This gives an instructor an opportunity to ask students to project 1999 shingle and dollar market demand and make a sales forecast using the "predicted market shares." It is here that students will realize that the highest dollar sales arise when Afton keeps the price at $44.50, regardless of market growth scenario. At this time, the class should be asked to vote again: (1) keep the price; (2) drop the price. An instructor will note that the number of students, who originally favored dropping the price, switch to the keep the price action. In some instances, the switch has been dramatic, which the instructor might note. This vote should lead an instructor to ask, "what about profit?" This question leads to the contribution analysis described in the teaching note. The discussion should lead students to realize that the keep/drop price alternatives produce very different contributions, depending on the market growth scenarios. It is here where decision analysis is applied, yielding a decision to drop the price.

Specific questions that are useful for case preparation or discussion purposes are:

1. How would you characterize the asphalt shingle market in Afton's region?

2. What is Afton's competitive position?

3. Why do you think competitors did not follow Afton's lead in raising the price on asphalt singles?

4. What price recommendation would you make to Afton's president? Why?

Areas for Discussion/Analysis

A. How would you characterize the asphalt shingle market in Afton's region?

    1. The market for asphalt shingles in Afton's region has been growing for seven years with shingle square volume more than doubling since 1991 (case Exhibit 2). A seven-year expansion period is uncommon since the asphalt shingle industry is traditionally cyclical—three to four years of sales growth followed by a sales slowdown and decline.

    2. Demand for asphalt shingles is **derived**. Asphalt shingles demand is driven by the incidence of new residential construction (which accounts for 20% of shingle volume), and reroofing activity which accounts for 80% of shingle volume. Furthermore, the type of asphalt shingle used is dictated by climate: organic-based shingles fare better in cold weather regions while fiberglass-based shingles fare better in warm weather regions.

    3. The marketing channel for asphalt shingles is shown below:

Manufacturer ⟶ Roofing Material Distributor ⟶ Roofing Contractor ⟶ Buyer

    4. Consumers play a relatively minor role in the brand purchase decision for asphalt shingles due to a lack of knowledge. Brand (manufacturer) choice is dominated by roofing contractors, provided the price and manufacturer's warranty are acceptable to the buyer.

    5. The growth of the asphalt shingle market over the past seven years has attracted many "fly-by-night" roofing contractors who benefited from demand not satisfied by more reputable roofing contractors. These roofers were believed to be pricing jobs to pick up business, exiting the market when demand declined, and reappearing in boom times. In addition, some "marginal" roofers tended to buy lower-priced shingles and mark them up so that the price differential between manufacturers was actually described as price parity, at least from the final buyers point of view. These roofers then pocketed the difference. "Fly-by-night" and "marginal roofers" have apparently grown in numbers during the economic expansion. Their presence in the regional shingle market has presumably contributed to Afton's present pricing situation, according to company management.

B. What is Afton's competitive position?

    1. Afton has been the traditional price leader in its regional market; that is, when the company announced its price on asphalt shingles, competitive shingle manufacturers followed. It is reasonable to assume that this price leadership arose from Afton's market share position. As recently as 1997, Afton captured 49 percent of the asphalt unit sales volume in its regional market. No large, national shingle manufacturer of asphalt shingles had a plant in Afton's region.

2. Afton's asphalt shingles and service are highly regarded by roofing material distributors and among established, reputable roofing contractors in the region. These factors also account for its competitive position. According to research conducted by the National Roofing Contractors Association, shingle performance (i.e., quality) and level of manufacturer service were the dominant choice considerations in selecting an asphalt shingle brand (manufacturer), followed by shingle warranty and then price. It is unlikely that "fly-by-night" contractors view anything other than price when making a brand choice/recommendation, providing the brand warranty is acceptable to the buyer.

3. The growth of the asphalt market in Afton's region had led to plant expansion by Afton and its competitors thus increasing their production capacity. Two of Afton's major competitors engaged in capacity expansion sooner than Afton, having added capacity in 1997. Afton's capacity expansion was completed in 1998.

4. Afton announced an average price increase in January 1998 that raised its average shingle price from $40.50 per square to $44.50 per square. The price increase was one of several changes directed by Afton's board of directors to improve the company's working capital position. The $4.00 average price increase (about 9.9%) was comparable to Afton's two previous price increases (about 10%) over the past seven years. Contrary to the past, Afton's major competitors did not follow.

5. The unwillingness of Afton's two major competitors to follow the price increase coupled with the pricing practices of "fly-by-night" and "marginal" roofing contractors have presumably contributed to a decline in Afton's market share in its region from 49 percent in 1997 to 44 percent in 1998. It is reasonable to speculate that without the presence of established and reputable roofing contractors, Afton's market share might have decreased further.

6. Even with a decline in unit market share to 44 percent, Afton probably remains the major shingle manufacturer (brand) in its region. However, the case states that no competitor, Afton included, has a (product) cost advantage. Given its $44.50 average price per square versus its competitor's lower (but not given in the case) prices, Afton is likely to be more profitable than its competitors on a per square basis and in terms of total company profitability.

C. Why do you think competitors did not follow Afton's lead in raising the price on asphalt shingles?

1. Afton's senior management believes that its competitors, with added capacity, are seeking to increase their market share, hence unit volume. This is plausible.

2. It is also possible that competitors, with capacity expansion (and most likely plant modernization), believe they have a product cost advantage. This advantage will allow them profitable margins at the existing (lower) price. Moreover, competitors are likely to believe

that higher unit volumes, with an attendant lower cost per unit, like Afton's cost projection (case Exhibit 3), will yield even higher profit margins. Of course, this reasoning is now questionable given that Afton too has completed its capacity expansion and plant modernization. There is no competitive cost advantage in 1998, according to Afton's management.

3. It is also possible that competitors believe market growth will continue. Shingle unit volume growth in the market did increase 11 percent in 1998. This growth, coupled with a market share gain, certainly increased the unit sales volume of competitors. There was no incentive to raise prices and they didn't.

4. To the extent that market growth continues and "fly-by-night" and "marginal" roofers continue to populate the regional shingle market, competitors will benefit from lower average prices and an exaggerated price differential from Afton.

5. However, 1999 presents a potentially different economic picture. If market growth slows, or actually declines, as the projections seem to indicate, competitors' pricing might also need to be revised.

D. **What price recommendation would you make to Afton's president? Why?**

1. A thorough student response to this question will involve a regional unit (square) volume projection under two different market growth scenarios and two price scenarios followed by a cost-volume-profit analysis and decision analysis. An instructor should be prepared to offer some direction in this phase of the class discussion and transparencies of Exhibits 1 - 4 in this note should be brought to class.

2. Experience teaching the case indicates that unit volume estimates for the two growth projections should be arrived at first, followed by Bob Shearer's speculation about Afton's market shares. These calculations are shown in Exhibit 1 in this note, based on case information.

Some discussion might arise concerning both market growth and market share estimates. Points to make in this discussion include:

- All of Bob Shearer's 1999 market share estimates—45%, 46%, 47%, and 49% are higher than the current 44 percent market share. Shearer is obviously aggressive and students may dispute the estimates and the reasoning behind them. However, they serve as a starting point for a cost-volume-profit analysis and should be viewed in this context.

EXHIBIT 1

REGIONAL SHINGLE VOLUME PROJECTIONS AND AFTON'S MARKET SHARE AND SALES ESTIMATES UNDER DIFFERENT PRICING SCENARIOS

Given in case:

1. 1998 Regional Market Shingle Square Volume: 1,610,000 squares

2. Market Growth Projections and Volume Forecast:

   - 2% Growth: 1.02 x 1,610,000 =   1,642,200 squares

   - 5% Decline: .95 x 1,610,000 =   1,529,500 squares

3. Afton Market Share and Sales Volume Estimates with Different Prices

   - 2% Growth and

     ... Keep Price (Market Share = 45%): .45 x 1,642,200 =   738,990 squares
         x $44.50
     Projected Sales $32,885,055

     ... Drop Price (Market Share = 47%): .47 x 1,642,200 =   771,834 squares
         x $40.50
     Projected Sales $31,259,277

   - 5% Decline and

     ... Keep Price (Market Share = 46%): .46 x 1,529,500 =   703,570 squares
         x $44.50
     Projected Sales $31,308,865

     ... Drop Price (Market Share = 49%): .49 x 1,529,500 =   749,455 squares
         x $40.50
     Projected Sales $30,352,927

- The likelihood of a slowing growth market (2% growth) and a declining market (5% decline) are roughly the same in Dan Egan's view. He stated, "I tend to think there is a 50 to 60 percent chance of two percent growth in 1999 and a 40 to 50 percent chance of a five percent decline." It is worth noting again that the shingle market has experienced a seven-year period of expansion when history shows a three to four year growth-decline cycle. Is slowed growth or an actual decline in demand on the horizon?

- All 1999-unit volume estimates, except one (703,570 squares), are higher than Afton's 1998 volume of 715,000 squares due to the market share estimates. Furthermore, one market-price scenario described by Shearer recaptures the 49 percent market share lost in 1998 (a 5% decline in shingle volume with a price drop to $40.50 per square).

- Dollar sales projections for the "Keep Price at $44.50" option are higher regardless of market growth scenario:

Pricing Option	Market Growth	
	2% Growth	5% Decline
Keep Price at $44.50	Sales Projection: $32,885,055	Sales Projection: $31,308,865
Drop Price to $40.50	Sales Projection: $31,259,277	Sales Projection: $30,352,927

An immediate response from some students is "Keep the price at $44.50, sales are higher." An instructor might respond: "Yes, but are profits higher?" [Note: A student might say that the sales dollars do not compare favorably with Afton's 1998 sales of $32 million. However, these sales projections only apply to shingles, not roofing accessory products which Afton also sells.]

3. A natural transition from the market growth–price–sales–share discussion is an analysis of cost-volume-profit relationships. It is here when the class discussion can bog down. An instructor may wish to assume a discussion-leader role by showing Exhibit 2 in this note, which is based on case Exhibit 3. This exhibit shows how variable costs per square change with output volume using standard cost as a guide. The approach used for estimating costs is straightforward. It is important to note that only unit variable costs are adjusted (excluding material), not unit fixed cost items, and the emphasis is placed on estimating unit contribution. That is, **only the variable costs–direct labor, direct material, scrappage, and product line direct expense–are relevant costs for the pricing decision.**

Some students will say that all costs, including fixed costs, need to be incorporated into the pricing decision. Others might note that there appears to be some volume sensitivity in the per-unit fixed costs, i.e., the per-unit costs for product line indirect expenses and selling and general administrative expense decrease as volume increases. On

EXHIBIT 2

PRICE, COST, MARGIN ESTIMATES AT DIFFERENT UNIT VOLUMES

	At $44.50 Price Per Square			At $40.50 Price Per Square	
	At 738,990 Squares	At 703,570 Squares		At 771,834 Squares	At 749,455 Squares
Price	$44.50	$44.50		$40.50	$40.50
Variable Cost:					
Direct Labor	$14.49*	$17.25		$11.50	$13.55
Direct Material	7.00**	7.00		7.00	7.00
Scrappage	2.02*	2.09		1.96	2.00
Direct Expense	3.42*	3.47		3.38	3.40
Unit Variable Cost	26.93	29.81		23.84	25.95
Square Contribution	$17.57	$14.69		$16.66	$14.55

*Case Exhibit 4 shows that direct labor, scrappage, and direct expense cost items decrease on a per unit basis as volume increases. Assuming a constant (linear) decline within a volume range, the per unit (square) cost can be estimated at volume levels within a range.

**A straightforward estimation method is shown for Direct Labor at the projected 738,990 square forecast. Other variable cost items at different projected volume levels are calculated in the same way.

$$\begin{pmatrix} \text{Direct} \\ \text{Labor} \\ @725{,}000 \end{pmatrix} - \left[\left[\begin{pmatrix} \text{Direct Labor} \\ @725{,}000 \end{pmatrix} - \begin{pmatrix} \text{Direct Labor} \\ @750{,}000 \end{pmatrix} \right] \div \begin{bmatrix} 25{,}000 \\ \text{Units} \end{bmatrix} \right] \times \left[\begin{pmatrix} \text{Projected} \\ \text{Volume} \end{pmatrix} - \begin{pmatrix} \text{Standard} \\ \text{Volume} \end{pmatrix} \right] = \begin{pmatrix} \text{Direct Labor} \\ @738{,}990 \end{pmatrix}$$

$$\$15.75 - \left[\left[(\$15.75) - (\$13.50) \right] \div \begin{bmatrix} 25{,}000 \\ \text{Units} \end{bmatrix} \right] \times \left[(738{,}990) - (725{,}000) \right] = \$14.49$$

EXHIBIT 3

CONTRIBUTION TO OVERHEAD AND PROFIT CALCULATION

Afton Actions	Market Demand	
	2% Growth	**5 % Decline**
Keep Price at $44.50 per square	<u>45% Market Share</u> 738,990 Squares x $17.57 Unit Contribution $12,984,054 Contribution to Overhead & Profit	<u>46% Market Share</u> 703,570 Squares x $14.69 Unit Contribution $10,335,433 Contribution to Overhead and Profit
Drop Price to $40.50 per square	<u>47% Market Share</u> 771,834 Squares x $16.66 Unit Contribution $12,858,754 Contribution to Overhead & Profit	<u>49% Market Share</u> 749,455 Squares x $14.55 Unit Contribution $10,904,570 Contribution to Overhead and Profit

the first point, the tenets of managerial accounting favor treating fixed costs in its full dollar amount, rather than as a per-unit cost. On the second point, total product line indirect expense actually varies little over the 700,000 to 775,000-volume range. Selling and General Administrative Expense (SG & A) includes a wide variety of expense items (executive, clerical, and sales salaries, insurance, etc.) probably varies somewhat, but are generally insensitive to volume. Yes, they will go down on a per unit basis because the denominator (Dollar SG & A ÷ unit volume) is going up. However, **fixed overhead costs differ little between the alternatives under consideration, and are irrelevant for the decision at hand.**

4. Exhibit 3 in this note shows the contribution to overhead calculation generated by each market-growth-price scenario. This exhibit shows that:

- Afton generates a higher total contribution if it keeps its price at $44.50 and the market records a two-percent growth than if it drops its price to $40.50; however,

- Afton generates a higher total contribution if it drops its price to $40.50 and the market declines by five-percent than if it keeps its price at $44.50.

Clearly, a cost–volume–profit analysis yields a different conclusion than a sales analysis. The previous sales projections showed that the "Keep Price at $44.50" option produced higher sales regardless of market growth (2% increase vs. 5% decline) scenario.

5. The cost–volume–profit analysis yields total contribution estimates that can be portrayed in a payoff table, like that described in Chapter 3, where the choice of an alternative (pricing action) depends on the likelihood of occurrence of uncertainties (market growth/decline) in the environment. Exhibit 4 in this note shows the payoff table, including the probabilities of occurrence for market growth and decline and the Expected Monetary Value (EMV) calculation for both pricing options. The probability of a two-percent market growth is set at Prob. = .55 which is the midpoint of Dan Egan's 50 to 60 percent probability estimate. The Prob. = .45 for the five-percent decline is based on his 40 to 50 percent probability estimate.

6. The EMV calculation shows that "Drop Price to $40.50" yields the highest average total contribution. Therefore, decision analysis suggests that this action be taken. [Note: The same conclusion results if the two-percent market growth projection is given a 50 percent or 60 percent probability and the five-percent market decline is given a 40 percent or 50 percent probability.]

At his juncture, an instructor may ask students to list the factors that produced the EMV calculation and decision:

- The market growth/decline forecast made by Dan Egan,
- The market share projection and reasoning offered by Bob Shearer,
- The standard cost estimates prepared by Pat, Afton's controller.

EXHIBIT 4

PRICE DECISION ANALYSIS

	Market Demand	
Afton Actions	**2% Growth**	**5 % Decline**
Keep Price at $44.50 per square	$12,984,054 Contribution	$10,335,443 Contribution
Drop Price to $40.50 per square	$12,858,754 Contribution	$10,904,570 Contribution
	Prob. = .55	Prob. = .45

$EMV_{\$44.50}$ = .55 ($12,984,054) + .45 ($10,335,443) = $11,792,179

$EMV_{\$40.50}$ = .55 ($12,858,754) + .45 ($10,904,570) = $11,979,371

Decision Based on Decision Analysis:

Choose The Pricing Action with the Higher Expected Monetary Value

Drop the Price to $40.50 Per Square

Changes in any of these factors will alter the EMV calculation and may change the decision. In fact, the two EMV's are very close to each other and are quite sensitive to these assumptions.

7. **Assuming** students generally concur with the market forecasts, share projections, and cost estimates, an instructor might ask: "How sensitive is the EMV calculation to the probability estimates made by Dan Egan?" This question gives the class an opportunity to identify the probability "break-point" where the decision **would** change. This can be done by setting the two price options equal to each other and solving for **P** using simple algebra, where **P** = probability of a two-percent market growth:

Keep Price at $44.50 per square		Drop Price to $40.50 per square
P($12,984,054) + 1 − P ($10,335,433)	=	P($12,858,754) + 1 − P ($10,904,570)
	P = .82	

In words, if the probability of a two-percent market growth is greater than .82, then the "Keep Price at $44.50 per square" pricing option should be chosen on the basis of total contribution. Students then can be asked how likely that the probability of a two-point market growth is greater than .82. Most will say "not likely."

E. Epilogue

Bob Shearer and Dan Egan recommended that Afton Industries (disguised name) should announce an across-the-board price cut on its shingles to $40.50 in January 1999. However, Tom Afton, the company president did not immediately act on their recommendation, saying that he needed to think about it. Two days later, a company salesperson reported that one of Afton's two major competitors had informed roofing material distributors that it was raising its prices by 9.9 percent across-the-board, effective immediately. The effect of the competitor's price increase was to return the region to traditional price tiers and differentials among at least two major competitors. Afton's second major competitor followed the next day. Tom Afton subsequently decided to keep Afton's average price at $44.50

Shingle demand in Afton's region evidenced a slowdown in 1999, beginning February 1999. In April 1999, construction of new houses declined 7.2 percent, the sharpest decline in more than five years ["New-Home Construction Plunged 10.1% in April," Wall Street Journal (May 19, 1999), p. A2.] By the end of 1999, new home construction was down 5 percent in Afton's region, reducing the demand for asphalt shingles. However, reroofing and remodeling demand was up 3.75 percent. The net growth given the 80/20 split between reroofing and new construction translated to an overall 2 percent market growth for the region. This growth rate is the same as one of the market scenarios identified by Dan Egan.

Afton's market share improved to 46 percent in 1999, a share that was slightly higher than the one (45%) estimated by Bob Shearer. By mid-2000, Afton's sales volume was trending toward 47 percent. Reputable roofing contractors, which had been ignoring the reroofing and remodeling business in 1998 due to excess demand and a shortage of labor to satisfy the demand, were again in this market and Afton was a preferred manufacturer and brand. As expected, "fly-by-night" roofing contractors that had fed on excess demand exited the market.

Tom Afton said afterward, "I was seriously considering a price reduction given Bob and Dan's recommendation. If I had, all of the major competitors would have been pricing low in a slow market, since I doubt that our competitors would have raised their prices. All of us would have been feeling a lot more pain given the slowdown in shingle volume. As it turned out, by not reducing our price, I looked like a genius. I know that it's better to be lucky than good sometimes."

F. Summary Points

1. Price determination requires a careful assessment of demand, cost, and competition.

2. Price determination is often affected by organizational objectives
   ... increase unit volume
   ... increase market share
   ... increase dollar sales
   ... achieve a certain level of profitability

A specific price level will often differ depending on organizational objectives.

3. Price reductions at the manufacturer level do not always reach the ultimate buyer. Resellers sometimes increase their margins rather than passing along the lower price.

4. Decision analysis is useful for articulating alternative courses of action, expected market and competitive response, and financial outcomes. However, the "quality" of any decision analysis lies in the accuracy of projected responses and financial outcomes, and the confidence one has in the probability estimates.

AUGUSTINE MEDICAL, INC.
THE BAIR HUGGER PATIENT WARMING SYSTEM

Synopsis

In early 1988, executives at Augustine Medical Inc. had to determine how to price The Bair Hugger Patient Warming System. This system was designed to treat patient post-operative hypothermia, a condition defined as a body temperature of less than 36° Centigrade or 96° Fahrenheit. Sixty to eighty percent of surgery patients suffer from this condition.

Pricing this system is made complex by the fact that two components of the system must be priced: (1) a heater/blower unit and (2) warming covers or blankets. The heater/blower unit is a durable good with a long life, say 15 years. Warming covers are disposable plastic blankets that are discarded after patient use for sanitary reasons. Company executives must determine pricing objectives, strategies, and a list price for the heater/blower unit and warming covers which will achieve a profitable initial level of hospital penetration and long-term profitability from continued sales of warming covers or blankets.

Students will quickly draw the analogy to razors and razor blades and talk about skimming and penetration price strategies. However, as the case unfolds, careful consumer analysis, competitive analysis, and cost analysis will play a part in arriving at objectives, strategies and a list price for the unit and blankets. In addition, the concepts of derived demand, innovation diffusion in hospitals, market segmentation/targeting (large vs. small hospitals), and market potential must be considered.

Teaching Objectives

This case has five teaching objectives:

1. To set forth the classic distinction between skimming and penetration pricing for an innovative "industrial" product.

2. To introduce students to the difficulties inherent in pricing complimentary products, and particularly where the long-term sales of one product (warming covers) is **contingent** on the initial purchase and ultimate penetration of another product (heater/blower units).

3. To give students an opportunity to consider demand, cost, and competition simultaneously in the determination of a list price.

4. To illustrate a common pricing problem, particularly prevalent to business-to-business marketing, where there is broad latitude in pricing, difficulty for a new company in gaining market penetration, and frequently unanticipated barriers to entry.

5. To assess alternative "system" prices and its components using sensitivity analysis.

Teaching Suggestions

This case is best suited for analysis later in the course. The costs underlying the pricing decision are simple enough to lay out, but students soon realize that there is much more involved in a pricing decision than cost behavior. Instructors should emphasize this point during the case analysis.

An issue that arises in a case analysis/discussion is the practice of price discounting. Students correctly note that competitors offer quantity discounts of 40% to 50% of their list prices. Students then conclude that The Bair Hugger heater/blower unit and blanket price analysis should factor this practice into the list price determination. However, as the analysis (should) unfold, the "everyday" list price for the heater/blower unit and blankets can be set more than 40% to 50% below competitor products and still produce a significant margin. In short, price discounting is not a substantive issue even though students will make a "big deal" about it!

The case is suitable for examination purposes and particularly for a take-home examination where students can perform a sensitivity analysis on their personal computers. The case has also proven to be an effective group presentation case. Specific questions which instructors might pose to students either before or during a case analysis include:

1. How would you characterize the prevailing technologies and products for preventing and treating post-operative hypothermia?

2. What factors will influence the market potential for The Bair Hugger Patient Warming System?

3. What is the annual cost to hospitals of competitive technologies or products?

4. What should be the pricing objectives and strategies for The Bair Hugger Patient Warming System?

5. What list price to hospitals should Augustine Medical set for The Bair Hugger Patient Warming System and what short-run profit impact can be expected from this decision?

6. What is the likely long-run profit impact of your pricing decision?

Areas for Discussion/Analysis

A. **How would you characterize the prevailing technologies and products for preventing and treating post-operative hypothermia?**

1. A wide variety of technologies exist for preventing and treating post-operative hypothermia. The case describes ten technologies categorized by surface warming and internal warming:

Surface Warming	Internal Warming
• Warmed hospital blankets • Water-circulating blankets • Air-circulating blankets/mattresses • Thermal Drapes • Infra-red heating lamps • Partial water immersion • Increased room temperature	• Heated and humidified inspired air • Warmed intravenous (I.V.) fluids • Drug Therapy

2. Warmed hospital blankets are the simplest, cheapest, and most frequently used "technology" for treating hypothermia. Water-circulating blankets are the second most used technology and quite similar to The Bair Hugger.

3. Water-circulating technology has the largest number of competitive products. As shown in case Exhibit 2, competitive products typically have a unit of some type and either reusable or disposable blankets, not unlike The Bair Hugger Patient Warming System which uses warmed air, rather than water. Only the Hosworth-Climator, which uses warmed air could compete directly with Bair Hugger. However, it is not yet available in the U.S.

4. It would seem that the "level of technology" for treating hypothermia is "low-tech," not "high-tech," despite the prevalence of this condition. Reasons for this situation are not made evident in the case. However, it would seem that familiarity with existing technologies, cost, skepticism about different technologies and the lack of better technology would contribute to this situation. Also, it may be that treating post-operative hypothermia is low on the priority list for hospitals despite the statement made in the case that the humanitarian ethic is "to make the patient feel more comfortable."

B. **What factors will influence the market potential for the Bair Hugger Patient Warming System?**

1. A number of factors will influence market potential, e.g.:

   • Number of hospitals and post-operative recover beds
   • Number of operations performed annually
   • Incidence of hypothermia
   • Hospital buying process

- Features of Bair Hugger over competing technology/products
- Distributor "push" -- sales effort
- Price or cost to hospitals

2. At the outset, students should recognize that all hospitals will not necessarily purchase Bair Hugger. Specifically, the 1,608 hospitals without post-operative recover beds and those with fewer than seven beds (3,602 hospitals) were not seen as potential users (at least by consultants hired by Augustine Medical). In short, 5,210 hospitals would/may not be prospective users. This leaves **1,888** hospitals that are prospective buyers. These hospitals perform 80 percent of the surgical operations in the U.S. Parenthetically, this calculation reveals another version of the "80-20 rule," -- i.e., 80 percent of the surgical operations are performed by 26.6 percent of the hospitals.

3. **Market potential** for the Bair Hugger heater/blower unit can be calculated from information in the case. A reasonable estimate of market potential is 2,737 heater/blower units (see Exhibit 1 in this note). **Note that this figure is simply potential and not an annual sales forecast.** Moreover, given the presumed long-life of this unit, there is not an immediate replacement market.

4. **Market potential** for the disposable warming blankets is much larger. The case notes that 21 million surgical operations are performed annually and 60-80 percent of all postoperative recovery room patients are clinically hypothermic. Moreover, as noted above, 80 percent of all operations are performed in hospitals that would be in the target market for the Bair Hugger. Therefore, **one estimate** of annual market potential for warming blankets is between 10,080,000 and 13,440,000 blankets:

21 million x .60 x .80 = 10,080,000 blankets, or

21 million x .80 x .80 = 13,440,000 blankets

A second estimate can be made by using the 2,737 heater/blower unit potential calculated in Exhibit 1 in this note. Since the warming time for a patient was two hours, four patients would use the system per day (assuming an 8 hour day). The case states that 84,000 operations are performed daily. Since 21 million operations are performed annually, this means that 250 days are "operating days" (21 million/84,000 = 250). Therefore, a **second estimate** of annual market potential for warming blankets is 2,737,000:

2,737 units x 4 patients/day x 250 days = 2,737,000 blankets

Clearly, a wide disparity exists in the market potential for warming blankets. The second estimate seems to be more realistic since blanket sales are contingent on heater/blower unit penetration/installation.

5. The **hospital buying process** will also affect potential for the Bair Hugger. The case notes that budget committee approval would be needed if equipment purchase price exceeded $1,500.00. Therefore, demand is clearly price sensitive.

EXHIBIT 1

ESTIMATING MARKET POTENTIAL FOR BAIR HUGGER HEATER/BLOWER UNITS

Post-Operative Beds	Number of Hospitals	x	Estimated % of Surgical Operations	x	Systems per 8 Beds per Hospital	=	Estimated Market Potential
0	1,608		0%		0		0
1 - 6	3,602		20%		0		0
7 - 11	1,281		40%		1.1		1,409
12 - 17	391		20%		1.8		704
18 - 22	135		10%		2.5		338
23 - 28	47		6%		3.2		150
29 - 33	17		2%		3.9		66
> 33	17		2%		4.1		70
					Total		**2,737**

Moreover, multiple parties are involved in the purchase decision: (1) physicians, (2) Head Nurse, (3) Chief Anesthesiologist. An unanswered question is who is (are) the gatekeepers, influencers, decision-makers, etc. If budget committee approval is required, then the Hospital Administrator and possibly the purchasing agent would participate in the purchase process. The buying process could slow down the hospital adoption process -- particularly at higher prices for the heater/blower unit.

6. **Bair Hugger features** will also affect market potential. We have found it useful to organize this discussion/analysis around the material in Chapter 6 on product factors that help or hinder the diffusion of an innovation. For example:

- **Felt Need**: It would seem that the treatment of hypothermia is important given its incidence. But present technologies do exist, which leads to the second factor.

- **Relative Advantage**: Dr. Augustine identified four benefits of the Bair Hugger over water-circulating blankets:

    a. Warm air makes patients feel warm and stop shivering.

-
  b. Will not cause burns and electrical problems with water leakage avoided.

  c. Disposable blankets prevent cross contamination.

  d. Lifting/rolling patients unnecessary.

- **Compatibility**: Bair Hugger would seem compatible for hospitals using the water-circulating blanket technology. Some learning will be necessary for hospitals using other technologies.

- **Simplicity**: Bair Hugger would seem simple to operate.

- **Testability**: Initial demonstrations and interviews indicated that actual use would be necessary before a hospital purchase commitment was made: "No one today...ever buys a pig in a poke."

- **Immediacy of Benefit**: Patient benefit should be seen quickly as would less work for nurses who would not have to constantly change warmed blankets. Cost benefits are not as immediate given the initial expense.

7. **Distributor effort** or "push" is a very important factor affecting market potential since Augustine Medical is at their mercy. However, the replacement market potential for blankets plus "competitive" margins would suggest that distributor effort might be present.

8. **Pricing** is the unknown as a factor affecting market potential. Indeed, this is the focus of the problem facing Augustine Medical. If the price of the blower/heater unit is too high, then the blanket potential will be affected because hospitals may not buy. If the blanket prices are too high, the total annual cost to the hospital might be seen as too high.

C. **What is the annual cost to hospitals of competitive technologies or products?**

1. Competitive prices are implicit in the analysis of market potential. Exhibit 2 in this note shows the list prices of competitive units and blankets. Also, the annual (12 month) cost to hospitals is shown including the assumptions made.

2. The price and annual cost range is shown below:

   Unit Price: $2,995 - $4,735

   Disposable Blanket Price: $20 - $24

   Annual Hospital Cost:

   Year of Purchase: $22,995 - $28,735

   On-going Cost: $2,730 - $24,000

EXHIBIT 2

PRICES AND ESTIMATED ANNUAL COSTS TO HOSPITALS
OF COMPETITIVE TECHNOLOGIES/PRODUCTS

Product/Technology	Unit List Price	Cost to Hospital for Disposables Unit & Blankets[1]	Blankets Only[2]
Blanketrol 200			
Manual Unit	$2,995	$2,995 + $20,000 = $22,995	
Automatic Unit	$4,895	$4,895 + $20,000 = $24,895	
Reusable Blanket	$165 - $305		
Disposable Blanket	$ 20		$20,000/12mo.
MTA 4700			
Unit	$4,735	$4,735 + $24,000 = $28,735	
Reusable Blanket	$139		
Disposable Blanket	$ 24		$24,000/12mo.
Aquamatic			
Unit	$4,479		
Climator			
Unit	$4,000		
"Warmed Blankets"			$ 2,730/12mo.[3]

[1]Unit & Blankets is the 12 month cost in the first year of using the system assuming 1,000 patients use the system every 12 months (2 hr. warming time) patient = 4 patients/day; 4 patients/day x 250 days = 1,000 patients/12 months).

[2]Simply the 12 month on-going cost.

[3]This is an equivalent cost for 1,000 patients: 1,000 patients x 7 (blankets/ application) x 1.5 applications = 10,500, blankets; 10,500, blankets x .$26/blanket for warming = $2,730.

The "cheapest" technology on an annual basis is "warmed blankets" at $2,730 per 12 month (year) period.

D. What should be the pricing objectives and strategies for The Bair Hugger Patient Warming System?

1. At the outset, students should consider the pricing objective(s) for Bair Hugger. Such objectives might include:

    a. Maximize (long-, short-run) sales volume

    b. Maximize (long-, short-run) dollar profit rate of return (ROI)

    c. Gain hospital penetration as quickly as possible (market share)

    d. Achieve break-even sales volume

    e. Achieve adequate cash flow

2. Depending on which objective(s) students chose, appropriate pricing strategies must be determined. These strategies should focus on some combination of demand (particularly price elasticity), cost, and competition.

3. **Demand**. Price elasticity of demand and cross-elasticity (unit and blankets) must be considered. Unfortunately, there is little data in the case to make any judgments on the elasticity question. However, students must consider the price of substitute products (technologies). Exhibit 3 in this note displays representative prices.

4. **Cost**. Cost data in this case is straightforward. The direct cost of the heater/blower unit is $380. The cost of material, manufacturing, and packaging of blankets is $.85 per blanket. Both costs are variable. Fixed costs were $500,000, which also represented the initial capitalization for the company. Therefore, the **minimum price** for the heater/blower unit (to cover its variable costs) is $380. The **minimum blanket price** is $.85.

5. **Competition**. Competitive prices for units and blankets are given in Exhibit 2 in the case. As shown in Exhibit 3 in this note, the price range is extremely broad.

6. Based on demand, cost and competitive, a pricing strategy must be adopted. Based on demand, should Augustine Medical use a "skimming" strategy or a penetration strategy, for units, for blankets? Based on cost, should Augustine Medical use some sort of cost-plus strategy for units, for blankets? Finally, based on competition, should Augustine Medical use an at-, below-, or above competitor price strategy?

EXHIBIT 3

BAIR HUGGER SYSTEM PRICE RANGE

	Heater/Blower Unit		Disposable Blanket
Blanketrol 200 (Automatic Unit)	$4,895	MTA 4700	$24
MTA 4700	$4,735	Blanketrol 200	$20
Aquamatic	$4,479		
Climator	$4,000		
Blanketrol 200 (Manual Unit)	$2,995	"Warmed blankets"	$2.73/application
Buying Committee Jurisdiction	$1,500		
Bair Hugger Direct Cost	$380	Bair Hugger Direct Cost	$.85

E. **What list price to hospitals should Augustine Medical set for The Bair Hugger Patient Warming System and what short-run profit impact can be expected from this decision?**

1. This question can be approached from two different angles. Some students will focus attention on individual components (units, blankets) while others will focus on the **system** by looking at combinations of unit and blanket prices.

2. Whatever list prices are recommended, students must consider distributor margins to arrive at manufacturer's selling price. Distributors will receive a 30 percent margin on the delivered price to hospitals for the heater/blower unit and a 40 percent margin on the hospital delivered price for blankets.

3. A convenient way to examine the list price question is to model the "contribution per system" for the Bair Hugger where:

Heater/Blower Unit Contribution	+	Blanket Contribution (x1000)	=	System Contribution
(Price - Direct Cost)	+	(Price - Direct Cost)		

and: 1. Heater/Blower Unit Contribution = Price - $380

2. Blanket Contribution = Price - $.85 x 1000 blankets per year assuming a unit is used at full capacity (250 operating days x 4 patients/day)

Exhibit 4 in this note shows the contribution produced by different prices for units and blankets. This analysis illustrates what students should have surmised: System profitability is driven by blanket price x volume, not by heater/blower unit price x volume. Consider for example, a heater/blower unit price of $1,500 (mftr. price = $1,050) and a blanket hospital price of $20.00 (mftr. price = $12.00). The system contribution is $11,820, of which 94 percent of contribution is produced by blankets (see case Exhibit 4):

Heater/Blower Unit Contribution	+	Blanket Contribution (x1000)	=	System Contribution
(Price - Direct Cost)	+	(Price - Direct Cost)		
$1,050 - $380		($12.00 - $.85)		$11,820

4. Assuming the $500,000 initial capitalization represents company's fixed cost, then a break-even analysis can be performed at different heater/blower unit and blanket prices, where:

$$\text{Break-even Systems (Units)} = \frac{\$500,000}{\text{Contribution per system}}$$

EXHIBIT 4
SYSTEM CONTRIBUTION AT DIFFERENT UNIT AND BLANKET COMBINATIONS

Price Per Blanket		Blower Unit Price																							
Retail	Manufct	$0	$250	$500	$750	$1,000	$1,250	$1,500	$1,750	$2,000	$2,250	$2,500	$2,750	$3,000	$3,250	$3,500	$3,750	$4,000	$4,250	$4,500	$4,750	$5,000	$5,250	$5,500	$5,750	$6,000 Retail
		$0	$175	$350	$525	$700	$875	$1,050	$1,225	$1,400	$1,575	$1,750	$1,925	$2,100	$2,275	$2,450	$2,625	$2,800	$2,975	$3,150	$3,325	$3,500	$3,675	$3,850	$4,025	$4,200 Mftr.
1.00	0.60	(3630)	(3455)	(3280)	(3105)	420	245	420	595	770	945	1,120	1,295	1,470	1,645	1,820	1,995	2,170	2,345	2,520	2,695	2,870	3,045	3,220	3,395	3,570
2.00	1.20	(30)	145	320	495	670	845	1,020	1,195	1,370	1,545	1,720	1,895	2,070	2,245	2,420	2,595	2,770	2,945	3,120	3,295	3,470	3,645	3,820	3,995	4,170
3.00	1.80	570	745	920	1,095	1,270	1,445	1,620	1,795	1,970	2,145	2,320	2,495	2,670	2,845	3,020	3,195	3,370	3,545	3,720	3,895	4,070	4,245	4,420	4,595	4,770
4.00	2.40	1,170	1,345	1,520	1,695	1,870	2,045	2,220	2,395	2,570	2,745	2,920	3,095	3,270	3,445	3,620	3,795	3,970	4,145	4,320	4,495	4,670	4,845	5,020	5,195	5,370
5.00	3.00	1,770	1,945	2,120	2,295	2,470	2,645	2,820	2,995	3,170	3,345	3,520	3,695	3,870	4,045	4,220	4,395	4,570	4,745	4,920	5,095	5,270	5,445	5,620	5,795	5,970
6.00	3.60	2,370	2,545	2,720	2,895	3,070	3,245	3,420	3,595	3,770	3,945	4,120	4,295	4,470	4,645	4,820	4,995	5,170	5,345	5,520	5,695	5,870	6,045	6,220	6,395	6,570
7.00	4.20	2,970	3,145	3,320	3,495	3,670	3,845	4,020	4,195	4,370	4,545	4,720	4,895	5,070	5,245	5,420	5,595	5,770	5,945	6,120	6,295	6,470	6,645	6,820	6,995	7,170
8.00	4.80	3,570	3,745	3,920	4,095	4,270	4,445	4,620	4,795	4,970	5,145	5,320	5,495	5,670	5,845	6,020	6,195	6,370	6,545	6,720	6,895	7,070	7,245	7,420	7,595	7,770
9.00	5.40	4,170	4,345	4,520	4,695	4,870	5,045	5,220	5,395	5,570	5,745	5,920	6,095	6,270	6,445	6,620	6,795	6,970	7,145	7,320	7,495	7,670	7,845	8,020	8,195	8,370
10.00	6.00	4,770	4,945	5,120	5,295	5,470	5,645	5,820	5,995	6,170	6,345	6,520	6,695	6,870	7,045	7,220	7,395	7,570	7,745	7,920	8,095	8,270	8,445	8,620	8,795	8,970
11.00	6.60	5,370	5,545	5,720	5,895	6,070	6,245	6,420	6,595	6,770	6,945	7,120	7,295	7,470	7,645	7,820	7,995	8,170	8,345	8,520	8,695	8,870	9,045	9,220	9,395	9,570
12.00	7.20	5,970	6,145	6,320	6,495	6,670	6,845	7,020	7,195	7,370	7,545	7,720	7,895	8,070	8,245	8,420	8,595	8,770	8,945	9,120	9,295	9,470	9,645	9,820	9,995	10,170
13.00	7.80	6,570	6,745	6,920	7,095	7,270	7,445	7,620	7,795	7,970	8,145	8,320	8,495	8,670	8,845	9,020	9,195	9,370	9,545	9,720	9,895	10,070	10,245	10,420	10,595	10,770
14.00	8.40	7,170	7,345	7,520	7,695	7,870	8,045	8,220	8,395	8,570	8,745	8,920	9,095	9,270	9,445	9,620	9,795	9,970	10,145	10,320	10,495	10,670	10,845	11,020	11,195	11,370
15.00	9.00	7,770	7,945	8,120	8,295	8,470	8,645	8,820	8,995	9,170	9,345	9,520	9,695	9,870	10,045	10,220	10,395	10,570	10,745	10,920	11,095	11,270	11,445	11,620	11,795	11,970
16.00	9.60	8,370	8,545	8,720	8,895	9,070	9,245	9,420	9,595	9,770	9,945	10,120	10,295	10,470	10,645	10,820	10,995	11,170	11,345	11,520	11,695	11,870	12,045	12,220	12,395	12,570
17.00	10.20	8,970	9,145	9,320	9,495	9,670	9,845	10,020	10,195	10,370	10,545	10,720	10,895	11,070	11,245	11,420	11,595	11,770	11,945	12,120	12,295	12,470	12,645	12,820	12,995	13,170
18.00	10.80	9,570	9,745	9,920	10,095	10,270	10,445	10,620	10,795	10,970	11,145	11,320	11,495	11,670	11,845	12,020	12,195	12,370	12,545	12,720	12,895	13,070	13,245	13,420	13,595	13,770
19.00	11.40	10,170	10,345	10,520	10,695	10,870	11,045	11,220	11,395	11,570	11,745	11,920	12,095	12,270	12,445	12,620	12,795	12,970	13,145	13,320	13,495	13,670	13,845	14,020	14,195	14,370
20.00	12.00	10,770	10,945	11,120	11,295	11,470	11,645	[11,820]	11,995	12,170	12,345	12,520	12,695	12,870	13,045	13,220	13,395	13,570	13,745	13,920	14,095	14,270	14,445	14,620	14,795	14,970
21.00	12.60	11,370	11,545	11,720	11,895	12,070	12,245	12,420	12,595	12,770	12,945	13,120	13,295	13,470	13,645	13,820	13,995	14,170	14,345	14,520	14,695	14,870	15,045	15,220	15,395	15,570
22.00	13.20	11,970	12,145	12,320	12,495	12,670	12,845	13,020	13,195	13,370	13,545	13,720	13,895	14,070	14,245	14,420	14,595	14,770	14,945	15,120	15,295	15,470	15,645	15,820	15,995	16,170
23.00	13.80	12,570	12,745	12,920	13,095	13,270	13,445	13,620	13,795	13,970	14,145	14,320	14,495	14,670	14,845	15,020	15,195	15,370	15,545	15,720	15,895	16,070	16,245	16,420	16,595	16,770
24.00	14.40	13,170	13,345	13,520	13,695	13,870	14,045	14,220	14,395	14,570	14,745	14,920	15,095	15,270	15,445	15,620	15,795	15,970	16,145	16,320	16,495	16,670	16,845	17,020	17,195	17,370
25.00	15.00	13,770	13,945	14,120	14,295	14,470	14,645	14,820	14,995	15,170	15,345	15,520	15,695	15,870	16,045	16,220	16,395	16,570	16,745	16,920	17,095	17,270	17,445	17,620	17,795	17,970
26.00	15.60	14,370	14,545	14,720	14,895	15,070	15,245	15,420	15,595	15,770	15,945	16,120	16,295	16,470	16,645	16,820	16,995	17,170	17,345	17,520	17,695	17,870	18,045	18,220	18,395	18,570
27.00	16.20	14,970	15,145	15,320	15,495	15,670	15,845	16,020	16,195	16,370	16,545	16,720	16,895	17,070	17,245	17,420	17,595	17,770	17,945	18,120	18,295	18,470	18,645	18,820	18,995	19,170
28.00	16.80	15,570	15,745	15,920	16,095	16,270	16,445	16,620	16,795	16,970	17,145	17,320	17,495	17,670	17,845	18,020	18,195	18,370	18,545	18,720	18,895	19,070	19,245	19,420	19,595	19,770
29.00	17.40	16,170	16,345	16,520	16,695	16,870	17,045	17,220	17,395	17,570	17,745	17,920	18,095	18,270	18,445	18,620	18,795	18,970	19,145	19,320	19,495	19,670	19,845	20,020	20,195	20,370
30.00	18.00	16,770	16,945	17,120	17,295	17,470	17,645	17,820	17,995	18,170	18,345	18,520	18,695	18,870	19,045	19,220	19,395	19,570	19,745	19,920	20,095	20,270	20,445	20,620	20,795	20,970
31.00	18.60	17,370	17,545	17,720	17,895	18,070	18,245	18,420	18,595	18,770	18,945	19,120	19,295	19,470	19,645	19,820	19,995	20,170	20,345	20,520	20,695	20,870	21,045	21,220	21,395	21,570
32.00	19.20	17,970	18,145	18,320	18,495	18,670	18,845	19,020	19,195	19,370	19,545	19,720	19,895	20,070	20,245	20,420	20,595	20,770	20,945	21,120	21,295	21,470	21,645	21,820	21,995	22,170
33.00	19.80	18,570	18,745	18,920	19,095	19,270	19,445	19,620	19,795	19,970	20,145	20,320	20,495	20,670	20,845	21,020	21,195	21,370	21,545	21,720	21,895	22,070	22,245	22,420	22,595	22,770
34.00	20.40	19,170	19,345	19,520	19,695	19,870	20,045	20,220	20,395	20,570	20,745	20,920	21,095	21,270	21,445	21,620	21,795	21,970	22,145	22,320	22,495	22,670	22,845	23,020	23,195	23,370
35.00	21.00	19,770	19,945	20,120	20,295	20,470	20,645	20,820	20,995	21,170	21,345	21,520	21,695	21,870	22,045	22,220	22,395	22,570	22,745	22,920	23,095	23,270	23,445	23,620	23,795	23,970

Exhibit 5 in this note shows the results of the break-even analysis. This analysis will prove useful in determining list prices for heater/blower units and blankets **and** for assessing the likelihood of profitable hospital penetration. Some students will argue that some profit objective should be incorporated into the analysis. This can be done easily by simply adding the profit objective to fixed cost. For example, if a pricing objective is to achieve a return on investment before tax of, say, 20 percent, then fixed costs would be $600,000. Students can then calculate the number of systems that have to be sold to achieve this figure. Exhibit 6 shows the number of systems at different prices for units and blankets given a 20 percent return on investment.

5. What then should be the list price for the heater/blower unit? A variety of prices are possible ranging from nothing ("Give it away!") to just under $1,500 (to overcome hospital buying committee approval), to $4,000 to be price competitive with the Climator, to $6,000 ("Let's skim the market given our innovative technology!"). Pros and cons can be developed for probably any list price. However, several important considerations deserve attention:

- a. Which price will gain the fastest penetration in hospitals? (Probably $0 to just under $1,500).

- b. Which price will distributors prefer? (Probably just under $1,500 since they will make some profit and not have to deal with buying committees).

- c. Which price will help cash flow for Augustine Medical (Probably just under $1,500 since cash will come from the unit immediately, while blanket revenue will come in over time).

- d. What will be the competitive reaction if the price is **too** low?

6. What should be the list price for blankets? Again, a variety of prices are possible. The prices range from $2.73 (the cost per application for warmed hospital blankets) to, say, $15.00 (or some figure below the $20 and $24, charged by competitors) to $25.00 or more ("Let's skim the market."). Pros and cons can be developed for probably any list price. However, three important considerations warrant attention.

- a. Since blanket volume will produce a long revenue stream, what blanket price will sustain the firm after the hospital market is saturated with heater/blower units? (See the analysis in F below).

EXHIBIT 5

SYSTEM BREAK-EVEN AT DIFFERENT
UNIT AND BLANKET COMBINATIONS

Price Per Blanket		Blower Unit Price																								
		$0	$250	$500	$750	$1,000	$1,250	$1,500	$1,750	$2,000	$2,250	$2,500	$2,750	$3,000	$3,250	$3,500	$3,750	$4,000	$4,250	$4,500	$4,750	$5,000	$5,250	$5,500	$5,750	$6,000 Retail
Retail	Manufact	$0	$175	$350	$525	$700	$875	$1,050	$1,225	$1,400	$1,575	$1,750	$1,925	$2,100	$2,275	$2,450	$2,625	$2,800	$2,975	$3,150	$3,325	$3,500	$3,675	$3,850	$4,025	$4,200 Mftr.
$1.00	$0.60	NA	NA	NA	NA	7,143	2,041	1,190	840	649	529	446	386	340	304	275	251	230	213	198	186	174	164	155	147	140
2.00	1.20	NA	3,448	1,563	1,010	746	592	490	418	365	324	291	264	242	223	207	193	181	170	160	152	144	137	131	125	120
3.00	1.80	877	671	543	457	394	346	309	279	254	233	216	200	187	176	166	156	148	141	134	128	123	118	113	109	105
4.00	2.40	427	372	329	295	267	244	225	209	195	182	171	162	153	145	138	132	126	121	116	111	107	103	100	96	93
5.00	3.00	282	257	236	218	202	189	177	167	158	149	142	135	129	124	118	114	109	105	102	98	95	92	89	86	84
6.00	3.60	211	196	184	173	163	154	146	139	133	127	121	116	112	108	104	100	97	94	91	88	85	83	80	78	76
7.00	4.20	168	159	151	143	136	130	124	119	114	110	106	102	99	95	92	89	87	84	82	79	77	75	73	71	70
8.00	4.80	140	134	128	122	117	112	108	104	101	97	94	91	88	86	83	81	78	76	74	73	71	69	67	66	64
9.00	5.40	120	115	111	106	103	99	96	93	90	87	84	82	80	78	76	74	72	70	68	67	65	64	62	61	60
10.00	6.00	105	101	98	94	91	89	86	83	81	79	77	75	73	71	69	68	66	65	63	62	60	59	58	57	56
11.00	6.60	93	90	87	85	82	80	78	76	74	72	70	69	67	65	64	63	61	60	59	58	56	55	54	53	52
12.00	7.20	84	81	79	77	75	73	71	69	68	66	65	63	62	61	59	58	57	56	55	54	53	52	51	50	49
13.00	7.80	76	74	72	70	69	67	66	64	63	61	60	59	58	57	55	54	53	52	51	51	50	49	48	47	46
14.00	8.40	70	68	66	65	64	62	61	60	58	57	56	55	54	53	52	51	50	49	48	48	47	46	45	45	44
15.00	9.00	64	63	62	60	59	58	57	56	55	54	53	52	51	50	49	48	47	47	46	45	44	44	43	42	42
16.00	9.60	60	59	57	56	55	54	53	52	51	50	49	49	48	47	46	45	45	44	43	43	42	42	41	40	40
17.00	10.20	56	55	54	53	52	51	50	49	48	47	47	46	45	44	44	43	42	42	41	41	40	40	39	38	38
18.00	10.80	52	51	50	50	49	48	47	46	46	45	44	43	43	42	42	41	40	40	39	39	38	38	37	37	36
19.00	11.40	49	48	48	47	46	45	45	44	43	43	42	41	41	40	40	39	39	38	38	37	37	36	36	35	35
20.00	12.00	46	46	45	44	44	43	42	42	41	41	40	39	39	38	38	37	37	36	36	35	35	35	34	34	33
21.00	12.60	44	43	43	42	41	41	40	40	39	39	38	38	37	37	36	36	35	35	34	34	34	33	33	32	32
22.00	13.20	42	41	41	40	39	39	38	38	37	37	36	36	36	35	35	34	34	33	33	33	32	32	32	31	31
23.00	13.80	40	39	39	38	38	37	37	36	36	35	35	34	34	34	33	33	33	32	32	31	31	31	30	30	30
24.00	14.40	38	37	37	37	36	36	35	35	34	34	34	33	33	32	32	32	31	31	31	30	30	30	29	29	29
25.00	15.00	36	36	35	35	35	34	34	33	33	33	32	32	32	31	31	30	30	30	30	29	29	29	28	28	28
26.00	15.60	35	34	34	34	33	33	32	32	32	31	31	31	30	30	30	29	29	29	29	28	28	28	27	27	27
27.00	16.20	33	33	33	32	32	32	31	31	31	30	30	30	29	29	29	28	28	28	28	27	27	27	27	26	26
28.00	16.80	32	32	31	31	31	30	30	30	29	29	29	29	28	28	28	27	27	27	27	26	26	26	26	26	25
29.00	17.40	31	31	30	30	30	29	29	29	28	28	28	28	27	27	27	27	26	26	26	26	25	25	25	25	25
30.00	18.00	30	30	29	29	29	28	28	28	28	27	27	27	26	26	26	26	26	25	25	25	25	24	24	24	24
31.00	18.60	29	28	28	28	28	27	27	27	27	26	26	26	26	25	25	25	25	25	24	24	24	24	24	23	23
32.00	19.20	28	28	27	27	27	27	26	26	26	26	25	25	25	25	24	24	24	24	24	23	23	23	23	23	23
33.00	19.80	27	27	26	26	26	26	25	25	25	25	25	24	24	24	24	24	23	23	23	23	23	22	22	22	22
34.00	20.40	26	26	26	25	25	25	25	25	24	24	24	24	24	23	23	23	23	23	22	22	22	22	22	22	21
35.00	21.00	25	25	25	25	24	24	24	24	24	23	23	23	23	23	23	22	22	22	22	22	21	21	21	21	21

EXHIBIT 6

SYSTEM VOLUME TO BE SOLD TO ACHIEVE 20 PERCENT ROI AT DIFFERENT UNIT AND BLANKET COMBINATIONS

Price Per Blanket Retail / Manufct	Blower Unit Price																										
Retail / Mfctr.	$0 / $0	$175 / $250	$350 / $500	$525 / $750	$700 / $1,000	$875 / $1,250	$1,050 / $1,500	$1,225 / $1,750	$1,400 / $2,000	$1,575 / $2,250	$1,750 / $2,500	$1,925 / $2,750	$2,100 / $3,000	$2,275 / $3,250	$2,450 / $3,500	$2,625 / $3,750	$2,800 / $4,000	$2,975 / $4,250	$3,150 / $4,500	$3,325 / $4,750	$3,500 / $5,000	$3,675 / $5,250	$3,850 / $5,500	$4,025 / $5,750	$4,200 / $6,000
$1.00 / $0.60	MA	MA	MA	MA	MA	2,449	1,429	1,008	779	635	536	463	408	365	330	301	276	256	238	223	209	197	186	177	168
2.00 / 1.20	MA	4,138	1,675	1,212	896	710	588	502	438	388	349	317	290	267	248	231	217	204	192	182	173	165	157	150	144
3.00 / 1.80	MA	1,053	805	652	548	472	415	370	334	305	280	259	240	225	211	199	188	178	169	161	154	147	141	136	131
4.00 / 2.40	513	446	395	354	321	295	270	251	233	219	205	194	183	174	166	158	151	145	139	133	128	124	120	115	112
5.00 / 3.00	339	308	283	261	243	227	213	200	189	179	170	162	155	148	142	137	131	126	122	118	114	110	107	104	101
6.00 / 3.60	253	236	221	207	195	185	175	167	159	152	146	140	134	129	124	120	116	112	109	105	102	99	96	94	91
7.00 / 4.20	202	191	181	172	163	156	149	143	137	132	127	123	118	114	111	107	104	101	98	95	93	90	88	86	84
8.00 / 4.80	168	160	153	147	141	135	130	125	121	117	113	109	106	103	100	97	94	92	89	87	85	83	81	79	77
9.00 / 5.40	144	138	133	128	123	119	115	111	108	104	101	98	96	93	91	88	86	84	82	80	78	76	75	73	72
10.00 / 6.00	126	121	117	113	110	106	103	100	97	95	92	90	87	85	83	81	79	77	76	74	72	71	69	68	67
11.00 / 6.60	112	108	105	102	99	96	93	91	89	86	84	82	80	78	77	75	73	72	70	69	67	66	65	64	63
12.00 / 7.20	101	98	95	92	90	88	85	83	81	80	78	76	74	73	71	70	68	67	66	65	63	62	61	60	59
13.00 / 7.80	91	89	87	85	83	81	79	77	76	74	72	71	69	68	67	65	64	63	62	61	60	59	58	57	56
14.00 / 8.40	84	82	80	78	76	75	73	72	70	69	67	66	65	64	63	61	60	59	58	57	56	55	55	54	53
15.00 / 9.00	77	76	74	73	71	70	69	67	66	65	63	62	61	60	59	58	57	56	55	54	53	52	52	51	50
16.00 / 9.60	72	70	69	68	67	65	64	63	62	61	60	59	58	57	56	55	54	53	52	51	50	50	49	48	48
17.00 / 10.20	67	66	65	64	63	62	61	60	59	58	57	56	55	54	53	52	52	51	50	49	49	48	47	47	46
18.00 / 10.80	63	62	61	60	59	58	58	57	56	55	54	53	52	52	51	50	49	49	48	47	47	46	45	45	44
19.00 / 11.40	59	58	58	57	56	55	54	54	53	52	51	51	50	49	49	48	47	47	46	45	45	44	44	43	43
20.00 / 12.00	56	55	54	54	53	52	52	51	50	50	49	48	48	47	46	46	45	45	44	44	43	42	42	41	41
21.00 / 12.60	53	52	52	51	50	50	49	48	48	47	47	46	46	45	44	44	43	43	42	42	41	41	40	40	39
22.00 / 13.20	50	49	49	48	48	47	47	46	46	45	45	44	43	43	42	42	41	41	41	40	40	39	39	38	38
23.00 / 13.80	48	47	47	46	46	45	45	44	44	43	43	42	42	41	41	41	40	40	39	39	38	38	38	37	37
24.00 / 14.40	45	45	44	44	44	43	43	42	42	42	41	41	40	40	40	39	39	38	38	38	37	37	36	36	36
25.00 / 15.00	44	43	43	42	42	42	41	41	40	40	40	39	39	39	38	38	37	37	37	36	36	36	35	35	35
26.00 / 15.60	42	41	41	41	40	40	40	39	39	39	38	38	38	37	37	37	36	36	36	35	35	35	34	34	34
27.00 / 16.20	40	40	39	39	39	39	38	38	38	37	37	37	36	36	36	36	35	35	35	34	34	34	33	33	33
28.00 / 16.80	39	38	38	38	38	37	37	37	37	36	36	36	35	35	35	35	34	34	34	33	33	33	33	32	32
29.00 / 17.40	37	37	37	37	36	36	36	36	35	35	35	35	34	34	34	34	33	33	33	33	32	32	32	32	31
30.00 / 18.00	36	36	36	35	35	35	35	35	34	34	34	34	33	33	33	33	32	32	32	32	31	31	31	31	30
31.00 / 18.60	35	35	35	34	34	34	34	34	33	33	33	33	32	32	32	32	32	31	31	31	31	30	30	30	30
32.00 / 19.20	34	34	33	33	33	33	33	33	32	32	32	32	31	31	31	31	31	30	30	30	30	29	29	29	29
33.00 / 19.80	33	33	32	32	32	32	32	32	31	31	31	31	30	30	30	30	30	29	29	29	29	29	28	28	28
34.00 / 20.40	32	32	31	31	31	31	31	31	30	30	30	30	30	29	29	29	29	28	28	28	28	28	27	27	27
35.00 / 21.00	30	30	30	30	30	29	29	29	29	29	29	28	28	28	28	28	27	27	27	27	27	26	26	26	26

    b.   How does the annual cost of Bair Hugger blankets compare with competitors? (At $20 - $24 per blanket, Bair Hugger is at parity with competitors, but below these prices a price advantage exists.)

    c.   How will competitors react to the price set? (If competitors have large margins like Bair Hugger, they have considerable latitude to cut prices if Bair Hugger prices are **too** low.)

F. What is the long-run profit impact of your price decision?

1. Long-run implications of the pricing decision must be considered, particularly as regards blanket prices. Blanket prices/volume must sustain the Bair Hugger System long after the hospital market has been penetrated with heater/blower units.

2. Students should be asked to consider the long-term profit impact of different blanket prices given different levels of heater/blower installations. A conservative approach to this question is to assume that Augustine Medical again operates with a fixed overhead cost of $500,000 for the subsequent 12 months **and** blanket volume must produce most of the company's sales revenue.

3. Break-even heater/blower unit figures for different blanket prices are shown below:

(1) Blanket Price to Hospitals	(2) Selling Price to Dealer less Cost	(3) Contribution per Installation	(4) B/E Units: $500,000÷(3)
$10	$ 6.00 - $.85	$ 5.15 x 1000	97
$15	$ 9.00 - $.85	$ 8.15 x 1000	61
$20	$12.00 - $.85	$11.15 x 1000	45
$25	$15.00 - $.85	$14.15 x 1000	35

The break-even figures can be compared with the system break-even figures in Exhibit 5 in this note. Assuming the heater/blower unit is sold for $1,500 and blankets for $25.00, the first year break-even point is 34 units. Augustine Medical will have about the same annual break-even at a blanket price of $25.00. For each of the other blanket prices, the long-term break-even is higher than the initial system break-even levels (see Exhibit 5 in this note). This means that Augustine Medical might find it difficult to achieve long-term profitability if the blanket price is too low, say $10.00.

G. Epilogue

In February, 1988, Augustine Medical decided to list price the heater/blower unit at $995.00. The blanket list price was set at $12.00. The Bair Hugger Patient Warming System was introduced in March, 1988.

Given the information in the case, the number of systems necessary to break-even over a 12-month period would be 75 units. By the end of April, 1988, 40 heater/blower units had been sold. By March, 1989, 90 units had been sold. The company had exceeded break-even. The Hosworth-Climator was not introduced to the U.S. market.

According to an executive at Augustine Medical, the heater/blower unit price was about right to gain market acceptance. However, the blanket price might have been too low. In 1991, the company introduced several other models of the blanket including a size for children and an even more portable blower unit. The new blankets were priced at $20.00 and the new blower unit was priced at $1,399. These new products have been favorably received.

By 1993, Augustine Medical recorded sales of $15 million and was projecting 1994 sales of $20 million. This growth placed Augustine Medical at Number 72 in Inc. magazine's 500 list of the fastest-growing U.S. companies. In addition, the company has recorded consistent profits since 1989. (Source: "Augustine Medical, Inc. Thriving with 'Overgrown Hair Dryer' Bair Hugger," Minneapolis Star Tribune, November 10, 1993).

H. Summary Points

1. Demand (Market Potential), Cost (Fixed and Variable), and Competition (Companies and Substitute Technologies) must be considered simultaneously when determining price levels.

2. A critical first step in arriving at a price strategy is to determine price objectives for the firm. These objectives might include:

- Maximize unit or dollar sales volume
- Gain market share (hospital penetration)
- Achieve adequate cash flow
- Achieve certain rate of return
- Achieve break-even

3. Cross-elasticity is a consideration when pricing complimentary products. In this case, blanket volume was **contingent** on heater/blower unit penetration which makes the pricing decision even more complex. Blanket volume is **derived**.

4. Numerous "pricing strategies" can be examined, depending upon the focus of attention:

Demand	Cost	Competition
• Skimming • Penetration	• Cost-Plus	• Above-the-market • At-the-market • Below-the-market

5. Case illustrates an important point in pricing. That is, cost is often the least important issue to be resolved or overcome when setting prices. Demand and competition are often more important.

6. The case raises important issues previously considered:

- **Buying Group**: Who were the gatekeepers, influences, users, buyers, and decision-makers?

- **New Product Adoption**: To what extent did Bair Hugger meet basic Considerations?

    ... Felt Need
    ... Relative Advantage (over current technology)
        ... Compatibility (with current procedures)
    ... Simplicity (to operate)
    ... Testability (trial use)
    ... Immediacy of Benefit (for nurses, patients)

- **Role of Distributors**: Desire for margins, long-run profits. Willingness to "push" products

SEAGRAM IN TAIWAN: SCOTCH AND COGNAC PRICING

Synopsis

In January 1998, Ian Swanson, vice-president of finance at Seagram Greater China, was contemplating what actions to take in light of the proposed changes to the duty rates that applied to imported scotch and cognac in Taiwan. Given that the Taiwanese spirits market had become very competitive in recent years, careful management of the duty rate changes was critical for ensuring future market share and profitability in Taiwan. This left Swanson with the task of trying to determine what pricing levels to recommend for Seagram's scotch and cognac products based upon the proposed duty regime.

The case is intended to help students develop an understanding of the importance of pricing strategy and its impact on sales growth and profitability as well as certain financial analysis tools useful in marketing decision-making. Cost-volume-profit analysis is useful in this situation as a tool to help analyze the impact of various pricing strategies available to Seagram in Taiwan as a result of prospective changes in the duty rates. The potential impact of transfer pricing on profitability can also be examined.

The case also gives students an opportunity to examine pricing actions in a "prisoner's dilemma" context. According to Ian Swanson:

> This situation is very similar to a "prisoner's dilemma" in that we need to protect our downside risk, yet be prepared to exploit any upside potential. On the one hand, if the competition drops its prices when the duties change, we will need to move immediately or else risk a loss of market share, the cost of which can be tremendously expensive to reacquire. On the other hand, if we drop our prices, we risk destroying our highly valued brand equity in our premium and super premium categories. This leaves us with four possible scenarios: we hold prices while the competition cuts prices; we cut prices while the competition holds; we both hold; or we both cut. Clearly, there is no way to precisely predict what will happen, but educated guesses can be made upon the strategies and competencies of our competitors and ourselves, as well as trends in the marketplace.

This feature of the case, which links directly to the discussion of "Pricing and Competitive Interaction" in Chapter 8, provides a rich framework for discussing pricing strategy and management in the international arena.

This teaching note is based on an analysis plan prepared by Tom Gleave under the supervision of Professor Claude Lanfranconi as an aid to instructors in the classroom use of the case Seagram in Taiwan: Scotch and Cognac Pricing. This teaching note should not be used in any way that would prejudice the future use of the case. Copyright © 1998, Ivey Management Services. Used with permission.

Teaching Objectives

This case has four teaching objectives:

1. To introduce a common issue in international marketing; namely, the role that duties play in pricing.

2. To engage students in a competitive game setting—the "Prisoner's Dilemma"—that forces them to consider short- and long-run actions and reactions of players.

3. To give students practice in using cost-volume-profit analyses when examining alternative price levels.

4. To raise for consideration issues related to interdivisional conflict and transfer pricing within a multinational company such as Seagram, if time permits.

Teaching Suggestions

This case is best suited for that portion of the course that emphasizes pricing strategy, or a module on global (international) marketing. The case can be used for examination purposes later in the course, or as a group presentation. It is advisable that the instructor carefully familiarize him/herself with the cost-volume-profit calculations.

As a class discussion case, the discussion can be separated into two distinct parts. The first part should be dedicated to a qualitative analysis of the situation so that the significant issues impacting Seagram in Taiwan can be flushed out. Given the limited information in the case, this process should not take any more than 15-20 minutes. Once the key issues have been identified, the instructor can then proceed to ask students to quantitatively demonstrate the impact of duty changes within the context of the salient issues facing Seagram.

A useful way to frame the "competitive-pricing interaction" dimension of the case is to use the following diagram:

Seagram	Competitors: Pass on Duty Savings by Dropping Prices	Competitors: Retain Duty Savings and Improve Margins
Pass on Duty Savings by Dropping Prices		
Retain Duty Savings and Improve Margins		

The following questions can be posed prior to or during a class discussion:

1. How would you characterize the Taiwanese scotch and cognac markets? What is your assessment of Seagram's competitive position in these markets?

2. What is the potential impact of the duty changes on the Taiwanese spirits market?

3. As Ian Swanson, what new price levels would you recommend for Seagram's products in Taiwan based upon the available alternatives? (Note: Focus most of your analysis on the premium scotch and standard cognac categories.)

4. (If time permits) How does the pricing decision affect other divisions in Seagram, e.g., Seagram Hong Kong or Greater China, or even worldwide? What additional financial data would be useful to address this issue?

Areas for Discussion/Analysis

A. How would you characterize the Taiwanese scotch and cognac markets? What is your assessment of Seagram's competitive position in these markets?

1. Although the Taiwanese government has imposed burdensome duties on imported spirits, scotch and cognac are still highly sought products as demonstrated by their significant market share. For example, imported scotch comprises about 32 per cent (482,000/1,522,000 cases) of the market, while premium and standard cognac combine to capture 12 per cent (183/1,522 cases). The primary competitor to these two types of spirits is Japanese whisky, a relatively late entrant into the market, but one that has achieved much success due to low pricing. The success of Japanese whisky (as well as the so-called "lookalike" brands) is one of the main reasons behind the Importers Association's push for duty reforms in Taiwan. The level of effort required to lobby for change in government policy suggests that the powerful spirits importers view the cheaper spirit producers as a genuine threat to the market over the long term.

2. Overall, the spirits market is expected to grow by a modest 17 per cent during the 1996 to 2000 period. Therefore, all factors remaining the same, scotch and cognac importers have limited opportunities for generating additional sales revenues through the growth of entire product categories. This means that an increasing reliance would need to be placed on capturing market share from competitors in order to sustain growth, in turn raising the possibility of a price war as rivals seek to gain a "bigger piece of the same pie." However, the prospect of significant reductions in duty rates presents a tremendous opportunity for generating growth in the scotch and cognac categories at the expense of Japanese whisky and the "lookalikes." This is because scotch and cognac duties will drop substantially, while duties on Japanese whisky will increase by about 32 per cent. (See Exhibit 1 in this note - Changes in Duty Structure.) This will be discussed in detail during part two of the class.

EXHIBIT 1

CHANGES IN DUTY STRUCTURE

	Super Premium Scotch		Premium Scotch		Premium Cognac		Standard Cognac		Other
Cost per Bottle (NT$)	Seagram Royal Salute	UD/Henn. J.W. Premier	Seagram Chivas Regal	UD/Henn. J.W. Black	Seagram XO	UD/Henn. XO	Seagram VSOP	UD/Henn. VSOP	Japanese Whisky
CIF Costs	832	832	272	272	976	976	464	464	180
Current Duty	*330*	*330*	*330*	*330*	*750*	*750*	*750*	*750*	*149*
Total Current Costs	1,162	1,162	602	602	1,726	1,726	1,214	1,214	329
Current Target Price	2,170	2,300	680	650	2,080	2,200	1,100	1,100	480
Current Target Margin	1,008	1,138	78	48	354	474	(114)	(114)	151

Proposed Duty

CIF Costs x 12.5%	104	104	34	34	122	122	58	58	23
+ NT $170X.75	128	128	128	128	128	128	128	128	128
+ 5% VAT	12	12	8	8	13	13	9	9	8
Proposed Duty	*244*	*244*	*170*	*170*	*263*	*263*	*195*	*195*	*158*

Potential Savings—NT$	86	86	160	160	488	488	555	555	(9)
Potential Savings—US$	2.61	2.61	4.82	4.82	14.70	14.70	16.73	16.73	(0.27)

Note: It is important to remember that the current duty rates are applied on a per litre basis, yet Seagram's sells bottles containing 750 ml. Therefore, the current duty rates need to be multiplied by 0.75 in order to derive the current bottle rate.

3. Seagram is a global powerhouse in the spirits industry with a well-established presence in most Western economies. It has also made significant in-roads in various emerging markets in recent years, including Asia Pacific. Given the mature nature of the Western markets, the emerging markets hold the best sales and volume growth potential for the company. Although Seagram has been able to increase profits during a period of declining revenues, disturbing trends have emerged in Asia and Europe pointing to increased pressure on the company to sustain its sales volumes. The recent 1997 and 1998 downturn in Asia is particularly problematic for Seagram Greater China since sharp declines in currency and equity markets indicate a fundamental restructuring of economies will need to take place before a full recovery is realized. This begs the question of whether or not Seagram Greater China should draw upon the considerable resources of head office to support the company's scotch and cognac brands in Asia at this time.

4. In the scotch category, Seagram dominates the premium and super-premium segments with its Chivas Regal and Royal Salute brands, while UD/Hennessy enjoys the largest share in the standard segment. The fact that Seagram does not participate in the standard segment places additional pressure on the company to maintain it leadership position in the two segments in which it does participate. The management and positioning of Chivas Regal (premium segment) is particularly critical given its status as the company's "key financial driver."

5. In the cognac category, Seagram has a slight lead in the premium segment over UD/Hennessy (41 per cent vs. 37 per cent); however, UD/Hennessy completely dominates the standard segment (56 per cent vs. 18 per cent), apparently because of its "price leadership and heavy marketing spending." Interestingly, the seemingly permanent decline in premium cognac sales may translate in modest sales growth opportunities in the standard segment as consumers switch to lower-cost alternatives. This presents Seagram with an additional problem it must take into account.

6. It is interesting to note the different advertising and promotion responses taken by Seagram and UD/Hennessy in addressing the issue of increased competitiveness and low product loyalty in Taiwan. Whereas UD/Hennessy has decided to invest more money in brand building, Seagram has chosen to slightly decrease its advertising expenditures; the rationale being that gains in market share are becoming disproportionately expensive. Additionally, it appears crucial that the Greater China division meets the pre-established profit targets it has set with Seagram's head office. Although the lowering of fixed advertising costs might yield over greater profits over the short term, it is highly debatable how effective this strategy will be in the long run. Given the impending changes to Taiwan's duty structure, major players like Seagram and UD/Hennessy will likely have the opportunity to reap some level of greater contribution, and still be able to invest more proceeds in brand building. Therefore, in considering his pricing recommendations, Ian Swanson must also factor in the implications of investing in greater advertising expenditures in order to sustain and build the company's brands in Taiwan.

7. Business executives are cited as one of the main consumer groups of scotch and cognac in Taiwan. Their behavior is characterized by their strong image consciousness and low brand loyalty. Given that about 20 per cent of Seagram's customer base consumes about 80 per cent of the sales volume, we can reasonably assume that business executives make up a significant portion of this core-drinking group. Since these executives likely have above average incomes compared with average Taiwanese, it is easy to understand why scotch and cognac sales have fared so well in Taiwan, despite their comparatively high prices. Presumably, a substantial amount of the spirits consumed by executives is done within the context of a "business entertainment" setting. This means that the sharp downturn in Asia's economies will have an adverse effect on on-premise sales as executives will be more inclined to curb spending on prestige goods like premium cognac. This demonstrates, yet again, the considerable pressures that are being felt by spirits importers in Taiwan.

8. Seagram's previous arrangement with five different distributors proved unsuccessful, causing the company to move toward a single distribution relationship with Formosa Trading. The successful management of this relationship could yield numerous benefits, including stabilized prices for Seagram products and a reduction in unauthorized commercial activity. The challenge for both Seagram and Formosa Trading will be to manage the relationship in such a way that both partners consider the situation mutually beneficial. This may become more difficult as the hypermarkets gain greater power and influence in Taiwan. This is because retailers (such as Wal-Mart) often prefer to deal directly with suppliers in order to achieve its marketing strategy of offering customers "everyday low prices." By dealing directly with suppliers, retailers can reduce the costs associated with intermediaries (such as distributors). This raises the spectre that Seagram may need to re-evaluate its distributor relationship in Taiwan whereby it services the hypermarkets directly and Formosa Trading services all other distribution channels.

B. What is the potential impact of the duty changes on the Taiwanese spirits market?

1. The impending changes to duty rates offers importers an opportunity to recoup substantial contribution margin (in the form of duty savings) after the proposed legislation takes effect. To demonstrate the impact of the duty changes, the instructor should ask one or two students to calculate and compare the new duty rates against the old rates for the premium scotch, standard cognac and other whisky categories.

2. As shown in Exhibit 1 in this note—Changes in Duty Structure, the duty for premium scotch will change from NT$330 per bottle to NT$170. The potential savings that Seagram could gain from this change, if it were to retain the entire difference, is NT$160 ($330 − $170). In the standard cognac category, the duty will fall NT$750 per bottle to $195, offering a savings potential of $555 ($750 - $195) per bottle. At the same time, Japanese whisky producers (like Suntory) will need to factor in a NT$9 increase into their prices, since the duties for this category will increase from NT$149 to $158. Given the growing price pressures that have been building up in the Taiwanese market, these modifications will be a welcomed change to players likes Seagram and UD/Hennessy since they will be able to drop

their prices substantially while retaining the same or even greater unit contribution levels. Japanese whisky producers, on the other hand, must face the prospect of increasing their prices by the full amount of the duty change or else be prepared to accept less unit contribution margin if they decide to absorb some of the increase.

C. **As Ian Swanson, what new price levels would you recommend for Seagram's products in Taiwan based upon the available alternatives? (Note: Focus most of your analysis on the premium scotch and standard cognac categories.)**

Seagram essentially has two possible responses to the changes in the duties, yet it must face four possible scenarios due to different possible competitive responses. These scenarios are as follows:

a. Seagram passes on duty savings by dropping prices by various amounts while its competitors retain the duty savings.

b. Seagram retains the savings while competitors pass them on.

c. Both Seagram and the competition retain the duty savings.

d. Both Seagram and the competition pass on the duty savings.

Even though he cites four possible scenarios, it is fairly clear to Ian Swanson that all major importers will drop their prices on both premium scotch and standard cognac. Therefore, the critical task for Swanson is to try to either establish the benchmark market price or else adequately predict the magnitude of the drop. It is important to recognize the need for balance in this situation, given that an inadequate price drop may result in lost market share, the cost of which is very steep to recover. On the other hand, too much of a price drop may dilute the brand equity associated with the premium and super premium categories. Swanson acknowledges that "there is no way to precisely predict what will happen," however he does offer specific scenarios based upon "educated guesses." **Therefore, the students should determine the effect of the duty changes on Seagram's profitability based upon the possible outcomes suggested by Swanson.**

1. Possible Outcomes—Premium Scotch (see Exhibit 2 in this note)

- In the premium scotch segment, Swanson believes that passing on 100 per cent of the duty saving would result in as much as a 25 per cent increase in the sales volume currently consumed by Japanese whisky drinkers (400,000 cases x 25% = 100,000 cases). As shown in Exhibit 2 in this note--Chivas Regal Potential Outcomes, by transferring all duty savings to the consumer, the target retail price will drop to NT$520, the unit margin of NT$78 would be maintained, and sales volumes would go from about 2.4 million to 3.6 million bottles. This would increase total contribution in Taiwan by about

EXHIBIT 2

CHIVAS REGAL POTENTIAL OUTCOMES:
VARIABLE TARGET PRICES AND SALES VOLUME

Price per Bottle	Current Scenario	Pass 100% Volume +25%	Pass 100% Volume +15%	Pass 75% Volume +10%	Pass 75% Volume 0%	Pass 50% Volume −50%
Transfer Price	242	242	242	242	242	242
+ Other Costs	30	30	30	30	30	30
= Sub-Total	272	272	272	272	272	272
+ Duty	330	170	170	170	170	170
= Landed Costs	602	442	442	442	442	442
Target Price	**680**	**520**	**520**	**560**	**560**	**600**
Unit Contribution NT$	78	78	78	118	118	158
Unit Contribution US$	2.35	2.35	2.35	3.56	3.56	4.76
Sales Volume						
Current Volume – Cases	199,800	199,800	199,800	199,800	199,800	199,800
Added/Lost Volume (from Japanese whisky)		100,000	60,000	40,000		(99,900)
New Volume – Cases	199,800	299,800	259,800	239,800	199,800	99,900
New Volume – Bottle	2,397,600	3,597,600	3,117,600	2,877,600	2,397,600	1,198,800
Contribution Calculations						
Taiwan Contribution (NT$)	187,012,800	280,612,800	243,172,800	339,556,800	282,916,800	189,410,400
Taiwan Contribution (US$)	5,639,710	8,462,388	7,333,317	10,239,952	8,531,870	5,712,014
Offshore Contribution @ 25% Margin (US$)	4,374,391	6,563,776	5,688,022	5,250,145	4,374,391	2,187,195
Offshore Contribution @ 50% Margin (US$)	8,748,782	13,127,551	11,376,043	10,500,290	8,748,782	4,374,391
Offshore Contribution @ 75% Margin (US$)	13,123,172	19,691,327	17,064,065	15,750,434	13,123,172	6,561,586
Total Contribution @ 25% Margin (US$)	10,014,101	15,026,164	13,021,339	15,490,097	12,906,261	7,899,210
Total Contribution @ 50% Margin (US$)	14,388,492	21,589,940	18,709,361	20,740,241	17,280,651	10,086,405
Total Contribution @ 75% Margin (US$)	18,762,883	28,153,715	24,397,382	25,990,386	21,655,042	12,273,601

US$1.00 = NT$33.76
The price per bottle calculations can be derived from the data provided in case Exhibit 2.
Base volume is 333,000 x 60% = 199,800 cases per case Exhibit 1. Each case is 9 litres – 12 bottles x 750 milliliters.
Base Japanese whisky volume = 400,000 cases.
Other costs include freight, handling and insurance – these costs are assumed fixed at NT$30 per bottle.
Potential duty savings: 100% savings – NT$330 – $214 = $116; 75% savings = NT$116 x 0.75 = $87;
50% savings = NT$116 x 0.50 = $58
Offshore contribution calculations are based upon the transfer price multiplied by the appropriate margins.

NT$94 million (US$3.2 million). Additional contribution would also be realized on the units transferred from Hong Kong in an amount equivalent to: 1.2 million bottles of incremental volume x transfer price x contribution margin. Therefore, if Seagram transferred Chivas Regal into Taiwan at a 25 per cent unit contribution rate, the increase in incremental sales volume would yield an increase of NT$74 million, US$2.2 million in contribution to the Hong Kong operation. The overall net effect would be that Seagram Greater China would realize an increase in contribution of NT$166 million, or US$5.0 million.

- Using the alternative scenario of passing on 75 per cent of the duty savings in the hopes of gaining 10 per cent of the current Japanese whisky volume (40,000 cases), contribution from Taiwan would increase by about NT$153 million (US$4.6 million), and offshore contribution would increase by NT$29 million (US$0.87 million). Interestingly, if Seagram passes on 75 percent of the duty savings and yet fails to gain any incremental sales volume, contribution from Taiwan would still rise by about NT$96 million (US$2.9 million), while the offshore contribution would remain stable at NT$145 million (US$4.4 million).

- At this point, it is interesting to note that even though Seagram's overall profitability increases and Seagram Taiwan is better off than the first two scenarios, 'Offshore Contribution' is less than under the two previous scenarios. This potential for interdivisional conflict is referred to in the conclusion.

- **Overall, the prognosis for the premium scotch segment looks promising for Seagram so long as it passes on a substantial portion of the duty savings to the consumer (on the presumption that UD/Hennessy will do the same). Essentially, the worst-case scenario for the company would be if UD/Hennessy led a price drop and Seagram responded by failing to drop prices adequately, consequently resulting in substantial sales volume that overshadows any increase in unit margin. However, it is important to recognize that different profit centers in the company are not indifferent to the allocation of the overall profit that is a function of the transfer price.**

2. Potential Outcomes—Standard Cognac (see Exhibit 3 in this note)

- In calculating the possible outcomes for the standard cognac segment, students should observe that, under the current duty structure, Seagram Taiwan is "losing" money for each bottle of VSOP that it sells in Taiwan. This is because the total costs per bottle is NT$1,214, whereas the current target price is NT$1,100, a shortfall of NT$114. It is important to

EXHIBIT 3
MARTELL VSOP POTENTIAL OUTCOMES
VARIABLE TARGET PRICES AND SALES VOLUME

Price per Bottle	Current Scenario	Pass 100% Volume +10%	Pass 100% Volume +/-0%	Pass 75% Volume +/-0%	Pass 75% Volume −25%	Pass 50% Volume −50%
Transfer Price	434	434	434	434	434	434
+ Other Costs	30	30	30	30	30	30
= Sub-Total	464	464	464	464	464	464
+ Duty	750	195	195	195	195	195
= Landed Costs	1,214	659	659	659	659	659
Target Price	1,100	545	545	684	684	823
Unit Contribution Margin NT$	(114)	(114)	(114)	25	25	164
Unit Contribution Margin US$	(3.44)	(3.44)	(3.44)	0.75	0.75	4.93

Sales Volume

Current Volume – Cases	11,700	11,700	11,700	11,700	11,700	11,700
Added/Lost Volume (from Japanese whisky)		1,170			(2,925)	(5,850)
New Volume – Cases	11,700	12,870	11,700	11,700	8,775	5,850
New Volume – Bottle	140,400	154,440	140,400	140,400	105,300	70,200

Contribution Calculations

Taiwan Contribution (NT$)	(16,005,600)	(17,606,160)	(16,005,600)	3,474,900	2,606,175	11,477,700
Taiwan Contribution (US$)	(482,678)	(530,946)	(482,678)	104,792	78,594	346,131
Offshore Contribution @ 25% Margin (US$)	459,391	505,330	459,391	459,391	344,543	229,695
Offshore Contribution @ 50% Margin (US$)	918,782	1,010,600	918,782	918,782	689,086	459,391
Offshore Contribution @ 75% Margin (US$)	1,378,172	1,515,990	1,378,172	1,378,172	1,033,629	689,086
Total Contribution @ 25% Margin (US$)	(23,287)	(25,616)	(23,287)	564,183	423,137	575,826
Total Contribution @ 50% Margin (US$)	436,104	479,714	436,104	1,023,574	767,680	805,522
Total Contribution @ 75% Margin (US$)	895,495	985,044	895,495	1,482,964	1,112,223	1,035,217

US$1.00 = NT$33.76

The price per bottle calculations can be derived from the data provided in case Exhibit 2.
Base volume 65,000 x 18% = 11,700 cases per case Exhibit 1. Each case is 9 litres – 12 bottles x 750 milliliters.
Other costs include freight, handling, and insurance – these costs are assumed fixed at NT$30 per bottle.
Potential duty savings: 100% savings = NT$1100 – $589 = $511; 75% savings = NT$511 x 0.75 = $383
50% savings = NT$511 x 0.50 = $255.50
Offshore contribution calculations are based upon the transfer price multiplied by the appropriate margins.

remember, however, that Seagram's offshore operation (in Hong Kong) is realizing a contribution for each bottle sold. Some students may recognize that Seagram Greater China may be motivated for a number of reasons to arrange its affairs for this to occur, e.g. trying to minimize its taxable profits in Taiwan. This situation highlights the need to take into account the impact that price or volume changes will have on Seagram's offshore contribution and the nature of its transfer pricing strategy.

- According to Swanson, passing on 100 per cent of the duty savings could potentially increase the sales volume of standard cognac by only 10 per cent, presuming UD/Hennessy does not pass on the full amount of its duty savings. In such a situation, Seagram Taiwan would in fact enlarge its "losses" in Taiwan, since the negative unit contribution margin of NT$114 will not have changed but the numbers of bottles sold would increase. However, it must be borne in mind that a 10 per cent increase in volume, which equates to 14,040 bottles (1,170 cases x 12), will generate greater contribution in Hong Kong, depending on the offshore unit rate contribution. For example, presuming that Seagram realizes a 50 per cent margin on the VSOP it transfers to Taiwan, each additional bottle sold adds NT$217 (transfer price NT$434 x 50%) to 'Seagram's Hong Kong's contribution. Therefore, the net effect would be an overall gain of NT$217 − $64 = $153 per unit sold in Taiwan.

- According to Swanson, the most likely scenario to expect would be for Seagram to pass on 75 per cent of the duty savings to the consumer without realizing an immediate increase in sales volume. The increase would come after 25 per cent duty savings is recouped by Seagram and reinvested in the VSOP brand. The results, under this scenario would be that Seagram would increase its overall contribution by NT$18 million (US$0.54 million), all of which would be from Taiwan, since the volume from Hong Kong, and the transfer prices, are assumed to be steady.

- It is interesting to note the results of the scenario suggested by Swanson whereby sales volumes would decrease by 50 per cent or more if Seagram passed only 50 per cent of the duty savings. If this situation were to materialize, the contribution generated in Taiwan would increase from a deficit of NT$16 million to a gain of NT$13.2 million. Naturally, a 50 per cent volume decline would mean that the contribution realized in the Hong Kong office would be halved if the current transfer price and the unit margins were held steady. Overall, this situation would be beneficial to Seagram if its unit margin from Hong Kong was 75 per cent *or less*! However, the higher the unit margin charged by the Hong Kong office, the more contribution it will lose as sales volumes decline.

D. (If time permits) How does the price decision affect other divisions in Seagram, e.g., Seagram Hong Kong or Greater China, or even worldwide? What additional financial data would be useful to address this issue?

1. The foregoing analyses are based upon the premise that the transfer prices from Hong Kong into Taiwan are fixed. In fact, there is nothing in the case to suggest that these prices must be held at specific levels. It must be recognized, however, that changes to the transfer prices will have varying effects on the contribution realized by the Hong Kong office, depending upon the offshore unit contribution rate. However, some students may recognize that, by lowering its transfer prices into Taiwan, Seagram would not have to pay as much duty, although the offshore contribution would naturally be less. For example, the proposed duty rate of NT$170 for Chivas Regal would drop to NT$161 if the Hong Kong office decided to lower its transfer price from NT$242 to NT$200. This would yield a further duty savings of NT$9. The net effect would be that Seagram's Hong Kong office would realize NT$42 less contribution per bottle sold in Taiwan, but the Taiwan office would have a NT$51 price band to play with when jockeying for market position.

2. Most students should do a reasonably thorough and correct analysis of the basic marketing issues and the differential contribution that would accrue to Seagram Taiwan under the different pricing scenarios. The next analytical leap would be the recognition of the potential losses to Seagram as a whole if the increased contribution to Seagram Taiwan occurs with a decline in overall volume. That is, the students need to consider the corporate contribution not just Seagram Taiwan's incremental contribution. The more subtle issue has to do with the potential interdivisional conflict. This could occur if one division, i.e. Hong Kong, has a volume decline and, as a result, loses some of its total contribution. This could occur even if overall corporate profitability increases and if the amount of Taiwan's total additional contribution, due to not passing on 100 per cent of the decline in duty, is greater than the amount of lost contribution due to the decline in volume of sales. This problem will be accentuated if the management control system rewards divisional managers for their divisional contribution. The rewards could be bonuses and promotions based on divisional profitability.

3. Clearly, there is no right answer to Ian Swanson's dilemma, at least not an economically optimal one. One would need a lot of additional data, which may not be available. We would expect that at the very least the students would be trying to address the pricing question using both qualitative and financial analysis of the data in the case. The decision should be consistent and aware of the unknowns. The pricing strategy suggestions should also recognize that an optimal decision will require analysis of the overall impact on Seagram.

E. **Summary Points**

1. Duties play an important role in pricing in the global marketplace.

2. The situation facing Seagram in Taiwan highlights the concept of competitive interaction in a pricing context. Seagram essentially has two possible responses to the changes in the duties, yet it must face four possible scenarios due to different possible competitive responses. These scenarios are as follows:

- Seagram passes on duty savings by dropping prices by various amounts while its competitors retain the duty savings.

- Seagram retains the savings while competitors pass them on.

- Both Seagram and the competition retain the duty savings.

- Both Seagram and the competition pass on the duty savings.

3. Contribution (cost-volume-profit) analysis is a useful technique to assess the profit impact of actions and reactions of competitors.

TEXAS INSTRUMENTS: GLOBAL PRICING IN THE SEMICONDUCTOR INDUSTRY

Synopsis

In early 1995, John Szczsponik, Director of North American Distribution for Texas Instruments' Semiconductor Group, scheduled a meeting with Kevin McGarity, Senior VP and Manager of Worldwide Marketing at TI. The purpose of the meeting was to discuss the matter of global pricing of TI's semiconductors which its largest distributor -- Arrow Electronics -- was advocating. Global pricing meant that large distributors and some original equipment manufacturers (OEMs) would buy semiconductors from their manufacturers at one worldwide price with common pricing terms. TI, like other semiconductor manufacturers, operated production facilities around the world. This often resulted in different regional manufacturing costs arising from differential wage rates and other costs of doing business. TI's contracts with its distributors prevented distributors from selling semiconductors outside of the region where they were purchased thus resulting in different prices in different regions due to different costs. Global pricing would eliminate this practice.

The matter of global pricing also was driven by the commodity status of semiconductors where little differentiation between competitors' products existed. Distributors and large OEMs routinely "shopped" semiconductor manufacturers to get the best price since no difference existed in semiconductors. Manufacturers, in turn, focused on low-cost, high-volume production.

On February 14, 1995, TI and Arrow executives were scheduled to meet to discuss global pricing. In anticipation of the meeting, John Szczponik believed TI had to address a variety of questions mentioned at the end of the case. These questions were: (1) who held the power in the relationships TI had with its distributors?; (2) what was the source of negotiating strength each party would bring to the meeting?; (3) what position should TI's Semiconductor Group take with its distributors regarding global pricing?; and (4) what organizational implications would such a policy imply?

On a more general level, the case setting provides students with an opportunity to negotiate a mutually beneficial price policy from the perspective of two members of a marketing channel; namely, a supplier and its major distributor. The opportunity to simulate a negotiation meeting is a unique feature of the case and a valuable learning experience in its own right.

Teaching Objectives

This case has four teaching objectives:

1. To expose students to the worldwide semiconductor industry, and particularly its distribution practices and pricing policies.

2. To reaffirm basic considerations in price setting, namely the role of demand, cost, and competition, and their application in a high technology, business-to-business marketing setting.

3. To give students an opportunity to consider matters of power and influence in a marketing channel, trade relations, and how these matters affect pricing to and through a marketing channel.

4. To provide students with an opportunity to negotiate a price policy from the perspective of two members of a marketing channel; namely, a supplier and a distributor.

Teaching Suggestions

This case is suited for use in the pricing, business-to-business marketing, or international marketing module of a marketing management course. The case is suitable for undergraduate and graduate courses.

The case can be assigned as a group presentation or as a simulated negotiation meeting between TI and Arrow executives. If the case is taught as a negotiation exercise, divide the students into two teams: one group is assigned the task of preparing a negotiating strategy for TI's position, the other is to prepare Arrow's negotiating strategy. Each group will elect three representative "executives" to attend the negotiation meeting and to attempt to win agreement for its position from the other team. Both TI and Arrow negotiating teams will need to prepare:

- Historical data on the mutual beneficial relationship they have had to date with the other party;
- Numerical data and examples illustrating their positions on the global pricing issues at hand;
- Your team's desired negotiated results;
- Your team's arguments for why your point of view should prevail;
- Alternative approaches to pricing for Arrow--areas of common interest between the two firms; and finally
- Fall-back positions.

The students who are not elected to participate as representative "executives" on the negotiating team play an important role in preparing their team for an effective meeting. They should consider themselves in the role of supporting managers and specialists within the two organizations, responsible for gathering the right data and the most logical rationale for presenting their company's case. This of course simulates real business negotiating situations, where the meeting participants (often executives or managing directors) are prepared by their staffs for important pricing negotiations such as this one.

If the case is assigned for class discussion purposes, the following questions can be posed to students prior to or during a class discussion:

1. How would you characterize the semiconductor industry and TI's competitive position in this industry?

2. What is TI's current approach to the pricing of semiconductors?

3. What is meant by global pricing and why are large distributors and some original equipment manufacturers advocating it?

4. What would be the implications for TI of adopting global pricing?

5. How important is it for TI to negotiate the matter of global pricing with Arrow Electronics, if at all?

Areas for Discussion/Analysis

A. How would you characterize the semiconductor industry and TI's competitive position in this industry?

1. Semiconductors are silicon chips that transmit heat, light and electrical charge and perform critical functions in virtually all electronic devices. They are a core technology in industrial robots, computers, office equipment, consumer electronics, the aerospace, telecommunications, and automobile industries, and the military.

2. Demand for semiconductors is **derived**. Sales volume is driven by the application and use by original equipment manufacturers (OEMs) for the products they sell. Furthermore, these products were readily available from suppliers worldwide and were treated as commodity products by most buyers. Semiconductors manufacturers competed for market share primarily on the basis of the price offered to OEMs and distributors.

3. To a large extent, the competitive environment for commodity semiconductors reflects many of the characteristics of pure competition. An instructor may remind students that pure competition assumes:

- A very large number of buyers and sellers exist, none of which controls a substantial portion of either supply or demand;

- Essentially identical or homogeneous products so that no one seller can influence demand by any unique product features;

- All buyers and sellers are fully informed about the product and condition of supply and demand; and

- Existence of a recognized market where all market participants can compete freely in both buying and selling.

4. Manufacturers of semiconductors seek to gain a competitive advantage by becoming low-cost producers, developing closer relationships with their customers, and creating differentiated semiconductors which could be sold at a premium price.

5. Semiconductors are distributed directly to large OEMs and indirectly through electronics distributors which serve primarily mid-sized and small OEMs. Consolidation has been occurring among electronics distributors with 7 or 8 distributors capturing a majority of indirect sales to OEMs. Arrow Electronics and Avnet alone captured 39.6 percent of distributor sales in 1994 (see case Exhibits 5 and 6). Arrow, in particular, has demonstrated the most aggressive growth in sales and market share.

6. TI is a major semiconductor manufacturer with production facilities throughout North America, Asia, and Europe. TI, along with Intel and Motorola, is ranked among the top 6 semiconductor manufacturers (see case Exhibit 2 for 1992 data). Some 90 percent of TI's semiconductor sales were in standard products --those that were deemed commodities; 10 percent of sales were accounted for by differentiated products -- those for which TI was the sole supplier.

7. TI markets its semiconductors direct to OEMs and distributors. Some 73 percent of TI sales are direct; 27 percent are through distributors. According to TI's John Szczponik:

50% of TI sales are sold direct to the top tier of 100 electronic manufacturers (OEMs)
23% of TI sales are sold direct to 1,400 mid-sized companies
 0% of TI sales are sold direct to 150,000 smaller companies
73% of TI sales are direct

23% of TI sales are sold through distributors to mid-size companies
 4% of TI sales are sold through distributors to 150,000 smaller companies
27% of TI sales are through distributors

Since the case states that TI's 1994 semiconductor sales were $2 billion, the dollar sales breakdown by direct vs. distributor channel can be calculated as follows:

$1.46 Billion   Direct Sales   ($2 Billion x 73% = $1.46 Billion)
$ .54 Billion   Distributor Sales   ($2 Billion x 27% = $540 Million)
$2.00 Billion

B. What is TI's current approach to the pricing of semiconductors?

1. TI's current approach to pricing semiconductor is best described as a **flexible-price policy**. A flexible-price policy involves offering the same product and quantities to similar customers but at different prices in light of demand, cost, and competitive conditions. TI's flexible-price policy gives the company discretion in setting the final price at which it sells its semiconductors.

2. The case describes (a) how TI uses a learning curve to predict production cost decreases and yield improvements as production volumes increased; (b) how TI "meets the competition" where appropriate, and (c) how TI considers available supply and market demand in setting prices. In short, there is no single price for even its "commodity" semiconductors. Rather, prices are set based on conditions prevailing at a point in time and negotiations.

3. A unique feature of its pricing policy was how TI links pricing to distribution. As noted in the case, "Texas Instruments current contracts with its distributors prevented them (distributors) from selling semiconductors outside of the region in which they were purchased..." This meant that if distributors bought semiconductors in say, Japan, they had to sell these semiconductors in Japan and not in Europe. This contractual aspect meant that prices reflected the costs of production, demand and competition in a particular geographical area.

C. What is meant by global pricing and why are large distributors and some original equipment manufacturers advocating it?

1. It is important that students and the instructor "flesh-out" what global pricing means. In effect, global pricing means a **one-price policy** rather than a flexible-price policy. It also means that a common set of pricing terms be applied worldwide--discounts, payment policies (payment in 30 days or 60 days), and geographical pricing practices (i.e., the extent to which shipping or freight costs are included in a price structure). These pricing terms determine the "effective price" for semiconductors.

Global pricing could also mean less volatility in semiconductor prices. That is, prices might be set for a particular time period and adjustments made on a quarterly or semi-annual basis.

2. Large distributors and some OEMs are advocating this policy for a variety of reasons, some of which are described in the case, and other reasons that can be inferred from the case. Likely reasons for advocating global pricing include:

- Distributors and OEMs with operations in different parts of the world will be able to have a common price (cost) for their "raw material." This will remove part of the differences in cost arising from geography.

- Planning and budgeting for global distributors and OEMs could be simplified and some uncertainty could be removed.

- Less time will be required determining the "market price" or "going rate" and the attendant administrative costs associated with price searching and negotiation.

- Accounting for "phantom inventory" (described in the case) and frequent price adjustments could be reduced; hence, elaborate record-keeping systems and attendant costs.

D. What would be the implications of TI adopting global pricing?

1. Global pricing has favorable and unfavorable implications for TI. Some examples include the following:

    - **Favorable implications of global pricing**

        ... reduce the administrative costs associated with making price decisions on almost a case-by-case basis.

        ... could reduce some price volatility; that is, "sticky prices" made possible by, say, guaranteed prices for a specific time period might reduce the incidence of lowered prices. On the other hand, upward price movements are also limited which doesn't benefit TI.

        ... provides a common set of pricing terms worldwide; hence, complexity is replaced with simplicity, broadly speaking.

    - **Unfavorable implications of global pricing**

        ... By definition, TI loses flexibility in its pricing and particularly in "meeting the competition" in specific cases.

        ... Buying (pricing) practices and terms aren't global. The case states that customary payment practices differ across countries as do geographical pricing practices. TI would not be consistent with local/regional business customers.

... Manufacturing cost differences for semiconductors across regions (countries) are apparently large. It could be a cost accounting nightmare making internal adjustments to reflect a single price and very different costs.

... How would a single price be set? For example, a global price to Arrow will need to be higher than or equal to that given TI's large to mid-sized OEM customers; otherwise TI risks losing the OEM business to Arrow and other large distributors. Also, less visible pricing terms would have to be monitored.

... TI will not be able to quickly adapt to supply and demand conditions.

... TI loses access to market information pertaining to competitor pricing practices and product movements.

... If TI adopts global pricing, the contractual terms with distributors which limits them to selling semiconductors in the region where they bought would not hold. Is this in TI's best interest?.

2. In general, students might be asked whether or not global pricing will result in a competitive advantage for TI? Will it improve its cost position relative to competitors? Will customers see sufficient "value" in this practice to stop shopping competitors and buy more from TI?

3. In a related manner, students might be asked: "What might TI do if a major competitor, such as Motorola, introduced global pricing? If a competitor introduced global pricing, as Motorola is apparently rumored to do, TI would probably be forced to follow suit, at least for the commodity (standard) chips it sells. Its differentiated specialty chips would be less vulnerable to pressure from competitors' pricing. Ask students however, if they can identify any factors which would make it possible for TI to avoid following competitor's introduction of a global pricing strategy, such as a distinctive competence or processes which justifies a higher TI price for its commodity chips. Can TI be the one to take the first action in this area, thus avoiding becoming the "reactive" follower, thereby forcing its competitors to follow its lead?

E. **How important is it for TI to negotiate the matter of global pricing with Arrow Electronics, if at all?**

1. Global pricing clearly favors Arrow over TI. However, there are other matters to consider that have to do with channel relationships and access to small and mid-sized electronics manufacturers typically serviced by distributors such as Arrow. In short, TI should not necessarily dismiss Arrow's overtures.

2. There are at least six reasons why TI should engage in negotiations with Arrow:

- Arrow is the largest electronics distributor and apparently the fastest growing of the top electronics distributors (see case Exhibit 5).

- A quick calculation suggests that Arrow may be TI's largest electronics distributor. As noted in the case, Arrow recorded sales of $4 billion in 1994 (case Exhibit 5 shows a figure of $3.973 billion). TI products accounted for 14 percent of Arrow sales, or $560 million ($4 billion x .14 = $560 million). As estimated earlier (see the calculation in A7 above), TI records $540 million in sales through distributors. Acknowledging the presence of distributor margins, it is reasonable to conclude that Arrow is probably the principal TI distributor. Therefore, Arrow's overtures cannot be dismissed.

- It is in TI's interest to uncover what Arrow is actually looking for when it talks about global pricing.

- Relatedly, TI would benefit from knowing how global pricing links to Arrow's own international expansion. Perhaps there is common ground for both to grow their international businesses through accommodation on certain elements of global pricing.

- If Arrow is promoting the idea of global pricing with other semiconductor manufacturers, such as Motorola, it is in TI's best interests to be at least in a discussion stage.

- Assuming TI markets its differentiated products through Arrow along with standard (commodity) semiconductors -- which it probably does -- there is no need to strain trade relations by not discussing this matter.

3. If time permits, an instructor might ask students to speculate on what they believe Arrow really wants. Although purely speculative, it would seem Arrow wishes to further reduce price volatility, continue in what appears to be a mutually beneficial relationship, grow its own international business, reduce its costs, and simplify its cumbersome inventory valuation process apparent in price adjustments.

F. Epilogue

Global pricing in the semiconductor industry continued to be discussed at TI and with its customers. However, despite frequent mention of the practice by Arrow and other electronic distributors, TI and other semiconductor manufacturers (including Motorola) have not adopted this practice on a large scale (at least as of January 1997).

Instead, TI has elected to apply global pricing for customer-specific engagements. That is, for high volume, mature products with little price volatility, TI establishes a global price annually for major OEM customers and major distributors so that both are quoted the same price. This price is revised quarterly, if necessary, to reflect supply and demand factors. This practice applies only in Europe and North America and not in Japan and Asian countries.

TI has been the most responsive to the notion of global pricing among semiconductor manufacturer. Other manufacturers as Motorola do not use global pricing in any form.

Electronic distributors do source TI semiconductors from, say Singapore, for sale in Europe occasionally. This action is frowned upon by TI. However, this practice occurs on an exception basis due mostly to short-term shortage situations.

(Source: Interview with John Szczponik, Texas Instruments, January 6, 1997.)

G. Summary Points

1. Pricing in business-to-business marketing settings is often based on negotiations between sellers and buyers. Even so, fundamental issues related to demand, cost, and competition need to be considered.

2. Global pricing, in the case of standard (commodity-type) semiconductors, does not benefit buyers <u>and</u> sellers equally. There are numerous advantages to OEMs and distributors:

- Distributors and OEMs with operations in different parts of the world will be able to have a common price (cost) for their "raw material." This will remove part of the differences in cost arising from geography.

- Planning and budgeting for global distributors and OEMs could be simplified and some uncertainty could be removed.

- Less time will be required determining the "market price" or "going rate" and the attendant administrative costs associated with price searching and negotiation.

- Accounting for "phantom inventory" (described in the case) and frequent price adjustments could be reduced; hence, elaborate record-keeping systems and attendant costs.

TI does not benefit from global pricing:

- By definition, TI loses flexibility in its pricing and particularly in "meeting the competition" in specific cases.

- Buying (pricing) practices and terms aren't global. The case states that customary payment practices differ across countries as do geographical pricing practices. TI would not be consistent with local/regional business customers.

- Manufacturing cost differences for semiconductors across regions (countries) are apparently large. It could be a cost accounting nightmare making internal adjustments to reflect a single price and very different costs.

- How would a single price be set? For example, a global price to Arrow will need to be higher than or equal to that given TI's large to mid-sized OEM customers; otherwise TI risks losing the OEM business to Arrow and other large distributors. Also, less visible pricing terms would have to be monitored.

- TI will not be able to quickly adapt to supply and demand conditions.

- TI loses access to market information pertaining to competitor pricing practices and product movements.

- If TI adopts global pricing, the contractual terms with distributors which limits them to selling semiconductors in the region where they bought would not hold. Is this in TI's best interest?

3. In general, an important underlying question percolates below the surface when considering global pricing. That is, "will global pricing result in a competitive advantage for TI?" If so, how?

- Will it improve TI's cost-price position relative to competitors?

- Will customers see sufficient "value" in this practice to stop shopping competitors and buy more from TI?

PEAPOD: MOVING TO THE INTERNET

Synopsis

In March 1998, Peapod was the world's largest online grocer. The company's 1997 sales revenue was $43.5 million, representing an unknown market share because the case does not report a market total for that year. However, sales revenue for 1996 ($22 million) can be divided by a reported market total ($27.5 million) to produce an estimate for 1996 market share of 80 percent. Peapod has yet to show a profit. In fact, Peapod's loss of $9.6 million for 1996 actually grew in 1997 to $13.0 million, an increase of some 35 percent. However, Peapod's loss as a percent of revenue fell for the two years, from 32.8 percent to 21.8 percent. The case hints that losses cannot be sustained much longer. Quite likely, shareholders are dissatisfied with the 60 percent decline in Peapod's stock price since 1997 when the company went public.

Peapod faces a major change in the way it does business (described succinctly in the case title). That is, the company has decided to replace its current business platform (proprietary software) and move all of its customer contact activities to the Internet. Only a few companies will find themselves exactly in Peapod's situation. However, many (almost all?) companies in developed countries will find themselves adding an Internet component to their current marketing activities. Thus, students will find the case to have widespread applicability.

Peapod faces numerous operational problems and opportunities as described throughout the case. It is building warehouses to consolidate and better control the fulfillment side of its business. It needs to devote attention to other operational activities, such as purchasing, delivery, and customer service. From a strategic point of view, the company needs to think carefully about demand building, partnering (both existing and future partners), and exactly how it will provide value on the Internet in the face of increasing competition. The opportunity in on-line grocery retailing is great. Although not given in the case, a 1998 Andersen Consulting study estimated that on-line grocery shopping will be a $60 billion to $85 billion business by 2007 ("Market for on-line supermarkets," USA Today, January 6, 1999, p. 1D).

The Peapod case is central to students' understanding of the "under-belly" of interactive marketing and electronic commerce. However, because the case is long and complex, it may require two 75-minute class periods to treat important issues adequately. Alternatively, the instructor may devote one class session to discussion and then use a follow-up assignment (either a written exercise or an exam) to bring the case to closure.

This teaching note is based on an analysis plan prepared by Professor James E. Nelson, University of Colorado at Boulder.

At the time of case assignment, the instructor should direct students to questions (or a subset of questions) appearing later in this note as the best way to structure preparation and discussion. **It is important to note that to answer questions two and three, students will need to understand the concepts of a value chain, value web, and value proposition**. Thus, the instructor should have covered these topics in a previous lecture or have distributed a handout (or done both) before class discussion or an exam begins.

Teaching Objectives

The case may be used to meet several teaching objectives, depending on questions chosen for discussion and time devoted to the case. Students should learn that:

1. A value web illustrates more vividly than a value chain how marketers on the Internet provide value to their customers.

2. A value web describes the network of relationships between independent organizations whose aim is to satisfy a number of common buyer segments. Technologies, information, decision-making, trust, and reward link organizations in a value web.

3. A fundamental problem facing new firms is how to build brand awareness and brand equity.

4. A fundamental problem facing infant web sites is how to generate traffic, economically, and rapidly. This problem is intensified when the firm lacks brand equity and resources (capital, people, facilities, technology).

5. The duties and responsibilities of a value web broker form the basis of the broker's marketing strategy.

6. Marketing on the Internet and marketing in its "traditional" sense show far more similarities than differences. Examples of similarities include first mover advantage, brand equity, market segmentation, value creation and value propositions, relationship marketing, and sustainable competitive advantage. Examples of differences include the value web, increasing returns from scale, and the emphasis on digitalization and knowledge as the basis for competition.

The instructor might present these and other insights taken from class discussion as summary points at the end of the class session.

Teaching Suggestions

This case is best suited for use in the course when the instructor wishes to address issues in interactive marketing and electronic commerce. The case is suitable for both graduate and undergraduate classes and makes for an excellent group presentation case.

The six questions below can be used to direct student preparation before class and their discussion in class. However, unless the class period is very long (at least two hours), it may not be possible for students to discuss all six questions in great depth and detail. Moreover, instructors may want to include one or two questions of their own to address either fundamental ideas (e.g., company strengths, weaknesses; environmental opportunities, threats) or topics of special interest (e.g., consumer behavior on the Internet, web business models, principles of internet marketing, web site design, etc.).

1. What does the Peapod brand represent today and what should it represent in the future?

2. Compare the existing value chain of today's grocery industry to the value web that could be created in the future. Draw a picture of the value web. Who are the major players? What are the value propositions offered by the different companies in the value web? Are the sources of value sustainable?

3. Which relationships in the value web are most critical? Which relationships can Peapod pursue based on its capabilities?

4. Given the value propositions and the priorities and capabilities for implementation, what content and/or applications should Peapod put on its Web site first?

5. What content and applications for Peapod's Web site may be sustainable and what may be quickly initiated?

6. If Peapod implements many of the activities you suggest, what capabilities and competencies will the company need? Which of these should Peapod develop in-house? Which should Peapod partner for?

Areas for Discussion/Analysis

A. What does the Peapod brand represent today and what should it represent in the future?

1. This question is a good way to begin discussion because it highlights Peapod's strengths and weaknesses from the viewpoint of the consumer. Briefly, "Peapod" is **inherently** a good brand name because it is memorable, easy and pleasant to pronounce,

connotes food, and is protected by law. However, the name is not particularly well known outside of its seven metropolitan markets (Chicago, San Francisco/San Jose, Columbus, Boston, Houston, Atlanta, and Dallas) and it may not be particularly well known even in these markets. Quite likely, the Peapod brand name represents a somewhat mixed bag of mental associations.

2. A good way to get these associations out is for the instructor to ask students to take out a piece of paper and a pen or pencil. He/she should tell them that they will have 60 seconds to write down all the words and phrases that come into their mind when the instructor says "   ." When students are ready, the instructor can shout "PEAPOD" and begin timing the activity. When time is up, volunteers or designated individuals can be asked for their top of mind associations, which then should be put on the board. Here's what should come out (column on the left):

Peapod now
- Young, unknown
- Broke
- Inconsistent service
- Errors in my order
- Weak, vulnerable company
- Convenient
- Now, modern
- Expensive
- A "novel" alternative to traditional stores
- Good for buying name brands
- Not good for perishable food
- The same as Jewel/Osco (in Chicago)

Peapod in the future
- Young in some markets, older in others
- Profitable in some markets, not in others
- Errorless, quick service in all markets
- The model or ideal Internet grocery
- A brand extender, putting its name on . . .
- A place where I can buy with confidence
- "My" grocery store
- A "smart" alternative to traditional stores

In general, the instructor should simply put the "Peapod now" associations on the board, with a minimum of evaluation or discussion from the class. The instructor might take care to solicit/list both positive **and** negative associations.

When this activity is finished, the instructor should ask students to state associations for Peapod in the future, say five years from the time of the case (1998). In other words, what **should be** the ideal set of brand associations for Peapod? Words and phrases in the right column should surface (without using any top of mind exercise).

3. A good way to end what should be a short discussion would be to note that Peapod looks to have a long way to go in moving from its existing brand associations to an ideal set in the future. Time permitting, the instructor could note that the topic being discussed is really **brand equity** (addressed in chapter 5) and that brand equity is an issue facing almost any firm moving all or some of its customer contact activities from conventional means to the Internet. Following Keller's conceptualization (*Strategic Brand Management*, Prentice-Hall, 1998) brand equity associations always should be strong, favorable, and unique—in that order. A unique association does its brand no good unless it is favorable. A favorable association is of little worth unless it is strong.

B. Compare the existing value chain of today's grocery industry to the value web that could be created in the future. Draw a picture of the value web. Who are the major players? What are the value propositions offered by the different companies in the value web? Are the sources of value sustainable?

1. This is a technical question that is the very heart of the case. Students will need to understand three concepts: value chain, value web, and value proposition. Here are three definitions:

A *value chain* for a firm describes the relative importance of five primary activities (inbound logistics, operations, outbound logistics, marketing and sales, and service) and four support activities (procurement, technology development, human resource development, and firm infrastructure) in producing a competitive advantage either by cost or by differentiation. (Porter, *Competitive Advantage: Creating and Sustaining Superior Performance*, The Free Press, 1985.) See Exhibit 1(A) in this note.

In contrast, a *value web* is a network of independent firms having shared: goals, expertise, decision-making, responsibility, trust, and reward. Each firm in the network has a unique, reliable capability that it attempts to maintain at a "state of the art" level (Snow and Miles, "Managing the 21st Century Network Organization," *California Management Review*, 1986). The network becomes a virtual corporation based on relationships between network nodes (independent firms), as described by formal alliances, working agreements, and information transfers. See Exhibit 1(B) in this note.

Major differences between a value chain and a value web appear in Exhibit 2 in this note (see Stabel and Fjelstad, "Configuring Value for Competitive Advantage: on Chains, Shops, and Networks," *Strategic Management Journal,* 1998).

A *value proposition* is a statement describing the benefits that a firm offers to served customer segments (either consumers or other businesses) as the basis to build a lasting relationship. Benefits derive from the physical product (or intangible service), augmented product, any bundled (physical and augmented) products, product delivery and usage instruction, after-sale service, and the buyer/user's emotional experiences with the product. Sources of a customer value proposition in marketspace include convenience, cost, choice, customization, customer service, and coordination (see Chapter 9, pp. 463-465).

2. Experience teaching the case indicates that some instructors simply make transparencies of Exhibits 1 and 2 in this note and present them to the class followed by discussion. **The discussion should focus principally on the Value Web Network and draw on the case text description (pp. 484-488).**

3. Alternatively, some instructors expect the class to actually draw a picture of the value web. Listed below are some suggestions when drawing the value web in the class:

EXHIBIT 1

(A) GENERIC VALUE CHAIN

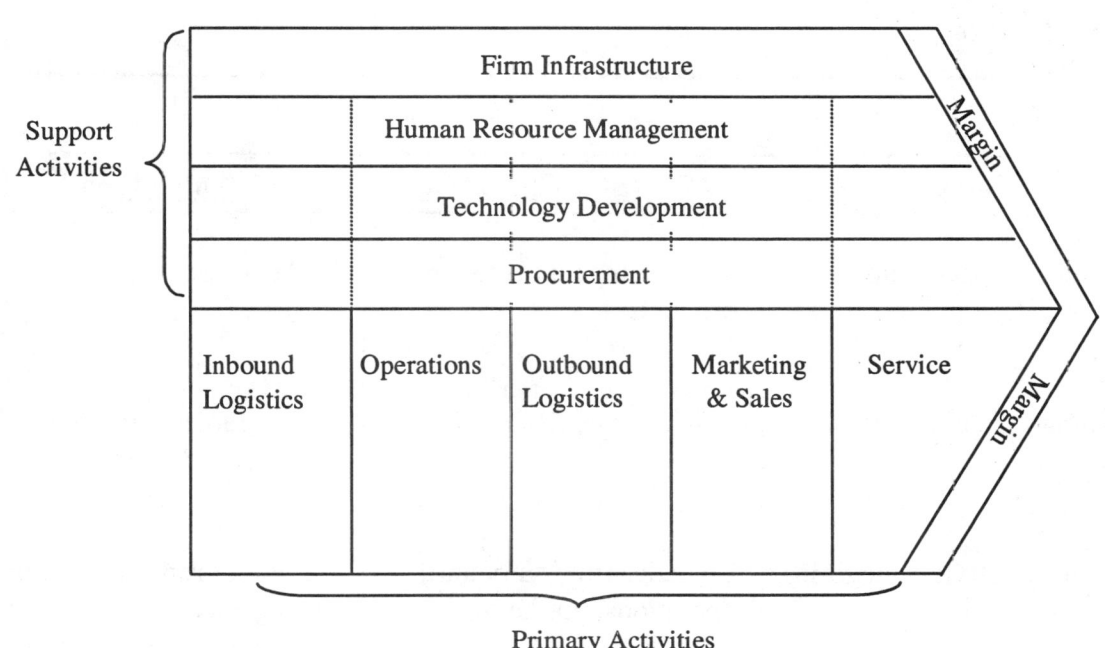

Source: Michael E. Porter, Competitive Advantage, (New York: The Free Press, 1985), p. 37.

(B) VALUE WEB NETWORK

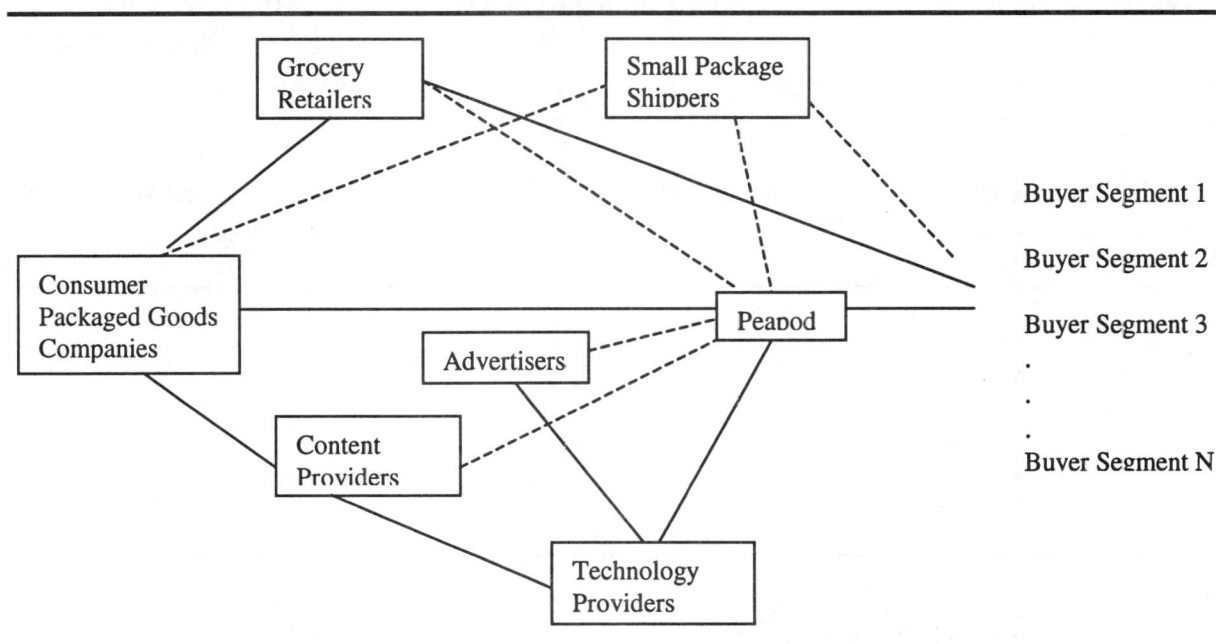

EXHIBIT 2

DIFFERENCES BETWEEN A VALUE CHAIN AND

A VALUE WEB NETWORK

Feature	Value Chain	Value Web
Value creation logic	Transforms inputs to products	Links buyers
Primary technology	Long, sequential links	Short, pooled, simultaneous, parallel, and reciprocal links
Primary activity categories	Logistics (in-, outbound) operations, marketing, service	Network promotion, contract management, service offerings, network operation
Cost drivers	Scale, capacity utilization	Scale, capacity utilization
Value drivers	The firm's strategic choices	The network's: design, operation, scale, and capacity utilization
Value system structure	Interlinked chains	Interconnected networks, layered networks

a. Put grocery retailers, small package shippers, and consumer packaged goods companies toward the top of the value web to highlight their proximity to the value chain: a necessary set of activities to move product from producer to consumer.

b. Put content providers, technology providers, and Internet advertisers at the bottom of the value web to indicate their distance from the "old" way of doing things.

c. Solid lines can be used to indicate mandatory relationships while dashed lines can indicate potential relationships.

d. Students will have little trouble isolating key nodes in the value web, except perhaps for the small package shippers. Some students will think FedEx or UPS will represent a mandatory node while others may hold for using only Peapod vehicles and drivers. The latter is, of course, more expensive but makes the company closer to the consumer and offers additional opportunities for building brand equity. Students usually agree that a mix of the two strategies, depending on market potential and order size, would be best.

There are several implications that can be drawn from the diagram:

a. A value chain describes activities that take place **inside a single firm**. A value web describes activities within and between several firms. Peapod should locate as the **value web broker**, a data-driven intermediary immediate to the served segments that satisfies trial, repeat, and loyal customer segments and that organizes, grows, and maintains all value web relationships. The value web broker will seek new customer segments, research and anticipate consumer preferences, and assemble a knowledge base that is itself a source of value. The broker should communicate regularly with served segments. The broker should anticipate and block competitive threats to the value web. The broker should lead and direct development of the value web.

b. **Electronic markets** operate as part of each solid or dashed line. That is, part of any relationship is arms-length, economic buying and selling.

c. Value webs work best when **relationships are long-term yet capable of dissolution** in the event of poor performance.

d. **Economic power** in a value web is reflected by relationship duration, value source singularity, and prices charged. Powerful nodes can bargain for long, exclusive relationships that produce high margins.

e. Firms located at each node attempt to **stay small, flexible, responsive, and profitable—based on exploiting the firm's particular knowledge and skill set**.

f. The value web **grows in terms of transaction volume and becomes more valuable** to its members because of revenue growth (due to the web's ability to reach new customer segments) and cost savings (due to function specialization and function proficiency, economies of scale, synergies, and information sharing).

4. Students now can formulate value propositions for players at each node in the value web. The value proposition for Peapod is given in item (a), immediately above. Value propositions for the remaining nodes appear below:

a. **Consumer packaged goods companies** provide value from performing the five primary and four support activities in a value chain. Value is achieved either through cost or differentiation, both of which are sustainable in the long run. However, cost advantages eventually diminish even when the leading firm holds a dominant position. This holds true for two reasons: the slope of the experience curve eventually flattens and cost reductions can be achieved only at greater and greater increases in experience. Value from differentiation also diminishes, unless the firm can regularly improve its offering in a proprietary manner.

b. **Grocery retailers** provide value by assembling collections of merchandise, inventorying and displaying merchandise, promoting and selling, providing credit, and resolving problems that consumers may have with their purchases. Retailers attempt to differentiate themselves from competitors by offering exclusive products, personalized services, and convenient locations. Retailers are further differentiated on their images, based on store layout and ambiance, point of contact personnel, variety and quantity and quality of merchandise carried, prices, promotion activities, customer service, and location. Retail images lead to a clientele or a group of patrons appearing in a store, with many customers forming long-term relationships with their favorite retailers. A retailer's value proposition is sustainable based on location, merchandise exclusivity, cost, image, personnel and training, name, and location.

c. **Small package shippers** provide value through physical delivery of product and reduction of uncertainty surrounding product shipment (tracking, pickup and delivery appointments, insurance). The proposition is sustainable based on investment entry barriers, proprietary knowledge, contractual agreements, and cost structure.

d. As the case notes, **advertisers** provide value to Peapod as a means to build the Peapod brand and to provide the company with a source of revenue. Advertisers also provide value to consumers and to the sponsoring company by providing information, creating image and brand equity, and reducing purchase uncertainty and risk. Both value propositions are sustainable to the degree that advertised information is timely, relevant, accessible, and credible and that image and equity are relevant and favorable.

e. **Content providers** provide value to consumers by finding, presenting, and linking subject matter that is relevant to one or more target segments, as the segments use the Internet. The subject matter creates value for target segments by solving problems, entertaining, educating, and titillating. Large content providers (e.g., Yahoo!, Netscape, MSNBC, CNN) often become portals or convenient starting points to a user's Internet session. A content provider's value proposition is sustainable to the degree that its content for consumers is unique, fresh, and accessible (including the ability to search for specific content). Content must be available quickly and conveniently, at an acceptable price. If time permits, the instructor could develop the idea of the "price" of using an Internet content provider. This price would be a function of site unreliability, delays in page loading times, page clutter, vague and confusing instructions, outdated links, anxiety over privacy concerns, clumsy navigation within the site, slow downloads, timeouts, site subscription fees, etc.

Content providers provide value to Peapod by creating Peapod brand awareness and by generating secondary associations for the Peapod brand. This latter type of value stems will from Peapod's Internet proximity to the content provider's own strong brand (much like a magazine or newspaper ad is perceived in the context of its publisher and within-issue location). Content providers can deliver customers and potential customers to the Peapod site. Peapod, in turn, can reciprocate and provide sustainable value for content providers by building high awareness and strong secondary associations for their sites. To build awareness and maintain strong associations will require substantial commitment of resources.

f. Students might note that Peapod needs the services of two types of technology providers. **Web technology providers** provide value at an elementary level simply by making sure that the value web system works as it should. However, web technology providers must go beyond this minimal operational concern by providing value from software and web site designs that are creative and that will amaze and delight users. Web technology providers that do this in a fashion that is proprietary—either by patent or by control of technology—will provide the greatest value to Peapod. Web technology providers can focus on Peapod's site to make shopping faster, more pleasant, more creative, higher volume per purchase, more profitable per order, etc. Or, web technology providers can focus on other nodes in the value web or on relationships between Peapod and the important nodes.

In contrast, **database technology providers** provide value by identifying consumer target segments whose purchase behaviors can be leveraged for greater volume and profit. Most often the leverage will be promotional in nature, to encourage purchase in larger volumes or to stimulate purchase of new products, products that are complementary in some fashion to ordered products, or products associated with special occasions (holidays, birthdays, parties, anniversaries, etc.). Database technology providers provide value to consumer packaged goods companies as well, to the extent that they stimulate greater consumption of a firm's products.

Value propositions for the two types of technology providers are sustainable to the degree that their technologies function correctly and creatively, meaning that technology providers must understand value propositions for players at each of their linked nodes as well as staying at the forefront of their respective technologies.

C. Which relationships in the value web are most critical? Which relationships can Peapod pursue based on their current capabilities?

1. Critical relationships in the value web are those that **directly touch buyer segments**. Thus, **Peapod's relationships with consumers and those of the small package shippers with consumers (in markets where shippers are used) will be critical**. Why? Students should respond that direct relationships with buyer segments have a big influence on buyer satisfaction and on repeat purchase rates. These relationships permit loyalty to develop and will reduce the effectiveness of competitors' activities. Further, these relationships are central to Peapod's understanding of its customers.

2. Another response identifying critical relationships will be to note the mandatory (solid line) relationships in the value web are more important that the potential (dashed line) relationships. That is, Peapod will thrive, merely survive, or die, depending on (1) the value it receives from its packaged goods suppliers and its technology providers and (2) the value it provides to its buyer segments. (<u>Note</u>: Some discussion of the 6-C framework from chapter 9 might be appropriate here.)

3. Other relationships in the value web are less critical to Peapod. Relationships between Peapod and grocery retailers will disappear as the company moves to using its own warehouses. Relationships with advertisers are less important because of advertisers' tangential importance to Peapod's core business and the limited potential of advertising to generate revenue. However, advertisers are important to the degree that they impact Peapod's image and brand equity. Content providers, too, probably fall into the less critical category. The number of content providers is likely quite large, although the better ones may be "captured" quickly by Peapod's competitors in their own value webs. Still, content providers are less central to Peapod's core business than those noted above.

4. Peapod needs to strengthen and to enhance critical relationships in the value web, particularly those that fall within the company's capabilities. The case states that **Peapod's primary strength lies in its strategic use of database technology rather than in its ability to maintain relationships with buyer segments. (The present operations and logistics systems that supported buyer segment relationships was flawed by stock-outs (up to 10% of ordered items) and by picker error (2% of ordered items).) These two shortcomings affect the very core of Peapod's value proposition—customer service and customer convenience—and are reflected by the high churn rate in Peapod's customer base.** If these shortcomings persist, Peapod will lose its position as the value web broker and the company would necessarily fold (or exist in dramatically altered form). In short, Peapod needs to pursue the database technology provider relationship because it can build on an existing strength. Moreover, Peapod may be able to exploit this technology by marketing its expertise to other web retailers, located either on Peapod's web site or elsewhere.

D. Given the value propositions and the priorities and capabilities for implementation, what content and/or applications should Peapod put on its site first?

1. The case identifies four types of content providers that Peapod was considering for its web site: cooking-enthusiast, diet and nutritional, iVillage (currently associated with a Peapod competitor, OnCart), and consumer packaged goods companies. Rather than rush headlong into a discussion of the relative advantages and disadvantages of each type, **students should be pushed back to Peapod's value proposition and the idea that the most important relationship in the value web from Peapod's point of view is its relationships with its buyer segments.** The term is stressed here to emphasize the idea that Peapod satisfies more than just one segment and that different segments will value different types of content. Case Exhibit 13 identifies eight different types of applications that Peapod could include on its web site: transaction engine, coupons offer, ingredients database, recipes database, chat rooms/message boards, personal meal planner, idea generator, and deliver meals (not just groceries). **Of the eight, only the transaction engine must be present on the Peapod site (assuming that Peapod maintains its online grocery role).** Discussion of the relative advantages and disadvantages of the other seven applications again will depend on just which buyer segment students have in mind.

2. However, thinking at a more fundamental level, students should conclude that this question is somewhat of a red herring. Peapod cannot hope to answer this question until it understands its buyer segments more completely and it articulates its mission, vision, or purpose. If time permits, discussion could focus on "just why would you buy from Peapod?" to see what sorts of buyer segments result. Students easily describe segments outlined in case Exhibit 9 (cost-conscious searcher, variety-seeking/chatter, convenience seeking, and health seeking) and the instructor can devote some space on the board to details. However, students should note the need for more formal marketing research (beyond that conducted by the Northwestern MBA students) to understand existing and potential Peapod segments. At a minimum, this research should focus on the relative attractiveness of each basic segment

(market potential, growth rates, receptivity to online shopping, and level of competition) and on reactions of each segment to the four different types of content and the seven types of applications.

3. Students should be pressed to add richness and understanding to buyer segments beyond information given in the case. Peapod should segment its markets into existing and potential customer segments. Pertinent concepts for existing segments include the ideas of trial and repeat purchasers, order size and the concept of the heavy user, and conversion rates. The latter concept represents the number of visitors during a specified period who take action at a site (purchase, register, provide information, request information, etc.) divided by the total number of site visitors. Conversion rates offer a useful metric for evaluating site features and overall site performance. Conversion rates rather than click-through rates will show the value of Peapod advertising placed on other web sites (an Internet advertisement is not effective unless something is sold?). Conversion rates form the basis for estimating segment profitability and the long-term or lifetime value of a customer segment. Pertinent concepts for trial or first-time purchasers also will include order size and conversion rates, along with other ideas. These include customer satisfaction and intention to buy again, how the first-time purchaser found the Peapod site, and their likes and dislikes of web site content and navigation..

4. At an equally fundamental level, Peapod must articulate what it wants to be. Decisions on content and applications can be made more easily once this vision is debated, adopted, and communicated. Again, if time permits, students could discuss alternative vision statements based on their view of the eventual nature of online grocery retailing. The instructor might ask "just what the market for online grocery retailing will look like in 2010?" Quite likely, the online grocery market will evolve to parallel the existing grocery market with a few large firms dominating the mass market and a large number of smaller, specialty grocers satisfying the needs of geographic, demographic, and behavioral segments (ethnic foods, health and diet, convenience stores, etc.). However, some students may note the potential for large and small consumer packaged goods companies to bypass retailers completely and deal directly with the most attractive segments. The trend in 2000 has clearly begun and students should be able to supply numerous examples drawn from the computer, automobile, travel, and other industries. The term used in value-web parlance is "cherry picking," a firm's selection and capture of the more profitable and faster growing buyer segments and its leaving of the less attractive segments to others.

E. **What content and applications for Peapod's web site may be sustainable and what may be quickly imitated?**

1. Discussion works best here if students focus first on the four types of content providers and then turn their attention to the seven potential applications. From an "advertising alone" perspective, the four types of content providers (cooking-enthusiast, diet and nutritional, iVillage, and consumer packaged goods companies) appear to be unsustainable for three reasons. First, the number of content providers is immense and the

advertising task itself is complex. That is, Peapod must identify, attract, and contract for advertising with the top 50 (100?, 200?) sites in each of the four content types. Then, Peapod must develop banner ads, co-branded/sponsorship ads, text links, or other communications with each selected content provider that are creative, uniquely positioned, and effective. These activities will be too expensive and time consuming for Peapod to undertake without the help of yet another node in the value web, a net advertising agency or web site designer. Second, each advertised site then must deliver sufficient traffic and conversion rates that Peapod will cover its fixed and variable advertising costs and will earn an acceptable return on sales. This requirement implies that Peapod will need to develop measures of advertising effectiveness and to monitor each content provider for performance. Third, all of Peapod's advertising relationships will be temporary and vulnerable to attack from competing grocery retailers who will drive up advertising costs at the best content providers in their desire to imitate Peapod's success. Thus, the only sustainable basis for advertising/linking with content providers is via long-term partnering (three years or longer in term) where Peapod sponsors messages that are integrated into the editorial content of selected providers.

2. The picture changes considerably when discussion focuses on the seven potential applications listed in case Exhibit 13, because the seven applications require none, one, or just a few new value web relationships. Moreover, many of the applications would use software that creates a sustainable advantage for Peapod, via either patents or proprietary knowledge. Students can spend a bit of time discussing the relative advantages and disadvantages of each of the seven. The recipes database, personal meal planner, and idea generator applications seem especially suited for Peapod because they require few new web relationships and could be sustainable. The coupons offer, ingredients database, and chat rooms/message board applications seem to fall into the "necessary, expected, and me-too" sort of category. That is, one, two, or all three of these applications will appeal to many consumers but the applications will not differentiate Peapod from competitors. Finally, the deliver meals application probably should remain on the drawing board for the time being. This application seems a bit removed from Peapod's core business and would require a huge investment of resources to identify restaurants in the seven metropolitan markets (and elsewhere?) that could deliver tasty, wholesome meals on a profitable basis. This application would be best left to the horde of existing competitors that are only a phone call away from each urban household.

3. As a last point here, students should suggest that Peapod aggressively pursue a number of relatively low cost Internet communication activities. Examples include affiliate programs that refer visitors at other web sites to Peapod's site, public relations (in traditional media and on the Internet), e-mail messages to existing customers targeted by past purchase behavior, and e-mail messages to potential customers who visit the Peapod site to encourage trial. Peapod also could use sales promotion activities on its web site to stimulate trial or to increase their order size. Throughout all these activities, Peapod must monitor results to see which content, applications, and promotion activities drive traffic to the web site and produce transactions.

F. **If Peapod implements many of the activities you suggest, what capabilities and competencies will the company need? Which of these should they develop in-house? Which should they partner for?**

1. This is a good question to end the discussion or to use as a follow-up assignment or examination as it summarizes much of the preceding discussion and points direction for the future.

2. Peapod needs to exhibit a wide range of capabilities and competencies in both a strategic and tactical sense. From a tactical perspective, Peapod needs to be able to **run its business efficiently and effectively**. This means that items ordered from Peapod are in stock and shipped without errors or substitutions. It means that high quality grocery items are delivered as scheduled at competitive prices. It means that existing and potential customers can communicate with knowledgeable Peapod personnel to answer questions, respond to complaints, and suggest alternatives to solve customers' problems. It means that Peapod's web site meets users' expectations for ease of use, reliability, privacy, novelty, and personalization. Finally, it means that the Peapod business model will produce acceptable profit, happy customers, discouraged competitors, and satisfied investors. Obviously, these are core capabilities and competencies that Peapod must have to exist in its present business form and structure.

3. From a strategic perspective, Peapod needs to **exercise the duties and responsibilities of the value web broker.** These duties and responsibilities were identified earlier in this note and are repeated here for convenience. A value web broker satisfies trial, repeat, and loyal customer segments and organizes, grows, and maintains all value web relationships. A value web broker will seek new customer segments, research and anticipate consumer preferences, and assemble a knowledge base that is itself a source of value. The broker should communicate regularly with served segments. The broker should anticipate and block competitive threats to the value web. The broker should lead and direct development of the value web. Peapod must develop these capabilities itself or the company will lose much of its ability to shape and control its destiny.

4. Some other needed strategic competencies at Peapod lie in the areas of brand building and brand management, competitive monitoring, and technological competency. On this last area, Peapod needs its own research and development capabilities for its core transaction engine because the engine is the company's very basis for existence. Some other needed research and development activities would be more applied such as in new product development (a Peapod private label perhaps?), tracking advertising effectiveness, inventory control, and logistics, for example. Peapod executives need the strategic ability to anticipate the future in such areas as buyer behavior, hardware (Internet appliances), media convergence, emerging and latent competition, and regulation. Executives need skills to identify attractive merger and acquisition partners, negotiate equitable agreements, and work closely and harmoniously with partners. At some point soon, executives will need skills to control business activities, to improve operating efficiency and produce profits.

5. Still other strategic competencies can be developed with organizations found in Peapod's value web. Web technology providers can help Peapod make online grocery shopping faster, more pleasant, and more economical from the buyer's point of view. Technology providers can develop Peapod's capability to mine transaction data in order to understand buyer segments, streamline a buyer's shopping experience, suggest new or untried items for trial, and ultimately produce profits for Peapod.

6. Students' opinions regarding which skills are needed inside Peapod and which can be found in partnerships with value web players will differ to some degree, as might be expected. The instructor might recognize that no right answer exists for some of these skill areas and simply call for arguments supporting each point of view.

G. Epilogue

The instructor might encourage students to visit Peapod's web site (www.peqpod.com) as a way of introducing them to the case. Students will see that site appearance and operation depend on visitors' zip codes. If visitors provide a zip code located in the **eight** served market area (as of May 2000), they will be directed to the full line of Peapod shopping aisles. However, visitors providing codes outside the eight markets will be directed to a Peapod Package Store, where they can purchase a limited number of non-perishable items delivered by UPS.

At either site, visitors will see and experience little beyond an online grocery store. That is, they will see no links to the four types of content providers described in the case and limited use of several applications listed in case Exhibit 13. Specifically, visitors can click to use a sort function to rank competing products in a category (by price, calories, grams of fat or sugar, or other criteria), find upwards of 40 recipes, and find a few ideas for meals and snacks. They will see no coupon offer, chat room/message board, or deliver meals applications.

A click on "About Peapod" will direct visitors to a brief company history, a listing of partners and sponsors (no e-commerce, content provider, or technology partners listed), and a listing of recent press releases. The release dated April 14, 2000 describes the purchase by Royal Ahold of Peapod convertible (to common) preferred stock in the amount of US$73 million, equal to 51 percent of Peapod's outstanding common stock. Ahold is a Dutch firm (1999 sales of US$20.3 billion), operating five supermarket companies along the eastern seaboard (1063 stores). Ahold's Stop & Shop (Boston area) and Edwards (New York area) were Peapod partners before the stock purchase. Ahold's extensive retail facilities will streamline Peapod's picking and logistic operations. Ahold also will bring to the partnership its grocery management expertise, massive buying power, and financial strength. Peapod will provide its home shopping expertise, web-based software, and web marketing skills-all attractive capabilities for expansion to the European market.

AMAZON.COM: WINNING THE ON-LINE BOOK WARS

Synopsis

In January 1998, Jeffery Bezos, the CEO of Amazon.com was reflecting on the company's 1997 year-end financial and operating results and the challenges that lay ahead. Amazon.com had recorded sales of $147.8 million in 1997—a 938 percent increase over 1996—and posted an operating loss of $27.6 million, an amount five times greater than its operating loss in 1996.

Two issues are prominent in the case:

1. How can Amazon.com fine-tune its current business model to achieve or more closely approach profitability?

2. How can Amazon.com profitably grow?

Students should have little difficulty isolating these issues. They appear at the end of the first paragraph on p. 495 and again at the end of the case.

The case provides an excellent vehicle for students to examine the origins, operations, and opportunities (challenges) of a marketspace pioneer in early 1998—a critical point in Amazon.com's development. The company is considering several different growth strategies—market penetration, market development, new offering development, and diversification. At the same time, students will need to consider how retailers, in general, generate revenues and profits, how retailers grow, and how retailers compete. Moreover, students should come to understand the nature of retail competition in e-commerce and articulate Amazon.com's customer value proposition, distinctive compentenc(ies), and core marketing strategy.

Teaching Objective

This case has four teaching objectives:

1. To introduce students to the origins, operations, and future opportunities and challenges facing a marketspace pioneer.

This teaching note is based on an analysis plan prepared by Professor James E. Nelson, University of Colorado at Boulder.

2. To illustrate that the fundamental tenets of strategic marketing management apply in the new marketspace just as they do in the traditional marketplace.

3. To give students an opportunity to consider and evaluate profitable growth opportunities for essentially a single product company (books) in the new marketspace.

4. To challenge students to consider how a company in the new marketspace can make a profit.

Teaching Suggestions

This case has multiple uses. It can be assigned as a Market Opportunity case, as a Comprehensive Marketing Programs case, or in course module featuring Interactive Marketing and Electronic Commerce. The case has been assigned as a group analysis and presentation case in both undergraduate and graduate courses.

Class discussion should be lively for several reasons. Amazon.com's current situation and the dynamic nature of e-commerce demand quick, decisive action (but not "Ready. Fire. Aim!"). Moreover, opportunities for Amazon.com are huge while missteps may be disastrous, if not fatal. Most students in the class will have purchased something from Amazon.com or its major "brick and mortar" competitor, Barnes & Noble. Most students will have little difficulty finding additional information about the company, its competitors, and current market statistics and practices.

Indeed, both the abundance and availability of information that summarizes events occurring after the time of the case may seem detrimental to the case's learning potential. For example, students can quickly find from company records and the popular business press "what happened," what caused "it" to happen, and what Amazon.com might possibly do in the future. However, as instructors know, cases are meant to be more than a vehicle for literature reviews. Cases are opportunities for students to develop decision-making skills, based on their qualitative and quantitative analyses of "facts" as found in the case, and as developed by the give and take of classroom discussion.

Still, the instructor should be aware of students' fascination with "answers to the case" as they think might be found from two hours of search time in the library. Comments like these might be appropriate at the time of Amazon.com's assignment:

> You can find LOTS of information about Amazon.com in the library or on the Web. In fact, if you search for an hour or so, I am sure that you'll find information that will take you at least another hour or two to digest. However, none of this information will be relevant to our discussion next class session. Instead, I want a discussion as of January, 1998 based on facts as they appear in the case.

The following questions can be posed to students either before or during a class discussion:

1. Amazon.com is a retailer. How, in general, do retailers generate revenues and profits, grow, and compete?

2. Describe the nature of competitive rivalry in e-commerce retailing for consumer products in early 1998. How do e-commerce retailers (e-tailers) compete, thrive, survive?

3. How would you describe Amazon.com's customer value proposition, distinctive competency, and core marketing strategy?

4. Can Amazon.com tweak its business model to make a profit on book sales in 1998? What can the company do?

5. How can Amazon.com grow profitably? What strategy do you recommend for a two- to five-year horizon?

Areas for Discussion/Analysis

A. Amazon.com is a retailer. How, in general, do retailers make revenues and profits, grow, compete?

1. This is a good question to begin discussion. The topic matter is important, students should be quick to respond, and their answers should take only a few minutes. Retailers satisfy consumer wants by assembling collections of merchandise, inventorying and displaying that merchandise, promoting and selling, providing credit, and resolving problems that consumers may have with their purchases. Retailers attempt to differentiate themselves from competitors by offering exclusive products, personalized services, and convenient locations. Retailers possess images based on their store layout and ambiance (including merchandise displays), point of contact personnel, variety and quantity and quality of merchandise carried, prices, promotion activities, customer service, and location. Retail images lead to a clientele or a group of patrons appearing in a store, with many customers forming long-term relationships with their favorite retailers. Sales at many retailers show strong seasonal variations, with perhaps half of all sales generated in the last quarter of each calendar year.

2. Retailers make money via unit margins, merchandise turnover, and cost control. Some retailers focus on margins, others emphasize turnover, and still others focus on costs. Retailers lose money by failing to understand their customers, by underestimating competitors, by inadequately controlling (inventory, expenses, security, customer credit, sales personnel, etc.) and by locating in a poor site. Retailers may buy the "wrong" merchandise or insufficient quantities of the "right" merchandise (because they must anticipate consumer demand by several months). Unlike manufacturers, retailers spend relatively small amounts

of their sales revenues on research and development activities. Retailers perform a time-honored economic activity whose essential activities change slowly.

3. When most of these ideas are out, the instructor might pose a summary question: In one sentence, **what is the "essence of successful retailing**?" The instructor might give students three minutes with a piece of paper to collect their thoughts and then ask students for their response. Responses can be put on the board to end the discussion. A good sentence would be something like this: Successful retailers satisfy their chosen customer targets, repeatedly, conveniently, at competitive prices. This is "all" that Amazon.com needs to do.

B. Describe the nature of competitive rivalry in e-commerce retailing for consumer products in early 1998. How do e-commerce retailers compete, thrive, survive?

1. The e-commerce retail market for consumer products in early 1998 was in its introductory or early growth stages. Thus, competitive rivalry was less intense than would be expected when the industry matures.

2. Rivalry in a retail market's introductory and early growth stages can be characterized by the following. Retailers try to obtain awareness, trial purchase, and then repeat purchases from chosen consumer segments. Attractive segments include innovators, opinion leaders, younger consumers who have not formed enduring relationships with existing retailers, older consumers who are less than satisfied with existing retailers, novelty and variety seekers, consumers who are comfortable buying at a distance (mail-order), consumers who are sensitive to shopping time and stress, and potentially heavy users. Because consumers already buy merchandise from traditional retailers based on established store images, e-commerce retailers must offer a relative advantage (price, selection, convenience, service, customer familiarity) sufficient to change existing patterns of behavior.

3. Thus, to compete successfully in e-commerce retail markets rivals must understand and satisfy chosen consumer segments. They must undertake marketing research on potential customers, on first-time customers, and on repeat purchasers. They will want to know how customers found their Web site, how first time and returning customers use the Web site, and what aspects of the buying experience lead to satisfaction and dissatisfaction. Rivals will need to test retailing strategies to see which activities are more effective than others.

4. Once such knowledge has been obtained, e–commerce rivals will race to induce information seeking and trial purchase behaviors, because initially **the marginal cost to acquire a new customer decreases with sales volume**. That is, an e-commerce retailer may spend millions to attract the first one or two percent of its patrons. However, these expenses can be spread over the next 10 or 20 percent of patrons, who follow based on word of mouth and from general knowledge, as the innovation diffuses into society, as the retailer achieves economies of scale, and as experience curves show their greatest effects in reducing costs. **However, at some point, the marginal cost to acquire a new customer can only go up**. To acquire late adopters and laggards will require more effort. New rivals will enter the

market and force customer acquisition costs upward. To summarize this idea, the instructor might put a U-shaped cost curve on the board and note sagely that both legs of the U support quick, decisive actions. The left leg implies "Acquire more customers because our marginal costs will go down." The right leg implies "Acquire more customers before our marginal costs inevitably go up." See Exhibit 1 in this note.

5. Rivalry also centers on retailers' business practices. Business models and plans will emphasize advertising and public relations to generate awareness, with advertising concentrated on the Internet medium because these consumers already are Web-connected. Later promotion experience will emphasize different media to attract late adopters and laggards. Business models and plans will stress the development of proprietary products and services that afford a haven from destructive competition. They will be unique and distinctive, given the embryonic nature of the e-commerce retailing industry. Models and plans also will be flexible, skeletal, and based on speed and first-to-market. A window of opportunity is open, perhaps widest to firms that lack established protocols and policies for doing things. In this regard, business models and plans will stress operational effectiveness over operational efficiency. The immediate and ultimate aim of e-commerce retailers in 1998 is to become **a "standard" that eliminates or minimizes competition before it can develop**.

6. To conclude discussion here, the instructor should call for implications. Students might note that a successful e-commerce retailer in 1998 must be:

- First, fast, and favored by consumer innovators and early adopters;

- Aggressive and predatory, to eliminate rivals before they can be born, grow, or mature;

- Future-oriented, looking at how decisions and activities made now will affect its market position some two to five years later;

- Focused on sales growth-customer acquisition costs, possible experience curve effects; and

- Able to exploit is proprietary operational knowledge.

All of these argue for expansion as soon as possible!

C. **How would you describe Amazon.com's customer value proposition, distinctive competency, and core marketing strategy?**

1. The case's first page contains a statement by Jeff Bezos that succinctly describes Amazon.com's customer value proposition as three things:

EXHIBIT 1

MARGINAL COST CURVE

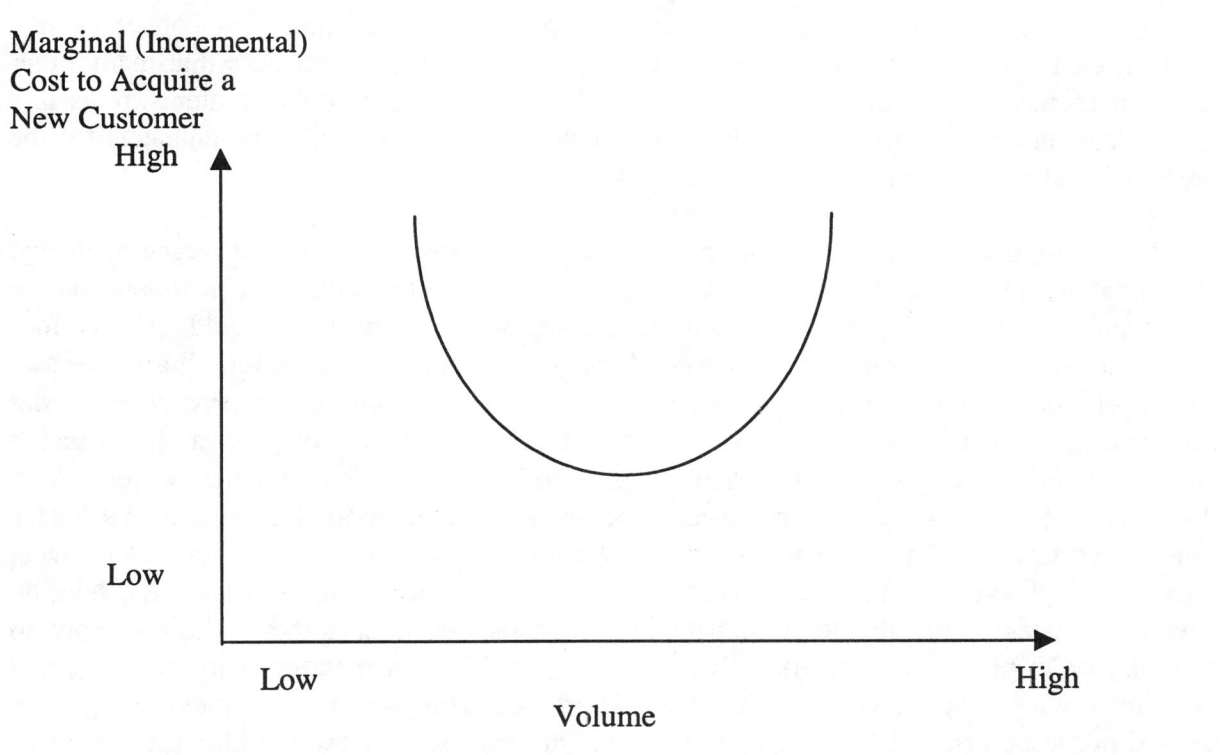

> One is having a larger selection than anyone else. The second is having lower prices or competitive prices. And the third is making the store as easy as possible to use and very convenient. So you save time when you are buying. Also the books get shipped to your home or office. That also saves you time. People are busy in the late 20th century.

These three things—vast electronic selection, competitive prices, time saving convenience—will provide value to many consumers but not to all. Students might note that many other consumers may desire a physical setting where they can browse a book's contents, relax in a cozy place, and talk to friends or a knowledgeable clerk. Thus, traditional channels for the retail sales of books should remain for many years to come.

2. At this point, discussion should turn to Amazon.com's distinctive competency. Just what aspects of Amazon.com's strategy provide value to book buying consumers and are not capable of being copied by book selling competitors? Students should identify four things. First, **Amazon.com has more knowledge of e-commerce operations than does any other retailer.** This knowledge extends to Web site design, order processing, order fulfillment, logistics, payment, privacy, Internet advertising and links (via the Amazon Associates Program), and inventory control (soon to be enhanced with the new warehouse in Delaware). Second, **Amazon.com understands consumer behavior on the Internet better than anyone else.** The company knows how consumers like to shop electronically, what pleases and displeases customers, what types of promotions and links work well, how an electronic sales agent should anticipate and stimulate each customer's desires, how to simplify ordering details (with one-click shopping, an idea not mentioned in the case), and how to provide superior customer service. Third, **Amazon.com has the most recognized brand name and the strongest equity** of all its Internet rivals. New and old customers will go to Amazon.com first (drawn either by reputation or by habit) and avoid a time-consuming, tiring search to save only a few dollars on their purchase. Fourth, by virtue of its premier position in the market, **Amazon.com has a cost advantage based on its economies of scale, experience curve position, and volume purchasing behavior.** Any following competitor must follow Amazon.com into the e-commerce arena at a less advantageous cost position and be prepared to be outspent.

3. Amazon.com's essential marketing strategy must be based on leveraging its distinctive competencies, quickly, to take advantage of existing and new opportunities in the new marketspace. This is a good way to discuss the marketing strategy question, i.e., existing vs. new opportunities. The existing book retailing business needs to be approached from a defensive position, retaining satisfied customers and appeasing disgruntled customers. Key consumer concepts in the strategy would include segments based on repeat purchasing behavior, heavy users, variety and novelty seeking consumers, and habitual and loyal consumers whose switching costs to other sites form a barrier. The existing book retailing business itself needs to be fine tuned and tweaked for profit and for export (to overseas opportunities)—see questions D and E below. Essentially, students should conclude that the

book retailing business to Amazon.com is rapidly becoming a cash cow that should be nurtured and utilized for cash flows needed elsewhere in the company.

4. New opportunities represent offensive strategies. The case identifies three possibilities—international expansion, online music sales, and backward integration into self-publishing (the details of which are discussed in question E in this note). In general, new opportunities present Amazon.com with greater reward and allow the company to realize a first-mover advantage and pre-empt competition. New opportunities offer potential for revenue increasing and cost reducing synergies in terms of company Internet and warehouse operations. New opportunity synergies extend also to consumers, who will develop a stronger, broader bond with the Amazon.com brand. However, students should understand the risks associated with most new opportunities. The new opportunity may fail, disappointing customers who may take their book buying business elsewhere (not so much a problem for the international expansion opportunity). A failed opportunity will consume resources over a protracted period of time, jeopardizing Amazon.com's core business. A failed opportunity could lead to shareholders and creditors becoming disenchanted and pessimistic, threatening the viability of the firm.

D. Can Amazon.com tweak its business model to make a profit on book sales in 1998? What can the company do?

1. This question can be posed to students at the time of case assignment, with an instruction that they should be prepared to present and discuss their own pro forma income statement for Amazon.com's 1998 operations. Three or four students might be selected to put their estimates on the board and to explain how they arrived at their numbers.

2. Alternatively, a good way to begin this discussion is to ask students, "Who has converted data in case Exhibit 2 from dollars to **percentages**?" Results appear below (ignoring interest income and net income) and should be put on the board in some abbreviated fashion:

	4Q 1997	4Q 1996	FY 1997	FY 1996
Net Sales	100.0	100.0	100.0	100.0
Cost of Sales	80.5	78.7	80.5	79.1
Gross Margin	19.5	22.3	19.5	21.9
Operating Expenses				
Marketing and Sales	24.7	34.7	26.4	38.7
Product Development	6.8	10.6	8.4	14.7
General and Administrative	2.9	5.3	4.4	6.6
Total Operating Expenses	34.5	50.6	39.3	59.9
Proft(Loss) from Operations	(14.9)	(28.3)	(19.8)	(38.0)

Students should make four interpretations (based on either FY data or 4Q data):

a. Amazon.com's gross margin fell slightly more than two percentage points from 1996 to 1997.

b. Amazon.com's operating expenses (fixed costs) as a percent of net sales fell dramatically from 1996 to 1997.

c. Amazon.com's operating loss as a percent of net sales fell dramatically from 1996 to 1997 (despite its rise in dollar terms).

d. Book sales at retail are probably quite seasonal, peaking in the fourth quarter.

A nice next step might be to ask, "Suppose Amazon.com simply continues its present operational activities and plans, what might percentage results for FY 1998 look like?" Students simply might extrapolate from percentages above and estimate a gross margin of 20 percent, operating expenses of (say) 15 to 25 percent, and a profit of plus or minus 5 percent.

3. An alternative approach would be to forecast Amazon.com's revenue for 1998 based on its growth rate for 1997. Case Exhibit 2 shows revenues grew at a rate of 938 percent from FY 1996 to FY 1997. However, students should question whether Amazon.com could grow this fast in 1998. Indeed, Exhibit 2 shows a **fourth quarter** growth rate for revenues from 1996 to 1997 of "only" $66,011/$8,468 or 780 percent. Based on these data, students might estimate that Amazon.com would produce revenues for 1998 that are some five to seven times greater than its revenues in 1998, resulting in forecasts that range from $750 million to $1.05 billion.

4. Other pertinent information in the case is a statement attributed to analysts at Morgan Stanley that Amazon.com should reach "a $200 to $300 million revenue run-rate sometime in 1998/99 and can potentially become profitable in 1999 after burning $25-50 million in cash." The "$200 to $300 million revenue" statement is repeated again in case Exhibit 11, showing Amazon.com with pretax margins that range from 3 percent to 10 percent, depending on gross margin scenario.

In sum, the three approaches outlined in the preceding paragraphs all indicate that Amazon.com should be profitable or at least breaking even in 1998, if it simply continues to follow its present operational activities and plans.

5. However, the case notes that Amazon.com began to depart from its present operational activities and plans in September 1997 by moving aggressively into self-distribution, expanding its Seattle warehouse and leasing a new warehouse in Delaware. Self-distribution would allow Amazon.com to buy some 200,000 to 300,000 titles directly from the publisher and capture the six to eight percentage points of margin (based on the book's **retail** price) normally given to wholesalers. Of course, Amazon.com's operating

expenses would increase as well but the result should be a net profit on sales of perhaps 2.0 percent. That is, the case states that the **average** book wholesaler achieved a net profit of "between 1 and 1.5 percent." However, the 200,000 to 300,000 titles that Amazon.com would warehouse would be the more popular, better selling books. These books would be bought in large quantities and warehoused efficiently and should produce a "warehousing" net profit of 2.0 percent. Referencing a 20/80 principle, students might estimate that the 10 percent of Amazon.com's 2,500,000 titles that would be stocked in its warehouses would account for upwards of 40 to 50 percent of total sales. Thus, warehousing would improve the company's gross margin by almost a percentage point (40 to 50 percent of sales times a 2 percent warehousing net profit). Finally, if Amazon.com's warehouse operations work efficiently while maintaining or improving customer satisfaction, self-distribution achieves an additional competitive advantage that competing bookstore chains will find difficult to match. Their warehousing and payment operations are geared toward shipping larger volumes of books to their own retailers.

6. Despite self-distribution activities, Amazon.com will need to continue its relationship with Ingram Book Group and many of its other wholesalers for the less popular titles. However, Amazon.com's foray into warehousing will put wholesalers on notice that they can be replaced and will serve to keep distribution costs down. Amazon.com probably should **try** Ingram's new "drop shipping" service and monitor it closely to see the impact on cost, delivery time, and customer satisfaction. Drop shipping should add an additional fraction of a percentage point to Amazon.com's gross margin.

7. Students should note that all this discussion reflects a "sales revenue" business model described in Chapter 9. However, gross margins at Amazon.com also can be improved by cost reductions—at some point, the company can consider itself "established" and reduce its efforts to build brand awareness. It may be able to reduce its expenditures on "product development" activities to be more in line with brick-and-mortar book retailers. Also at this point, Amazon.com can exploit its brand equity and begin to sell advertising on its Web site to less well-known businesses, perhaps offsetting as much as half of its own communication expenditures. Suppose, just suppose, that these ideas could be realized in 1998—results might look something like this:

Net Sales	100.0
Cost of Sales	79.0
Gross Margin	21.0
Operating Expenses (same as B&N)	
Marketing and Sales	10.0
(20 percent, but offset by advertising sales)	
Product Development	3.0
General and Administrative	3.0
Net Operating Expenses	16.0
Profit(Loss) from Operations	5.0

This sort of result should end discussion on this question. Most students should agree with a summary point that Amazon.com is close to profitability—if it pursues a "status quo" sort of direction for 1998. However, the company is unlikely to take such an unassertive position—see discussion below.

E. **How can Amazon.com grow profitably? What strategy do you recommend for a two to five year horizon?**

1. A good way to begin discussion here is reference to Chapter 1, Exhibit 1.1, Product-Market Strategies. That is, Amazon.com can grow by using one or more basic strategic approaches: market penetration, market development, new offering development, and diversification. Students usually recognize a fifth possibility, forming strategic alliances via mergers and acquisitions.

2. Concerning **market penetration**, Amazon.com already seems to be doing a good job. A statement in the case says that Amazon.com enjoyed a 58 percent repeat business rate at the end of 1997, superior to barnesandnoble.com's 40 repeat percent rate. Amazon.com can capitalize on its superior customer satisfaction by offering volume discounts, loyalty programs, special promotions, and the like to increase order size and order frequency. However, at some point, the market penetration strategy will cease to produce growth because of market saturation and Amazon.com's sales revenues will stabilize. Perhaps its overall market share will exceed that of Barnes & Noble; perhaps it will not. The conclusion, though, is inescapable—at some point, the market for books purchased on the Internet will mature and any additional sales growth for Amazon.com will be tied to current economic conditions and to long-term population, entertainment, and educational trends.

3. Moreover, **a focus only on increasing book sales to Amazon.com's existing target segment ignores the strategic window open to pursue growth via new offerings or new markets**. Taking the latter idea first, students should reference a statement in the case that the $82 billion market worldwide easily dwarfs the $18 billion market for books in the U.S.. Amazon.com can expand to Europe and perhaps to some other regions where e-commerce is nascent. The company's transfer of customer service and warehousing technology to overseas operations should be relatively easy. Delivery of books to buyers will depend on the postal system and on the private, small parcel delivery infrastructure. Perhaps the two biggest problems will be establishing relationships with overseas book publishers and establishing brand awareness. Thus, Amazon.com's general and administrative costs and its communication costs for a start-up overseas operations would imply that break-even volumes would take at least as long to achieve as it did in the U.S. Also, students should conclude that Amazon.com's expanding to new geographic markets is as much a defensive move as offensive: If the company does not exploit its proprietary knowledge of e-commerce in attractive overseas markets, other firms will achieve a first mover position in markets that are at least as lucrative as the U.S.

4. Again, however, Amazon.com will see its growth rate and its revenues flatten as it achieves a steady state share of the worldwide market for books. Students might be pressed for some number here—maybe Amazon.com can be one of 10 (50?) major players in the sales and distribution of books worldwide. Students might estimate a share of two to 10 percent, achievable in 10 to 20 years.

5. Thus, **the biggest opportunities for growth lie in either new offerings or diversification**. The case describes two possible new offerings: online music sales and backward integration into self-publishing. An interesting way to begin discussion is to call for a vote on the two options. Students should choose online music over self-publishing by a huge margin. In fact, the case itself effectively rules out self-publishing by listing important drawbacks (Publishing books is a low-margin, high risk business that requires skills that Amazon.com does not have; Amazon.com would upset publishers both in the U.S. and overseas if it attempted to compete with them for authors.).

6. The sale of music online is another matter. The case notes that the market for music is more than twice as big as that for books and that online sales would offer buyers: large selections, flexible searching, audio samples, and convenience. Further, no company has as yet established itself on the Internet as a major player with high brand awareness. Amazon.com's customer service and warehousing technology probably could be applied without much difficulty to online music sales. Online music sales would attract visitors to Amazon.com's Web site who might buy books, either at the same time or at some point in the future. However, the case notes two negative points that students might discuss for a bit—would consumers buy music online and would major record labels be too powerful as suppliers? Discussion of these points might conclude that some portion of consumers could easily be induced to buy music online because perceived risk is low, the Web site is convenient, Amazon.com is a trusted brand name, and trial before purchase is easily accomplished. Major record labels may welcome the additional channel for various reasons—sales and profits may increase, distribution and communication costs may decrease, and the channel power possessed by large record chains should decrease. Major labels may recognize the hurdles to e-commerce and be eager to take advantage of Amazon.com's expertise in customer service and warehousing.

7. A good way to structure discussion at this point is simply to pose the question, "What should Amazon.com do with respect to the online music sales opportunity?" These sorts of recommendations should surface:

   a. Understand what buyers of music want—just how important are large selection, low price, and products delivered to a buyer's home or office?

   b. Identify attractive market segments in terms of market potential, socioeconomic characteristics, purchase behavior, and Internet experience.

   c. Research the CDNow site to see if Amazon.com can offer superior customer service.

d. Plan and execute a concept test (based on an Amazon.com online music offering) among several target segments.

e. Develop a business plan(s) and forecast performance under different scenarios.

However, speed is of the essence before CDNow or someone (Barnes & Noble? Musicland Stores? Virgin? AOL/Time Warner?) attains a first or early mover advantage. Decision-makers at Amazon.com might reason that "if we build it, consumers will come" and that the only real issue is "do we have a customer service and warehousing advantage that can extend to music?" If the answer to this question is favorable, then "let's go for it!"

A good way to end discussion is to note that Amazon.com's choice between market development and new offerings strategies hinges more on the company's vision than on its resources. Does Amazon.com want to be the biggest book retailer in the U.S.? In the world? Or, does Amazon.com instead wish to be the biggest hard goods retailer in the U.S.? World? The answer to "that vision question" as of early 2000 (the time of this note) is that Amazon.com wants to become the biggest e-commerce merchant, selling hard goods and infomediary services (aggregation and auction platforms) to worldwide markets.

F. Summary Points

1. Retailing on the Internet has inherent advantages and disadvantages over conventional channels of distribution. Retailing on the Internet has tremendous potential.

2. Successful retailers satisfy their chosen customer segments, repeatedly, conveniently, at competitive prices. In this respect, retailing on the Internet is no different than retailing in a department store, discount store, or specialty store.

3. In theory, value propositions, distinctive competencies, and marketing strategies come together to achieve sustainable competitive advantage. In practice, execution is everything.

4. Efficiency and effectiveness are competing criteria to evaluate marketing strategies and tactics. Efficiency is the appropriate measure for slower growth, more mature operations. Effectiveness is better for dynamic market conditions.

5. Strategic windows of opportunity remain open only so long. The window is more attractive to some firms than others, depending on company resources and distinctive competencies.

6. A paradigm shift in a market offers first-mover advantages to nimble firms equipped with vision. These advantages are accompanied by outstanding opportunities for risk and reward.

G. **Epilogue**

Instructors should recognize that many (all?) students are only a mouse click or two away from Amazon.com's current Web site. Thus, most students will know that since January, 1998 Amazon.com has rapidly expanded into music, DVD and video, electronics, toys, video games, home improvement products (!), auctions, aggregator services, etc. So, students face no challenge at all in finding out what the company did. The trick or focus here is on how decisions on new offerings should be made.

Profitability is a nagging issue that plaques Amazon.com and other companies that market exclusively via Internet/Web-based technology. Amazon.com was not profitable in FY 1998 or FY 1999, despite growing sales (see the chart showing Amazon.com sales and profit/losses), even though book sales did achieve profitability in 1999. In early 2000, Amazon.com and investment analysts projected continuing losses in FY 2000 and FY 2001, even as sales were projected to grow rapidly. However, Amazon.com is expected to record a profit in FY 2002.

Amazon.com expects to register a profit in FY 2002 by focusing on five areas:

1. Improve operational efficiency: On January 28, 2000 Amazon laid off 2% of its staff whose job demands outpaced their skills. By streamlining processes in its distribution centers, Amazon.com expects to cut operational losses from 20% of sales in FY 1999 to 5% or less by FY 2000.

2. Continue to expand product offerings to spur customers to spend more: The amount each of its customers spends is expected to rise from $116 in FY 1999 to $150 in 2002.

3. Keep the cost of acquiring customers down: With its brand among the most recognized on the Web, Amazon.com will lessen its advertising and marketing spending from 25% of sales in FY 1999 to 13% of sales in 2002. As a result, its cost of acquiring each customer is expected to fall from an industry-leading $19, to $16 in 2002.

4. Charge other e-tailers for exposure on its site: Amazon.com has signed six deals since November, 1999 that will net a total of $606.5 million at profit margins of 80% or more.

5. Consider a new revenue streams: It could focus on advertising revenue, providing Internet service for a monthly fee, offering memberships that include extra services, and providing logistics services to other e-tailers.

Sources: "Suddenly, Amazon's Books Look Better," Business Week (February 21, 2000), pp. 78-84; "Marketer of the Year: Amazon.com," Advertising Age (December 13, 1999), pp. 1, 36.

AMAZON.COM SALES AND PROFIT/LOSSES

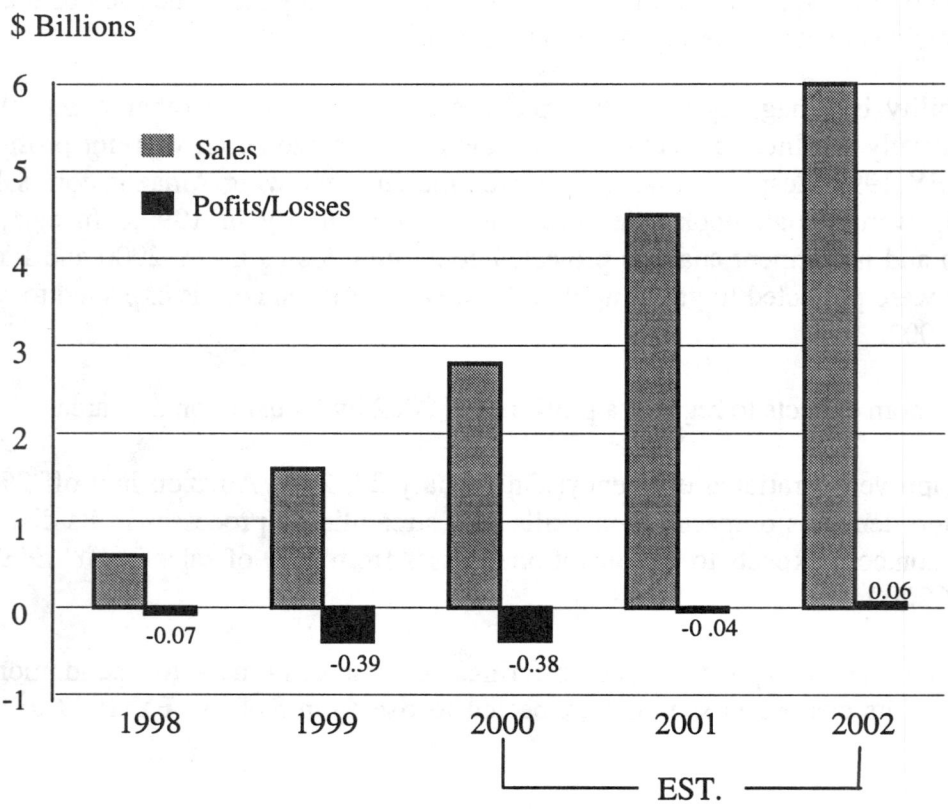

NOTE: Profits are net before noncash items such as minority investments in other companies. Data: Amazon.com, Goldman, Sachs & Co. estimates.

ARROW ELECTRONICS, INC.

Synopsis

In the spring of 1997, Jan Salsgiver, president of the Arrow/Schweber division of Arrow Electronics, a distributor of semiconductors and other electronics components, must decide whether or not to sign onto Express Parts' new Internet broker service. With over $2 billion in 1996 sales, Arrow/Schweber represents the largest division of Arrow Electronics. Salsgiver's boss Steve Kaufman, the President and CEO of Arrow Electronics, wants Arrow to keep its margins above 15% so that Arrow can continue to meet its financial goals.

Because of the structure of manufacturers' incentives, Arrow/Schweber (Arrow) has developed a selling strategy of subsidizing its value added services to ensure margins obtained from commodity product (BAS) sales. The Express proposal presents an opportunity to sell commodity products through a new electronic bidding site. It appears that this new channel has the potential to attract incremental sales to new customers that Arrow had never served. However, there is the risk that the new channel can break down Arrow's current business model by siphoning off the lucrative high margin product sales as well.

This case also deals with the issue of cross-selling and managing a portfolio of products and services offered to customers ranging from transactional customers to relationship customers. Arrow supplies customers in both market segments with commodity, "book and ship" (BAS) products, and with "value added" (VA) products that include services such as programming, field application engineering, etc. It uses its value added services and products as loss leaders to ensure sales of the high margin BAS (or standardized) products. Express threatens to undermine this cross-subsidization model by cannibalizing the high margin commodity product sales from relationship purchasing into a competitive Internet-based auction channel.

This case provides an avenue for discussing the role of electronic commerce in a business marketing firm's channel strategy. The electronics industry has become accustomed to doing business in a highly structured way, with a careful balance of power between manufacturer and distributor. The emergence of the Internet presents a challenge to Arrow's (a traditional distributor) value proposition. Arrow has to decide on how it wants to respond to the Internet-based electronic commerce.

This note was prepared by Professor Das Narayandas for the sole purpose of aiding classroom instructors in the use of Arrow Electronics Inc. It provides analysis and questions that are intended to present alternative approaches to deepening students' comprehension of business issues and energizing classroom discussion. Copyright © 2000 by the President and Fellows of Harvard College. Used with permission.

Teaching Objectives

This case has five teaching objectives.

1. To introduce students to issues present in business-to-business (B2B) electronic commerce and particularly the response of incumbent firms to the advent of the Internet.

2. To examine how Internet/Web-based technology might alter a distributor's approach to creating long-term and mutually beneficial exchange relationships with suppliers and customers.

3. To give students an opportunity to consider twin threats commonly faced by incumbent companies as the marketplace and marketspace converge; namely, cannibalism and disintermediation.

4. To challenge students to make a GO/NO GO decision concerning its presence in the new marketspace.

5. To illustrate that fundamental marketing and financial analyses are necessary when making marketing channel-related decisions, regardless of whether the channels are traditional "brick-and-motor" or electronic marketing channels.

Teaching Suggestions

This case has multiple uses. It can be assigned as a Marketing Channel Strategy and Management case or as a case on Interactive Marketing and Electronic Commerce. The case is particularly suited for graduate courses and, with more direction, undergraduate courses. The case can be used as a group presentation case or as an examination case.

The action orientation of the case lends itself to a spirited and detailed discussion of whether or not Arrow should accept Express's proposal. It is best to take as much time as required to surface all the viewpoints. Those that have run the numbers (the instructor can make sure that this happens by giving student preparation questions that walk students through the numbers) are likely to say "NO GO." Students that support **GO** will say that the Net is here to stay, that distributors are going to vanish (disintermediation), and that Arrow should do it before anybody else. They are likely to say that Express allows Arrow to be anonymous and therefore Arrow will not be compromised.

Before going any further, it is important for the instructor to get the Express business model on the board (see Exhibit 1 in this note which outlines the Board Plan). The instructor needs to make sure that there is consensus on the following issues regarding the Express business model.

EXHIBIT 1

BOARD PLAN

Front board:

      Action   What should Arrow do in the long-term?
GO   NO GO

Middle board:

Arrow's selling approach to customers   Where & how does Arrow Create value for its customers?   The changing nature of VA.

Back board:

Arrow's relationship with its suppliers like Intel.

Where & how does Arrow create value for Intel and other suppliers?

What does Express offer that Arrow cannot?

Left side board:

1. Margin calculation under optimistic and pessimistic scenarios.
2. Break-up of Arrow business.

Right side board:

1. Express model step by step – how does the Express model work?

- What is the flow of information?

- What is the flow of product?

- What does the customer want?

- What does the customer get?

The instructor can then pose the question, "Is Express justified in asking for 6% as its cut?" Given the complexity of issues, it is unlikely that this question will be resolved at this point. The instructor can leverage the lack of resolution by moving the discussion to the next two themes of Arrow's relationships with its customers and its suppliers.

The focus of the discussion on Arrow's relationship with its customers revolves around several issues including the fact:

- that Arrow has a portfolio of customers ranging from transactional to relationship customers

- that the Arrow sales force tends to use VA products to sell BAS products (which means that the students need to understand why BAS product margins are high and VA margins are low)

- the changing nature of Arrow's value added activities (the instructor should push the students to answer the question of whether Arrow is creating enough value for customers to ensure its position in the channel and thereby prevent "disintermediation" or "displacement."

- the impact of accepting the Express proposal on Arrow's sales force.

Having covered these issues, the instructor can circle the discussion back to the questions of whether Express is justified in asking for 6 percent as its cut, and whether it makes sense for Arrow to go with the Express proposal. Here again, it is unlikely that the group will reach a consensus on whether or not Arrow should accept the Express proposal.

Having covered Arrow's relationship with its customers, the instructor can then migrate the discussion to Arrow's relationship with its suppliers focusing on the following issues/questions:

- What is a BAS product? What is a VA product?

- Why is an Intel x86 considered to be a BAS or commodity product?

- How does Intel manage its relationship with Arrow?

- How does Intel manage price? What are design wins? How are they different from jump balls? How does Intel use these different sales situations to keep its suppliers in check?

- Does this mean that Intel is all-powerful in the relationship, and that distributors are at the supplier's mercy at all times? Is there any way in which distributors like Arrow can counter the power of suppliers like Intel?

Having covered these issues, the instructor can now come back to the question of what Arrow should do with the Express proposal. By this time, a majority of the students are likely to be in the "NO GO" camp. They are likely to say that Arrow should not do it with Express but should be ready (or even go ahead) to do it itself.

Student Preparation Questions

The following questions can be distributed to students prior to the class discussion. Their purpose is to focus student attention on relevant case issues and provide guidance in developing a financial analysis.

1. How do the Arrow/Schweber (Arrow) salespeople build their relationship with their customers? Specifically, how do they leverage Arrow's product line BAS versus VA products to add value to their customers?

2. What is Arrow's business model? What value does it add for its suppliers? What value does it provide its customers?

- In order to understand the Arrow's customer management model, it is important that we have an answer to the questions of "what does Arrow sell to whom," and "where does it make money." The following information should provide you with some directions to develop a matrix of sales of book and ship and value added products to transactional and relational customers.

- Arrow sales are $2.31 billion as shown in case Exhibit 7 (first dollar column).

- The case mentions that, under the optimistic scenario, Arrow would lose all its transactional customers. In case Exhibit 7, we find that under the optimistic scenario Arrow will cannibalize $293 million of BAS sales.

- The case mentions that, under the pessimistic scenario, Arrow would lose all of its transactional customers and 40 percent of its relationship customers. In case Exhibit 7, we find that under this scenario, Arrow will cannibalize $601 million of its BAS sales.

- With the matrix of what Arrow sells to whom, and the fact that Arrow makes 10 to 15 percent gross margins on VA products (for your analysis, you could take an average of 12.5 percent). The case states that Arrow makes 20 to 25 percent on standardized (or BAS) products (assume an average of 22.5 percent). You can now calculate the impact on Arrow's profitability under different scenarios if it were to work with Express.

3. How does Express affect Arrow's business model and its selling effort? Will Arrow be able to keep its margins above 15 percent – the objective set by Steve Kaufman?

4. Do you think the Internet is a friend or a foe to Arrow? In what ways can Arrow leverage the Internet to facilitate its sales effort?

5. What is your action plan? How should Arrow respond to the Express proposal? Should they accept or reject it? What other measures should they?

Class Discussion Flow Questions

The following questions suggest the flow of an in-class discussion:

1. What is your action plan? How should Arrow respond to the Express proposal? Should they accept or reject it? What other measures should they take?

2. What is the impact of Express on Arrow's profitability?

3. What is the relationship between Arrow and its major suppliers like Intel, Motorola?

4. What value does Arrow add for customers?

5. What does "value-added" mean in this business? What is the changing nature of value added by Arrow?

6. How would you characterize the supplier-distributor relationship? What value does Arrow add for suppliers?

7. What is the role of franchised distributors? How do suppliers leverage their relationship with franchised distributors?

8. What is Arrow's sales strategy? How does Express affect Arrow's sales force?

These questions are posed on the Board Plan in Exhibit 1 in this note.

Areas for Discussion/Analysis

A. **What is your action plan? How should Arrow respond to the Express proposal? Should they accept or reject it? What other measures should they take?**

    1. The argument for accepting the Express proposal is given in the case as follows. First, Express provides access to customers that Arrow has previously not been able to reach. A related point is that Arrow currently gets about 25% of its sales from transactional customers. If Arrow remains aloof from Internet brokers while its competitors join, the transactional sales may be in jeopardy.

    2. A second argument in favor of the Express proposal has to do with the potential for using the alternate channel for the purposes of segmentation. Value added products attract a different sort of customer from the BAS products sold over the Internet. Currently, Arrow spends sales dollars on obtaining BAS orders. If Express were to channel these orders away from the inside sales force, Arrow might be able to eliminate some of the inefficiencies involved in marketing to transactional customers.

    3. Arguments against the Express proposal are given in the case as follows: First, Express presents all customers, relationship buyers included, with the opportunity to cherry-pick products from different channels at the best possible prices. This has the potential to destroy the cross-subsidization that allows Arrow to reap the benefits of the value added engineering services it provides to its customers.

    4. A second problem with the Express proposal has to do with Arrow's position as a distributor. Given the pricing structure of microelectronics, adding another intermediary has the potential to cut into Arrow's profits. Arrow pursues customers in exchange for better prices from its suppliers. If the only value being added is the presence of a market, Arrow may be in danger of being disintermediated by its suppliers.

    The discussion of advantages and disadvantages of accepting the Express proposal will turn sooner or later to a discussion of the current sales figures and the optimistic and pessimistic scenarios for cannibalization under the accept-Express plan.

B. **What is the impact of Express on Arrow's profitability?**

    1. In order to understand the impact of accepting the Express proposal, the analysis needs to cover.
- Arrow's sales to relationship customers.
- Arrow's sales to transactional customers.
- Sales of BAS products.
- Sales of VA products.

Note: The student preparation questions are very helpful in directing students.

2. Exhibit 2 in this note shows the breakdown of Arrow sales of $2.31 billion. Exhibit 3 in this note shows the step-by-step process used to arrive at the sales breakdown.

3. Now, calculating the base case margins. From the case, we know that gross margins for VA products vary between 10 to 15 percent (with an average of 12.5 percent) and those for BAS products vary between 20 and 25 percent (with an average of 22.5 percent).

Base case overall gross margins =

$$\frac{\$1.443 \text{ bil.} \times 12.5\% + \$.867 \text{ bil.} \times 22.5\%}{\$2.31 \text{ bil.}} = 16.23 \text{ percent}$$

Given that products purchased on the Internet are those where customers are looking for price and do not want any additional support and service, Arrow is likely to lose its BAS products to the Express channel if it accepts the Express proposal.

4. Under the optimistic scenario, case page 534 states that all transactional customers are likely to switch to the Express channel. Exhibit 3 in this note tells us that $293 million is the total BAS business that will be lost. We can therefore conclude that BAS business with transactional customers amounts to $293 million.

The new gross margins under the optimistic scenario are

Optimistic scenario gross margins =

$$\frac{\$1.443 \text{ bil.} \times 12.5\% + \$.293 \text{ bil.} \times (22.5\% - 6\%) + \$.578 \text{ bil.} \times 22.5\%}{\$2.31 \text{ bil.}} = 15.53\%$$

This is still above the corporate objective set by Steve Kaufman.

5. However, things are different under the pessimistic scenario. Now, Arrow will lose not only all the BAS business with transactional customers but also 40 percent of the current BAS business with relationship customers.

Pessimistic scenario gross margins =

$$\frac{\$1.443 \text{ bil.} \times .125\% + \$.601 \text{ bil.} \times (22.5\% - 6\%) + \$.206 \text{ bil.} \times 22.5\%}{\$2.31 \text{ bil.}} = 14\%$$

This level is below Steve Kaufman's objective.

EXHIBIT 2

BREAKDOWN OF ARROW SALES

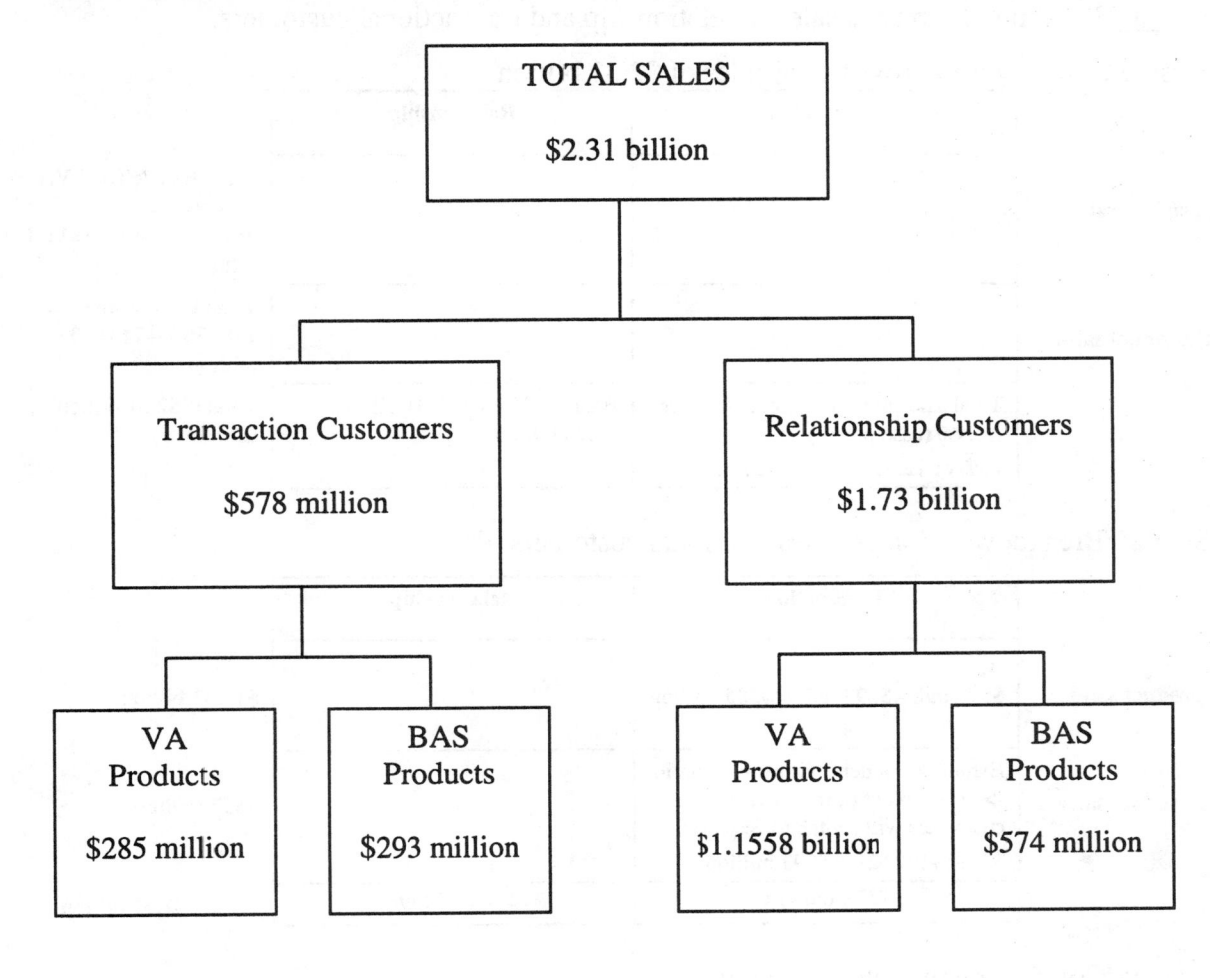

EXHIBIT 3

CALCULATIONS USED TO BREAK DOWN ARROW SALES

Step 1: Breakup of Arrow's sales to relationship and transactional customers.

First, we begin with Arrow's total sales of $2.31 billion.

	Transaction	Relationship	
VA product sales			From Exh 7: Total VA Business = 262+936+5+240 = $1.443 billion
BAS product sales			Total BAS business = 198+364 + 245+60 = $867 million
	Total sales to transaction customers is 25% (case p. 530) 25% of $2.31 billion = $578 mill	Balance 75% of $2.31 billion = $1.73 billion	Total = $2.31 billion (Exhibit 7)

Step 2: Breakdown of sales to transactional customers.

	Transaction	Relationship	
VA product sales	$578 mil. - $293 mil. = $285 million		$1.443 billion
BAS product sales	Exhibit 7: under optimistic scenario -> 100 percent of transactional customers will switch to Express: 59+91+122+21 = $293 million		$867 million
	$578 million	$1.73 billion	$2.31 billion

Step 3: Completing the sales breakdown.

	Transaction	Relationship	
VA product sales	$285 million	$1.443 bill – $285 mil. = $1.1558 billion	$1.443 billion
BAS product sales	$293 million	$867mil. – $293 mil. = $574 million	$867 million
	$578 million	$1.73 billion	$2.31 billion

6. At this point, the following diagram can be used to capture the relationship between product type, gross margins and costs to serve in this business. The Express question has everything to do with the influence of the new channel on the cross-subsidization used by Arrow to maintain the profitability of its business.

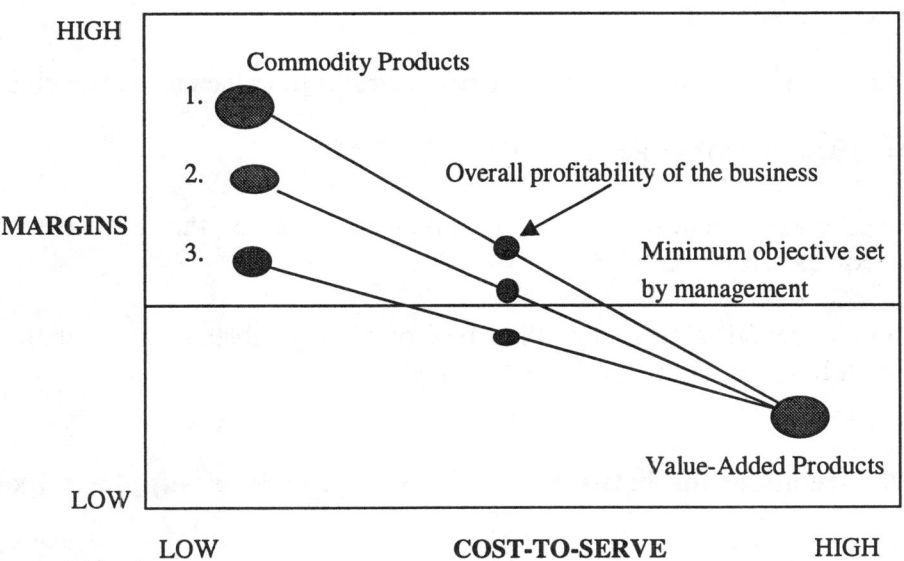

ARROW ELECTRONICS

1. Current Position
2. New position under an optimistic consumption on cannibalization by the Internet channel
3. New position under a pessimistic consumption on cannibalization and current sales by the new Internet channel

7. It is important to take some time out to discuss the counter-intuitive nature of this business with the students. Arrow is making more money with BAS products as compared to VA products. Usually, one would expect firms to make more money on VA or specialty products as compared to BAS or commodity products. Clearly, there is something special about this channel that needs to be understood before any major decisions regarding the Express proposal are made.

8. Despite the numbers suggesting a "NO GO" approach, some students may argue that it is possible that no major distributor will sign on with Express. They will point out that in this case, Arrow is unlikely to lose any sales. This is a natural springboard for the discussion of Arrow's relationship with suppliers, customers, and the nature of value added.

The analysis discussed above does not consider the issue of incremental sales to Arrow from Express. The instructor should be prepared for students that go beyond the numbers presented in the case and consider the issue of Arrow being able to obtain incremental sales. This analysis is likely to proceed as follows[1]:

Letting BAS = current book and ship volume, M be the Arrow book and ship margin, Me be the Arrow Margins through Express, p be the percent of current business that now moves through Express, and x be the incremental volume that access to Express will provide, then the break even condition for using the Express channel is given by

Current Profits =< Profits with Express

Current Profits =< Profits from Existing Customers + Profits from Incremental Customers

BAS * M =< [BAS*(1-p)*M + BAS*(p)*(Me)] + BAS*x*Me

Substituting case values and solving (see Exhibit 4 in this note), the break even condition becomes x/p >= 0.364

When incremental sales are less than 10% or so, any substantial cannibalization of current sales through Express will result in lost money[2].

C. What is the relationship between Arrow and its major suppliers like Intel, Motorola?

1. Arrow's relationship with Intel is the same as that with Motorola, TI, and other major suppliers. Here are some important issues that need to be understood by the students:

- Intel wants to keep track of who uses its products.

- Intel wants to manage price through the channel.

- Intel doesn't want to serve smaller customers directly.

- Intel wants its distributors to provide value added services (logistics, credit, and other traditional distributor functions).

---

[1] This analysis was provided by Professor Carl Mela of Duke University.
[2] Note: this analysis assumes Arrow will not lose sales by staying off the net. Were that to happen, another term would be needed on the left hand side.

EXHIBIT 4

COMPUTING THE BREAK EVEN CONDITION FOR USING THE EXPRESS CHANNEL

Let: BAS = current book and ship dollar sales volume ($867 million)

M = Arrow book and ship margin (22.5%)

Me = Arrow margin through Express (22.5% − 6% = 16.5%)

p = percent of business that moves through Express

x = incremental volume that access to Express will provide

Break even

Current Arrow Profit $=/<$ Express Profit

Current Arrow Profit $=/<$ Profit from Existing Customers + Profit from Incremental Customers

$$(BAS)(M) =/< [(BAS)(1-p)(M) + (BAS)(p)(Me)] + [(BAS)(x)(Me)]$$

$$(867)(22.5\%) =/< [(867)(1-p)(22.5\%) + (867)(p)(16.5\%) + [(867)(x)(16.5\%)]$$

Solving for the break-even condition:

$$x/p >/= 0.364$$

D. **What value does Arrow add for customers?**

1. The instructor can draw the following chart to help students understand Arrow's role in the channel:

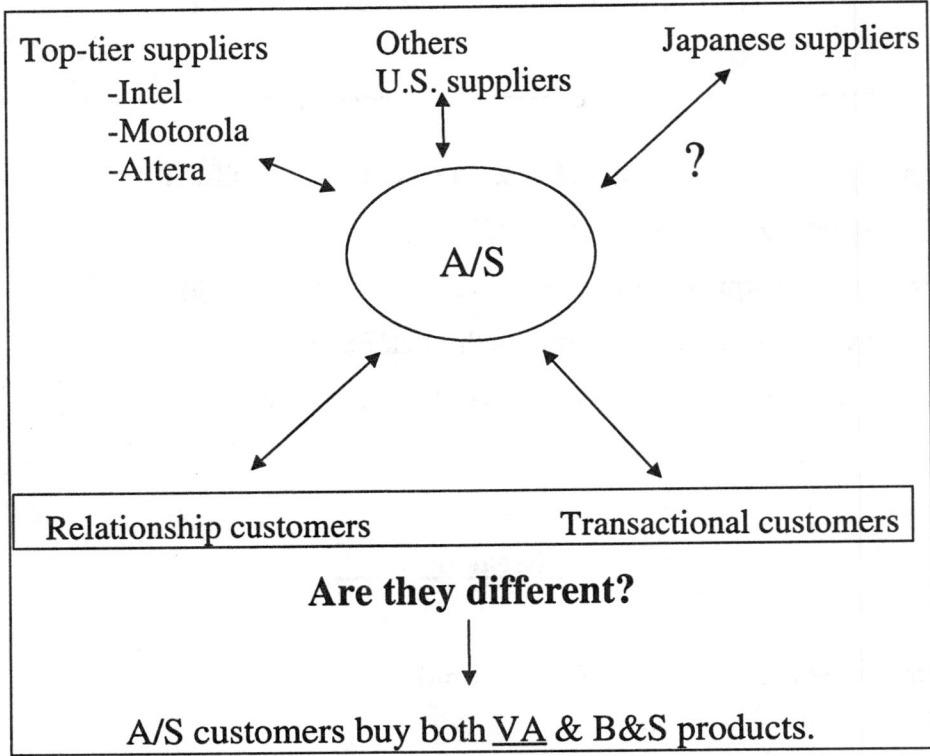

The central part of this discussion revolves around the fact that the nature of the value that Arrow adds has changed over time – Case Exhibit 3.

2. Students are also likely to further divide value added according to the type of customers.

- Small OEMs: small quantity orders with short lead times, credit, kitting, JIT procurement systems.

- Large OEMs: materials management services.

- Contract Manufacturers: programming, supply chain management, delivery service.

- X86 customers: delivery and credit.

- ICP customers: field engineering for highly customized solutions.

3. **What needs to emerge from this part of the discussion is an opinion on whether Arrow has a sustainable position. If the value that it provides is something that the customers want but the suppliers cannot provide, then there is reason to believe that Arrow will be able to keep its place in the channel. If, on the other hand, the consensus is that all the functions provided by Arrow are things that the suppliers can provide directly, Arrow is in danger of being disintermediated.**

In order to be able to make this call, it is important to understand the relationship that Arrow has with its suppliers.

E. **What does "value added" mean in this business? What is the changing nature of value added by Arrow?**

1. The definition of value added may represent a point of confusion for students, as the term can be construed both broadly and narrowly. One place to begin is with the quote from Skip Streber on page 527 of the case describing the evolution of value added services from credit to programming to kitting to the construction of virtual organizations. From this, the students can gather that the act of programming a chip to meet customer specifications represents a value added service on the part of Arrow/Schweber, while the type of chip that requires programming is called a value added product.

2. Over the years, Arrow has not only enhanced the value it adds to the end customer but also the nature of the value added. It has focused on this course of action in response to the demands of both its customers and its suppliers.

3. Using case Exhibits 3, 4, and Streber's comment on page 527, the instructor can explore the question of how, and more important why, has the nature of value added by Arrow changed over time.

4. It is important for the students to recognize that the activities undertaken by Arrow are those that are unlikely to be taken up by its suppliers. Over time, Arrow has enhanced the value it adds to customers by taking on those functions that its suppliers are either not capable of, or, more important, not interested in providing to customers. Unlike products that can offer gross margins of 60 percent or higher, gross margins for value added services are in the low teens or twenties. If these firms were to begin providing value added services, they are likely to face an erosion in their overall gross margins – a fact that would not be very highly appreciated by the financial markets. To suppliers like Intel, distributors like Arrow are invaluable.

5. Given that the case does not provide detailed information on gross margins of products versus value added services, students are unlikely to have thought this issue through. Given the importance of this issue (from the angle of establishing Arrow's role in the channel), I explore this issue in class with those students that suggest that suppliers are likely to take over Arrow's functions and roles. Specifically, I ask questions like .

- What are typical gross margins for products and value added services?

- What would happen to Intel's overall margins if it were to assume the responsibility of providing value added services?

- From the profitability standpoint, how does a supplier like Intel look at Arrow's role in the channel?

F. How would you characterize the supplier-distributor relationship? What value does Arrow add for suppliers?

1. The case discusses several ways in which Arrow adds value for its suppliers, some of which represent the general value proposition presented by distributors to suppliers, and other of which are more specific to the microelectronics industry. One place to begin is the quote on page 525 of the case in which Salsgiver explains the two fundamental needs that suppliers want distributors to fulfill: "to win business in their commodity products to help them grow and gain both profit and market share" and "to represent their new technologies and products to our customers."

The main areas discussed in the case are listed below from general to specific.

- Aggregating small customer demand. Microelectronics manufacturers generally serve only their larger customers directly, finding it more cost effective to let distributors maintain the order processing capacity necessary to address the multitude of small orders originating from small customers.

- Providing credit. Suppliers generally do not see providing credit as a core competency and are therefore reluctant to maintain the facilities necessary to support that service in-house.

- Providing value added services that customers want but that are not cost effective for suppliers to provide. This includes not only logic programming but materials management for large OEMs as well (see case page 4).

- Providing data on small customers for suppliers. On case page 7, Salsgiver comments that "an operation in someone's garage this year could be the multi-billion dollar giant five years from now," a situation that makes suppliers very interested in who is buying what.

- Generating demand as customers move from transactional buying to relational buying.

2. The supplier's power over the distributor is first and foremost the power of the franchise: without the brand-name products that the customers desire, the distributor is out of the game. The supplier exercises this power when the customer asks for a referral by

prioritizing among its recommended distributors; and when the distributor calls for a price, by returning the call in a timely fashion or not.

3. The distributor's power is in its knowledge of the customer and control over information about them. The distributor is particularly powerful when providing value added services to the customer in conjunction with a purchase. Here, the distributor will often have multiple sources for a BAS product, and exercises power in its selection of a supplier. As well, distributors are the ones who discover the garage operations that have the potential to grow into large future customers by cultivating a taste for a particular manufacturer's product among such customers. Arrow maintains some measure of control over the future demand for their suppliers' products.

G. What is the role of franchised distributors? How do suppliers leverage their relationship with franchised distributors?

1. Intel has few franchised distributors – only products bought through these distributors will carry warranty. By doing so, Intel reduces inter-distributor rivalry. Also, by making Arrow & Avnet & other franchised distributors call in each time to obtain discount from Intel, Intel is able to obtain critical customer-related information. This is a great example of how the firm can control its markets even when using an indirect channel of distribution. Also, Intel is able to control PRICE & prevent any PRICE war that leads to price erosion[3].

2. From Intel's viewpoint, if Arrow went on Express's auction site, then Intel loses complete control over customer data. Also, it risks PRICE EROSION. Finally, if all that Arrow provides is a listing on Express's Web-site, then Intel doesn't need Arrow. Therefore, from a strategic viewpoint, Arrow shouldn't work with Express since it risks losing its FRANCHISED distributor status. Express is good for non-franchised distributors who don't have access to Intel products.

3. Interestingly, why is Express coming to Arrow rather than going directly to suppliers like Intel? They tried. It did not work. Suppliers did not want to do business with them.

---

[3] There are interesting implications of how suppliers like Intel manage pricing. Some students are likely to question the legality of this structure.

H. What is Arrow's sales strategy? How does Express affect Arrow's sales force?

1. Arrow and other franchised distributors know that suppliers like Intel are going to work hard to prevent BAS product margins from going down. With that in mind, Arrow <u>or</u> Avnet goes to its customers (who buy BAS and VA products) with the following proposal:

> If you buy your BAS products from me (and you know that you are not likely to get a better price from any other distribution), then I will give you a discount on the VA programming services, etc., to you.

2. It is easy to see how, between Arrow and Avnet, there will be a complete erosion of margins on VA products. Very soon, the incumbent distributor is giving away VA services (leading to low margins on VA products) to ensure their BAS business.

3. Imagine now what happens when Arrow goes to Express. Arrow's salesforce lose their major (actually, only) trump card. From this angle, Express once again is a bad idea.

I. Epilogue

Arrow decided not to go ahead with the Express proposal. But they did decide to develop their own Internet strategy and set up ChipCenter.com (www.chipcenter.com) along with Avnet and other large distributors. Express was not able to get the support of other franchised distributors and this dramatically affected the degree of their success. The limited business conducted on Express's site was limited to products made by second tier (and lower) suppliers and they have now got niched as an electronic broker of low volume, low margin commodity components.

At this point the instructor can distribute the company press release that discusses the formation of Chipcenter, a joint venture set up by Arrow Electronics, Aspect Development, Avent, and CMP media. The press release is available at .

http://www.chipcenter.com/about/pr_042699_0.html

Arrow and its main competitors want to develop a <u>PORTAL</u> for electronic designers. In essence, the distributors are now trying to use the web to educate customers, provide product info, etc. The instructor can challenge the students by asking the following questions:

- Is this a good move by Arrow?
- What do you think Arrow is trying to achieve by setting up Chipcenter?
- Is this the next level in the changing nature of value added by distributors like Arrow?
- If you are a supplier to Arrow, do you like this move?

VECTOR MARKETING CORPORATION: "CUTCO, THE WORLD'S FINEST CUTLERY"

Synopsis

In early 2000, executives from ALCAS Corporation and Vector Marketing Corporation were considering whether to use the Internet (specifically the World Wide Web or "Web") as an additional channel for marketing company products. ALCAS Corporation is a privately held company with four wholly owned subsidiaries, of which Vector Marketing Corporation is one. Collectively, the companies manufacture and market CUTCO cutlery, extremely high quality and distinctive cutting utensils, tableware, and gardening tools.

To date, CUTCO products were primarily marketed through direct selling—person-to-person selling away from a fixed business location—although this approach was supplemented by selective catalog marketing. (See Robert A. Peterson and Thomas Wotruba, "What is Direct Selling? Definition, Perspectives, and Research Agenda," *Journal of Personal Selling and Sales Management*, 16 (Fall), pp. 1-16, for insights on direct selling as a marketing strategy.) For a variety of reasons, the issue of whether to use the Web to market CUTCO cutlery and, if so, how, was a very critical and complex one for ALCAS and Vector executives.

The issue was critical because Michael Lancellot, CEO of Vector Sales North America, and Erick Laine, Chairman and CEO of ALCAS Corporation, were committed to doubling Vector's revenues in the next five years. While revenues were increasing, the rate at which they were increasing was decreasing and in the last two years was less than that of the direct selling industry as a whole. Unless some change was made in marketing strategy, the corporate revenue target would probably not be achieved.

The issue was complex because of the nature of the direct selling process. The direct selling process is very fragile, and any disruptions can be very de-motivating to a sales force, especially one like Vector's that consists of independent contractors. To the extent that any Web-based marketing channel is perceived by the sales force as a competing channel or as a potential replacement for it, sales force morale would be damaged and corporate revenues might actually decline. Thus, an underlying theme in the case is that of **channel disintermediation**, the partial or complete elimination or bypassing of channel intermediaries (the sales representatives in this instance).

Teaching Objectives

This case has three general teaching objectives:

1. To introduce students to a ubiquitous yet often ignored approach to marketing consumer goods and services—direct selling.

2. To provide an opportunity for students to contrast two diametrically opposed approaches to marketing—a "person-to-person" approach (i.e., direct selling) and a "machine-to-person" approach (i.e., Web-based marketing).

3. To emphasize the importance of taking nonquantifiable factors into account when considering a new marketing strategy.

Teaching Suggestions

Students find this case to be enjoyable for several reasons. The primary decision issue to be addressed, whether to add a Web-based marketing channel (and, if so, how to employ it), is fairly straightforward. (Even though the case opens with mention of two other decision issues, how much emphasis to place on international versus domestic marketing programs and what new products to add to the corporate portfolio, the focus of the case is unequivocally on the Web.) Moreover, the case is relatively brief, and the level of quantitative analyses required is minimal (and somewhat transparent, although illuminating). Thus, because of these characteristics, the case is perhaps more appropriate for undergraduate students than for graduate students. Also, because of these characteristics, the case can serve as the basis of either a midterm or a final examination.

A second reason students enjoy the case is that it deals with the Web (and/or Internet). They are faced with a very relevant and deceptively simple issue: is it necessary for an established firm to add a Web-based marketing capacity to be successful in the future? Because of the current allure and popularity of the Web (and/or Internet) as a potentially powerful marketing tool, students tend to react positively to the possibility of Vector's immediate adoption of it as a revenue enhancer or generator. What tends to be downplayed is the potential effect of a Web-based marketing channel on the present marketing approach of direct selling. Note: students should be encouraged to visit the various websites mentioned in the case. Doing so increases involvement (but may sidetrack the case discussion!).

However, perhaps the main reason that students enjoy the case is that (1) they are likely to know someone who has sold CUTCO products, (2) their parents or relatives may have purchased CUTCO products, and/or (3) they have personally sold CUTCO products. In a class of thirty or more marketing students (particularly undergraduate students), it is common for someone to have sold CUTCO products or to have a roommate or friend who sold CUTCO products. Consequently, a good way to begin discussion of the case and "warm up" students is to ask if anyone in the class has sold CUTCO cutlery. (Note: Vector Marketing Corporation is very amenable to having a representative speak to a class and perform some of the demonstrations mentioned in the case.)

Often students approach this case by immediately delving into the Web decision. This approach should be discouraged because it leads to a superficial analysis. Experience with the case suggests that initiating the analysis with a discussion of direct selling provides a necessary foundation or context for highlighting three important facets of the case: the relatively unique marketing approach used (i.e., direct selling using college students), the corporate emphasis on quality, and the nature of the target market. Specific questions that might be used to guide an analysis and discussion include the following:

1. What is direct selling?

2. How would one respectively characterize ALCAS Corporation and Vector Marketing Corporation?

3. How is CUTCO cutlery marketed?

4. What factors should be considered when making the Internet decision?

5. Should a Web-based marketing channel capacity be added? Why or why not?

Areas for Discussion/Analysis

A. What is direct selling?

1. Direct selling is a strategy for marketing to consumers that is a form of nonstore retailing. More specifically, direct selling is person-to-person (face-to-face) selling away from a fixed business location. Seventy percent of all direct sales are made in a residence.

2. Because direct selling is not "brick and mortar" retailing, it has no obvious physical presence. Further, as a "push" marketing strategy, direct selling does not utilize advertising. Consequently, with few exceptions (e.g., AMWAY, Avon, Mary Kay, or Tupperware), direct selling firms are relatively small, privately owned, and not well known by the general public.

3. Of the approximately 9.7 million individuals who are direct sellers in the United States, nearly all are independent contractors (not firm employees), 90 percent only work part-time, and three quarters (73 percent) are women. Approximately 81 percent of all direct sellers are associated with a multi-level or network marketing program (such as that of AMWAY).

4. During the 1990s direct selling industry revenues increased steadily, with the average increase being about 8.7% per year.

5. Although a wide range of products is marketed through direct selling (in Japan—the country with the largest direct selling revenues—even automobiles are marketed through direct selling), the best-selling products seem to be consumables—cosmetics, vitamins and dietary supplements, and cleaning products.

6. The "typical" direct selling consumer is an affluent female 35-54 years of age. Note that the nature of the typical customer is intuitively consistent with the best-selling products in the industry (cosmetics, vitamins and dietary supplements, and cleaning products).

B. How would one respectively characterize ALCAS Corporation and Vector Marketing Corporation?

1. ALCAS Corporation was established as a joint venture between two large, well known, and presumably respected companies (ALCOA and Case & Sons) to manufacture high quality cutlery.

2. ALCAS is presently a privately held company (analogous to the majority of firms in the direct selling industry). It has been in existence for more than 50 years. For more than 20 years the same individual, Erick Laine, has been the company's chief executive. According to its vision statement, a major corporate goal is to be the "most respected and widely recognized cutlery company in the world." These facts, plus the company's history, would suggest that the company is relatively stable and perhaps conservative when making marketing decisions (anecdotal evidence of conservatism includes the fact that ALCAS and Vector executives had been studying the issue of what role, if any, the Internet should play for more than three years).

3. Probably the defining characteristic of ALCAS is its emphasis on product quality. This emphasis is reflected in several ways. It is reflected in the company's stated intent in 1948 to "manufacture high-quality kitchen cutlery." It is reflected in the fact that, over time, the company has virtually eliminated out-sourcing of product components and manufactures its entire cutlery line in-house to ensure consistently high quality products. It is also reflected in the company's lifetime ("forever") product guarantee.

4. The emphasis on quality carries over to marketing CUTCO products. In 1985 ALCAS acquired several independent distributorships that sold company products (the first being Vector Marketing Corporation) so that it could better control and coordinate the marketing process (and, by implication, have higher quality marketing).

5. The mantra of quality in the ALCAS culture is an important feature that would seem to permeate all corporate decision-making, including that relating to the Internet.

6. Vector Marketing Corporation is one of four wholly owned subsidiaries of ALCAS. It is responsible for marketing CUTCO cutlery through direct selling in the United States and Canada and through a catalog in the United States.

7. In 1999, ALCAS corporate sales totaled $130.1 million, which represented a 5.1% increase from 1998. Vector direct selling revenues in 1999 totaled $106.7 million, which represented 82.1 percent of ALCAS revenues and a 4.5% increase over 1998.

8. Exhibit 1 presents the percentage revenue contributions of ALCAS profit centers for the period 1995-1999. Exhibit 2 presents percentage revenue changes for the same period. Both of these exhibits are drawn from case Exhibit 1.

9. Collectively, case Exhibit 1 and Exhibits 1 and 2 here contain insights into the financial performance of ALCAS and Vector. For example, the exhibits illustrate the importance of direct selling as a revenue generator as well as the spurt in revenue that occurred in 1996. They also quantitatively document the changes that occurred organizationally and the changing environments faced by ALCAS and Vector, especially in the international arena.

10. However, even though ALCAS revenues and Vector direct selling revenues steadily increased from 1995 to 1999, Exhibit 2 shows that the rates of increase declined every year. Moreover, when the 5% price increase in 1999 is taken into account, it appears that Vector's direct selling unit sales may have been flat or even decreasing in 1999 since revenue only increased 4.5% over 1998. (Note that the 5% price increases in odd-numbered years were generally equivalent to the annual 3% increases in consumer prices mentioned in the case.)

11. Given the sales and sales trends observed, together with the fact that the sales of Henckels (a major competitor) in the United States had just exceeded ALCAS's domestic sales for the first time, it would appear that Lancellot and Laine were "right on target" when they stated that sales growth was the fundamental issue facing Vector (and ALCAS). The (somewhat optimistic) statements in the case about revenue growth and employee profit sharing, although accurate, should be tempered by the figures contained in the exhibits.

12. Inspection of the operating margins within ALCAS reveal major differences across three major revenue generators. In 1999 CUTCO International had an operating margin of 2.5% (which, based on information in the case, suggests it was at best marginally profitable). The operating margin of the catalog component of Vector was 15%, some six times greater than that of CUTCO International. The direct selling component of Vector had an operating margin of 10.5%. These latter numbers are useful when assessing the viability of a Web-based marketing channel.

EXHIBIT 1

ALCAS PERCENTAGE REVENUES, 1995-1999

Profit Center	1995	1996	1997	1998	1999
Vector (direct sales)	84.6%	82.2%	82.9%	82.5%	82.1%
Vector (catalog)	7.2%	7.4%	7.2%	7.6%	8.2%
CUTCO Int'l	5.6%	8.8%	8.3%	8.0%	7.0%
Misc. Sales	2.6%	1.6%	1.6%	1.9%	2.7%
Total	100%	100%	100%	100%	100%

EXHIBIT 2

ALCAS REVENUE CHANGES, 1995-1999

Profit Center	95-96	96-97	97-98	98-99	Average An. Change
Vector (direct sales)	23.6%	12.3%	8.5%	4.5%	12.0%
Vector (catalog)	30.3%	8.6%	14.9%	13.6%	16.6%
CUTCO Int'l	101.4%	4.3%	6.1%	-8.4%	19.5%
ALCAS	27.2%	11.4%	9.0%	5.1%	12.9%

C. How is CUTCO cutlery marketed?

1. CUTCO cutlery has been marketed through direct selling since the inception of ALCAS. (As mentioned above, direct selling revenues are the largest part of corporate revenues.) This sets the company apart from its major competitors (e.g., Henckels, Chicago Cutlery, and Wusthoff-Trident) that sell through more traditional indirect channels, such as department stores and specialty stores.

2. Initially CUTCO cutlery was marketed by an ALCOA direct-selling subsidiary (WearEver). Subsequently, about 100 small, independent firms marketed CUTCO cutlery through direct selling. With the acquisition and integration of the largest of these 100 independent firms into Vector Marketing Corporation, ALCAS gained direct control over all aspects of the marketing process.

3. Vector has organized the marketing effort geographically. There are four sales regions in the United States, each managed by a vice president and a director of sales. Within each of these regions are approximately 8-9 divisions, and spread across these divisions are some 200 "permanent" district offices that function year round and another 200 branch or summer ("temporary") offices that function only during the summer months. Professional direct sellers manage district offices, whereas college students manage branch offices.

4. Like other direct selling firms, the Vector sales force consists of independent contractors, nonemployee sales representatives whose only compensation consists of commissions from the sales that they make. However, the composition of the Vector sales force differs from those of other direct selling firms in a number of ways. For example, Vector sales representatives are primarily college students who typically only sell during their summer vacations. This means sales and revenues are concentrated in May-August. It also suggests that most of the Vector sales representatives view their selling experience as a temporary job such that they focus on immediate sales; repeat sales and the notion of relationship marketing are not of concern. Indeed, according to the case, 90% of the Vector sales representatives sell only one summer, and only about one sixth of the sales are made to previous purchasers. Interestingly enough, a majority of the Vector sales representatives are males, nearly twice the proportion of males in other direct selling companies.

5. The "typical" CUTCO customer appears to be somewhat older and more affluent than the typical direct selling customer. This is logical for two reasons. First, Vector sales representatives often make their first sales to relatives (parents and/or aunts and uncles) and subsequent sales through referrals provided by customers. Hence, given that the Vector sales representatives tend to be college students, their parents, as well as the parents' referrals, tend to be older than the general population (and the typical direct selling customer). Second, CUTCO cutlery is relatively expensive cutlery. Consequently, it probably has more appeal to affluent individuals than to non-affluent individuals.

D. What factors should be considered when making the Internet decision?

1. There are many factors to consider when deciding whether to add a Web-based marketing channel. Among the general factors that need to be considered are the following.

- **Possible market.** The age and income characteristics of individuals who access the Internet and/or Web seem to be similar to those possessed by CUTCO customers. This would auger in favor of offering a Web-based marketing channel because it suggests that such a channel could reach potential as well as past and present CUTCO customers.

- **Compatibility of CUTCO cutlery with a Web-based marketing channel.** According to the case, products that at least superficially possess characteristics similar to CUTCO cutlery—durability and homogeneity, for example, and tend to be one-time purchases (e.g., books, computer software and hardware)—are among the best Web sellers. This would seem to weigh in favor of using the Web to market CUTCO cutlery. At the same time, however, Vector management strongly believes that CUTCO cutlery needs to be personally demonstrated for its quality and distinctiveness to be fully appreciated. The need for personal demonstrations would seem to weigh against using the Web to market CUTCO cutlery.

- **Competitive activities.** Competitive cutlery manufacturers, such as Henckels and Wusthof-Trident, are already marketing their products on the Web in a variety of ways. It is noteworthy that the major competitor of ALCAS, Henckels, is said to be marketing its products on the Web at a 30% discount to its retail or list price. Although this might indicate a low-price Web strategy, the discount is not much less than Henckels' street price (25% less than its retail or list price). The existence of competitive activities on the Web needs to be considered but is probably not determinative of a decision in this instance.

- **Acceptance of the Web as a marketing channel.** Several major, highly respected retailers ranging from Neiman Marcus to Wal-Mart have recently started offering their products on the Web. The actions of such firms tend to legitimize the Web as a marketing channel and should be viewed positively by ALCAS and Vector executives.

- **Uncertainty.** Several leading direct selling companies, including AMWAY, Avon, and Tupperware, have opened websites to market their products. Each of these companies has taken a different approach to using the Web. That other direct selling companies are in effect endorsing the Web as a marketing channel should be considered a positive sign by ALCAS and Vector executives. Simultaneously, though, that these companies are approaching the Web in very different ways implies considerable uncertainty about the "best" way for a direct selling firm to use the Web as a marketing channel. Unfortunately, because the other direct selling companies only recently started using the Web as a marketing channel, there is little to be learned from their experiences.

- ALCAS experience. Vector is already using the Web as an information channel to communicate with potential customers and to recruit sales representatives. The latter use is very logical given that the sales representatives being sought are college students and most college students have ready access to, and are comfortable using, the Web. Furthermore, Ka-Bar Knives has an operational (albeit somewhat modest) website through which it is marketing its product line. These two experiences with the Web, both of which seem to be encouraging, should provide ALCAS and Vector executives with insightful information and should be viewed positively.

2. The major concern and "big unknown" of the ALCAS and Vector executives regarding the addition of a Web-based marketing channel relates to the reactions of "the field." How would Vector sales representatives and regional, division, and district managers perceive a Web-based marketing channel? Because of the dependency on independent contractors as sales representatives and the personal nature of recruiting, training, and selling, a direct selling organization, especially one like Vector's, is very fragile, and even a rumor can produce havoc. Already the field has heard rumors about company discussions and is worried about the consequences of a possible Web-based marketing channel. If the field believes that a Web-based marketing channel will compete with it for sales or that the company is even thinking about eliminating the direct selling channel, any Web-based effort is likely to fail. The entire direct selling function is likely to suffer if the company is perceived as not supporting the direct selling channel. In brief, the field is concerned about the possibility of disintermediation.

3. Although there is not sufficient financial information available in the case to permit a full-scale analysis, it is possible, by making certain assumptions, to undertake a limited financial analysis. While certainly not definitive, even a limited analysis serves a useful purpose in that it forces consideration of financial boundaries. Three useful assumptions are that (1) all funding for a website will come only from Vector (i.e., ALCAS will not fund website development), (2) website purchases will only be permitted from the United States, and (3) the current operating margin of the catalog component of Vector can be applied as a surrogate for the potential contribution margin of a Web-based marketing channel when calculating an approximate breakeven point. These assumptions seem reasonable given case information. For example, the case states that products sold through a website would have fulfillment costs similar to those of the catalog operation, and a question was raised as to what to do if an order originated from outside of the United States.

4. The case states that the construction cost of a website would range from $200,000 to $500,000, depending on whether it was constructed internally or by outsourcing. (The

issue of timing—how urgent the need was—control, and capabilities of Brett Trent's staff would have to be considered when determining whether to "make or buy.") Can Vector afford to build a website?

5. In 1999, Vector revenues totaled $117.4 million, $106.7 million from direct selling and $10.7 million from catalog sales. However, $7.8 million of the direct selling revenues came from the Canadian organization (6% of ALCAS revenues), leaving a net of $98.9 million in U.S. direct selling revenues. Given that a website would only be operative in the United States, any financial analysis should exclude Canadian revenues. With operating margins of 10.5% for the direct selling component and 15% percent for the catalog component, this means that Vector could conceivably (and optimistically) have up to $12 million that might be available for website construction ($10.4 million from direct selling revenues and $1.6 million from catalog revenues) on an annual basis. (More funds might be available if Trent's staff constructed the website internally, since construction would be spread over a longer time period.) Thus, it would seem, at least theoretically, that Vector could afford to construct a website.

6. What is the breakeven point for a website? At this time there is insufficient information to make any revenue projections, either from internal data or from external sources (i.e., analogous situations faced by other direct selling firms). Besides, any revenue projection would require specifying how the website would be positioned (i.e., accessible by anyone or only CUTCO customers), something that has yet to be determined.

7. According to John Whelpley, the technical overhead (fixed cost) of a website alone would be about $250,000 per year. This means that, assuming the operating margin of the catalog operation can be used as a reasonable estimate of a website's contribution margin, the breakeven point, in dollars, is $1.67 million (i.e., $250,000/.15) for technical overhead, **without** or **before** taking into account marketing overhead. (Although Vector would experience some marketing overhead, many of the marketing costs associated with a website, such as telephone operators and training, would be a function of demand and hence variable.) How likely is it that this breakeven point can be achieved? .

8. Vector filled 509,000 orders in the United States resulting from direct selling in 1999. Since U.S. direct selling revenues were estimated to be $98.9 million (see point 5 above), the average direct selling order in the United States in 1999 was $194.30 ($98.9 million/509,000 orders). In 1999, Vector filled 97,000 catalog orders that generated revenues of $10.7 million. Thus, the average catalog order size was $110.31 ($10.7 million/97,000 orders), about 57% of the size of a direct selling order. This results in an average operating contribution of $20.40 per direct selling order and $16.55 per catalog order. (The implications of these differences for the company are obvious.) Note that approximately 3.5 catalog orders were generated for every 100 customers mailed catalogs (97,000 orders/2.8 million customers).

9. If the breakeven point of a Web-based marketing channel in dollars is $1.67 million and the average catalog order is $110.31, this means that, on average, Vector must

generate 15,140 orders to cover technical overhead. Is a Web-based marketing channel likely to achieve this number of orders? An interesting point of reference is the following. The case notes that the 509,000 orders filled in 1999 effectively represent 509,000 new customers. If these new customers were mailed catalogs according to the existing mailout strategy, and the existing numbers hold (i.e., 3.5 orders per 100 customers and an average catalog order size of $110.31), approximately 17,633 incremental catalog orders valued at $1.95 million would be expected from these customers. Would this happen if a Web-based marketing channel were available?

E. Should a Web-based marketing channel capacity be added? Why or why not?

1. If the Vector goal of doubling revenue in the next five years is to be achieved, it is clear that "something" must be done. It is apparent from the case that the projected increase in the number of households through 2010, 1.1% annually—a possible indicator of market growth—will not "naturally" lead to a doubling of revenue. Doubling 1999 revenue would require revenue of $234,790 in 2004. Even assuming (somewhat optimistically) that its 12.0% and 16.6% average annual growth rates for, respectively, the direct selling and catalog operations can be maintained (a questionable assumption given the last two years' growth rates), revenue will not double. (Applying the 12.0% and 16.6% growth rates to the respective 1999 revenues yields estimated revenue of $211,079 in 2004.)

2. The primary potential benefit of marketing CUTCO cutlery on the Web is increased revenue. For example, since 90 percent of the sales representatives only sell for one summer, the possibility of repeat sales is low and the likelihood that future sales to their customers will be lost is high. Furthermore, any incremental sales through a website would be relatively "inexpensive" since the operating margin would most likely be similar to that of Vector's catalog operation, which is nearly 50% greater than that of its direct selling operation. The primary potential drawback of marketing CUTCO cutlery on the Web is the negative reaction of the field—the regional, division, and district Vector managers as well as the sales representatives.

3. The qualitative analysis generally supports a decision for Vector to move forward with a Web-based marketing channel, even though there obviously is uncertainty present. And, although the results of the limited financial analysis are somewhat equivocal, the most important consideration is the potential negative reaction of the field, a possibility that cannot be ignored or, unfortunately, easily quantified.

4. Apart from the potential problem with the field, the major "downside" to a decision to move forward with a Web-based marketing channel would be its construction cost and the attention that it would require from top executives. For example, both ALCAS and Vector executives would probably have to actively participate in field meetings to assuage the concerns of sales representatives and Vector field managers.

5. Given that Vector should proceed with a Web-based marketing channel, the issue becomes one of not offending the field. Perhaps the best way to proceed is to replicate the process followed when implementing the catalog operation. This means that, at least initially, (1) only past customers should be permitted to purchase from the website, and (2) sales representatives (if active) and their managers should be given some sort of commission if one of their customers purchases from the website, regardless of whether they directly influenced the purchase.

F. Epilogue

There were several major decisions made at the executive meeting. One was to immediately involve key representatives from the field so that they would have input into, and hopefully "buy into," all aspects of the decision. A second was the general agreement to somehow pursue the idea of using the Internet or Web to assist in the marketing of CUTCO cutlery. A third was the decision to build a website internally, with some assistance from consultants, rather than outsourcing the project. (Note that this latter decision is consistent with the corporate philosophy to "make" versus "buy" to ensure high quality standards.)

Subsequent to the meeting, an "e-commerce philosophy statement" was proposed. This statement, which is reproduced at the end of this teaching note (and is suitable for class presentation by means of an overhead), basically affirms that (1) Internet-related marketing activities will only be ancillary and complementary to Vector's current direct selling approach, (2) Internet-related marketing activities will be limited to current CUTCO customers, and (3) Internet-related sales will be commissionable for the sales representative (if active) originating the customer and his or her manager.

In brief, ALCAS and Vector executives decided to create a synergistic marketing strategy wherein the sales representatives serve as the "engine" to acquire new customers, whereas the Internet, in conjunction with the catalog operation, would efficiently service current customers. This strategy was viewed as providing benefits for all parties—customers, sales representatives, and the company.

In March 2000 a pilot test was initiated. A representative sample of CUTCO customers mailed the spring catalog was invited to shop www.cutco-online.com (a special entry code and PIN were required). The test was designed to assess customer reaction to buying CUTCO cutlery on-line and the company's ability to properly service those customers buying on-line. Initial indications were that sales exceeded the expectations of company executives. A second, large-scale test is being planned for fall 2000.

G. **Summary Points**

1. The decision to add a new marketing channel is very complex. Although financial considerations are important, it is often difficult to obtain relevant financial data.

2. The potential impact of a new marketing channel on present firm capacities must be carefully evaluated. Nonfinancial considerations, many of which may be subtle and nonquantifiable, often are the determining factors when deciding on a new marketing channel.

3. Without question, the emergence of the Internet has "changed the face of marketing." Virtually all firms, whether established or new, must address how they will harness and manage the capabilities created by the Internet. Stated simply, the question is not **whether** a firm will utilize the Internet. Rather, the question is how a firm will utilize the Internet.

4. A major issue raised by the prospect of using the Internet or Web as a new marketing channel is that of **disintermediation**, the complete or partial elimination of channel intermediaries (in this instance the independent contractors who serve as sales representatives). The potential implications of disintermediation need to be carefully considered before adopting the Internet or Web as a marketing channel.

VECTOR MARKETING CORPORATION
E-COMMERCE PHILOSOPHIES

E-commerce is a rapidly growing segment of the retail marketplace. In response to this reality, it is important for Vector Marketing Corporation to examine customer interest along with the possibility of increased sales growth and earnings potential that e-commerce could have for both the field sales organization and the company.

Vector's e-commerce philosophies are as follows:

- It is our belief that on-line sales should be ancillary and complementary to our current person-to-person, direct sales method. This primary approach has and will continue to enable us to build a vibrant and successful business because of benefits such as:

    - The ability to generate new customers
    - High impact visual demonstrations
    - Personal contact with customers
    - Creative selling approach
    - Increased average order

For all of these reasons, we feel it is critically important to maintain this existing method as our primary source of distribution.

- It is our commitment to support the field sales organization by having them share in the profits of these e-commerce sales in a meaningful way.

- E-commerce activity will be limited to current CUTCO customers only.

- A first-time buyer will be directed to the field in the traditional manner. Our Internet presence will increase the likelihood of such leads becoming available for field follow-up.

Reproduced with permission.

PHARMACIA & UPJOHN, INC.: ROGAINE HAIR REGROWTH TREATMENT

Synopsis

On February 9, 1996, the U.S. Food and Drug Administration (FDA) approved Rogaine Hair Regrowth Treatment for sale without a physician's prescription. Rogaine, the only medically proven hair regrowth treatment at the time for men and women with common hereditary hair loss, had been sold as a prescription drug in the United States since 1988. Cumulative U.S. sales of Rogaine since its introduction exceeded $700 million. Worldwide cumulative Rogaine sales exceeded $1 billion.

With Rogaine's patent about to expire in four days, FDA approval of Rogaine as a nonprescription, or over-the-counter (OTC), drug was welcome news to Pharmacia & Upjohn, Inc., the manufacturer of the product. The company also requested the FDA to approve a three-year period of marketing exclusivity for nonprescription Rogaine under provisions of the Waxman-Hatch Amendment to the U.S. Food, Drug and Cosmetic Act. These provisions allow pharmaceutical companies to petition the FDA for a three-year marketing exclusivity if they paid for new research that was necessary to convert a prescription drug to nonprescription use. Anticipating FDA approval for nonprescription Rogaine and a favorable FDA response to its petition for a three-year marketing exclusivity, company officials outlined an aggressive marketing program for the Rogaine brand scheduled for an April 1996 launch.

On April 5, 1996, the FDA notified Pharmacia & Upjohn, Inc., that its request for a three-year period of marketing exclusivity for nonprescription Rogaine had been denied. The FDA also approved three competing generic versions of Rogaine containing a 2-percent solution of minoxidil -- the active chemical ingredient in Rogaine that stimulates hair regrowth--for sale without a prescription. Generic products, which are supposed to be medically equivalent to brand-name products, are typically priced 25 percent to 50 percent less than brand-name products and not advertised. On April 12, 1996, Pharmacia & Upjohn, Inc. filed a lawsuit against the FDA. The company asked the Court to reverse the FDA's ruling on the matter of market exclusivity for nonprescription Rogaine and to order the FDA to defer approval of competing nonprescription products containing minoxidil. On April 30, 1996, the Court ruled in favor of the FDA. This meant that Rogaine would not have a three-year marketing exclusivity and three competing generic products had approval for sale without a prescription in the U.S.

The conversion of Rogaine from a prescription to nonprescription status, the FDA's denial of a three-year marketing exclusivity for Rogaine, and FDA approval of generic products, raised a variety of related market and marketing questions. First, what unit and dollar sales potential for the product (minoxidil) category as a whole might be expected now that a minoxidil treatment for hair regrowth no longer required a prescription and "generic" products could become available? Second, how will the loss of U.S. patent protection and marketing exclusivity that Rogaine had enjoyed and competition from generics affect sales of the Rogaine brand? Third, would the U.S. marketing strategy developed for nonprescription Rogaine prior to the FDA's recent rulings need to be modified? If so, how? Nonprescription Rogaine was already being shipped to retailers and the consumer advertising and sales promotion program was ready to be implemented.

This case challenges students to assess the market(ing) opportunity for Rogaine both as a prescription and a nonprescription drug. Market segmentation and targeting play an important role in assessing the market(ing) opportunity. Case information allows students to segment the market on the basis of sex, age, and income. Also, behavioral considerations in the purchase and use of Rogaine can be addressed, including the concepts of perceived risk and the consumer adoption process. These factors combine to allow students to examine the **effective demand** for Rogaine (the ability and willingness of consumers to buy) in both a qualitative and quantitative sense and the role marketing mix elements play in stimulating effective demand. In addition, the role of government in promoting monopolies by granting patents and marketing exclusivity arrangements might be addressed.

Teaching Objectives

This case has four teaching objectives.

1. To expose students to product development and marketing practices in the U.S. prescription and nonprescription pharmaceutical industry.

2. To illustrate how a market(ing) opportunity can be affected by governmental regulations and actions and a company's market segmentation and marketing mix effort.

3. To reify the concept of effective demand; namely, the willingness and ability of prospective buyers to purchase and use a product or service.

4. To challenge students to consider creative applications of the chain ratio method for estimating market potential and product sales for an innovative offering, and perform sensitivity analyses.

Teaching Suggestions

This case has proven to be a challenging assignment in both undergraduate and graduate classes. The case has been used as a marketing opportunity analysis case and as a product management and strategy case. It has been assigned as a group presentation and a take-home examination case.

Previous classroom teaching experience with the case indicates that attention to the immediate issues posed in the case should be postponed until students have dissected Rogaine's performance as a prescription drug. Once done, class discussion can then turn to the "marketing opportunity" for Rogaine as a nonprescription drug. A 75-minute class is necessary to teach the case.

Instructors should read the teaching note carefully to familiarize themselves with the "numbers" in the case. Special attention should be given to case Exhibits 3, 4, and 5 and the accompanying discussion in the teaching note. It is helpful to prepare transparencies of Exhibits 2, 3, 4, 5, 6, 8, 9, 10 and 11 in this note should students get bogged down in the conceptual underpinnings of the chain ratio approach and/or the calculations. **It is important that instructors emphasize that the "numbers" illustrate reasonable and defensible estimates; however other estimates can be made when employing a chain ratio approach for estimating market potential and forecasting sales. Indeed, students should be encouraged to use different estimates, provided they can provide reasonable and defensible assumptions for doing so.**

Specific questions that can be posed to students prior to or during a class discussion are:

1. How would you characterize the various treatments for balding? Why do people use these treatments?

2. How effective is Rogaine as a treatment for balding and for whom?

3. How will the buying process for nonprescription Rogaine differ from the buying process for prescription Rogaine?

4. Describe and explain the U.S. sales performance of Rogaine through 1995. Was the marketing objective of "maximizing" sales of Rogaine in the U.S. market achieved?

5. How realistic is the belief, expressed by Pharmacia & Upjohn officials, that nonprescription Rogaine (minoxidil) sales of $1 billion were possible over five years given the marketing program for the brand?

6. How might the loss of U.S. patent protection and marketing exclusivity enjoyed by Rogaine since its introduction and competition from generic products affect sales of the Rogaine brand?

7. Will the U.S. marketing strategy developed for nonprescription Rogaine prior to the FDA's recent rulings need to be modified? If so, how?

Area for Discussion/Analysis

A. **How would you characterize the various treatments for balding? Why do people use these treatments?**

   1. Treatments for balding and thinning hair is a $1.3 billion-a-year business in the U.S.. There are three major treatments. Hairpieces or wigs represent $400 million in annual sales, including periodic cleaning and styling. Hair transplants represent another $800 million in annual sales. Finally, prescription drugs represented by Rogaine, produce annual sales of $96 million (in 1995). In addition, some $300 million is spent annually for "hair-thickening" products such as shampoos, lotions, and conditioners. Another $100 million is spent for elixirs, teas, horse-hoof ointments and the like to treat hair loss!

   2. Only one treatment has been shown to stimulate hair growth in men and women. Until 1996, Rogaine was the only drug approved by the FDA that could make this claim.

   3. There are a variety of reasons why people with thinning hair or with male pattern baldness (men) and diffuse hair loss (women) might use these treatments. For instance, people undergoing medical treatment might experience temporary hair loss from medication or therapy. For them, hairpieces or wigs are typically used. For the bulk of treatments, however, the purchase is made by healthy men and women. The treatment is a **discretionary purchase** made to address a common hereditary condition. Most treatments are cosmetic and the purchase motive(s) are many and varied. An instructor might ask students why someone might purchase this product and other treatments (hairpieces or hair transplants).

B. **How effective is Rogaine as a treatment for balding and for whom?**

   1. This question focuses student attention on data in the case that is somewhat contradictory depending on the time and the source, e.g. Pharmacia & Upjohn and the FDA. For example, early company studies (pre-1982) indicated that 48 percent of 18-49 year old white men in good health reported "moderate to dense hair growth" after one year of use. However, clinicians and the FDA judged that 39 percent of the patients had achieved "moderate to dense hair growth."

   2. Exhibit 1 in this note summarizes more recent clinical studies reported in the case. Instructors will recognize these as "after-only with control group" experimental designs. These experiments indicate that a large percentage of men and women report minimal hair regrowth using a placebo. These percentages are very close to the percentages for those using Rogaine. A noticeable difference exists in the reported incidence of "moderate to dense hair regrowth" between the experimental and control group for men and women. Therefore, the sex of the user appears to determine "effectiveness."

   3. It is noteworthy that the FDA in 1996 approved Rogaine as a nonprescription drug noting that Rogaine resulted in "meaningful" hair growth in 25 percent of men and 20 percent

EXHIBIT 1

SUMMARY OF ROGAINE "EFFECTIVENESS" STUDIES

Pharmacia & Upjohn Male Study

Experimental Group	Control Group
Among mostly white men between the ages of 18 and 49 with moderate hair loss...	Among mostly white men between the ages of 18 and 49 with moderate hair loss...
26% reported moderate to dense hair regrowth using Rogaine for 4 months	11% reported moderate to dense hair regrowth using a Placebo for 4 months
33% reported minimal regrowth using Rogaine for 4 months	31% reported minimal regrowth using a Placebo for 4 months

Pharmacia & Upjohn Female Study

Experimental Group	Control Group
Among mostly white women between the ages of 18-45 with mild to moderate hair loss ...	Among mostly white women between the ages of 18-45 with mild to moderate hair loss...
19% reported moderate hair regrowth using Rogaine for 8 months	7% reported moderate hair regrowth using a Placebo for 8 months
40% reported minimal hair regrowth using Rogaine for 8 months	33% reported minimal hair regrowth using a Placebo for 8 months

of women. These figures are very close to the moderate to dense hair regrowth percentages for women and men in Pharmacia & Upjohn studies.

4. On a final note, instructors might find it useful to digress on the notion of "perception" with respect to reported hair regrowth. It is likely that the reported hair growth represented some perceptual bias on the part of users. This is evident in the control group studies described in Exhibit 1 in this note with the incidence and nature of reported hair regrowth using a placebo.

5. Other variables, in addition to sex, also influence Rogaine's effectiveness:

- Rogaine appears to be more effective for younger people who are just beginning to evidence hair loss. According to the case, "Hair growth appeared to be more pronounced for patients under 30 years of age and those in the early stages of male pattern baldness progression."

- Rogaine only treats male pattern baldness, a condition that accounts for 95 percent of hair loss cases among men and women in the U.S.

- Rogaine is a life-time treatment. If Rogaine is not applied twice daily, hair loss results.

C. How will the buying process for nonprescription Rogaine differ from the buying process for prescription Rogaine?

1. The purpose of this question is to get students thinking about how prospective Rogaine buyers actually go about making a purchase decision. For either a prescription or a nonprescription drug the buying process is triggered by **problem recognition** -- the difference between an actual state (thinning hair) and a desired state (full head of hair). Problem recognition might cause individuals to seek out and attend to information that provides a solution such as advertising for "hair-thickening" products or Rogaine. In this setting, the "consumer adoption process" is worth considering:

Awareness → Interest → Evaluation → Trial → Adoption

2. For prescription Rogaine, buyers become **aware** of Rogaine through brand advertising (or word-of-mouth). If their **interest** is perked, due to claims made for the product, they will seek the advice of a physician at which time a physician **evaluation** is made as to whether Rogaine might be an appropriate treatment. If the physician does not think so, no prescription is given and product trial doesn't happen. However, **trial** will result if the physician evaluation is positive. If there is perceived hair regrowth, visits to physician coupled with renewed prescriptions makes for **adoption**. "Perceived risk" also plays a role. That is, uncertainty about the efficacy of the treatment and the amount at stake (financial cost) will also dictate trial and adoption. The greater the perceived risk, the less likely that consumers will try the product or continue usage.

3. This outline highlights the role of a physician with a prescription drug. A physician can affect consumer evaluation of the product. They also can act as an influencer and/or gatekeeper in terms of encouraging or discouraging product trial.

4. For nonprescription Rogaine, the "consumer adoption process" remains the same, but the physician is removed as an evaluator of the product and a patient's condition and as an influencer and/or gatekeeper in terms of product trial. This could mean that product trial will increase without physician involvement. Furthermore, without a prescription, the consumer cost of Rogaine drops because the cost (and "hassle") of physician visits is eliminated.

D. **Describe and explain the U.S. sales performance of Rogaine through 1995. Was the marketing objective of "maximizing sales of Rogaine in the U.S. market" achieved?**

1. Case Exhibit 1 displays Rogaine U.S. sales through 1995. As shown, Rogaine sales grew through 1992. In 1992, Rogaine was introduced for women after FDA approval in 1991 which produced an 18 percent sales jump and a sales peak. Sales declined in 1993 by about 31 percent, then increased by 14 percent and plateaued at $96 million in 1994 and 1995.

2. After describing the Rogaine sales history, students might be asked: "What factors can you identify that might explain Rogaine's sales performance?" It is here where students will draw on information contained in the case under the heading: Prescription Drug Marketing Program for Rogaine Hair Regrowth Treatment. This discussion details the target market(s) sought and elements of the marketing mix. Students can be expected to comment on the advertising program and pricing, in particular. We have found it helpful in a class discussion setting to frame student comments/observations within the "consumer adoption process" sequence described in "C" earlier.

3. The behavioral discussion should naturally lead to recognition of other factors that help explain Rogaine's sales performance. These factors will (and should) include:

- The estimated number of balding men (40 million) and women (20 million) in the U.S.

- The type of balding (male pattern baldness) for which Rogaine is applicable: 95 percent of balding in men and women is attributed to male pattern baldness.

- The incidence of seeking treatment among balding men (9.9%) and women (13.3%)

- The incidence of achieving "meaningful" hair regrowth among men (25%) and women (20%) according to the FDA.

- The annual consumer expenditure for Rogaine treatment (one-year supply is $600 to $720 at retail less pharmacist margin of 10 percent, say $540 to $648), is say $594 at manufacturer prices.

- Consideration of a potential users' income, or ability to pay $600 to $720 per year plus physician visit fees which brings the total annual cost to $800 to $900 per year. This factor relates to a consumer's ability to buy.

These factors, coupled with Rogaine's broadening target market -- 25 to 49 year old men first, then 25 to 49 year old women -- also help to explain Rogaine's sales performance. How?

It is reasonable to assume that Rogaine sales volume is a function of the number of men and women with male pattern baldness who try the product and find that it produces "meaningful" hair regrowth. Unit volume results from the trial and continued use of Rogaine on a regular basis - one bottle per month or 12 bottles per year. Dollar sales volume is then annual unit volume times the annual expenditure (about $594 at the manufacturer price).

However, because this expenditure added to physicians' fees brings the annual cash outlay to $800 to $900, it is also reasonable to assume that an income constraint will limit trial and use to those individuals with incomes high enough to pay for the product. Medical insurance does not cover Rogaine.

It is further reasonable to assume that the incidence of trial among the target population (which is linked to the incidence of seeking treatment by men and women) will grow over time due to Rogaine advertising and favorable word-of-mouth activity, but will ultimately reach a point where incremental trial becomes very small (see Exhibit 2A in this note). Further, all triers will not become repeat users since "meaningful" hair regrowth occurs in 25% of men and 20% of women (according to the FDA).

Therefore, sales volume in any one year for a target population comes from new triers and (accumulated) repeat users. Over time, the percentage of sales volume due to new triers decreases while the percentage of volume attributed to repeat users increases. Exhibit 2B in this note illustrates what this phenomenon might look like for Rogaine.

Since more frequent usage among many repeat users does not promote more hair regrowth, the opportunity for sales growth is most likely to come from expanding the target market (population) and building trial. This was done when Rogaine was marketed to women in 1992 following FDA approval.

It is likely that most Rogaine sales in 1994 and 1995 were repeat sales among men and women users since sales have plateaued.

EXHIBIT 2

ILLUSTRATIVE CUMULATIVE TRIAL AND TRIAL AND REPEAT SALES FOR ROGAINE

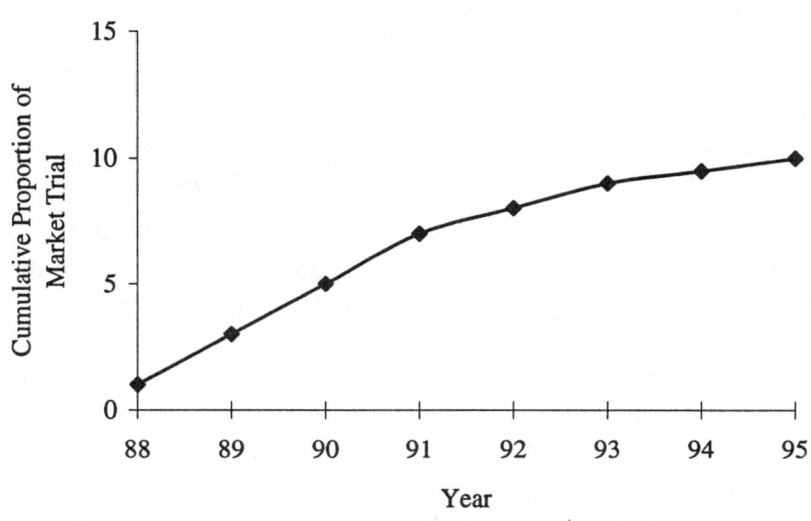

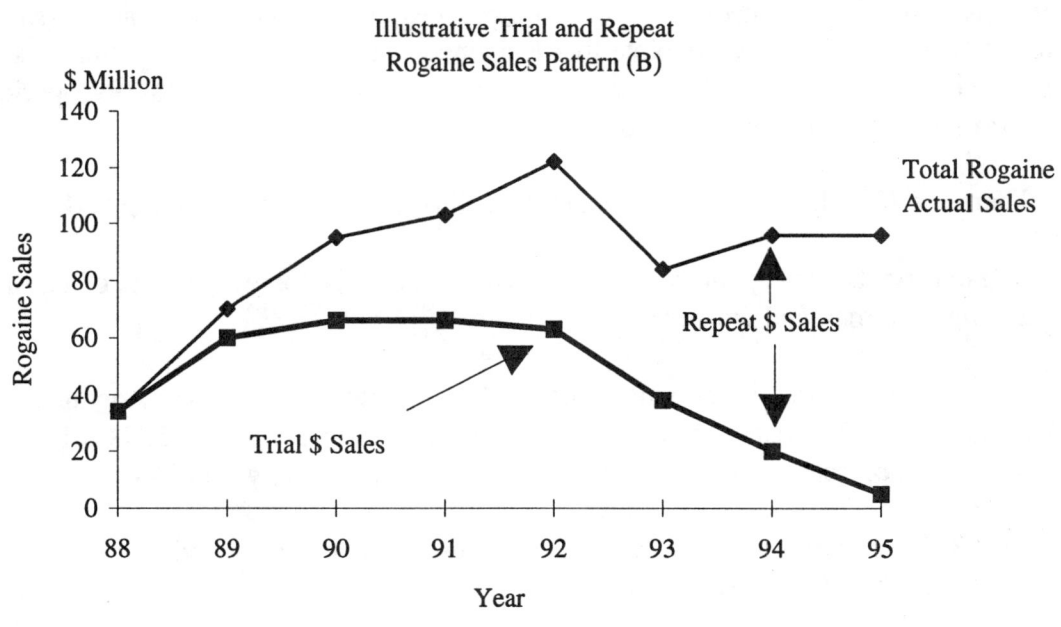

4. Once the discussion related to describing and explaining sales performance is concluded, an important question to pose to students is:

> The announced marketing objective for Rogaine when it was first introduced was "to maximize sales of Rogaine in the U.S. market." Was this objective met?

This question is important for two reasons. First, this wording illustrates "how not" to state an objective. What does "maximize" mean? Second, if the objective was to "maximize sales," then some reference point with respect to what and when is needed, such as maximize sales with respect to its market potential over the life of the patent (through 1995). This, of course, leads to another question: "What was (is) the market potential for Rogaine?"

The case states that Wall Street analysts believed annual sales for Rogaine for men alone could be $400 to $500 million. This has clearly not happened. Cumulative Rogaine U.S. sales of $700 million and cumulative worldwide sales of $1 billion through 1995 are considerable less than Wall Street analysts' estimates. (Note: Although not stated in the case, some industry analysts began referring to Rogaine as "no-gain" in the early 1990s.)

5. The question relating to sales maximization provides an opportunity for students to estimate market potential for Rogaine as a prescription drug for men and for women through 1995. Such an analysis is critical for it provides a basis for assessing market potential for Rogaine as a nonprescription drug as well. Students should be asked to estimate Rogaine market potential using a variation of the **chain ratio method** which is described in Chapter 4.

Several assumptions are necessary to estimate prescription Rogaine market (sales) potential for the period 1988 to 1995. Note that Rogaine's market potential is the same as its sales potential since Rogaine was the only product available during the 1988-1995 period. Each assumption is based on case information:

- There are 40 million balding men and 20 million balding women in the U.S.

- Rogaine treats male pattern baldness, which accounts for 95 percent of balding among U.S. men and women.

- A person's income level will affect a balding person's use of Rogaine. A reasonable and **conservative** assumption is that people with a $50,000 income will be the **primary users** of Rogaine given its cost, plus physician fees.

- The Rogaine target market, and primary user age category, will be men and women in the 25 - 49 year old age bracket.

- Using information in case Exhibit 5, Exhibit 3 in this note shows the calculation for estimating the number of men and women aged 25 - 49 with incomes $50,000 and over, respectively.

- The following application of the **chain ratio method** shows the number of men and women who are likely purchasers of Rogaine:

Male Calculation

40 Million	:	Balding U.S. men (given in case)
x .95	:	95% of balding men have male pattern baldness (given in case)
x .16	:	16% represents the percentage of males aged 25-49 with incomes equal to or greater than $50,000. See calculations in Exhibit 3 in this note.
6,080,000	:	Total number of balding males in U.S. with incomes equal to or greater than $50,000.

Female Calculation

20 Million	:	Balding U.S. women (given in case)
x .95	:	95% of balding women have male pattern baldness (given in case)
x .0282	:	2.82% represents the percentage of males aged 25-49 with incomes equal to or greater than $50,000. See calculations in Exhibit 3 in this note.
535,800	:	Total number of balding females in U.S. with incomes equal to or greater than $50,000.

- Male "triers" will spend $178.00 for four months of trial ($594 for one year's use, therefore four months usage equals $594 ÷ 3= $178.20). Note: Males see results after four months of use.

- 25 percent of male triers will find Rogaine to be effective and continue usage; 75 percent will not benefit from Rogaine per FDA estimates. Male "repeaters" will spend $594 for one-year's treatment with Rogaine, exclusive of physician's fees. These males will become life-time users.

EXHIBIT 3

ESTIMATING THE PERCENTAGE OF MALES AND FEMALES
WITH INCOME EQUAL TO OR GREATER THAN $50,000
(Based on U.S. Census figures in case Exhibit 5)

Calculation for Males

Age Group	Persons in Age Group	x	% with Income ≥ $50,000	=	# of Males
25 - 34	21.3 MM	x	6.4%	=	1.36 MM
35 - 44	19.0 MM	x	17.8%	=	3.38 MM
45 - 49*	6.2 MM	x	22.0%	=	1.36 MM
	46.5 MM				7.46 MM

7.46/46.5 = 16.0%

*6.2 Million men represents one-half of total men in the 45-54 year old age group reported in case Exhibit 5.

Calculation for Females

Age Group	Persons in Age Group	x	% with Income ≥ $50,000	=	# of Females
25 - 34	21.6 MM	x	1.6%	=	.35 MM
35 - 44	19.6 MM	x	3.7%	=	.73 MM
45 - 49*	6.65 MM	x	4.0%	=	.27 MM
	47.85 MM				1.35 MM

1.35/47.85 = 2.82%

*6.65 Million women represents one-half of total women in the 45-54 year old age group reported in case Exhibit 5.

- Female "triers" will spend $396 for eight months of trial ($594 for one year's use, therefore eight months usage equals $594 x .667 = $396). Note: Females see results after eight months of use.

- 20 percent of female triers will find Rogaine to be effective and continue usage; 80 percent will not benefit from Rogaine per FDA estimates. Female "repeaters" will spend $594 for one-year's treatment with Rogaine, exclusive of physician's fees. These females will become life-time users.

- Survey results indicate that 9.9 percent of adult males will seek treatment for their balding; 13.3 percent of adult females will seek treatment. These percentages can be viewed as "cumulative trial rates." These percentages represent cumulative figures as of 1995; that is, they represent a "building" of trial over time. This "building" was depicted earlier in Exhibit 2A in this note.

6. Exhibits 4 and 5 shows the calculation of Rogaine market potential for men and women, respectively, through 1995. As shown:

- The base figures for balding men is 6,080,000; for women, 535,800. These figures were calculated earlier.

- An initial trial in the first year of introduction for men (2%) and women (11%) was set. This trial figure grows with each succeeding year and peaks at 9.9 percent for men and 13.3 percent for women. Note: "Incremental" trial is higher in the earlier periods and becomes smaller over time.

  Although apparently arbitrary, the initial and incremental trial figures are reasonable. The 2 percent male trial figure reflects the initial launch of a new product in 1988 and seems reasonable, particularly since the case notes the initial company concern that Rogaine's prescription sales were low. The 11 percent female trial figure in 1992 is reasonable in that considerable advertising, word-of-mouth, and "hype" has already preceded the Rogaine launch for men. Also Rogaine was supported by a $20 million marketing expenditure for women.

- The number of Rogaine triers is obtained by first multiplying the initial trial percent in the year introduced (for men, for women) and then multiplying the incremental trial times the number of balding males (females) in the target market. Trier dollar volume is calculated by multiplying the trial expenditure for males ($178 for 4 months) or females ($396 for 8 months) times the number of triers. Note: The number of triers decreases in each succeeding year as does trier dollar volume.

- The number of Rogaine repeaters is obtained by multiplying the number of triers times .25 for men and .20 for women. This figure represents FDA estimates on the effectiveness of Rogaine: 25 percent of men and 20 percent of women will

EXHIBIT 4

ESTIMATING ROGAINE POTENTIAL FOR MEN: 1988 - 1995

Year	Cumulative % Trial		Target Mkt. Size	# of Triers	Trier Sales (# of Triers x $178)	Repeat Users (# Triers x 25%)	Repeat Sales (Repeat Users x $594)	Total Sales (Trier + Repeat Sales)	Cumulative Sales
1988	2.0%	x	6,080,000	121,600	$21,644,800	30,400	$18,057,600	$39,702,400	$ 39,702,400
Incremental Trial		3% x	6,080,000	182,400	$32,467,200	45,600	$27,086,400 + $18,057,600		
1989	5.0%						$45,144,000	$77,611,200	$117,313,600
Incremental Trial		2% x	6,080,000	121,600	$21,644,800	30,400	$18,057,600 + $45,144,000		
1990	7.0%						$63,201,600	$84,847,000	$202,160,600
Incremental Trial		1% x	6,080,000	60,800	$10,822,400	15,200	$ 9,028,800 + $63,201,600		
1991	8.0%						$72,230,400	$83,053,400	$285,214,000
Incremental Trial		.5% x	6,080,000	30,400	$5,411,200	7,600	$ 4,514,400 + $72,230,400		
1992	8.5%						$76,744,800	$82,156,600	$367,370,600
Incremental Trial		.5% x	6,080,000	30,400	$5,411,200	7,600	$ 4,514,400 + 76,744, 800		
1993	9.0%						$81,259,200	$86,671,000	$454,041,600
Incremental Trial		.45% x	6,080,000	27,360	$4,870,080	6,840	$ 4,062,960 + $81,259,200		
1994	9.45%						$85,322,160	$90,192,840	$544,234,440
Incremental Trial		.45% x	6,080,000	27,360	$4,870,080	6,840	$ 4,062,960 + $85,322,160		
1995	9.9%						$89,385,120	$94,255,200	$638,486,640
Totals				601,920	$107,141,760	150,480	$531,344,880	$638,486,640	

EXHIBIT 5

ESTIMATING ROGAINE POTENTIAL FOR WOMEN: 1988 - 1995

Year	Cumulative % Trial		Target Mkt. Size	# of Triers	Trier Sales (# of Triers x $178)	Repeat Users (# Triers x 25%)	Repeat Sales (Repeat Users x $594)	Total Sales (Trier + Repeat Sales)	Cumulative Sales
1992	11%	x	535,800	58,938	$23,339,448	11,788	$7,002,072	$30,341,520	$30,341,520
Incremental Trial	1%	x	535,800	5,358					
1993	12%	x		5,358	$2,121,768	1,072	$ 636,768 + $7,002,072	$ 9,760,608	$ 40,102,128
Incremental Trial	1%	x	535,800	5,358			$7,638,840		
1994	13%	x		5,358	$2,121,768	1,072	$ 636,768 + $7,638,840	$10,397,376	$50,499,504
Incremental Trial	.3%	x	535,800	1,607			$8,275,608		
1995	13.3%			1,607	$636,372	320	$ 190,080 + $8,275,608 $8,465,688	$ 9,102,060	$ 59,601,564
Totals				71,261	$28,219,356	14,252	$31,382,208	$59,601,564	

achieve "meaningful" hair regrowth. Repeat dollar sales is calculated by multiplying the estimated annual Rogaine expenditure for regular users ($594) times the number of Rogaine repeaters. Since regular users (repeaters) will continue to use Rogaine, the cumulative repeat dollar volume grows by adding repeat volumes from previous periods.

- Total dollar sales in each year is the sum of trier dollar sales and accumulated repeat dollar sales (for each year and previous years).

7. Inspection of Exhibits 4 and 5 in this note reveals the following conclusions related to Rogaine's market (sales) potential, given the assumptions stated:

- A total of 601,920 male triers were estimated to use Rogaine; trial dollar sales volume since introduction was $107,141,760. Rogaine repeaters numbered 150,480; repeat dollar sales volume was $531,344,880. Total estimated Rogaine sales for men were $638,486,640 over the period 1988 - 1995.

- A total of 71,261 female triers were estimated to use Rogaine; trial dollar sales volume since the 1992 introduction was $28,219,356. Rogaine repeaters numbered 14,252; repeat dollar sales volume was $31,382,208 from 1992 through 1995. Total estimated Rogaine sales for women were $59,601,564.

- The estimated market potential for Rogaine for the period 1988 through 1995 is therefore $638,486,640 + $59,601,564 = $698,088,208. Actual cumulative sales for this period were $700 million. **Rogaine's market (sales) potential was realized given the assumptions made!**

- When the yearly total sales figures for men and women in Exhibits 4 and 5 in this note are combined and plotted alongside actual U.S. sales, the pattern shown in Exhibit 6 in this note appears. As shown, the yearly estimates track the actual figures closely. Moreover, these estimates could have been made before Rogaine was ever launched!

- Finally, Exhibits 4 and 5 in this note lend credence to the view (see case Exhibit 2B) that almost all of Rogaine sales in 1994 and 1995 for men and women were repeat sales. As will be addressed next, this observation has implications for launching nonprescription Rogaine.

E. **How realistic is the belief, expressed by Pharmacia & Upjohn officials, that nonprescription Rogaine (minoxidil) sales of $1 billion were possible over five years given the marketing program for the brand?**

1. On the surface, this expressed belief essentially says that nonprescription Rogaine (minoxidil) dollar sales will more than double from $96 million in 1995 to $200 million for each of the next five years on average. Why might this happen?" Exhibit 7 in this note

EXHIBIT 6

ACTUAL AND ESTIMATED ROGAINE SALES: 1988 - 1995

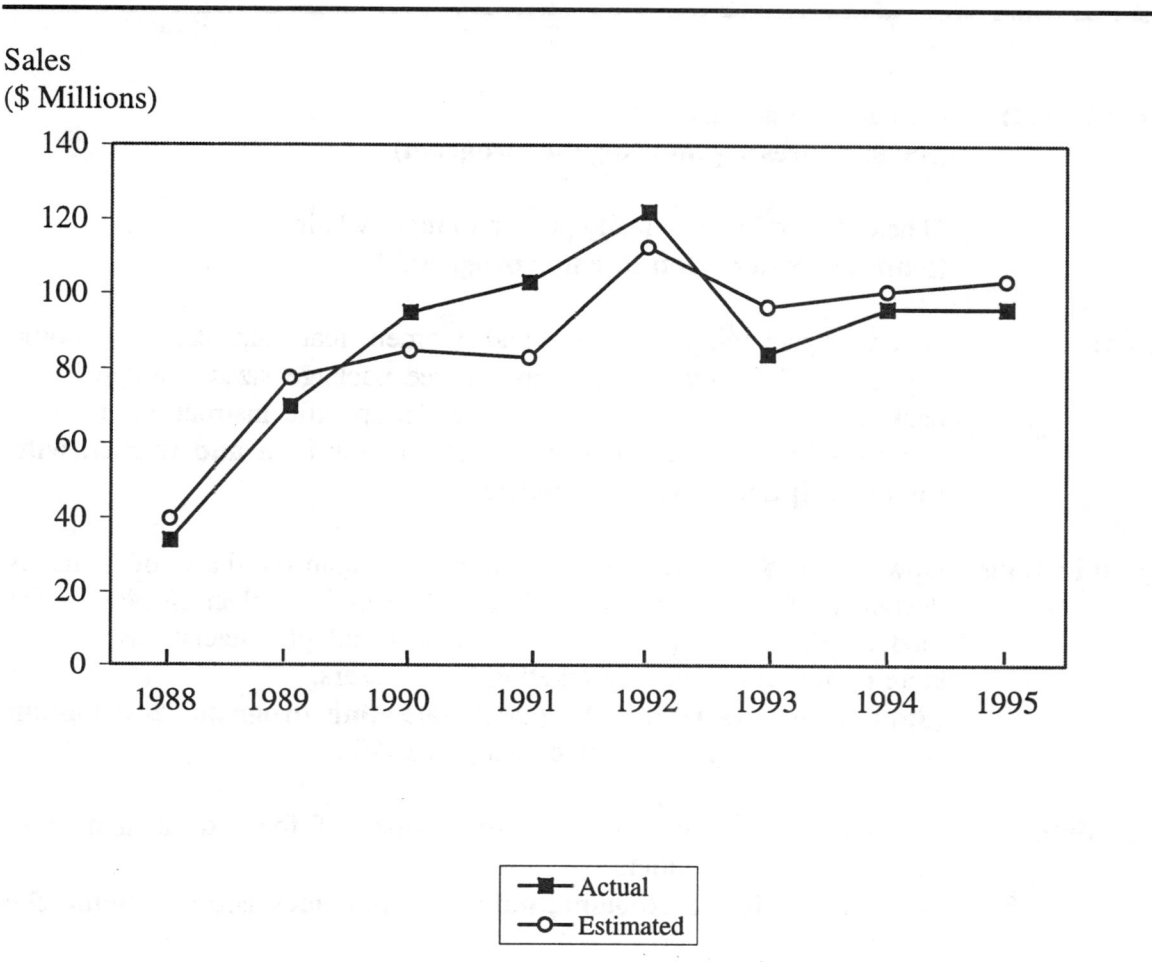

EXHIBIT 7

MARKETING PROGRAM OUTLINE FOR NONPRESCRIPTION ROGAINE

Target Market: Men and women aged 25 to 49.
(Same as prescription Rogaine program)

Positioning: "The only product medically proven to regrow hair"
(Same as prescription Rogaine program)

Product: Separate packaging for men and women featuring different bottle applicators for men and women. Three package sizes: single bottle pack, twin-pack, and triple-pack. Gender-specific instructions for use.
(Presumably no difference in packaging for men and women with the prescription Rogaine program.)

Communications: Upwards of $75 million expenditure, more than one-half of which is designated for consumer advertising. Use of both electronic and print media. Extensive mailings to physicians and pharmacists as well as store promotions. Direct marketing to new users.
(Similar to prescription Rogaine marketing program: $40 million was spent for consumer advertising in 1995).

Distribution: Focus on pharmacy and hair care sections of food, drug, and mass merchandise retail outlets.
(With prescription Rogaine, only the pharmacy could provide the product.)

Pricing: Nonprescription retail price for a single-pack would be $29.50, for a twin-pack, $55.00, and for a triple-pack $75.00.
(Prescription Rogaine retail price was $50 - $60 per bottle, or one-month supply. Note further that pharmacist margin on prescription Rogaine was 10%. Retail margin on nonprescription Rogaine is 20%.)

outlines the introductory marketing program for nonprescription Rogaine. Comparisons with the prescription Rogaine program are highlighted in bold type.

We have found it useful to couch the discussion related to this question in terms of **effective demand** (see Chapter 4). Effective demand is a function of a consumer's willingness and ability to buy.

Factors that Promote Willingness to Buy

- Without a prescription, prospective and current users will no longer need to visit a physician. The "hassle" plus the accompanying cost could have limited initial trial of the product. In addition, physicians served as "gatekeepers"; that is, if they didn't believe a prospective user would benefit from minoxidil (Rogaine) they probably wouldn't prescribe the product. With this factor eliminated, increased trial is possible as prospective users "self-prescribe."

- Without the need for a physician's evaluation and prescription, prospective users can self-prescribe based on their perceived condition. This should also increase trial. Advertising can create awareness and interest in the product and can have a more direct influence on trial without a physician as a gatekeeper. This should also increase trial. However, it is possible that people who self-prescribe will actually experience less positive results than those who sought a medical evaluation and received a prescription. Why? "Hope springs eternal!"

- The lower retail price ($29.50) for nonprescription Rogaine (vs. $50 - $60 for prescription Rogaine) is likely to promote initial trial among a larger percentage of "self-prescribers."

Factors that Promote Ability to Buy

- A lower price should increase Rogaine affordability among a larger number of prospective users. Total annual out-of-pocket costs to consumers for prescription Rogaine could be as high as $800 - $900 per year, including physician visits, according to the case. Nonprescription Rogaine would cost consumers $354 annually (12 x $29.50, the cost of one-month's supply), or even less if purchased in multi-packs. This should increase the likelihood of trial among a larger (male and female) income group, say, those with an income in the $25,000 to $49,999 bracket.

- More widespread distribution, to include hair care sections of food, drug, and mass merchandise stores, beyond store pharmacies, increases product availability, purchase convenience, and the potential for product trial.

Summary on Willingness/Ability to Buy

- It should be emphasized that creating new product trial among a broader user group is the key to growing sales volume. Exhibit 8 in this note shows the broadening of Rogaine's target market by Pharmacia & Upjohn, Inc.

- The nonprescription Rogaine marketing plan essentially seeks to promote willingness to "try" and ability to "try" through advertising/promotion, broadened distribution, and lower prices.

2. An increase in Rogaine dollar sales will prove to be a challenge, particularly since Rogaine's price has been cut substantially. As noted earlier, the annual prescription cost (at manufacturer price) to patients was $594. (Remember that the average price was $600, less the 10% pharmacist margin). The lower non-prescription Rogaine price, coupled with a higher retail margin (20%) represents a significant price cut to $21.86, or $262.32, say $262, for a year's supply (12 x $21.86 = $262.32):

   Nonprescription Rogaine Price Estimate

   - 1-bottle pack = $29.50, or $29.50/bottle
     2-bottle pack = $55.00, or $27.50/bottle
     3-bottle pack = $75.00, or $25.00/bottle

   - The average bottle retail price (1 bottle = 1 month supply) equals [$29.50 +$27.50 + $25.00] ÷ 3 = $27.33. This retail price becomes $21.86/bottle when the 20% retail margin is deducted, or $262 per year.

This price cut meant that the average Rogaine price declined by 44.1 percent ($262 ÷ $594 = 44.1%). This also means that almost all of the 1994 and 1995 dollar volume, which was repeat volume, would be reduced by 44.1 percent. Therefore, the $96 million in prescription Rogaine sales becomes $42.24 million as current users begin buying nonprescription Rogaine (44.1% x $96 million = $42.34 million). The implication is clear. Real Rogaine dollar sales will have to increase almost five-fold for Rogaine to achieve $200 million in sales ($200 million ÷ $42.34 million = 472%). Similarly, unit sales must also increase by this amount.

3. Where will this dollar sales growth come from? The most likely source of new volume will come from prospective users who now believe Rogaine's cost is affordable. It is reasonable to assume that the lower nonprescription Rogaine price has opened up a new user segment -- balding men and women with incomes in the $25,000 to $49,999 bracket. Using the same approach as before, 14,478,000 men and 3,800,000 women now might become possible users, or 2.76 times more potential users than with prescription Rogaine.

EXHIBIT 8

POSSIBLE SEGMENTATION OF "ROGAINE" MARKET BY SEX, AGE, AND INCOME

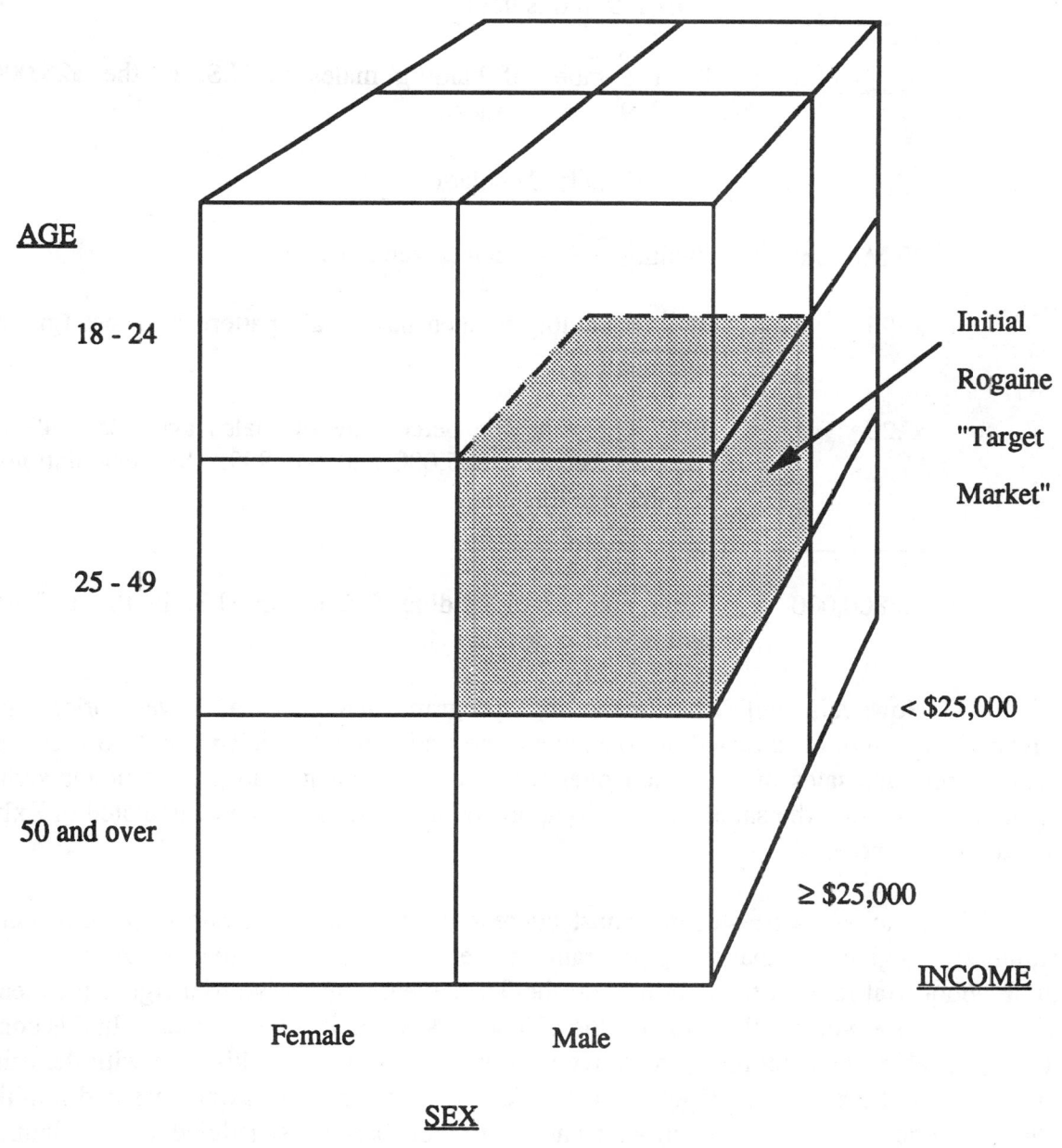

Male Calculation

40 Million	:	Balding U.S. men (given in case)
x .95	:	95% of balding men have male pattern baldness (given in case)
x .381	:	38.1% represents the percentage of males aged 25 - 49 with incomes between $25,000 and $49,999. See calculations in Exhibit 9 in this note.
__14,478,000__	:	Total number of balding males in U.S. in the $25,000 - $49,999 income bracket.

Female Calculation

20 Million	:	Balding U.S. women (given in case)
x .95	:	95% of balding women have male pattern baldness (given in case)
x .20	:	20% represents the percentage of males aged 25 - 49 with incomes between $25,000 and $49,999. See calculations in Exhibit 9 in this note.
3,800,000	:	Total number of balding females in U.S. in the $25,000 - $49,000 income bracket.

4. However, will the marketing program featuring a lower price, heavy advertising/promotion directed at consumers, the trade, and physicians, and no prescription actually produce sales of $1 billion over five years? Students can project nonprescription Rogaine sales using the same chain ratio approach detailed earlier and calculated in Exhibits 4 and 5 in this note.

The principal issue students must address is the likely trial rate -- incremental and cumulative -- given the marketing program directed at a larger target market. A useful way to think about trial rates is to again rely on the 9.9 percent cumulative trial figure for men and 13.3 percent for women, this time for the $25,000 - $49,999 income segment. In this context, it is reasonable to expect that cumulative trial will occur more quickly than with the original introduction of prescription Rogaine due to (a) existing consumer awareness and familiarity with Rogaine and (b) the advertising and promotion barrage scheduled for the launch of nonprescription Rogaine.

EXHIBIT 9

ESTIMATING THE PERCENTAGE OF MALES AND FEMALES

WITH INCOMES BETWEEN $25,000 AND $49,999
(Based on U.S. Census figures in Case Exhibit 5)

Calculation for Males

Age Group	Persons in Age Group	x	% with Income Between $25,000 - $49,999	=	# of Males
25 - 34	21.3 MM	x	34.4%	=	7.33 MM
35 - 44	19.0 MM	x	41.8%	=	7.94 MM
45 - 49*	6.2 MM	x	39.3%	=	2.44 MM
	46.5 MM				17.71 MM

$$17.71/46.5 = 38.1\%$$

* 6.2 million men represents one-half of total men in the 45-54 year old age group reported in case Exhibit 5.

Calculation for Females

Age Group	Persons in Age Group	x	% with Income Between $25,000 - $49,999	=	# of Females
25 - 34	21.6 MM	x	17.2%	=	3.72 MM
35 - 44	19.6 MM	x	22.2%	=	4.34 MM
44 - 49*	6.65 MM	x	22.2%	=	1.48 MM
	47.85 MM				9.55 MM

$$9.55/47.85 = 20\%$$

* 6.65 million women represents one-half of total women in the 45-49 year old age group reported in case Exhibit 5.

5. Exhibits 10 and 11 in this note shows a Rogaine (minoxidil) sales forecast for the five-year period 1996 - 2000. The sales forecast uses the same approach as before (see Exhibits 4 and 5 in this note) with certain changes:

- Trial rates are accelerated. For example, the 1996 trial rate for men is 4 percent, the 1996 trial rate for women is 11 percent.

- The annual price to consumers is $262 as calculated earlier, with the trial cost to men being $87.33 for a 4-month trial and $175 for women for an 8-month trial.

- **An important inclusion in Exhibit 10 is the Rogaine sales volume from 1995. This volume appears in the Repeat Sales column in Exhibit 10 as $42,340,000 reflecting the lower Rogaine price. The dollar volume assumes that all of 1995 Rogaine volume was repeat sales volume carried forward, but at a lower price.**

6. Summing across the total sales for men and women for each year yields $907.78 million in sales (rounded) for Rogaine over five years:

Year	Male Sales (millions)	+	Female Sales (millions)	=	Total Sales (millions)
1996	$130.85		$95.05		$225.90
1997	$146.65		$30.54		$177.19
1998	$130.85		$28.22		$159.07
1999	$140.33		$29.21		$169.54
2000	$147.60		$28.48		$176.08
	$696.28	+	$211.50	=	$907.78

F. **How might the loss of U.S. patent protection and marketing exclusivity enjoyed by Rogaine since its introduction and competition from generic products affect sales of the Rogaine brand?**

1. The analysis thus far has assumed Rogaine would retain its monopoly status as the only hair regrowth treatment available in the U.S. Even with expiration of its patent, the three-year marketing exclusivity would have maintained Rogaine's monopoly status. However, with the FDA's denial of a marketing exclusivity <u>and</u> approval of substitute generic products containing minoxidil, Rogaine faces a very different competitive context.

EXHIBIT 10

MALE SALES PROJECTION OF ROGAINE (MINOXIDAL)

FROM 1996 THROUGH 2000 WITHOUT GENERIC COMPETITION

Year	Cumulative % Trial		Target Mkt. Size	# of Triers	Trier Sales (# of Triers x $87.33)	Repeat Users (# of Triers x 25%)	Repeat Sales (Repeat Users x $262)	Total Sales (Trial & Repeat Sales)
1996	4%	x	14,478,000	579,120	$50,574,549	144,780	$42,340,000* + $37,932,360 $80,272,360	$130,846,909
Incremental Trial	3%	x	14,478,000	434,340	$37,930,912	108,585	$28,449,270 $80,272,360 $108,721,630	$146,652,542
1997	7%							
Incremental Trial	1%	x	14,478,000	144,780	$12,643,637	36,195	$ 9,483,090 + $108,721,630 $118,204,720	$130,848,357
1998	8%							
Incremental Trial	1%	x	14,478,000	144,780	$12,643,637	36,195	$ 9,483,090 $118,204,720 $127,687,810	$140,331,447
1999	9%							
Incremental Trial	.9%	x	14,478,000	130,302	$11,379,273	32,576	$8,534,912 $127,687,810 $136,222,712	$147,601,985
2000	9.9%							
Totals				1,433,322	$125,172,008	358,331	$571,109,232	$696,281,240

*1995 Rogaine sales adjusted for lower price. This figure includes sales to both men and women.

EXHIBIT 11

FEMALE SALES PROJECTION OF ROGAINE (MINOXIDAL) FROM 1996 THROUGH 2000 WITHOUT GENERIC COMPETITION

Year	Cumulative % Trial		Target Mkt. Size	# of Triers	Trier Sales (# of Triers x $87.33)	Repeat Users (# of Triers x 25%)	Repeat Sales (Repeat Users x $262)	Total Sales (Trial & Repeat Sales)
1996	11%	x	3,800,000	418,000	$73,150,000	83,600	$21,903,200	$95,053,200
Incremental Trial		3% x	3,800,000					
1997	12%			38,000	$16,650,000	7,600	$1,991,200 + $21,903,200 = $23,894,400	$30,544,400
Incremental Trial		.5% x	3,800,000					
1998	12.5%			19,000	$3,325,000	3,800	$995,600 + $23,894,400 = $24,890,000	$28,215,000
Incremental Trial		.5% x	3,800,000					
1999	13.0%			19,000	$3,325,000	3,800	$995,600 + $24,890,000 = $25,885,600	$29,210,600
Incremental Trial		.3% x	3,800,000					
2000	13.3%			11,400	$1,995,000	2,280	$597,360 + $25,885,600 = $26,482,960	$28,477,960
Totals				505,400	$88,445,000	101,080	$123,056,160	$211,501,160

2. The presence of generics presents a marketing challenge primarily because of their lower prices -- typically 25 to 50 percent below brand name products such as Rogaine. To the extent that price is a major determinant in product/brand choice, generics can be expected to draw sales from branded products. On the other hand, generics are not advertised. Accordingly, their availability may not be known to the "typical" new buyer. Instructors might ask students to recall the last time they had a prescription from a physician and then ask them whether or not the pharmacist asked them if they would accept a generic substitute. Many will say that they were not aware of a generic substitute. It is also instructive to ask students if they accepted the generic substitute.

This digression helps make a point. That is, according to the case, "patented prescription drugs lose up to 60 percent of their volume within six months after their patent expired due to generic competition." Some of this loss could very will be due to physicians/pharmacists promoting generic drugs over prescription drugs. The conversion of Rogaine from prescription to nonprescription status reduces this source of influence.

3. All things considered, Rogaine is likely to lose sales to generics and branded competitors. The case notes that sales outside the U.S. suffered as a result of competition from generic brands and substitute products in non-U.S. markets. The issue facing the student is to consider <u>who</u> will likely use generics, <u>how</u> <u>large</u> a sales loss is likely, and <u>when</u> Rogaine will feel the impact of generics and branded competitors. A series of questions can be used to focus this discussion.

- Who will likely use a generic minoxidil product?
  ... existing users of Rogaine or prospective new users?
  ... lower income users? Those with incomes at the lower end of the $25,000 - $49,999 income bracket?

- How large of a sales loss is likely?
  ... up to 60% of Rogaine volume? Based on loss of patent protection for prescription drugs given in the case.
  ... less than 60% of Rogaine volume? See the earlier discussion.

- When will Rogaine feel the impact of generics?
  ... within 6 months? Somewhat since generics are not advertised and no physician/pharmacist influencer can affect the purchase discussion.
  ... after one year? Probably very likely. Generic sales and brand competitor effects could be clearly seen by 1997.

4. Students should be expected to come up with a sales loss estimate (in percentage and dollar terms) and the date (year) when Rogaine will begin to feel the effect of generics and branded products between 1996 and 2000. Armed with these two pieces of information, an instructor can direct the discussion back to Rogaine's sales forecast from 1996 through 2000 (see the calculation in item #6 earlier). If students conclude that Rogaine's sales loss will be less than that for prescription drugs -- say 30% -- and this effect will be incurred in

1996, grow to 40% in 1997, and stabilize at 50% beginning in 1998, the sales loss will be $390.68 million, or 43 percent:

Year	Total Est. Sales	x	Competitive Effect	=	Revised Sales
1996	$225.90	x	70%		$158.13
1997	$177.19	x	60%		$106.31
1998	$159.07	x	50%		$ 79.85
1999	$169.54	x	50%		$ 84.77
2000	$176.08	x	50%		$ 88.04
	$907.78				$517.10

Sales Loss: $907.78 − $517.10 = $390.68; $390.68 ÷ $907.78 = 43%

* Note: This calculation assumes that generics and branded products will capture 30% of forecasted 1996 sales, 40% of 1997 sales, and 50% of 1998-2000 sales.

G. Will the U.S. marketing strategy developed for non-prescription Rogaine prior to the FDA's recent rulings need to be modified? If so, how?

1. Yes, the marketing strategy developed for nonprescription Rogaine will have to be modified following the FDA's recent rulings. But only modestly.

2. Rogaine positioning will have to alter its positioning immediately from "the only product medically proven to regrow hair," to, say, "Rogaine ... medically proven to regrow hair."

3. The 1996 advertising/promotion program and expenditure focusing on building awareness and trial among the new user group should be continued. However, consideration should be given to placing even greater attention on "retention" direct marketing to recent triers and current users to encourage compliance with the Rogaine usage regimen. An increase in advertising/promotion spending over the $40 million planned expenditure may be required.

4. Lowering price to match generics is not a viable option. Decreasing price will serve to reduce margins even further -- margins necessary to pay for advertising and promotion designed to generate trial and retention ... the principal drivers of subsequent sales volume.

5. Overall, the nonprescription Rogaine marketing strategy seems well-suited to confront the threat of generics and branded versions of minoxidil.

H. Epilogue

Pharmacia & Upjohn Company, Inc. launched nonprescription Rogaine in April 1996 as originally planned. The introductory marketing strategy was identical to that described in the case except that the positioning statement was modified to eliminate "the only product" phrase. Rogaine's positioning was modified to say, "Rogaine ... medically proven to regrow hair," to reflect the presence of competing suppliers of minoxidil. Advertising spending for Rogaine in measured media was $42.6 million for the period January through September 1996. Annualized, this figure approaches $56.8 million for 1996 -- a sizable increase over spending when Rogaine was a prescription drug.

The company recognized that generics and branded competitors would reduce the projected sales of nonprescription Rogaine. In testimony before the Federal District Court, the company estimated that Rogaine U.S. sales would be $660 million over five years (New York Times, May 1, 1996) and not the $1 billion figure that was originally announced. Note that the teaching note projected sales of $517.10 million over five years.

U.S. sales of Rogaine were estimated to be $155 million for 1996. This figure includes prescription Rogaine sales for the period January through March 1996 and nonprescription Rogaine sales for the April through December 1996 period. The 1996 sales figure is very close to the projected sales of $158.13 million in the teaching note. Estimated sales in 1997 were $92 million. Generic competition and competition from branded products emerged quickly. For example, Bausch & Lomb offered its minoxidil treatment under the Healthguard label by in mid-1996. Merck & Company introduced Propecia, a prescription pill to treat hair loss in early 1997. Overall dollar sales in the U.S. hair regrowth category decreased 13.5% between 1996 and 1997 (Advertising Age, August 31, 1998, p. 32).

By early 1997, Rogaine promoted using "Starter Kits" which reflected a price discount and offered a refund of $135 to consumers if they were dissatisfied with results after four months use. Also, advertising to women was being given greater emphasis.

I. Summary Points

1. A "market" consists of prospective buyers who are willing and able to purchase an existing or potential offering of our organization. The willingness and ability to buy refers to effective demand for a product or service.

2. Market segmentation is an invaluable tool for identifying market opportunities and effective demand. Identifying appropriate segmentation variables involves finding those variables that relate to purchase, consumption, or use behavior. In this case ...

- Age and sex affect the success of Rogaine, hence "willingness to buy" reflected in trial purchases and repeat purchase behavior

- Income affects the "ability to buy" Rogaine

3. Quantitative estimates of market (sales) potential are often difficult to make even for the seasoned executive. Reasonable and defensible assumption about what drives market (effective) demand are often required and judgment and creativity are important. The chain ratio method is a useful tool for assessing market (sales) potential.

4. The market (sales) potential for a product or service is influenced by the target market sought and the effectiveness of the marketing mix supporting the offering.

5. Market opportunities are made possible by government regulations, in this case, patent protection and marketing exclusivities for drugs. Both serve as barriers to entry for competitors. The opportunity made possible by governmental regulation creates "window of opportunity" that can be opened and closed.

3M TELECOM SYSTEMS DIVISION: FIBRLOK™ SPLICE

Synopsis

In early 1996 Denny Hamill, a business director in the Telecom Systems Division of 3M, was faced with a strategic marketing decision regarding the company's Fibrlok™ Splice. The splice was used by telecommunications firms to splice optical fibers when installing and repairing telephone lines to households. Introduced in August 1988, the splice initially exceeded 3M's sales expectations, but in recent years sales had been flat, and Hamill was assigned the task of determining if, and how, sales could be stimulated. 3M had earlier (1959) pioneered a similar splice (the Scotchlok™ Connector) for copper wire that was the industry leader and consequently believed that the Fibrlok™ Splice would be as or even more successful than the copper wire splice.

After reviewing considerable material relating to the Fibrlok™ Splice, Hamill attempted to estimate the market size for the splice. He did so by estimating the rate at which new telephone lines were being installed and three possible rates at which copper telephone lines were being converted to fiber optic lines. He then developed three general marketing alternatives. The first was essentially a status quo strategy—do nothing dramatic and continue with the current strategy. The second possible marketing strategy was more proactive and assumed that the size of the market would grow significantly. The third possible marketing strategy was for 3M to try to drive market growth through product redesign and aggressive marketing, with a special emphasis on pricing.

Teaching Objectives

This case has three teaching objectives:

1. To familiarize students with the concept of derived demand and its influence on strategic marketing alternatives in the context of business-to-business marketing.

2. To illustrate some straightforward analyses that are useful in evaluating alternative marketing strategies.

3. To present issues that often arise when trying to revive or stimulate products whose sales have declined from earlier levels or are stagnant.

Teaching Suggestions

This is a relatively enjoyable and interesting case to teach, in part because of the issues involved and in part because of the company featured. 3M is one of the most well-known and respected corporations in the world. At the same time, the case is conceptually straightforward, and few difficult quantitative analyses are required. Consequently, the case is more appropriate for undergraduate than graduate students. Although the case is designed for that portion of the course where reformulation strategies and management issues are addressed, it can easily be used elsewhere because of its emphasis on the issues of derived demand and environmental uncertainty. Finally, because of its length the case can be used as the basis of an in-class examination.

Specific questions that might be used to guide an analysis and discussion include the following:

1. How would one characterize 3M?

2. How would one respectively characterize 3M's Telecom Systems Division and the Fibrlok™ Splice?

3. What major environmental factors does 3M need to consider when developing a marketing strategy for the Fibrlok™ Splice?

4. What should 3M do, and why?

Areas for Discussion/Analysis

A. How would one characterize 3M?

1. 3M is one of the largest corporations in the world. In 1995 corporate revenues totaled $13.46 billion, which represented an increase of 10.8% from 1994 and 21.8% from 1993. Hence, over the period 1993-1995 corporate revenues were growing at an average annual rate of 10.4%. Fifty-four percent of corporate revenues, $7.3 billion, were derived from international operations in 1995.

2. 3M is a manufacturing company that appears to have distinctive competencies in research and new product development. It can be argued, through example and policy, that the company is not obsessively market-driven or market-oriented with respect to product development. In other words, rather than conducting research to determine what its various markets say they need or want, 3M builds on the product development interests of its own researchers and engineers. This is illustrated by Art Fry's search for a solution to stop his bookmark from falling out of his hymnal, Dick Patterson's interest in connectors, and the corporate policy of letting technical and engineering staff members spend up to 15 percent of

their time pursuing their own pet projects. Indeed, it can be argued that 3M cannot rely on the marketplace for ideas if it wishes to be a pioneering company, since the marketplace is only reactive and does not possess any foresight.

3. At the same time, the 3M culture is very oriented toward innovation and entrepreneurship. A corporate goal is to obtain 30 percent of sales from products that are less than four years old, and policies such as bootlegging time and venture-team development foster creativity and initiative.

4. Although 3M is a large corporation, it is important to realize that it can perhaps best be characterized as consisting of many small, often independent, businesses. It consists of 50 different entities that collectively produce more than 60,000 different products. Although product revenues are not normally distributed, it is instructive to note that the revenue of an "average product" in 1995 would have been about $223,333 ($13.4 billion/60,000). In brief, the company is highly decentralized and, as the case points out, focuses on "niche markets with niche products."

5. Consistent with its goals and policies, 3M spends a considerable amount of money on research and development. In 1995 it spent $883 million, about 6.6% of its revenues on research and development. Even so, research and development expenditures have been increasing at an average annual percentage rate (5.5%), slower than that of revenues.

6. Over the last three years (1993-1995) 3M's cost of goods sold has averaged 57% of revenues. In 1995 it was 57.3%.

B. How would one respectively characterize 3M's Telecom Systems Division and the Fibrlok™ Splice?

1. The Telecom Systems Division manufactures and distributes industrial products. Because its marketing efforts are business-to-business, its customers are typically very large organizations (with customer decision makers presumably consisting of engineering-type individuals), and its products technical, the division primarily employs selective communication strategies in trade publications, trade shows, and the like. Mass media are not used.

2. The division has been in existence for 30 years (note that 3M developed and introduced the Scotchlok™ Connector for splicing copper telephone wires in 1959, before the division was formed). The division is part of the Industrial and Consumer sector, which accounted for 62% of corporate revenues ($8.31 billion) in 1995. Although division revenues are not given explicitly in the case, for analysis purposes it can be assumed that they are approximately $1.47 billion (from case Exhibit 2, "connecting and insulating products"). Thus division revenues are a substantial percentage of both corporate revenues (10.9%) and sector revenues (17.7%), although they are not growing as fast, on average (8.4% annually), as corporate revenues in general.

3. Approximately 60% of the division's revenues come from international operations. This is more than the company as a whole (54%).

4. The Fibrlok™ Splice was introduced into the marketplace in August 1988. It was designed for splicing a single fiber optic telephone cable running to a household, although in 1995 a six-fiber splice (twelve fiber pairs divided by two) was introduced. For reasons mentioned later, this splice does not play a large role in the analysis.

5. Individual splices were initially priced at $12, and splice kits, which contain an assembly tool and 55 splices, were priced at $755 (case Exhibit 5) for both distributors and large customers. Three sizes of splices were produced (for optical fibers respectively having diameters of 125, 250, or 900 microns).

6. The factory cost of each splice in 1988 was $6 (50% of the price). Although 3M believed that the cost could be reduced substantially as demand increased, this has not happened. Thus the cost remains at approximately $6 per splice (and, consequently, the price remains at $12). Note that the cost is somewhat less than the cost of goods for the company as a whole (hence the splice's gross margin is higher than that of the "average" 3M product—50% versus 42.7% in 1995).

7. According to the case, about 5 million single-fiber mechanical splices were sold globally in 1995, with 3M's Fibrlok™ Splice holding a 30 percent market share. This suggests that, in 1995, 3M sold about 1.5 million splices. At $12 per splice, this means that fiber optic splices generated $18 million in revenues for the company in 1995.

8. Thus, the Fibrlok™ Splice generated a relatively small percentage of the division's revenues (1.2%). Simultaneously, though, fiber optic splices generated considerably more revenue than the "average" 3M product (nearly 81 times more revenue). Overall, the Fibrlok™ Splice would seem to be an important product for 3M.

C. What major environmental factors does 3M need to consider when developing a marketing strategy for the Fibrlok™ Splice?

1. Although the demand for 3M's optical fiber splice appears to have reached a plateau, it would seem that the demand for optical fiber is increasing. The case states that as of 1995 more than 60 million miles of optical fiber had been installed worldwide. Assuming that 1982 marked the beginning of demand for optical fiber, this would imply that the average annual growth rate in the installation of fiber optic cable is about 37%. This, in turn, would suggest that about 16 million miles of fiber optic cable was installed in 1995. Note that this number is consistent with other case information, namely that Corning produced 5.2 million miles of optical fiber in 1995 and possessed a market share of 32% (hence, 5.2 million miles/.32 = 16.25 million miles).

2. An average annual growth rate of 37% for optical fiber cable installation, if it continued, would mean that in the two-year planning horizon that Hamill faced, 22.2 million miles would be installed in 1996 and 30.4 million miles would be installed in 1997.

3. Through 1995 there were more than 600 million identifiable telephone lines in the world. This means that, on average, there were 10 identifiable telephone lines per mile of installed fiber optic cable.

4. Hamill estimated that telephone lines were being constructed globally at a rate of 8 percent per year (using the 600 million installed lines as a base). This means that 48 million new telephone lines should be in existence by the end of 1996, and nearly 100 million new telephone lines by the end of 1997 (48 million + 52 million constructed in 1997), for a total of 700 million lines. However, no information is given in the case regarding the extent to which the new telephone lines being constructed were copper lines or optical fiber lines.

5. Hamill assumed that three annual copper wire-to-optical fiber conversion or change-out rates were possible over the next few years—two percent, six percent, and ten percent. These rates probably formed the basis for the three alternative marketing strategy scenarios he was considering. When the three rates are weighted by their respective probabilities of occurrence (.65, .25, and .10), the expected growth rate is 3.8% (.02 x .65 + .06 x .25 + .10 x .10), which is closest to his minimal conversion rate (and minimal growth scenario).

6. All things considered, it would appear that the growth in installation of optic fiber cable worldwide has been due to its use when constructing (new) long haul or major telephone lines, commonly referred to as the backbone of a telephone system. Data in the case support this contention. On average, 5 to 10 splices are required for bringing fiber to the home. But, in 1995, there were only .313 mechanical splices produced for every mile of fiber optic cable installed (5 million mechanical splices/16 million miles of fiber optic cable installed) and only .104 mechanical splices produced for every new telephone line (copper as well as fiber) installed (5 million mechanical splices/44 million new telephone lines, assuming the 8% growth figure since 556 = 600/1.08 and 600-556 = 44). This would explain the stagnant demand facing 3M, since its splices are used primarily in local loops and, by inference, primarily in restoring damaged lines that had been previously installed. Fusion splices, which tend to be used in constructing new telephone lines (and major lines in particular), outnumber mechanical splices such as the Fibrlok^{TM} Splice by a factor of 8 to 1 (thus it can be assumed that 40 million fusion splices were produced in 1995). The case implies that fusion splices are more popular than mechanical splices in "high volume" applications, such as would be found in other-than-local loop applications. One reason may be that the incremental cost of a fusion splice only includes labor; there is no physical splice, and, hence, additional cost, involved. (The cost of the fusion splicing instrument, while potentially large, can be amortized over the splices made. Thus, the more splices, the less expensive each individual one.) This may be a reason why the multi-fiber Fibrlok^{TM} Splice has been less successful than anticipated, since it was designed for large-scale splicing operations and competes directly with fusion splices.

7. Bringing optical fiber cable to homes was estimated in the case to cost as much as $2,000 per home. The total cost of making a mechanical splice was stated as being between $7 and $20. The loaded labor rate of a telecom technician was given in the case as $60 per hour, and the time required to prepare and make a mechanical splice is about 2-3 minutes. Given that the cost of a Fibrlok^{TM} Splice to one of 3M's customers is $12 (the cost would be more if the splice were sold through a distributor), the total cost of making a splice with 3M's splice would be about $14.50. If the expected number of splices to be made between a central telephone office and a home is 7.5 (averaging the 5 and 10 numbers presented in the case), the cost of splices would be about $108.75, or 5.4% of the total cost of bringing fiber optic cable to the home. This, though, assumes that all splices would be mechanical, a somewhat dubious assumption. Therefore, the estimate should be considered an upper bound.

C. What should 3M do, and why?

1. Hamill set forth three possible marketing strategies that 3M could pursue:

- Continue to follow the present strategy. This alternative is based on the assumption that the market will grow very slowly (perhaps the two percent rate previously mentioned). 3M would employ its current product, pricing, and communications strategy. The focus would be on maintaining the company's market share.

- Modify the marketing mix to maintain the company's market share but increase revenues in an absolute sense. This alternative is based on the assumption that there will be significant growth in the penetration of optical fiber to the home (perhaps in the range of 6 percent annually).

- Attempt to drive or stimulate the rate of growth in the provision of optical fiber to the home by improving productivity in mechanical splicing through significant product redesign, price (and cost) reductions, and different kinds of market support than currently used. This alternative is based on the assumption that 3M, by itself, can influence the rate at which fiber optic cable is brought to the home, and that it would be possible to reduce the cost of a Fibrlok^{TM} Splice to $.50 or less.

2. There are two general considerations that must be addressed when determining which marketing strategy to pursue. One is environmental uncertainty. As noted in the case, whether fiber optic cable will ever be installed to the home is a looming question. Even though consumers may want fiber so that their facsimile machines can operate faster and they can better access the Internet, the questions of (a) who will pay for the installation and (b) to what extent are there viable optical fiber substitutes (such electronic enhancements and wireless capabilities) remain unanswered.

3. The second general consideration relates to the demand for mechanical splices. There is no primary demand for mechanical splices; no one would buy a mechanical splice "just to have one." Mechanical splices are purchased for what they offer—a way to quickly and simultaneously connect and insulate optical fibers. The resulting splice must be high quality and lasting (too much money depends on the splice for it to be anything else); cost—within reason—is probably of secondary concern. In brief, **the demand for mechanical splices is derived**; it is dependent on or contingent on the demand for optical fiber to the home. Recognizing this fact is critical to properly analyzing the situation facing 3M

4. Given that demand for the Fibrlok™ Splice is derived, to what extent can 3M influence the demand for optical fiber to the home? Copper wire is still dominant in the telecom industry: 10 <u>billion</u> copper wire splices were produced in 1995 whereas 5 <u>million</u> mechanical optic fiber splices were produced that year. Even if the cost of a fiber optic splice could be reduced to as low as $.50 with, say, a commensurate price of $1.00 (maintaining the current price-to-cost ratio), would this make a difference in the installation rate of fiber to the home? Assuming the same labor rate and average number of splices as before, the splice-related cost of bringing fiber to the home is $26.25 (7.5 x ($2.50 + $1.00) = $26.25) or 1.3% of the total cost. This represents a cost savings of $82.50 (4.1%) per home, the equivalent of 1.38 hours of labor. Is this enough of a cost reduction to drive the market? Probably not.

5. Even if 3M wanted to drive the market, it probably would not be able to do so. The company, while large, operates as small business units and, although the Telecom Systems Division has sizable revenues, it probably would not want to expend the resources that would be required to affect primary demand, especially given the relative importance (i.e., revenues) of the Fibrlok™ Splice. Commitments by telecoms, governments, and the general public are required before optical fiber will be brought to the home. How likely is it that 3M can effectuate these commitments?

6. Moreover, 3M is a manufacturing company with distinctive competencies in research and development, not marketing. In turn, the Telecom Systems Division has no expertise in consumer marketing, and, since consumers will ultimately determine whether there will fiber optic cable to the home (by their willingness to pay for it), it will be necessary for someone to persuade them to adopt fiber optic cable. Consequently, the third marketing strategy alternative, driving the growth of the market, does not seem to be viable. Indeed, that 3M was able to grow the market for copper wire splices may be an overstatement.

7. The second marketing strategy alternative hinges on whether there will be significant "natural" growth in the market. There are several indications that "significant" growth in the demand for mechanical splices will not occur in the near future. Consider the following points. In general, the growth in the construction of new telephone lines (100 million in the next two years, although many, perhaps most, will be copper) and the expected copper wire-to-fiber optic cable conversion rate (3.8% annually, producing a market potential of nearly 45 million lines in the next two years) would seem to suggest demand will increase substantially (bearing in mind previous caveats). Even so, previous experience suggests such estimates may be a bit optimistic. At the same time, given the likelihood of increased

demand and its nature (the fact that it is derived), there would seem to be no reason to substantially change the current marketing mix.

8. When all things are considered—the uncertainty in the environment and the nature of the product, the industry, and the demand—it would seem that the Telecom Systems Division should be prepared for a moderate increase in demand, but should not attempt to make major changes in its current marketing strategy. Thus the status quo alternative would appear appropriate.

9. Currently the Fibrlok™ Splice contributes about $9 million to the division's fixed costs ($6 per unit x 1.5 million units). If the splice were produced at $.50 and sold at $1 per unit (assuming the price-cost ratio that now exists), 3M would need to sell 18 million units, a 12-fold increase, for the 1995 contribution to be maintained. How reasonable is this, given that 45 million total fiber optic splices (5 million mechanical and 40 million fusion) were produced in 1995?

E. Epilogue

After considerable reflection Denny Hamill recommended that the Telecom Systems Division continue the current strategy but gradually prepare for increasing demand. He recommended no changes in product pricing but did recommend that the division initiate discussions with its largest customers, such as NTT, to determine whether it would be able to build partnerships and better manage demand in the future. Hamill also recommended that a formal mechanism be established to monitor the marketplace for fiber optic cable so that 3M would be prepared if demand were to suddenly increase. No information was available at the time this case was written as to what marketing actions were taken on the Fibrlok™ Splice.

F. Summary Points

1. Marketing success requires understanding what drives the demand for a brand as well as a product category. Different strategies are required when demand is primary as compared to when it is derived. Not appreciating the type of demand being faced could lead to major errors when creating an appropriate marketing strategy.

2. The existence of considerable marketplace uncertainty typically requires a conservative marketing strategy and careful, continuous monitoring of that marketplace. Both overreaction and underreaction are common mistakes that must be avoided in times of uncertainty.

THE CIRCLE K CORPORATION

Synopsis

The Circle K Corporation is the second largest convenience store chain in the United States and the 30th largest retailer. Since fiscal 1984 (year-end April 30), when the company embarked on an aggressive acquisition program, Circle K saw its sales volume grow almost four-fold from $1 billion to almost $3.7 billion in fiscal 1990.

On May 15, 1990, Circle K filed for protection under Chapter 11 of the U.S. Bankruptcy Code. This action was taken because of the company's deteriorating financial condition. Circle K's operating loss of $819,370 in fiscal 1990 was attributed to the company's heavy debt (interest) burden, the negative effect of merchandise and price policies instituted in 1989, and a highly competitive environment in the convenience store industry.

The case focus is on the turnaround strategy announced by Circle K officials. The announced strategy consisted of (1) a change in merchandising practices, (2) increased promotional efforts, (3) an aggressive pricing program, and (4) closing or selling unprofitable stores. The student's task is to examine this strategy given Circle K's situation and competitive setting and assess the likelihood of its success. Ample case information is provided to perform both a qualitative and quantitative (financial) analysis.

Teaching Objectives

This case has five teaching objectives:

1. To introduce students to marketing issues faced by one of the largest retailing segments in the U.S., the convenience store retailing.

2. To explore patronage behavior for convenience stores.

3. To address issues involved in the formulation of a corporate turnaround strategy where a comprehensive marketing program is the centerpiece.

4. To explore subtleties in the development of a comprehensive marketing program, namely program-market fit, program company fit, and program-competitor fit.

5. To consider marketing mix sensitivities where changes in merchandise mix, pricing, and promotion can be assessed in terms of sales volume and profit impact.

Teaching Suggestions

This case is best suited for the portion of the course that emphasizes comprehensive marketing programs. However, some instructors have used the case to focus on cost-volume-profit analyses and assigned it as a pricing case. Still others have focused on matters related to strategic and operations control and strategy reformulation and assigned it as a case on marketing control. The case is suitable as a written case for final examination purposes.

Previous experience teaching the case indicates that students are very familiar with convenience stores. Student patronage of these stores (including Circle K) usually means that class discussions are spirited. Many students express surprise when learning of Circle K's predicament in 1990.

A useful way to begin a class discussion to ask students directly:

"Will Circle K's announced turnaround strategy return the company to profitability as envisioned by its president?"

The following questions might be posed to students prior to or during a class discussion:

1. How would you characterize the convenience store industry in 1990?

2. How would you characterize Circle K's situation?

3. What are the pros and cons of the announced turnaround strategy for Circle K?

4. What is the likely sales and profit impact of Circle K's announced turnaround strategy and your assessment of the strategy's potential success?

Areas for Discussion/Analysis

A. **How would you characterize the convenience store industry in 1990?**

1. Students should focus their attention on two major topics: (a) industry structure and performance and (b) consumer demographics and patronage behavior.

2. Several aspects of industry structure and broad trends have been identified as affecting the performance of the convenience store industry:

- The industry is highly fragmented with 1,353 companies. Small convenience store chains with fewer than 50 stores account for a sizable percent of stores (42%) and industry sales (31%).

- Convenience stores compete for customers from a variety of other types of retailers, including gasoline stations ("g-stores"), supermarkets, and fast food outlets. This has happened because convenience stores have engaged in scrambled merchandising - the practice of offering numerous unrelated product lines in a single store. Unfortunately, convenience stores have become "stuck in the middle" between g-stores and supermarkets.

- There is some evidence (Exhibit 4 in the case) that the convenience store industry is maturing. This is apparent in the year-to-year changes in industry sales and the number of total stores in operation. Also, little differentiation between stores exists. According to a 7-Eleven executive, "The thing to overcome is the battle of sameness."

- Competition for customers is increasing and gross and net profit margins have declined (see case Exhibit 4).

- Five product categories account for 80 percent of convenience store total sales. They are gasoline, tobacco, alcoholic beverages, soft drinks, and prepared foods.

- The convenience store sales mix is changing with merchandise sales declining and gasoline sales increasing. In 1989, 60 percent of sales were for merchandise versus 82 percent in the late 1970s.

- The industry is driven by a large number of store visits (transactions) with a small average transaction of $2.29 for merchandise.

3. Consumer demographics and patronage behavior are also noteworthy in the assessment of the convenience store industry. For example:

- Based on case Exhibit 6 and the text, convenience stores attract a disproportionate percentage of younger (18-34) male customers.

- There is a general belief that women, particularly working women, and older consumers represent an untapped market for convenience stores and their numbers are growing.

- There is general belief that the rise in one- and two-person households (the "8 items and under segment"), will find convenience stores attractive. To date, however, these households have not patronized convenience stores to a degree desired by convenience store executives.

- Convenience, or more specifically time available for shopping, will become an even greater determinant in store patronage decisions.

4. Overall, industry structure statistics, industry executive perceptions, and trends coupled with consumer demographics and patronage behavior data provide a rich context for

the analysis of the convenience store industry. Interpretation of this information, with respect to the future, is not an easy task. Instructors should solicit student views on the patronage issues since they are major customers.

B.   How would you characterize Circle K's situation?

1.   Clearly, the situation is tenuous since Circle K has filed for Chapter 11 bankruptcy protection. However, students should be asked to elaborate on specific marketing and financial issues.

2.   Circle K operates about 6.5 percent of all convenience stores in the U.S. and captures about 5 percent of total convenience store industry sales. However, it is clear that numerous marketing-related issues exist:

- **Customer Alienation**. Circle K has apparently alienated customers by promoting high-profit-margin products that traditional customers did not want.

- **History of "Price Gouging."** According to the Circle K president, "... we had the attitude of gouging the customer for what we could get." This practice produced the highest gross profit margins in the industry. However, the practice alienated customers and sales volume slipped.

- **Lack of Differentiation**. Circle K probably suffers from a lack of differentiation from convenience store competitors in terms of merchandise assortment, store characteristics, etc.

- **Curtailed Advertising**. Circle K has curtailed advertising when the case suggests that the industry has stepped up its advertising (promotion) efforts. Note: Advertising as a percent-of-sales for the industry was .6 percent in 1989. Circle K spent .1 percent in 1989 and virtually stopped advertising in 1990.

- **Location**. About 84 percent of Circle K stores are situated in sunbelt states ranging from Florida to California. The case states that the southwestern, southeastern, and western U.S. are potentially over-store and saturated with convenience stores.

- **Sales Mix**. The sales mix for merchandise and gasoline suggests that Circle K has outpaced industry averages in its movement away from merchandise to gasoline. Merchandise as a percent of total sales has steadily declined (62% in 1988; 56% in 1989; 50% in 1990) to where Circle K is "becoming" a high cost g-store (see case Exhibit 3). Moreover, the changing sales mix toward gasoline means lower overall gross profits.

3. The financial situation facing Circle K does not bode well for the company. **Indeed, the financial situation was likely brought about by the marketing situation described above.** Students should recognize several important aspects of Circle K's financial condition:

- Circle K recorded a **net loss** of $772,869 in fiscal 1990 on sales of about $3.69 billion (see case Exhibit 1).

- Circle K's operating loss (Revenues - Cost of Sales and Expenses) was $819,370 in fiscal 1990. Note that 78 percent of the **operating loss** can be attributed to the $639,310 Reorganization and Restructuring charge incurred. This charge is a one-time expense.

- Circle K's **gross profit margin** in fiscal 1990 was 24.1 percent (vs. 25% in 1989; 27.6% in 1988). Note: Gross Profit = Sales minus Cost of Sales divided by Sales from case Exhibit 1. Identical percentage figures can be obtained by calculating the weighted average gross profit from case Exhibit 3.

- **Working Capital** (Current Assets - Current Liabilities) as a measure of liquidity was $89.9 million as calculated from case Exhibit 2. Circle K has $50.2 million in cash and short-term investments. These figures become important when issues related to funding the turnaround strategy arise for discussion.

4. The immediate financial and marketing challenge facing Circle K is to achieve break-even for fiscal 1991. That is, Total Revenue = Total Cost. As a practical matter, **break-even** can be viewed as:

Sales Revenue - Cost of Sales - Operating Expenses = 0.

The Reorganization and Restructuring charge is a one-time cost and not a relevant cost for calculating break-even in fiscal 1991.

5. **Assuming** that the remaining overhead expenses remain unchanged in fiscal 1991, then overhead expenses which are mostly fixed costs are (from case Exhibit 1):

Operating and Administrative	$865,602,000
Depreciation and Amortization	127,652,000
	$993,254,000

Note: Interest and debt expense of $126,799,000 are not included because under a Chapter 11 bankruptcy, the firm is stayed from paying interest, except on certain debt which is authorized under the bankruptcy terms. Typically, a bankrupt firm will only pay interest and debt that is paid currently. For purposes of analysis, this interest and debt is omitted. **Students often overlook or are not knowledgeable**

of bankruptcy law and the instructor might have to inform them of this provision.

If, as the case states, Circle K will no longer pay lease costs on 400 stores that have been shut down, then $1.5 million per month will be saved for a total of $18 million in fiscal 1991. This saving will reduce overhead expenses to $975,250,000. If, say, the savings from further store closings and the potential gain from store sales produces another $18 million, operating expenses will decline to $957,254,000.

6. For Circle K to break-even, gross profit dollars (Sales - Cost of Sales) must equal or exceed the operating expenses described above. These expenses will be in the range of $975,250,000 to $957,254,000.

Circle K's gross profit dollars in fiscal 1990 were $889,755,000 ($3,686,314,000 - $2,796,559,000) based on case Exhibit 1. This means that if Circle K reduces operating expenses, but does not increase dollar sales volume or improve its gross profit margin percentage, then it fails to achieve break-even.

7. Three implications become apparent from the above analysis:

- Circle K must increase dollar sales volume and/or decrease operating expenses if the gross profit percent remains unchanged at 24.1 percent (the gross profit achieved in fiscal 1990).

- Circle K must increase its gross profit percent if dollar sales and operating expenses remain unchanged.

- Some combinations of an increase in dollar sales, higher gross profit percent and decrease in operating expense is necessary.

Marketing has an important role to play in the areas of pricing (gross profit), sales mix (gross profit change due to the relative percentage of merchandise vs. gasoline), advertising or promotion (operating expenses), and sales volume stimulation.

8. Somewhere at this stage in the analysis, students should consider what drives sales volume. One perspective is that

Sales = f (Average dollar transaction size x number of customers)

This relationship indicates that if either transaction size or customer count increases with the other variable staying constant, then dollar sales increase. Furthermore, students should consider what affects transaction size and customer counts. For example:

Increase Average Dollar Transaction Size	Increase Number of Daily Customers
• Increased prices overall • Alter the product category sales mix to emphasize more expensive items • Increase amount purchased per visit	• Increase patronage frequency of present customers • Attract new customers

C. **What are the pros and cons of the announced turnaround strategy for Circle K?**

1. Shortly after the bankruptcy filing, Circle K president Robert A. Dearth, Jr. announced that he was determined to reposition the company so it could return to profitability and pay its debt in fiscal 1991. Key elements of the plan to revitalize Circle K included a change in merchandising practices, increased promotional efforts, and an aggressive price program, all of which were designed to improve customer service and increase sales. Two other points were made:

   a. Opportunities to close or sell unprofitable stores would be pursued.

   b. Mr. Dearth expressed no intention of downsizing the company or laying off any of the company's 27,000 employees.

These latter two points are inconsistent. If students mention this inconsistency, instructors should acknowledge it and move on.

2. The announced turnaround strategy contains each element of the marketing mix:

   - **Price**: Overall price reduction of 10 percent

   - **Product**: Merchandise to reflect socio-economic characteristics of individual store trade areas.

   - **Advertising/Promotion**: $100 million advertising/promotion program

   - **Distribution**: Eliminate unprofitable Circle K outlets.

Aspects of each marketing mix element is addressed below.

3. **Pricing: Overall price reduction of 10 percent.**

   - This seems like a good idea given that Circle K had "the attitude of gouging the customer for what we could get," according to the Company's president. Apparently, this practice alienated customers. After raising its merchandise prices in 1989 by 6 to 7 percent and watching sales decline 8 to 10 percent, the company rolled back prices to where prices are now about 5 percent above the competition.

- Given that present prices are 5 percent above competition, a 10 percent across-the-board price reduction would mean that Circle K would be priced 5 percent **below** the competition. However, is price a **critical** store patronage criterion for convenience outlets?

- Students should be expected to calculate a "rough" estimate of the price elasticity of demand based on Circle K's experience with price changes:

$$E = \frac{\text{Percentage Change in Quantity Sold}}{\text{Percentage Change in Price}}$$

$$E = \frac{-8\% \text{ (in sales)}}{+6\% \text{ (in price)}} = -1.33$$

$$E = \frac{-10\% \text{ (in sales)}}{+7\% \text{ (in price)}} = -1.43$$

Clearly, merchandise sold by Circle K is price elastic (E is greater than 1). Therefore, it **may be** concluded that a 10 percent **decrease** in price across-the-board should **increase quantity sold** (sales). However, students should be alerted to the fact that price elasticity is not the same over the demand curve.

- It is noteworthy that gasoline sales also declined 1 to 6 percent with the increase in merchandise prices (6 to 7%) indicating **cross-elasticity of demand**. Cross-elasticity is defined as

$$E_c = \frac{\text{Percentage Change in Quantity Sold of Product A}}{\text{Percentage Change in Price of Price of Product B}}$$

where Product A = Gasoline

Product B = Merchandise

Given these figures cross-elasticity of demand is in the range of
$E_c = -.14$ to $E_c = -1.0$.

- An important calculation relates to profitability since Circle K needs funds to cover its operating expenses. If Circle K reduces its prices 10 percent across-the-board, this means that the gross profit margin (Sales - Cost of Goods Sold/Sales) will decline from 24.1 percent (calculated previously) to 15.7 percent as calculated below:

Original Prices	New Prices
$1.000	$.900 (10% decrease in price)
-.759 (CGS)	.759 (CGS remains unchanged)
$ .241 or 24.1%	$.141 or $.141/$.90 = 15.7%

For Circle K to reduce its prices 10 percent **and not suffer** a loss in gross profit dollars, sales must increase 54 percent as shown below:

$$\frac{\text{Fiscal 1990 Gross Profit Margin}}{24.1\%} \times \frac{\text{Fiscal 1990 Sales (approx.)}}{\$3.7 \text{ Billion}} \times \frac{\text{Fiscal 1990 Gross Profit Dollars}}{\$89.7 \text{ Million}}$$

$$\frac{\text{Fiscal 1991 Gross Profit Margin}}{15.7\%} \times \frac{\text{Fiscal 1991 Sales}}{X} = \frac{\text{Fiscal 1991 Gross Profit Dollars}}{\$891.7 \text{ Million}}$$

Solving for "X", or fiscal 1991 sales,

.157(X) = $891.7 Million

X = $5.68 Billion

Sales increase = $5.7 Billion - $3.7 Billion

= $2 Billion

= $2 Billion/$3.7 Billion

= 54 percent

Sales will probably increase with a 10 percent across-the-board price reduction (say a 13%-14% increase in sales given the elasticity calculated earlier). This will not be enough to offset the loss in gross profit. However, the merchandise program and advertising/promotion program may contribute to the sales increase.

4. **Product Program: Targeted Merchandise for Store Trade Areas**

- Tailoring merchandise for specific socio-economic groups also seems like a good idea when implemented at the individual store level. This is a classic example of "market targeting," or "regional marketing."

- The case states that National Convenience Stores, Inc., with its Stop N Go stores, has already done this with some success. This merchandising program could increase sales 4 to 5 percent according to the case. Circle K's merchandise sales were $1,869.4 million in fiscal 1990 (see case Exhibit 3). If nothing else were done and strategy were implemented, **merchandise sales** could increase in the range shown below:

1.04 x $1,869.4 Million = $1,944.2 Million

1.05 x $1,869.4 Million = $1,962.9 Million

If gasoline sales do not increase, then Circle K total sales would only increase about 2 percent.

5. **Advertising/Promotion Program: $100 Million Investment**

   - Students will need to consider advertising and promotion "elasticity's" and costs. On the surface, more aggressive advertising/promotion could stimulate store patronage. When combined with lower prices overall, synergies are possible.

   - Nevertheless, two points are worth considering:

     ... Where will the funds come from? Circle K does not have the cash to pay for this program. However, assuming that the program does stimulate patronage, it is possible that increased merchandise turnover could produce cash - a form of "pay as you go." Also, some funds might be forthcoming from store unit sales.

     ... Is the advertising/promotion elasticity large enough to stimulate sales in the magnitude necessary to recoup this expenditure? The case notes that Circle K competitors (e.g., 7-11) have their own promotion programs - frequent buyer programs, give-away programs - that have had mixed success.

6. **Distribution: Store Elimination**

   - Circle K intends to close or sell unprofitable stores. This action will show improvement in Circle K's "bottom line" - sales of units, closing of unprofitable stores.

   - However, a subtle issue needs consideration. Circle K will need increased sales volume from existing stores. Stated differently, retained stores will have to sell disproportionately more to achieve the sales gains required from the price decrease and increased advertising/promotion.

D. What is the likely sales and profit impact of Circle K's announced turnaround strategy and your assessment of the strategy's potential success?

1. The previous analysis suggests that each element of the announced turnaround strategy has the potential to influence sales and profits. Most important, **it is incumbent upon the elements and potential synergies.**

2. In addition, students will find it necessary to also consider the broader overhead expenses of Circle K (discussed previously).

3. Exhibit 1 in this note provides an illustration of what the sales and profit impact of Circle K's announced turnaround strategy might look like. This worksheet shows (a) incremental sales volume gains and losses, (b) projected gross profit (in percentage and dollar terms), and (c) projected expenses.

- **Sales Volume Changes.** The worksheet shows what the incremental gains from each of the announced changes in the marketing mix. Changes due to the price decrease and new merchandise policy have been discussed previously. The 5 percent change due to advertising/promotion is a "guesstimate." The decline in sales of 10 percent due to store closings reflects the 400 units sold which are about 10 percent of Circle K units. These changes produce an estimated 10.5 percent increase in sales volume for fiscal 1991.

- **Projected Gross Profit.** The figure of 15.7 percent is the estimated gross profit percent with a 10 percent decrease in prices. This figure was derived previously.

- Expense Change. Changes in overhead expenses exclusive of interest and debt expense - see earlier comment on Chapter 11 provisions) reflect "guesstimates" of cost savings. Although rough, these estimates provide a basis for arriving at a projected operating profit impact.

4. This worksheet is for illustration purposes only. Instructors will find that students provide different projections. This is fine, providing they provide a rationale for their projections.

5. It is clear from this illustrative analysis that Circle K's announced turnaround strategy is unlikely to produce the necessary sales volume and gross profit to result in break-even. Circle K will continue to incur a loss in fiscal 1991.

EXHIBIT 1
REVENUE AND EXPENSE WORKSHEET FOR CIRCLE K'S
ANNOUNCED TURNAROUND STRATEGY
(Illustration)

		Fiscal 1990 Figure ($000)	Percent Change	Fiscal 1991 Projection ($000)
A.	**Sales Volume Change**			
	Due to Price Decrease (includes Merchandise & Gasoline)	$3,686,314	+13%	$ 479,221
	Due to Merchandise Policy (omits Gasoline Sales)	$1,869,400	+5%	93,470
	Due to Advertising/Promotion (includes Merchandise & Gasoline)	$3,686,314	+5%	184,316
	Due to Closed Stores (includes Merchandise & Gasoline)	$3,686,314	-10%	(368,631)
B.	**Incremental Change in Sales**			$ 388,375
C.	**Base: Fiscal 1990 Sales** (given in case Exhibit 1)			$3,686,314
D.	**Projected Fiscal 1991 Sales** (Item B + Item C)			$4,074,689
E.	**Percentage Sales Increase** (Item B ÷ Item C)			10.5%
F.	**Projected Gross Profit Percent in Fiscal 1991**			15.7%
G.	**Projected Fiscal 1991 Gross Profit in Dollars** (Item D x Item F)			$ 639,726
H.	**Expense Change**			
	Operating & Administrative (net effect of store closings, increase advertising/promotion and presumably other cost cutting)	$ 865,602	No Change	$ 865,602
	Depreciation and Amortization (reflects primarily store closing)	$ 127,652	-10%	114,887
	Projected Expenses (Total)			$ 980,489
	Projected Operating Profit (Loss)			($ 340,763)

E. Epilogue

The Circle K Corporation saga subsequent to the date of this case continues. Students welcome seeing the financial results for Circle K in fiscal 1991 (year end April 30, 1991). Sales revenue, gross profits, operating expenses, and operating profit figures are shown in case Exhibit 2.

Other noteworthy developments during fiscal 1991 include:

1. Circle K closed 779 stores and opened 7 stores during fiscal 1991 bringing its year-end store total to 3,859. (**Note:** The case analysis projected that about 10 percent of Circle K stores would close. In actuality, 17 percent of stores were closed.)

2. Stores that were not closed had merchandise and gasoline sale increases of 2 percent and 1.9 percent in fiscal 1991. (**Note:** These figures are far below the expectations for a price decrease. Apparently, price **is not a major criterion** for store patronage - see the case analysis on this point.)

3. The overall gross percent fell to 20 percent with the price program (**Note:** This figure is less than that appearing in the analysis - 15.7% - because a 10 percent across-the-board price decrease was not actually implemented; however, substantially price cuts existed for selected items.) Operating expenses declined as expected. (The figures presented in the case illustrative analysis are quite close if the store closings were higher, that is 17 percent of stores rather than 10 percent.)

4. In June, 1991, Robert A. Dearth resigned as president of The Circle K Corporation. In September, 1991, John Antioco, a former senior vice-president of store operations for Southland Corporation (7-11), assumed the presidency.

5. In December, 1991, The Circle K Corporation announced the adoption of a 5-year strategic plan. This plan included reduction of Circle K stores to 2,200 units by 1993 and withdrawal from 14 of the 32 states in which it operated. In addition, a Circle K spokesperson said that the company hopes to "be an aggressive competitor in the convenience store industry for years to come" (*Wall Street Journal*, December 6, 1991, p. A7).

In June, 1992, an investor group that included partners from the Middle East, Spain, and the U.S. made an offer to acquire The Circle K Corporation for $375 million and the assumption of certain liabilities. The offer was not accepted. In July, 1993, Circle K emerged from bankruptcy with its purchase by Investcorp, a holding company based in Bahrain, for $399.5 million. Circle K sales in fiscal 1991 were $3.6 billion and in fiscal 1992, $2.9 billion. The company had not yet recorded a net profit. (*Wall Street Journal*, February 11, 1993, p. B6)

EXHIBIT 2

THE CIRCLE K CORPORATION

SELECTED FINANCIAL DATA:

FISCAL 1990 vs. FISCAL 1991

	Fiscal 1990	Fiscal 1991	Change
Sales ($ millions)			
Merchandise	$1,869.4	$1,697.6	-9.2%
Gasoline	$1,817.0	$1,852.1	+1.9%
Total	$3,686.4	$3,549.7	-3.7%
Gross Profit (Percent)			
Merchandise	37.2%	32.8%	-11.8%
Gasoline	10.8%	8.4%	-22.2%
Overall	24.1%	20.1%	-17.0%
Overhead Expenses ($000)			
Operating & Administrative	$865,602	$845,360	-2.3%
Depreciation & Amortization	127,652	91,002	-28.7%
Total	$993,254	$936,362	-5.7%
Operating Profit ($000)	($819,370)	($111,840)	+98.7%

Source: The Circle K Corporation, Form 10K, Fiscal 1991.

F. Summary Points

1. A comprehensive marketing program is often the centerpiece of a larger corporate turnaround strategy.

2. While cost control and management are important considerations in returning firms to profitability, revenue considerations are equally important. A useful way to think about the determinants of sales revenue is the relationship:

$$\text{Sales Revenue} = f \begin{pmatrix} \text{Average Dollar Transaction Sale} \\ \times \\ \text{Number of Customers} \end{pmatrix}$$

Retailers can increase sales revenue by increasing one factor while keeping the other constant, or ideally, increasing both. Circle K attempted to use pricing, promotion, and tailored merchandising to focus mostly on increasing the number of customers patronizing their stores.

3. Marketing mix "sensitivities" and "synergies" should be considered when gauging the sales and profit consequences of marketing decisions. Estimates of sensitivities and synergies are important considerations when making sales volume projections for pro forma income statements.

MARSHALL MUSEUM OF ART

Synopsis

In early 2000, Ashley Mercer, Director of Development and Community Affairs, and Donald Pate, Director of Finance and Administration of the Marshall Museum of Art (MMA) met to discuss what had transpired at a meeting the previous afternoon. The meeting, attended by the senior staff of the museum and several members of the museum's Board of Trustees, had focused on the financial status of the museum. The Marshall Museum recorded its third consecutive annual loss in 1999 and Mercer and Pate were assigned responsibility for making recommendations that would reverse the situation.

This case introduces students to marketing issues related to the not-for-profit service sector, and particularly museum marketing. Specific issues raised include matters of museum image, visitation, and membership, the role and profitability of "retail operations" associated with the museum, and specific proposals for reversing the museum's deteriorating financial condition. A subtle issue implicit in the case relates to the mission of the museum and the providing of "high culture" for the community.

A major aspect of the case analysis focuses on an "audit" of museum practices and auxiliary activities as each relates to the expressed mission of the Marshall Museum. The audit involves both a qualitative (image issues) and quantitative (financial) appraisal of the museum and allows for the assessment of specific proposals. In addition, the audit should uncover potential problems with proposals made in the case and lead to recommendations not specified in the case.

Teaching Objectives

This case has four teaching objectives:

1. To expose students to marketing challenges in the not-for-profit service sector, and particular issues in museum marketing.

2. To give students an opportunity to conduct a "strategic audit" and an "operations audit" of a not-for-profit organization in the context of its mission statement and operating practices.

3. To illustrate the concept of product/service bundling and bundle pricing.

4. To examine price-cost-profit issues in a not-for-profit organization and their implications for delivering benefits to its constituencies.

Teaching Suggestions

This case has multiple uses and has been assigned in both graduate and undergraduate courses. Instructors have assigned the case early in the course when product and service management and strategy issues are addressed and much later in the course as an integrative case. Still others have used the case in the pricing portion of the course given the revenue-cost-profit analyses embedded in the case analysis as well as issues related to (1) admission pricing, (2) benefit discount allowances given to members, and (3) product/service bundle pricing. We have placed the case in Chapter 10 to focus attention on marketing strategy reformulation and control issues; namely, matters of strategic and operations control and the challenges of performing a marketing audit.

Questions that can be assigned to students prior to or during a class discussion are:

1. What exactly is the Marshall Museum of Art?

2. What is the "image" of the Marshall Museum of Art? Why is image important for a museum?

3. How would you rate the overall performance of the Marshall Museum of Art?

4. What are the roles and financial expectations for a museum's auxiliary activities and how are these activities performing?

5. What recommendations should Ms. Mercer and Mr. Pate make to the Marshall Museum's Board of Trustees?

6. Prepare a pro forma income statement like that shown in Exhibit 2 in the case which includes expected revenues and costs for 2000.

Areas for Discussion/Analysis

A. **What exactly is the Marshall Museum of Art?**

1. The purpose of this question is to direct student attention to the many points of view expressed about the Marshall Museum. Students might note that the museum is ...

- A museum (what is an museum?).

- A gallery featuring artworks put into a historical context.

- A culturally-oriented social or community organization.

- A sponsor of unique special exhibitions.

- An educational institution.
- A great place to have lunch or brunch and do a little browsing.
- Situated close to exceptional parking downtown for shopping.
- A place to buy unique gifts.
- A place for private corporate, foundation, and fund-raising events.

2. Some students might refer to the museum's charter (its mission):

> To provide an inviting setting for the appreciation of art in its historical and cultural context for the benefit of this and successive generations of Fannel County citizens and visitors.

Students might be asked what this charter (mission) means.

B. What is the "image" of the Marshall Museum of Art? Why is image important for a museum?

1. Considerable case commentary relates to the image of MMA.
Randall Brent III, the museum's director, says:

> "It is basically correct to say that, in the mind of the public, the MMA has no image."

Janet Blake, staff assistant in charge of membership, noted:

> "Among our membership, MMA is viewed as a community organization that has a cachet of class. It is exciting, educational, convenient, and inviting. It is a great place to bring visitors to our city for an afternoon of lunch and browsing."

Ashley Mercer, Director of Development and Community Affairs, said:

> "Based on our marketing research, I think there are two distinctly different images. One is a non-image. People don't know what the museum is. They also don't know what we have to offer in the way of lunch, dinner, brunch, shopping, movies, etc. They are not familiar with our collections. They are probably proud, however, that their community has a beautiful art and history museum.
>
> The other image is that we are only for specific people. This image is probably based on our membership. About 85 percent of members are college educated (vs. 70% of the county population of 2.5 million), 60 percent have household

incomes in excess of $60,000 (vs. 25% of the county population), half are over 40 years old (vs. 25% of the county population), and 98 percent are white (vs. 75 percent of the county population)."

A MMA critic said:

> The MMA has a definite image in my opinion. It's a great place to have lunch or brunch, buy an art or history book for the coffee table, and see a few things if time permits. It's parking facility is strategically located to allow its members to park conveniently for downtown shopping, particularly during the Christmas holidays.

2. Two conclusions might be drawn from these observations made by MMA officials. First, MMA does not have an image. Second, if MMA has an image it may be defined as "an institution for upper middle income educated white individuals around 40 years old who like having a place to show others they have some class or culture." An interesting question to pose to students is: "Which 'image' is better?"

3. Image is important to a museum for a variety of reasons. In particular, a image affects museum visitation, membership, grants, and contributions.

4. Some instructors might expand on the discussion of image by asking students: "How is a museum's image created and how easy is it to change a museum's image?"

C. How would you rate the overall performance of the Marshall Museum of Art?

1. This is a wide-open question. However, student observations typically fall into three categories: (a) museum activities, (b) membership, and (c) overall finances.

2. **Museum Activities**. The MMA would seem to be fulfilling its community mission. That is, its efforts "to provide an inviting setting for the appreciation of art in its historical and cultural context for ... Fannel County citizens and visitors" seem to be consistent with its mission. The physical facility, collection, and display would seem to be inviting. The MMA's efforts to publish features about art and history in the local media and its various education and outreach programs also seem consistent with its mission. In short, MMA is probably a fine institution and its efforts to make Fannel County citizens artistically and historically literate are noble indeed.

Students might note that total museum attendance has more than doubled since 1991 (see case Exhibit 1). Furthermore, 1999 marked the second highest attendance level at the museum -- the highest attendance was in 1995 (the first year the new museum opened).

3. **Membership**. Personal membership at the MMA is down over 4,000 members since 1995 -- the inaugural year for the new facility (see case Exhibit 4). The 1999 total personal membership revenue is at a four-year low (1996-1999). There are several observations worth noting about personal members and memberships:

- About 15 percent of MMA attendance can be attributed to members. The remaining 85 percent of attendance results from non-members.

- Personal member revenues were $2,298,449 in 1999 (case Exhibit 4). These members "cost" the museum $932,224 (**Note:** The case shows a figure for member benefit cost of $1,057,800. However, the corporate member cost of $125,576 needs to be subtracted.) Therefore, personal members "contributed" $1,366,225 over their "cost."

- Membership, particularly at the "regular" $50.00 membership level, exhibits extremely high-turnover. MMA records indicate that 70 percent of $50 members do not renew after their first year. This is a classic example of "high trial-low repeat" purchasing behavior indicative of "novelty purchase behavior." Furthermore, one-half of $50 members do not renew each succeeding year. Stated differently, for every 100-$50 members recruited in any one year, fewer than eight are members four years later.

4. **Overall Finances**. According to the case, MMA has recorded three (1997-1999) consecutive years of losses following seven consecutive years of either break-even or profitable years. The cumulative loss since 1997 of $794,066 had depleted the museum's reserves. The case states and case Exhibit 2 shows that MMA has experienced a sizable loss in operating income; however, auxiliary activities have shown a profit. Nevertheless, profit from auxiliary activities (special exhibitions, gift shop, restaurant, parking, museum association) has not kept pace with operating losses. Students should observe that:

- The most significant change in finances in the operations area is in personnel costs. MMA's personnel expenses increased almost $900,000 from 1998 to 1999.

- Membership revenue represented the largest single operating revenue source.

- Auxiliary activities have grown substantially both in terms of revenue generation and expenses. Auxiliary activities in 1999 accounted for 39.2 percent of MMA revenue and about 31 percent of total expenses. These figures compare with 22.8 percent of revenue and 21.9 percent of expenses in 1998. Clearly, auxiliary activities warrant attention.

- Special exhibition revenue (an auxiliary activity) accounted for the great bulk of auxiliary revenue. The benefits of special exhibitions are clearly indicated:

    ... They produce revenue (see case Exhibit 2).
    ... They increase museum attendance (see case Exhibit 1).
    ... They create traffic/revenue for the gift shop, the restaurant, and parking.
    ... They probably also convert visitors into members.

D. What are the roles and financial expectations for a museum's auxiliary activities and how are these activities performing?

1. The previous observations should logically move to a discussion of a museum's auxiliary activities. The case mentions that auxiliary activities "were intended to produce a profit."

2. It is important for students to consider auxiliary activities in the context of each's contribution to MMA's overall mission and financial expectations for such activities. Exhibit 1 in this note provides a mechanism for an instructor to organize the class discussion related to auxiliary activities. Students might be asked to assign the various auxiliary activities to the appropriate "cells." Exhibit 2 in this note shows what students typically conclude.

3. Class discussion can then turn to evaluating the various auxiliary activities from a financial perspective. Exhibit 3 in this note (based on case Exhibit 2) shows that

... Special Exhibitions are highly profitable

... Museum Parking is highly profitable

... the Museum Association operates slightly below break-even

... the Museum Gift Shop and the Skyline Buffet are highly unprofitable.

Clearly, the MMA will need to address the operations of its restaurant and gift shop. Costs will have to be reduced or revenues must increase. The matter of member discounts at both might require attention.

E. What recommendations should Ms. Mercer and Mr. Pate make to the Marshall Museum's Board of Trustees?

1. This question is designed to focus attention on the numerous and somewhat disjointed proposals discussed by Ms. Mercer and Mr. Pate at the end of the case.

2. Students (and the instructor) should initially describe the proposals "to get them on the table" and outline the revenue and expense expectations for 2000. This is done in Exhibit 4 in this note.

3. The revenue and expense expectations provide a basis for assessing the 2000 financial condition for MMA. Exhibit 5 in this note shows the revenues, expenses, and

EXHIBIT 1

ALIGNING MUSEUM MISSION AND ACTIVITIES

WITH FINANCIAL EXPECTATIONS

Financial Expectations

Activity-Mission Fit	Profit-Oriented	Break Even	Loss as "Investment"
Activities that actively advance institutional mission			
Activities that are compatible with institutional mission			
Activities that are unrelated to institutional mission			

Source: Adapted from Christopher H. Lovelock and Charles B. Weinberg, Public and Nonprofit Marketing, 2nd ed. (Redwood City, CA: The Scientific Press, 1989), p. 480.

EXHIBIT 2

ALIGNING MUSEUM MISSION AND ACTIVITIES WITH FINANCIAL EXPECTATIONS

	Financial Expectations		
Activity-Mission Fit	Profit-Oriented	Break Even	Loss as "Investment"
Activities that actively advance institutional mission	Special Exhibitions	Museum Association	Publications/ Public Info./ Education
Activities that are compatible with institutional mission	Museum Gift Shop	Museum Parking	
Activities that are unrelated to institutional mission	Skyline Buffet		

EXHIBIT 3

PROFIT AND LOSS OF AUXILIARY ACTIVITIES:
1997-1999

Special Exhibitions

	1999	1998	1997
Revenue	$1,655,200	$510,415	$451,347
Expense	814,741	313,057	137,680
Profit (Loss)	$ 850,459	$197,358	$313,667

Museum Gift Shop

	1999	1998	1997
Revenue	$1,596,775	$606,503	$810,123
Expense	1,679,294	662,685	990,090
Profit (Loss)	($ 82,519)	($ 56,182)	($179,967)

Skyline Buffet

	1999	1998	1997
Revenue	$ 515,843	$305,952	$418,960
Expense	592,051	457,841	462,475
Profit (Loss)	($ 76,208)	($151,889)	($ 43,515)

Museum Parking

	1999	1998	1997
Revenue	$ 131,512	$ 45,068	$ 64,651
Expense	31,168	16,528	16,536
Profit (Loss)	$ 100,344	$ 28,540	$ 48,115

Museum Association

	1999	1998	1997
Revenue	$ 337,136	$305,910	$342,850
Expense	344,955	292,877	353,016
Profit (Loss)	($ 7,819)	$ 13,033	($ 10,166)

Source: Case Exhibit 2

EXHIBIT 4

MARSHALL MUSEUM EXPECTATIONS CONCERNING REVENUES AND EXPENSES AND PROPOSALS FOR CONSIDERATION

Revenue/Expense Expectations	Proposals for Consideration
1. A 10 percent reduction in personnel and administration costs.	1. Institute a $1.00 admission charge for non-member museum visitors.
2. Special exhibitions to generate revenues of $1.2 million and cost $675,000.	2. Create new $30 membership categories for students and senior citizens.
3. Museum parking revenues and expenses to remain the same.	3. Improve the benefit package for members:
4. Non-member museum visitors would stay the same.	• Raise Skyline Buffet membership discount to 20 percent.
5. Museum education programs budgeted at $500,000.	• Raise Museum Gift Shop membership discount to 20 percent.
6. Appropriation from Fannel County, contributions, grants, investment income, endowment earnings, and other income would be 15 percent less than 1999 levels.	• Free admission for members (assuming non-members pay a $1.00 admission charge).
7. Expenditures for publications/public information would not change.	

EXHIBIT 5
INCOME AND EXPENSE WORKSHEET FOR MARSHALL MUSEUM

OPERATIONS

INCOME

	1999	2000
Appropriations - Fannel County	$ 1,786,929	
Contributions	338,664	
Grants	763,581	$3,179,271
Investment Income	27,878	
Earnings from Endowment	673,805	
Other	149,462	
Memberships	$2,917,325	(_____)
Total Revenue	**$6,657,644**	(_____)

EXPENSES

	1999	2000
Personnel	$1,973,218	$1,775,896
Publications/Public Information	594,067	594,067
Education	616,828	500,000
Administration	3,777,042	3,399,338
Memberships	854,461	(_____)
Total Expenses	**$7,815,616**	( )
OPERATING INCOME	**($1,157,972)**	

AUXILIARY-ACTIVITIES

Revenue from Auxiliary

	1999	2000
Special Exhibitions	$1,655,200	$1,200,000
Museum Gift Shop	1,596,775	(_____)
Skyline Buffet	515,843	(_____)
Museum Parking	131,512	131,512
Museum Association	337,136	(_____)
Revenue from Auxiliary	$4,236,466	(_____)

Expenses from Auxiliary

	1999	2000
Special Exhibitions	$ 814,741	$ 675,000
Museum Gift Shop	1,679,294	(_____)
Skyline Buffet	592,051	(_____)
Museum Parking	31,168	31,168
Museum Association	344,955	(_____)
Expenses from Auxiliary	$3,462,209	(_____)
PROFIT FROM AUXILIARY ACTIVITIES	**$ 774,257**	(_____)
NET INCOME	**($ 383,715)**	(_____)

income for MMA in 1999. Also shown are the revenue and expense expectations for individual "line items" for 2000, leaving certain "line items" blank where no explicit case information is provided. Students should recognize that MMA will "lose" **$568,368** in 2000 **if** the expected revenues **and** expenses materialize and revenues and expenses for memberships, Skyline Buffet, Gift Shop, and the Museum Association remain unchanged. Actually, with fewer special exhibitions planned, it is likely that Skyline Buffet and Gift Shop revenues will decline. **This overview indicates that something must be done.** Mr. Pate's opinion that changes in the Skyline Buffet and Gift Shop were not planned is inappropriate.

4. **Museum a $1.00 Admission Charge for Non-Member Visitors.** This proposal has the potential to increase revenue by $343,607:

- 85% of attendance is from non-members. Since special exhibitions already have paid admissions, special exhibition attendance should be subtracted from total museum attendance (628,472 - 284,863 = 343,607).

- Revenue from $1.00 admission change = $1.00 x 343,607 = $343,607 **assuming** non-member visitor attendance **does not** decline.

- It is important to note, however, that an admission charge is contrary to the "free access" view expounded by Mr. Brent, the MMA director. However, as noted in the case, "free admission" for MMA members can then become another item for the member "benefit bundle."

5. **Membership Categories.** The proposal to add a $30 membership category to attract student and senior citizen members/visitors could increase revenue and traffic at the museum. This option is therefore a positive proposal, although it is not likely to produce significant revenue. Also, the "benefit" package will have to be designed.

However, membership categories and particularly dollar levels require a closer look. The $50 membership category is a case in point. Exhibit 6 in this note shows the rough economics of the $50 category. Two figures are worth noting:

- The $50 member category "costs" the museum $46.15 in benefits. Therefore, each member "contributes" $3.85.

- These $50 members turnover quickly and need to be replenished. Direct mail solicitations typically cost $43.40 per new member. When benefit "costs" are included, these memberships actually "cost" the MMA $34.54!

More broadly, the "contribution" of different membership categories warrant attention. Exhibit 7 in this note plots the membership category revenues (from case Exhibit 4) and benefit "cost" (from the text). As shown, the $50 category "contributes" very little; the $1,500 and $5,000 categories "contribute" the most to MMA. An interesting question to

EXHIBIT 6

ECONOMICS OF DIRECT MAIL SOLICITATION FOR NEW MEMBERS
(August 1999 Case Study)

Revenue

Total Membership Revenue:	$84,280.00	
÷ Total Memberships Obtained:	÷ 1,532	
Average Membership Amount:		$55.01

Cost

(A)	Total Direct Mail Cost:	$66,488.80	
	÷ Total Memberships Obtained:	÷ 1,532	
	Average Direct Mail Cost:	$43.40	
(B)	Annual Benefit "Cost" of $50 Members:	$631,016	
	÷ Total $50 members	÷ 13,672	
	Average Annual Cost of $50 member	$46.15	$89.55
		First Year Loss	($34.54)

EXHIBIT 7

MEMBERSHIP REVENUE AND COST BY MEMBERSHIP CATEGORY

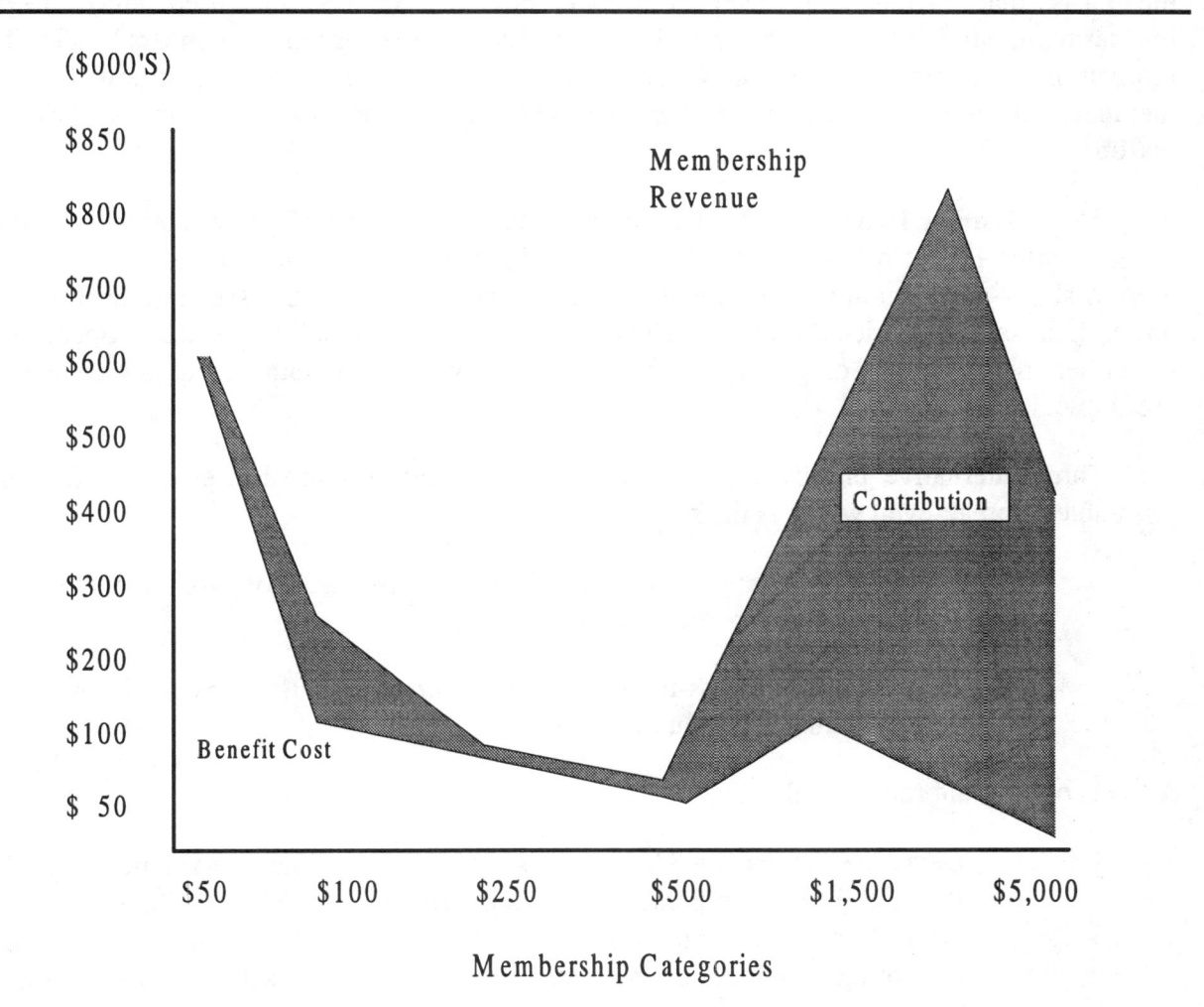

pose to students is: "Is the "benefit bundle" price and cost at the $50 level appropriate? Is the price too low or are the benefits too numerous or expensive?"

A possible counter proposal is to increase the dollar value of membership categories, i.e., $50 becomes $75, $100 becomes $150 and so forth. This proposal can be supported on the basis that membership category dollar values have not increased since 1995. Furthermore, students might be asked: "Why do people become members?" Is the motivation altruistic or utilitarian (benefit) based?" It is conceivable that lower ($50) members are joining for benefits; higher levels ($100+) may become members for altruistic reasons.

6. **Member Discounts**. MMA members currently receive 15 percent price discounts at the Skyline Buffet restaurant and Gift Shop. Furthermore, as noted previously, both are unprofitable -- they should be profitable given their role at the MMA (see Exhibit 3 in this note). Increasing the price discount to 20 percent is unlikely to result in profitable operations for either the restaurant or gift shop. It could very well make both operations even less profitable.

Three alternative proposals are possible to make the Skyline Buffet and Gift Shop profitable or break-even which is their purpose.

- Decrease operating costs (reduce labor expense, use more volunteers, etc.). Eliminate the 15 percent member discount.

- Increase prices across-the-board for restaurant and gift items and keep the 15 percent member discount.

Aspects of each alternative follow.

a. **Decrease Operating Costs**. This option is possible as evidenced by Mr. Pate's ability to cut personnel costs by 10 percent. Most of these costs are probably staff cuts, unrelated to the delivery of auxiliary services, however. Assuming revenues for the restaurant and gift shop will be stable in 2000, then the Gift Shop must cut $82,519 in expenses (5% of expenses) and the Skyline Buffet must cut $76,208 or 13 percent of expenses (see Exhibit 4 in this note). In either instance, these auxiliary activities will still only break-even, and not be profitable. However, some cost cutting might be necessary.

b. **Eliminate the 15 Percent Member Discount**. This option runs contrary to the proposal to increase member discounts at the restaurant and gift shop to 20 percent. It is instructive for students to consider the profit impact of eliminating discounts. Exhibits 8 and 9 in this note show that by removing discounts, the Gift Shop shows a $100,641 profit given specific assumptions. The restaurant shows a loss of $17,038 given specific assumptions. In both instances, the auxiliary activities show a profit improvement over 1999.

EXHIBIT 8

PROFIT IMPACT OF ELIMINATING THE 15 PERCENT MEMBER DISCOUNT FOR THE GIFT SHOP

1999 Total Revenue:	$1,596,775	(case Exhibit 2)
Revenue on 15% Discount:	$1,037,904	(65% of Gift Shop Revenue)
Non-discount Revenue:	$ 558,871	(35% of Gift Shop Revenue)
Full Revenue Equivalent of 15% Member Discount (i.e., items sold at list price)	$1,221,064	($1,037,904 = .85x, x = $1,221,064)
Gift Shop Revenue w/o 15% Discount:		
Full Revenue from Members	$1,221,064	
Non-Member Revenue	+ 558,871	
Total Revenue	$1,779,935	
Less: Cost	- 1,679,294	(case Exhibit 2)
Profit	$ 100,641	

Assumptions:
1. Number of transactions remain unchanged.
2. Cost does not change.
3. Prices do not change.
4. Mix of gifts sold does not change (sales mix).

EXHIBIT 9

PROFIT IMPACT OF ELIMINATING THE 15 PERCENT MEMBER DISCOUNT FOR SKYLINE BUFFET

1999 Total Revenue:	$515,843	(case Exhibit 2)
Revenue on 15% Discount:	$335,298	(65% of Restaurant Revenue)
Non-discount Revenue:	$180,545	(35% of Restaurant Revenue)
Full Revenue Equivalent of 15% Member Discount: (i.e., items sold at list price)	$394,468	($335,298 = .85x; x = $394,468)

Skyline Buffet Revenue w/o 15% Discount:

Full Revenue from Members	$394,468	
Non-member Revenue	180,545	
Total Revenue	$575,013	
Less: Cost	- 592,051	(case Exhibit 2)
Profit (Loss)	($ 17,038)	

Assumptions:
1. Number of transactions remain unchanged.
2. Cost does not change.
3. Prices do not change.
4. Item mix sold does not change (sales mix).

It is important that instructors familiarize themselves with the calculation of **full revenue sales**; that is, revenue obtained had the 15 percent discount not been offered.

Eliminating the 15 percent discount reduces the "benefit bundle" for MMA members. To eliminate it might reduce the value of the benefit bundle. On the other hand, if a $50 member working downtown has a $25.00 lunch/brunch for two six times a year, buys a single item from the Gift Shop at a list price of $50.00 (the price of a reasonably attractive "art" book), and attends two special exhibitions (average admission $5.00), that $50 member has "cost" the MMA $40.00.

c. **Increase Prices Across-the-Board for Restaurant and Gift Items and Keep the 15 Percent Member Discount.** This option was not stated in the case. It retains the same member discounts, but the dollar contribution per purchase transaction increases. If prices increase 15 percent, then for every $10 purchase transaction by a member which produced $8.50 in sales for the Museum in 1999, $9.77 in sales will result in 2000:

	1999	2000
Purchase transaction at list price:	$10.00	$11.50
Less: 15% Discount	1.50	1.73
Sales Revenue	$ 8.50	$ 9.77

Exhibits 10 and 11 in this note show the effects of a 15 percent price increase for the Gift Shop and Skyline Buffet. As indicated, Gift Shop profit becomes $156,988; the Skyline Buffet slightly exceeds break-even, given the assumptions shown.

Raising prices might be viewed cautiously by MMA officials. However, these two auxiliary activities are "supposed" to be profit-oriented! An important issue is whether a 15 percent price increase will reduce sales activity in one or both auxiliary activities. It would appear that a decline in traffic will be more than offset by a price increase.

F. **Prepare a pro forma income like that shown in Exhibit 2 in the case which includes expected revenues and costs for 2000.**

1. The previous analysis allows students to make "informed and defensible assumptions" concerning likely 2000 revenues and expenses for the Marshall Museum. Specifically, students, based on their analyses, could:

EXHIBIT 10

PROFIT IMPACT OF AN ACROSS-THE-BOARD 15 PERCENT PRICE INCREASE IN THE MUSEUM GIFT SHOP WITH A 15 PERCENT MEMBER DISCOUNT

1999 Total Revenue:	$1,596,775	(case Exhibit 2)
2000 List Price Increase of 15%:	x 1.15	
Total Revenue	$1,836,291	
Less: Cost	1,679,294	(case Exhibit 2)
Profit	$ 156,997	

ALTERNATIVE CALCULATION

Member Revenue

Full Revenue Equivalent of Member with 15% Discount	$1,221,064	[Members acct. for 65% of business; therefore .65 x $1,596,775 = $1,037,904. Full rev. equivalent: $1,037,904 = .85x; x = $1,221,064]
Times 2000 List Price Increase of 15%	x 1.15	
	$1,404,224	
Less: 15% member discount:	210,634	
Revenue from MMA Members	$1,193,590	
Plus: 1999 Non-member Revenue times 1.15	642,702	[Non-members account for 35% of business; therefore .35 x $1,596,775 = $558,871]
Total Revenue	$1,836,292	
Less: Cost	1,679,294	(case Exhibit 2)
Profit	$ 156,998	

Assumptions: 1. Number of transactions and sales mix is unchanged.
2. Cost does not change.

EXHIBIT 11

PROFIT IMPACT OF AN ACROSS-THE-BOARD 15 PERCENT PRICE INCREASE AT THE SKYLINE BUFFET WITH A 15 PERCENT MEMBER DISCOUNT

1999 Total Revenue:	$515,843	(case Exhibit 2)
2000 List Price Increase of 15%:	x 1.15	
Total Revenue	$593,219	
Less: Cost	592,051	(case Exhibit 2)
Profit	$ 1,168	

ALTERNATIVE CALCULATION

Member Revenue

Full Revenue Equivalent of Member with 15% Discount:	$394,468	[Members acct. for 65% of business; therefore .65 x $515,843 = $335,298. Full Revenue equivalent: $335,298 = .85x; x = $394,468]
Times 2000 List Price Increase of 15%	x 1.15	
	$453,638	
Less: 15% Member Discount	68,046	
Revenue from MMA Members	$385,592	
Plus: 1999 Non-member Revenue times 1.15	207,627	[Non-members acct. for 35% of business; therefore, .35 x $515,843 = $180,545]
Total Revenue	$593,219	
Less: Cost	592,051	
Profit	$ 1,168	

Assumptions: 1. Number of transactions and sales mix is unchanged.
2. Cost does not change.

- Make a revenue and expense forecast for memberships (perhaps a trend extrapolation).

- Incorporate a revenue estimate assuming a $1.00 admission fee for non-MMA members (see previous analysis).

- Make revenue and expense forecasts for the Skyline Buffet and Gift Shop (see Exhibits 8-11 in this note).

- Project Museum Association revenues and expenses (i.e., make revenues and expenses equal to break-even, or $337,136).

- Incorporate planning assumptions for revenues and expenses described in the case itself (i.e., 10% reduction in personnel costs, spending for education, parking revenues/expenses, etc.).

2. We have found that the discussion concerning the income statement moves along nicely if Exhibit 5 in this note is reproduced for students, or made into a transparency.

3. The **pro forma** income statement should ideally show that MMA can break-even in 2000. Furthermore, policies that will ensure future auxiliary activity revenue producing opportunities should be indicated.

G. Epilogue

The Marshall Museum of Art (disguised name) Board of Trustees adopted the following proposals for 2000:

1. A $30 membership category for students and senior citizens was added. This category added a total of 2,455 new members by mid 2000 (increased membership revenue by a modest $74,000).

2. Across-the-board price increases of 12 percent was introduced for the Skyline Buffet and the Gift Shop. An audit of purchase transactions indicated that 1999 and early 2000 transactions were virtually identical. Expenses for each were reduced 5 percent through increased volunteer participation.

3. A $1.00 admission charge for non-members was instituted. No material decline in non-member visits was observed.

4. Membership dollar category levels were not changed. However, this matter was again examined in mid-2000. A change would be instituted in 2000. The $50 category would become $60 and the $100 category would become $125.

Projected revenue and expenses made in the case were generally quite accurate.

The Marshall Museum was projected to operate at break-even in 2000 and museum officials believed a slight surplus was possible for 2001, due in part to favorable general economic conditions and the changes that were made.

H. Summary Points

1. Effective management of arts organizations is a challenging assignment. The Marshall Museum situation is common and illustrates that not-for-profit institutions must consider revenue and cost issues in the marketing of their service offering.

2. Image is an important factor in museum marketing. Image affects visitation, membership, and contributions and gifts. Images are often difficult to change.

3. Auxiliary activities of not-for-profit organizations are typically "for profit" endeavors. They must be managed and marketed like any commercial enterprise.

4. Pricing is a difficult and sensitive issue for not-for-profit organizations. Determining what to price and how much often involves considerations of the organization's mission. Some pricing issues raised in this case were:

- What is the appropriate price for membership categories given the specific benefits provided (bundle pricing)?

- Should a "public institution" charge admission?

- What should be the pricing objectives for auxiliary activities?

    ... break-even

    ... percent return on revenue

    ... specific dollar profit

FRITO-LAY, INC.: SUNCHIPS MULTIGRAIN SNACKS

Synopsis

In mid-1990, Dr. Dwight R. Riskey, Vice President of Marketing Research and New Business at Frito-Lay, Inc., assembled the product management team responsible for SunChips Multigrain Snacks. SunChips had been in test market for 10 months in the Minneapolis-St. Paul, Minnesota, area and recommendations related to future action on the brand were eminent. The options, stated in the case, were to (1) continue the test for another six months, (2) expand the test to other geographical areas with the same marketing strategy or some modification, or (3) ready SunChips for a national introduction using the test market strategy or some modification.

The challenge facing the SunChips product team is articulated by Riskey on the first page of the case:

> "We will have to do heavy-duty selling [to top executives] because SunChips™ Multigrain Snacks required a new manufacturing process, carried a new brand name, and pioneered a new snack chip category. There is a huge capital investment and a huge marketing investment that could be financially justified only with a product that could be sustainable for an extended time period."

The case describes the development of SunChips through the first ten months of its test market. As such, students are given an overview of how product concepts emerge, are examined, and test marketed. This case forces students to forecast first-year volume given product trial and repeat data, consider the sustainability of volume, and assess the effects of cannibalism. It also requires students to assess cost and profitability issues as related to the marketing and manufacturing investment in the product, the value of additional market and consumer information, and opportunity costs.

Teaching Objectives

This case has six teaching objectives:

1. To introduce students to a common marketing problem encountered by product managers; namely, the go/no go decision on a new product.

2. To explore challenges market pioneers face when creating new product-markets.

3. To illustrate the kinds of marketing research data product managers in large consumer products firms have and use when making new product decisions.

4. To give students practice in using trial, repeat, and depth of repeat purchase data to determine first-year sales volume and sustainable volume for a consumer packaged good.

5. To raise for consideration the assessment of product cannibalism in a new product introduction and its effect on product profitability.

6. To expose students to matters relating marketing and manufacturing investments in the face of demand uncertainty.

Teaching Suggestions

This case is suitable for that portion of the course when the instructor wishes to examine new product decisions. Experience with this case indicate that it is well received by students, presents a rigorous treatment of new product issues for consumer package goods firms, and alerts students to the perils and payoffs from market pioneering.

The numerical work in this case can be challenging for the average student and laborious for all students. Average students typically struggle with computing sales volume forecasts from trial and repeat rate data and conducting a profitability analysis. However, better students will deal with these matters. Accordingly, this case has been found to be an excellent examination tool and group presentation assignment both for undergraduate and graduate students.

Experience teaching the case indicates that several issues arise. First, students will often extrapolate the cumulative trial and repeat data shown in case Exhibit 10 for 13 periods. They do this to estimate annual cumulative trial and repeat percentages. This action will obviously increase sales volume forecasts. This practice isn't completely correct. If students extrapolate using linear or logistic regression analysis, they should be reminded that the data are cumulative. Therefore, it isn't surprising that they get "high R-square" values given the cumulative progression. Moreover, they often overlook the behavioral processes driving trial and repeat and do not consider that advertising and merchandising dollars have been all but spent by the tenth period. While it is possible that the percentages will increase, it is unlikely the percentages actually conform to the projection. In actuality, the cumulative trial and repeat percentages in the tenth, 4-week reported in Exhibit 10 did not increase in subsequent periods.

Students also tend to prepare pro forma income statements that incorporate depreciation expense using an arbitrary 5, 7, or 10 year straight-line manufacturing life for the $20 million investment in SunChip plant and equipment. This is incorrect since depreciation is already factored into the calculation of gross profit (see case footnote 4). By incorporating depreciation into the gross profit estimate, Frito-Lay uses a "units-of-production" depreciation method which is a form of accelerated depreciation. In short, by subtracting depreciation, students are effectively double-counting this expense.

Another issue for instructors to be aware of is the tendency for students to assume that the beliefs and views expressed by product management team members concerning strategy options are fact. They are not! These views are only useful for performing sensitivity analyses.

This note contains numerous transparency masters in exhibit form that have proven useful in moving the discussion along when the case is taught in a class discussion setting. Instructors might bring these transparencies to class on the day the case is taught.

Specific questions that may be posed to students prior to or during a class discussion are:

1. How would you characterize the snack chip category and Frito-Lay's competitive position in this category?

2. What specific challenges and risks does Frito-Lay face in marketing SunChips and what are the implications of each?

3. What insights can be drawn from Frito-Lay's prior experience with multigrain snacks?

4. What conclusions can be drawn from research on SunChips' consumer acceptance and sales potential prior to the Minneapolis-St. Paul test market?

5. What is your assessment of the SunChips' test market results?

6. Given your assessment of the test market results, what actions should Dwight Riskey recommend to Frito-Lay's top executives?

Areas for Discussion/Analysis

A. How would you characterize the snack ship category and Frito-Lay's competitive position in this category?

1. The snack chip category consists of potato, corn, and tortilla chips, pretzels, and ready-to-eat popcorn. This category generated retail sales of snack chips were $9.8 billion in 1990 - a 5 percent increase over 1989.

2. U.S. consumers bought 3.5 billion pounds of snack chips in 1990, or nearly 14 pounds per person. Per capita consumption of snack chips in 1986 was less than 12 pounds.

3. Three types of competitors serve the snack chip category: (a) national brand firms, (b) regional brand firms, and (c) private label firms. National firms include Frito-Lay, Borden, Procter & Gamble, RJR Nabisco, Keebler, and Eagle Snacks (a division of Anheuser-Busch). Regional firms include Snyder's, Mike Sells, and Charles Chips. Private label manufacturers produce chips for major supermarket chains (e.g., Kroger).

4. Competition in the snack chip industry is intense:

- 650 snack chip products are introduced each year by national and regional brand firms; most products are flavor extensions.

- Pricing is very competitive and price deals are frequently used to attract consumers.

- Heavy use of advertising, price deals and consumer and trade promotions.

5. The new product failure rate for snack chips is high. Fewer than one percent of new products generate more than $25 million in first-year sales. (**Note:** The case states that Frito-Lay's sales goal for new products is $100 million.)

6. Frito-Lay is a dominant player in the snack chip category with a 50 percent market share. The company markets eight of the top-selling snack chips in U.S. supermarkets.

B. What specific challenges and risks does Frito-Lay face in marketing SunChips and what are the implications of each?

1. The purpose of this question is to get students thinking early in the discussion about the unique issues related to SunChips.

2. Three challenges should immediately become apparent. These were mentioned by Dr. Riskey on the first page of the case:

- Multigrain snack chips represent a new product category.

- Frito-Lay is introducing a new brand name.

- Frito-Lay must develop and implement a new manufacturing process.

Each challenge translates into a "huge capital investment and a huge marketing investment" according to Riskey. Students should be asked to articulate the implication of these challenges (see Exhibit 1 in this note).

3. There is considerable **risk** in the undertaking. Using the notion of **Perceived Risk = f (Uncertainty x Amount at Stake)**, students should be asked to identify contributors to both:

EXHIBIT 1

CHALLENGES AND IMPLICATIONS FOR SUNCHIPS MULTIGRAIN SNACKS

	Challenge	Implications
1.	Multigrain snack chips represent a new product category (class) for consumers <u>and</u> Frito-Lay.	• Frito-Lay will be a "market pioneer" meaning that SunChips will have to establish the product category.
		• Frito-Lay must differentiate this category from other categories (e.g., potato, tortilla, and corn chips) by demonstrating a unique, and sustainable value proposition for consumers.
2.	Frito-Lay is introducing a new brand name.	• Frito-Lay will need to create awareness of the SunChips name among snack chip users. **Note:** This requires more effort than simply introducing a line extension in the form of a new flavor, e.g., Ranch Flavor Ruffles Potato Chips.
		• Frito-Lay will need to link SunChips with the multigrain snack chip category. In effect, make the name and the category synonymous by creating the "prototype" multigrain snack chip that subsequent brands must be compared to.
3.	Frito-Lay must develop and implement a new manufacturing process.	• Frito-Lay must invest in new plant and equipment to produce multigrain snack chips - upwards of $20 million to serve a national market.
		• Frito-Lay must engage in quality assurance to insure product integrity given a new manufacturing process technology.

Uncertainty	Amount at Stake
• Initial Consumer Acceptance (trial)	• Heavy marketing dollar investment ($22 million advertising/promotion expenditure-first year)
• Sustainability of Consumer Acceptance (repeat, depth of repeat)	• Heavy capital investment in plant and equipment (upwards of $20 million for full scale production)
• Usage Characteristics (Everyday Snack vs. Occasional Snack, e.g., treat)	
• Competitor Reaction (timing, nature of response)	• Opportunity cost (investment in other projects/products, whether new or existing)
• Manufacturing Capability (Production volume, quality, product consistency given new product/process technology)	• Derivatives of a major new product failure - external image, internal stress, etc.

C. What insights can be drawn from Frito-Lay's prior experience with multigrain snacks?

1. Students should acknowledge that the multigrain snack idea has existed at Frito-Lay since the early 1970s. The first multigrain chip, called Prontos, was introduced in 1974, but withdrawn from the marketplace in 1978. Reasons given for the poor performance by Frito-Lay executives were:

- "noncommittal copy, a confusing name, and a too narrow target market" (all marketing issues);

- "The difficulty of the manufacturing process" (process technology presumably that did not produce a quality product); and

- "Invented and introduced before its time" (the consumer wasn't ready for a "healthy" snack chip - the marketing environment was not favorable).

2. Research conducted in the early 1980s also failed to identify consumer enthusiasm for wholesome snacks.

3. This experience with multigrain snacks indicates that **primary demand** for wholesome snacks did not exist in the 1970s and early 1980s. Equally noteworthy, a conscious effort to stimulate primary demand for multigrain snacks by the world's premier snack chip producer failed. If time permits, an instructor might use this example to illustrate that marketing doesn't necessarily create consumer wants.

D. **What conclusions can be drawn from research on SunChips' consumer acceptance and sales potential prior to the Minneapolis-St. Paul test market?**

1. Two pieces of research are relevant to this question: (a) the concept test and (b) the premarket test.

2. **Concept Test.** The case text and case Exhibit 3 describe the results of the concept test. Conclusions from this test indicate:

    - Consumers viewed all three flavors as healthy snacks when exposed to the concept (triers), but none were viewed as appropriate for everyday snacking.

    - Consumers who indicated intention to repeat purchase reported that the Natural and French Onion flavor would be for everyday snacking. The Mild Cheddar flavor, while showing evidence of being a everyday snack among repeaters, was not as likely to be viewed as such.

    - Nonrepeaters of all three flavors rated the product much less favorably. These consumers were considerably less likely to view the product as "healthy" and less likely to view it as an everyday snack.

    - Exhibit 2 in this note (based on case Exhibit 3) displays pre-trial expectations and post-use perceptions for the three flavors and visually illustrates the changes described.

3. Two implications arise from the concept test:

    - The Natural and French Onion flavors have potential as an everyday snack among those that intended to make a repeat purchase; therefore, the potential for **repeat** volume is high as is **depth of repeat** (repeats-per repeater).

    - Nonrepeaters have equally pronounced perceptions. After use, they were much less likely to view the product as healthy and less likely to be an everyday snack - a double whammy for multigrain snacks!

4. **Premarket Test.** Summary statistics for the simulated market test commissioned by Frito-Lay are shown in case Exhibit 5. Conclusions from this study indicate:

    - Regardless of flavor combination introduced (Natural/Mild Cheddar vs. Natural/French Onion), projected dollar sales are virtually the same.

EXHIBIT 2

PRE-TRIAL EXPECTATIONS AND POST-USE PERCEPTIONS OF FRITO-LAY MULTIGRAIN SNACKS

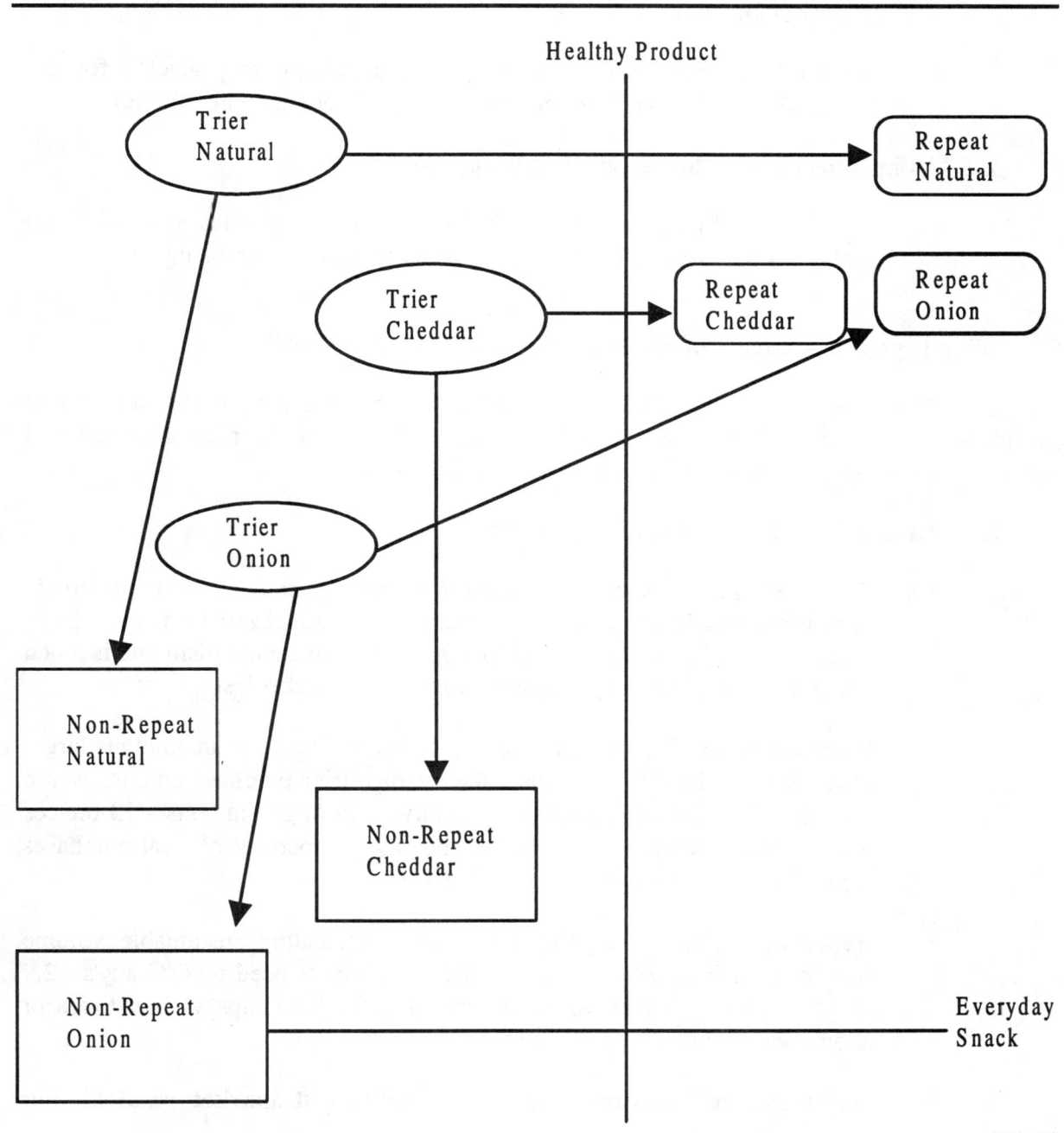

Based on Case Exhibit 3

- Higher sales for the larger advertising and merchandising budget ($22 million) are expected, regardless of flavor combination.

- Higher product trial and initial repeat purchases are projected for the Natural/Mild Cheddar flavor combination, but slightly higher number of purchases (repeats-per-repeater) are projected for the Natural/French Onion flavor combination.

- Greater incremental volume (i.e., less cannibalism) is projected for the Natural/French Onion flavor combination (58% incremental volume).

5. An important implication arises from the premarket test:

- SunChips is likely to achieve Frito-Lay's first-year sales goal of $100 million, **if** $22 million is spent in advertising and merchandising.

E. What is your assessment of the SunChips' test market results?

1. There are several pieces of data that are "good news" and other data that might be considered "bad news." The "good news-bad news" is based on the premarket test and comparisons with O'Grady's, Frito-Lay's last $100 million brand.

2. **Favorable test market results include:**

- **Cannibalism.** The source of volume for SunChips indicates that 70 percent of volume was incremental; 30 percent was cannibalized from Frito-Lay's potato, tortilla, and corn snack chips. A 30 percent cannibalism rate is much lower than the 42 percent estimated from the premarket test.

- **Purchase Rate.** Consumers appear to be trying SunChips in amounts larger than the trial size (2¼ oz.) since the average trier purchase amount was 6 ounces. Furthermore, repeaters were buying in large amounts - 13-ounces per purchase occasion. As noted in the case, 87 percent of total purchases were of the 7-ounce and 11-ounce package.

- **Repeats-per-Repeater.** Depth of repeat, indicating sustainable volume from consumer adoption, is higher than that experienced by O'Grady's - 2.9 times or about 3 times on an annual basis for SunChips vs. 1.9 times or about twice annually for O'Grady's.

3. However, there are also **important unfavorable test market results**. For example:

- **Brand Awareness.** Brand awareness is lower than projected from the premarket test for the Natural/French Onion flavor combination with a $22 million advertising and merchandising equivalent expenditure (33% vs. 48%

- see case Exhibit 5). However, the 33 percent brand awareness level is higher than the 28 percent recorded for O'Grady's potato chips.

- **Brand Trial.** The cumulative household trial rate of 19.9 percent is much lower than projected by the premarket test (25%) and lower than the trial rate for O'Grady's (roughly 23-24% from case Exhibit 11).

- **Brand Repeat Purchasing.** SunChips cumulative household repeat rate of 41.8 percent is lower than the premarket test projection (57%) and slightly lower than that achieved by O'Grady's (roughly 44% from case Exhibit 11).

4. SunChips awareness, trial, repeat, and depth-of-repeat allows for a projection of first-year national sales volume. Not surprisingly, SunChips falls short of the $100 million sales goal for new products. Exhibits 3 and 4 in this note shows the appropriate calculations. As indicated, SunChips projected first-year dollar sales are $83,826,859; total gross profit is $40,361,080.

Note: Students will sometimes base their calculations on the Minneapolis-St. Paul market. As shown in Exhibit 5 in this note, the pound volume results are comparable (as will be dollar sales and gross profit estimates).

5. **Incremental Analysis: Cannibalization.** SunChips will produce a total gross profit of $40,361,080. However, it is necessary to consider incremental gross profit since SunChips requires an incremental increase in advertising and merchandising support ($22 million). A cannibalism assessment is therefore necessary.

As noted in the case footnote 4, SunChips will produce a higher gross profit per pound ($1.30/lb.) than other Frito-Lay potato, tortilla, and corn chips ($1.05/lb.). Therefore, for every pound cannibalized by SunChips, Frito-Lay gains $.25. However, this gain is not free. It is appropriate to match incremental gross profit with incremental expenses. Exhibit 6 in this note shows the analysis for determining incremental gross profit given the cannibalism of other Frito-Lay snacks. As indicated, SunChips produces an incremental brand contribution, exclusive of incremental capital investment, of $8,581,279:

$30,581,279	Incremental Gross Profit (after cannibalism)
22,000,000	Incremental Advertising/Merchandising
$ 8,581,279	Incremental Brand Contribution (exclusive of capital investment costs)

6. **Sustainability of Volume.** A critical concern to Frito-Lay management is the sustainability of the sales volume for SunChips given the need to invest in new product and process technology. In actuality, the issue of volume sustainability relates to the presence of **adopters** - those households that will buy SunChips on a regular basis - reflected in the depth-of-repeat data gathered during the test market and the amount purchased per purchase occasion.

EXHIBIT 3

CALCULATION OF SUNCHIPS NATIONAL POUND VOLUME

I. **Inputs**

Given: (1) <u>Cumulative Trial Rate</u>: 19.9% of U.S. snack chip households (case Exhibit 10)

(2) <u>Cumulative Repeat Rate</u>: 41.8% of U.S. snack chip households (case Exhibit 10)

(3) <u>Depth of Repeat</u>: Each repeater purchased the product 2.9 times or 3 times annually after the first initial repeat.

(4) <u>Average Purchase</u>: 6 ounces for triers; 13 ounces for repeaters.

(5) <u>Households</u>: 90 million snack chip user households in the U.S.

II. **Volume Calculation**

Trial Volume: 19.9% x 90 mm HH x 6 oz = 107,460,000 oz.
+
Repeat Volume: 41.8% x 17.91 mm HH x 13 oz = 97,322,940 oz.
+
Repeater Volume: 7,486,380 HH x 3 repeats x 13 oz = <u>291,968,820</u> oz.
496,751,760 oz.

<u>Conversion to Pound Volume</u>:
496,751,760 oz ÷ 16oz = 31,046,985 lbs.

EXHIBIT 4

CALCULATION OF SUNCHIPS NATIONAL DOLLAR SALES VOLUME AND GROSS PROFIT

I. <u>Sales Volume</u>

Given: (1) 15% of purchases were 2¼-oz size at $0.385/pkg.
(2) 47% of purchases were 7-oz size at $1.240/pkg.
(3) 38% of purchases were 11-oz size at $1.7321/pkg.

Weighted Average Price Per Ounce (Pound) at List Price to Retailer (from case Exhibit 7):

- 15% x ($0.385/2¼ oz)   = $0.0257 oz.
- 47% x ($1.240/7 oz)   = $0.0833 oz.
- 38% x ($1.732/11 oz)   =   <u>$0.0598</u> oz.
                                                $0.1688 oz.

Conversion to Dollars/Pound:

(16 x $0.1688)   = $2.70

National Dollar Sales Projection: $83,826,859

($2.70 x 31,046,985 lbs)

II. <u>Gross Profit (based on case footnote 4)</u>

$1.30 GP/lb x 31,046,985 lbs = <u>$40,361,080</u>

EXHIBIT 5

CALCULATION OF SUNCHIPS VOLUME USING MINNEAPOLIS-ST. PAUL DATA

Using only the Minneapolis-St. Paul data, which many students do, a national forecast for SunChips can be made. The same figures apply except that the number of households is 1.98 million households and the test market volume is extrapolated to the entire U.S.

The calculations are as follows:

Trial Volume:
19.9% x 1.98 mm HH x 6 oz = 2,364,120 oz.

Repeat Volume:
41.8% x 394,040 Trier HH x 13 oz = 2,141,213 oz.

Repeater Volume:
164,709 Repeat HH x 3 repeats x 13 oz = 6,423,651 oz.
10,928,984 oz.
÷ 16
683,062 lbs.

Since Minneapolis-St. Paul contains 2.2 percent of U.S. snack chip user households, annual volume can be estimated as follows:

683,062 lbs/.022 = 31,048,272 lbs.

This figure is roughly equivalent to the 31,046,985 lbs. calculated in Exhibit 3 in this note.

EXHIBIT 6

CANNIBALISM ANALYSIS FOR SUNCHIPS
(Incremental Gross Profit Effect)

---

1. Frito-Lay gains $.25 per pound each time SunChips diverts a pound away from other Frito-Lay snack chips (potato, tortilla, and corn chips). SunChips Gross Profit: $1.30/lb. Gross Profit for potato, tortilla, and corn chips: $1.05/lb. (See case footnote 4.)

2. Given that 30 percent of SunChips volume was cannibalized from other Frito-Lay snack chips (or 30% x 31,046,985 lbs. = 9,314,096 lbs.), Frito-Lay gross profit increased:

    $.25 x 9,314,096 = $2,328,524

3. SunChips will sell an incremental 21,732,889 lbs. (70% x 31,046,985 lbs.), which means that SunChips addition to Frito-Lay gross profit is:

    $1.30 x 21,732,889 lbs. = $28,252,755

4. Therefore, a net positive incremental increase in gross profit is produced:

    $28,252,755 + $2,328,524 = $30,581,279

Note: Total SunChips gross profit calculated from Exhibit 4 in this note is $40,361,080. However, $9,779,801 in gross profit arose from sales cannibalized from other Frito-Lay snack chips (9,314,096 cannibalized lb. volume x $1.05 lb./gross profit = $9,779,801). Total SunChips gross profit:

$30,581,279	Incremental gross profit
9,779,801	Cannibalized gross profit
$40,361,080	SunChips total gross profit

It is also important to note that the cannibalized gross profit will always be 24.1 percent of the projected SunChips total gross profit of the different options considered later in the case, **except** for the flavor extension. A flavor extension could raise the cannibalization rate to 35 percent or the equivalent of 28.3 percent (actually 28.269%).

SunChips recorded a depth-of-repeat of 2.9 times or 3 times annually with an average purchase of 13 ounces. Note that this depth-of-repeat figure is higher than O'Grady's Potato Chips depth-of-repeat of 1.9 times or about twice per year.

Exhibit 7 shows a calculation for sustained dollar volume. This calculation is conservative for a variety of reasons, some of which are:

- It does not consider that adopters will buy any more frequently or more per purchase occasion. They probably will.

- There is a reasonable likelihood that later triers will purchase the product (e.g., laggards), some will repeat, and still others will become adopters.

- This calculation does not consider actions by Frito-Lay such as line (flavor) extensions, price increases, different packaging, etc., all of which could increase dollar sales.

The sustained dollar sales volume estimate of $49,269,737 and gross profit estimate of $23,722,466 therefore represent only "working" estimates for considering subsequent actions to be taken by Frito-Lay.

F. Given your assessment of the test market results, what actions should Dwight Riskey recommend to Frito-Lay's top executives?

1. Riskey and his product management team's presentation to senior Frito-Lay executives would have to conclude with his recommendations for the future marketing of SunChips. He could recommend that:

- the test market be continued for another six months in Minneapolis-St. Paul;

- the test market be expanded to other geographical areas with the same introductory strategy or some modification;

- SunChips be readied for a national introduction with the same introductory strategy or some modification.

Possible modifications in the SunChips market entry strategy include those stated in the case:

- Increase advertising and merchandising spending to the national equivalent of $30 million

- Add a larger package size - 15 ounces

- Certain combinations are possible:
  ... Increase A&M spending **and** add a larger package
  ... Increase A&M spending **and** add another flavor

EXHIBIT 7

CALCULATION OF ESTIMATED SUSTAINED VOLUME AND GROSS PROFIT
(Conservative Estimate)

I. <u>Sustained Dollar Volume</u>

    Given: (1)   Repeater Volume Calculation (adopters) from Exhibit 3 in this note:

                        291,968,820 ounces or 18,248,051 lbs.

              (2)   Weighted Average Price Per Pound: $2.70

<u>Sustained Volume</u> = 18,248,051 lbs. x $2.70 = <u>$49,269,737</u>

II. <u>Sustained Gross Profit</u>

    $1.30 GP/lb x 18,248,051 lbs = <u>$23,722,466</u>

Students might make other suggestions. However, they will have to justify them. Exhibit 8 in this note shows a possible decision tree to structure the decision-making (class discussion) process.

2. **Continue Testing for Six Months in Minneapolis-St. Paul.** Continued testing is justified only if it will provide worthwhile diagnostic information for management action.

   Pros

   - Will allow Frito-Lay to further track trial, repeat, depth-of-repeat and average purchase amounts for repeaters. This might help assess the sustainability issue.

   - Cannibalism potential can be studied further.

   Cons

   - The fundamental strategy has been implemented. **Note:** 70 percent of advertising/merchandising money was spent in the first 6 months.

   - Competitors are probably monitoring Frito-Lay's test market and may even be "reverse engineering" the SunChips multigrain snack. The opportunity to be "first-to-market" might be lost.

   - Probably small incremental dollar expenditure - mostly cost of further tracking by research firm. However, an **opportunity cost** exists assuming the incremental information is only marginally useful.

3. **Expand Test Market to Other Geographical Areas with the Same Strategy or a Modified Strategy.**

   Pros

   - Will allow Frito-Lay an opportunity to assess possible geographical differences in multigrain snack purchase behavior. Perhaps the Minneapolis-St. Paul market is not "typical" with respect to multigrain snack purchase behavior and competitive activity.

   - Will give Frito-Lay another chance to "work-out the bugs" in execution, if any existed.

   - If a modified strategy is used and proves to generate higher volume, Frito-Lay might get a "better fix" on the sales potential for SunChips.

EXHIBIT 8

SUNCHIPS DECISION TREE

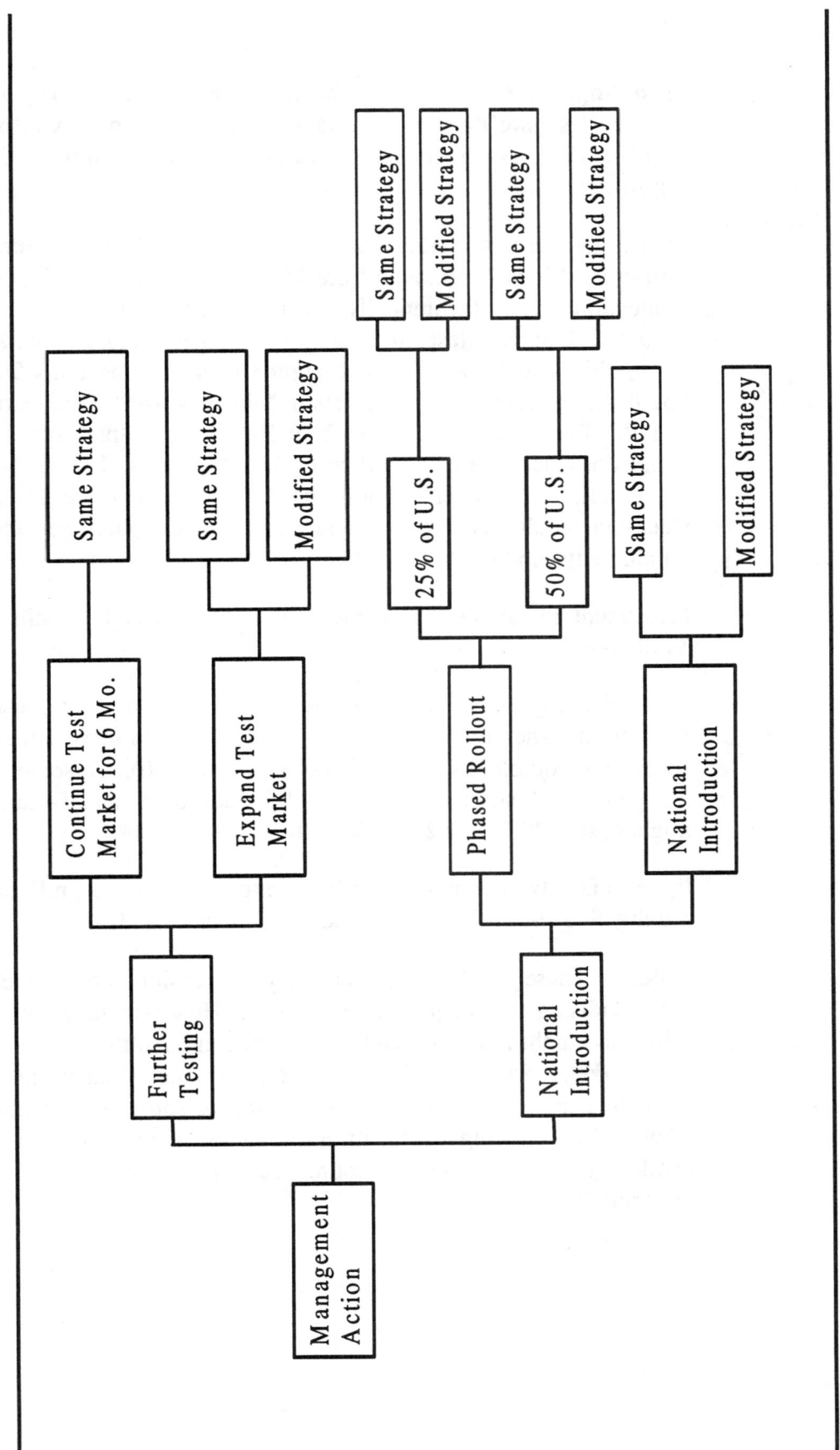

Cons

- **Most important, it may not be possible for Frito-Lay to expand to another test site due to manufacturing limitations. Another test will require the investment in another production line.** Consider the following:

    Expanding the test market will require additional manufacturing capacity **unless** SunChips is removed from Minneapolis-St. Paul. The one existing production line is theoretically capable of producing one million pounds annually. If another test site of comparable size is chosen (i.e., 2.2% of U.S. snack chip users), sales volume approximates Minneapolis-St. Paul (683,062 lbs.), and repeat volume exists in Minneapolis-St. Paul (estimated to be 401,457 lbs.: 18,248,051 lbs. from Exhibit 7 in this note x .022), total pounds produced annually will be 1,084,519 pounds. If the new test is more successful, then the production shortfall becomes more severe. Indeed, stock-outs could result which would affect repeat purchases and distort the purchase dynamics data.

- Investment in another production line can be roughly estimated to cost $440,000:

    Production capacity to serve 25 percent of U.S. snack chip households costs $5 million. Therefore, it costs roughly $200,000 to serve 1 percent of U.S. snack chip households ($5 million ÷ 25 = $200,000). To serve an additional 2.2 percent of snack chip households additional manufacturing capacity might cost $440,000 (2.2 x $200,000).

- If the same advertising/merchandising expenditure of $22 million is applied, roughly $484,000 will be spent: .022 x $22 m = $484,000.

- **Note:** These figures for capacity expansion and advertising and merchandising are rough approximations. However, they demonstrate that Frito-Lay might have to spend almost another $1 million for expanding the test market. Students might be asked to state whether the incremental marketing information is worth $1 million or some similar amount. Also, what dollar value might students assign to time (an opportunity cost); that is, another year spent market testing SunChips. Will the first-to-market opportunity be lost?

4. **Ready SunChips for a National Introduction using the Test Market Strategy or a Modified Strategy.**

   Pros

   - SunChips appears to have created a following as evidence by the depth-of-repeat data.

   - Multigrain snacks appear to be differentiated from other Frito-Lay snack chips as evidenced by the cannibalism rate.

   - SunChips has sales and profit appeal as evidenced by projected annual dollar sales from the test market and incremental gross profit.

   - If introduced, SunChips has a window of opportunity to introduce a pioneer brand thus creating the "prototype" multigrain chip and can build production capacity ahead of competitors. Competitors may "reverse engineer" SunChips, but they may not have the process technology to produce a multigrain snack.

   Cons

   - SunChips is not projected to achieve the $100 million sales goal given the Minneapolis - St. Paul test market.

   - Important issues remain:

     ... Brand awareness is low - would increased advertising and merchandising help? Probably yes.

     ... Trial is lower than expected. Probably due to low brand awareness. That is,

     Brand Awareness → Brand Trial

     Advertising and merchandising drives brand awareness, assuming the message creates attention and is compelling.

5. If Dwight Riskey and his product management team advocates a national introduction, then two important questions remain:

   - Should the introduction be immediate thus requiring a manufacturing investment of $20 million to serve the entire U.S., or phased - add $5 million in manufacturing capacity to serve 25 percent of the U.S., then another $5 million to serve 50 percent of the U.S.?

- Should the market entry strategy be the same as that tested in Minneapolis-St. Paul, or should the strategy be modified? If modified, what modifications are probably necessary?

6. **Market Entry: Capacity Expansion**

At least two questions must be addressed related to the market entry/capacity expansion issue:

- Do the test market strategy and extrapolated results warrant a full-scale introduction?

- Are there benefits to preempting possible competitors such as creating the prototype multigrain chip, building capacity to create possible cost advantages, etc.?

7. **Market Entry: Strategy Change or No Change.**

There seems to be a need to modify the market entry strategy given that test market results do not indicate a sales volume of $100 million in the first year. **It is important for the instructor (and students) to recognize that the quantitative assessments of strategy changes are based almost solely on product management team members' beliefs, perspectives, and assumptions. Students should not take these views as fact!**

It is equally important to note that all of the views expressed are researchable. That is, further testing would shed light on the effect of increased advertising and promotion on household trial, the effect of a flavor extension on repeat buying (and trial) and cannibalism, the effect of a larger package size on stimulating average purchase amounts for repeat households.

a) **Increase Advertising & Merchandising Budget to $30 Million**

Pros

- Should increase brand awareness among snack chip households.

- Increased brand awareness should lead to an increase in brand trial, hence volume.

Cons

- It is not altogether clear that a $30 million expenditure alone will produce the necessary trial level to produce $100 million in sales. Exhibit 9 in this note plots the relationship between A&M spending and brand awareness and brand trial based on the pre-market test (case Exhibit 5). Also shown is SunChips' experience. It is possible to extrapolate pre-market test data assuming a linear relationship. Similarly, it is reasonable to assume decreasing returns to advertising/merchandising (an "S" function). In either instance, SunChips

EXHIBIT 9

PROJECTING SUNCHIPS BRAND AWARENESS AND TRIAL

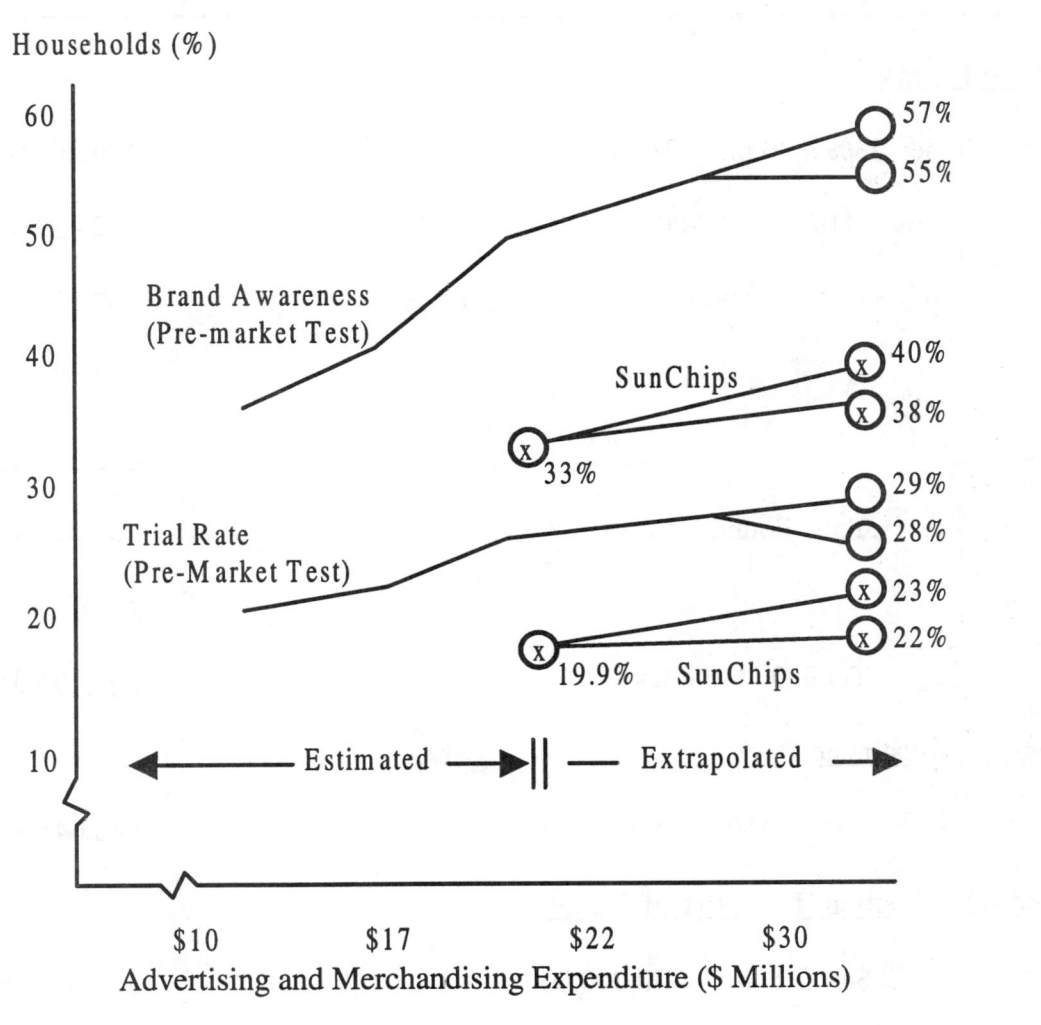

Source: Based on Case Exhibit 5 (Simulated Test Market) and SunChips Test Market Results

EXHIBIT 10

CALCULATION OF SUNCHIPS NATIONAL VOLUME/PROFITABILITY WITH INCREASED ADVERTISING AND MERCHANDISING SPENDING

Volume Estimate

Trial Volume: 23% x 90 mm HH x 6 oz.	124,200,000 oz.
+ Repeat Volume: 41.8% x 20,700,000 HH x 13 oz.	112,483,800 oz.
+ Repeater Volume: 8,652,600 HH x 3 repeats x 13 oz.	<u>337,451,400</u> oz.
	574,135,200 oz.
	÷ <u>16 oz/lb.</u>
Total Pound Volume:	35,883,450 lbs.
	x <u>$2.70/lb.</u>
Total Dollar Sales:	<u>$96,885,315</u>

Gross Profit Estimate

$$35{,}883{,}450 \text{ lbs.} \times \$1/30/\text{lb.} = \$46{,}648{,}485$$

Brand "Contribution" Exclusive of Cannibalism

$$\$46{,}648{,}485 - \$30{,}000{,}000 = \$16{,}648{,}485$$

Brand "Incremental Contribution" after Cannibalism*

$$\$16{,}648{,}485 - \$11{,}303{,}286 = \$5{,}345{,}199$$

---

*Cannibalism calculated as follows:

$$30\% \times 35{,}883{,}450 \text{ lbs.} \times \$1.05 = \$11{,}303{,}286$$

awareness and trial fails to produce $100 million in sales. Exhibit 10 in this note shows that at a trial rate of 23 percent, all other things being equal, projected annual first year sales are $96.9 million and incremental brand contribution is $5.34 million.

b) **Add a larger package size - 15 ounces**

Pros

- Some executives believe this action will provide an opportunity to increase average purchase amount per repeat/repeater purchase occasion, particularly among adopters.

- The net effect is assumed to increase the average purchase amount by one-half ounce among repeat/repeater households who buy three times per year.

Cons

- Adding a larger package is not expected to increase the average gross profit per pound sold. It will, however, increase the SKUs from six to eight. This may possibly affect manufacturing.

- Even though pound volume is expected to increase, the increase does not alone produce sales of $100 million for SunChips (see Exhibit 11 in this note).

c) **Add another flavor - Mild Cheddar**

Pros

- Another flavor would increase variety, thus increasing the likelihood of more "repeats per repeater" - 3½ times as some executives expressed in the case.

- Although not mentioned in the case, a flavor extension might also increase trial, again due to variety.

Cons

- A flavor extension at this stage in commercialization might stretch the product and process technology for multigrain snacks. Frito-Lay has not yet manufactured the Mild Cheddar flavor on a large scale. Note also that another flavor in three sizes increases the SKUs from six to nine.

- It is worth noting from case Exhibit 2 that the Mild Cheddar flavor **did not** score as well as an "everyday snack" as did the other two flavors.

- Another flavor could increase the cannibalism rate to 35 percent from the test market experience of 30 percent as notes by a Frito-Lay executive.

EXHIBIT 11

CALCULATION OF SUNCHIPS VOLUME/PROFITABILITY ASSUMING A 15-OUNCE PACKAGE

Volume Estimate

Trial Volume: 19.9% x 90 mm HH x 6 oz.	107,460,000 oz.
Repeat Volume: 41.8% x 17,910,000 HH x 13½ oz.	101,066,130 oz.
Repeater Volume: 7,486,380 HH x 3 repeats x 13½ oz.	<u>303,198,390</u> oz.
	511,724,520 oz.
	÷ 16 oz./lb.
Total lb. Volume:	31,982,782 lbs.
	x $2.70/lb.
Total Dollar Volume:	$86,353,511

Gross Profit Estimate

    31,982,782 lbs. x $1.30 = $41,577,616

Brand "Contribution" Exclusive of Cannibalism

    $41,577,616 - $22,000,000 = $19,577,616

Brand "Incremental Contribution" after Cannibalism*

    $19,577,616 - $10,074,576 = $9,503,040

---

*Cannibalism calculated as follows:

    30% x 31,982,782 lbs. x $1.05 = $10,074,576

EXHIBIT 12

CALCULATION OF SUNCHIPS NATIONAL VOLUME/PROFITABILITY ASSUMING A FLAVOR EXTENSION

Volume Estimate

Trial Volume: 19.9% x 90 mm HH x 6 oz.	107,460,000 oz.
+	
Repeat Volume: 41.8% x 17.91 mm HH x 13 oz.	97,322,940 oz.
+	
Repeater Volume: 7,486,380 HH x 3½ repeats x 13 oz.	340,630,290 oz.
	545,413,230 oz.
	÷ 16 oz./lb.
Total Pound Volume:	34,088,326
	x $2.70/lb.
Total Dollar Sales:	$ 92,038,480

Gross Profit Estimate

    34,088,326 lbs. x $1.30/lb. = $44,314,823

Brand "Contribution" Exclusive of Cannibalism

    $44,314,823 - $22,000,000 = $22,314,823

Brand "Contribution" after Cannibalism*

    $22,314,823 - $12,527,459 = $ 9,787,364

---

*Cannibalism calculated as follows:

    35% x 34,088,326 lbs. x $1.05 = $12,527,459

- Assuming that the executives are correct as regards the repeats-per-repeater of 3½ times, first-year sales volume still does not achieve $100 million. Exhibit 12 in this note shows calculated sales of $92 million and an incremental brand contribution of $9.8 million.

d) **Increase advertising & merchandising budget to $30 million and introduce a flavor extension**

Pros

- Presumably this action will increase both household trial and depth of repeat (repeats-per-repeater).

- Assuming a 23 percent cumulative trial is achieved and the repeats materialize projected first-year sales become $106.4 million. However, incremental brand contribution becomes $6.7 million (see Exhibit 13 in this note).

Cons

- A modification in advertising & merchandising will be necessary to incorporate the Mild Cheddar flavor. This will represent either an incremental expense or be subtracted from the planned $30 million media and trade budget.

- Another flavor could place an additional burden on manufacturing. It will require the addition of three SKUs (i.e., Mild Cheddar in 3 sizes).

e) **Increase advertising & merchandising budget to $30 million and introduce a larger package**

Pros

- Presumably will increase household trial and increase the amount purchased per occasion by repeats and repeaters.

- Projected sales are almost $100 million ($99.8 million) as shown in Exhibit 14 in this note.

Cons

- Even though dollar sales are generated, the incremental brand contribution is less than the test market strategy.

- A larger package adds two additional SKUs which may cause manufacturing problems.

EXHIBIT 13

CALCULATION OF SUNCHIPS VOLUME/PROFITABILITY WITH INCREASED ADVERTISING AND MERCHANDISING EXPENDITURE AND A FLAVOR EXTENSION

Volume Estimate

Trial Volume: 23% x 90 mm hh x 6 oz.	124,200,000 oz.
+ Repeat Volume: 41.8% x 20,700,000 x 13 oz.	112,483,800 oz.
+ Repeater Volume: 8,652,600 x 3½ repeats x 13 oz.	393,693,300 oz.
	630,377,100 oz.
	÷ 16 oz./lb.
Total Pound Volume:	39,398,568 lbs.
	x $2.70/lb.
Total Dollar Sales:	$106,376,130

Gross Profit Estimate

39,398,568 lbs. x $1.30/lb.   = $51,218,138

Brand "Contribution" Exclusive of Cannibalism

$51,218,138 - $30,000,000   = $21,218,138

Brand "Incremental Contribution" after Cannibalism*

$21,218,138 - $14,478,972   = $ 6,739,166

---

*Cannibalism calculated as follows:

35% x 39,398,568 lbs. x $1.05   = $14,478,972

EXHIBIT 14

CALCULATION OF SUNCHIPS VOLUME/PROFITABILITY WITH INCREASED ADVERTISING AND MERCHANDISING EXPENDITURE AND A LARGER PACKAGE

Volume Estimate

Trial Volume: 23% x 90 mm HH x 6 oz.	124,200,000 oz.
+ Repeat Volume: 41.8% x 20,700,000 x 13½ oz.	116,810,100 oz.
+ Repeater Volume: 8,652,600 HH x 3 repeats x 13½ oz.	350,430,300 oz.
	591,440,400 oz.
	÷ 16 oz./lb.
Total Pound Volume:	36,965,025 lbs.
	x $2.70/lb.
Total Dollar Volume:	$99,805,567

Gross Profit Estimate

36,965,025 lbs. x $1.30/lb. = $48,054,532

Brand "Contribution" Exclusive of Cannibalism

$48,054,532 - $30,000,000 A&M = $18,054,532

Brand "Incremental Contribution" after Cannibalism*

$18,054,532 - $13,584,645 = $ 4,469,887

---

*Cannibalism calculated as follows:

35% x 36,965,025 x $1.05 = $13,584,645

G. Further Considerations Pertaining to the Recommendation

1. Exhibit 15 summarizes the sensitivity analyses pertaining to the strategy change options. As indicated:

- Two strategy options generally satisfy the first year $100 million sales goal

    ... Increase A&M Budget and Add a Larger Package ($99.8 mm)

    ... Increase A&M Budget and Add a New Flavor ($106.4 mm)

- Two strategy options result in the highest first-year incremental brand contribution:

    ... Introduce a Flavor-Extension ($9.78 mm)

    ... Add a 15-ounce package ($9.5 mm)

2. Two possible questions can be posed to students at this juncture:

"Would you continue testing, spend another $1 million, and wait another year to find out what product-promotion strategy should be pursued given what you have done so far?"

Alternatively,

"Does your analysis thus far suggest a phased national introduction, building manufacturing capacity in $5 million increments and extending the roll-out over, say two years, rather than launching the product nationally which would involve $20 million capital investment and a $30 million advertising and merchandising expenditure?"

H. Epilogue

Dwight Riskey and his product management team recommended that SunChips Multigrain Snacks be launched nationally in the fall of 1990 supported by a $30 million advertising and merchandising expenditure. In effect, a $50 million investment was recommended. The recommendation was approved by senior Frito-Lay management.

SunChips achieved first year sales of $100 million. It is worth mentioning to students that the first-year sales projection based on a $30 million advertising and merchandising expenditure only (see Exhibits 9 and 10 in this note) was $96.9 million. In the fall of 1991, a flavor extension was introduced called "Harvest Cheddar" which was the Mild Cheddar. Second year sales were $190 million. Third year sales topped $200 million.

EXHIBIT 15

SUNCHIPS SALES AND PROFIT SUMMARY FOR MODIFIED STRATEGY OPTIONS

	Increase A&M Budget to $30 Million	Add 15-oz Package	Introduce Flavor Extension	Increase A&M Budget and Add Large Package	Increase A&M Budget and Add Flavor
Sales	$96,885,315	$86,353,511	$92,038,480	$99,805,567	$106,376,130
Gross Profit	$46,648,485	$41,577,616	$44,314,823	$48,054,532	$51,218,138
Cannibalization	($11,303,286)	($10,074,576)	($12,527,459)	($13,584,645)	($14,478,972)
A&M Budget	($30,000,000)	($22,000,000)	($22,000,000)	($30,000,000)	($30,000,000)
Incremental Brand "Contribution"	$ 5,345,199	$ 9,503,040	$ 9,787,364	$ 4,469,887	$ 6,739,166

TEST MARKET RESULTS: BASE CASE	
Sales	$83,826,859
Gross Profit	$40,361,080
Cannibalism	($ 9,779,801)
A&M Budget	($22,000,000)
Incremental Brand "Contribution"	$ 8,581,279

Frito-Lay executives opted to spend $30 million in A&M spending because it was felt that brand awareness and trial needed to be bolstered to establish the brand and category - which it did. Concerns related to manufacturing affected the decision not to add another flavor for the national introduction or add a larger package size.

In 1993, a larger package size was introduced. In 1995, SunChips underwent a major ingredient change to reduce the chip's fat content. As of early 1997, SunChips was regarded as a Frito-Lay "core brand."

Frito-Lay executives interpreted the successful launch of SunChips to mean that the "better-for-you" category of snack chips could represent a viable category for Frito-Lay to vigorously pursue. In 1995, Frito-Lay launched Baked Lay's low-fat potato chips for the "better-for-you" category. Baked Lay's posted sales of $250 million in its first full year on the market.

I. Summary Points

1. This case introduces the fundamental decision when test marketing new products:

    - Continue testing
    - Expand the test to other locations
    - Introduce the product
    - Kill the product

    The decision often revolves around the sales volume forecast given test market data.

2. Trial, repeat, and depth of repeat purchase data can be used to forecast new product sales volume for frequently purchased consumer goods. Each type of purchase data provides important data by itself. For example:

    - Trial rates provide an assessment of promotional activity.
    - Repeat rates provide information on the incidence of new product acceptance.
    - Depth-of-repeat data provide information on long-run viability of the product.

3. Product cannibalism is almost always present in new product introductions and must be considered. It is necessary to calculate the incremental sales produced by the new product and the incremental cost of introducing the new product.

4. Marketing and manufacturing considerations often must be considered in new product introductions. In this case, production capacity and production capability, in the form of product and process technology, had to be jointly factored into the decision-making process.

5. A detailed financial analysis is always necessary in new product introductions, particularly during the business analysis phase of the product development process.

UNITED STATES CENSUS BUREAU: MARKETING SERVICES OFFICE

Synopsis

In late 1999, Jack Campbell (a pseudonym), Chief of the Marketing Services Office (MSO) in the U.S. Census Bureau, scheduled a meeting with the managers of the four work units in the office. The Marketing Services Office is a small (49 employees at the time of the case) but visible office in the Census Bureau. Its primary mission is to provide marketing support for more than 30 program areas in the Census Bureau. An implicit issue in the case relates to the future role and position of the MSO in the Bureau.

The purpose of the meeting is to begin developing a long-range marketing strategy for the Marketing Services Office. Campbell is a bit concerned that the meeting will be dominated by discussion of the marketing campaign currently being run to increase public participation in the 2000 population census. For the first time ever, the Census Bureau is employing a comprehensive, professionally managed marketing campaign in an attempt to increase response rates to mailed census questionnaires and facilitate the jobs of census enumerators. Although the Marketing Services Office will be involved in certain post-census marketing activities, Campbell wants to develop a comprehensive marketing strategy that extends beyond its census-related responsibilities.

The meeting produces an open discussion and provides a lively exchange of ideas. Numerous strategic marketing issues and initiatives are identified in the meeting, and the meeting ends with Campbell requesting that the managers address the **fundamental** strategic marketing issues facing the MSO and recommend what markets, products, and services the MSO should focus on as well as how to focus on them. In general, the case is concerned with coalescing strategic marketing issues and prioritizing strategic marketing initiatives in the context of a nonprofit (government) agency.

Teaching Objectives

This case has three general teaching objectives:

1. To remind students that marketing is employed by all organizations, whether private or public, and to emphasize its importance in accomplishing organizational objectives.

2. To provide insights into a major marketing event—marketing the 2000 population census—that is likely to influence the application of marketing in government agencies in the future.

3. To communicate the idea that developing marketing strategies can be a "messy business" involving many, often competing, ideas, agendas, and priorities.

4. To illustrate distinctions between strategic marketing issues and strategic marketing initiatives and suggest a framework for identifying strategic marketing issues.

Teaching Suggestions

This case is best utilized at the beginning of a course to generate discussion of the role of marketing and emphasize the fact that all organizations, in one fashion or another, use marketing to achieve their objectives. Because of the recency of the 2000 population census and especially the publicity it received regarding response rates and advertising, as well as the controversy over methodology (census versus sample) and whether households receiving the long version of the census questionnaire were required to answer all questions, most students will be aware of it. Moreover, most students will be able to relate some personal experience or communicated anecdote regarding the census. Consequently, when used at the beginning of a course, the case often leads to stimulating discussions regarding the 2000 population census per se and/or the Census Bureau's marketing and marketing expenditures relating to it. As an aside, it is interesting to note that the Census Bureau's measured media advertising in the first quarter of 2000 placed it in the upper 1% of all entities (i.e., brands) advertising in that period.

Due to the absence of detailed quantitative analyses, the case is best suited for an undergraduate course. A pedagogical approach that seems to "work" is to have groups of students independently role-play the work unit managers and (1) identify the strategic marketing issues facing the MSO and (2) prioritize the strategic marketing initiatives addressing the issues. Following this, each of the groups can be asked to present and defend the strategic marketing issues and initiatives identified as well as the prioritization of the latter to the remaining groups. There is usually considerable discussion and disagreement among students as to what actually constitutes "strategic" (as opposed to "tactical") marketing issues and initiatives, and how the two differ. A major part of the class discussion may center on respectively disentangling strategies and tactics and issues and initiatives.

In certain instances it is appropriate to ask students to visit the Census Bureau website (www.census.gov) prior to discussing this case in class. Many students will visit the site on their own, simply because it is mentioned in the case. Asking students to visit the website facilitates classroom discussions since all will then have been exposed the contents of the site. Besides, the site contains a wealth of information that students may find helpful in other contexts. Instructors who follow this approach may find it worthwhile to begin discussion of the case by inquiring about what is on the Census Bureau's website.

Specific questions that might be used to guide an analysis and discussion include the following, organized from general to specific:

1. What are the activities and responsibilities of the Census Bureau?

2. What distinguishes the 2000 population census from previous censuses?

3. What is the role of the Marketing Services Office within the Census Bureau?

4. What are the major strategic issues being proposed in the meeting?

5. What should the MSO's strategic marketing initiatives be, and why?

Areas for Discussion/Analysis

A. What are the activities and responsibilities of the Census Bureau?

1. The predecessor to the United States Census Bureau was formally established in 1890 to coordinate population censuses. Prior to that time population censuses were carried out under the supervision of United States marshals or a temporary agency. In 1913 the Census Bureau was formally named and placed under the direction of the Department of Commerce.

2. Over time the activities and responsibilities of the Census Bureau have expanded from only conducting the population census every ten years to conducting dozens of censuses and surveys for federal, state, and government agencies as well as other organizations. Even so, the population census remains the Bureau's most critical responsibility, daunting task, and visible activity. To illustrate, the Census Bureau's budget for 2000 was $4.6 billion, of which $4.5 billion was dedicated to the 2000 population census. This budget was nearly ten times the average annual budget for years in which a population census was not conducted.

3. The expanded activities and responsibilities of the Census Bureau are reflected in its official mission statement: "To be the preeminent collector and provider of timely, relevant, and quality data about the people and economy of the United States." Case Exhibit 2 contains examples of data products resulting from the censuses and surveys that the Census Bureau conducts. The exhibit reveals that the Census Bureau produces a wide range of data products, from reference books, to data on imports and exports, to economic and demographic data, and even geographic data.

B. **What distinguishes the 2000 population census from previous censuses?**

1. The United States Constitution requires that a census of the population be carried out every ten years. The principal purpose of the census is to provide information that can be used to determine the number of congressional representatives that will be allocated to each state. Other purposes include providing information for determining local voting district boundaries, allocating federal funds, and defining the socioeconomic characteristics of the population.

2. In the three most recent population censuses (1970, 1980, and 1990), the percentage of the population returning mailed-out census questionnaires declined from 78 percent to 65 percent. In an attempt to increase the mail return rate and facilitate the jobs of census enumerators, Census Bureau employees who personally interview individuals not returning mailed questionnaires, the Census Bureau initiated a comprehensive, professionally managed marketing campaign. (Instructor note: Previously the Bureau had used PSAs, public service announcements or free advertisements appearing at the convenience of the media and often on late-night television, to communicate information about a population census).

3. The comprehensive, paid marketing campaign was a "first" for the Census Bureau. Never before had the Census Bureau been allocated funds by Congress to "market a census." The Bureau hired an advertising agency, Young and Rubicam, conducted research, and developed a demographic and attitudinal segmentation scheme in order to focus on increasing the likelihood that "hard-to-enumerate" groups (e.g., Hmongs) would complete and return census questionnaires mailed to them.

4. The marketing campaign consisted of five interrelated components:

- Partnerships between the Bureau and more than 32,000 government agencies and for-profit and not-for-profit organizations to personally communicate the benefits of the census and encourage participation.

- Media public relations to obtain as much publicity as possible for the census.

- A "census in schools" program that distributed teaching kits to more than 300,000 elementary and secondary school teachers for classroom presentations and discussion (with the hope that students would urge their parents to participate in the census).

- Special promotions and events (e.g., parades) to increase awareness.

- An advertising program.

5. The advertising program consisted of three different temporal phases, each with a different purpose (creating awareness, motivating behavior, and encouraging cooperation). It employed virtually all advertising media and respectively focused on all English-speaking people and the demographic and attitudinal segments defined by research as hard-to-enumerate. The unifying theme or tagline of the advertising program, which appeared on or in every advertisement (albeit in a modified form for some segments), was "This is Your Future. Don't Leave it Blank." Nearly $167 million was budgeted for the advertising program.

C. **What is the role of the Marketing Services Office within the Census Bureau?**

1. The Marketing Services Office (MSO) is a small, 49-employee office within the Census Bureau. (The number of permanent employees in the Census Bureau is more than 12,000.) However, even though it is small, MSO is relatively visible because of some of the activities it performs (see below).

2. Although not explicitly mentioned in the case, it would seem that the role (and position) of the Marketing Services Office in the Census Bureau is at least somewhat uncertain and perhaps a bit tenuous. This observation is based on several pieces of information in the case. First, case Exhibit 4 indicates that the office has had a rather tortuous history. It originated as the Data Services Division and "morphed" into its present form after a series of offices, branches, and divisions were respectively created, abolished, and/or combined.

3. Moreover, in its various forms the MSO has reported to a variety of positions, with the most recent reporting relationship apparently representing a "demotion." Second, the MSO does not appear to have its own mission statement. Although it originally (see case Exhibit 4) was visualized (in 1993) as having responsibility for "marketing the Census Bureau, its programs (especially large-scale surveys for other federal agencies), and data products," its responsibility seems to be limited to the latter activity. Third, many of the MSO's responsibilities seem unrelated to "marketing." Fourth, the revenue produced by the office is miniscule compared with that obtained from conducting reimbursable studies for various agencies and organizations. Finally, the comments in the case imply that the office needs to better market itself inside the Census Bureau or else it risks becoming obsolete. The chance that the office may face a tight budget once the 2000 population census has been completed suggests MSO managers are aware of potential problems.

4. The Marketing Services Office is organized into four work units, each headed by a manager reporting to Jack Campbell:

- The Customer Service Center (CSC) work unit, managed by Harrison Leslie, processes off-the-shelf data product orders, answers questions on a wide variety of topics, and is frequently the first point of contact for customers external to the Bureau.

- The Research, Planning and Evaluation (RP&E) work unit, managed by Carol Ford, is responsible for the MSO's in-house customer database, conducts sales analyses, and is generally responsible for market and data product research.

- The American Community Survey (ACS) work unit, managed by Maureen Chalsonte, is responsible for all aspects of marketing the newly developed annual survey (i.e., the American Community Survey) of population characteristics designed to replace the administration of the long version of the population census questionnaire.

- The Promotions work unit, managed by Ralph Brown, is responsible for a variety of activities ranging from direct mail campaigns to conference and event coordination and publication management and distribution.

(Note: all managers' names are disguised.)

5. One of the primary responsibilities of the Marketing Services Office is marketing various Census Bureau data products and services. In fiscal 1999, the MSO produced revenues of approximately $1.2 million, which represented a decrease of 8% from fiscal year 1998 and a decrease of 25% from fiscal year 1997. As the case notes, the decreases were probably due at least in part to the cyclical nature of demand for Census Bureau data products. For example, products based on 1990 census data were virtually obsolete in 1999 and sales of them would be expected to be relatively minor. Case Exhibit 5 confirms this expectation.

6. Since 11,009 products were shipped in fiscal 1999, the average product was priced at approximately $109 ($1.2 million/11,009 products), whereas the average order was $115 ($1.2 million/10,434 orders). (The average product price is intuitively logical given that 60% of the MSO's data-products revenue was derived from the sale of CD-ROMs.) Further, the average order consisted of 1.06 data products, which indicates that the vast majority of customers only purchased a single data product.

7. Three factors probably constrain the revenues that the MSO could be expected to generate (apart from the data products themselves). First, the MSO is required to market its data products at cost. Second, many of the Census Bureau's data products are sold by and through the Government Printing Office (GPO), not the MSO. Since the Government Printing Office is a separate entity from the Census Bureau, the MSO receives no revenues from GPO sales. Third, many of the Census Bureau's data products are made available without charge to a variety of state data centers, libraries, universities, federal agencies, and other organizations (including the media), detracting from potential sales.

D. What are the major strategic issues being proposed in the meeting?

1. Successful analysis of this case requires that strategic marketing issues be recognized and initiatives to address these issues identified and prioritized. Careful consideration of the various discussion points in the meeting in the context of broader issues in the case reveals four major classes of strategic issues that coincidently relate to marketing's "four p's."

- Pricing issues
- Product issues
- Distribution issues
- Promotion issues

These issues were discussed both directly and indirectly in the meeting and from a variety of perspectives. For several of these issues strategic initiatives were suggested. Other issues set forth in the meeting either did not possess a strategic orientation or were idiosyncratic to an individual or work unit. Examples of such issues were reflected by questions regarding entrepreneurial activities and the forthcoming centennial anniversary of the Census Bureau.

2. Pricing issues were reflected by decisions that have to be made regarding the appropriate prices to charge for the various data products. Should the Census Bureau simply make data products available to everyone at no cost? If there is a charge, the questions then become how to price products (for example, cost recovery versus attempting to achieve a "surplus" or profit) and whether quantity discounts should be offered.

3. Product issues were reflected by decisions that have to be made about data products to offer—for example, whether the Census Bureau should offer a print-on-demand service and customized data products—and the form in which data products should be offered. Additional product issues include how to control product development time and time lags between product announcements and product availability and whether it was possible to obtain exclusivity on certain data products through copyrights or the like.

4. Discussions of distribution issues primarily revolved around the role of the Internet in disseminating data products. Considerable uncertainty was expressed regarding the extent to which the Internet would or could be employed in disseminating data products from the 2000 population census. The issue of whether and how to distribute Census Bureau data products internationally was also one identified as needing attention.

5. Communication issues were represented by questions relating to how the MSO could better market itself internally, better communicate with external customers, and better manage its events and exhibits programs.

6. There is an additional issue that subsumes the other four. This is the issue of marketing forthcoming 2000 population census data products. Although there was limited

overt discussion of this issue in the meeting, most likely it was on the minds of all meeting participants.

E. What should the MSO's strategic marketing initiatives be, and why?

1. Without question, the principal Marketing Services Office strategic initiative must be marketing the forthcoming 2000 population census data products. This initiative will undoubtedly require considerable MSO resources and managerial attention because of its importance and visibility. Consider the following example. According to the case, in the previous fiscal year the MSO processed 10,434 product orders. It is anticipated that in 2002 the Customer Services Center will process more than 60,000 orders. This represents about a six-fold increase in the number of orders that must be processed and indicates a need for considerable planning and an increase in personnel. Note that the projected increase in the number of orders implies that the MSO will also be generating considerably more revenue than it does presently.

2. There is probably no need for a pricing initiative. The Marketing Services Office is very constrained regarding pricing options. Offering products at a "zero" price (that is, giving them away) would seem to inconsistent with the alleged mandate to be more entrepreneurial and the opinion that the MSO's budget will become tighter after the 2000 population census has been completed. Market-based pricing or pricing to achieve a surplus is not permitted. The Census Bureau can only price to recover costs. Quantity discounts may be questionable since they may imply that the original price was something other than a cost-recovery price.

3. Similarly, there is probably no need for a data product initiative. The Marketing Services Office has no formal control over product development and the time between product announcements and product availability. Indeed, because of its size, the Marketing Services Office probably does not have much informal influence over such activities and occurrences either. Likewise, since the Census Bureau cannot have copyrights or exclusive rights to data products, there is nothing that the Marketing Services Office can do in this regard. Product resellers will continue to purchase data products from the Census Bureau at a minimal cost and resell them at some higher price.

4. There does seem to be a need for a strategic initiative relating to the distribution of data products. In particular, the role of the Internet in distributing data products needs to be explicitly addressed. It is clear that the Internet is already affecting the manner in which individuals communicate with, interact with, and purchase products from, the Census Bureau. For example, the case states that the Census Bureau's website was experiencing more than one million "hits" **per day**. Moreover, although the MSO only started marketing data products through the Census Bureau's website in July 1999, already nearly 25% of the orders it processes originate from the website. (The fact that 40% of the website orders have originated during nonbusiness hours, as well as the fact that 60% of the orders are from new customers, suggests that the purchasers are not traditional businesses.) Attempts to market

Census Bureau products internationally should be considered in the context of an Internet-based marketing effort.

5. Finally, both internal and external communication initiatives probably deserve attention. Given the MSO's differing assignments and perhaps somewhat nebulous responsibilities, together with its position in the Census Bureau and relative size, an internal communication initiative would seem appropriate. Communicating 2000 population census data products to potential customers would also seem to be an appropriate strategic initiative.

6. In brief, marketing data products from the 2000 population census should be accorded the highest priority of the initiatives identified. The second-highest priority—and obviously one related to the first initiative—should be the development of an Internet-based marketing strategy. Attention should also be given to a communication initiative. Because of both internal and external constraints, neither a pricing initiative nor a product initiative appears warranted at this time.

F. Epilogue

Subsequent to the meeting with the unit managers, Campbell drafted a marketing strategy for the Marketing Services Office. As might be expected, the strategy emphasized issues relating to marketing 2000 population census data products. The strategy noted that the MSO had little discretion in pricing and that cost recovery would likely be the major determinant when setting individual data product prices. Although pricing decisions were not finalized, it was likely that there would be no charge for American Factfinder. No new pricing initiatives were recommended.

The strategy established a task force to investigate how to integrate the various new data products that would be offered as a consequence of the 2000 population census. It was anticipated that relatively more customized data products would be requested by users when the 2000 population census data products became available. The strategy recognized that the MSO had no control over product development time schedules and that federal data are by definition in the public domain and hence, for example, printed data products were not copyrightable. No major data product initiatives were incorporated into the strategy.

The strategy emphasized distributing data products over the Internet. This emphasis was viewed as a major strategic initiative and the Internet was viewed as a strategic imperative. Simultaneously, an expanded array of CD-based products was contemplated and an investigation into the use of DVDs as a distribution medium was recommended.

No strategic communication initiatives were planned. Because the focus of the strategy was on marketing 2000 population census data products, it was thought that communication issues would resolve themselves. As Campbell often reiterated after the meeting, "It's all decennial [census] at this point."

In early 2000, the Marketing Services Office was assigned additional responsibilities. For example, it was tasked with responding to residual inquiries regarding the 2000 population census. In April alone more than 10,000 emails and telephone calls relating to the 2000 population census were processed by MSO. It also was tasked with coordinating the Census Bureau's move to a new order entry and inventory system and procuring call center software and additional CD-ROM hardware. (These assignments suggest that the role of the MSO in the Census Bureau has yet to be finalized.)

G. Summary Points

1. All organizations have a marketing function, even a government agency that has as its mission the provision of data and information. Because organizations have a marketing function, they must have a marketing strategy.

2. All marketing strategies must begin with the identification of strategic issues. Often this is a difficult task that requires considerable creativity. Using the four p's as an organizing framework frequently facilitates identifying fundamental strategic marketing issues.

3. Once strategic marketing issues have been identified, it is necessary to develop and prioritize strategic initiatives to address the issues. Doing so typically requires the input of individuals who will implement the initiatives or be affected by the initiatives.

BIOPURE CORPORATION

Synopsis

Biopure Corporation is a small biopharmaceutical firm with $200 million invested in the development of a revolutionary new "blood substitute" designed to replace the need for donated blood. To date, the company has developed two (and only two) products—"Oxyglobin" for the veterinary market and "Hemopure" for the human market. These products are nearly identical in physical properties and production processes. Oxyglobin has just recently been approved for commercial release by the U.S. Food and Drug Administration while Hemopure is still two years away from final FDA approval.

The tension in the case involves what to do with Oxyglobin. Conventional wisdom suggests that the market for Oxyglobin is small and price sensitive, while the market for Hemopure is large and price insensitive. Further, due to the physical similarity of the two products, there is a fear that Oxyglobin will create an unacceptably low price expectation for Hemopure if released first. As a result, Biopure is questioning whether to immediately release Oxyglobin or to delay its release until after Hemopure has established itself in the marketplace? And if Oxyglobin is released now, how should it be brought to market?

As a comprehensive marketing programs case, Biopure illustrates the challenge of determining where to compete, how to compete, and when to compete in the development of a marketing strategy. As such, the case links directly to the discussion in chapter 11

Teaching Objectives

This case has three multi-faceted teaching objectives.

1. **Marketing Potential.** Students should consider how large a market needs to be before it is attractive in its own right. A detailed analysis reveals (1) that the animal market is larger and that the human market is smaller than initially expected and (2) that Biopure faces little competition in the vet market and substantial competition in the human market.

2. **Reference Pricing.** What is the most important benchmark when deciding how to price a new product? While Biopure worries about the impact of Oxyglobin on Hemopure, other benchmarks in the human market may be more important (e.g., the price of donated blood, the price of competitor's blood substitutes, the value of a life).

This note was prepared by John T. Gourville for the sole purpose of aiding classroom instructors in the use of BIOPURE Corporation, HBS No. 598-150. It provides analysis and questions that are intended to present alternative approaches to deepening students' comprehension of business issues and energizing classroom discussion. (Copyright © 1999 by the President and Fellows of Harvard College. Used with permission.

3. **Going to Market.** When starting from scratch, how does one decide on price, distribution and a target market? Being a technology-based company, Biopure has spent little to no time thinking about these marketing issues.

Teaching Suggestions

This business-to-business case has multiple uses. It can be used as an Opportunity Analysis and Targeting case, a Pricing Strategy case, and as a Comprehensive Marketing Programs case. The case is suitable for both undergraduate and graduate students and can be used for examination or group presentation purposes, ideally toward the end of the course.

Given the strong "Go" vs. "No Go" focus in the case, students likely will have formed an opinion about whether Oxyglobin should be launched immediately. As such, it is recommended that instructors start with a "What would you do?" type of opener with the expectation that the student will provide a rationale for either launching or not launching Oxyglobin. Based on the first student's response to this opener, the instructor should look to solicit the opinion of other students who either agree or disagree with the first student's viewpoint. The instructor should avoid being too directive during this initial discussion and should merely attempt to capture the various students' comments on the blackboard under the headings "Reasons to Launch" and "Reasons to Not Launch". This initial discussion should last about 15 minutes.

Four themes will likely emerge from this initial discussion. The four themes involve (1) the uncertainty surrounding Hemopure's FDA approval, (2) the potential of the animal versus the human market, (3) the potential impact of Oxyglobin's pricing on Hemopure, and (4) the challenge faced by Biopure in "going to market". In all likelihood, the first of these themes is self-contained and need not be expanded upon further. The remaining three themes, however, deserve further attention and should be addressed in turn.

After the opening discussion, the instructor should focus the class's attention on theme (2): relative market potential. The goal of this discussion should be to highlight the fact that the animal market is larger than it first appears and that the human market is smaller and more competitive than it first appears. This discussion might take 20 minutes. Next, the instructor should focus the discussion on theme (3): potential impact of Oxyglobin's pricing on Hemopure. This discussion might take 15 minutes.

With about 20 minutes left in class and after having addressed themes 1, 2 and 3, the instructor may wish to ask for a show of hands as to whether Biopure should launch or not launch Oxyglobin. Experience with the case suggests that at least 75% of the students will want to launch citing the market potential of Oxyglobin and the risks associated with Hemopure as the primary reasons. With this being the case, the instructor should transition to a marketing plan for Oxyglobin, perhaps with the question, "So, most of you want to go ahead with Oxyglobin. How would you go about doing it? What would the details be?" This should lead naturally to a discussion of target marketing, price and distribution. A suggested board plan for the class discussion is provided in Exhibit 1 in this note.

EXHIBIT 1

SUGGESTED BOARD PLAN

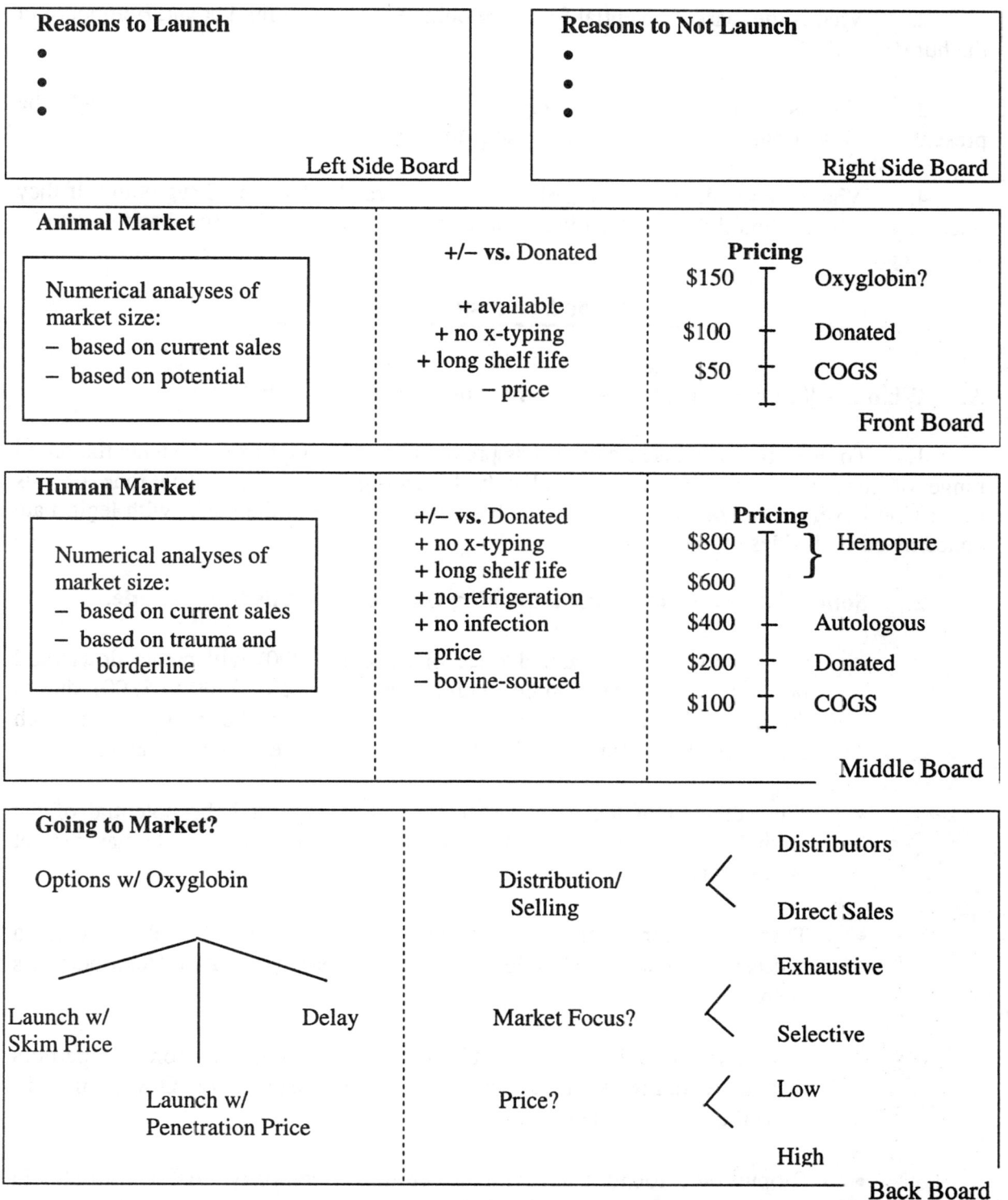

Specific questions that can be posed to students either before class or during a class discussion are:

1. What are likely reasons for and against launching Oxyglobin?

2. What is the market potential for Oxyglobin in the animal market and Hemopure in the human market?

3. What is the likely impact of Oxyglobin's pricing on Hemopure? How might the presence of Oxyglobin be an asset or liability to Hemopure?

4. What should Biopure do regarding the commercial release of Oxyglobin? If they release, what price should they set? How should Oxyglobin be sold/distributed and to who?

Areas for Discussion/Analysis

A. What are likely reasons for and against launching Oxyglobin?

1. To open the case discussion, it has proven useful to elicit from students the broad range of reasons for and against immediately launching Oxyglobin. The tone of this discussion is very much one of "a bird in the hand is worth two in the bush" with legitimate concerns on both sides of the argument.

2. **Some of the reasons for not launching Oxyglobin at this time include:**

- Oxyglobin (with a planned price of $100 to $200) will create downward price pressure on Hemopure (with a planned price of $600 to $800), due to the physical similarity of the two products. Given that margins are much greater for Hemopure, this downward price pressure is unacceptable.

- The potential of the human market is very large and the potential of the animal market is small. Why do anything to jeopardize the human market opportunity?

- There is no foreseeable competition in the animal market, allowing for a successful launch of Oxyglobin in several years (i.e., after Hemopure has been launch).

- Hemopure is bovine-sourced and will be prone to attacks from competitors that have human-sourced products. The existence of Oxyglobin will exacerbate this problem.

- Biopure was founded as a "human products" company. As such, it should not do anything to jeopardize that focus or image.

- Biopure has limited capacity to produce either Oxyglobin or Hemopure. Given that the expected margins on these two products strongly favors Hemopure, why take up valuable production capacity with Oxyglobin.

- A recent round of venture capital financing ($50 million) is sufficient to support operations for the next two years, until Hemopure is projected to gain FDA approval.

3. **At the same time, other students will generate a host of reasons for immediately launching Oxyglobin. These include:**

- The timing of Hemopure's FDA approval is still uncertain and there are reasons to believe that Hemopure will take longer than the projected two years to launch. First, Baxter is experiencing difficulties with its human blood substitute. Second, some recent high-profile product failures demonstrate that no biotech product is guaranteed FDA approval. Third, Biopure has yet to receive approval for Phase 3 clinical trials.

- Delaying Oxyglobin means giving up two to three years of revenues, revenues that would help in the launch of Hemopure.

- Oxyglobin and Hemopure were designed for distinctly different markets. While the products may be physically similar, they are not interchangeable, decreasing the potential for cross-market price pressures.

- Oxyglobin will greatly expand the current animal transfusion market, making the animal market very attractive in its own right.

- Oxyglobin has a 2+ year **first-mover advantage** in the animal market. If launched now, Oxyglobin could gain acceptance among veterinarians and lock up a substantial portion of the market before any competitors can enter.

- Biopure has no experience launching a product of any type and Oxyglobin will allow them to gain some experience in going to market. As stated by Andy Wright, "would you rather make a mistake now with Oxyglobin, or in two years with Hemopure?"

- The Oxyglobin marketing team is in place and ready to go.

4. In summarizing these points, four themes emerge. These themes involve (1) the uncertainty surrounding Hemopure's FDA approval, (2) the potential of the animal versus the human market, (3) the potential impact of Oxyglobin's pricing on Hemopure and (4) the challenge faced by Biopure in "going to market".

5. The first of these issues—i.e., uncertainty surrounding Hemopure's FDA approval – is rather straightforward and should be adequately addressed in the initial "launch vs. don't launch" debate. In particular, students should recognize and agree that Hemopure is not a sure bet to gain FDA approval within two years and factor that uncertainty into their subsequent decision-making. The remaining issues are more complex and demand further attention.

B. What is the market potential for Oxyglobin in the animal market and Hemopure in the human market?

1. The case is written to suggest that the animal market is much less attractive than the human market. On page 1, Ted Jacobs' states that the "... veterinary market is small and price sensitive. We'll be lucky to get $150 per unit ..." while the "... human market ... is many times larger and we can realistically achieve price points of $600 to $800..."

2. Students should be expected to critically analyze this claim. Based on preliminary analyses that use current levels of animal and human blood transfusions, Jacobs' argument seems to hold. However, more complete analyses suggest that Oxyglobin greatly expands the market for animal transfusions while Hemopure might replace donated blood only in select applications.

3. **The Market Potential for Oxyglobin.** There are several different approaches for estimating the market potential for Oxyglobin:

- **Based on Current Transfusion Levels.** Some students will mistakenly gauge the potential for Oxyglobin based on the existing levels of animal transfusions. If so, these students should estimate a potential market of 300,000 to 350,000 units per year, as shown below. At the suggested price of $150 per unit, this would imply a market potential of $45 to $53 MM (million) per year:

    <u>Estimate #1:</u> (based on statistics given in the case):

        15,000 practices   (number of veterinary practices)
    x 800 dogs/yr./practice (dogs/yr./practice suffering from acute blood loss)
    x 2.5%   (% of those dogs who receive a transfusion)

    = 300,000 units/year
    x $150 per unit

    = $45 MM per year

Estimate #2: (based on transfusions at primary care vs. emergency care facilities given in the case):

    242,250 units/year   (= 15,000 practices x 95% primary care x 17 units/year)
+ 112,500 units/year   (= 15,000 practices x 5% emergency care x 150 units/year)

= 354,750 units/year
x $150 per unit

= $ 53.2 MM per year

- **Based on Potential to Expand the Market.** Other students will recognize that 300,000 to 350,000 units per year is a very conservative estimate. In particular, they will note that while 30% of the dogs suffering from acute blood loss would benefit from a transfusion, only 2.5% currently receive one. More generally, they will argue that the use of transfusions in the vet market is currently very constrained due to:

  – the lack of an adequate donor supply.

  – the potential for negative reaction.

  – a 84% user dissatisfaction with current transfusion alternatives.

These students will argue that by eliminating these problems, Oxyglobin should expand the animal transfusion market by a factor of 12 (30% vs. 2.5%), bringing demand to 3.6 to 4.3 MM units per year, as shown below. This would imply a much larger market of $540 to $638.5 million per year.

Estimate #3: (based on application rate of 30% instead of 2.5% referred to in the case):

    15,000 practices   (number of veterinary practices)
x 800 dogs/yr./practice (dogs/yr./practice suffering from acute blood loss)
x 30%   (% of those dogs who receive a transfusion)

= 3,600,000 units/year

x $150 per unit

= $540 MM per year

Estimate #4: (similar to Estimate #2, but adjusted upward by a factor of 12 = 30% / 2.5%).

    242,250 units/year   (= 15,000 practices x 95% primary care x 17 units/year)
+ 112,500 units/year   (= 15,000 practices x 5% emergency care x 150 units/year)

= 354,750 units/year   (total number of units transfused per year)
x   12   (ratio between actual and potential = 30% / 2.5%)

= 4,257,000 units/year
x $150 per unit

= $638.5 MM per year

As a final caveat, the case identifies Oxyglobin as a canine blood substitute (with dogs representing 50% of the vet market). Some students will speculate that Oxyglobin also may be appropriate for other small animals, especially cats (35% of the vet market), thereby doubling the potential for Oxyglobin. While a possibility (and in reality, Biopure's hope), there is no data in the case to support this assertion.

4. **The Market Potential for Hemopure.** There are also different approaches and perspectives on the market potential for Hemopure.

- **As a Wholesale Replacement for Donated Blood.** In the same way that some students will mistakenly look to current transfusions in the vet market to gauge the potential for Oxyglobin, some students will mistakenly look to current transfusions in the human market to gauge the potential for Hemopure. Building off of Case Exhibit 5, these individuals may argue for a potential market of 11.3 MM units per year (8.1 MM units for acute blood loss cases and 3.2 MM units for chronic anemia cases). At a price of $600 to $800 per unit (assume $700), this implies a potential market of $7.9 billion per year.

  At a minimum however, these students should recognize the shortcomings of Hemopure for chronic anemia cases. In particular, the high price and short half-life of Hemopure make it inappropriate as a replacement for the 3.2 MM units of donated blood used to treat chronic anemia. Nevertheless, if they view Hemopure as a wholesale replacement for donated blood in all acute blood cases, this still implies a potential market of 8.1 MM units and $5.67 billion per year.

- **As an Alternative in Select Applications Only.** Other students should argue that $6 to $8 billion vastly overstates the opportunity offered by Hemopure. They will argue that the human market is satisfied with donated blood for most applications. In particular, donated blood is:

  – well-entrenched and widely accepted in modern human medicine.

  – readily available through a well-established network of blood collection groups (e.g. the American Red Cross).

  – relatively inexpensive, at $125 to $225 per unit (vs. $600 to $800 for Hemopure).

  – relatively safe, with little chance of infection (e.g. 1 in 500,000 chance of AIDs).

  As a result, these students will argue that Hemopure is only appropriate for applications where donated blood is not readily available <u>and</u> where the loss of blood is life threatening. A good argument can be made trauma cases fall into this category. Some students will want to argue that borderline transfusion cases represent a potential market for Hemopure, but the cost effectiveness of Hemopure for these cases is suspect.

Trauma cases. There are 500,000 trauma cases each year where there is the immediate and unplanned need for blood at the scene of the accident (e.g., car accidents, shootings). Currently, in 90% of these cases, the transfusion of blood is delayed until the patient reaches the hospital. This delay is at least partly responsible for the 30% fatality rate in these cases. This delay is due to the inability of the paramedic units to efficiently store, type and administer blood "in the field".

Importantly, Hemopure is well-suited for use "in the field" across these 500,000 trauma cases:

- Ease of use by paramedics (e.g., no need for blood typing).

- Easy storage by paramedics (e.g., long shelf life, no refrigeration needed).

- Low price sensitivity of consumer (i.e., trauma victim faces chance of death).

In the 10% of trauma cases where blood was administered "in the field," patients required an average of 4 units of blood each [i.e., 200,000 units administered (Case Exhibit 5) to 50,000 patients]. Assuming that the patients for whom a transfusion was delayed also would have required 4 units, this implies a potential market of 2 MM units and $1.4 billion per year, as shown below.

Estimate for Human Trauma Market:

    500,000 case/year
x   4 units/case   (average for those who receive blood "in the field")
= 2,000,000 units/year

x $700 per unit   (avg. of $600 and $800)

= $1.4 billion/year

Borderline Transfusion cases. Some students will argue that Hemopure is appropriate in "borderline transfusions" cases, described as surgeries in which blood loss is one to two units. The case states that in spite of its potential benefit, blood is typically not transfused in these surgeries for fear of disease transmission or negative reaction to the transfusion.

While Hemopure is a disease-free alternative to donated blood, the fact that donated blood is not used in these cases suggests that the cases are not "life-threatening". This calls into question the cost-effectiveness of a $700 per unit blood substitute. Nonetheless, if this demand were to materialize, it could result in 1.5 MM units (1 MM cases x 1.5 units/case) and $1 billion per year.

Together, these two applications suggest a potential market for Hemopure of between 2.0 MM and 3.5 MM units per year and $1.4 billion and $2.45 billion per year. While attractive, these numbers suggest that the market for a human blood substitute is far smaller than might first appear.

5. **Competitive Environment Effects.** The final bit of analysis that is useful to explore when discussing market potential is the competitive environment facing Biopure in both the animal and the human markets.

- **Animal Market.** We have estimated the potential animal market to be about 3.6 MM units and $500 million per year. Adding to the attractiveness of these estimates, there are at least two reasons to believe that Biopure will have this market to themselves for the foreseeable future:

    ... Given the lengthy FDA approval process (that no competitor has yet begun), Biopure anticipates a 2 to 5 year first-mover advantage.

    ... Biopure's most likely source of competition in the animal market would come from its human market competitors--Baxter and Northfield. However, both employ a design that relies on human blood. It is unlikely either company would divert this scarce resource from the production of a high-margin human product to a low-margin animal product.

As a result, students should recognize that Biopure faces no current competition and little threat of future competition in a market that may grow from its current annual demand of about 300,000 units of donated blood to about 3.6 million units of blood substitute. This is reflected in Exhibit 2 in this note.

- **Human Market.** In contrast to the animal market, Biopure faces stiff competition in the human market:

    ... Two competitors have developed products that have already entered Phase 3 trials.

    ... One of these two competitors is Baxter International, a company with instant credibility in the human blood market due to its past successes with blood related products.

    ... The products of the two competitors are human-sourced as opposed to bovine-sourced, a fact they likely will highlight when trying to sell customers on their products.

EXHIBIT 2

MARKET ANALYSIS SUMMARY OF THE ANIMAL AND HUMAN MARKETS

Animal Market:

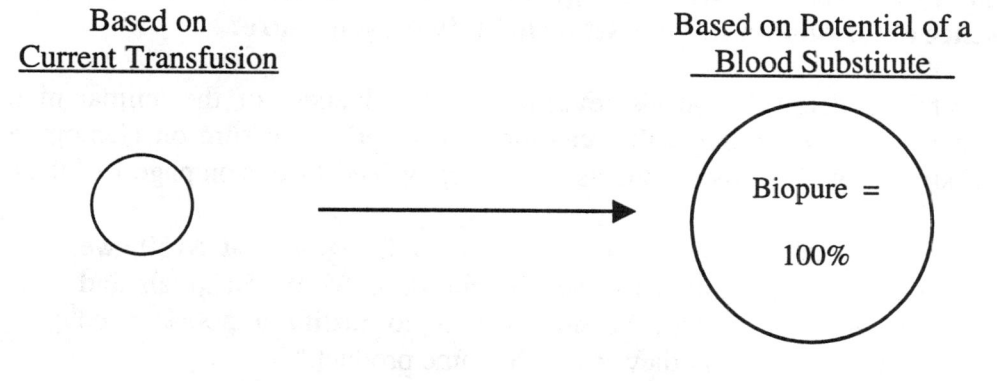

300K to 350K units/year
$45 MM to $53 MM/year

3.6 MM to 4.3 MM units/year
$540 MM to $640 MM/year

Human Market:

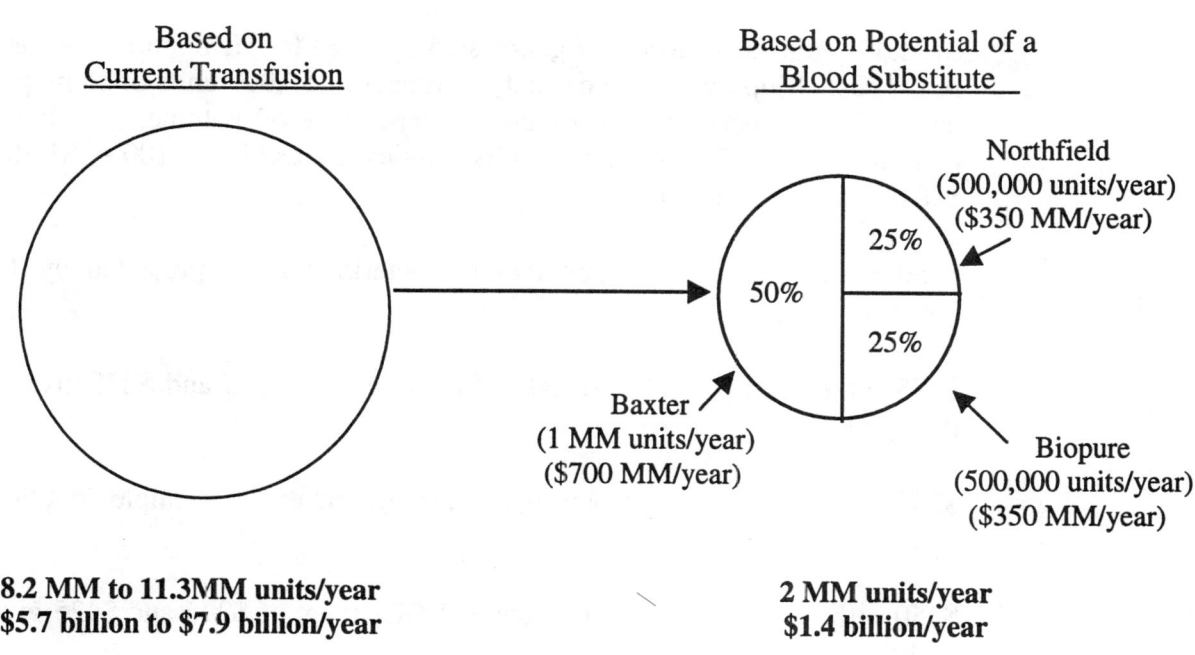

8.2 MM to 11.3MM units/year
$5.7 billion to $7.9 billion/year

2 MM units/year
$1.4 billion/year

These reasons suggest that Biopure will be fighting for a share of the 2 million unit per year trauma market. While only speculation, one might guess that Baxter has the size and credibility to capture the largest share of this market (say 50% share), leaving Northfield and Biopure to split the remainder (say a 25% share for each). With a 25% share of the human trauma market, Biopure could expect an annual demand of 500,000 units and $350 million as shown in Exhibit 2 in this note.

C. What is the likely impact of Oxyglobin's pricing on Hemopure? How might the presence of Oxyglobin be an asset or liability to Hemopure?

1. While a detailed analysis reveals the attractiveness of the animal market, the concern remains that Oxyglobin will create downward price pressure on Hemopure due to the physical similarity of the two products. As stated by Ted Jacobs on page 1 of the case:

> "... as soon as we come out with Oxyglobin at $150, we jeopardize our ability to price Hemopure at $800. Hospitals and insurance firms will be all over us to justify a 500% price difference for what they see as the same product."

Implicit in this statement is the assumption that Oxyglobin is the appropriate benchmark for Hemopure. Students should challenge this contention. In doing so, it is useful to establish the potential **reference prices** for a human blood substitute.

2. In assessing the price of Hemopure, there are several relevant prices and/or costs that might act as a benchmark. These **reference prices** include:

- $101.50 = the variable cost of goods sold (COGS) for Hemopure. As stated in the case, Biopure has the capacity to produce 150,000 units of Hemopure per year at a cost of $15 million, independent of volume. With raw materials adding $1.50 per unit, this implies a COGS of $100 + $1.50 = $101.50 at full production.

- $150 = the price of Oxyglobin to the veterinarian (as projected by Ted Jacobs).

- $175 = the average cost of donated RBCs (avg. of $125 and $225 given in the case)

- $300 = the price of Oxyglobin to the pet owner, given a simple "doubling rule".

- $350 = the average cost of autologous RBCs (avg. of $275 and $425 given in the case)

- $600-$800 = the planned price of competitor's human blood substitutes.

- $$$ = the value of a human life—non-quantifiable, but important to consider.

Other relevant reference points for Hemopure might include the COGS for the competing products. Performing a similar calculation to that shown for Hemopure, one could calculate that the projected COGS is $58 for Baxter's Hem-Assist and $125 for Northfield's Poly-Heme.[1]

3. Having considered various reference prices of Hemopure, students should begin to realize that Oxyglobin is one of many benchmarks consumers could use in assessing the price of Hemopure. Arguably, Oxyglobin may be among the least salient of these benchmarks and have little impact on the price acceptance of Hemopure as a result. Support for this contention include:

- For most human blood recipients and transfusion providers, the most visible benchmark will be donated human blood, which is priced at $175 per unit.

- For risk-averse blood recipients, a more appropriate benchmark might be autologous blood (both eliminate the risk of infection), which is priced at $350.

- For trauma victims in need of blood "in the field," there currently is no alternative to Hemopure and, thus, no appropriate point of reference. Given the significant risk of death, willingness-to-pay among trauma victims and emergency care providers should be very high and unaffected by the pricing of Oxyglobin.

- Assuming Baxter and Northfield successfully launch their products, these products will become the relevant comparison for Hemopure. Currently, they plan to price at $600 to $800 and there is no reason to believe their pricing will be influenced by Oxyglobin.

For these reasons, it appears Biopure's fears may be unfounded. In particular, Biopure appears to be using a "Cost-Plus" mentality when considering price acceptance for Hemopure. In this regard, they fear that consumers will use Oxyglobin's price to infer the COGS for Hemopure.

4. However, in practice, consumers (both medical providers and patients) will likely evaluate the price of Hemopure in the context of potential and acceptable alternatives. As such, a price of $600 to $800 makes sense in cases of trauma, where (1) acceptable

---

[1] As an interesting side note, one could predict that the competitor's COGS will rise significantly over time, due to a rising cost of raw material. Currently, Baxter and Northfield use relatively inexpensive outdated human blood as their source material. However, given the relative scarcity of human blood, a market should develop for outdated human blood as production of HemAssist and PolyHeme increase. This should lead to a price increase in their cost of raw material (possibly to that of the cost of fresh whole blood) which will raise their final COGS significantly.

alternatives currently do not exist and (2) alternatives under development will also be priced in the $600 to $800 range. At the same time, a price of $600 to $800 is probably unacceptable in the cases of planned surgeries given the ready supply of donated RBCs priced at $125 to $225. In both cases, price acceptance of Hemopure should hinge on the price of alternative treatments and not on the price of Oxyglobin. To make this thinking salient, it is difficult to imagine a paramedic refusing to administer a potentially life saving transfusion of Hemopure because they feel that Hemopure is priced too far above its COGS.

5. In leaving this issue, students should recognize that the pricing of Oxyglobin and Hemopure are relatively independent. This is especially true given the fact that these two products are not interchangeable in use. As such, Oxyglobin should be priced so as to optimize financial returns in the animal market and Hemopure should be priced (independently of Oxyglobin) so as to optimize financial returns in the human market.

D. What should Biopure do regarding the commercial release of Oxyglobin? If they release, what price should they set? How should Oxyglobin be sold/distributed and to who?

1. After a thorough discussion of market potential and of impact of Oxyglobin's pricing on Hemopure, most of the class will argue that Oxyglobin should be launched immediately. What remains to be determined is how to go to market with Oxyglobin. In this regard, the challenge facing Biopure should not be underestimated. In particular, there are many reasons to suggest that a successful launch of Oxyglobin is anything but a "sure thing":

- The company has never brought a product to market.

- The company is new to veterinary medicine, having been founded as a human products company.

- The company is dominated by engineers and manufacturing types, as evidenced by the organization chart in case Exhibit 2.

- The company has only recently hired someone to take on the role of marketing Oxyglobin and, to date, only seven people have been hired to support him.

- Traditionally, the veterinary market is price sensitive, with veterinarians playing the role of gatekeeper when it comes to recommending treatments to pet owners.

In terms of a target market, the question facing Biopure is how large a net to cast in the veterinary market. Specifically, do they want to be comprehensive or do they want to be selective in their initial marketing Oxyglobin.

2. **Target Market for Oxyglobin.** In terms of a target market, the question facing Biopure is how large a net to cast in the veterinary market. Specifically, do they want to be comprehensive or do they want to be selective in their initial marketing of Oxyglobin.

- **Comprehensive Approach.** Some students will argue that Oxyglobin will have immediate appeal across all 15,000 veterinary practices in the United States. As a more convenient alternative to donated animal blood, Oxyglobin eliminates the need for donor animals and for animal blood banks. While this might be true, students should be forced to consider the likelihood of rapid adoption among the broad cross-section of veterinary practices. In particular, given that the vast majority (i.e., 95%) of practices perform an average of only 17 transfusions per year, it is not clear how willing these practices will be to try a revolutionary new blood product.

- **Selective Approach.** A more compelling case can be made for Biopure to initially focus it efforts on those practices that perform the greatest number of transfusions. Specifically, while an average of 17 units of canine blood was transfused each year by each primary care practice, an average of 150 units of canine blood was transfused each year by each emergency care practice. In addition, the case states that 15% of practices handled 65% of all canine surgeries and that 10% of all practices handled 55% of all canine trauma cases (two examples of the "80-20 rule"). These "high incidence" practices tended to be the emergency care practices and large primary care practices.

By initially focusing on these "high incidence" practices, Biopure accomplishes several things. First, they reduce the scope of their efforts from 15,000 practices to about 1,500 practices. Second, given their significantly greater reliance on blood transfusions, these practices will see greater value from Oxyglobin than will "low-incidence" practices. Third, these practices are likely to be thought leaders and lead users when it comes to adopting new emergency medical techniques. As such, they may be more receptive to the Oxyglobin sales pitch. Finally, the cost of treatment at an emergency care practice is usually many times greater than at a primary care practice, suggesting lower price sensitivity for Oxyglobin at these locations. **These factors suggest that Biopure should be selective in its initial target marketing effort.**

3. **Sales/Distribution Strategy for Oxyglobin.** The second issue that needs to be addressed is how best to sell and distribute Oxyglobin. Two alternatives are on the table—going through an independent distributor or going direct with a direct sales force.

- **Independent Distributors.** Going through an independent distributor has the advantages of speed and scale—these distributors have established relationships with the 15,000 veterinary practices and can very quickly introduce Oxyglobin to these practices. For instance, a national distributor with 100 sales reps can reach the 15,000 veterinary practices in far less time than can Biopure with its 3 sales reps. In addition to selling, these distributors would take on the responsibility of physically distributing Oxyglobin to the veterinary practices.

However, there are several drawbacks to going through an independent distributor. First, they typically receive 30% of the selling price of a new product, implying a $30 to $60 charge for selling Oxyglobin. Second, they introduce about 100 new products each year, suggesting that any one new product receives very little attention in their weekly 15-minute meetings with veterinarians. Third, Biopure would still be required to educate these sales reps on the technical specifications and merits of Oxyglobin.

- **Direct Salesforce.** In contrast to the intense distribution offered by an independent distributor, Biopure could take on the selling and distribution responsibility itself. Such an effort has several advantages over an independent distributor. First, any time spent with veterinarians would be fully dedicated to Oxyglobin. Second, a Biopure sales rep would have far greater knowledge about Oxyglobin than a distributor's sales rep could ever have. Given the unique and complex nature of Oxyglobin, this added knowledge could be critical in product acceptance by the veterinarians.

  One potential drawback in using a direct sales force is the length of time it would take to reach the 15,000 veterinary practices. However, by choosing to be selective in their initial marketing efforts, as suggested above, they can limit themselves to about 1,500 practices. Assuming 4 full-time sales reps (i.e., 3 full-time sales reps + 2 half-time efforts from Andy Wright and his director of marketing) each making 4 sales calls per day, this implies that the targeted 1,500 practices could be called upon within a relatively short 20-week window.

  Another potential drawback of going direct is that Biopure would take on the responsibility of physical distribution. However, Biopure estimates that they could satisfy this requirement at a cost of $10 to $15 per unit, which is far cheaper than the $30 to $60 that would be charged by an independent distributor.

  In the end, given the sophisticated sales pitch required to sell Oxyglobin, the selective distribution that Biopure might initially follow, and the relatively low cost to physically distribute the product themselves, it makes sense for Biopure to go direct with their own sales force.

4. **Oxyglobin Pricing.** A third decision facing Biopure is how to price Oxyglobin. There are several categories of price that students may propose for the Oxyglobin, including:

- Price low (e.g., $100), in response to the high price sensitivity of the broad market.

- Price high (e.g., $200), in response to the lower price sensitivity in the emergency care market.

- Price very high (e.g., $400) so as to limit sales to all but the most price insensitive customers and, in the process, eliminate any lingering fears of negatively impacting Hemopure.

The third option only makes sense if students are still convinced that Oxyglobin's low price will negatively impact Hemopure. If students have convinced themselves that this is not a problem, the pricing decision will likely revolve around the first two options—price low to penetrate the broad market or price high to skim the emergency care market.

In arriving at a price for Oxyglobin, it is helpful to factor in the per unit cost of Oxyglobin. The case states that Biopure has the capacity to produce 300,000 units of Oxyglobin per year at a cost of $15 million, independent of volume. With raw materials adding $1.50 per unit, this implies a COGS of $51.50 at full production. In addition, the case states that Biopure can ship Oxyglobin at a cost of $10 to $15 per unit (assume $12.50). Combined, this results in a per unit cost of $64, implying a $36 gross margin if Oxyglobin is priced at $100 and a $136 gross margin if Oxyglobin is priced at $200. Based on a simple breakeven analysis, this difference in gross margin favors pricing at $200 as long as demand at $200 is at least 27% of demand at $100 ($36/$136 = .264).

It is also helpful to consider the consumer's willingness to pay. Two patterns emerge from the case. First, it appears that veterinarians are more price-sensitive than pet owners, especially in non-critical cases. This heightened price sensitivity among veterinarians is important given the "gate-keeper," role that many veterinarians play. Second, when priced at $100, veterinarian's willingness to try Oxyglobin is high for both critical and non-critical cases. However, when priced at $200, willingness to try drops to 5% in non-critical cases, but remains high (60%) in critical cases.

On first glance, this pattern of sensitivity among veterinarians suggests that a $100 price might make more sense than a $200 price. However, when one considers that the workload of the 1,500 "high incident" practices is heavily skewed toward "critical" cases, the 5% willingness to trial in non-critical cases seems less relevant.

In summary, if Biopure wishes to target the entire 15,000 veterinary practices in the United States, a $200 price might be prohibitively high. However, if they wish to pursue a more selective strategy and focus on the 1,500 "high incidence" practices that handle predominantly critical cases, a $200 per unit price seems to make sense.

E. Epilogue

Oxyglobin was launched in April of 1998 at a price of $150. Rather than go through a distributor, Andy Wright and his sales team sold Oxyglobin directly to the veterinarians, initially focusing on the 750 emergency care veterinary practices and the 750 largest primary care practices. This was done for two reasons. First, these 1,500 practices handled a disproportionate number of canine surgeries and trauma cases and second, the veterinarians in these practices were believed to be the thought leaders in the veterinary community. Product shipment to these practices was handled via Federal Express at a cost of about $10 per shipment.

Among the 1,500 target practices, initial sales were promising and the product received praise from the veterinarians. However, a follow-up investigation revealed that these veterinarians viewed Oxyglobin in one of two fashions. About half viewed Oxyglobin as an everyday replacement for donated animal blood, resulting in the reordering of Oxyglobin on an ongoing basis. The other half viewed Oxyglobin as an "emergency" alternative to donated animal blood. These vets put Oxyglobin on their shelves and only used it in special cases. By the end of 1998, sales of Oxyglobin were approaching an annualize rate of 50,000 units and a coverage across 15 – 20% of veterinary practices.

F. Summary Points

1. The challenge facing the manager responsible for formulating and implementing a comprehensive marketing program divides into three related decisions and actions…

- Decide where to compete: Product-Market Choice
- Decide how to compete: Marketing-mix Design
- Decide when to compete: Timing

Biopure Corporation had to make all three decisions in its launch of a revolutionary new "blood substitute" designed to replace the need for donated blood.

2. A quantitative estimate of market sales potential is crucial in determining whether or not a marketing opportunity exists. In its most basic form, market sales potential is the product of three variables: (1) the number of prospective buyers (B) who are willing and able to purchase an offering; (2) the quantity (Q) of an offering purchased by an average buyer in a specific time period; and (3) the price (P) of an average unit of the offering.

$$\text{Market Sales Potential} = B \times Q \times P$$

Variations of this simple expression were applied in the various market potential estimates for Oxyglobin and Hemopure.

3. When pricing a new product or service, a manager can employ a skimming pricing strategy, a penetration pricing strategy, or an intermediate pricing strategy. The decision to use one of three strategies is apparent for Oxyglobin. On balance, the following conditions support a skimming pricing strategy, and apply to Oxyglobin:

- Demand is likely to be price inelastic.

- There are different price-market segments, thereby appealing first to buyers who have a higher range of acceptable prices.

- The offering is unique enough to be protected from competition by patent, copyright, or trade secret.

- Production or marketing costs are unknown.

- A capacity constraint in producing the product or providing the service exists.

- An organization wants to generate funds quickly to recover its investment or finance other development efforts.

- There is a realistic perceived value in the product or service.

4. Whereas a pricing strategy establishes a general price level, it does not necessarily set a price point. A reference price—the price of a competitive product or service or a substitute that satisfies the same need—is often used to benchmark a specific price point. The reference price will vary by market segment as was observed for Oxyglobin in the animal market and Hemopure in the human market.

CIMA MOUNTAINEERING, INC.

Synopsis

Cima Mountaineering is a strategic marketing case on selecting a marketing strategy for expansion in the recreation footwear market. Students will have the opportunity to evaluate a strategy for expanding the sales of a product they are quite familiar with, hiking boots. Additionally, the case is designed to allow the instructor to use student teams to conduct marketing research, make a presentation, and apply the concepts of financial analysis, product design and advertising, sales forecasting, discounting to present value and payback to evaluate a marketing proposal. The Internet can also be used to gather some of the information.

The case is nicely suited for a course project near the end of an undergraduate marketing management course. The issue centers on the evaluation of two marketing opportunities competing for the resources of the firm. The instructor can form project teams of 3 to 5 students and assign each team to research and evaluate one of the two marketing proposals. (See case Exhibits 1, 2 and 3) Following the research, student teams prepare a written report on the assigned proposal and present it to the class. Following the presentations, class discussion centers around selecting the most reasonable alternative for the company.

Teaching Objectives

This case has four teaching objectives:

1. To introduce students to an important strategic issue in marketing management; selecting a marketing strategy for future growth.

2. To teach students teamwork and enable them to gain experience using marketing research to guide the development of marketing strategy.

3. To reinforce the interrelationship of marketing, accounting, and finance in the marketing management process.

This teaching note was prepared by Lawrence M. Lamont, Professor of Management and Eva Cid and Wade Drew Hammond, seniors in the Class of 1995 at Washington and Lee University. Copyright © 1995, Washington and Lee University, Lexington, Virginia. Used with permission.

4. To develop quantitative skills by using a computer spreadsheet to evaluate the profit implications of a marketing proposal.

Teaching Suggestions

As a project-based case, matters related to project teams and project presentations are important considerations in assigning the case. The following approach has proven to be effective.

Forming Project Teams

If Cima Mountaineering is assigned as a course project, teams of 3 to 5 students work very well for the case study. Instructors should form teams comprised of students having the skills to complete the projects. In addition to marketing, each team should have students with some accounting and finance skills and computer spreadsheet capabilities. All will be needed to complete the assignment.

Assign the Cima Mountaineering case to students and instruct them to read it carefully. The text of the case provides the necessary background while the case tables, figures and exhibits provide some of the information needed to complete the projects.

Student teams should be assigned to work on Project 1 **or** Project 2. Case Exhibit 1 provides additional background on Project 1, while Exhibit 2 gives similar information on Project 2. Exhibit 3 defines the scope of each project and the work to be completed. Students will need to read the case and study these exhibits carefully.

Each project requires about 10-15 hours for a team to complete if some of the work is divided among team members. **It is important to assign the case three to four weeks before the written reports are due and the case presentations are to be made.** This is desirable because each project requires some consumer marketing research.

Instructors should encourage student teams to supplement the case information and consumer research by using the Internet and visiting retail outlets to gather product brochures, observe retail prices, talk with sales people and examine the mountaineering and hiking boots stocked. The products are very popular with students, so most college communities should have one or more retailers carrying backpacking and hiking equipment.

Most of the hiking boot manufacturers are privately owned or they are divisions of larger companies. Experience indicates that they generally will not disclose much information that cannot be gathered from other sources. However, many advertise to consumers using specialized magazines such as **Backpacker.** Reviewing current issues of these magazines can be helpful to students in stimulating advertising and product design ideas.

Project Presentations

A creative option that can be considered by the instructor is to have the student teams video tape their presentations. This option can be a valuable experience for students because of the increasing use of teleconferencing and the opportunity it provides for some exposure to the camera. Additionally, it provides the student teams an opportunity to edit and polish their presentations and to see how they present themselves as a member of a marketing **project** team. Students find this option challenging and they develop some very creative presentations using the various possibilities available with modern video cameras. The video tape presentation can be used instead of live classroom presentations in instances where classes are large and the instructor does not want to utilize class time for several presentations. In this instance, the video tape presentations provide a visual record for students and for purposes of assigning a grade to this part of the project. Alternatively, instructors may decide to ask student teams to complete the case analysis, prepare the designs, advertisements, and spreadsheets and present their findings on video tape or in class without preparing a formal written report.

Instructors may also decide not to use presentations and simply ask for written student reports. This latter option will not be as effective because student designs and advertisements will vary considerably and the visual presentations are a valuable learning experience for the other student teams.

Other possibilities certainly exist, and instructors are encouraged to consider them. However, the case was designed specifically to provide students with a **team** learning experience in marketing management. In addition to helping students address marketing strategy and marketing management issues, the case will help students develop research skills, teamwork, and improve oral and written communication skills.

The following questions and assignments have been found useful in directing student analysis of the case and completing the project.

1. What is the financial condition of Cima Mountaineering?

2. What is the current marketing situation at Cima Mountaineering?

3. Appraise Margaret's proposal to enter the "week-ender" segment of the hiking boot market.

4. Appraise Anthony's proposal to extend existing product lines.

Areas for Discussion/Analysis

A. What is the financial condition of Cima Mountaineering?

1. As part of each project, student teams should be instructed to assess the ability of Cima to finance the product development and capital expenditures. The analysis here is designed to assist the instructor in evaluating the written reports and presentations.

2. An analysis of the financial statements and cash flow from operations is summarized in Exhibit 1 in this note. It indicates that Cima is not in particularly strong financial condition, but is certainly capable of funding one of the two projects. The issue is which project will have the greatest impact on the future of the firm.

3. The company generated $408,633 of operating cash flow in 1995. However, Cima is a highly leveraged company with a debt to asset ratio above 81 percent. About 25 percent of the debt is classified as long-term. It is unlikely that Cima will be able to take on much additional debt to finance any expansion.

4. From case Table 1, it can be determined that Cima sales have increased 54 percent since 1990 at an average rate of 9.0 percent annually. However, sales increases have been declining over the past two years. Revenues were up 8.4 and 7.2 percent in 1994 and 1995 compared to a 10.7 percent increase in 1993. It appears that Cima is losing the momentum in its growth, which increases the urgency to develop new marketing opportunities.

5. The 1995 profit margin of 4.27 percent, although higher than the industry average, has been gradually declining over the past three years. Cima's profit margin had reached nearly 5 percent in 1992. The decrease is due in part, to the higher costs and the smaller sales increases.

6. The current ratio of 1.14, is low due to the high accrued liabilities. The quick ratio of 0.59 is also low because of the inventory buildup. Cima's return on assets and equity has declined from 1994 and the return on assets is below the average for the footwear industry. However, cash flow from operations is reasonably strong.

7. Instructors should note that Margaret and Anthony are the sole owners of the company. They each draw a salary but the profits from operations are reinvested in the business.

B. What is the current marketing situation at Cima Mountaineering?

1. This assessment is helpful for instructors as background for leading the class discussion to select a marketing strategy after the team presentations have been completed.

EXHIBIT 1

SUMMARY OF FINANCIAL STATEMENT ANALYSIS

Financial Ratio Analysis

	1995	**1994**	**Industry**
Current Ratio	1.14	1.08	3.2
Quick Ratio	0.59	0.55	1.3
Inventory Turnover	3.24	3.52	2.0
Days Sales Outstanding	84	78	65
Times Interest Earned	10.34	10.91	
Asset Turnover	1.11	1.22	1.8
Debt to Asset Ratio	81.2%	83.5%	80.0%
Profit Margin	4.27%	4.32%	4.2%
Return on Assets	4.7%	5.3%	6.3%
Return on Equity	25.3%	32.0%	10.2%

Operating Cash Flow

Net Income	$ 857,134
Depreciation	$ 259,727
Change in Current Assets	
Receivables	($ 719,652)
Inventories	($ 867,717)
Other Current Assets	$5,429
Change in Current Liabilities	
Accounts Payable	$183,226
Accrued Liabilities	$690,486
Operating Cash Flow	$408,633

Source: Cima financial statements in case Tables 2 and 3. Industry comparisons obtained from comparative financial statement published by Robert Morris Associates on the Footwear Industry. Financial ratios and operating cash flow was derived from computer software provided by **Quattro Pro for Windows**, version 5.0, Borland International, Inc.

2. Cima Mountaineering is a business owned and operated by two members of a family. Typically, family businesses pursue niche markets and emphasize high quality products. Family members are often risk averse, but they take enormous pride in their business and are willing to work long and hard to preserve its traditions and market position. Cima is not an exception. The company has high quality products, a strong brand franchise, a reasonably good position in two segments of the market and a strong regional focus.

3. Cima has been a fairly progressive company in some ways and slow to change in others. The implementation of computer-assisted design and the use of work teams to improve product quality and reduce costs would be evidence of innovative behavior. However, Cima has been slow to change its products. Historically, it has relied on classic styling and traditional construction materials. The industry has moved to boots with nylon and leather construction, selling through mail order catalogs and offering fashionable designs for uses other than mountaineering and hiking. Now, confronted with strong foreign competition, the recent loss of two large customers, and a market where consumer preferences seem to be changing, Cima must decide whether to stay with its present target markets or move the company into a new market. The case presents a "classic" decision often faced by the niche marketer when margin and profit growth begins to slow. The projects described in case Exhibit 3, are designed to provide information for this decision.

C. Appraise Margaret's proposal to enter the "weekender" segment of the hiking boot market.

1. Student teams assigned Project 1 should address items 1-10 in case Exhibit 3 in their reports and presentations.

2. The product design should utilize the results of the research conducted with consumers and retailers of mountaineering and backpacking equipment. Students usually present the design on a large posterboard or color transparency but other visual presentations should be acceptable. The important part of the assignment is to give students experience using information from marketing research to design a new product. Exhibit 2 in this note shows a student design. Note how the design also lists the important features and benefits of the hiking boot, but mistakenly uses welt construction to attach the uppers to the sole and heel. Following the presentations, students should be expected to defend their designs. Check to make sure the design has most of the features specified in Margaret's proposal.

3. Product designs should specify a type of leather and two colors for the nylon to be used in the construction. Again, the student teams should use the results of their marketing research in making these decisions. The leather and color options are presented in case Exhibit 1. They should be those preferred by the consumers in the weekender market segment.

4. The brand name student teams select for the proposed boots should have appeal to the consumers in the weekender market segment. TREKKER was used by the students that

EXHIBIT 2

Student Team Product Design for Hiking Boot
The Trekker

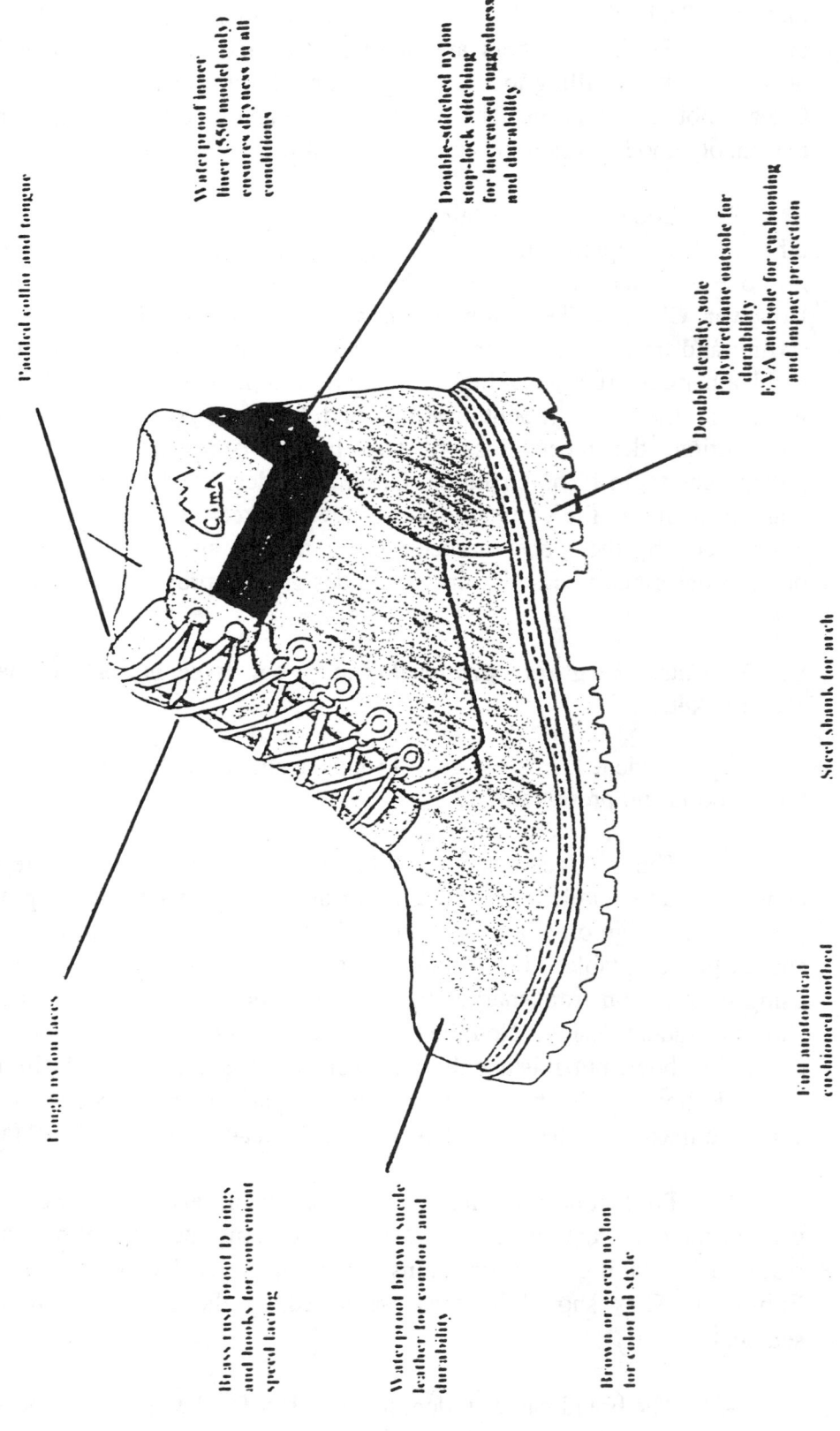

prepared the design shown in Exhibit 2 in this note. Look for the rationale in the choice of a brand name and the brand mark on the boot design.

5. The retail prices proposed for the VX 550 and WX 450 are $89.00 and $69.00 respectively. Student teams should verify the acceptability of these prices through their marketing research. Retailers and mail order catalogs are helpful sources of information here.

6. The preparation of a four color print advertisement for the WX 550 (or WX 450) hiking boot, enables student teams to explore additional creative aspects of marketing strategy.

7. Student teams usually prepare the advertisement on a large posterboard or color transparency and it generally features the product design they developed earlier in the project along with other illustrations and advertising copy. Some student teams will use the services of a student artist to give the advertisement a professional appearance. To evaluate the advertisements, check the illustrations and copy to make certain they fit the target market and convey the desired positioning for the new product. Ask the student teams to provide the rationale for their creative approach.

8. Students enjoy this part of the case analysis and become actively involved in the creative process. The teams will produce some excellent, creative advertising. Instructor's Note, Appendix A provides an example of a two-page centerfold advertisement developed for a **mountaineering** boot with a different company and different brand name. Student team advertisements for the Cima hiking boots will be somewhat similar except they will feature **hiking boots** for a different market segment.

9. Student teams can assess the before-tax profitability of Margaret's proposal by using the sales forecasts presented for WX 550 and WX 450 in case Table 5 and the cost information in case Table 6. A summary of the appropriate computations is provided in Exhibit 3 in this note. Students can prepare the analysis using a personal computer and spread sheet software such as EXCEL or QUATTRO PRO. Student solutions may differ slightly from Exhibit 3 depending on the assumptions and the number of significant digits carried in the analysis and the resulting rounding error.

10. Probably the easiest way to construct the spreadsheet is to work with unit prices, costs and profits. Begin with the 1997-1998 suggested retail prices of $89.00 for WX 550 and $69.00 for WX 450 and remove the 50 percent retail markup to arrive at the Cima selling price. Then apply the appropriate percentages from Table 6 to determine the unit costs for sales commissions, sales promotion, materials and labor, OHD, and transportation. Subtract the unit costs from the Cima unit price to arrive at the before-tax profit margin; $6.67 for WX 550 and $5.16 for WX 450. The computations are shown on the top portion of Exhibit 3 in this note. **Instructors: review the markup concept used here with your students prior to assigning the case.**

EXHIBIT 3

PROPOSAL TO ENTER WEEKENDER SEGMENT OF HIKING BOOT MARKET
PRESENT VALUE ANALYSIS

	WX 550	WX 450
Retail Price	$89.00	$69.00
Cima Price	44.50	34.50
Sales Commissions	4.45	3.45
Sales Promotion	2.23	1.73
Materials	18.69	12.08
Labor, OHD, Transp.	12.46	12.08
Unit Profit	$6.67	$5.16

WX 550

	1997-98	1998-99	1999-00	2000-01	2001-02
Unit Price	$44.50	$48.28	$48.13	$50.06	$52.06
Unit Cost	37.83	38.96	40.13	41.34	42.58
Profit Margin	6.67	7.32	8.00	8.72	9.48
Sales Forecast (units)	4,050	5,590	8,420	14.104	16,420
Profit, before-tax	27,014	40,919	67,360	122,987	155,662
Present Value (15%)	23,490	30,941	44,290	70,318	77,392
Cumulative	23,490	54,431	98,721	169,039	246,431

WX 450

	1997-98	1998-99	1999-00	2000-01	2001-02
Unit Price	$34.50	$35.88	$37.32	$38.81	$40.36
Unit Cost	29.34	30.22	31.13	32.06	33.02
Profit Margin	5.16	5.66	6.19	6.75	7.34
Sales Forecast (units)	6,160	8,430	12,605	21,115	24,590
Profit, before-tax	31,786	47,714	78,025	142,526	180,491
Present Value (15%)	27,640	36,078	51,303	81,490	89,736
Cumulative	27,640	63,718	115,021	196,511	286,247
Cumulative Total	$51,130	$118,149	$213,742	$356,550	$532,678

11. The before-tax profits for 1997-98 are calculated by multiplying the unit profit margin for each product by the sales forecast for the same period. The before-tax profits are then discounted one year to present value (1996-1997) in the same spreadsheet using a discount rate of 15 percent.

12. For the remaining four years, 1998-99 through 2001-2002, the unit sales price for each product is increased by 4.0 percent each year (price increases) and the unit costs are increased by 3.0 percent each year (cost increases). The new profit margin is determined and the before-tax profits are calculated as before. The profits are discounted to present value for each year and the totals are cumulated as shown in Exhibit 3 in this note. The cumulative total for the five-year projection is shown at the bottom of the exhibit.

13. **Note: Instructors using the case study in years beyond 1996-97** should instruct students to complete the financial analysis for the case in the 1996-1997 to 2001-2002 time period, as it is written. The base year for purposes of discounting to present value should be 1996-1997. Thus, the before-tax profits for 1997-1998 should be discounted one year, two years for 1998-1999, three years for 1999-2000, and so forth.

14. The payback period for the proposal occurs when the product development costs of $350,000 and the capital expenditures of $150,000 are offset by the cumulative present value of expected before-tax profits. The proposal costs should be recovered sometime in 2001-2002 if everything goes as expected. This is a long payback period.

15. To determine the acceptability of the student product designs to mail order catalog companies, students should explore the issue with consumers and review the catalogs of firms like L.L. Bean, Eddie Bauer, Gander Mountain, REI, Cabela's, etc. Sales through the catalog marketers are an attractive way of expanding distribution and eventually they could account for about 5-10 percent of the sales of the new product line. A good resource here is **The United States Mail Order Industry**, by Maxwell Sroge, published by NTC Business Books, 1994. Historically, about 4 percent of footwear sales are made through mail order.

16. Student reports for this project are usually 5-6 pages in length excluding tables and exhibits. In addition to items listed in case Exhibit 3, reports should discuss the advantages and disadvantages of Margaret's proposal and the sources of information used to prepare the report. Some of the advantages include:

- Margaret's proposal is consistent with the changing market. Consumer preferences are shifting to more casual boots and the new products better **fit** the emerging consumer needs.

- The weekender market segment has a large share of the total market and a high growth rate.

- The new line will enable the company's retail dealers to offer an expanded line of Cima boots. The new line should help to prevent the further loss of retail customers.

- Some of the boots will be sold in sporting goods stores; a new type of retail customer for Cima.

- Assuming the designs and prices are acceptable to the mail order companies, the new products should enable Cima to expand sales and distribution into new geographic markets.

17. The proposal is not without disadvantages. Some of these include:

- Potential damage to the Cima Mountaineering image because of the low price points on the new products. Probably not very significant.

- Entry into a market segment where large athletic shoe firms (Nike, Reebok and recently Adidas and New Balance) have the potential to provide aggressive price and design competition.

- If the project begins in 1996-1997, it has a payback period of more than 5 years. This period is quite lengthy.

- Cima has no previous marketing experience in the weekender market segment.

18. Classroom presentations should last about 15 minutes, with each team member having about 3 or 4 minutes to present part of the team's report. Presentations should cover the major areas mentioned in the project proposal. Students often prefer to omit the disadvantages of the proposal, so listen carefully to make certain this aspect is included. Before reading and grading the report and presentations, check the bibliography and the summary of the research to determine the scope of the team effort. The research should focus on recreational users and ask questions that will help the project team make the required decisions.

D. Appraise Anthony's proposal to extend existing product lines.

1. Student teams assigned Project 2, should address items 1-9 in case Exhibit 3 in their reports and presentations.

2. Student teams should provide separate designs for HX 100 and HX 50 since they are different items in the same line. Look for a design that combines leather and nylon since that is the construction specified in the memorandum. Referring again to Exhibit 2 in this note, the design for the TREKKER uses classic welt construction to stitch the uppers to the sole. This is a design error for both projects. The boot should be constructed using the

contemporary method to join the uppers to the sole and heel. It is less expensive and perfectly acceptable to the customers in both the weekender and serious hiker market segments. Refer to case Figure 4 for an example of the contemporary method which shows a molded rubber outsole as specified in case Exhibits 1 and 2.

3. Product designs should specify a type of leather and two colors for the nylon to be used in the construction. Again, the student teams should use the results of the marketing research in making these decisions. The leather and colors selected should reflect ruggedness and quality. The leather and nylon options are presented in case Exhibit 2.

4. No brand name is needed for Project 2. The mountaineering boot for women, MX 3507 will be branded with the name Glacier and the HX 100 and HX 50 hiking boots will be branded with the name Summit.

5. The retail prices proposed for the MX 350, HX 100 and HX 50 are $219.00, $119.00 and $89.00 respectively. Students should verify the acceptability of these prices through their marketing research.

6. The magazine advertisement should feature both the HX 100 and the HX 50 boots. Advertising copy should introduce and position the boots as new additions to the Summit line of hiking boots. To evaluate the advertisements, check the illustrations and copy to make certain that they are appropriate for the target market and convey the desired positioning. Ask the student teams to provide the rationale for their creative approach.

7. Students can assess the before-tax profitability of Anthony's proposal by using the sales forecasts presented for MX 350, HX 100 and HX 50 presented in case Table 5 and the cost information in case Table 6. A summary of the appropriate computations is provided in Exhibit 4 in this note. Students should prepare the analysis using a personal computer and spreadsheet such as EXCEL or QUATTRO PRO.

8. The methodology for constructing the spreadsheet and conducting the analysis is exactly the same as used for Margaret's proposal, Team Project 1. (See the previous comments in this note.)

9. The payback period for the proposal occurs when the product development costs of $400,000 and the capital investment of $150,000 is offset by the cumulative net present value of before-tax profits. Payback should occur sometime in 2001-2002.

10. To determine the acceptability of the student hiking boot designs to mail order catalog companies, students should explore the issue with consumers and review the catalogs of firms previously mentioned. Most of the catalog companies stock hiking boots for serious hikers as well as boots for more casual, weekend wear. Careful study of the catalogs should enable the students to make the distinctions between the products targeted to consumers in the different markets. Sales through the catalog marketers are an attractive way of expanding

EXHIBIT 4

PROPOSAL TO EXTEND EXISTING LINES OF MOUNTAINEERING AND HIKING BOOKS
PRESENT VALUE ANALYSIS

	MX 350		HX 100		HX 50
Retail Price	$219.00		$119.00		$89.00
Cima Price	109.50		59.50		44.50
Sales Commissions	10.95		5.95		4.45
Sales Promotion	5.48		2.98		2.23
Materials	38.33		24.99		15.58
Labor, OHD, Transp.	38.33		16.66		15.58
Unit Profit	$16.41		$8.92		$6.66
MX 350	**1997-98**	**1998-99**	**1999-00**	**2000-01**	**2001-02**
Unit Price	$109.50	$113.88	$118.44	$123.17	$128.10
Unit Cost	93.09	95.88	98.76	101.72	104.77
Profit Margin	16.41	18.00	19.68	21.45	23.33
Sales Forecast (units)	414	538	897	1,778	2,249
Profit, before-tax	6,794	9,684	17,653	38,138	52,469
Present Value (15%)	5,908	7,322	11,607	21,806	26,086
Cumulative	5,908	13,230	24,837	46,643	72,729
HX 100	**1997-98**	**1998-99**	**1999-00**	**2000-01**	**2001-02**
Unit Price	$59.50	$61,88	$64.36	$66.93	$69.61
Unit Cost	50.58	52.10	53.66	55.27	56.93
Profit Margin	8.92	9.78	10.70	11.66	12.68
Sales Forecast (units)	4,049	5,470	10,078	13,285	15,420
Profit, before-tax	36,117	53,497	107,835	154,903	195,526
Present Value (15%)	31,406	40,451	70,903	88,566	97,211
Cumulative	31,406	71,857	142,760	231,326	328,537
HX 100	**1997-98**	**1998-99**	**1999-00**	**2000-01**	**2001-02**
Unit Price	$44.50	$46.28	$48.13	$50.06	$52.06
Unit Cost	37.84	38.98	40.14	41.35	42.59
Profit Margin	6.66	7.30	7.99	8.71	9.47
Sales Forecast (units)	3,813	5,049	9,169	11,733	12,897
Profit, before-tax	25,395	36,858	73,260	102,194	122,135
Present Value (15%)	22,082	27,870	48,170	58,430	60,722
Cumulative Total	$22,082	49,952	98,122	156,552	217,274
Cumulative Total	$59,396	$135,039	$265,719	$434,521	$618,540

distribution and eventually they could account for about 5 to 10 percent of the sales of the Summit line.

11. Student reports for this project are usually 5-6 pages in length excluding tables and exhibits. In addition to the items listed in case Exhibit 3, reports should discuss the advantages and disadvantages of Anthony's proposal and the sources of information used to prepare the report. Some of the advantages include:

- Cima would be entering markets where they have an established product line and a recognized brand name.

- The new products would enable Cima to expand its market share in its existing market segments.

- The existing retail outlets can be used. The new products should help Cima retain its retail dealers because the Glacier and Summit lines will now meet a wider range of customer needs and provide price points at the low end of the line.

- According to the sales forecasts, a demand exists for a women's mountaineering boot. The MX 350 designed for women would strengthen the Glacier line.

12. Anthony's proposal also has some disadvantages. Some of these include:

- The existing market segments, mountaineering and serious hiker, are small and not growing very rapidly. In the long-term, it may be better to commit resources to more rapidly growing markets.

- The Cima brand image may be damaged by adding boots to the Summit line at lower price points. Probably not very significant.

- The payback period is about 5 years, about the same as Project 1. However, the present value of before-tax profits is higher.

Classroom presentations for tells working on Project 2 should last about 15 minutes, with each team member having about 3 or 4 minutes to present part of the team's report. Presentations should cover the major areas mentioned in the project proposal. Students often prefer to omit the disadvantages of the proposal, so listen carefully to make certain this aspect is included.

APPENDIX A

BLAIR WATER PURIFIERS INDIA

Synopsis

Blair Company is a small U.S. manufacturer (1996 sales expected to be $400 million) of products designed to make water safe and palatable for human consumption. The company is considering entering the Indian market for home water purifiers with its "Delight" purifier. According to Blair Company engineers, the Delight purifier should outperform anything currently on the market.

Students are introduced to Rahal Chatterjee who is employed as an international market liaison for Blair Company. Chatterjee's assignment, and that facing the student, is to determine whether or not Blair Company should enter the Indian market. However, before they can answer "yes" or "no," students should consider the mode of market entry (license, joint venture, acquisition) and examine advertising, pricing, sales and channel possibilities. Students must undertake both qualitative and quantitative analyses to assess entry options and market mix questions to arrive at a reasoned and defensible decision and position.

Teaching Objectives

This case has five teaching objectives:

1. Develop an awareness of global marketing opportunities and challenges.

2. Understand the nature of a marketing opportunity in a less developed country (LDC).

3. Compare and contrast licensing arrangements, joint ventures, and acquisition as strategies to enter foreign markets.

4. Examine the merits of different marketing mix strategies in qualitative and quantitative terms and take a reasoned and defensible position.

5. Explore the nature of a strategic international alliance.

This teaching note was prepared by Professor James E. Nelson, University of Colorado at Boulder. Used with permission.

Teaching Suggestions

This case has multiple uses. It can be assigned early in the course as a market opportunity analysis case, as part of module on international marketing, or later in a course as a comprehensive marketing programs case. The case is suitable as a group presentation case and as an examination case for undergraduate and graduate students.

The following questions can be posed to students prior to or during a class discussion.

1. Compared to a developed country like the U.S. or Germany, what is different about marketing in a less developed country? What is the same?

2. How attractive is the Indian market for home water purifiers?

3. Compare the three modes of market entry available to Blair Company in India. How do decisions related to the marketing mix factor into the comparison among market entry modes?

4. What should Chatterjee recommend to Blair Company regarding the market opportunity in India?

Areas for Discussion/Analysis

A. Compared to a developed country like the U.S. or Germany, what is different about marketing in a less developed country? What is the same?

1. Students will find it easy to identify differences in marketing between developed countries and LDCs. The two types of countries show marketing environments that differ in every fundamental aspect--political, technological, social, competitive, and economic. Infrastructure in LDCs is less advanced than in developed countries, making marketing communications, movement of goods and money, and change more difficult. Compared to a developed country, rural and urban consumers in LDCs will show greater contrasts in income and lifestyles. Governments and people in LDCs often fear or mistrust multinational corporations and even smaller foreign companies. Governments may also limit the company's ability to remove profits. LDCs offer far greater potential for rapid growth in many product categories (e.g., automobiles, telephones, household appliances) than do developed countries.

2. After these and other relevant points come out in discussion, the instructor can turn to marketing similarities between developed countries and LDCs. After perhaps an awkward silence, someone might volunteer that good marketing strategy in LDCs still must consider consumers, competitors, and environments in a creative fashion. Marketers still must attempt to satisfy consumers while accomplishing organizational objectives. Marketers

still must develop strategic alternatives, analyze each in a detailed fashion, and then choose one to implement. In short, after a few minutes of thought, students might conclude that differences in marketing between developed countries and LDCs are more ones of detail and degree rather than ones of principle and procedure.

B.   How attractive is the Indian market for home water purifiers?

1.   This is a good question to continue the discussion. The topic matter is important, the analysis complex, and the answer neither obvious nor unanimous among students. Students might note the following.

2.   The Indian market for home water purifiers is attractive for several reasons. The market is huge and growing—see case Exhibit 1. Moreover, if the market could be expanded to India's rural areas, forecasts in case Exhibit 1 would increase by some six to ten times (Note: Chatterjee estimated that "existing manufacturers were reaching only ten to fifteen percent of the entire population.") In addition, India's extremely low wage rates and central location offer the possibility of export sales to a number of nearby LDCs. Indian consumers are aware of problems with their water quality and are favorably disposed to Western products in general. The Indian government is actively seeking foreign investment into the economy. Water filters and purifiers currently on the market appear inferior to Blair Company's Delight purifier. India represents almost a prototypical case with respect to Blair Company's goal of thriving in LDCs (case's first paragraph). Finally, as will be seen in C. below, India can be entered with relatively little investment of Blair Company resources.

3.   The Indian market for home water purifiers is unattractive for three reasons. First, India is a large, complex, distant nation considerably removed from Blair Company's established "comfort zone" of countries whose business practices and cultures are much more Westernized. Second, the market may be mature with its numerous established competitors, who will not look the other way should Blair Company enter. Finally, the Indian government may reverse its position regarding the attractiveness of foreign investment.

C.   Compare the three modes of market entry available to Blair Company in India. How do decisions related to the marketing mix factor into the comparison among market entry modes?

1.   **Joint Working Arrangement or License.**

   a.   The joint working arrangement or license mode of entry represents relatively low risk: Blair Company would invest almost nothing and would occupy a very low political profile. Likely the product could be placed quickly on dealers' shelves and royalty payments soon would flow to Blair Company. However, Blair Company would have limited control over product quality and nothing at all to say about the nature and level of marketing mix activities. Blair Company would establish no brand awareness among consumers and develop no trade relationships among channel members. It would learn little about consumers, competitors, and business practice in India.

b. Breakeven quantities for the joint working arrangement or license depend on the hiring of an Indian national who would manage the arrangement. Annual fixed costs <u>before</u> hiring this individual are given in the case as $40,000; fixed costs <u>after</u> hiring drop to $15,000. The average royalty paid to Blair Company in both cases is given as Rs.300. For breakeven quantities, we have:($40,000 x 35)/Rs.300 = 4,667 units before hiring the Indian manager, and ($15,000 x 35)/Rs.300 = 1,750 units after. [Note: The U.S. dollar figures are multiplied by 35 because U.S. $1.00 = 35 Indian Rupees (Rs.) as noted in the case.]

c. These quantities can be compared to market forecasts for 1998 or 1999 (the expected first year of operation) in case Exhibit 1 to estimate necessary market shares. Using the "realistic scenario" forecasts from Exhibit 1, we have for 1998, 1,750 units/430,000 units = 0.4 percent of the market and 4,667 units/430,000 units = 1.1 percent. Both percentages are based on nationwide demand. If the licensee restricts operations to just two regions (market potentials shown in case Exhibit 5), the same market shares for 1998 would be 1,750/55,000 or 3.2 percent and 4,667/55,000 or 8.5 percent. Some students may want to recover the $25,000 cost of the field study in the first year or two of operations and their breakeven quantities and share percentages will be a bit higher. However, the $25,000 is more appropriately treated as a "sunk cost."

d. Students also might examine the upside aspect of licensing. Suppose that Blair Company actually achieves a 10 or a 20 percent market share in 1998. Using the same realistic scenario forecasts from Exhibit 1, profits for a 10 percent share of the national market would be (.10)(430,000 units)(Rs.300) - ($15,000)(Rs.35) = Rs12.375 million or approximately $354,000. For a 20 percent share, profits would be (.20)(430,000 units)(Rs.300) - ($15,000)(Rs.35) = Rs.25.275 million or approximately $722,000. If operations focus only on two regions, profits for 10 and 20 percent market shares reduce to Rs.1.125 million and Rs.2.775 million, respectively ($32,140 and $79,285).

e. On balance, the joint working arrangement looks extremely attractive--little is at risk and the opportunity is present for huge rewards--if Blair Company can find and motivate a licensee.

2. **Joint Venture**.

a. When Blair Company partners with an Indian firm, the resulting joint venture will occupy a more visible position in the political arena and place more capital at risk (in the form of investments and annual fixed costs). Another concern is that Blair Company may find it difficult to find and convince an Indian firm to commit to the partnership. Blair Company also may find it difficult to establish day-to-day work rules, policy, and strategic direction with the partner. Still other potential thorny issues include the distribution of profits versus their reinvestment, transfer of technology, access to dealers, and product research and development–all possibly leading to mistrust and early dissolution of the joint venture.

b. On the plus side, the biggest gain that Blair Company realizes with a joint venture entry is increased control over all business activities, including procurement, production, finance, marketing and distribution. Blair Company also can take advantage of the Indian partner's expertise in these activities. (As one expert put it, "An international joint venture essentially reduces to a race between the two partners to see which one can learn the most from the other in the least amount of time."). And, while political and economic risks are increased, these risks will be shared between the two partners. However, so, too, will be the rewards.

c. The amount at economic risk for a joint venture depends on operational scope, as shown in case Exhibit 5. Exhibit 5 also shows that annual fixed costs depend on whether the entry strategy will use dealers or a direct salesforce. Unit contribution margins depend as well on the choice between dealers and a direct salesforce and further on whether a skimming or a penetration price strategy will be used. Estimated unit contribution margins for the channel and price options can be found in the case's last section and are summarized below:

	Channel Strategy	
Price Strategy	Dealers	Direct Salesforce
Skimming	Rs.650	Rs.500
Penetration	Rs.300	Rs.200

Essentially, Chatterjee has figured for the skimming strategy that Rs.1050 are available to cover unit contribution, plus either the dealer's margin (Rs.400) or the salesman's commission (Rs.550). For the penetration strategy, he has allowed Rs.600 to cover unit contribution, plus either the dealer's margin (Rs.300) or the salesman's commission (Rs.400). Thus, in both pricing strategies, the dealer margin per unit is less than the direct salesforce's commission per unit. The dealer option also ties up less money in inventory and incurs lower inventory carrying costs.

d. Beyond the four contribution margins above, student calculations for breakeven are complicated by the need to estimate advertising and promotion expenditures (next to last paragraph in the case). Chatterjee thinks that Eureka Forbes will spend about Rs.1 million in 1996 on advertising for Aquaguard and that Ion Exchange will spend a total of "around Rs.3 million" for <u>all marketing</u> activities associated with ZERO-B. Given this meager information, most students will estimate annual advertising and promotional expenditures somewhere between Rs.500,000 and Rs.2 million and recognize that their calculations are quite crude. More skillful students may include a return on investment in their breakeven calculations, applying an annual target return of around 20 to 25 percent to investments shown in case Exhibit 5.

e. Because students will use different estimates for advertising and promotion expenditures and different rates for ROI (including 0.0), classroom discussion will produce a range of breakeven quantities and market share percentages. At the end of discussion, some students will be uncomfortable with the absence of a single, agreed upon answer. The case is purposely vague in terms of permitting a single answer, for two reasons. First, the opportunity itself is known to Blair Company only to the precision described in the case (indeed, many at Blair Company would hold that the case is much too exact and that more ambiguity, not less, actually characterizes the situation). Second, the case should be assigned very late in most courses, at a time when students should recognize that interesting marketing phenomena almost never are known to the penny or Rupee and that the whole idea of breakeven analyses is for students to demonstrate their analytical judgment.

f. Exhibit 1 in this note contains data from case Exhibit 5, along with estimates for a 20 percent return on investment, estimates for expenditures on advertising and promotion, unit contribution margins for the various distribution and pricing options as given in the case, and resulting breakeven quantities. Student results will differ based on their assumptions for ROI and expenditures for advertising and promotion.

Students should compare breakeven quantities above with the three estimates of market size, shown on the first line above and in case Exhibit 5. The range for breakeven market share is (14,770 units)/(110,000 units) = 13.4 percent for the skimming price and dealer channel combination to (480,000 units)/(430,000 units) = 111.6 percent for the penetrating price and direct salesforce combination.

g. When these or similar numbers have been placed on the board, the instructor can ask for a summary interpretation. A good activity at this point is to stop discussion and give the class three to five minutes to jot down their interpretations. The following integration should arise.

EXHIBIT 1

ANALYSIS OF JOINT VENTURE OPTION USING DIFFERENT CHANNEL AND SALES STRATEGIES AND DIFFERENT PRICING (SKIMMING VS. PENETRATION) STRATEGIES

	Operational Scope		
	Two Regions	Four Regions	National Market
1998 Market Potential	55,000 units	110,000 units	430,000 units
Initial Investment (Rs.000)	4,000	8,000	30,000
20% Return on Initial Investment (Rs.000)	800	1,600	6,000
Advertising and Promotion (Rs.000)	500	1,000	2,000
Analysis for Dealer Channels			
Fixed Overhead (Rs.000)	4,000	7,000	40,000
Total Fixed Costs (Rs.000)	5,300	9,600	48,000
Skimming Unit C.M. (Rs.)	650	650	650
Skimming Breakeven Qty.	8,155 units	14,770 units	73,850 units
Penetration Unit C.M. (Rs.)	300	300	300
Penetration Breakeven Qty.	17,670 units	32,000 units	160,000 units
Analysis for Direct Salesforce			
Fixed Overhead (Rs.000)	7,200	14,000	88,000
Total Fixed Costs (Rs.000)	8,500	16,600	96,000
Skimming Unit C.M. (Rs.)	500	500	500
Skimming Breakeven Qty.	17,000 units	33,200 units	192,000 units
Penetration Unit C.M. (Rs.)	200	200	200
Penetration Breakeven Qty.	42,500 units	83,000 units	480,000 units

1. The penetration price and direct salesforce combination should be rejected out of hand.

2. Breakeven quantities for the skimming price and direct salesforce combination are about the same as the penetration price and dealer channel combination.

3. Breakeven quantities for the skimming price and dealer channel are the smallest.

4. Contribution margins for all combinations using penetration pricing make licensing a preferred alternative.

5. Licensing is a preferred alternative if actual sales quantities stay small.

On this last point, one or two students may see a way to compare the economic aspects of licensing with a joint venture. Students can calculate critical values for quantities such that sales below these levels make licensing look more attractive than a joint venture and that sales above which make the reverse true. The calculations actually are quite simple. From the two region, dealer channel, skimming price data from case Exhibit 5, we can write an equation where the left side represents total contribution for licensing and the right the total contribution for a joint venture. We have [(Rs.300)(Q) - (Rs.15,000)] = [(Rs.650)(Q) - (Rs.4,500,000)], and Q = 12,814 units. For the four region, dealer channel, skimming price data, we have [(Rs.300)(Q) - Rs.15,000)] = [(Rs.650)(Q) - (Rs.8,000,000)], and Q = 22,814 units. For the entire national market, dealer channel, skimming price data, we have [(Rs.300)(Q) - Rs.15,000)] = [(Rs.650)(Q) - (Rs.42,000,000)], and Q = 119,957 units. All three calculations assume that Blair Company would receive 100 percent of the contribution and such is the case only for licensing. If Blair Company were to receive just half of the contribution (as might be stipulated in the joint venture agreement), then the three critical quantities above would double.

h. Finally, one or two students may comment on the idea that a lot of time is being spent on "crunching numbers" and that many other considerations need to be discussed. Besides, they might argue, Blair Company seems a bit old fashioned here—shouldn't a target segment and market demand drive cost such that the final product meets market expectations rather than existing price levels? This is an excellent point that the instructor should be prepared to stress before moving on.

i. Discussion now might shift to qualitative concerns: What else can be said regarding Blair Company's choice between skimming and penetration price strategies? Skimming is an excellent way to "feel out" demand and to learn about the market as events take place. In addition, some Indian consumers probably associate price with quality and others exhibit inelastic demand. Skimming permits Blair Company to field a large salesforce and to control customer contact. Skimming encourages competitors to enter or to stay in the market. On the other hand, a penetration strategy would permit Blair Company to realize economies of scale and experience curve effects more quickly. These efficiencies will enlarge the market and may pave the way for the joint venture to enter India's rural market. Finally, a penetration strategy will discourage competitors from entering or staying in the market.

What else might be said regarding Blair Company's choice between using dealers or using a direct salesforce? Dealers are attractive because they take title and possession of goods, thereby reducing economic risk to the joint venture. Dealers may provide service for damaged or old units; they will stock and sell related products. Both activities offer convenience to consumers. Dealers already are in place and can begin sales of Delight purifiers almost immediately. Dealers offer instant credibility and image, if they are chosen and trained properly. Dealers know their customers and trading areas very well. Dealers are independent businesses, not under the thumb of the joint venture's managers. In contrast, the direct salesforce can be more easily trained, motivated, and controlled. Moreover, many consumers will need an education about the product category that a salesforce can best supply. Like life insurance, the product may be such that it needs to be pushed. However, a direct salesforce represents a huge investment and large fixed costs—should the market contract for any reason, the joint venture may not produce a profit. A large salesforce would be difficult to manage and control. A disgruntled salesman would reflect poorly on the joint venture, not the independent dealer.

3. **Acquisition.**

   a. The acquisition mode of entry represents the greatest political risk to Blair Company. The resulting operation, even if it is given an Indian name, will be known to politicians and social activists as a U.S. (ferengi) owned and managed operation. Thus, it will be vulnerable to the sorts of difficulties recently encountered by such U.S. firms as Cargill, Enron, MacDonalds, and KFC.

   b. In terms of economic risk, the acquisition mode of entry probably will have greater exposure than a joint venture (and certainly greater exposure than licensing). However, the case points out that the amount of investment actually may be lower for acquisition than a joint venture entry because it depends on exactly what will be acquired. For example, Blair Company might buy only a medium sized manufacturing facility, not an entire company, and the investment could be less than that for a joint venture. About the best that students can do here is to recognize these ideas and move on. The case simply lacks sufficient information for a more complete economic analysis.

D. **What should Chatterjee recommend to Blair Company regarding the market opportunity in India?**

This is the most interesting question in the case. Unfortunately, given the depth and breadth of preceding discussion, many 80-minute classes will lack sufficient time to attack this question. If this happens, the question makes an excellent take home quiz or extra credit assignment. The question has essentially two answers.

1. One answer is that Chatterjee should recommend that Blair Company forget about India for the time being. Mostly this position is based on the idea that India is simply too exotic and that "there is too much at risk." Before leaving this answer, the instructor should tease out just what students mean. Clearly, India represents a major challenge to Blair Company's International Division and other LDCs may be easier to enter and offer greater opportunities. However, initial investments and annual fixed costs for the joint working arrangement in India are so small as to be negligible to Blair Company. Still, a troubled joint venture in India might tie up managers at Blair Company and represent a hidden opportunity cost.

2. The second answer is more adventuresome and would have Chatterjee recommend market entry, either via a joint working arrangement or a joint venture. Licensing is the easier answer and students see it as essentially a no risk decision. Licensing has economic advantages, particularly if initial sales levels are small. Licensing is consistent with Blair Company's present level of international expertise; it lets Blair Company start small and learn to walk before it learns to run. Many students reason that Blair Company's operation in India will be that of a single product firm whose product has never seen a moment's use in the field—in India or in any other country. How could the company consider investing even a small amount of resources in a joint venture with such (in)experience? What joint venture partner in India would see Blair Company as attractive, given the lack of a track record?

Students favoring a joint venture take a longer term view. After all, they reason, many well-managed firms selling consumer durable goods recently have entered India. The market is huge, labor costs low, and political and economic risk of reasonable magnitudes. Why not enter with a joint venture? Blair Company managers undoubtedly will make some mistakes but they should try to learn from these mistakes and avoid repeating them. A vigorous entry now may deter one or more other entrants from entering in the very near future.

As should be obvious, the choice between licensing and a joint venture entry has no right answer. Perfectly legitimate positions may be taken on either side, depending on the students' tolerance of risk and decision horizon. Students who are risk averse and short-term oriented should favor licensing. Students who are risk tolerant and long-term oriented should choose the joint venture. The most important point for students to recognize is not "Any answer will do" but rather that "Both positions have strengths and weaknesses that must be understood before managers can make a good decision."

Regardless of mode of entry, operations in India probably should use a skimming price strategy. Skimming offers the lowest breakeven quantities. It permits the use of a large (or a small) salesforce. Most importantly, skimming generates cash for a variety of strategic purposes, all relevant to Blair Company operations in India. Cash will be needed to educate consumers via advertising and promotion and to attract, train, and support dealers (should the dealer option be chosen over the direct salesforce). Cash will be needed to expand market areas from two regions to four, from four regions to the entire nation, and, finally, to rural areas where market potential is huge. Cash also will be needed for new product development, to expand the Delight product line, and to add new lines. Line extensions will be needed when geographic expansion slows because sales increases cannot easily come from increased usage of the Delight purifier among existing owners.

Regardless of mode of entry, operations in India probably should emphasize a dealer network based on reasons outlined in part C. of this Note. Still, some large urban areas may use a direct salesforce who can prospect their neighborhoods and sell, deliver, and service products. The salesforce also can educate new users (and nonusers) and collect payments, if units are sold via hire purchase. Finally, the limited use of a direct salesforce or a factory owned retail outlet system may help Blair Company control dealers, much like the role of factory outlet stores in the U.S.

E. Epilogue

In summary, India seems a very nice fit for Blair Company's international goals. However, the company decided to enter Brazil first, via a joint venture. The company chose Brazil largely because of geographic proximity—Brazil lies only two time zones and just a few thousand miles away from Blair Company headquarters. If things go well in Brazil, Blair Company then will enter Argentina—again because of proximity (and similarity with Brazil). India has been put on the "back burner" for the time being.

Students usually are disappointed to hear this. However, managers at Blair Company received favorable reports on the markets for water purifiers in all four countries mentioned in the case—Argentina, Brazil, India, and Indonesia. Political concerns ruled out Indonesia for market entry but the company still faced a difficult choice. The Indian market (not counting the rural areas) was bigger than Brazil and Argentina combined. However, managers viewed India as too challenging, beyond their capabilities to understand and to perform well in. Still, Chatterjee and a few other managers at Blair Company believed that a license arrangement to enter India would have been a better decision.